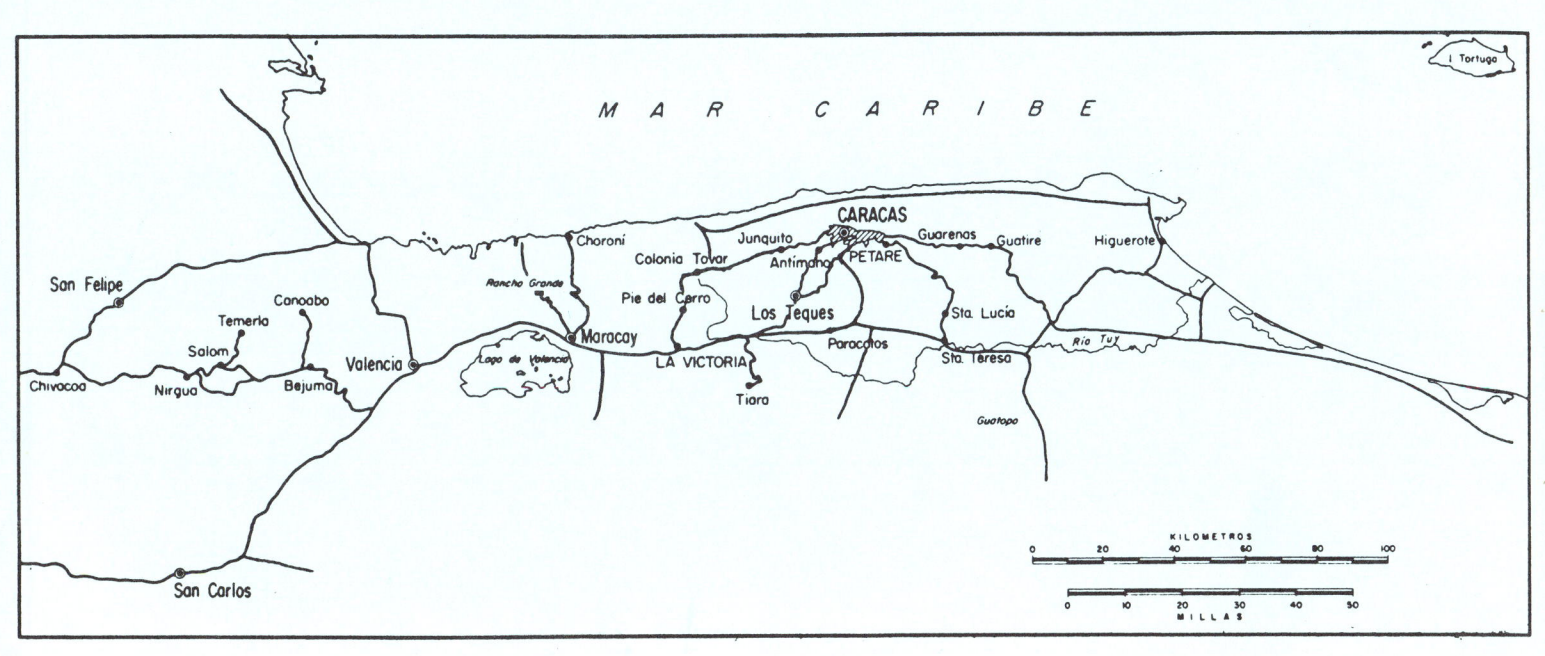

VENEZUELA

Orchid Hunting in the Lost World

jacket illustration (front)

Front Cover: *Acineta superba,* which occurs in cloud forests above the Venezuelan coast, produces spectacular, pendent inflorescences of waxy, maroon-spotted flowers.
(*Photo:* G. C. K. Dunsterville)

frontispiece

With binoculars Nora Dunsterville scans the densely forested mountains in the southern part of the boundary between Venezuela and Guyana. From this region comes *Phragmipedium lindleyanum, Phragmipedium klotzscheanum, Lepanthopsis pulchella,* and many other orchid species.
(*Photo:* G. C. K. Dunsterville)

jacket illustration (back)

Back Cover: The mist-shrouded base of Angel Falls, highest single-jump waterfall in the world (3,000 feet), is home to several species, including *Hexadesmia bifida* and *Chaubardiella tigrina.*
(*Photo:* G. C. K. Dunsterville)

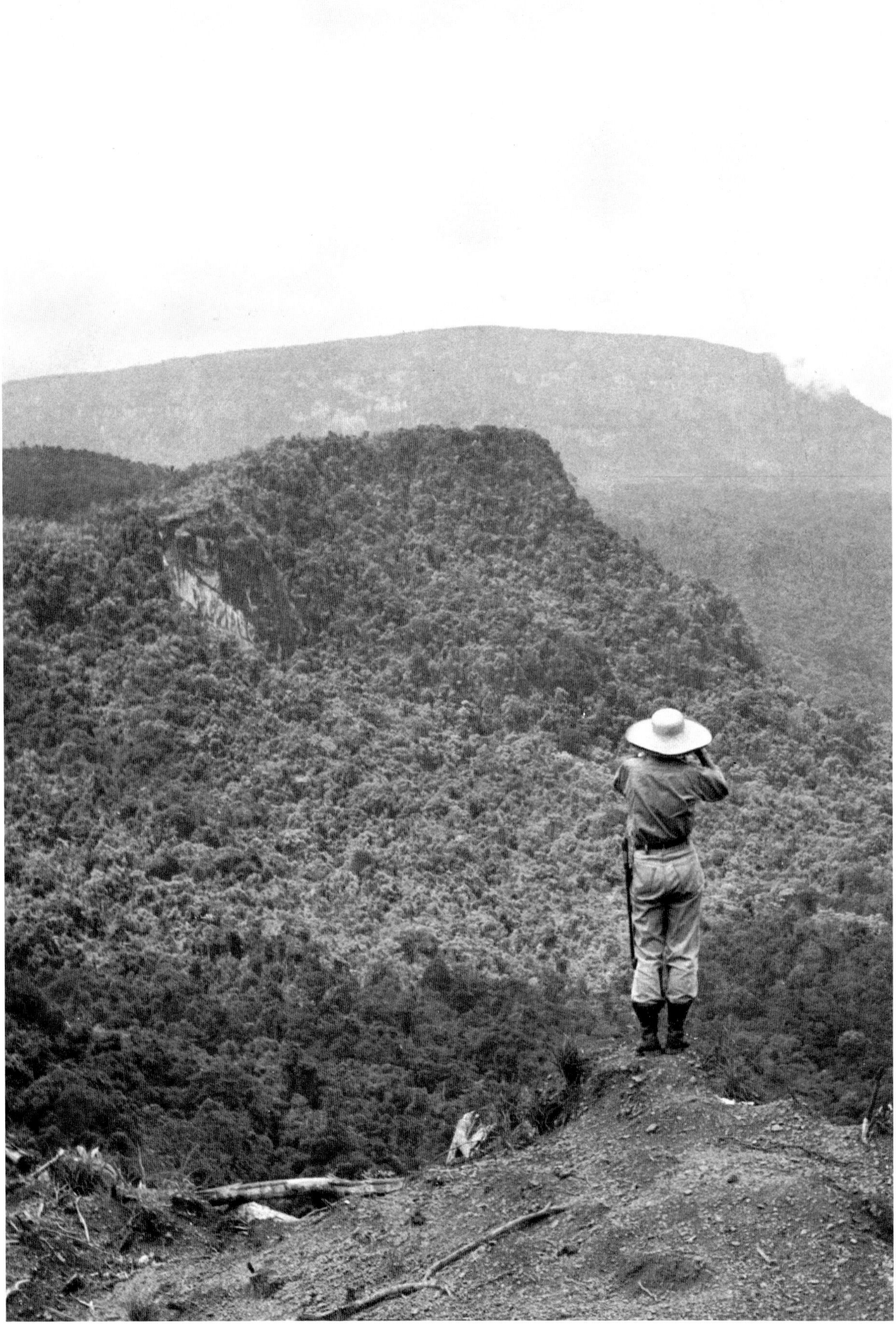

ORCHID HUNTING IN THE LOST WORLD

(and Elsewhere in Venezuela)

G. C. K. DUNSTERVILLE
and
E. DUNSTERVILLE

Edited by:
Alec M. Pridgeon

AMERICAN ORCHID SOCIETY, INC.
WEST PALM BEACH, FLORIDA

Copyright © 1988 by American Orchid Society, Inc.
All rights reserved

Printed in the United States of America
by Southeastern Printing Company, Stuart, Florida
Dustjacket designed by KY Design, West Palm Beach, Florida

Published by the American Orchid Society, Inc.
6000 South Olive Avenue, West Palm Beach, FL 33405, U.S.A.

ISBN # 0-923096-00-0

Text material appeared in different form in the *American Orchid Society Bulletin* from 1959 to 1986 periodically. The Botanical Museum of Harvard University has generously permitted the reprinting of many line drawings by G. C. K. Dunsterville from *Orchids of Venezuela: An Illustrated Field Guide,* 1979. *The Orchid Review* permitted the second reprinting of "Jaua, Sarisariñama, and Holes in the Ground," which originally appeared in different form in *The Orchid Review,* volume 82, pages 205-213, 1974.

Contents

Foreword		ix
Preface		xi
Acknowledgments		xiii
In Memoriam		xiv
Introduction		xv
1.	Orchids for Retirement	1
PART 1		
2.	Orchids — What They Are and What They Do	4
3.	Orchids of Venezuela	12
4.	Rain Forest, Cloud Forest, and Jungle (?) in Venezuela	17
5.	Orchids of Caracas	22
6.	Auyántepui, Home of 50 Million Orchids	27
7.	Orchids of Cerro Autana, Venezuela	34
8.	Helicoptering for Orchids in an Unknown Part of Venezuela's Amazonas	40
9.	Some Venezuelan Orchids of the Sierra de Perijá	46
10.	Jaua, Sarisariñama, and Holes in the Ground	50
11.	Tepui-top Hopping by Helicopter	58
12.	100 Orchids (and 37 Snakes) Up the Orinoco	65
PART 2		
13.	The Flowering Seasons of Some Venezuelan Orchids	73
14.	Finding Phragmipedium caudatum	80
15.	Oncidium meirax	85
16.	Some Maxillarias of Venezuela	87
17.	Some Venezuelan Sobralias	92
18.	Some Venezuelan 'Monospecific' Genera	98
19.	Bifrenaria maguirei, Zygosepalum tatei, and Otoglossum arminii — Three Fine Orchids Safe in Venezuela's Hinterlands	104
20.	The Chondrorhyncha Alliance in Venezuela	109
21.	Some Small Venezuelan Orchids — 1	117
22.	Some Small Venezuelan Orchids — 2	123
23.	Epidendrum nocturnum, a Schizoid Species	129

24.	Some Venezuelan Endemic Orchids	135
25.	Octomeria steyermarkii	144
26.	Some Venezuelan 'Monospecific' Genera — II	147
27.	Two and a Half Paphinias of Venezuela	153
28.	Anguloas of Venezuela	157
29.	Cattleya jenmanii — Late to the Party, Early to Leave?	161
30.	Some Venezuelan Elleanthus Species	164
31.	Zygosepalums of Venezuela	170
32.	Some Venezuelan Notylias	175
33.	Some Pleurothallis Species from Venezuela's Western Andes	178
34.	Galeottia into Mendoncella	184
35.	Some Venezuelan Catasetum Species	187
36.	Altensteinia, Bifrenaria, Chrysocycnis, and Dichaea of Venezuela	192
37.	New Names for Old	195
38.	Cleistes rosea	198
39.	Sobralia sessilis — An Orchid Hunt in an Orchid Herbarium	200
40.	Four Odd P(eas) from Venezuela	203
41.	Epidendrum tigrinum and Epidendrum pamplonense — Old Species Restored to Life	208
42.	Epidendrum leucochilum	211
43.	Selenipedium steyermarkii — A 'Commodius' Orchid	213
44.	Shady Business with Maxillaria callichroma	216
45.	Brassia bidens from 'Dumpleen Camp'	219
46.	Sobralia ruckeri — a Jinx-afflicted Beauty Queen	222
47.	Polycycnis vittata, Polycycnis ornata, and a Night with the Virgin	228
48.	Masdevallia sprucei	228
49.	Barbosella cucullata and Barbosella orbicularis — Chalk and Cheese	231
50.	Pleurothallis perijaënsis Dunsterv.	233
51.	Octomeria flaviflora	235
52.	Apatostelis garayi — A Thank-you Orchid	238
53.	Pleurothallis sclerophylla	241
54.	Maxillaria lepidota Lindl. — or How Silly Can an Orchid Name Be?	243
55.	The 'Ochroleuca Group' of Venezuelan Maxillarias	245
56.	Trichocentrum cornucopiae	248
57.	Houlletia tigrina and Serendipity	251
58.	Hunting Phragmipedium klotzscheanum — An Agony in Eight Fits	254
59.	Psychopsis and Psychopsiella — One Old and One New Genus	257
60.	Comparettia falcata and Psygmorchis glossomystax — Miniature Orchids for a Very Large Christmas Tree	261
61.	Aa, Aha, Aha ha — and What Next?	264
62.	Kefersteinia Species in Venezuela	267
63.	Solenidium racemosum — The Return of a Prodigal Son	271

AFTERWORD:

64.	Conservation in an Overpopulated World	274
	Index to Names of Orchidaceae	278

Foreword

The whole collection of Kipling stories about the childhood exploits of Beetle, Stalky, and McTurk (e.g., *Stalky & Co., Something of Myself For My Friends Known and Unknown*), who strenuously tried their best to undermine the disciplinary efforts of their prep school headmaster, held little immediacy for me until I fell into the employ of the American Orchid Society and began corresponding with G. C. K. Dunsterville. I was aware of the scores of fascinating articles that he and his wife Nora had written for the *American Orchid Society Bulletin* and other orchid periodicals, and, as the new Editor, wrote to ask — beg — for more accounts of their exploits. Alas, he replied, the well had run regrettably dry, and signed his letter "Stalky." Curious about what the initials G. C. K., cloaked in secrecy, represented and even more so why he always signed his correspondence simply, "Stalky," I brazenly broached the tender subject matter-of-factly in one letter and anxiously awaited the revelation. It was not to arrive with his next note, for reasons which were arcane and only served to ante up the suspense level.

Finally, in a letter dated 27/10/84 with the postscript, "10/27/84 if you drive on the right," he disclosed the awful, unspeakable truth. He was born on February 18, 1905, in Devon, England, and "christened Galfrid Clement Keyworth without anyone begging my permission. Galfrid is an old family name derived from the Norman form of Geoffrey (in line with the original DeNestanville ancestors who invaded England in 1066). Clement was in honour of a close friend of my father's youth. And Keyworth was my mother's maiden name. When it came time for me to go to a boarding prep school (my parents being away in India), I rapidly developed a hatred for those names. Who wants to be called 'Gaalfrid' at the age of eight by a bunch of young hooligans? So I refused to answer to any of these names, and became known by more sensible ones such as Tubby (a slander, as I was not fat, only round-faced), Brainy (intended sarcastically), etc., until as I grew older someone started calling me Stalky and that has stuck ever after, becoming the name by which Nora first met me as a co-student at Birmingham University in 1923 or thereabouts.

"There was a spell when I first started my oil career with Shell as a trainee in California (1925) when, having refused to divulge my 'proper' names, my fellow workers decided to call me 'Jim,' and there are still some who call me Jim nearly 60 years later. But Stalky is the name that has become universal, though it is not a name to which I have any legitimate rights since its origin rests with Rudyard Kipling who, as a fellow schoolmate of my father, wrote his famous book *Stalky & Co.* about the iniquitous exploits of Rudyard Kipling himself (nicknamed Beetle), my father (nicknamed Stalky), and a certain boy named Beresford (nicknamed McTurk), all trying to make life difficult for such masters as they disliked. Although this was a pure work of fiction, other Kipling stories about the subsequent military exploits of 'Stalky' took such firm hold that my father was never able to convince people that the whole book was invention. And partly because certain friends seemed to see relics of Stalky-like behaviour on my part as I approached years of discretion, 'Stalky' gradually took over, to the degree that it was no longer possible for me to adopt any other name, however 'false' its origin may have been.

So now you know why it is Stalky who signs this letter

                  Sincerely,

                  Stalky"

After graduation, Nora, maiden name Ellinor Freeman, went to Canada to teach, at the same time Stalky was in California as a trainee for Royal Dutch Petroleum-Shell. They married in 1929 — in Egypt — and traveled the world in the oil business: Holland, Rumania, the United States, Trinidad, England, Egypt again, England again, Colombia, finally alighting in Venezuela in 1947. They met Ernesto Foldats, Venezuelan orchid specialist, who one day showed them a flowering specimen of *Platystele ornata* under the microscope. They were now victims of the orchid fever that envelops us all.

Every three years Shell would allow the Dunstervilles a three-month holiday. It was then and during Christmas and New Year's vacations that they would make intrepid expeditions to the lost worlds of Arthur Conan Doyle and Professor Challenger, those isolated sandstone table mountains called tepuis. The most famous of these and one of the largest is Auyántepui, on the summit of which Jimmy Angel first set down in his light plane in 1937.

Their month-long assault on Auyántepui in 1963 required months of planning and mapping of the summit from aerial photos. This flat-topped mass of rock is 180 miles south of the Orinoco, 140 miles north of Brazil, and west-northwest of the tepui named Roraima on which Arthur Conan Doyle based his story of the Lost World and which was first climbed in 1885. All in all, the summit stretches over 300 square miles. Cliffs as high as 3,000 feet have helped to isolate the flora for centuries and hold civilization in abeyance.

Another dramatic expedition, full of mystery and the fancy of prehistoric monsters lurking about, was to Meseta de Sarisariñama, which was reported to have massive, unexplored holes in it. Try to imagine a flat expanse of rock, 200 square miles in size, broken into deep chasms up to 1,000 feet deep and 1,500 feet in diameter, filled with tall forest with the promise of many species new to science. Forty species of orchids, including two new ones, rewarded Stalky and Nora for their efforts.

Helicoptering among other tepuis in the Amazonas Territory, they collected more spectacular specimens of species such as *Zygopetalum lindeniae* despite vicious, ceaseless attacks by hungry sandflies (or *plaga*, as the natives know them) that can drive a man insane, despite sleeping in the oozing mud created by nighttime cloudbursts, and despite the threat of becoming a jaguar's brunch.

During their expeditions into such remote and basically inaccessible places, several platitudes took on real meaning, such as "Look before you leap," "All that glitters is not a safe handhold," and "Stand not upon thy dignity but slide upon thy butt."

River crossings were always treacherous, and river travel was much more uncomfortable than hopping about tepuis by helicopter. Though the journey might begin benignly, ultimately the heat, the insects, and sun would take their toll. Compared to the orchid diversity at higher elevations, there were few orchids in the lowlands. Instead, Stalky and Nora found an endless variety of birds, fish, monkeys, alligators, giant lizards, and snakes.

In the intervening years Stalky and Nora made some 1,055 collections of orchid species, quite an accomplishment given an estimate of only 1,200 species in all of Venezuela. Stalky amassed a bibliography of some 250 articles, not counting books. Beginning in 1959, Stalky and Dr. Leslie Garay described and illustrated 1,000 of these species in six volumes of *Venezuelan Orchids Illustrated*. Stalky was later to add another 55 species in *Orchids of Venezuela: An Illustrated Field Guide*.

The standard of artistry that Stalky brought to the world of orchids is asymptotic — it may be approached in the years to come but never equaled. Stalky's superb photography will continue to appear in the *A.O.S. Bulletin*, just as it has for the past 25 years. The framing, exposures, and fine focus reflect a reverence and affection not just for orchids but for the whole of nature. His carefully executed line drawings will demonstrate to the world of the future that these species were once here, before the encroachment of man and accelerating deforestation. The illustrations become even more remarkable when one considers that many were sketched out in exquisite detail in the field while the flowers were still fresh, but also while the *plaga* were still biting and a netting was necessary.

In many of the dramatic halftone photographs that Stalky made on their journeys, Nora's straw hat is prominent. Like its owner, that hat has suffered many hardships and bruises through the decades and has been taped and retaped to prove it. It betrays the thrilling lives that Stalky and Nora have led and signifies their tireless efforts to leave something of worth behind for future generations. We shared their romantic ventures vicariously in their photographs and words and learned something about life from Socrates through them, namely that the unexamined life is not worth living.

Alec M. Pridgeon

Preface

In my preparation and editing of more than 60 articles that previously appeared in the *American Orchid Society Bulletin* from 1959 to 1986, the changes made necessary by the ravages of time were more extensive than I ever realized. Not only had the style of the Dunstervilles' works been treated differently over four decades by four different editors, but the names of many species had been changed by orchid taxonomists (some names two or three times). Knowing that these and other names will change in the future as well, I have relied on common and accepted usage as the main criterion for the nomenclature herein.

This volume, however, is not meant to serve primarily as a systematic treatise. There are enough books with that *raison d'etre,* particularly the magnificent six-volume set of *Venezuelan Orchids Illustrated* by G. C. K. Dunsterville and Leslie A. Garay and published by Andre Deutsch. Rather, it is enough to focus on the search for the unknown by two remarkable individuals the likes of which the world will never witness again. Their dauntless exploits bring to mind the hardships faced by orchid collectors of the nineteenth century — hunger, thirst, snakebite, primitive transportation, cloudbursts, floods, mud, biting insects, exposure, and disease. To suffer these hardly minor inconveniences, strength of character and a sense of humor are prerequisites, both held in abundance by Stalky and Nora Dunsterville as they challenged the world around them.

Although the arrangement of the chapters is fundamentally chronological, they seem to fall naturally into two categories. The first part of the anthology introduces the diversity and evolutionary complexity of orchids, the geography and climatic regimes of Venezuela, then enlists the reader on expeditions to remote, lost worlds such as Auyántepui. The second part comprises chapters focusing more on the orchids themselves — their habitats, taxonomy, and cultivation.

By this arrangement into the general and the specific, the Dunsterville's works are made, I think, even more accessible to the reader unfamiliar with Venezuela and/or orchids. The wit and language of the Dunstervilles in presenting their world view, however, transcends even the most specialized subjects, an ability that characterizes great men and women.— Alec M. Pridgeon

ACKNOWLEDGMENTS

The interest of the American Orchid Society in this book is understandable but my wife and I are nevertheless very grateful for the Society's help in publishing and, in particular for that of Dr. Alec Pridgeon, Director of the Society's Education and Research affairs, who spent arduous hours collating and editing our articles, selecting the illustrations, and overseeing the printing. The initial impetus and sizable financial grant also came from the Stanley Smith Horticultural Trust in Scotland directed by Sir George Taylor, a trust whose purpose is to encourage the publication of botanical writings which might not otherwise see print. We are not only grateful but honored to receive the support of such dedicated groups.

Many of the articles collected in the present book arose from the fieldwork we made for a specialized orchid series published by Andre Deutsch Ltd. of London, *Venezuelan Orchids Illustrated.* And finally we wish here to express a very special debt of gratitude to the Fundación Shell, which helped this series (eventually six volumes) with a publishing loan.

G.C.K. and E. Dunsterville

In Memoriam

It is one of the great tragedies of the orchid world, and a personal tragedy for so many, that G. C. K. "Stalky" Dunsterville died on November 26, 1988, after a brief illness. He is survived by his wife Nora, who shared the experiences in this volume, by daughters Hilary Branch and Jenny Fernandez, and by two grandchildren.

Though he never saw this anthology, he received updates on its production and was thrilled by its progress. We hope that this, the record of his and Nora's exploits and their love affair with orchids, will preserve his memory in the heart of man.

Alec M. Pridgeon

Introduction

We have been married some 60 years and our life together has been immensely enriched by orchids. Through this book we hope to share with plant lovers some of the beauty and excitement of the orchids and orchid habitats that Venezuela has in such abundance.

Nora and I began life with the advantage of plant-loving parents, British-born. At the early age of three in India where my father was then in service with the Indian Army, I was taught to recite "*Potamogeton polygonifolia.*" I understood it was the name of a miserable water weed, but with that handle attached to it as a parlor trick to demonstrate my infantile prowess, I have never forgotten it. Some people have asked if my nickname, Stalky, refers to a plant or to plant-hunting but, no, I inherited it from my father, Lionel Charles, who was almost universally known as Stalky, as he was dubbed by his schoolmate Rudyard Kipling (see *Stalky & Co.*).

Nora learned much from her father, Bertram Freeman, who at over 90 years of age was still winning gold medals in England for his alpine plants. The care and love that she invests in transporting the plants from the wild and potting them up in the "civilized" garden of our home in Caracas stems from the sensitivity to microclimates that marks a great alpine or tropical horticulturist.

We met at the University of Birmingham in the UK and afterwards our interests branched into oil, via digging ditches and latrines in California, and into teaching classics to Toronto schoolchildren. After we married in Egypt in 1929, my career with Shell Oil carried us around the world until we finally alighted in Venezuela. There I was told that many of my carefully executed paintings of flowers were rejected by orchid experts as being "very nice on the wall but useless for identification." So I threw out my brushes and took up botanical drawing with pen and ink instead. For this work I found I needed a microscope, many orchids being truly and exquisitely minute. This led us to an interest in ever smaller species and ever more remote rivers and tepuis in this fascinating country of Venezuela.

This book covers a period of time and range of forests which we fear will never return. We have been fortunate enough to collect more than 1,055 species, including two new genera and many other species bearing our names. But many orchids native to Caracas were already elusive or extinct 40 years ago and many species have disappeared since then, along with their habitats. Sadly, this is true not only for Caracas but for the Andes, the Guayana highlands, the Coastal Range. In this sense, this book is not only a record but also an appeal to the rising generation of orchidists, regardless of nationality, to take steps to safeguard our fields and forests everywhere.

G.C.K. and E. Dunsterville

Introduction

Orchids for Retirement[1,2]

WE HAVE BEEN ASKED to do something rather embarrassing — write an article about ourselves or, better, to explain the reasons which made us incurable orchid fanciers. Being different from the poet Stephen Spender, who a few years ago wrote his autobiography when he was only 30 (supposing that this work would be of tremendous interest to all the world), we, who are twice his age, are not convinced of the necessity of publishing autobiographical notes. Nevertheless, we are people who find it difficult to say no to friends, so we decided to accede to the request. This way, at least, there is the possibility of suppressing certain disagreeable truths.

Our interest in orchids did not begin until the 1950s, when we were employed (or rather badly employed) for many years looking for oil in countries where we could have been looking for orchids. For example, in Trinidad we must have come face to face many times with orchids without recognizing them or, in Colombia, where we collected wildflowers in the savanna of Bogotá and took pictures of them only to realize many years later that these pictures were of orchids.

When we arrived in Caracas in 1947, we had no interest in orchids and even less knowledge of them — except that when we saw a *Cattleya* flower, we could say with conviction, yes, it was an orchid. However, once we were established here, we had to keep on a par with our friends and, by chance, many of our Caracas friends had one or two beautiful orchid plants in their gardens and houses.

In those days, we went early in the morning to the Chacao market in Caracas, where there was a booth with all sorts of plants for sale, including orchids that were not cattleyas. We bought our cattleyas from an old man we called "the vagabond," who walked the streets of urban Altamira selling burlap bags of *Cattleya mossiae* brought down from the slopes of the mountains around Caracas. He also sold plants of the common lavender cattleyas in whose sheaths had been deftly inserted white cattleya flowers.

Little by little, our collection of non-*Cattleya* orchids grew, and at the same time grew our frustration with the fact that nobody could identify our orchids or sometimes even confirm that they were orchids. Nobody informed us until much later that there was a Botanical Institute, so it appeared to us that if we wanted information about orchids, we would have to look for it ourselves. We made pencil drawings which were sent to the Royal Botanic Gardens at Kew asking for information. Kew, in the person of the late Victor Summerhayes, was extraordinarily amiable and patient in dealing with two people as ignorant as we were in remote Caracas. Answering a question on the identity of a certain plant, he replied in January 1953 that it was *Stenorrhynchos nutans*, "described in 1848 from a plant in cultivation but apparently never seen again." Later, it was revealed that this name was a synonym for *Spiranthes speciosa* and, thus, was no rarity, but Summerhayes' letter served to light a flame that we now know was a strong, latent desire to make original investigations and, perhaps, leave something permanent in this world when the hour to leave for unknown destinies arrives. It seemed to us that if we could find such a rare orchid in a market, surely we could find others in the forests and possibly we could find some that were unknown until now.

From that time on, weekend excursions to places where there was a possibility of finding orchids not far from Caracas became a part of our lives, and our "orchid customs" took on the aspect of WE-SHE-HE which exists even today; a division of chores which resulted in an absorbing hobby, an ideal occupation for a retired couple. WE go together to the forests, plains, and mountains of this magnificent country looking for wild orchids to

[1] Originally appeared in *A.O.S. Bulletin*, Vol. 55, February 1986, Pages 135-139

[2] Translated with authors' permission from *La Orquidea Venezolana*, December 1975, by Marianne Ploch.

study. SHE is responsible for the packing, transportation, and care of the collected plants, and at times this involves personally carrying the bundle because it cannot be trusted to him, because HE is not careful enough. Once at home, SHE again is responsible for the cultivation of all the orchids (really all the plants in the house and garden), an interminable chore to which HE contributes nothing inasmuch as his sporadic efforts generally consist of doing something wrong at the most inconvenient moment. While SHE exercises her "green thumb," HE occupies himself with a considerable amount of correspondence with the whole world, which evolved from the first letters sent to Kew. HE writes all sorts of articles (like the present one) for various orchid publications, work that is essential to maintain the impression that we are expert orchidologists. When WE find an interesting flower on one of our trips, HE is responsible for making a sketch and preliminary observations and for placing the flower in a jar in order to study it in more detail at home. HE also does this work when SHE comes running in to show him a recently opened flower in the orchid house.

In our search for knowledge of orchids, we soon realized that if we wanted to consult experts abroad, we would have to find a more adequate way to draw the plants and flowers; it was impossible always to send live material. In those times, we did not know how taxonomists worked, and it did not seem reasonable to us that it was possible to identify plants from dried material. The artistic work was delegated to the masculine member of the team, and the first pencil drawings rapidly transformed into colored portraits which were far more ambitious and detailed. While these portraits were a good occupation and helped one forget business problems (and some were used later as postage stamps), it soon became evident that they were as useless for our purpose as colored photographs. When some experts courteously explained to us that if the tiny, internal details of the flower (such as pollinia, the crest of the labellum, details of the column, etc.) could not be seen at the same time as the external aspect, our drawings were lacking in practical use. Finally, when we did a drawing of a true miniature, *Platystele ornata,* we realized that we would need three things if we hoped to progress with our hobby. First, we would have to buy a good microscope, an expensive but durable item. We would have to acquire a certain knowledge of botany and a certain ability to dissect the flowers in an intelligent manner. Finally, we would have to learn a satisfactory way to draw the flowers, inasmuch as there were many parts of the flowers to illustrate, all to different scales, and afterwards the parts had to be assembled into a whole. We could not use photographs. Pencil drawings did not have sufficient luster and were difficult to reproduce. The solution was drawings done in China ink, for which we had to acquire the ability with much patience and practice.

After our first contact with Summerhayes, we had the good fortune to communicate with Leslie Garay during the time that he was studying orchids at the University of Toronto. Our friendship continued growing when he moved to Harvard and was named curator of the world-famous Orchid Herbarium of Oakes Ames. With Garay's help, our increasing number of orchid illustrations began to have botanical significance. When we started to pursue the knowledge of orchids, we decided that if we succeeded in acquiring a certain knowledge, we would do everything possible to share it with others. When we had 400 drawings, we felt the moment had arrived to do something in this respect. Therefore, with the essential collaboration of Garay, the series of books *Venezuelan Orchids Illustrated* was born. The first volume was published in 1959, just at the moment we retired from our "oil" life and were finally able to devote ourselves completely to orchids. Aside from looking for the material for these volumes, doing the drawings, and writing the descriptions, financing the series was a problem because we could not find a publishing house willing to publish the books except on the basis of self-financing. Notwithstanding, the books would not be worth anything without the essential collaboration of Garay, whose contribution transformed a collection of drawings into a work of real botanical merit. It is inevitable that we bask in the reflection of this botanical glory and that we are considered, falsely, expert orchidologists-botanists, but the truth is that it is unjust for Garay, and we are anguished by the fact that our name precedes his on the title of the books. It is really a collaboration where the contributions of the "field" and the "herbarium" are as essential as they are distinct, and it is only by the association with Garay that the author of the "field" could add certain truth to the idea, mistakenly and little convincing, that he is a botanist because he was named Associate of Investigations of the Botanical Museum of Harvard, forming a part of the faculty of Harvard University. What emotion could be greater for an old petroleum expert than to see a tourist taking a picture of his name included in the list of directors of the Museum, even though being a member absent and without salary?

During the first years, when we were bound to the oil industry, the opportunity to take trips to the remote parts of Venezuela had to be limited. We took advantage of the last part of our three-month vacation every three years, given to foreign employees of Shell Oil. We would hurry back from a trip to Europe having approximately three weeks left of vacation, assuring each other that no one was aware of our return before disappearing into the "interior" and assured that no one would call us from the office. We also used the "local vacations," which were a lot shorter but could be combined with the holidays, especially toward the end of the year. These created sometimes delicate situations, such as the time at the end of 1957 when the dictatorship of Perez Jimenez fell and we were far from reach in Icabarú, making it necessary to send a company plane to find us. Later, we had a similar rescue when, surprisingly, the income tax laws were changed in 1958 and we were again "incommunicados" at the base of Angel Falls.

Truly, it was not until our retirement in 1959 that we could start working seriously to try to find and know all the orchid species of Venezuela, which we now estimate at 1,200. It is a labor without end because although the number that we find continues to grow, it becomes more difficult to find the few that are missing. But the endless search is what fascinates us. We have explored the country by car where there are roads, by jeep on paths, by river where paths are lost and there are but fluvial ways, walking where there is no river or path, by mules and donkeys when our feet are tired, and finally, thanks to certain people, by helicopter to places where only helicopters can go.

Until now, we have collected about 1,050 Venezuelan orchid species, and we are very grateful to a small group of orchid enthusiasts without whose contribution we would be short of a good number of species that have been published in the six volumes of our "opus." With so many "trophies" hanging from our belt, it is not surprising that on the last expeditions we found very little new material. In the early days, on a first visit to a new place like the Guatopo forest, we could find in one day a dozen species that were new to us. Today, we are very happy on a 15-day trip if we find one plant that we have not seen before. Nevertheless, there are still 200 species in the jungle waiting for us. We know that they exist because they are described in the five volumes of *Orchidaceae* of *Flora de Venezuela,* an invaluable and authentic work compiled by Ernesto Foldats a few years ago. Some common plants like *Vanilla planifolia* continue to be elusive; we never find it in a flower, and it resists all our efforts to make it flower at home. *Palmorchis* is not a rare genus although it has only three species native to Venezuela, but it also resists cultivation. Just recently, after searching for 20 years, we found a plant in the jungle which amiably at least showed us its buds.

However, while these common plants elude us, in our search to find them many times we found new species, contributing to keep the flame of our enthusiasm lit. As an incentive to avoid dying for as long as possible, there are few passions comparable to orchids.

Part I

Orchids — What They Are and What They Do[1]

WE FIRST WROTE about the almost incredible story of the orchid family in our book *The World of Orchids*, published by Librería Lectura in 1962. Since then, well over two decades of orchid aficionados have grown up. Many of these "newcomers" may not realize fully just what a wonderful family of plants Orchidaceae is. The story of the orchids is well worth repeating, the more so because our book has been out of print for many years and the membership of the American Orchid Society has grown to more than 20,000 in the interim. There is nothing new in this story, the "science" of which is drawn mostly from that splendid book *The Orchids: Natural History and Classification* by Dr. Robert L. Dressler (Harvard University Press, 1981).

An article about the uniqueness of the orchid family seemed to be a good idea. We must consider how we can tell an orchid from any other flowering plants. And we must summarize (speaking anthropomorphically) the many very extraordinary "tricks" that orchids have developed in their anxiety to avoid self-fertilization while not discouraging fertilization by pollen from other flowers of the same species.

Writing this article has not been easy because the readership of the *A.O.S. Bulletin* is so extensive that it includes the expert taxonomist at one end of the "orchid knowledge scale" and the "greenest" beginner at the other. (The latter is perhaps so new to this fascinating subject that he or she has yet to discover that a taxonomist is a most important person in the orchid world and is by no means the same as the taxidermist who stuffed the hunting trophy adorning a neighbor's family room.) It also has not been easy to be sure that we have outlined the complete answer to how to distinguish an orchid because the composition of the orchid is so involved that, as will be described later, there is no one feature (or even two) that you can pin down as truly diagnostic.

First we must deal with the "uniqueness" of this wonderful family. It is unavoidable to get a bit "technical" by explaining that the orchid family (Orchidaceae) is a member of a higher and more extensive group (called an order) that is known as Microspermae because of its minute seeds, an order so specialized that it contains only two or three other plant families, each small and obscure. Yet other taxonomists place orchids in an even more exclusive order known as Orchidales, which contains just the orchid family, making the group a truly unique one — a verdict with which, we are sure, all aficionados will agree.

Apart from its uniqueness, the orchid family also rivals the daisy family (Compositae, or Asteraceae in modern usage) for the honor of being the largest family in the vegetable kingdom in terms of number of species. Estimates for Orchidaceae range from 15,000 to 35,000, depending on who does the counting. One taxonomist may consider certain "similar but different" orchids to have full species status where another may classify them as no more than "forms" or "varieties" of a single species. Moreover, as knowledge of the orchid family grows, more and more species (or even genera) are described as new discoveries are made.

Before considering the characteristics that orchids *do* have, it is worth a quick glance at the commonly reputed qualities that they do *not* have:

• As distinct from the "aphrodisiac" effect that a fine corsage of *Cattleya* flowers *might* have on the young lady of your choice, there are no proven aphrodisiac qualities in an orchid plant — even if you eat every bit of it.

• Orchids eat neither insects nor man, although (as described later) they do sometimes trap insects as part of their strategy for cross-pollination. In our

[1] Originally appeared in *A.O.S. Bulletin*, Vol. 55, June 1986, Pages 604-611

youth, we once read a horror story about a man-catching orchid. But unless some reader has direct experience with such a monster (with photos to prove it), we shall give this tale no credence.
• Orchids (at least the epiphytic ones) are by and large not overly difficult to grow. In fact, they are not normally very touchy in comparison to other plants. We found this out when smuggling into Venezuela a live orchid given to us by a friend in Colombia during a visit there. We carefully hid the plant in a clean shirt in a suitcase, and it was not rediscovered until the shirt was opened up several months later. The plant was still alive!
• Despite their Latin American name of *parásitos,* epiphytic orchids do not feed on the plant on which they grow. Thus, they are not parasites, although the sheer weight of a large clump might end up breaking a rotten branch.
• While a number of orchids do have extremely dark purple-brown or black-like spots, there is no truly black orchid.
• A rare wild orchid species might bring the discoverer some money if he uses it for propagation by meristem techniques, but no real fortune is likely to be made nowadays by a lucky find, quite the opposite of the situation in the early days of the orchid craze in the 19th century.

It is not the main purpose of this article to tell the reader what an orchid is *not* but to outline what an orchid *is* and what distinguishes it from other plants.

There is no simple, single reply to the often-heard question, "What is an orchid?" It can be answered only by listing the many strange features that, taken together, set the orchids apart from other plant families. These features, very briefly (and leaving out certain important but abstruse botanical features) are as follows:
• The stamens (pollen-bearing male parts) and pistil (stigma-bearing female part), which are separate sexual elements in most flowering plants, in the orchids are at least partly fused into a single central element called the column or gynostemium. While this element sometimes is columnar in shape, it often looks most *un*like a column, as illustrated by the columns of the 12 Venezuelan orchids shown in Figure 1.
• The seeds are truly minute. The *Kew Bulletin* for 1909 reports a scientifically determined figure of 3,770,000 seeds in a single capsule of the common Venezuelan orchid *Cycnoches chlorochilon.* Thus, it is easy to credit the figure we have seen in some now-misplaced book which worked out that the seeds would be so light that it would take 3,000,000,000,000 (yes, three million million) to weigh a kilogram!
• The flowers have an outer whorl of three sepals that often are very colorful. However, the inner whorl of floral parts does not (except in freak cases) contain the expected three identically shaped petals. Two of the petals resemble one another. But the third petal usually has been drastically modified into a structure called the labellum or, more commonly, just the lip (the English translation of the Latin *labellum*). This structure usually serves in some manner in the particular species' pollination mechanism. The sepals also may be separate or joined together in varying ways. When the two lateral sepals are joined completely, the united structure is called a synsepal. Such a structure is a feature of most "slipper orchids," including the popular paphiopedilums and the wild temperate species in the genus *Cypripedium.*
• The flower in bud starts in the "primordial" attitude, with the lip at the top in a "prone" position, that is, pointing upward parallel to the axis of the inflorescence. But as the flower bud matures, the stem or pedicel on which it is borne usually twists during its development, so that when the flower opens, the lip is "supine," pointing downward at the bottom of the flower, a position probably important in attracting pollinating insects or admiring orchid lovers. This 180° twisting action is called resupination. But there are some orchids, such as certain species of the genus *Malaxis,* in which the lip begins in the natural primordial attitude in the bud then twists through a full 360°, so that the lip once more comes back to its primordial prone or upward-pointing position when the flower opens. Sometimes labeled "super-resupination," this phenomenon may be an evolutionary response to changing pollinators.
• Where most other flowers have loose pollen grains, in orchids the pollen is stuck together in lumps of varied consistency. These are known as pollinia, and they usually are enclosed in a protective cap called an anther. They may be connected by a stipe or caudicle to a sticky element known as a viscidium. There is much scientific debate about the origin of each of these stuctures, but they all function in the pollination process. Between the pollinia and the sticky stigmatic surface, there is generally an important flap-like element called the rostellum. This also serves varying functions in the process of pollination.

While other flowers may have one or more of the features listed above, only orchids display all of these characteristics. But the orchid is still difficult to define because there always seem to be a few exceptions to every rule. Although we define orchids as having bisexual or "perfect" flowers (that is, they contain both the male and female organs of reproduction in a united structure, the column), there are some genera, notably *Catasetum* and its relatives, whose species usually produce unisexual flowers. They are usually either female (pistillate) or male (staminate), although bisexual flowers occur which have functioning male and female parts, and sterile flowers are not unknown. A plant of *Catasetum* may bear exclusively female flowers or exclusively male flowers at any one time (with sex expression apparently based on light intensities at the site where the plant grows). Other plants may produce a mixture of the two. We have found on a single raceme of *Catasetum longifolium* not only male and female flowers but the whole gamut of intermediate forms. What a mixed-up orchid!

What Do Orchid Flowers and Plants Look Like?

The orchid family is so large in numbers and variety of species that it is not possible to explain what an orchid flower or plant looks like. The size of the flower may vary from that of the head of a very small pin in, say, *Lepanthes steyermarkii* up to large *Cattleya* flowers and on up to such curiosities as some *Phragmipedium* species with their boat-shaped "slipper-type" lips and extremely long, narrow, ribbon-like petals that dangle for lengths up to 70 cm. In "oddness," we could point to the miniature *Platystele johnstonii*, with its absurdly long and slender apex of the dorsal sepal, or the flower of *Pleurothallis (=Myoxanthus) reymondii*, which looks like a dangerous insect armed with petals ending in "boxing gloves." Then there are the extremely queer flowers of *Scaphosepalum verrucosum*, which look like insects whose mothers had been taking LSD. Or consider the extraordinary *Porroglossum echidnum*, with its lip that snaps shut, trapping an insect inside. Add to this list of oddities the well-known *Oncidium papilio*, which gets its species name from its resemblance to a butterfly that has developed a third antenna. This flower is also an interesting "freak" because, while it seems to have three long, antenna-like sepals and two normal petals, in fact two of the "antennae" are petals and one is a sepal.

As far as the size of the complete inflorescence is concerned, we can cite *Dunstervillea mirabilis* as a real "shorty." Its peduncle and terminal raceme of 2 or 3 flowers scarcely measure 1 centimeter overall. On the other hand, an erect inflorescence of the terrestrial *Eulophia alta* can grow as tall as 3 meters. Then there are some of the epiphytic oncidiums with long, straggling inflorescences, such as *Oncidium volvox*, which has an inflorescence at least 5 meters long when straightened out.

We could go on quoting examples of the variability of flowers and inflorescences almost indefinitely, but let us pass on to the form of the orchid plant as a whole. Here again, the variety prohibits any effort to explain what an orchid plant looks like. In size, a whole adult plant may vary from the aforementioned *Dunstervillea mirabilis*, six of which could fit into a thimble, up to *Sobralia cattleya*, with plants that may exceed 5 meters in height. The size of a single leaf varies from 5 millimeters for *Chamelophyton kegelii* to almost 1 meter for the broad-leaved *Xylobium leontoglossum*. The very extraordinary terete leaf of *Scuticaria steelei*, which is little thicker than a pencil, dangles from the branch of a tree for a length of 1.5 meters.

Some orchids grow in clumps, while others have ever-lengthening rhizomes that clamber all over a tree. Some have no pseudobulbs, while others are almost too small to see, as in *Epidendrum manarae*. At the other extreme are plants such as *Cyrtopodium glutiniferum*, which as fusiform (cigar-shaped) pseudobulbs more than 50 centimeters tall. Still others, such as an as-yet unidentified *Acineta* from the Andes, have pseudobulbs the size of large fists (18 × 12 centimeters).

Mycorrhiza

The word mycorrhiza introduces a generally invisible but extremely important element in the growth of an orchid from seed. It already has been stressed that orchid seeds are produced by the millions and are extremely small. It also must be mentioned that a great many of them are equipped with a loose, rather papery coat that helps them to be windborne for long distances. Thus, we begin to wonder why the forests of the world have not already been smothered to death in orchids. The answer to this is that Nature, left to itself, has its own ways of avoiding excesses of this sort. In the case of the orchids, it is the very smallness of the seeds themselves that achieve this. A tiny seed, if it is to be airborne, cannot afford to travel encumbered with enough food supplies to start life elsewhere, and few would survive were it not for a complicated scheme of nature that helps the orchid begin its new life with the aid of a normally deadly enemy, a type of root fungus called a mycorrhiza.

When the seed lands where conditions are otherwise favorable for germination, the first stages of precarious growth may start in the absence of any fungus. But most seedlings are unable to continue growth without help from this fungus. Typically, the fungal hyphae enter the seed and penetrate the germinating embryo. Then one of three things can happen. In many cases, the fungus kills the orchid seed. But in other cases, the orchid turns the tables and kills the fungus — after which the orchid also dies for lack of food. But if the proper balance is established, the seedling is able to obtain enough sustenance from the fungus and will continue growing until it develops leaves, after which photosynthesis starts the plant on its permanent way.

Therefore, it is clear that the orchid seed begins life in a very touch-and-go manner, with a high proportion failing to survive and, thus, failing to swamp the forests with orchids.

Orchid "Tricks" and Mechanisms

In this final part of this article, we will be dealing with the "tricks," "ploys," or call them what you will that orchids indulge in, some of them simple and others so complicated that it is hard to believe that there is not a thinking mind behind them.

Because both male and female reproductive organs are united in the same structure within most species of orchids, a way must be found to avoid self-fertilization because, under most circumstances, outcrossing (cross-pollination with a genetically different individual) is preferable to self-pollination. Orchids generally achieve this by "desexing" one of the three stigmas incorporated into the original column and causing this sterile stigma to develop into a rostellum to form a barrier between the pollinia and active stigma at the end of the column. In certain plants of a species, this barrier may weaken and allow contact between the flower's pollinia and its own stigma, whereupon self-pollination will take place.

The desired cross-fertilization takes place when the right kind of insect (or bird in some instances) visits the flower. The pollinator is attracted to the flower by its scent, color, nectar, or other "lure." When it enters or leaves the flower, the "right" pollinator is so positioned by the flower's structure that it touches the viscidium and withdraws the pollinia as it exits. The anther cap which protected the pollinia falls away during this process or sometime shortly thereafter. The "wrong" kind of pollinator would be one to which the orchid denies entry or one which is too small to activate the pollination mechanisms. The means by which the orchid selects which pollinators are "right" and which are "wrong" are extremely ingenious and by themselves would need lengthy description, for which there is insufficient space in this article. But some space must be devoted to a very brief description of at least a few of the devices or "tricks" invented by Nature to aid cross-pollination and prevent self-fertilization:

Trick No. 1 — This trick is so simple that it is surprising the orchids ever bothered to "invent" other and far more complicated ones. In this trick, the rostellum depresses itself when the pollinia are removed, thus blocking access to the stigma for the same pollinator or others until after a prudent interval, by which time the first pollinator with its "cargo" of pollinia will have gone elsewhere. When this period is over, the rostellum lifts again, readying the flower to welcome a visit from another pollinator loaded with pollinia from another flower, thus achieving the required cross-pollination.

Trick No. 2 — This trick is used by the small Venezuelan orchid called *Porroglossum echidnum*. It has a sensitive lip with a hinge connecting it to the column-foot, as shown in Figure 2. When an insect lands on the open lip and touches the sensitive spot, the hinge contracts, and the lip sweeps up with considerable rapidity, imprisoning the insect between the lip and column in such a way that it can escape only by first passing the stigma, where it deposits its load of pollinia from an earlier flower (if any) then picks up a new load to take elsewhere. While so imprisoned, it cannot back up to put the new load of pollinia back on the stigmas and thus cause self-fertilization. By the time the lip opens again, the insect may be too exhausted to try revisiting the same flower before another insect appears on the scene.

Trick No. 3 — This involves the stipe attached to the pollinia. When the pollinator enters the flower and contacts the viscidium, thus removing the pollinia and the anther cap, the stipe immediately curls up in such a way that the anther cap is retained in place on the pollinia. The pollinator leaves with all this impedimenta on board. If the pollinator pays a quick return visit to the same flower, the anther cap effectively will prevent any fertilization. But after a lapse of time, the stipe dries, whereupon it uncurls, releasing the anther cap and exposing the pollinia in a position ready to pollinate the next flower visited. But by then the pollinator almost certainly will have gone elsewhere, forgetting its intention of making a second pass at the original flower.

Trick No. 4 — This one also involves the stipe. When the pollinator contacts the viscidium, it flies away with the pollinia stuck to its head or back in a poor attitude for contacting the stigma of the flower from which it has just removed the pollinia. Thus, an immediate return to the same flower will not effect self-pollination. Again, after a pause, the viscidium will lose some of its natural moisture, and the attitude of the stipe and pollinia will revert to the original position and thus be ready to enter the next floral column, contact the stigma, and effect the desired cross-pollination. The chances of the pollinator going back to the original flower still bearing the original pollinia are slim indeed.

Trick No. 5 — This trick is based on a most complicated formation of the lip and column of the flower. In this case, it is utilized by *Coryanthes biflora,* and it is a device which must have taken Nature untold ages to perfect. The lip of this species and some other species of *Coryanthes* is large and heavy and, as shown in Figure 3, hangs from the pedicel in the form of a sort of bucket, with the column hanging inside it. At the base of the column (now its upper end), there are two small glands, one on each side. These slowly secrete a fairly large amount of liquid, drop by drop. The base of the "bucket" thus accumulates a noticeable quantity of this liquid. Small bees, attracted by some desirable fragrances, eventually fall into the bucket. Because they are unable to fly out of the bucket with wet wings, they have to seek another exit. This exit is in the front of the bucket near its base, well-hidden behind the up-curling apex of the column. It is so placed that in escaping, the insect has to brush by the viscidium and collect a load of pollinia, having first deposited on the stigma any pollinia it may already have been carrying. It is most unlikely that the insect will try to repeat this process immediately. In the meantime, other pollinia-bearing bees will have passed through the flower. Scientific observations of this species showed that "sometimes there are so many bees assembled that there is a continual procession of them through the passage."

Trick No. 6 — This trick we have left to the last because it is quite unbelievable how it ever came to be discovered by unthinking plants. At some very early stage of its development, a species of the European terrestrial orchid genus *Ophrys* found that a hairy insect in the same part of the Mediterranean had the odd habit whereby the male of the species emerged from its burrow for a life in the open about a month before the females emerged for mating. The *Ophrys* orchid, whether by design or good management, not only has a lip that looks like the insect but also opens its flowers just at the time when the lustful male insects are appearing. The result is that the male is deceived into thinking that he has discovered a wife. He lands on the lip of the flower and does his best to mate with this ersatz "female" insect. In the process, the insect removes the orchid's pollinia and carries them to the next flower, where he may fulfill the orchid's need to effect cross-pollination. Self-pollination is avoided because the insect, thinking he has dealt with one female, obviously does not want to dally with her any longer, so he moves on to continue his amorous conquests elsewhere. This pollination mechanism is known as pseudocopulation. As incredible as it is, what is even more incredible is that it has been "discovered" and used by other orchids and insects in other parts of the world!

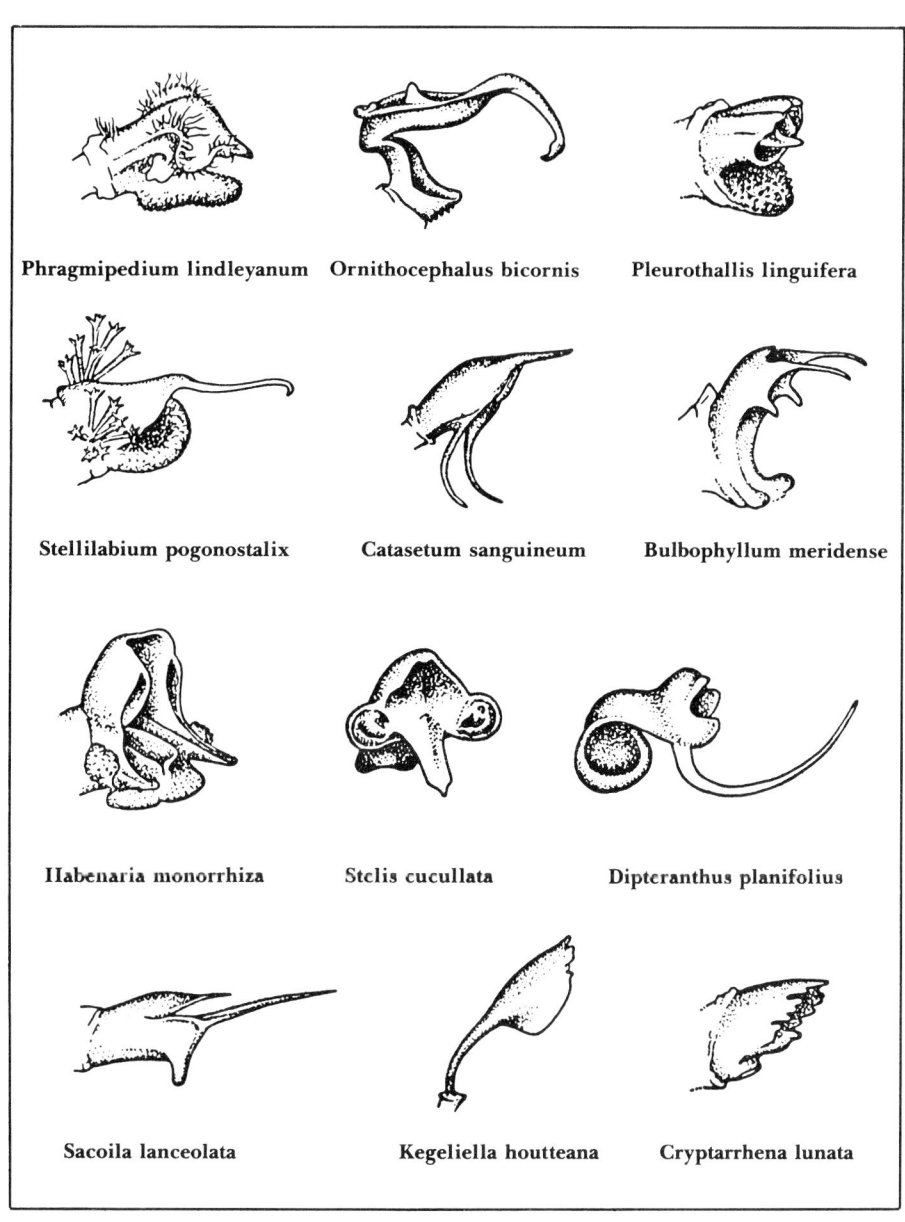

All illustrations: G. C. K. Dunsterville

Fig. 1. Columns of 12 Venezuelan orchid species.

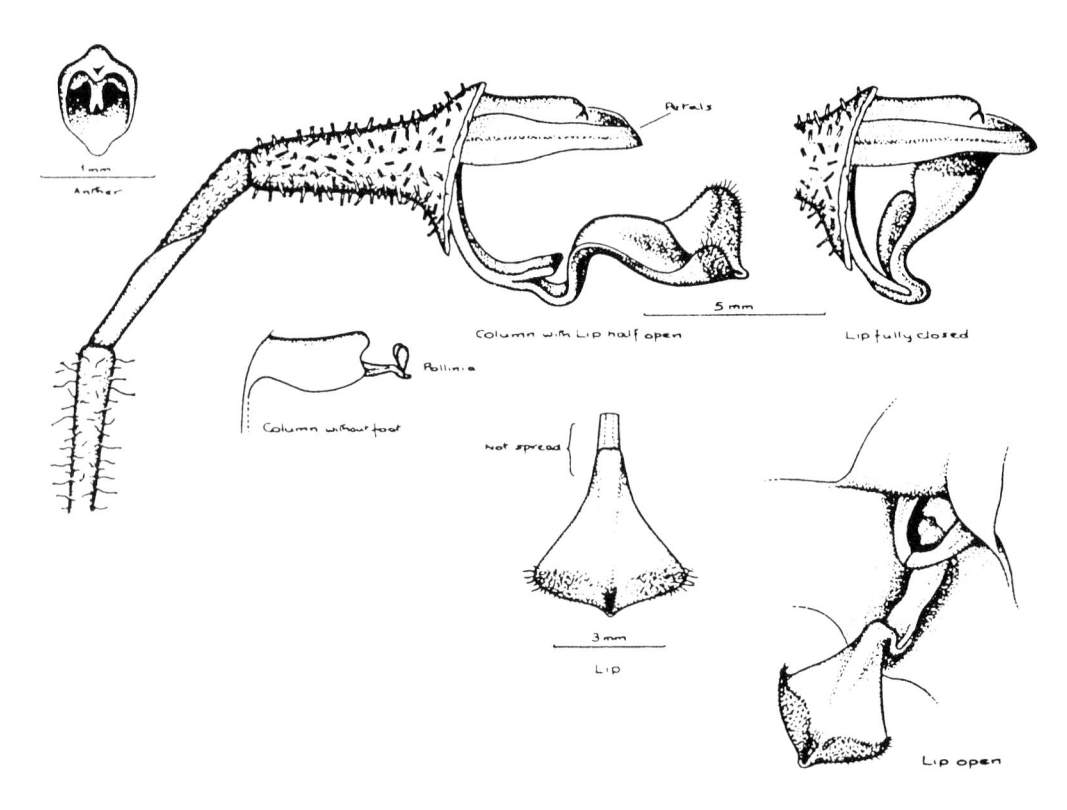

Fig 2. Column and hinged lip of **Porroglossum echidnum** from Venezuela. When a visiting insect touches the hinge/trigger, the lip snaps shut, trapping the potential pollinator. The only way out is past the stigma (where the insect deposits any pollinia from other flowers) and then the viscidium (where it picks up new pollinia.)

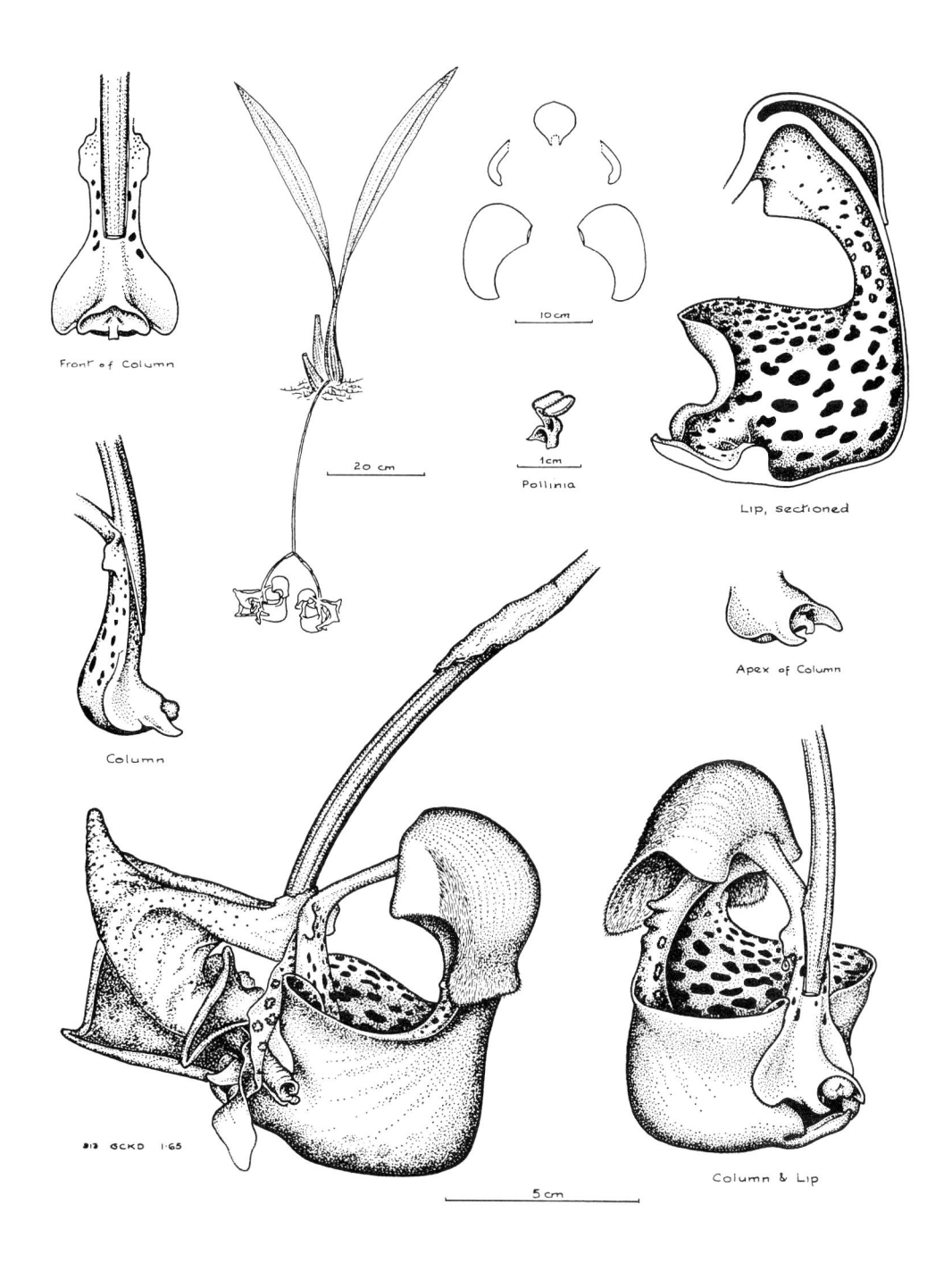

Fig. 3. Coryanthes biflora Barb. Rodr., Gen. et Sp. Orch. Nov. 1:103, 1877. — A.

Orchids of Venezuela[1, 2]

IN RECENT YEARS, Venezuela has grown from little more than a name on the map to one of the most up-and-coming of the South American nations, a country of very real importance in the world pattern of commerce and industry. A liberal attitude towards free enterprise and progressive government, backed by the generosity of nature, has made her, among other things, the largest exporter of oil in the world (nearly three million barrels a day) and a most important source of high-grade iron ore. However, while nature has equally blessed this country from the point of view of an orchidist — it is well known as the home of the *Cattleya mossiae,* foundation of so many valuable hybrids — investigation of her very prolific orchid flora has lagged and the available literature is very scanty indeed. The day is therefore ripe for Venezuela to be properly put on the orchid map, and it is hoped that the present paper will stimulate the interest of amateurs and professionals to this end.

Geographically, Venezuela occupies the central and eastern part of the north end of the continent of South America, lying between the parallels of 1° and 12° north of the equator, and covering an area about four times as large as the United Kingdom or 40% bigger than the state of Texas. Topography and climate cover a wide range from the heat of the Atlantic and Caribbean coasts to the cold of the eternal snows crowning the high Andes that reach to 16,500 feet; from the vast inland plains of the Llanos to great areas of floating forest covering the swamps at the mouth of the Orinoco; from sand-dune deserts to the high forests and dramatic tableland area of the Gran Sabana, inspiration of the "Lost World" fantasy of Conan Doyle and home of the stupendous three-thousand-foot leap of Angel Falls.

In the west, Venezuela shares with Colombia in the orchid-rich flora of the Andean ranges, a section of which sweeps north and northeast to surround Lake Maracaibo and then continues fitfully eastward along the coast to die out finally in Trinidad. In the southeast, again, Venezuela shares in the rich orchid flora of her neighbors, British Guiana and northern Brazil. The wonder, then, is not that Venezuela should, for her size, be so rich in orchid territory, but that so little has yet been studied and published on her orchids compared with those of Colombia and Brazil.

Excluding for the moment the mountain areas, where height above sea-level is the dominant factor governing the climate, the rainfall characteristics of the country from sea-level to around a thousand feet in elevation can be broadly expressed (*see map*) as follows. A wide central belt of moderate rainfall with marked dry season extends along the Orinoco and to the north to a width of some 150 miles. This band, which roughly corresponds to the Llanos, separates the country into two parts. On the part ly-

Map of Venezuela showing rainfall and climate.

[1] Originally appeared in *A. O. S. Bulletin,* Vol. 28, April 1959, Pages 272-277

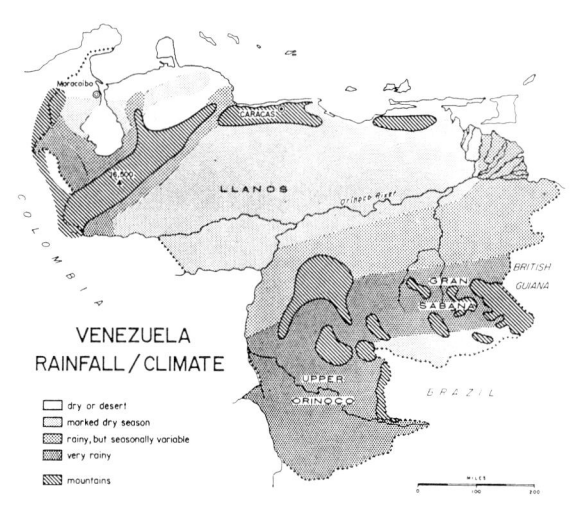

[2] Reprinted by permission from the "Proceedings of the Second World Orchid Conference," Cambridge, Mass., 1958

ing to the north and northwest of it, the westernmost end up against the Colombian border is rainy almost all the year 'round and is consequently an area of forest and swamp. This wet area grades north and northwest through regions of fair rainfall with seasonal fluctuations to areas of strong dry season and finally to sea-level coastal areas where there is very restricted rainfall, or even desert. South of the Llanos belt, which in effect means south of the Orinoco, the dry season conditions get progressively less severe and a rainy belt of seasonal fluctuation leads to a great expanse of forest which never has a real dry season, even though little of it can be classed as true rain forest. Squeezed between this region and the Brazilian border is again a patch where "seasons" intrude. The map shows hard lines between these areas but the transition from one zone to another is naturally gradual in most places and the whole pattern has, of course, been greatly simplified.

Superimposed on this low territory climate are the mountain climates where belts of cloud forest tend to develop from 3,000' to 10,000' altitude in the Andean and coastal range areas and on the summits of the "tepuis" or table-lands of the Gran Sabana, with some areas of greater cold, with cold rains or even snow, in the higher Andes of the west where heights exceed 10,000 feet.

In this range of climate and temperature, there is a home for every kind of tropical orchid. The most recent collation of data, a review made in 1953 by E. Foldats of the Caracas Botanical Institute, shows a total of 770 species divided among 107 genera, but there is little doubt that as search continues this total will reach 1,000 species. In the writer's own searches in the last few years, backed by identification by Leslie Garay[3] of Toronto University, about 80 out of some 350 species encountered have proven to be additions to the Foldats' list, and six previously unlisted genera have been picked up, namely *Barbosella, Bollea, Dipteranthus, Orleanesia, Platystele,* and *Scuticaria*. None of this is surprising in view of the geographic and climatic advantages enjoyed by Venezuela, but it is illustrative of the degree to which Venezuela's orchid wealth remains still largely unexplored in detail.

In common with her neighbors, Venezuela's most prolific genera (in terms of number of species in the Foldats' list) are:

Epidendrum	around 125 species
Pleurothallis	around 85 species
Oncidium	around 50 species
Stelis	around 40 species
Maxillaria	around 35 species

(Real numbers are probably some 50% higher than the figures quoted.)

Horticulturally, the most important genus is undoubtedly *Cattleya*. The National Flower, *Cattleya mossiae*, has already been mentioned, and although past and even present depredations are steadily stripping this magnificent flower from the forest of the coastal ranges, it is still to be found in some regions in fair abundance. *Cattleya gaskelliana, C. percivaliana*, and *C. lueddemanniana* are other well-known Venezuelan *Cattleya* species (or, if you prefer it, varieties of the *C. labiata* group), and one of the most wonderful wildflower sights is surely a great clump of any one of these orchids in

The Gran Sabana skyline, showing three tepuis, with Roraima on the right.

[3] Now past Curator of the Ames Orchid Herbarium at Harvard University.

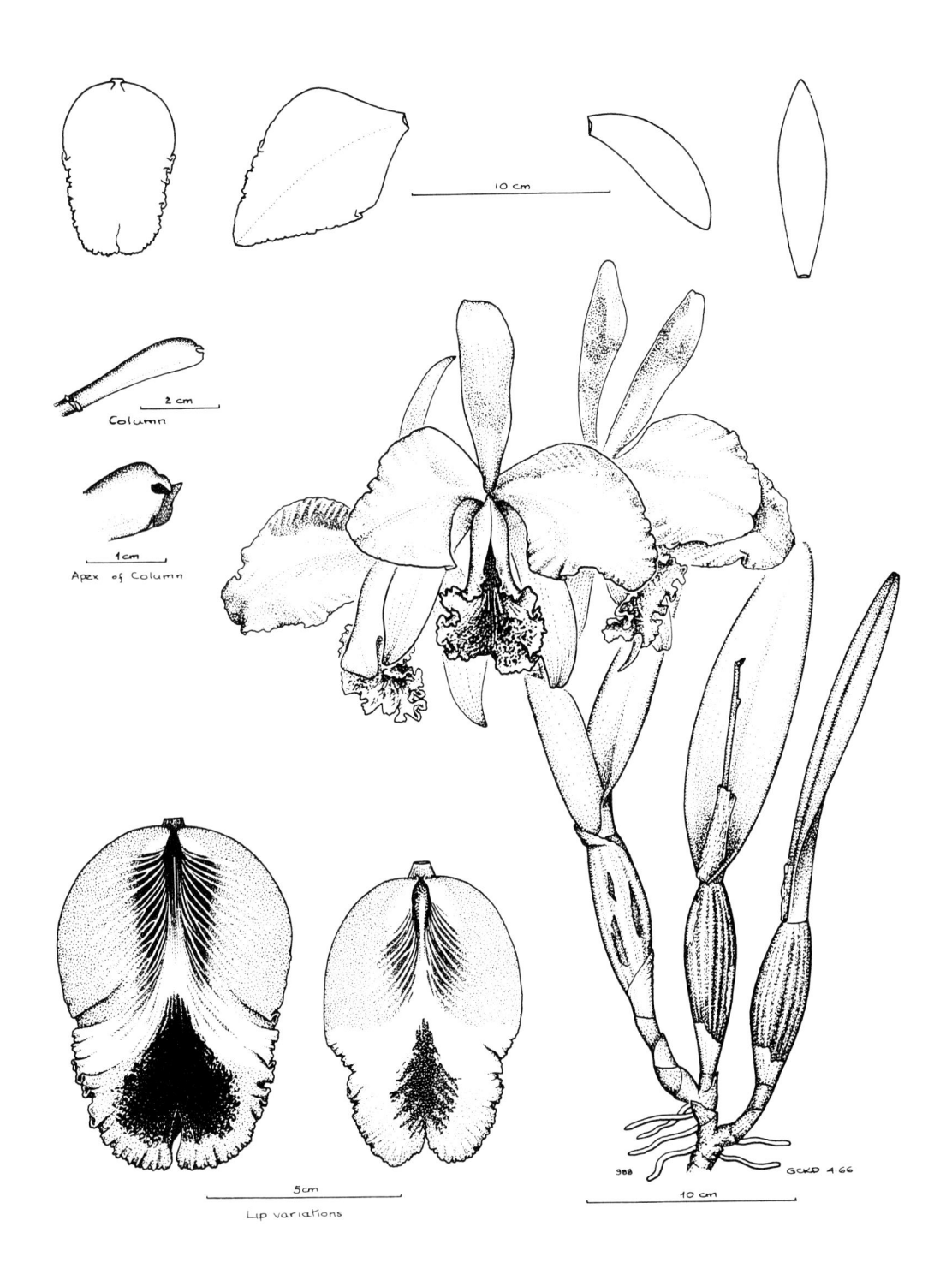

Cattleya mossiae Hook. in Bot. Mag. 65: t. 3669, 1838. — B.

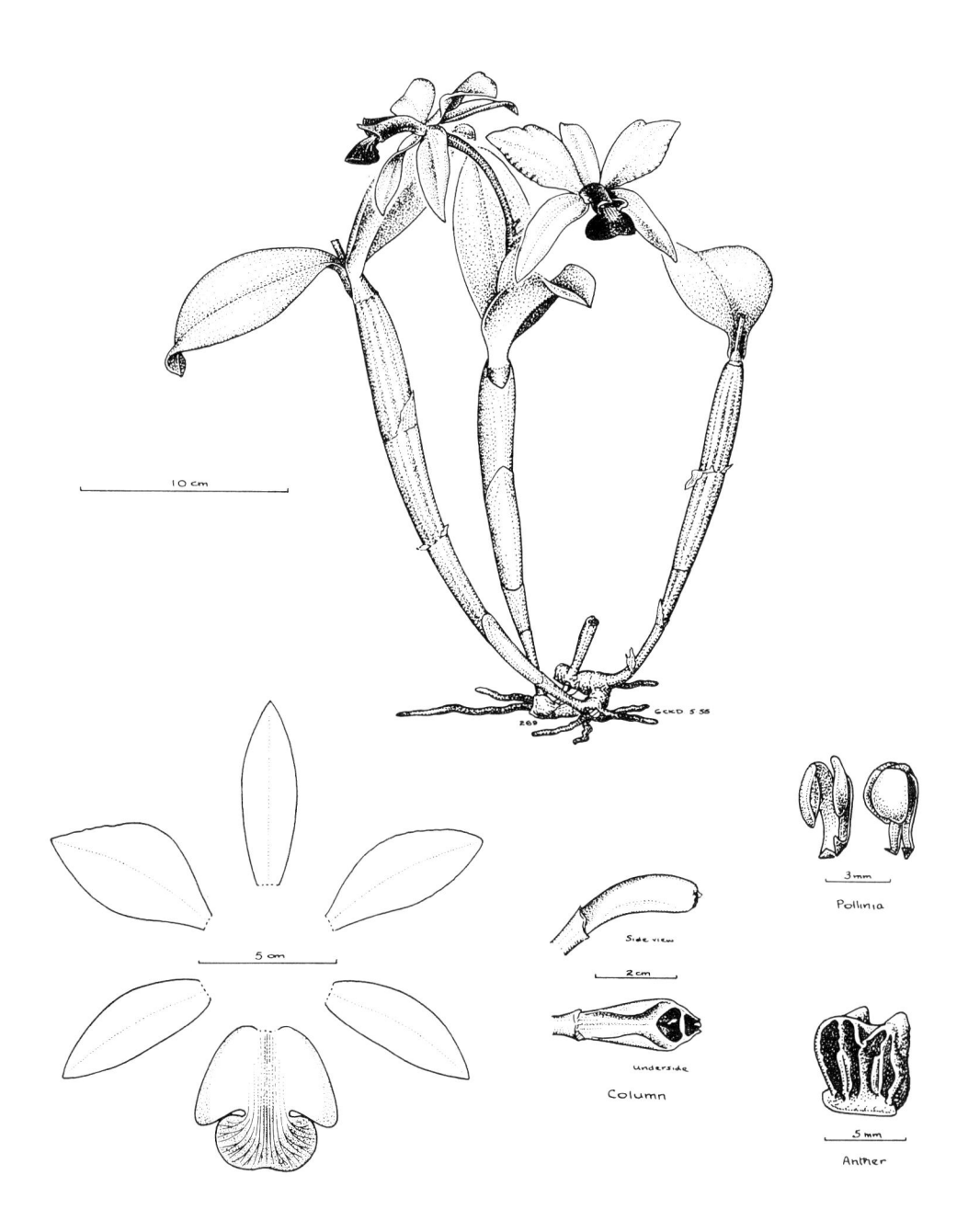

Cattleya violacea (H.B.K.) Rolfe in Gard. Chron. ser. 3, 5:802, 1889 — D.E.

full bloom way up high on the bare trunk or on a broad branch of a giant tree. Of the other Cattleyas, *C. patini, C. violacea (C. superba)* and *C. lawrenceana* are worthy of mention. The first of this trio is now very hard to find but the other two grow profusely, if in a somewhat limited area, in the "interior" south of the Orinoco. The exhibition for the first time of a white variety of *C. violacea* was the highlight of the 1957 Orchid Show in Caracas.

Another horticulturally coveted species is *Catasetum pileatum* which is still to be found, though with difficulty, in the region of the upper Orinoco and which comes in a whole gamut of varieties including some with very handsome purple-spotted flowers. *Cycnoches chlorochilon, C. maculatum,* and *C. loddigesii* are other interesting plants, the first-named being quite common. *Oncidium lanceanum*, with its strikingly colored flowers, is another prize but occurs only sparsely in the east and southeast of the country.

To the enthusiast, however, highly rewarding treasures are also to be found among some of the less spectacular species. "Minor" catasetums abound, such as *C. callosum, C. macrocarpum, and C.* × *splendens* (a natural hybrid) and in fact the whole *Catasetum* genus offers ground for a most interesting study since in its natural habitat the occurrence of female and various types of hermaphrodite flowers is common (sometimes all three types on one inflorescence)...so much so that it is a frequent complaint of those growing catasetums locally that the dull female flowers *will* keep cropping up in place of the much prettier male flowers. In the forest numerous yellow spray oncidiums can be found, such as *O. volvox* or *O. obryzatum,* along with many other epiphytes of interest, such as *Oncidium papilio, Epidendrum ciliare* and *E. atropurpureum* [now known as *Encyclia cordigera*], *Acineta superba, Gongora maculata, Stanhopea wardii, Masdevallia tovarensis,* and *Paphinia cristata.*

Terrestrials, which probably account for some 10% of all Venezuelan orchids, are frequently of the rather uninteresting *Habenaria, Spiranthes,* or similar genera, but such items as *Cyrtopodium cristatum, Bletia purpurea,* or *Cleistes rosea* add welcome color.

But to the really dyed-in-the-wool lover of orchid species, there are even greater delights to be found in the hundreds of smaller and often lesser-known (if not even sometimes despised) botanicals, many of which have very great beauty to make up for lack of size. *Hexisea bidentata,* for example, is an exciting and beautiful thing to find in the wild when in full bloom and there is a great wealth of other handsome plants such as *Maxillaria spilotantha* or *M. triloris, Rodriguezia secunda, Comparettia falcata,* to name but a few.

Going further down the scale of size, the miniature oncidiums such as *Psygmorchis pusilla* or the even smaller *Psygmorchis glossomystax* are sweet enough to charm the heart of even the hardest of hybrid horticulturists, while for those who have microscopes the miniature-miniatures of the Pleurothallidinae are an eternal fascination. Principally these rest in the genera *Stelis* and *Pleurothallis,* a number of which are also quite large, but lesser known genera such as *Lepanthes* and *Platystele* are strong competitors in interest if not in number of species. Of all the species in the writer's collection, the one from which he would find it hardest to part (were it not for the fact that he thinks he can find more of them) is *Platystele ornata,* which carries a spray of up to a dozen beautifully formed bright purple flowers. The entire plant fits easily into a thimble and the whole spray does not exceed a quarter inch in length, a perfect corsage for a bee.

It must be frankly confessed that this paper, which is written neither by a botanist nor a horticulturist but by a plain out-and-out amateur enthusiast with botanical leanings, has as its aim not only to draw some needed attention to Venezuela as an orchid country but to try to recruit more members yet to the growing numbers of people truly interested in orchid species. As many can attest, the orchid bug is a strange animal: its bite is gentle and subtle but the effects are cumulative and last a lifetime. Those so bitten who are lucky enough to live where orchids grow are most happily placed, as a whole new world of interest in their surroundings is opened up. Venezuela is *par excellence* such a place, as the rapidity of its recent development provides reasonable access to even the most distant and still virgin regions; the many new roads being constructed means the felling of many trees, bringing to the collector's hand many orchids that otherwise would remain tantalizingly far out of reach; and as background to it all is the fundamental richness of the local orchid life. Within a few hours by excellent road from Caracas can be found untouched forest inhabited only by howler monkeys and "tigres," where a single large tree will generally hold on its trunk and branches at least 10 and often as many as 20 or more different species. Within a few hours by plane one can reach areas of mountain, river and forest, spectacularly beautiful and so virgin as to be uninhabited. All this hinterland is crying out for intense exploration of detail, in a field where the serious amateur can not only have the time of his life practicing his most fascinating pastime, but also, in the process, can add his little bit to the common pot of knowledge and the final collation of all orchids of the country.

Rain Forest, Cloud Forest, and Jungle (?) in Venezuela[1]

IN THE PREFACE to his famous book *High Jungle* of 1949, describing zoological rather than botanical aspects of the Venezuelan Central Range forests, William Beebe explains that his use of the word "jungle" was intentional "as a convenient way of defining dense tree growths within the tropical zone. Such words as 'woods' and 'forests' seem appropriate to the more temperate regions. It is not my fault if jungle has become synonymous with low malarial growths, infested with ferocious mammals, noxious reptiles and ferocious insects. To us, as naturalists jungle is an epitome of beauty, comfort and intense scientific interest."

Which is where we part company, if only semantically, with Dr. Beebe. Our *Encyclopaedia Britannica* says — "Jungle; an Anglo-Indian term for a forest, a tangled wilderness. The Hindustani word *jangal* means waste, cultivated ground which tends to become covered with trees or long grass." So we feel that it is Beebe's fault if he considers jungles to be beautiful and comfortable. For us, despite the occasional use here of the "Spanglish" word *"jungla"* to denote "forest," the English word "jungle" applies only to the Old World phenomenon, romantic to read about in Kipling's "Mowgli" books, but probably filled with all the horrible things mentioned by Beebe, plus man-eating tigers or lions or even elephants running amok.

By contrast, in the New World we have *"selvas siempreverdes,"* or evergreen forests, which may not be comfortable but are filled with nice things like sloths and armadillos and kinkajous, and minor cats such as jaguars (known here as *"tigres"*), ocelots and pumas (known here as *"leones"*). And if you have to talk about snakes, what about our *"Reinita"* (*Leimadolphus zweifeli*) or our *"Sabanera"* (*L. melanotus)*, which the book says "are characterized by their good nature, ready to establish a certain degree of friendliness with man — one of the most inoffensive of snakes, they never try to bite and can be very useful as domestic pets for the children." Our domestic cats have unfortunately not heard about this, so our sitting room floor tends at times to be strewn with the corpses of dead but quite innocent baby snakes, whose duty in life would have been to eat the poisonous ones!

Ranging from sea level to the tree line at about 3,300 m (10,000 feet), Venezuela provides a home for many types of evergreen forest such as "riverine forest," "gallery forest," "rain forest," "tropical rain forest," "subtropical rain forest," "cloud forest," "montane forest," "montane rain forest," "lower montane rain forest," "subAndean rain forest;" you name it, we have it, provided only that you don't ask for "monsoon forest" as we have no monsoons in this hemisphere. But we do have what are called *"selvas alisias"*, or "trade wind forests", to make up. It is, however, one thing to name these types of forest and quite another to explain what these names mean or actually describe the forest types themselves. This should be the task of professional ecologists, but alas!, for reasons explained below, this does not seem to be feasible; hence our present effort to fill at least a part of the gap as best we can.

Probably the forest name most heard in discussing orchid habitats is the name "rain forest," a term invented by the botanist A.F.W. Schimper in 1903, when he gave it this brief description: "Evergreen, hygrophilous in character, at least 30 m high but usually much taller, rich in thick-stemmed lianas and in woody as well as herbaceous epiphytes." According to P.W. Richards in his excellent book *The Tropical Rain Forest*, "this definition fits the concept of tropical rain forest as used by most writers since Schimper, but in the narrower sense this term would be reserved for the

[1] Originally appeared in *A.O.S. Bulletin*, Vol. 52, October 1983, pages 1067-1072

almost completely non-seasonal forest with a very evenly distributed rainfall." We personally favor this narrower meaning, if only to avoid confusion with the many quite different "montane" types of forest, and particularly to maintain "cloud forest" as a concept entirely distinct from low-altitude "rain forest."

In truth, there is absolutely no consensus as to what is meant by the term "rain forest," a fact that is dramatically illustrated in an article by the Venezuelan ecologist, Volkmar Vareschi, in the Caracas *A.T. Botanica* of December 1968, in which he shows a series of small outline maps of Venezuela, illustrating what various important botanical authors consider, or have considered in the past, to be the limits of "rain forest" in this country. For the sake of simplicity we show here only the two most extreme of these maps:

Map Number 1, showing some 65% of the country covered by rain forest, is based on data of Schimper-Faber of 1935; Map Number 2, showing no rain forest at all, is based on data from Holdridge of 1966.

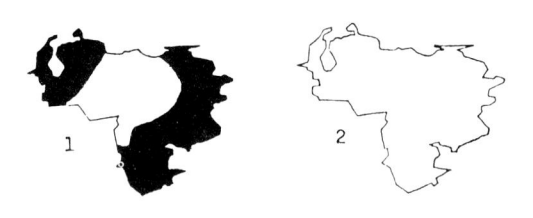

This does not mean that these specialists do not know what they are talking about, but does highlight the fact that there is no agreement in the botanical world as to what the term "rain forest" really means or how it should be defined, as this makes the general use of this term really rather meaningless!

In his book, Richards says, "The term Tropical Rain Forest has a fatal tendency to produce rhetorical exuberance in those who describe it. Few writers on the rain forest seem able to resist the temptation of the purple passage, and in the rush of superlatives are apt to describe things they never saw or misrepresent what was really there." As a result, it is scarcely surprising if the popular idea of a tropical rain forest is likely to be very far from the truth. By contrast, the forest ecologist's view will be free of false ideas, but, on the other hand, will seldom, it seems, agree with the definition given by another ecologist.

This lack of agreement is not really surprising when bearing in mind the extremely wide range of soil, climate, and altitude where forests exist in the tropics, and the fantastically rich variety and high volume of plant life in many such places. Where a given area of forest in temperate countries might contain a hundred species of plants, the same area in the tropics is likely to contain five times as many.

Obviously, under these conditions, a great variety of forest "types" can be defined and named, and this in turn leads to a great variety of expert opinion as to which of these types fall, or do not fall, within the scope of the words "rain forest." If an expert takes these words in the highly restrictive sense of an almost completely non-seasonal, low-altitude forest with extremely evenly distributed rainfall, he will probably consider that rain forests exist only in certain very limited parts of Africa, the Far East, or the heart of the Amazon Basin, and, like Holdridge, will paint no part of his map of Venezuela in black. By contract, the expert who paints more than half his map black, like Schimper-Faber, will be using the term "rain forest" in a very wide sense indeed, including in it much forest that is seasonal or only semi-evergreen, and, at the other extreme, will include large areas of high-altitude forest right up to the tree line.

As the start of this article we listed a dozen names for various types of evergreen forest in Venezuela, types whose definitions have seldom been clear to us but whose names we have seen in published works on the subject. We have no intention of getting involved in attempts to provide our own descriptions of all these forest types, if only because of our gross ignorance of the matter, but we do feel it important to make a clear distinction, amateur though it may be, between "rain forest" and "cloud forest." Our ideas on what is rain forest and what is cloud forest are outlined below.

Rain Forests

In Venezuela, these appear to be limited entirely to the Federal Amazonas Territory in the far south of the country, at the headwaters of the Orinoco and the Río Negro, which are interconnected by the Río Casiquiare. They are all low-altitude, hot forests on mainly flat terrain, frequently bearing many tall trees whose tops tend to exclude most direct sunlight from the forest floor, and, as there is also very restricted air movement inside the forest, there is a general absence of undergrowth apart from saplings. As we have once said elsewhere, the interior of such a forest is dark, damp, dismal, dripping, definitely depressing and devoid of orchids except in the tops of the trees where they are inaccessible. The trees themselves are usually straight and relatively slender, unbranched until near the top, and the base commonly provided with flange-like buttresses. Richards remarks in his book that the dimensions reached by trees in a rain forest have sometimes been exaggerated, the average height of the taller trees being rarely more than

150-180 feet. While trees over 200 feet have been reliably recorded, they never reach the gigantic dimensions of the California redwoods (*Sequoia sempervirens*, 360 feet) or the giant eucalyptus of Australia (*Eucalyptus regnans*, 350 feet).

The general climate of the rain forest is essentially non-seasonal, the average rainfall is high, and due to the almost negligible drop in elevation over the long distance between the forest and the sea, the runoff is slow and the forests are often flooded for long periods.

These forests are normally quite easy to get around in once one is away from the river banks where there is frequently a very dense and almost impenetrable barrier of tangled undergrowth and creepers. As stated by Richards, "in the interior of an old and undisturbed forest it is usually possible to see another person at least 20 feet away, and a cutlass is needed more to mark a path than to hack one's way." While there may not be danger from animals, apart from the ubiquitous snakes, this ease of movement does in itself present a risk because of the chance of failing to mark a path as one goes. With no slope to the terrain to guide one, and the sun seldom visible, one can lose one's way very quickly in a moment of inattention, when finding the trail again could be extremely difficult. Moreover, these forests are usually in "white water" areas so there will be no lack of painful flying pests to be dealt with, not forgetting the clouds of small non-biting flies that can create intense and immediate personal panic by crowding into one's ears or nose at most inconvenient moments.

In other words, therefore, one's orchid hunting in rain forest terrain is basically limited to the banks of rivers or forest streams. This does not mean that on a longish trip, with many stops at such places, one must return empty-handed. On one such trip, covering 600 km (400 miles) of the Upper Orinoco, we collected well over 100 species (unfortunately many not in flower and thus hard to identify with certainty), but none of these came from truly wet rain-forest conditions. However, a number of plants were very useful additions to our collections for botanical study, even if few of them could enjoy the change to our Caracas climate. Among such species we could name *Acacallis cyanea, Aspasia variegata, Bifrenaria longicornis, Cattleya violacea, Epidendrum ottonis, Galeandra stangeana, Lockhartia imbricata, Maxillaria violaceopunctata, Oncidium cebolleta, Psygmorchis glossomystax, Rodriguezia secunda, Scaphyglottis amethystina, Trigonidium acuminatum,* and *Zygosepalum lindeniae.*

Cloud Forests

Cloud forest is a very special part of the general evergreen montane forest complex that inhabits

Typical cloud-forest vegetation in Rancho Grande National Park near Caracas.

hilly or even mountainous country in most parts of Venezuela, a very extensive habitat indeed, as broadly speaking it covers nearly all the higher ground in Venezuela with the exception of cultivated and built-over parts, swampy ground, and the bare-rock tops of the great sandstone massifs of the Guayana and Amazonas regions. This general montane forest would, in our classification, include the limited amounts of fine forest that still survive in the Venezuelan Andes despite years of deforestation in the past, an activity that continues to make severe inroads into the remaining forests as the peasants continue to clear ground for cultivation and their cattle.

Mixed in with these generalized montane forests, cloud forests occur like plums in a plum cake. The size and quality of each plum can be extremely variable, depending on such localized factors as variation in soil, the lie of the land relative to local and prevailing winds, the steepness of slopes, actual altitude and so on. But essentially, these plums, large or small, occur where the topography and winds are sure that warm, moisture-laden air is forced rapidly up to cooler land and thus forms ground-hugging cloud and mist.

When we were young, or at least quite a bit younger than we are now, and were planning a move from an oil-based business life to an orchid-based retirement one, we searched for, and found, a suitable piece of ground on which to build a house. The requisites were that it should be close enough to Caracas not to lose all contact with doctors and dentists and old friends, but far enough to have few immediate neighbors and lots of peace and clean air. And cheap enough that we could buy plenty of space for house and future orchid shelters. And, of course, with adequate "facilities." In due course we found what we wanted (at a price about a twentieth of its present value) on a steep-sided ridge dipping gently to the east. Road access was tolerable and a power line was nearby, so we bought about two acres and built the house, despite a water supply that was initially so erratic that we had to buy frequent tank-truck loads to fill the house tanks; and it was 10 years before we got a much-needed telephone.

When we moved into the new house we congratulated ourselves on our good choice, and now, more than 20 years later, it is still a haven of peace and clean air while Caracas city has become a conglomeration of traffic and high-rise apartment buildings amid noise and air pollution. But our luck was better than for some considerable time we realized. One attraction to the site was that it adjoins a small remnant of natural forest that covers about 500 acres, of which a tiny bit falls within our boundary. At that time we imagined all tropical forest was called rain forest, so we had no idea we had acquired a piece of genuine cloud forest, nor did we have any real idea of what cloud forest was. Only later did we realize that its presence implied that we would be enjoying a climate very different from the general climate around us, and vastly more desirable.

At our altitude of about 1,300 m. (4,300 feet) (Caracas valley floor is some 300 m., 1,000 feet, lower), the countryside is mostly open, treeless and steeply hilly, and has a marked dry season that lasts, almost without any rain, from early January to late March; or in "dry" years from mid-November to mid-June, putting considerable strain on the city water supply and the tempers of its inhabitants. Yet the piece of steep hillside that bears our little forest (known as the "*Selva de la Virgen*") has a climate, almost throughout the year, of night and early-morning mists, or at times quite wet fogs, that are extremely localized. Approaching our home from the "village" El Hatillo some 120 m (400 feet) lower, we can see very clearly that in the early morning our ridge is actually hidden in the base of a cloud. The result is that the forest, whose humidity is further maintained by rains in the rainy season, is always cool and damp, and our immediately adjoining open grounds, where we keep most of our orchids, also benefit, though naturally in minor degree. This contrast with our relatively dry surroundings is strongly accentuated when the usual dry-season grass fires get going in our district, and ashes rain down on us to make a mess of our just-washed laundry hanging on the line, while at the same time we can see, and even hear, the condensed moisture dripping from the leaves of our mist-shrouded forest.

Dr. Beebe to the contrary, we are quite sure that our "virgin" forest is neither jungle nor even rain forest. The rains are most decidedly seasonal, and the total volume (perhaps 35 to 45 inches per year) is not great. Quite definitely it is cloud forest, and as such is enjoyed by the 20 or so epiphytic orchids growing there, including *Stanhopea wardii*, *Oncidium volvox*, *Oncidium zebrinum*, *Epidendrum recurvatum*, and *Pleurothallis chamensis*. Among an equal number of terrestrials (many of them *Habenaria* species) we have found the quite rare *Galeandra beyrichii*.

Our forest trees are not very tall (to about 60 feet) and branch from quite low down but have uncrowded and well-aerated crowns. The forest floor is very steep as it forms the flank of a fairly deep ravine (here known as a "*quebrada*"), and as the undergrowth is quite dense, the terrain is not by any means easy to get around in — the more so as we have made few paths, so as to avoid disturbance to the forest by visitors. The trees themselves mostly bear a fair load of often very decorative aroid creepers, bromeliads with long, tough, dangling roots reaching down to the soil, and many other epiphytes (including several families of sloths!). Mostly these do no great harm to the trees, but we note an increasing amount of parasitic plants of the mistletoe type, and these we do not welcome, not even at Christmas. The light inside the forest is mostly quite adequate and includes some direct insolation, but in misty hours it is subdued and the view, looking straight out from the steeply sloping forest floors, reveals only the outlines of the trees and their epiphytic burdens silhouetted against the light outside.

One can never afford to be dogmatic about exactly which is what and where when trying to define forest types, and we do not want to produce too rigid an idea of what, in our view, constitutes real cloud forest; there are many places where it exists in a form less clearly marked than in our "virgin" piece. There is a large area, for example, on the slopes of the Caroní Basin in the Guayana area, leading down from the north end of the Gran Sabana, and there are fine cloud forests in parts of the National Park of Guatopo east of Caracas, or of the National Parks of Yacambu or Terepaima not far to the west of the city.

As already mentioned, however, cloud forests grow where warm, moisture-laden air rises rapidly to cooler heights, and this is very much the case where steep slopes rise straight from the sea along the north coast of the Coastal Range. As one drives along the road to the west of Caracas, running parallel to and to the south of the dry, south flank of this range, one can nearly always see clouds spilling over the top of the ridge from the seaward side on the north, and this is nowhere better exemplified than at the Portachuelo Pass where the Rancho Grande building is located that Beebe used for his studies of the region. In fact, Beebe's own map of this locality in his book marks the crest of the ridge as bearing cloud forest, and makes no mention of jungle! Here, and on similar places along the whole length of the ridge, the cloud forest reaches maximum development, with much larger and taller trees than in our virgin's forest and with yet more magnificent development of undergrowth and aerial plants. Close to Caracas, the Coastal Range rises to a culmination about 3,300 m (10,000 feet) high, and the cloud forest on its seaward side rises to over 2,100 m (7,000 feet).

But high or low, in big plums or little ones, the character of the forest remains the same, and we are very fond of our own little piece.

As for the orchids of this Rancho Grande-Caracas coastal area, neither our readers nor the editors would thank us for a mere catalog of the species to be found there. Suffice it to say that in genera alone we have seen at least 30, and that the species range from enchanting miniatures such as *Dipteranthus obliquus,* through relative rarities like *Houlletia tigrina* or *Masdevallia verecunda* and pot-size items such as *Brassia keiliana* or *Gongora quinquenervis,* and so on up to the king (or queen?) of them all — Venezuela's national flower, *Cattleya mossiae.*

This very famous species grows in other parts of northern Venezuela and is understood to grow also in high, sea-facing cloudy slopes in the Avila Range above Caracas. In recent years, however, it seems to have been found only in the drier, south-facing slopes where the forests that still exist are not what we would ourselves call true cloud forest.

Orchids of Caracas[1]

FROM VERY EARLY DAYS in the history of cultivated orchids, Venezuela has enjoyed a well-merited reputation as one of the orchid-rich countries of the American tropics. Much of this fame rests, naturally, on the showy cattleyas with which it is endowed: *Cattleya mossiae, C. gaskelliana, C. lueddemanniana* (syn. *C. speciosissima), C. percivaliana, C. lawrenceana,* and *C. violacea* (or *C. superba,* as most Venezuelans, following instinct rather than international rules, prefer to call it). *Cattleya labiata,* recently located in the far southeastern corner of the country, and the rather disappointing *C. patini,* round out the list of Venezuelan cattleyas but do not enter into the list of those that put Venezuelan orchids on the map.

Without by any means making the claim that Venezuela is richer than all her neighbors in orchids, it is still true that despite intense stripping in the past, and despite the modern wave of ax and fire, it is still a treasure house for the orchid lover, and in particular for the *orquidiota* who can see beauty and excitement in the smaller "botanicals" and miniatures as well as in the larger commercial species. This wealth in orchids does not imply that as you drive swiftly (or even slowly) along Venezuela's excellent roads you will see orchids dripping from the trees, as some visitors seem to expect. Before the coming of the automobile, transportation speeds were more in line with ability to spot orchids while on the move; nevertheless, it is probably true that even in those days the finding of orchids still called for positive searching as distinct from mere looking, and that only in very few places would "dripping from trees by the roadside" have been more than imaginative fiction.

A question much in the minds of orchid lovers today is the possible extermination of certain orchid species by cement and asphalt, fire and ax, as well as by the commercial stripping that still goes on here and there or (in temperate climates) the depredations of the wildflower-picking public. When dealing with tropical orchids, and particularly those of the tropical forests, so many hundreds of square miles remain that have been at best only skimpily explored that it is rare indeed that one can point to a certain orchid and say that it is on the point of extermination. The very most one can say is that where it has previously been recorded it is now absent, or that if it was once prolific it is now rare.

With a view to studying the impact of asphalt and concrete on a small but once prolific zone, we have made as good an investigation as we can of the Caracas area. Caracas was for many years one of the magic names in the orchid trade and many orchid plants reached European growers and botanists with "Caracas" as their label. The present study is an attempt to see what now remains of the original Caracas orchid life. Unfortunately, no precise or even half-precise comparison can be made with the past, as the old records of where Caracas plants were found are, not unnaturally, much too vague to fit into any exact boundaries. An orchid with the general label of "neighborhood of Caracas" could have come from anywhere within 30 miles or more, or in the case of a commercial plant, perhaps have acquired the label only because Caracas was the shipping port for a trip to Europe that had begun far in the interior. Similarly, "above Caracas" could signify anything from the level of the valley at 3,000 feet to the top of the local mountains at 10,000 feet. All that now seems possible to do is to list the orchids that remain in Caracas and to note those that are entering the "very scarce" phase. For this purpose we have taken for the limits of modern Caracas a broadly sweeping line that encloses the present city, along with its outliers and suburbs. This constitutes an

---

[1] Originally appeared in *A.O.S. Bulletin,* Vol. 38, June 1969, pages 493-496

area about 13 miles from east to west, with a fairly straight northern boundary following the fire break at the foot of the steeply rising flank of the main Avila ridge, and with a rather irregular southern boundary. The extreme east and west ends are relatively narrow, and the maximum width about eight miles, giving a total area of roughly 100 square miles. There are indications from past records that as many as 160 species of orchids once inhabited this area, which is not surprising, as even 50 years ago 90 percent was field or forest. What is surprising is that despite the almost explosive spread of construction inside the area in recent years, and despite the very frequent fires that have swept much of the area not actually taken up by development, it has still been possible for us to locate as many as 87 orchid species still existing, albeit tenuously, within the area. Thanks to identifications very kindly made by Dr. Leslie A. Garay, Curator of the famous Oakes Ames Orchid Herbarium, we have been able to put names to all these species and a list of them is appended. It is, of course, very probable that quite a few more species are lurking in hidden corners, so the list is by no means final. To show how easy it is to miss things, some five years ago we found a small epidendrum a long way west of Caracas. This epidendrum was studied by Dr. Garay and proved to be a species new to science, receiving the name of *Epidendrum deltoglossum* when published in *Venezuelan Orchids Illustrated,* Volume IV. Quite recently, an enthusiastic orchid-hunting friend, Mr. W. Rodríguez, came upon far more prolific growths of this same species within the defined area, in some forest only a few hundred yards from our own Caracas home!

The Caracas area divides into two fairly distinct zones:—
1) The floor of the valley, at about 3,000 feet, in which the bulk of the city lies. This is relatively flat and has a number of fingers stretching alongside valleys that lead into the southern hills.
2) Higher and often steeply sloping ground, mainly along the southern boundary where it reaches a height of about 4,500 feet, and a very narrow strip along the northern edge. Part of this area is already urbanized and in much of the remainder bulldozers are busy shaping new hillside residential zones for present and future expansion.

As far as the first of these two areas is concerned, it is scarcely an exaggeration to say that it is now entirely overlaid by concrete and asphalt and its original orchid life finished. Here and there a lone tree, in what was a large verdant patch no more than 20 years ago, still remains to serve as a host for a scattering of orchid plants, but these scatterings are every day thinner and the trees themselves every day fewer. A very few of these trees and plants may linger for a great while yet, but it is not far from the truth to say that the valley floor is now finished as an orchid habitat. Pressure for housing, and the commercial incentives that go with it, have completely outstripped any measures there might have been to conserve enclaves of "wild" trees and greenery within the area. Zones until recently covered with large trees and dense vegetation have been turned into residential areas under boastful advertising slogans such as "The Pride of Humboldt." These now lie bare of all trees except the few "educated" ones being regrown along the avenues and in the gardens of the new houses. Many of the more appreciated orchids of Caracas grew originally in this valley-floor area, shunning the cooler slopes above, and these are now quite definitely condemned even if a few specimens may still survive for awhile. Principal among these are *Epidendrum atropurpureum, Epidendrum chacaoense* [now known as *Encyclia cordigera* and *Encyclia chacaoensis,* respectively,] *Epidendrum diurnum* [*Encyclia diurna*], *Epidendrum ceratistes,* [*Encyclia ceratistes,*] *Epidendrum ciliare, Cycnoches chlorochilon, Catasetum macrocarpum, Oncidium cebolleta,* and *Schomburgkia undulata.*

Rising from the valley floor to the second zone outlined above, the picture is happier. Despite the bulldozer, appreciable untouched areas still remain, principally where the hillsides are yet too steep to attract the builder and the customer, even if the architect may view them as a pleasurable challenge to his ingenuity. Some dramatic and doubtfully practical houses have built on semi-cliffs, but the cost of development and construction on such steep parts makes them economically risky — at least for today. These grassy slopes, and others not so steep but still just beyond the reach of present land development, are not infrequently swept by dry-season fires, but this is fortunately the period when their terrestrial orchid content will have died back, and the flashfire heat does not penetrate the roots. Strips of woodland in the ravines often escape fire by virtue of their more evergreen nature and by the fact that the fires climb up slopes, and thus follow the ridges, rather than creep downward into the ravines. But the dominant factor of survival in the orchid life of this higher suburban part of the city is the continued presence of a small remnant of once very extensive national forest that lies within the southern boundary at an elevation of around 4,000 to 4,500 feet. It is here that the bulk of the cooler-growing epiphytic orchids can still be found. Together with much wild bird and animal life, ranging from parrots and

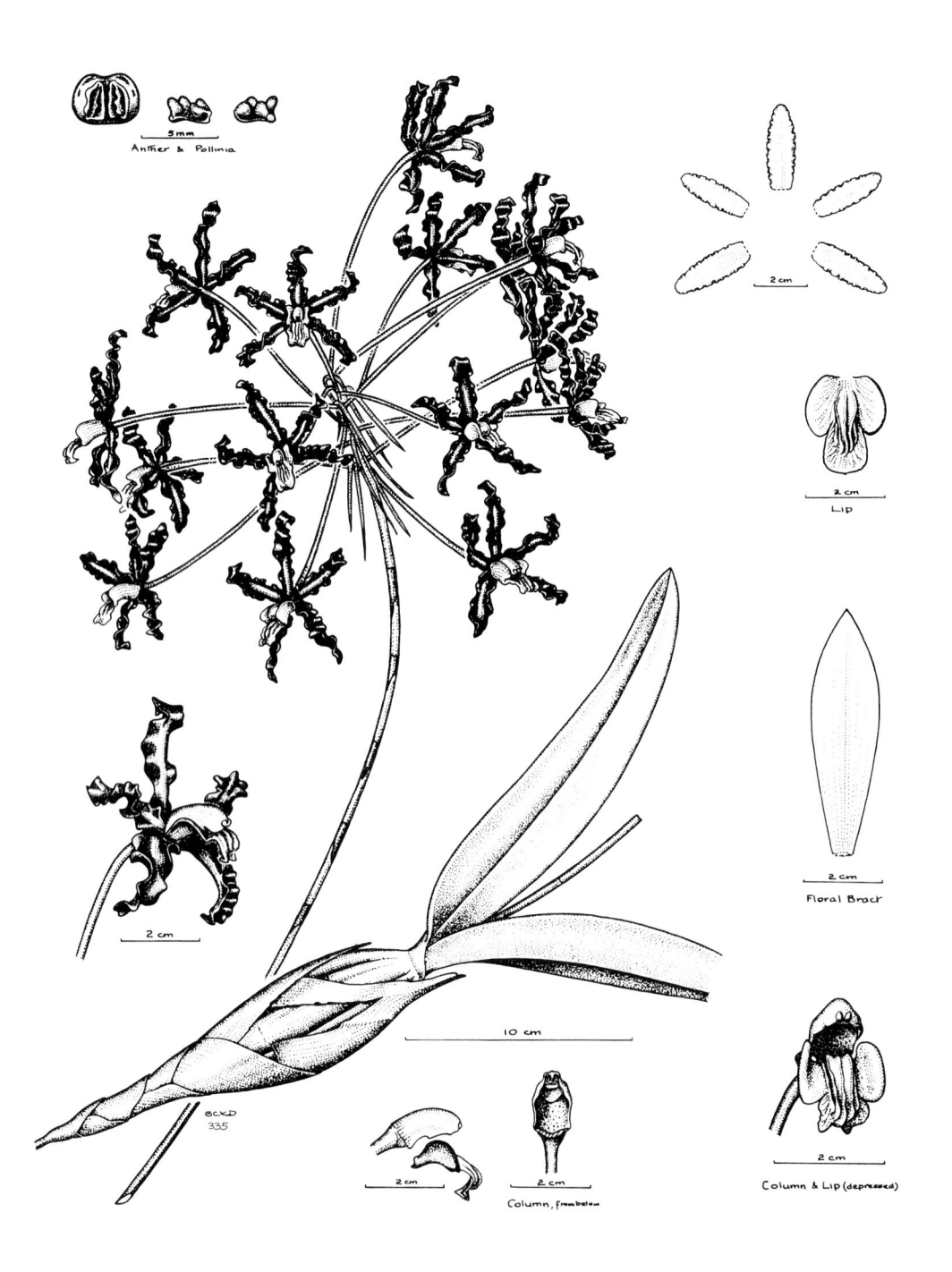

Schomburgkia undulata Lindl. in Bot. Reg. 30: Misc. p. 13, 1844. — B. C.

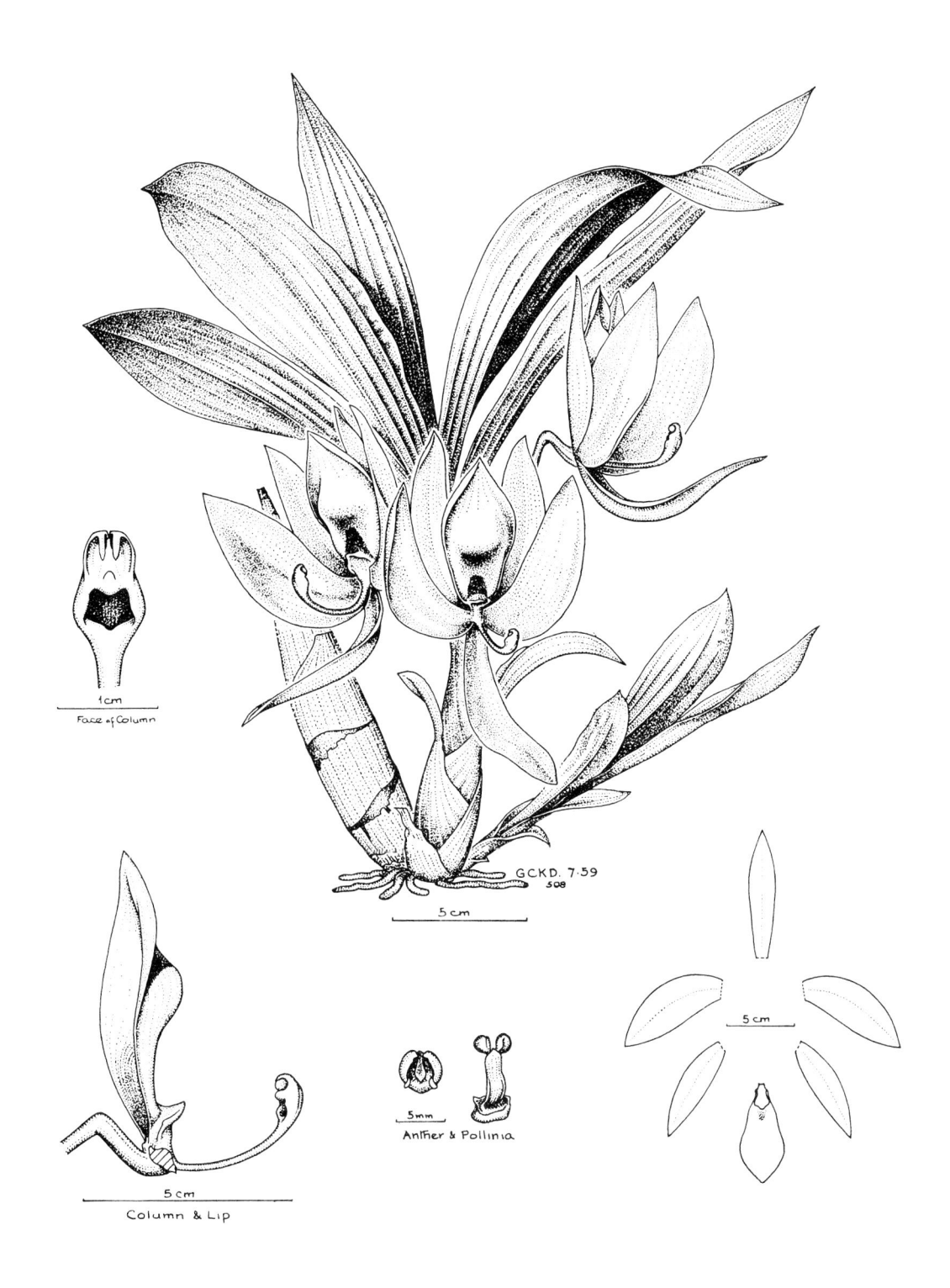

Cycnoches chlorochilon Kl. in Allgem. Gartenzeit. 6: 225, 1838. — A. B.

snakes to sloths and porcupines, they live a life not greatly different from that of their ancestors. But the keynote of modern life is urban progress, and only two things can conserve this natural little park for the enjoyment of the grandchildren of the city of today. The first is the much-hoped-for but most unlikely miracle of a quick, effective, and peaceable halt to the population explosion. The second is that the city fathers will have the foresight, wisdom, and courage to follow up suggestions already made by others to declare this piece of forest a national park, and having so declared it, to provide the necessary policing to ensure that its boundaries remain sealed against urbanizers and despoilers, however powerful the former and however cunning the latter. Caracas has just celebrated its Fourth Centenary. If this piece of forest reaches Caracas of the Fifth Centenary unharmed, the city fathers responsible will surely be worthy of a highly honored niche in the Fifth Centenary Hall of Fame.

Orchids of Caracas
(taxonomy updated from 1967 list)

Beadlea lindleyana (Link, Kl. & Otto) Garay & Dunsterv.
Bletia purpurea (Lam.) de Candolle
    stenophylla Schltr.
Brassia glumacea Lindl.
Catasetum macrocarpum L. C. Rich. ex Kunth
Caularthron bilamellatum (Reichb. f.) R. E. Schultes
Cladobium violaceum Lindl.
Cleistes rosea Lindl.
Comparettia falcata Poeppig & Endl.
Cycnoches chlorochilon Kl.
    maculatum Lindl.
Cyrtopodium cristatum Lindl.
Eltroplectris roseo-alba (Reichb. f.) Hamer & Garay
Encyclia ceratistes (Lindl.) Schltr.
    chacaoensis (Reichb. f.) Dressler & Pollard
    cordigera (H.B.K.) Dressler
    diurna Schltr.
    fragrans (Sw.) Lemée
    livida (Lindl.) Dressler
Epidendrum ciliare L.
    deltoglossum Garay & Dunsterv.
    densiflorum Hook.
    nocturnum Jacq.
    purum Lindl.
    recurvatum Lindl.
    secundum Jacq.
    serpens Lindl.
Eulophia alta (L.) Fawcett & Rendle
Galeandra beyrichii Reichb. f.
Govenia superba (L.) Lindl. ex Lodd.
Habenaria entomantha (Llave & Lex.) Lindl.
    mesodactyla Griseb.
    monorrhyza (Sw.) Reichb. f.
    obtusa Lindl.
    petalodes Lindl.
    repens Nutt.
    trifida H.B.K.
Hapalorchis cheirostyloides Schltr.
Hexadesmia fusiformis Griseb.
Isochilus linearis (Jacq.) R. Br.
Jacquiniella globosa (Jacq.) Schltr.
    teretifolia (Sw.) Britt. & Wils.
Kefersteinia sanguinolenta Reichb. f.

Leochilus labiatus (Sw.) O. Kuntze
Liparis nervosa (Thunb.) Lindl.
    vexillifera (Llave & Lex.) Cogn.
    wendlandii Reichb. f.
Lockhartia longifolia (Lindl.) Schltr.
Malaxis caracasana (Kl. ex Ridl.) O. Kuntze
Maxillaria ponerantha Reichb. f.
    ramosa Ruiz & Pavón
    rufescens Lindl.
    stenophylla Reichb. f.
Mormodes buccinator Lindl.
Oeceoclades maculata (Lindl.) Lindl.
Oncidium cebolleta (Jacq.) Sw.
    nudum Bateman
    volvox Reichb. f.
    zebrinum Reichb. f.
Pleurothallis ceratothallis Reichb. f.
    chamensis Lindl.
    ciliaris (Lindl.) L. O. Williams
    discoidea Lindl.
    erinacea Reichb. f.
    hemirrhoda Lindl.
    pruinosa Lindl.
    ruscifolia (Jacq.) R. Br.
    sicaria Lindl.
    testaefolia (Sw.) Lindl.
    velaticaulis Reichb. f.
Polystachya foliosa (Hook.) Reichb. f.
Ponthieva orchioides Schltr.
    racemosa (Walter) Mohr
Psygmorchis glossomystax (Reichb. f.)
    Dodson & Dressler
    pusilla (L.) Dodson & Dressler
Schomburgkia undulata Lindl.
Spiranthes tenuis Lindl.
Stanhopea wardii Lodd. ex Lindl.
Stelis braccata Reichb. f. & Warsc.
    porpax Reichb. f.
    trichorrachis Reichb. f.
Stenorrhynchos lanceolatus (Aubl.) L. C. Rich
    ex Spreng.
Trizeuxis falcata Lindl.
Vanilla pompona Schiede

Auyántepui, Home of 50 Million Orchids[1]

VIRGIN LAND FOR THE BOTANIST in the tropics of the New World is no longer as easy to find as it was a scant hundred years ago, but many areas still remain botanically almost untouched. Of these, none can be more enticing than the great sandstone table mountains or "tepuis" of the Venezuelan "Guayana" region. Despite noble work done by a handful of botanical explorers in recent years, much of the terrain is still virtually virgin. And of all these tepuis, the most enticing and dramatically impressive is surely the great mass called Auyántepui.

Lying in the heart of the Venezuelan Guayana, Auyántepui is about 180 miles south of the Orinoco, 80 miles west of British Guiana, and 140 miles north of Brazil. Its size can be expressed in figures, but its impressiveness escapes words. In the form of a gigantic thick-limbed V, with the narrow end at the south, it is an unimaginably enormous rock whose not-so-flat "flat top" covers an area of over 300 square miles, lifted up to an altitude of 8,000 feet on an unbroken coastline, hundreds of miles in length, of great vertical cliffs. These are nowhere less than 600 feet in sheer height and in many places far exceed 1,000 feet, reaching the fantastic figure of nearly 3,000 feet where Angel River pours from the top to form the world's highest one-jump waterfall.

This fascinating "Lost World" was practically unheard of until 1937, when a bush pilot named Jimmy Angel landed his small plane on the top near some very high falls in a vain search for gold and diamonds. His plane bogged down, never to rise again; he found no riches and, with his wife and two companions, was lucky to escape alive; but "Angel Falls" was thenceforward on the map. Auyántepui itself is still known to most people only as the background to the falls, but some day it will surely be known as one of the great natural marvels of the world.

Prior to Angel's exploit, and as part of the preparations for it, a way to the top had been searched for and found by two of Venezuela's foremost explorers, Felix Cardona and Gustavo Heny. So unbroken is the coast of cliffs, and so tough the forest-clad talus slopes below them, that today, nearly 30 years later, their route to the top remains the only access known.

Following close on Angel's visit, and inspired by the discovery of a way to the top, a scientific expedition (led by G. H. H. Tate of the American Museum of Natural History and financed by the well-known Venezuelan ornithologist, William Phelps, Sr.) spent more than three months on top from November 1937 onwards. Botanical exploration, however, was only lightly touched on, and only the southern section was explored. Since then, another party has done some light botanizing at the southern end, and three very small parties have ascended for non-botanical purposes.

In April of 1963, my wife and I made a fleeting visit to the top, but bad weather and lack of provisions for a prolonged stay made this botanically abortive though the drama of the scenery sparked an intense desire to return. Later, our friend Julian Steyermark, a dyed-in-the-wool botanical explorer if there ever was one, suggested a joint trip to start early in 1964 and agreement was reached in a matter of seconds. In the event, however, a number of factors such as possible limitations to the availability of Indian porters (who are often away looking for diamonds), problematic water supply on the rocky top in an exceptionally dry dry-season, etc., dictated the advisability of making the expedition in two separate parts, my wife and I going first to "do orchids" and Julian following later to do anything and everything that showed fruit or flower, seed or spores, with his usual extreme thor-

[1] Originally appeared in *A.O.S. Bulletin*, Vol. 33, August 1964, Pages 678-689

TOP LEFT — Jimmy Angel's plane on the summit of Auyántepui after it sank into the soft soil and could not take off again. Later it was removed by helicopter to a permanent exhibition in Ciudad Bolívar.

TOP RIGHT — A pause at the overhang of an enormous boulder halfway to the top provides a safe shelter for our tent.

MIDDLE LEFT — A campsite on the top of Auyántepui showing our porters on the (temporarily) dry stream bed. The "small" cliff in the background is typical of the "flat" surface of the summit.

BOTTOM LEFT — Crossing the run-off stream at the base of Angel Falls. Mist from the Falls can be seen in the background.

BOTTOM RIGHT — A section of the "flat" summit of Auyántepui, with our heavily laden porter doing most of the work.

TOP RIGHT — Stalky and Nora in the thick of real forest on Auyántepui. Is it an orchid or isn't it?

MIDDLE LEFT — A thirst-making part of the summit calls for a cupful of water from a handy bromeliad plant. Daughter Hilary pours for Stalky as Nora waits her turn.

MIDDLE RIGHT — Captain Felix Cardona, in his day Venezuela's foremost explorer of the Guyana area, rescued Angel's party from the summit of Auyántepui and left this mark along their escape route.

BOTTOM LEFT — **Eriopsis biloba** — the dominant orchid on the summit of Auyántepui.

BOTTOM RIGHT — At the base of the final (600-foot) vertical cliff guarding the summit of Auyántepui, the small group of porters is just visible at the very base of the cliff on the right. The way up to the top from where the porters are grouped is to the left and then through the gap to the right of the separate "tower."

oughness. Our own trip set off on February 28th and finished March 22nd, Julian's starting soon after we got back.

The results of Julian's work, based on the more than 1,000 specimens he collected, will clearly take much time to analyze. Our own orchid results are quickly known insofar as they rest on plants found in flower but as many species were not in flower and have been brought back alive for cultivation until they do flower, full results may also be a long time in becoming available. There is enough material, however, to provide the basis for a preliminary report.

One of the major difficulties of botanical exploration in completely unmapped areas such as Auyántepui, is how to pinpoint, for the record, the sites where the various species are found. Each explorer is forced to invent his own names to record localities and do his best to describe where these localities are, and as time passes, great confusion can arise. In the hopes of avoiding this in the case of Auyántepui, I studied air photos and did the best I could to produce a map before setting off on the trip. A very simplified version of this map appears here. On it I have incorporated such names as appear on the map of the Phelps-Tate expedition published in 1938 in the *Geographical Review*, plus one name (El Libertador) produced by a later expedition, plus such names as we and Julian Steyermark have found it necessary to invent for recording purposes. It is much to be hoped that until such time as a detailed map with names is produced officially, further explorers will use these names (or their Spanish equivalents) and not invent new ones for the same spots.

The sole access to the top is at the southern end of the mountain. Although this is the highest part in gross elevation, it has the lowest section (about 700 feet) of vertical barrier cliff. The rest of the elevation is built up from the 1,500-foot elevation of the surrounding savanna in two main shoulders separated by steep slopes. The first shoulder is a broad savanna where, at a point called Guayaraca, light planes can land. The second shoulder is at 5,000 feet (Danto), the intervening slope being covered with botanically very interesting and little-explored forest. Above Danto a talus slope stretches up to the base of the Top Cliff where, at something over 7,000 feet, there is a very convenient Rest Point. Above this point the final cliff rises sheer to the top, but here also is the entrance to the Access Crack, a wide, diagonal, steeply rising gash hidden behind impressive rock slabs and tall towers and filled with a tumbled mass of enormous boulders. At the very top of the crack one has to find a secret exit upwards through more of these boulders before stepping out into the relatively flat and bare rock mass at the top, near the point called El Libertador where patriotic fervor inspired a previous expedition to place a bust of Simón Bolívar.

From here the whole "inside" of the mountaintop slopes gently downwards towards the north while the flanks, guarded by Tate's First Wall on the left and East Wall on the right, rise even higher. The trail to Jimmy Angel's plane, the only trail yet made on this great summit, leads down and forward across the South Section to the southern end of the great central gash of the Churún Canyon, making wide sweeps to skirt the deep mile-long chasms that characterize this end of the mountain and which, in varying degree, play havoc with any attempt at straight-line travel wherever sandstone rock is exposed. Nearing Churún Canyon one is faced with the alternative of breaking new and difficult terrain to enter the so-far unexplored bare-rock expanse of the Northeast Arm, or climbing the 600-foot Second Wall that bars access to the Northwest Arm and Angel's plane. In dry weather this calls for no great mountaineering ability though a rope may be advisable at one point, but the labyrinthine mass of house-size boulders that crown the Wall in tumbled disorder for a depth of almost a mile demands the greatest care in following the faint signs of the old Angel Trail if one is not to be lost in hopeless wanderings for days on end.

Once through the labyrinth, the ground smooths out, but straight-line travel is still hindered by the need to make wide sweeps to avoid excessively boggy ground or tongues of extremely tough, dense dwarf-forest. Typical bare and broken sandstone country continues on the west, but beyond Drizzly Camp the eastern half of the Northwest Arm has a capping of igneous rock and is more or less smoothly rolling up to and beyond the point where Angel's plane stands axle-deep in boggy ground, its aluminum construction still unrotted. In contrast with the sandstone area which is largely bare rock, the igneous zone is extensively covered with savanna vegetation, shrubs and dwarf forest, with only very occasional exposures of rock surface. In the sandstone section the few forest patches or copses are also dwarf and very dense, and although the rock is — broadly speaking — bare, bromeliads, sedges, orchids, and even small shrubs thrive wherever even a faint skin of soil has been able to accumulate. At the bottom of the wider chasms, thick vegetation and trees have developed.

To describe and list in detail where the many individual orchid species were found would need far more space than here available. Some species appeared to be "rare" or "localized," but a great many were widespread, both across the top and down the southern slopes despite considerable changes of altitude. For the purposes of this preliminary note, therefore, only four main divisions have been taken:

Flying past Angel Falls to get a good view of the 3,000-foot drop, a view not often seen by passengers too busy using their "emergency" buckets.

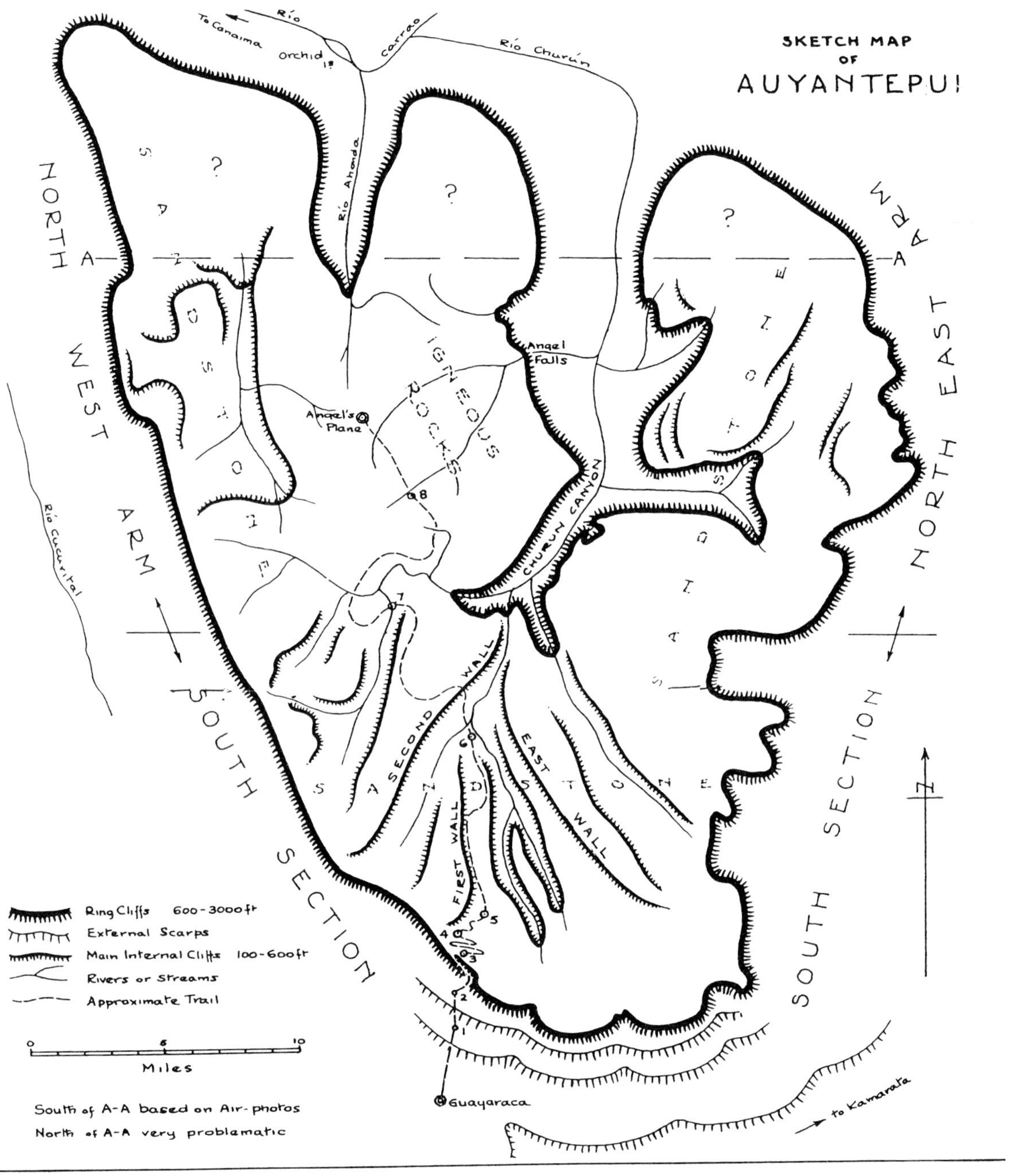

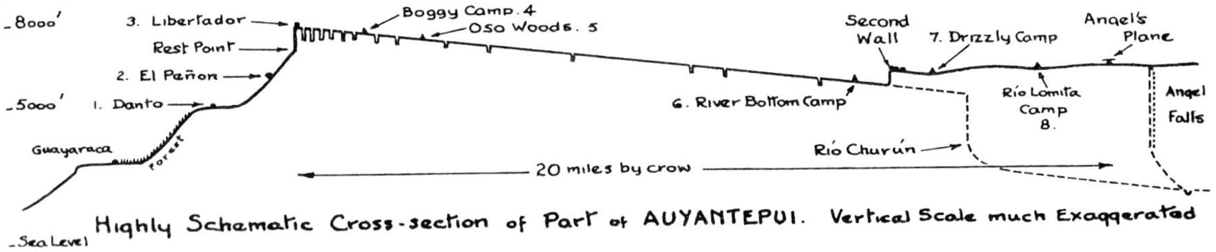

Highly Schematic Cross-section of Part of AUYANTEPUI. Vertical Scale much Exaggerated

A. **The First Shoulder Area,** including Guayaraca and the forested slope above it up to the edge, at 5,000 feet, of the Second Shoulder Area.
B. **The Second Shoulder Area,** including Danto at 5,000 feet and up to Rest Point at 7,000 feet.
C. **The Sandstone Area,** from Rest Point to El Libertador at about 7,700 feet and northwards across the top to Drizzly Camp at just under 6,000 feet (at the base of the Second Wall the altitude is about 5,500 feet).
D. **The Igneous Area,** from Drizzly Camp to Angel's Plane, ranging between 6,000 and 6,300 feet.

The area of search was limited to the route shown on the map, with trails radiating out from camp sites for a mile or so into the surrounding country. Clearly only a very small fraction of the enormous total area has thus been touched, but visibility all around is excellent and enough could be seen to lead us to believe that the ground we did search is fairly representative of the vast bulk of the 300 square miles. It will be surprising if further explorations in the years to come do not turn up much that we have missed, but I feel that this "preliminary canter" will prove to have covered a very representative section.

Due to the great expanses bare of trees (perhaps natural in some places but at others, and almost certainly on the flanks, due to past fires), the orchid life is dominantly terrestrial or lithophytic. The dense dwarf forests on top contain many epiphytic species (generally small in size), but the bulk of orchid life grows lithophytically everywhere and anywhere that there is the least trace of soil. Even acinetas, born surely to be epiphytes, can be found growing terrestrially in lush and abounding health with their inflorescences aborting uselessly in the soil below.

Despite the tough exposed conditions in many places — high winds, smashing rains, hot sun and cold nights — the terrestrial orchid life is amazingly prolific. Except where it thins out in truly boggy stretches, it grows so fruitfully anywhere there is soil (and even at times where there is not) that it is almost impossible to avoid treading on orchids at every step. Shut your eyes and walk 10 paces, and if you don't crack your skull against a boulder or break your neck falling into a chasm you will probably have trodden on at least five plants. By simple mathematics, and assuming the route traveled to be roughly representative of the whole, it is no exaggerated guesstimate that of the six major large-plant species alone, Auyántepui harbors some 50 million plants.

The undoubted King of the Castle is *Eriopsis biloba,* highly variable in form of leaf and pseudobulb but relatively constant in its two- to four-foot erect inflorescences. The Queen is probably *Oncidium nigratum*, with large clumps of big pseudobulbs and six-foot branched inflorescences. Princes are *Epidendrum nocturnum,* with flowers up to six inches in spread; *Oncidium warmingii* with enchanting sprays of delicate white-and-yellow flowers; *Zygopetalum burkei* with sometimes very pale and sometimes very dark flowers; and a large and beautiful new species of *Sobralia* that has yet to be "published."

For a complete listing and distribution of orchid species on Auyántepui, see the *A.O.S. Bulletin*, volume 33, pages 687-689—Ed.

Orchids of Cerro Autana, Venezuela[1]

IN A PROPERLY ORGANIZED SOCIETY all field orchidists working in undeveloped and uninhabited terrain would be provided with free, personal helicopter service to get around with, and thus be able to spend 90 percent of their time effectively on the spot instead of losing 90 percent of it getting there and back. Unfortunately, in this respect as well as in many others, modern society is sadly deficient and it is only on a spot-chance basis that helicopters come to the orchidist's aid. Such chances obviously need some degree of cultivation, a good growing medium being that formed by persons who own, control or in any way have influence over helicopters, this soil then being watered with a gentle rain of hints. By this means I have so far achieved two helicopter-aided orchid-hunting trips (and, by bad luck or prior irrevocable engagement, narrowly missed a third), and as a result am completely sold on the idea that the helicopter was expressly invented to assist botanical field workers, even if in practice its use has been degraded to less worthy purposes. The first of such trips, under the auspices of a Government boundary survey organization, was to the most remote of all Venezuela's high sandstone mountains known as tepuis. A free lift in military transport planes and helicopters condensed into a matter of hours a journey to a Brazilian mission near the base of the 10,000-foot-high tepui, a trip that by normal river transport up the Orinoco, down the Casiquiare, down the Negro and up the Maturacá rivers would have used up weeks and a mint of money, plus the same again for the return to civilization. From the mission, situated in low-level forest some miles from the tepui, it was going to take the heavily laden, main survey team about a week on foot to reach the principal survey camp near the top. By helicopter it took us 15 minutes.

The second trip was to a far smaller but much more spectacular summit, also in the Venezuelan "Amazonas" or Upper Orinoco territory, but less remote. This mountain, known as Autana-tepui or Cerro Autana, is only 4,000 feet high but has the fascination of complete isolation, of being very tall for its width, and of rising sheer out of the almost sea-level forests at its base. I had seen it first from the air some 20 years ago and wondered then if I would ever be able to set foot on its summit. A few years ago my wife Nora and I did get around to trying to reach its base (though with no intention of trying to climb its vertical faces), but were foiled by the dense forests surrounding it that were not dry enough for walking nor deep enough in flood waters for canoeing. An expedition of alpinists which also set out to make an attack on the tepui was not only equally defeated by the flooded forest but, to highlight the risks, was unfortunate enough to lose one of its members in some rapids. At this point it seemed that the top of Cerro Autana was out of reach and was going to stay that way. And then, quite unexpectedly, the chance came along. A young Venezuelan dentist-alpinist-explorer, Charles Brewer, whose quite extraordinarily patient patients apparently tolerate his frequent exploring absences from his dental drill, had also long had his eyes on the peak and in a close-up aerial reconnaissance had seen some fascinating caves that not only debouched on the sheer cliff faces some 500 feet from the summit but actually provided a peep-hole right through from one side to the other. Discussing these finds with Dr. Nyerges, Executive Director of CODESUR, a Government concern charged with the important task of opening up Venezuela's vast Amazonas territory, resulted in the setting up of a multi-objective expedition to visit the summit of Autana under the auspices of CODESUR who not only had a direct interest in such exploration but also had at their disposal the necessary aircraft. Out of this planning grew a large and mixed team of *Na-*

[1] Originally appeared in *A.O.S. Bulletin*, Vol. 42, May 1973, Pages 388-401

tional Geographic, alpine, cine, geological, biological, and botanical experts. The *National Geographic* and alpine section was to find a way down the cliff face to explore the caves; the biological and botanical sides were important because with such a small and completely isolated peak there was much speculation as to the degree of endemicity and new species that might have developed on top. The botanical side would be in the very thorough and competent hands of Venezuela's top field botanist, Dr. Julian Steyermark, and there seemed little reason on the face of it to squeeze an orchid maniac into such an already overcrowded party. But with Charles' recommendation and Dr. Nyerges' kind consent, for which I am extremely grateful, I finally got in as a sort of low man on the totem pole.

CODESUR took complete and most efficient charge of the very complicated logistics, flying the group first some 350 miles to Puerto Ayacucho, the main city of the Territorio Amazonas, and then to a small island strip on Isla Raton about 60 miles farther up the Orinoco. From here flights were made by helicopter and small slow-flying planes to the Cerro, 35 miles away, for purposes of general reconnaissance and photography by cine, still-photo, and alpine teams, the still photography being in the able hands of Señorita Angela Capriles with whose kind permission the view in this article is reproduced. Finally, all food supplies, camping material, alpine equipment, and general baggage, in fact everything except human bodies and delicate equipment, were hurled brutally, but with entire success, onto the top as the last step before shuttling "bodies" up in a series of short helicopter flights which afforded the passengers brief but spectacular views of the peak and close-ups of its great vertical cliffs running in many places sheer to the forests at its base.

Once settled, the party stayed for three days on the top. The non-alpinists were offered a chance of roping down to the cave but one look over the edge was enough and their decision to stay on top was unanimous, leaving Charles and David Nott (who had recently been one of a party of four making a first ascent of the vertical face of Auyántepui near Angel Falls), to help a heroic Bob Madden of the *National Geographic* reach the cave, where the trio stayed incommunicado until almost the end. As we helicoptered over the top prior to landing, I felt it could only need a few hours of work to check its possible orchid content, so small it seemed. In fact, its total area, which I would guess to be about 900 yards long by 250 yards wide, is only some 30 acres, nearly all of which seemed to be open savanna, easy to get around. But appearance belied the reality, and, as time passed, I began to realize how many tiny but distinct "ecological niches" or habitats were packed on the summit; by the time we left I was sure that another week could profitably have been spent on top. As a final send-off bonus, we had the unforgettable experience, when helicoptering off the top, of looking vertically down through the transparent floor of the machine as it passed over the cliff edge, when the boggy land only a few feet below the craft dropped in a split second to a view of forests 4,000 feet below, sucking one's heart and stomach with it.

The top of this tepui can best be compared to the deck of a liner, by far the largest part consisting of the fore and after decks, almost flat expanses of quite boggy ground littered with small boulders (which our dropped baggage had fortunately failed to hit) and bearing a fairly dense savanna-like covering of calf-high vegetation in which tall red-flowered heads of beautiful and extremely rare *Kuhnhardtia rhodantha* plants (regrettably not of the orchid family) livened up a duller background of the dominant *Brocchinia hechtioides* plants (bromeliad family), endemic to the tepuis. For the purposes of correlating orchids with their habitats, I will call this **Habitat A**. It was by no means poor in total orchid plants but was poor in variety. The first impression of the top was thus one of considerable orchid disappointment, but this quickly changed as other habitats showed up.

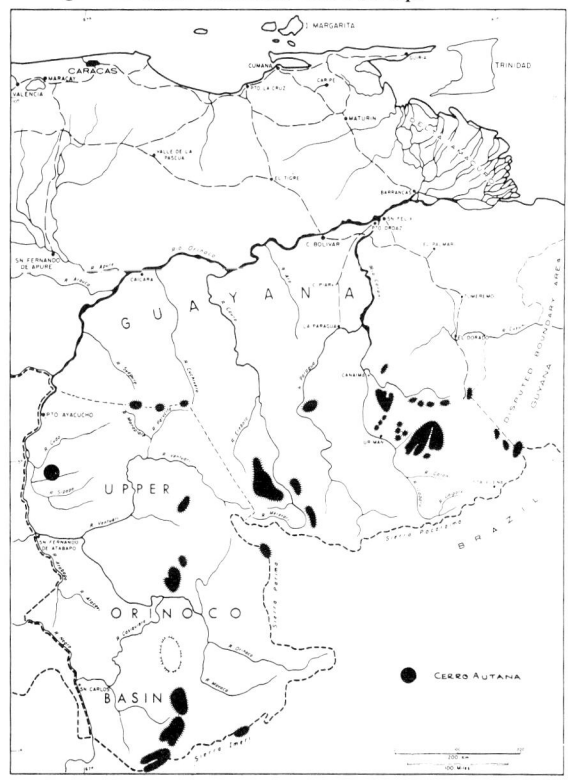

Map of Cerro Autana region in Venezuela

Habitat B was formed by the "Bridge" of the liner, a rounded hill rising 100 feet above the general level in the center of the summit, its sloping sides dropping on the starboard side to the very edge of the vertical cliffs and on the port side leaving only a narrow but important shoulder. The soil of this boulder-strewn hill was naturally much drier than in Habitat A, and the vegetation included many clumps of scrub; on the top the bushes graded into very small trees.

Habitat C was composed of tall scrub and very small trees covering the extreme end of the bow and stern sections, and a bit along the bow and stern scuppers. It differed from Habitat B principally by virtue of the fact that the soil was very damp, being only a shade less boggy than Habitat A.

Habitat D was formed by the extreme edge of the almost 4,000-foot vertical cliff, mostly on the port side from about midships to near the bow. This was an extremely narrow strip, at most five yards wide and in some places only a matter of feet, where the vegetation grew mainly lithophytically on bare rock, fully exposed to sun and wind, with comparatively little moisture retention at the base — an enormous contrast with Habitat A which in many parts it adjoined.

Habitats E and F were composed of deep, longitudinal cracks, widening into gulleys and then into very narrow valleys, cutting at a slight angle along the port side amidships and debouching onto the cliff face. In this compound habitat was growing the only "forest" that existed on the top, the cracks, gulleys, and valleys being filled with trees whose tops alone reached above the general level so that when viewed laterally the first impression was that of low woods, though the many trees were in fact quite reasonably tall. Here Habitat E consisted of the upper part of the trees, where drainage, insolation, and ventilation were all at a fairly high

Maxillaria reichenheimiana

Maxillaria ochroleuca

level, while Habitat F was made of the lower part of the trees and of the gulleys themselves, where conditions of drainage, light, and air movement were poor and utterly distinct.

One more niche, which I shall call **Habitat G**, though probably not really justifying so grand a title, came to light shortly before the end of the trip, a fine example of how easy it would be to miss such tiny but important enclaves unless one trod almost every square yard of the surface. This was a minute hollow, low down on the starboard side of the central hill, and only a few yards back from the edge of the cliff. Set in the typical scrub surroundings of Habitat B, this little hollow evidently had sufficient microclimatic difference to endow it with a character of its own, small trees being set in a dense undergrowth of a very pretty, sprawling, semi-climbing, and compoundly branching *Selaginella* that Steyermark tells me has proven to be a new species. It also gave us one of the two new-to-Venezuela species that resulted from this trip. How many more such tiny yet distinct zones exist on top must unfortunately remain a question until, if ever, another expedition goes up, but I am sure that with more time there is yet more to be found. It may sound odd that in three days such a small and generally open area as this top, even with its varied nature, could not be exhaustively covered, but with so much to be checked in detail, and with the going in some parts both slow and tricky, it takes a lot of time to cover even one acre properly, and probably not more than 20% of the surface was dealt with as thoroughly as one would wish.

As is natural, by no means all the orchid species seen on top were in flower, and a complete list can-

Cerro Autana (photo by Charles Brewer-Carías)

not be drawn up until and unless all the specimens of unflowering species brought back to Caracas flower in captivity. However, a number of such plants have indeed flowered by now, just one year later, so that a fairly close summary can be given. Thirty different species were collected, of which eight were in flower at the time and eight have flowered in Caracas, giving a total of 16 species whose identity can be determined positively. Of the remainder, another eight are vegetatively sufficiently distinct that there is really very little doubt about their identity, leaving only six species quite unidentifiable. One or more of these could yet produce a surprise, but none of them really look at all "unusual" and it would indeed be most surprising if something new turned up among them. Original hopes for a new species find never really amounted to an expectation as dispersion of the extremely fine orchid seed by air currents is so effective that this family does not go in very strongly for endemism. It is, however, distinctly gratifying that this one tiny area did, in a three-day search, produce two orchid species that are new to the record for Venezuela. The first of these is *Epistephium hernandii* Garay, the identification of which was made by Dr. Garay himself, whose patient help in the past has enabled me to accumulate such orchid taxonomic knowledge as I possess — a fact for which I am greatly in his debt. The second orchid new to Venezuela is *Maxillaria pendens* Pabst, not as beautiful as the epistephium but an interesting and pleasant plant all the same.

As regards the effectiveness of the various habitats in encouraging variety of orchid life, it is perhaps to be expected that the joint Habitat E-F, the only one with real scope for epiphytes, should be the richest, with 12 epiphytic and two terrestrial species. More surprising was the success of Habitat D, the tiny narrow strip along the cliff edge, which yielded 10 species, all but one growing as terrestrials in thin soil on rock or actually on the rock itself. The variety of orchid life here, in contrast to the lack of variety in the other, larger habitats, serves to highlight the fact that, besides their general preference for an epiphytic life, tropical orchids as a whole are not too fond of damp conditions while at the same time being quite surprisingly accommodating to considerable extremes of exposure to sun, wind, and rain, always provided that there is ample drainage around the roots. This latter factor, combined with a freedom from many terrestrial competitors, is presumably also an important element in the preference of so many tropical orchids for an epiphytic life.

For those interested in more detail, the orchids growing in each habitat were as follows:

Habitat A *(Main boggy area)*; all plants terrestrial

Bifrenaria maguirei C. Schweinf.?? The dominant orchid on the summit, growing prolifically here with its aggregate, unifoliate pseudobulbs frequently buried to their tops in the boggy soil. The erect leaves were up to 24 inches tall, of which half was a slender, petiolate base. From the general aspect of the plants and the very tall remains of old, erect inflorescences, I think there is very little doubt that these are plants of *Bifrenaria maguirei*, named after Dr. Basset Maguire of the New York Botanical Garden, who found specimens on other tepuis in his many explorations of the Venezuelan interior. If this tentative identification is correct we hope it will not be too long before we at last see this rare and fine specimen of the genus produce its four-inch flowers with faded-yellow sepals and petals and strongly purple-nerved lip: the plants brought back from the top seem to be well established in soil also brought from the top and are sending up new growths.

Eriopsis biloba Lindl.?? Fairly frequent, growing much as the bifrenarias: no flowers yet, but the identification is fairly certain.

Cleistes tenuis Reichb. f. One plant, with just enough flower for identification, growing more or less at the junction of habitats A and B.

Habitat B *(Central hill)*

Epidendrum nocturnum Jacq. Lithophytic; one smallish specimen of this species which in Venezuela is ubiquitous and common.

Habenaria trifida H.B.K. Terrestrial; one single plant, fortunately in flower.

Jacquiniella globosa (Jacq.) Schltr. Epiphytic on shrubs.

Habitat C *(Scrub in damp soil)*

Bifrenaria maguirei?? A few terrestrial plants.

Eriopsis biloba?? A few terrestrial plants.

Manniella americana C. Schweinf. & Garay. This makes a third known locality for this small and very rare Venezuelan orchid, previously found on Cerro Guaiquinima (Amazonas) by Maguire, and in the Southeast Guayana by Steyermark. The genus contains only two other species, both of which are in Africa. The Guayana specimens grow by mossy stream sides, at times submerged — conditions very different from those of Habitat G, though the elevation is about the same.

Maxillaria meridensis Lindl. A few plants epiphytic on small trees.

Habitat D *(Cliff edge)*

Bifrenaria maguirei?? Growing both terrestrial and lithophytic, the very hard pseudobulbs fully exposed, the leaves tending to be small and very rigid.

Elleanthus sp. Terrestrial in thin soil: no clues as to its identity.

Epidendrum dendrobioides Thunb.? Terrestrial. No flowers, but vegetatively fairly distinct and the identification "highly probable;" a fairly common orchid of the tepuis, often at much higher altitudes.

Epidendrum nocturnum. Epiphytic; a thick-leaved, stunted specimen on a small stunted tree.

Epistephium parviflorum Lindl. Terrestrial and lithophytic.

Eriopsis biloba?? Terrestrial and lithophytic.

Maxillaria amazonica Schltr. Lithophytic; flowered in Caracas. The very tough conditions in which this plant was growing resulted in both pseudobulbs and leaves being quite untypical of the normal form, the pseudobulbs largely sheathless and strongly tapering to the base, the leaves short and thick. It was one of the plants I was sure would be something new to us, so Nora got no thanks when she proved me wrong by flowering it, the flower itself being quite normal and typical for the species.

Maxillaria desvauxiana Reichb.f. Lithophytic. One rather stunted specimen of this species which in any case is very variable in size. This time Nora's success in flowering it was given due appreciation, as despite the smallness of the plant the flower proved to be by far the largest and most handsome of this species we have yet seen.

Sobralia sp. Terrestrial and lithophytic; a few clumps of what is most probably *S. infundibuligera* Garay & Dunsterv., a species recently found on Auyántepui and which has very characteristic, prominent, compressed, funnel-shaped, sheathing leaf bases.

Hexisea imbricata (Lindl.) Rchb.f. Terrestrial and lithophytic, the few plants very dry and sunburned but otherwise healthy enough for one of them to flower in Caracas.

Habitat E *(Upper part of trees in gulleys, etc.)* All epiphytic.

Dichaea sp. One small plant.

Elleanthus graminifolius (Barb. Rodr.) Løjtnant?? A few plants of this very common orchid, easily recognizable vegetatively.

Jacquiniella teretifolia (Sw.) Britt. & Wilson? As for *Elleanthus graminifolius*.

Lepanthopsis floripecten (Reichb.f.) Ames. A few plants of this pretty representative of this genus of mini-miniatures; the one brought back flowered in Caracas.

Maxillaria reichenheimiana Endr. & Reichb.f. Quite a number of plants with very characteristic white-spotted leaves; flowered in Caracas.

Maxillaria splendens Poepp. & Endl. Fairly frequent plants, with narrow leaves to 24 inches long. Flowered in Caracas with three-inch, white flowers on 10-inch-tall peduncles.

Maxillaria sp. Several plants somewhat similar to the above but smaller and with enough vegetative differences that they will hopefully turn out to be a different species when they flower.

Maxillaria sp. A repent rhizome with small, bifoliate pseudobulbs every two inches.

Maxillaria sp. A plant with small pseudobulbs and leaves and a repent, branching rhizome, rather like a large form of *M. notylioglossa* in appearance.

Pinelia sp. Almost certainly *Pinelia alticola* Garay & Dunsterv., a rare miniature from Auyántepui and Southeast Guayana with distinctive vegetative features.

Scaphyglottis sp. A few plants, none of which has yet flowered.

Stelis alata Lindl. A few plants in flower on the spot.

Habitat F *(Lower part of trees, and terrestrial, in gulleys)*

Epistephium sp. Several terrestrial plants, to about four feet tall, with rather smooth leaves.

Maxillaria pendens Pabst. A robust, epiphytic plant with a number of very long (six feet or more), semi-pendent rhizomes bearing distant pseudobulbs and upturned leafy terminals, producing in Caracas a number of half-inch, fasciculate flowers from the axils. The base of the plant was completely buried in the thick coating of bryophytes on the trunk of the tree; the gulley at this point was very deep and narrow so that direct insolation of the plant was extremely limited and for the most part the plant would be growing in deep shadow. Until very recently this Brazilian species was known only by its old name of *Camaridium pendulum* Rodr., being transferred to the genus *Maxillaria* in May 1972 by G. F. J. Pabst. The name *Maxillaria pendula* could not be used as this name had already been given by C. Schweinfurth to a distinct species, so the new name *M. pendens* was adopted. This Autana specimen is a first record for Venezuela.

Sobralia sessilis Lindl. Several plants, to about four feet tall, one of which later flowered in Caracas.

Habitat G *(Wooded hollow on starboard side)*

Epistephium hernandii Garay. Terrestrial; several scandent, suberect stems to about five feet tall. This handsome species was first discovered by Garay in the Colombian Amazonas at a fairly low level and published by him in the *A.O.S. Bulletin* for June 1971. This Autana specimen now adds it for the first time to the list of Venezuelan orchids and raises considerably its vertical range.

Maxillaria meridensis Lindl. Several healthy epiphytic plants in flower.

Helicoptering for Orchids in an Unknown Part of Venezuela's Amazonas[1]

HELICOPTERING TO THE TOPS of distant and otherwise inaccessible mountains is a "cheating" type of orchid exploration, in no way at all to be compared with proper botanical exploration on foot or by river either in the thoroughness of the work achieved or in the explorational merits accruing to the participants. It is the foot-sloggers who should be writing articles of this type; but, as is so often the case, the real workers remain unseen while the butterflies catch the eye. Which of course does not mean that opportunities to be butterflies should be rejected, the more so when they arise when one is at a stage in life when the bones are a bit creaky and the muscles not as eager as they once were. And it is only human to enjoy doing something that others would give their eyeteeth to be allowed to do but do not get the chance. So when we received an invitation to join a survey party using a helicopter to visit a very distant and basically unexplored part of Venezuela's Amazonas, we had no hesitation in signing on. This invitation came from a double source; firstly from Dr. Nicholas Nyerges, head of the government organization, CODESUR, that had so kindly provided the helicopter airlift to Cerro Autana described in the *A.O.S. Bulletin* for May 1973; and secondly from Ir. Georges Pantchenko, Chief Surveyor of the government's Border Survey Commission who had provided the helicopter airlift for a visit to Cerro de la Neblina in 1970. These two entities were collaborating with the government's mapping service to help the latter make a series of astronomic "fixes," gravity and magnetic readings, etc. in the upper half of the Río Siapa in a corner of the Amazonas area fairly close to the Brazilian border.

The Siapa River, about 200 miles long, has its source very close to that of the Orinoco itself, but it flows to join the Río Negro via the Casiquiare River and thus eventually joins the Amazon. For about the first 100 miles it flows west southwest as the Upper Siapa, then makes a quite illogical twist to cut steeply through a 20-mile gap between the sandstone-capped uplift of Cerro Avispa and a large extent of tangled igneous summits running from Avispa northwards. After the gap it becomes a winding river across flat, low (300-foot elevation), often flooded country until it joins the Casiquiare. This twisted course of the river had been correctly noted more than a hundred years ago by the celebrated mapmaker Codazzi, but in quite recent years it was somehow accepted that Codazzi must have been wrong — no river could take such a crazy course — and maps were changed to show the Upper Siapa as a part of the Río Mavaca which flows into the Upper Orinoco, the Lower Siapa being shown as a separate stream starting at the Avispa gap. Only very recently indeed, when all the Amazonas territory was submitted to a radar air survey by CODESUR, was Codazzi proved to be perfectly correct.

Until official and accurate maps are published of this region, some uncertainty must exist in the use of any of the current names for topographical heights. On the trip, the cerro where we camped for a while was referred to by all parties as Cerro Avispa. On most existing maps, however, C. Avispa is shown as a height more to the southwest and nearer to C. Neblina, with our camp site falling on a summit called C. Aracamuni. On the new radar airmaps it is apparent that these two cerros form one unit, with the former C. Avispa being a sort of southwest extension of the main block that on existing maps would be C. Aracamuni. Until some official pronouncement on this matter is made, the present tendency seems to be to call the *whole unit* Cerro Avispa, and if further definition is needed, to refer to the individual parts as the "Avispa sector" and the "Aracamuni sector" of Cerro Avispa. On this basis, our camp was on the Aracamuni sector of Cerro Avispa.

The Lower Siapa is reasonably well known and, in 1959, a field party from the New York Botanical

---

[1] Originally appeared in *A.O.S. Bulletin*, Vol. 43, July 1974, pages 576-583

Garden in the persons of botanists Wurdack and Adderley included the lower part of the Avispa gap in an extensive exploration of several Amazonas localities. The Upper Siapa and the summit of Avispa, however, remained virtually untouched; and this was the part where the survey party was to operate with a subsidiary objective of seeing how much Indian life inhabited the region. Along with Christa Lindemann, a lady coleopterist attached to the Munich Museum, we constituted a small, unofficial unit for whom transport and "upkeep" was most kindly provided, with an opportunity to search for our respective specialties both at river level and on top of the cerro. To say that every moment of the trip was wildly exciting or extremely enjoyable would be to veer considerably from the truth. The helicopter was, of course, at the prior disposal of the survey party and could only attend to us when not otherwise employed. This prevented it from hanging around at our pleasure, and, when it did come, it was only natural that "helicopter impatience" was frequently noticeable. In some places the machine apparently dared not rest its full weight on the soft ground (or feared its ability to restart if it once stopped?); on these occasions the unceasing fup-fup-fup of its rotor formed a terribly compelling call to hurry-hurry-hurry, whether disembarking or rushing to board it. Communication direct with the machine or anywhere else for that matter was impossible for us, so with only the vaguest of timetables to go by, many hours were inevitably spent in thumb-twiddling and most distressing idleness, waiting packed and ready to go for a machine that might perhaps not turn up today, nor tomorrow, nor even the day after; nothing was certain except that when it did, it would fup fup-fup at us in seeming rage at any delay. Despite this and various other complications, the three of us did enjoy the experience, did find interesting material and did gain the right to claim acquaintance with a hitherto unknown piece of Amazonas.

The areas we were able to explore were of three basic types: 1) the top end of the Lower Siapa and the falls and rapids at the lower end of the Avispa gap, at a level of about 500-600 feet; 2) the Upper Siapa, at a level of 1,500-1,700 feet, in the form of heliports and camp sites about 30 and 80 miles above the gap; and 3) the top of Cerro Avispa itself at about 5,000 feet. The Base Camp at the low end of the Lower Siapa had been selected as the farthest point upstream feasible for water transport of the special kerosene for the helicopter; with a fuel consumption of two gallons a minute, more than just a couple of drums were needed. Unfortunately this camp site and its forested surroundings formed one of the most painful places we have ever worked in and we must confess we did not by any means

The artist at work in the field, well protected from biting insects, commonly called *plaga* in Venezuela.

take full orchid advantage of all our hours on the spot. Nights were fairly cool (minimum 70°F) and pleasantly bug-free, but from dawn to after dusk a constant cloud of vicious and quite extraordinarily hungry *plaga* made life outside the protection of a mosquito net an indescribable misery; no repellent of any make was of any use as it washed off in copious sweat as quickly as it was applied. We can put no scientific name to any of these minute but powerful pests, commonly called "no-seeums," *jejenes, piums*, or what have you, and the non-scientific names we gave them are, even in these permissive days, not printable in the *A.O.S. Bulletin*. Wurdack, in extraordinarily restrained language, has confirmed to us his view that "the *Simulium* problem on the Siapa is the worst in Amazonas." He should know and we have no inclination at all to contradict him.

Going up or down river in an outboard-powered, inflatable-raft type of boat, for a couple of hours either way, extended the range of our searches and provided some bug relief. Around Base Camp itself, the most we could achieve was about four hours of blasphemous work from breakfast to midday, sweltering in the fug of a mosquito-netted hat to cover face and neck and with socks to cover hands, before leaping into our mosquito-netted jungle hammocks in a state of near hysteria. Once safely hammocked we could strip off almost all clothing and slowly relax as the bites wore off, eventually dozing or reading dime novels until nightfall brought blissful release, a chance for a cooling dip in the river and finally the only proper meal of the day. Orchids in this part did not seem to be overly varied, the miniatures very few indeed and the main items among the larger ones being *Clowesia warsewiczii, Caularthron bicornutum, Polycycnis vittata, Paphinia lindeniana, Zygosepalum lindeniae,* and a narrow-lipped form of *Brassia lanceana,* as well as various unflowered and thus unidentifiable plants of *Brassia, Batemannia, Maxillaria,* and possibly *Mendoncella,* none of which looked vegetatively unusual to us. Nothing, in fact, had turned up sufficiently exciting to compensate for the *plaga* and no member of the party was sorry when the time came to move elsewhere. That Wurdack and Adderley had managed to survive a considerable period at this spot borders on the incredible and speaks volumes for their devotion to botanical duty.

As already mentioned, the Lower Siapa flows through flat and largely uninteresting, low-lying country. The Upper Siapa, by contrast, lies in a large valley, about 100 by 30 miles in extent, at an elevation of 1,500 to 1,800 feet, bounded on the south by the relatively low range that forms the border with Brazil, and on the north by the jumbled, igneous (?) summits, mainly 3,000 to 5,000 feet high, of the Sierra de Unturán. The "flat" floor of this valley is in reality a tangled, close-packed mass of small, steep-sided hills and hillocks, like a giant sharkskin with pimples from 30 to 100 feet in height, all covered with dense forest that to a casual glance conceals the extreme complication of the topography. Looking at it critically from some 1,000 feet above it as the helicopter flew over, it impressed one deeply as a most beautiful but utterly impenetrable piece of country; and we have no desire to join any party that wants to explore it intensively on foot.

The camps on the Upper Siapa were, to the relief of everyone, less buggy as we went farther upstream, and the uppermost camp was really quite tolerable — the presence of an inextinguishable nest of the much-feared "24" ants in the base of the fallen tree that served as our dining table provided no more than the amusement of wondering who would get bitten first; the chief pilot gained this unenviable distinction. At this uppermost camp site the river had developed into a maze of small streams and little, forest-covered islands, one of which, scarcely larger than the spread of the helicopter's rotor, had been cleared as a heliport after a somewhat larger island had had to be abandoned due to an excess of snakes. No tale of heroic exploration is acceptable, of course, without snakes and tigers, but on this trip the best we could raise in the snake line was this hearsay report from the advance party. As for tigers (the local name for jaguars), Christa alone came anywhere near seeing one. Rejoining us after a search of a small section of forest-lined river bank she said that she had heard but not seen a tapir that she must have disturbed in the bush. Asked what sort of noise it had made, she did not produce the sharp whistle of the tapir but did produce a reasonable imitation of the jaguar's cough; the poor animal was probably scared almost to death by this human intrusion of his hunting grounds and had left in a hurry.

Concurrent with the decrease of *plaga* increasing signs of Indian life appeared the farther upstream we went. From the helicopter a number of Indian *shaponos* had been sighted, lean-to shelters built in a ring around a central patch of earth. While we sought orchids, Christa and some of the others made an effort to contact some of the Indians, reporting that they had finally achieved this at the only *shapono* where the Indians, instead of hiding in the forest, actually signaled the helicopter to descend. The reward to the poor Indians for this was the not unexpected one of seeing their flimsy dwelling blown to pieces by the helicopter's blast; but this did not prevent a cordial welcome for the visitors by the local chief and two visiting chiefs, all dressed in their best finery: namely girls' petticoats, which had no doubt passed from one admiring hand to another on a long chain from some Indians in contact with a far distant mission center.

Among the principal orchids provided by this part of the trip were *Peristeria aspersa* and *Epidendrum calamarium,* both new to us, and another epidendrum not yet identified, plus a number of more or less miniature orchids such as the very pretty *Ornithocephalus gladiatus, Trigonidium acuminatum,* and *Maxillaria uncata.* Among its many pleasant moments was an encounter with a nice, fat, 400-pound tapir, normally a most shy animal but here so tame and unsuspecting that it plowed about in the rocky stream bed for quite a time within a very gentle stone's throw before deciding to canter splashingly away. Luckily our Indians had no shotgun with them, as there is nothing they like better than to kill such prey even when, as was the case, more than enough tapir meat had already been shot.

The third part of the trip was our stay on the summit on Cerro Avispa at about 5,000 feet, where we spent a week in company with Felix Cardona, a dyed-in-the-wool explorer-surveyor whom we have known for many years and whose function now was to make an astronomic determination of a suitable spot on top of the cerro; i.e., the first small piece of hard rock he could find on which to set up

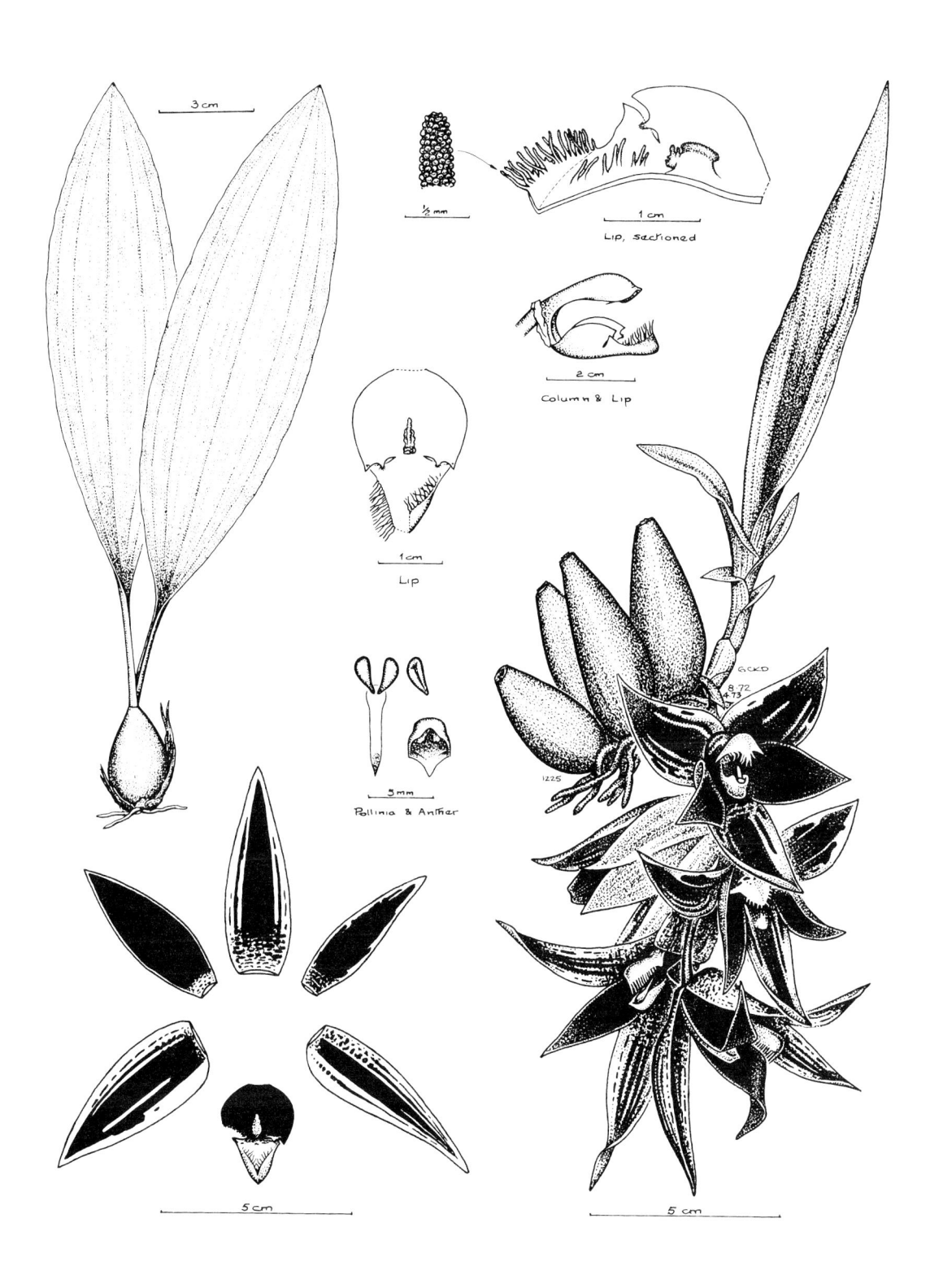

Paphinia lindeniana Reichb. f. in Flora 70:497, 1887. — D.

his theodolite. He made a separate camp and we saw little of him as his work was all nocturnal. The frequent cloudy, rainy, or stormy weather in the end defeated his efforts to get full star readings. Life on top for our own group of three was a combination of fun and misery, starting with misery and finally reaching the point where the misery is so bad that it turns out to be fun after all — a stage that is *never* reached with misery caused by *plaga* but can be attained where only general discomfort and frustration are concerned. On this occasion the misery started with the weather and the tent and ended with the weather without the tent. Christa had no tent and camping on the treeless summit would be impossible without one. We offered to share with her our inflatable "igloo" tent; with all our possessions kept inside to be out of the wet, the tent would be cramped but not intolerably so. Proudly we erected the rather ancient igloo, selecting a spot near the very top of the ridge where the ground was moderately flat and moderately dry; elsewhere it was not only sloping but soggy-boggy in the extreme. As we settled in before nightfall, a storm blew up. No sooner were we snugly beginning to snore than one of the increasingly violent gusts blew a kink into one of the inflated, tubular "legs" and the tent began to collapse inwards. Christa, nearest the affected corner, leaped to her feet to push it back into shape and to hold it there for a while until it seemed safe to go back to bed. Not long after, another violent gust repeated the process, and again and again, with the two ladies taking turns at holding the tent while the lone male, in his comfortable, downwind side, gave moral support and/or continued snoring. Finally, after the umpteenth crisis, the ladies found that if they lay flat and motionless the collapsed tent did not utterly crush them, only tickled their recumbent noses; the male was less affected though also pinned down. The rest of the night was spent with the tent collapsed on top of its occupants.

With stormy nights apparently the normal, nocturnal way of life on top, we moved the next day down the slope to a very squishy and not overly flat spot where the worst of the gales passed safely overhead. Later still, as each day we packed tent and all in expectation of the helicopter's impatient arrival to move us elsewhere, only to put it up again the next night, we decided to dispense altogether with the tent and sleep under a plastic tarpaulin in a small copse of thin trees where we had set up our kitchen. The first night this was tolerable even if the floor was muddy, but a semi-cloudburst then turned it into a stream of black mud. After rolling over into this guck off a blown-up mattress in the middle of the night, we took to sleeping cramped, but at least dry, on "tables" made of thin poles laid across stouter verticals sunk in the ooze. Our stay had been timed for a "couple of nights," but the helicopter got tied up elsewhere and day succeeded day. When our morale was at a very low point indeed, what with the mess and the enforced idleness and the exhaustion of almost all food supplies including last-ditch soda crackers and mayonnaise, hunger finally drove us to open a very unappetizing emergency package labeled "Combat Rations." To our surprise and joy these turned out to be excellent; neither cigarettes, lightly scented toilet paper, nor small wooden "dental stimulators" had been forgotten to keep the troops happy. When air rescue finally arrived, we were once more in fine and smiling fettle. Sharing close-quarter troubles with a complete stranger is always risky, but Christa turned out to be a fine and very *simpatico* morale-sustainer; conditions that might have fractured forever our budding friendship ended in mutual laughter. Our orchid rewards for this messy stay on top were not extensive but did include *Sobralia speciosa* that we had never met before in flower, and to our great joy gave us our first sight of the very striking *Bifrenaria maguirei* endemic solely to the Amazonas highlands from about 4,000 to 5,000 feet. The few, flowerless plants of this species we had previously collected from other places are still alive but do not seem to be working up any enthusiasm for flowering.

The original journey to Base Camp had been by a 700-mile helicopter flight, taken in a series of rather boring hops with slow, hand-pumped fueling stops in between. For the return trip, the helicopter made several lifts to the nearest "civilization," namely San Carlos on the Río Negro, our particular lift being a very crowded, just-get-off-the-ground one with three crew members, seven passengers, and heaven knows how much baggage. For us, the most important part of the latter was our plants. To make room for them we had to abandon other items such as the tent and hammocks which would come back via the long water route of the Lower Siapa, Casiquiare, and Orinoco. Even at that, everything that accumulated at San Carlos could not possibly continue by helicopter all the way home. When six of us finally got a ride to Caracas packed in a tiny plane, after several long days of waiting in San Carlos, we had with us no more than our plants and a spare handkerchief. After a long and anxious month all our left-behind bits and pieces finally caught up with us and we were once more ready for the next bush trip. Some of the plants may yet produce nice surprises for us when they flower; but even if they do not, we have at least got acquainted with four new-to-us species and have at last caught *Bifrenaria maguirei* in flower. We can count the trip an orchid success as well as having gathered some new and memorable experiences.

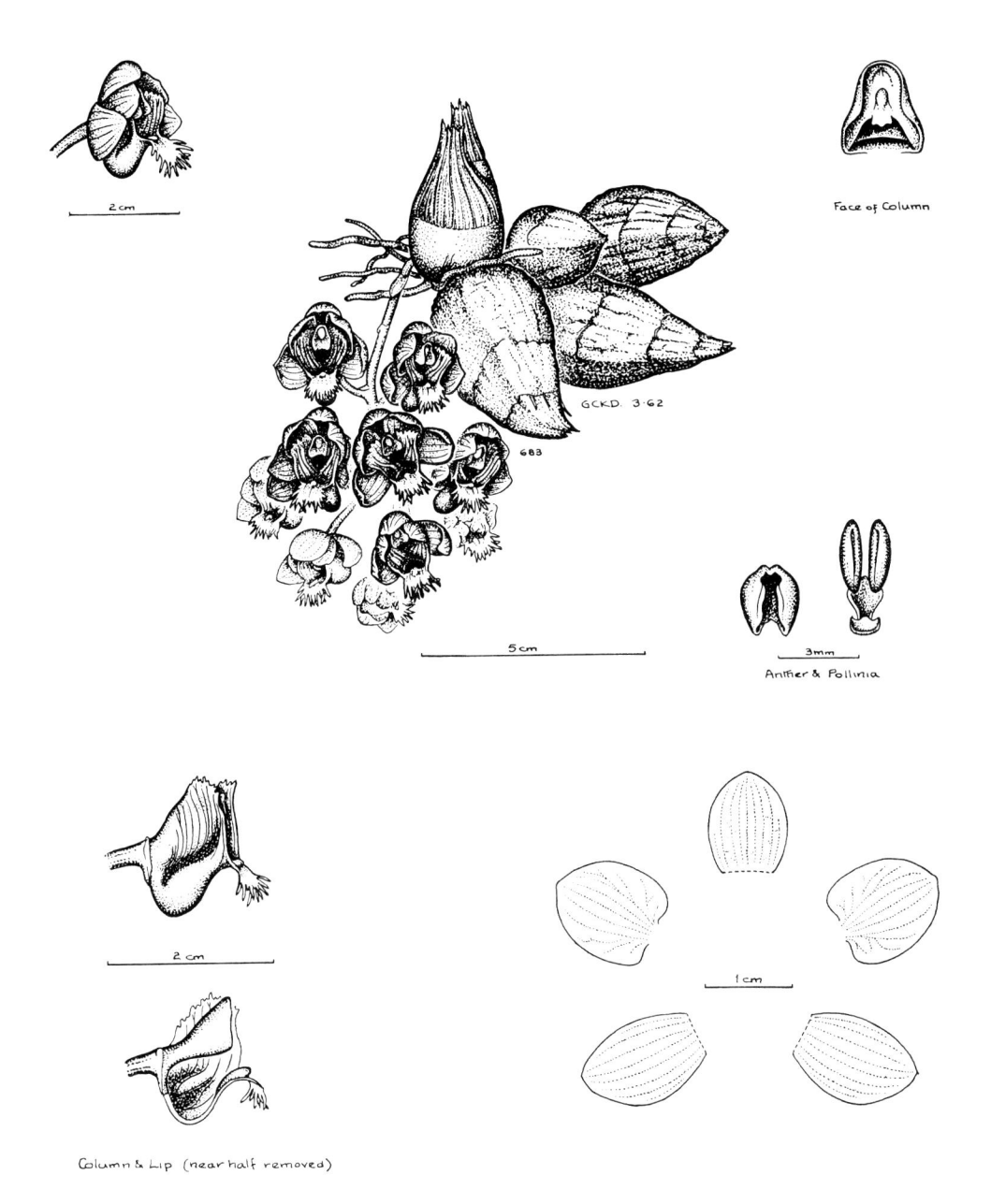

Clowesia warscewiczii (Lindl. & Paxt.) Dodson in Selbyana 1:136, 1975. — D.E.

Some Venezuelan Orchids of the Sierra de Perijá[1, 2]

IT IS NATURAL that areas of easy access should be the parts of Venezuela that have been most intensely explored from the point of view of plant life in general and orchids in particular. Thus it is no surprise to know that, although much work remains to be done, the orchids of the coastal zone and of the Andes have been catalogued, and their localities carefully noted, in a much more detailed manner than those of the scantily populated regions of Estado Bolívar and Territorio Amazonas, despite the attraction these later areas have long held for botanists and the many special expeditions that have been made to investigate their flora. But in considering the question of "remote and inaccessible" areas, there is a tendency to overlook one region that lies quite close to civilization and main roads, yet has been only scantily explored to date by comparison with what has been done elsewhere. This is the region of the Sierra de Perijá, the long range of hills and mountains that is shared with Colombia and which forms a large part of Venezuela's international boundary west of Lake Maracaibo.

That this region has so far been botanically explored in only a relatively light manner is not in any way due to lack of interest in its flora, but exclusively to two factors. The less important factor is that despite its proximity to main roads, there is no vehicular access, even by jeep, to its higher levels where the flora is richest. More important is the fact that until very recently a large part of the area has been virtually barred to extensive scientific investigation — or indeed any investigation at all — by the presence of the renowned Motilone Indians with their well-earned reputation for shooting arrows first and asking no questions afterwards, a habit for which, knowing the evils as well as the blessings of civilization, nobody could really blame them. Fortunately, largely due to courageous work by certain religious missionary explorers, these once dangerous Indians have recently been won over to being pacific, and travel is now largely free of serious dangers within their territory. The same applies to the rather less alarming Yupa Indians whose territory adjoins that of the Motilones on the north. But exploring these little-known forests up to the Colombian border at altitudes of 6,000 to 10,000 feet still requires plenty of physical effort, careful planning and, in the case of a prolonged stay, the use of a considerable number of Indian porters whose reliability is by no means always 100%. Some very recent Government boundary survey work using helicopters has, by the kindness of the organizers, also assisted in some quick botanical research, but such opportunities are likely to remain very scarce indeed. It will probably still be a long time before the fauna and flora of this range have been as intensively studied as, say, that of the Andes which lie not far to the south of it. Moreover, while the "Indian peril" is now very strongly reduced, a secondary danger still lurks along the forest trails, or *caminos verdes,* that cross the spine of the Sierra de Perijá. This danger lies in the presence of *vagabundos* and *maleantes* who, themselves frequently criminals in hiding, prey upon the infrequent traveler and the more frequent and relatively innocent *indocumentados* and *maleteros* (minor smugglers) who use these tracks as an unofficial way of sneaking from one country to the other.

The effect of these adverse factors is that, while the area is not remote in terms of distance, it is inaccessible enough that its orchids are still only skimpily known. It can, however, be said with confidence that its forests, as is to be expected, are the home of many species. This was confirmed by the fact that rather more than 70 species were located during a recent three-week exploration, along with Dr. J. A. Steyermark of the Caracas Botanical Institute, traveling by one *camino verde* to the Co-

[1] Originally appeared in *A.O.S. Bulletin,* Vol. 44, Dec. 1975, Pages 1075-1079
[2] Pronounced Perry-ha

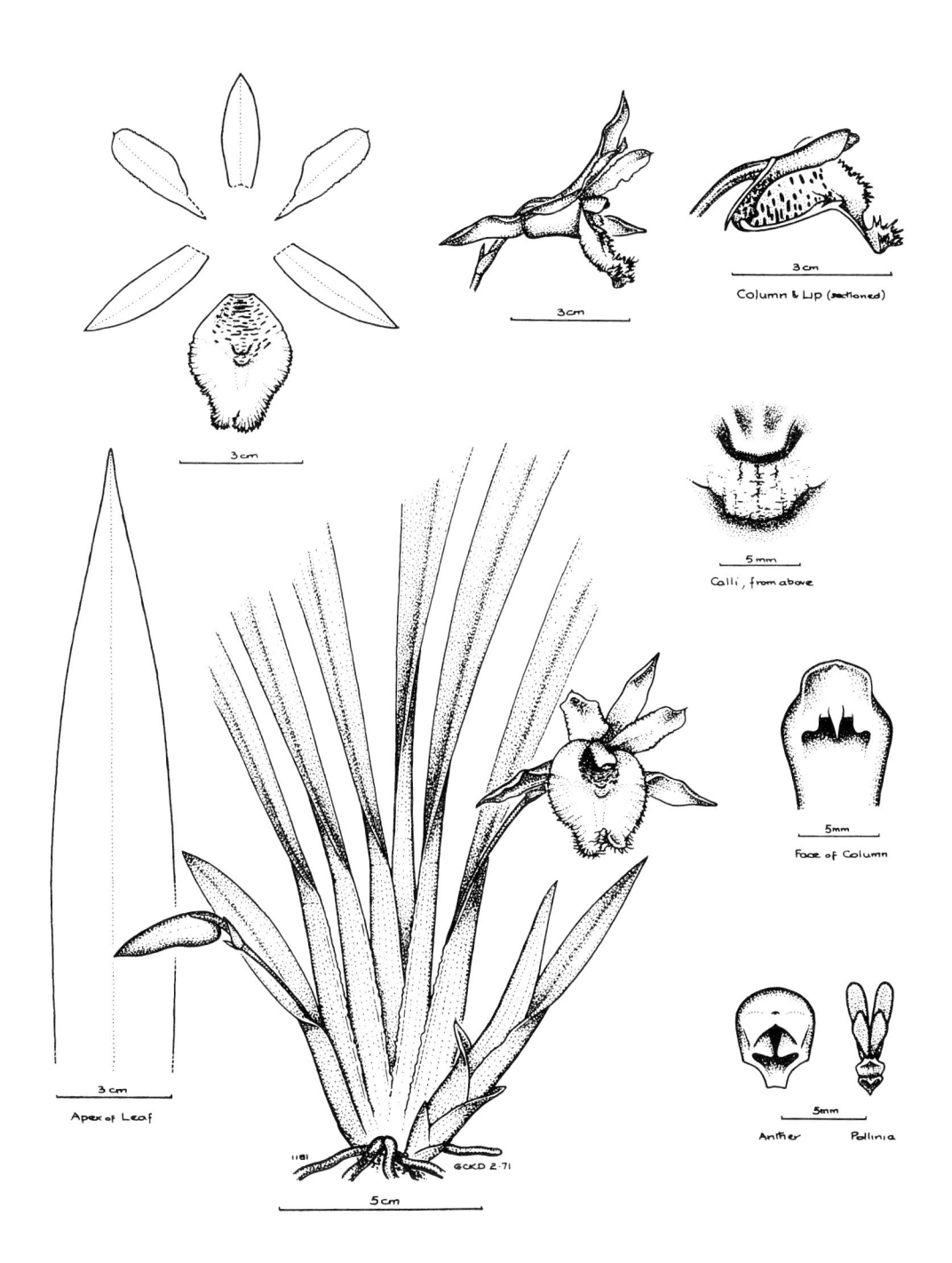

Chondrorhyncha flaveola (Lind. & Reichb. f.) Garay in Bot. Mus. Leafl. 21:256, 1967. — A.

lombian border west of the small Yupa settlement of Pishicacao and returning by a second, much more hidden *camino*. While, as always, a high proportion of the orchids we found were small and not very eye-catching, others were very attractive indeed. A few orchid species were in relatively open ground, but the great majority lay in the fine, dense forest that clothes these steep slopes between 4,500 and 7,000 feet.

Among these many orchids were the four discussed here. The most striking of these is *Odontoglossum hastilabium,* an orchid not common in Colombia and, until our expedition, unknown in Venezuela. Indeed it was almost an accident that it was found at all, our eyes being caught at a late stage in our travels by a fairly small plant of the "oncidium" type, growing epiphytically in the forest at about 5,000 feet elevation, and which we took along only because so few orchids of this type had been seen on the trip. It was therefore a great and pleasant surprise when the plant flowered at home above Caracas and showed itself to be this very beautiful rarity. The 2½" flowers are of a form that illustrates very well how confusing the rather artificial separation between the genera of *Odontoglossum, Oncidium,* and *Miltonia* can sometimes be, as the flower of this species has elements of all these in its form. It is no surprise to know that it started life being called *Oncidium hastilabium.* Our plant has been mounted on a block of tree-fern root and placed in a well-ventilated position of medium shade in our home. Here it has flowered for a second time and seems to be well-established, but it was a small plant when found and it will be long before it has the many-flowered, five-foot-long inflorescence which robust plants are understood to develop.

The second Perijá orchid illustrated here is not as rare as the odontoglossum but is nevertheless not at all common in Venezuela and is well worth a place in any collection. This is *Chondrorhyncha flaveola,* which only a short while earlier had been found for the first time in Venezuela in the forests above the towns of Guarico and Amzoategui in the State of Lara. On our Perijá trip (in the State of Zulia) it appeared in abundance at levels from 5,000 to 6,500 feet, so it is logical to expect it to prove eventually to be a fairly common orchid in the Sierra de Perijá forests and thus, one hopes, fairly safe from being rapidly collected out of existence. The flowers have a spread of about two inches and our plants have shown themselves to be remarkably floriferous, to the extent that while a single plant seldom has more than one flower at a time it will put out a succession of flowers for many months in succession. To date, one or other of our few plants have flowered in all months of the year except January, February, and March. The plants are cultivated in pots filled with well-compacted, chopped, tree-fern root which seems to suit them well despite their normal epiphytic way of life.

The third orchid species, *Cochleanthes marginata,* has a plant form very similar to that of the chondrorhyncha, consisting of more or less fan-shaped, leafy sprays with no pseudobulbs, the flowers appearing from the axils of the leaves. These species form part of a very confusing group of closely related genera that have long puzzled taxonomists and have gone through many changes, well reflected in the fact that *Chondrorhyncha flaveola* has at one time or another been placed in the genera of *Zygopetalum, Stenia,* and *Kefersteinia,* while *Cochleanthes marginata* has similarly formerly been allocated to the genera of *Warscewiczella, Huntleya, Warrea, Zygopetalum,* and *Chondrorhyncha.* Although it has been known in Venezuela longer than *Chondrorhyncha flaveola, Cochleanthes marginata* is nevertheless a quite recent newcomer to the records of Venezuela, having been found by L. Schnee in the Caracas area in 1952 and another plant picked up by us in a Caracas market in 1956. On a later occasion we found a large, dense mat of these very pretty plants growing in most surprising luxuriance in the leaf mold and debris on the floor of some rather dry woods in the Barquisimeto region of Lara State at perhaps 2,000 feet elevation. We collected a few plants from this mass, planning to leave the bulk undisturbed where they would quickly grow new plants to replace the ones we took, but, to our disgust, a commercial collector who was with us swept all the rest into a large sack on the excuse that if he did not take them all, then the next dry season would see them destroyed by fire — an obviously false argument because it was quite evident that many previous dry seasons had left them completely unharmed. It is examples such as these that have left us convinced that the "money motive" is at the root of much of the destructive collecting of Venezuela's showier orchids that goes on today and that will presumably remain unchecked until the eventual customers for such plants refuse to buy them, which is probably equivalent to saying "never." It was therefore with exceptional pleasure that we found this species growing (epiphytically this time) in fair profusion alongside the *Chondrorhyncha flaveola* plants in these isolated Perijá forests, where orchid hunters seldom penetrate and which are wet enough through the whole year to be reasonably safe from fire.

This species has, at least in Venezuela, three distinct color forms. The Perijá specimens, growing intermixed but not showing any intergrading color varieties, have either white lips with a narrow, light pink margin and heavy purple throat or have creamy white lips with heavy purple center but no marginal color change at all. The Barquisimeto plants were of the former type. Elsewhere in Lara we have also found a third quite distinct variety whose lip is purple-red throughout except for a white throat showing well-marked purple nerves. In all cases, the characteristic callus, hidden in the throat of the lip, is yellow.

"Tell me how a plant grows in Nature and I shall know how to grow it at home" is a boast one sometimes hears, particularly from those who express great disappointment if one cannot give them fullest year-round information on a plant's habitat and the micro-climate where it grows. But the orchid in nature is frequently not at all co-operative with the searcher for strict guide lines. We have, as mentioned, found the *Cochleanthes* species growing "dry and fairly low" in one place and "damp and fairly high" in another, and if you check it under its earlier name of *Chondrorhyncha marginata* in the 1949 *Flora of Panama,* you will see the note "Found in damp shaded locations usually at low elevations." In other words, it is not a desert xerophyte nor a lover of high *paramos*. All we can add is that the plants we brought home have taken hold surprisingly well, surprisingly because our previous experience with the Lara plants had indicated that it is a rather touchy species to cultivate. Grown similarly to the *Chondrorhyncha* plants, they are now very floriferous, putting out a number of flowers (often several at a time) over all months of the year except (so far) January, February, March, and April.

The fourth species, *Maxillaria spilotantha,* has been included to show that an orchid does not have to be large, or even medium-sized, to be most attractive: the individual flowers are about a half-inch in width. By contrast with the foregoing orchids, this *Maxillaria* species is relatively common, with a geographic range that spreads from Ecuador and Colombia down to Brazil. As it is by way of being a rather humble orchid plant it is presumably safe from over-collecting by enthusiasts, and, as it is an inhabitant of generally damp forest, it is probably also reasonably safe from fire. As regards danger to all the species mentioned here, from felling of their forest habitat, we hope that it will be long before this becomes a real threat in the upper reaches of the Sierra de Perijá although the levels below about 4,000 feet have already been largely deprived of forest cover in all except river beds and ravines.

Odontoglossum hastilabium

The humble *Maxillaria spilotantha* has the advantage of living also in the extensive Guatopo Forest near Caracas, which has passed from being one of the most severely threatened forest zones in the country to being one of the best protected since it has been converted to a properly cared-for National Park. Outside Guatopo and various places in the Coastal Range, this species is on record only for the limestone San Luis Range behind Coro in Falcón State, and now as mentioned, in the Sierra de Perijá. This is a relatively limited number of localities for such a widespread orchid and it must surely exist in many other places in northern Venezuela. In Perijá we found it growing almost within touching distance of the Colombian border at 6,500 feet. Elsewhere its habitat is generally recorded as between the limits of 3,000 and 5,000 feet, so the Perijá location may represent about its highest level in this country. One of its attractions is that it is one of a number of orchid species that show great variation in color. In the case of *Maxillaria spilotantha* this may range from the yellow form with dark-centered lip, to a dark but bright reddish maroon form with some green highlights at the apices of the sepals. The most common type is probably one with pinky yellow sepals and lip with red at their base. The plants are not difficult to grow on blocks of tree-fern root, and a happily growing plant can have 20 or more flowers open at a time.

Jaua, Sarisariñama, and Holes in the Ground[1, 2]

IT IS NOT NECESSARY for good orchid hunting that one should find oneself part of an expedition that receives press attention from London to Sydney, but it certainly adds to one's feeling of self-importance, however little deserved. That we have recently found ourselves in such a position is due to a happy combination of three main factors. Firstly, that we have long been good friends with Dr. Charles Brewer-Carías who, when not exercising his profession of dentist on extremely patient patients, is "Exploration Chief" of the Sociedad Venezolana de Ciencias Naturales, and we have been with him on earlier expeditions. Secondly, that to raise funds and other help for a full-scale expedition to a normally inaccessible part of Venezuela's hinterland calls for an objective with "sex appeal" well in excess of more normal objectives such as orchids or snakes. And thirdly, that Charles had laid eyes (from the air) on some spectacularly large and most intriguing holes in the top of a distant table mountain or *meseta,* first spotted by another friend of ours, Capt. Harry Gibson, in 1964, but never explored.

The appeal of these holes, holding out to the more unscrupulous press the promise of a sort of inverted "Lost World," prehistoric monsters still lurking in their depths, was irresistible. With all the publicity that ensued, effective help was soon promised from both public and private sources. The expedition was "on" and thanks to "firstly" above we were part of it. The general target would be near the Brazilian border, some 450 miles S.S.E. of Caracas, where a 50-mile-long uplift has two culminations rising to about 8,000 feet maximum, the *Meseta de Jaua* and the *Meseta de Sarisariñama.* If time and fuel permitted, a third meseta, *Guanacoco,* would be included. Sarisariñama, being the home of the large holes, was the main publicity target, but Jaua offered a greater variety of level and of habitats and could thus be at least as interesting from the general scientific point of view.

As the organization and fund raising progressed, so did the size of the party increase until finally it achieved a rather unwieldy total that varied from 25 to 35 persons, plus occasional visitors. Besides several Indians for general help, two radio experts, one medico, one camp boss, and frequently three helicopter crew, there were (putting ourselves bashfully first) two orchidists, one really-truly botanist (Julian Steyermark) and his helper, one herpetologist and one geologist from the Organization of American States in Washington, another geologist in Venezuelan Government service, two ornithologists with accompanying gun-man, one animal hunter, one speleologist, one anthropologist, a cinema team of four, and finally three alpinists (including Charles himself) to explore the holes. That one of these alpinists was David Nott, an English press correspondent resident in Caracas, may account perhaps for the speed with which word of the holes reached the outside world.

As always, one may query the need for two orchidists when botany as such was going to be well-cared for by a true botanist, and, as always we must explain, firstly that the botanist would have his hands full collecting and pressing flowering specimens for herbarium records with no time for plants not in flower, however intriguing their appearance, and secondly that, at least out here, orchids form a supremely dominant family that justifies special attention in the form of bring-'em-back-alive collectors so that such flowerless plants may in due course be also properly studied, a process that over the years has proved its worth by adding many species localities to the Venezuelan records and even a new species here and there. Also, we try to be useful by bringing back alive plants of other families where Julian feels that a flowerless plant looks particularly interesting, and we do have some non-orchid new species to our

[1] Originally appeared in *A.O.S. Bulletin,* Vol. 45, April 1976, pages 328-336

[2] Reprinted, with revision, from *The Orchid Review,* July 1974.

One of the many holes on Sarisariñama, this one the Big Hole. The alpinistically inclines members of the group ventured to the base, some 1,000 feet deep. Stalky and Nora stayed on the top.

credit. Anyway, justified or not, we were on the trip, and early in February were being flown in the cold and deafening interior of an unpadded C.123 *barrigón* (big belly) Venezuelan Air Force transport from near Caracas to a hot and distant open-savanna landing strip at Cacurí, a tiny Indian settlement way up the Upper Ventuari River in the Territoria Amazonas (upper Orinoco) region. Our target now lay some 50 to 100 miles to the east and southeast, on the other side of the relatively low but important Maigualida Range that separates the Upper from the Lower Orinoco basins. The next step therefore was to get ourselves, our baggage, and all the special helicopter fuel that had been *barrigón*-dumped at Cacurí over this divide to the rather modernized Indian village of Santa María on the Erebato River at about a 1,300-foot elevation. Light planes could also land here, and it was the most suitable low-altitude base close enough to the Jaua-Sarisariñama uplift for the final assault. Despite the size of our group and all the material that had to be moved, such is the capacity of the Bell gas-turbine helicopter at our service that before operations came to a halt for the day, most of us were concentrated in the large, circular, conical-roofed *churata* or communal house in Santa María. Hopes were high for an early move to the top of Sarisariñama.

Unfortunately at this stage we met a delay of several days, partly caused by the need for further shuttling to and from Cacurí to fetch over the many drums of fuel, and partly by what we have come to call Helicopter Hiccups, meaning that the helicopter "can't take off yet because it is too clouded-in here, or is probably too clouded-in there, but when it does clear there must be no delay so please just hang around (all day if necessary), ready to leap smartly on board at the first favorable moment." Luckily, advance parties would in any case have to go up first to clear a heliport and set up at least the rudiments of a camp. In other words, there would be a reasonable warning before our turn came, and, as a result, we were able to get in several days of useful, hot-country orchid hunting in the neighboring forests while waiting. Among the 30 or so seen-before species that showed their faces were some fine plants of *Polycycnis vittata, Maxillaria parkeri*, a pink-flowered *Mormodes buccinator,* a *Bollea hemixantha* (flowering later at home), and, in the village itself, a mango tree full of jewel-like *Psygmorchis pusilla* plants. As a final reward for braving the blazing sun and occasional drenching rain, we also came across a small, new-to-us pleurothallis in flower, the first trophy of the trip, which we are happy to say has arrived back in Caracas in fairly good shape.

Since the next step from here was to be up to a heliport and camp site near the famous holes on Sarisariñama, a word at this point about these very odd features is due. Imagine first a very approximately flat expanse of forest-covered rock, some 200 square miles in extent, seemingly smooth in places and broken into deep chasms in others, all lying at a 5,000- to 7,000-foot elevation and ringed by high cliffs and steep slopes to separate it from densely forested land at much lower levels. This is Sarisariñama. While in very broad terms this description would fit many of the flat-topped mountains of Venezuela's hinterland, each *meseta* has its own special characteristics, and in the case of Sarisariñama this is undoubtedly the remarkable holes that lie near its northern edge. Almost circular in outline, and with vertical or even overhanging sides, they look like enormous rocket-launching silos punched out (by von Dänikan's Gods from Outer Space?) in the almost horizontal bedding of the Roraima sandstone of which all these highlands are formed. The largest hole is about 1,000 feet deep and 1,500 feet in diameter, which places it among the largest and deepest holes known anywhere. How these holes came to be formed has not yet been officially explained, but, if one of the geologists on the trip is correct, they are probably the result of solution of the material cementing the sandstone by the very acid waters that are generated here, as on the top of almost all these highlands. Each hole is at the bottom of a wide, gentle depression which has concentrated the flow of water to a point where once there was extensive and very deep vertical fracturing at two distinct angles, forming, when viewed from above, a rectangular criss-crossing pattern, a feature common to many mesetas here. If this should then be cut by fault-fracturing at yet another angle, it is easy to see that a roughly circular pattern could be formed. These sandstone mesetas are often so strongly and deeply fractured that filtration of water "down and out" is common, and, if this happens at the base of a gentle depression, the concentrated down-and-out movement of acid waters could (says the theory) eventually break down the whole center of a "circle" of deep vertical fractures, leaving, after millions of years perhaps, a great, cylindrical, vertical-sided hole. It is certainly noticeable that as one approaches a hole the surface becomes increasingly fractured and the fractures and chasms increasingly wide, as if the surroundings were slowly trying to move into the hole and fall into it.

The bottom of these holes is filled with tall forest and, given a continual process of further plant material falling off the edge into the hole and the general mobility of much plant seed by air or bird transport, the expectation of finding a great number of new plant species that had developed in this tiny habitat due to complete isolation was perhaps

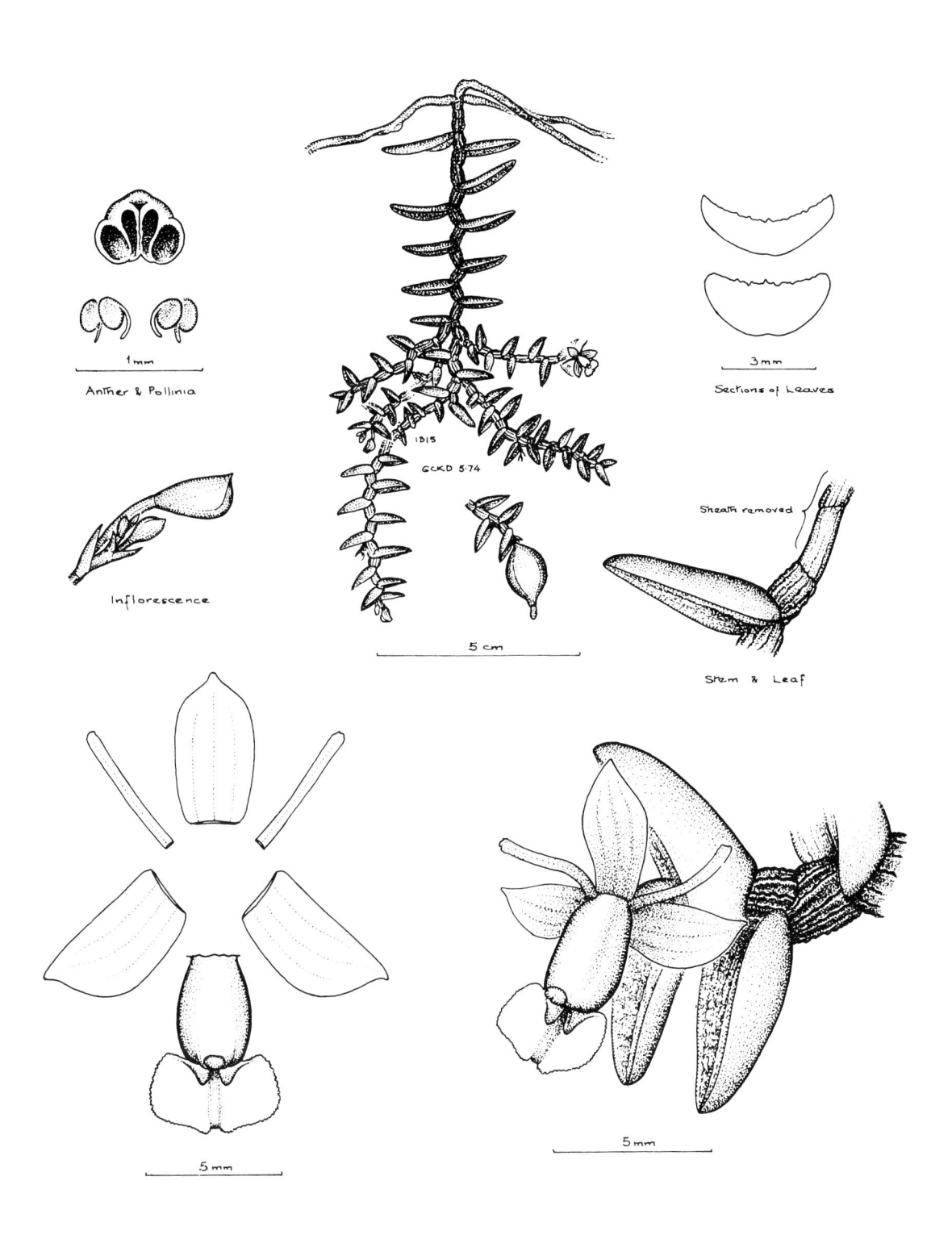

Epidendrum pachyphyton Garay in Orquideología 8: 182, 1973. — E.

not very high. The same sort of reasoning would apply to any animal life not completely trapped by the vertical walls; after all, what might be a neck-breaking cliff to a human could have routes presenting little difficulty to a lizard or small rodent and, in any case, there would be a continual, if accidental, in-fall of such things to keep some mixed breeding going on in the hole. Nevertheless, though prehistoric monsters were never in the picture outside the imagination of some reporters, there would certainly be a chance of at least some endemic items new to science.

Creating a heliport (a grand name for a relatively small clearing) is not exactly complicated, but unless an ample, open space exists it does call for considerable work. There may be helicopters that make a habit of landing and taking off, as we originally imagined, in a purely vertical fashion, but the fact is that all those we have met so far, while perhaps capable of such methods in an emergency, vastly prefer to come in and take off almost like an ordinary plane, with the difference that the first (or last) few yards are done at a crawling pace and from (or to) a static point about a foot above the ground. Thus besides a tiny cleared area for the final touchdown, a rough sort of runway is also needed in the form of a stretch devoid of major obstacles for a distance of maybe a hundred yards. Using manpower lowered from the hovering helicopter, a simple heliport had been cleared at the edge of the main hole, for the use of the down-the-hole party and cine team, etc., but the principal camp was set up about a mile away where a small open space made everything much easier and even allowed for two heliports to be established, a matter that assumed importance when the helicopter had trouble with a broken line and a second one had to come to the rescue with the necessary spare part.

Here, at this main camp, we spent the first week while the three alpinists went down the hole by "rappelling" with ropes, and eventually came out with the aid of special, steer-wire ladders suspended from the top. From the bottom they radioed progress reports and a small power-winch pulled up their specimens, many of these being plants for Julian to work on. While this was going on (and being filmed) the rest of us went about our own special lines of business. Ours was to go out "East and West and South and North," like Lars Porsena's messengers, to summon up what orchids we could, but we quickly found that if East was difficult, none of the other directions were much better. One was either faced with quite incredibly dense and tangled dwarf forest of mainly tough, twisted *Bonnetia* trees (endemic to these highland zones) with thickly tangled undergrowth through which hacking a way with machete was extremely slow, hard, and temper-losing work, or one went off over more open places covered with beautiful expanses of equally endemic knee- or hip-high terrestrial bromeliads, only to find that in a short distance one was having to jump ever wider and deeper crevasses, with an increasing risk that what jumps easily on the way out might prove a very tricky jump on the way back. But with perseverance we tracked down about 40 species, mostly small epiphytes on the gnarled shrubby trees, the remainder fairly large terrestrials including some healthy-looking plants of *Eriopsis* (presumably *E. biloba)*, and such ubiquitous things as *Epidendrum secundum* and *E. nocturnum.* Most plants were without flowers but only a very few showed vegetative characters promising something out of the ordinary, and the same applied to the orchids sent up by Charles from the bottom of the hole. However, having some 1,000 Venezuelan orchid scalps already under our belts, we can no longer expect a continual stream of new stuff to cross our path, even in such remote places, and we were at least adding to our locality records: when two certainly new-to-us plants came to light during the week, we felt things were progressing satisfactorily. One of these was a tiny pleurothallis (?) consisting of confetti-sized, circular, fleshy leaves sticking tightly to the bark of a small tree (we shall be most annoyed if it turns out to be a cool-growing plant of *P. nanifolia* from hot forest areas), and the other a very odd, pleurothallis-type plant with hairy capsules arising almost from the rhizome. This latter plant had been sent up from the hole by Charles, but whether it is endemic to that spot will only be known when the surface forests have received much more attention than we could give them in the short period of our stay. Submitting a sketch of the plant to Dr. Leslie Garay it appears that it is either *P. lappiformis* from Nicaragua, or something very similar, but only when and if the plant flowers for us in Caracas shall we know; so far it looks very healthy. In the meantime we can tickle our imaginations trying to figure out how maybe an orchid from 1,500 miles away has managed to drop its seed so neatly into such a remote hole-in-the-ground.

Despite lack of great orchid success and a certain amount of "kitchen trouble" due to food supplies being in one place and the camp in another, we had pleasant scrambles around the limited places we could reach, including a chasm-crossing visit to the edge of (but NOT into) the smaller hole. The flora of these summits is largely composed of a botanist's paradise of rare and endemic plants, and the extremely acid soil conditions calls for very special characteristics on the part of the plants that enjoy it, dominant among which in more open areas are large, terrestrial bromeliads. Our water supply started from a few, small holes dug in the sandy floor of the heliport where recent rains had soaked in, but with absence of rain (which we blessed) these holes dried up (which we cursed), and for several days we had to fall back on the usual emergency water source, namely the water stored in the bromeliads themselves. A good specimen of *Brocchinia acuminata* has a length of two to five feet (semi-reclining ones often much more), with aerial-like inflorescences reaching up a further four or five feet, and the one- to two-foot-long swollen part of the body can yield a quart or more of water. But supplying 20 to 30 thirsty people calls for quite a volume, and the neighborhood of camp soon began to look as if a Martian invasion, on landing here to capture the enormous rocket-launching silos that Charles was at the moment investigating, had got their information mixed and had decided as a first step to eliminate all these upstanding "humans" with their aerial top pieces. The water these plants contain frequently comes out black and opaque with fine debris, but this is easily filtered out through any old rag. The resulting water is clear and tasteless, and (subject to the cleanliness of the rag) is perfectly drinkable without further treatment, though its rather astringent nature does produce pretty awful tea.

Finally the alpinists finished their work in the large and then a smaller hole, the V.I.P. guests departed, and the party was ready to move over to the meseta of Jaua to continue work on such things as orchids, uninterrupted by urgent cries for more cine film or steel-wire ladders. In one thankfully cloudless day, the whole party was helicoptered in a series of flights over the 30-mile gap to the top of Jaua. Here, at 6,000 feet, the general aspect was very different from that of Sarisariñama. An easy heliport was found in a bromeliad savanna close to the bank of a fine, 20-yard-wide, red-water stream flowing shallowly over its sandstone bed, and fairly open horizons promised much easier mobility. The roughly 300 square-mile, narrowly triangular top of this meseta is in the unusual form of a gentle valley containing a thin, central ridge and bounded east and west by the high edges of the meseta. To the south, these edges meet at the 8,000-foot point of the triangle and drainage is thus lengthwise along the heart of the top from south to north.

There would now be no scarcity of water for drinking, cooking, bathing, or diluting Julian's formol. Adequate sites for the main and subsidiary "private" camps were easily available within reach of the river and, indeed, in some cases almost in it. These sediment-free, clear red or dark tea-colored waters are characteristic of most of the highlands of the interior and of the rivers that flow from them. They are acid by nature (one of our scientist members said its pH acidity was equal to that of household vinegar, though it did not taste so!), and

The outlying cliffs of Cerro Jaua

while such waters do not make good tea, so important to our English tastes, they are perfectly serviceable for all general purposes. The "acid as vinegar" pronouncement produced a rash of psychosomatic indigestion in the more susceptible members of the party who had not previously had experience of these so-called "black" waters and the cook was seen hurling quantities of bicarbonate into the soup to "cure" it, but if any indigestion afflicted the party it was more likely caused by eating, at very late hours, an unaccustomed diet extremely high in carbohydrates and low in fats and meat. This acidity of the water is said to be due to humic acid and produces results that stretch far beyond the banks of the rivers themselves. By contrast with the normal "white water" rivers, all mobile life — animal, reptile, and insect — in black water regions is on a very reduced scale and much of the plant life, while abundant, is highly specialized to compensate for an impoverished intake of nutrients. The rivers themselves contain very few fish, indeed, and the lack of fish seems to spread to a general reduction in all forms of mobile life. In particular, this has the great advantage of cutting down enormously on the quantity of *plaga* that can make the traveler's life a misery in other areas. On Sarisariñama, we had been only mildly plagued; here on Jaua we saw no sandfly at all and the mosquitoes appeared only during strict union hours of 30 minutes at sunrise and 30 minutes at sunset.

While the generally open aspect of our surroundings promised, and indeed in some degree fulfilled, greater mobility in our searches, all was not as easy to get around in as it first seemed likely. Much of the *Brocchinia hectioides* "bromeliad" savannas, beautiful as they were, were extremely boggy, and the intervening patches of scrub frustratingly dense and tough. Trail-making varied from what we call "four-to-one" in the boggy parts to at least "10-to-one" in the dense scrub, meaning that if it takes you four (or 10) minutes to make a given yardage of trail it will only take you one minute on the way back. In 10-to-one conditions a whole morning of hard work might not yield as much as a mile of trail. In some dry savanna and in some sections of tall forest, the going was much easier — indeed almost one-to-one — but these were exceptions.

From the orchid point of view, these bromeliad savannas were poor, with occasional *Duckeella alticola* and some *Zygopetalum* plants the most noticeable, but, on the other hand, they were full of non-orchid plants both beautiful and rare. Honor where honor is due, and though it may be sacrilege to comment in an orchid publication on the merits of non-orchid plants we will risk stating that it was a great pleasure to be wandering among such lovely rarities as (with botanical help from Julian) large, golden flowers on small shrubs of *Bonnetia triflora;* large, bright-yellow heads of a not-yet-identified species of *Stegolepis* on six-foot stems and brilliant blue flowers of an equally not-yet-identified species of *Abolboda,* both growing in the very sandy soil; bright-red, insectivorous "sundews" of various *Drosera* species, one of which was "new," growing in sand or on rocks, and plants of another insectivore, *Utricularia humboldtii,* with its large, purple flowers waving in the breeze while its bladder-wort roots enjoyed an aquatic life in water trapped at the base of bromeliad leaves.

Elsewhere, in the tough scrub, in the low forest at the river's edge, in the higher forest beyond or in the mixed scrub and savanna at the side of our own little private encampment, orchid life was extremely prolific, and in many places walking without crushing an orchid was not easy. The epiphytes ranged from strings of tiny, dark, globose pseudobulbs of what we believe will prove to be a new-to-us *Epidendrum serpens,* to large plants of a species of *Acineta,* one of which is about to flower and reveal its identity in Caracas. Another odd-looking epidendrum proved eventually (and to our disappointment) to be merely a depauperate form of *Epidendrum fragrans,* one of the commonest of all tropical American orchids. Plants of what we are sure must be the very beautiful *Odontoglossum arminii* were widespread, from dry, lithophytic places, through semi-terrestrial situations to fully epiphytic in the forest. But it was the terrestrials that were the most striking, evidently greatly enjoying their acid habitat and the presumably high annual rainfall. Plants of *Houlletia odoratissima* had leaves a yard long, and though Julian (with a nose full of formol fumes?) said he could smell no scent, for us they fully lived up to their name with a strong and most pleasant perfume. *Oncidium nigratum* plants were plentiful, with panicles of spotted, white flowers with brilliant, yellow centers reaching a full five feet tall; large-flowered specimens of the ubiquitous *Epidendrum nocturnum,* one plant of which had a terminal capsule so high it could only just be reached with a machete stretched up to full arm's length; the very pretty *Sobralia infundibuligera* (endemic to these hinterlands) with stems to six feet tall, and the equally striking *Epistephium duckei* with its thick, glossy, dark-purple stems and bright magenta flowers, even taller.

No trip, however, can be endless, and indeed when the purpose is to collect live material there is a point beyond which the pressure to get the material home in safety begins to conflict ever more strongly with the desire to stay on and collect more, so when the day of departure came it was not entirely a day of unalloyed mourning. In one day of helicoptering, much of it in thick cloud that, in this mountainous area, terrified us even if it did not scare the pilot, we were back in the heat of Santa María. The next afternoon we were switching from helicopter to *barrigón* at Cacurí, and that evening, four weeks from the start, were home again. There had been time and fuel for only one very quick side trip to Guanacoco, and even including an earlier visit by Julian to another corner of Sarisariñama we had physically examined less than a thousandth part of our target summits. To say we had explored these mesetas would thus be the sheerest of nonsense, but we had at least been privileged to see and touch a tiny fraction of their surface. Out of more than a hundred species seen, we had three new-to-us orchids in flower and the promise of several more if the plants brought back behave themselves. The herpetologist had failed to see a single snake but had a few interesting lizards and frogs and one most interesting, worm-size electric eel. The birders had a number of possible new subspecies; the animal man had a squirrel and some tiny opossums (and we had eaten two small monkeys: tasty but very tough and but a mouthful apiece among so many mouths); the geologist had some lumps of rock; the anthropologist had material from Santa María but (naturally) nothing from on top; the cine unit had enough film to reach from Caracas to Jaua and back; the spelunker, the alpinists, and (we hope) the occasional visitors had happy memories. Most successful of all, we feel, were Julian and Charles. Julian, busy from sunrise to sunset collecting, pressing and formolizing his specimens, had achieved a total of some 5,000 collections, covering more than 1,000 numbered species plus many "extra copies." By the time the trip was over, he had converted hundreds of pounds of concentrated formol and old newspapers into an enormous bulk of bundle after bundle of precious herbarium material, all backed by a good, broad grin. Charles had organized his party, got it financed, taken it to its objectives and brought it back again, and could look back with pride on a very considerable achievement. Nobody had died of thirst or starvation, nobody had been left at the bottom of a hole or on top of a mountain. The only real complaint was that nothing had gone wrong to form a basis for a thrilling account — as dear old Mr. Ramsbottom would say, "There was no wrecks, and nobody drownded; in fact, nothing to laff at at all."

All that now remains for us is to make sure that the plants brought back survive and flourish, particularly the possibly new ones. (Since writing the above, one of these has flowered, to show that Colombia has just beaten us by a short head in the finding of a new species. This is *Epidendrum pachyphyton:* our plant was found on Jaua in February 1974, the description of it as a new species for Colombia (with a very nice illustration) was published by L. A. Garay in *Orquideología* for December 1973.) On Jaua, at 6,000 feet, we had been mighty glad of our down-filled sleeping bags when the temperature dropped from roughly 80°F shaded maximum at noon to 44°F minimum at night, but though in our home above Caracas at some 4,000 feet, we do not get quite as cold as that, we do have good cool nights. The acidity and other secrets of the general habitat we can probably do little about, but all but one of the critical plants are epiphytes and, while we may fail with the terrestrial treasure, we hope to succeed with the rest.

Tepui-Top Hopping by Helicopter[1]

BY OURSELVES, or in company with others, we have been responsible for finding about 50 new species of orchids during the past 20 years. This record is by no means as wonderful as it may sound to the uninitiated as the fields and forests of the South American tropics are still largely unexplored in detail and it only needs a modicum of perseverance to come across species not yet on the record. The law of diminishing returns has naturally enforced a declining rate of discovery in recent years, but we were nevertheless very hopeful of finding at least one more new-to-us species during a recent expedition organized very expertly by Dr. Charles Brewer-Carías on behalf of the Venezuelan Ministry of Environment and Renewable Resources, with the essential cooperation of the Venezuelan Air Force to provide the helicopter transport. The expedition was set up to investigate the fauna and flora on the summits of a number of high, sandstone table mountains or mesas, locally known as tepuis, in the beautiful Gran Sabana region of southeast Venezuela. Apart from ourselves as "bring-'em-back-alive" orchidologists, there was botanist Julian Steyermark (and his helper, Victor Carreno) of the Ministry, an entomologist, a geologist, a geomorphologist, a limnologist, and an amphibiologist, plus Brewer himself who is an expert photographer as well as being a dentist and an explorer.

By the end of a week of helicoptering in the northern section of the Gran Sabana, in excellent weather most of the time, eight different tepui-summit sites had been visited. Four of these sites were on the much-publicized massif of Auyán-tepui. Part of this tepui had been investigated in detail about 15 years earlier by Julian for botany in general and by ourselves for orchids in particular, but the summit of this tepui is so enormous (covering about 700 sq. km.) that none of the highly broken and generally inaccessible eastern part had previously been touched, nor the extreme north end which forms an almost separate tepui, split off from the remainder by the gorge of the Río Aonda not far from the tourist resort of Canaima. Four sites at about 1,900 m on the eastern portion were visited on the present occasion, and in addition two sites at nearly 2,500 m were selected on the almost equally large (and much more broken-up) massif of Chimantá. The latter had been the object of a very thorough, eight-month study by Steyermark, but here again, with a target of this size and complexity, large sections still remained untouched. Among these were two culminations known as Tiripon and Amurí (or Toronto and Auroda, depending on which Indians produce the names for you — a habit most annoying to the botanist trying to label his precious plants correctly) and these summits were also included. The summit of the small but equally high Aprada-tepui, lying between the Auyán and Chimantá massifs, was landed on and investigated for the first time ever, and the top of the small but high (2,400 m) Ptari-tepui, the most easterly of them all, was equally virgin territory until the expedition landed there. Surrounded by an unbroken ring of high, vertical cliffs, this tepui had long been a magnet for Steyermark who some 30 years earlier had exhaustively searched its forested flanks up to the base of the final cliffs and ever since then had yearned to see the top.

With this background everyone, including ourselves, expected to find at least one "novelty" in his own discipline. Julian, having the whole plant kingdom to work on, and plants being available in abundance, could expect more. In the event, though he found many very interesting species, he ended up with only one single item that he believed would turn out to be new, and when the time came for the helicopter to return to its base we ourselves had only plants that were obviously well-known and typical inhabitants of the tepuis, or were

[1] Originally appeared in *A.O.S. Bulletin*, Vol. 48, March 1979, pages 222-228

ordinary-looking plants that would have to be cultivated at home until, if ever, they flowered and could be properly identified. Only one (flowerless) plant had a general aspect that was new to our eyes and this was almost certainly a species known from Roraima, *Octomeria connellii*. Our searches had naturally been limited by the hours the helicopter could afford to leave us on top (not forgetting a couple of hurried exits when in-rolling clouds threatened to pin us down overnight), and in lateral extent were frequently limited by large chasms or other obstacles, so our hunting had not been as extensive as we had hoped. But this did not mean that we would be rating our participation in the expedition as a failure. The hope of finding something new (and preferably with enormous flowers) on such untouched summits had been an exciting incentive, and success would have been welcome, but as Julian would confirm, a most important function of such an expedition is to add to the total knowledge of the flora (and fauna) and general ecology of the region, and in this respect the results we had obtained would have real value.

After we got back home there was an exciting moment with one of the plants we had brought back. This was apparently just a plant of the very common *Encyclia vespa*, so common that we almost did not bother to collect it, but when it developed an inflorescence and its flowers opened they were far from the usual dull green with dark markings — instead, they were a very handsome, unspotted yellow. We must surely have got a new-to-us species, we thought, perhaps an altogether new species that we could call "*breweri*" to reward Charles for all his help. Alas, when enthusiasm died down and we studied the flowers carefully we realized that all we had was a very unusual and remarkably pretty albino form of the large-flowered variety of *E. vespa* often known by its synonym of *E. tigrinum*.

In total, some 40 species of orchids were located, of which 25 with flowers could be identified with certainty: seven species were flowerless but had characteristic vegetative form allowing near-certain identification, and a further eight or nine species remain whose identification cannot be undertaken until and unless they show us their flowers in captivity. A good proportion of these latter "unknowns" are octomerias, a genus whose members often provide little clue to their identity when without flower, so one cannot even be certain just how many species one is dealing with. The final list is thus open-ended as far as the total number of species is concerned, but in general shows a fairly uniform orchid flora in line with the fairly uniform environment. Some sites yielded more species than others, but given more time and scope for seaching it seems probable that the orchid content of each summit would prove to be very similar to all the others. A possible exception to this might be the Auyántepui site D which was relatively sheltered in a low, fairly wide, shallow valley. All the other sites were open in character and showed a variable mixture of otherwise "standard" tepui-top habitats, unique to this part of the world but not exceptional within these small regional limits. These habitats (or at time microhabitats) were as follows:

A. Expanses of bare rock on which orchids (and other small plants) were growing in a truly lithophytic manner, or at most with a very thin layer of sand and old leaves, etc., the roots either clinging somehow to the exposed rock or thrusting themselves into cracks to find moisture and shelter. Plants growing in such conditions, exposed to the full extremes of temperature, sun, ultra-violet radiation, wind, and rain to which these summits are subjected, frequently develop characteristically hard (but not necessarily small) leaves and stems, with a very pronounced, almost black, dark purple color instead of what would normally be green. Other plants of identical species but with normal green leaves could occasionally be found intermixed with the almost black ones, a phenomenon for which we see no explanation. Cultivated at home, we always find these dark and hardened plants very difficult to keep alive as they seem to lack the will to produce roots, but we have no real clue as to why this should be when green plants from the same site behave properly.

B. Patches or expanses of thin sandy soil, bearing typical tepui-summit vegetation, often green but nearly always quite extraordinarily brittle, and characterized by the presence of bromeliads and tepui-endemic shrubs such as *Brocchinia hechtioides, B. acuta, Bonnetia roraimae, Maguireothamnus specio*, etc. These patches may also be the site of sparse growths of dwarf trees.

C. Occasional, generally small patches of boggy soil, very treacherous to the unsuspecting foot and characterized frequently by the very large and beautiful flowers of *Utricularia humboldtii*.

D. Numerous deep and generally parallel cracks (*zanjones*) that grade into deep chasms or at times into quite wide rock valleys with vertical or overhanging sides. These tend to be the home of small, brittle, scrubby trees (or dwarf forest in the wider cracks) composed mainly of tepui-endemic plants such as certain *Bonnetia* species. Such trees have a very rough and brittle bark that falls away at a touch and is thus basically unsuitable for epiphytic orchids however promising the tree may seem to be at first sight. In these places some epiphytic orchids do exist (notably the very beautiful *Zygosepalum angustilabium*), but with few exceptions the orchid life is terrestrial in its manner of growth and, in this habitat, lives mainly in the soil of the margin of these wooded patches or just inside the "forest" itself.

E. Rock ledges on the vertical face of chasms and cliffs, which provide mini-habitats enjoyed by rare ferns, occasional orchids, and other small plants.

At each site we visited, there were naturally varying proportions of these basic types of habitat, and the cracks and chasms varied from small to large enough to hem even the most agile expedition members in on all sides. The only exception, perhaps, was the Auyántepui site D, already mentioned, with its very shallow, black-water stream flowing over a flat, sandstone bed, and closed in by the usual cliffs and dense, dwarf forest of *Bonnetia* trees.

The dominant orchid species found on this expedition, and the types of habitat where they were growing, were as follows:

Eriopsis biloba Lindl. This handsome species was abundant underfoot everywhere we went and showed the usual variation between a few plants with relatively small, round, smooth, green pseudobulbs and the great majority with very different looking, strongly elongated pseudobulbs with a very dark, rough surface and of lengths up to 35 cm. While florally there is no clear and constant distinction between these two types the one with the long, dark pseudobulbs is also known as *E. grandibulbosa* Ames & Schweinf. Some of these latter plants, though not in flower, showed old erect inflorescnes up to 150 cm tall.

Sobralia infundibuligera Garay & Dunsterv. This orchid is characterized by the flat, wide, funnel-shaped, sheathing bases of its leaves, and by its very striking, large flowers with pale petals and very prominent bright purple lip.

Epidendrum nocturnum Jacq. This species of orchid has many varieties that at one time or another have been given separate names as species in their own right, as mentioned in our note on this

Ptari E. — closeup of habitat

Aprada C. — high ridge

species in the *A.O.S. Bulletin* for October 1977. Almost all the plants of this species found on this trip were of the erect type with stiff, suberect leaves and large flowers, all of which were at the moment withered and had developed large seed capsules. This type has recently been named *E. strictum* by Brieger & Bical.

Epidendrum dendrobioides Thunb. This orchid was common in many places, mainly in small form but with distinctive nutant inflorescences of pale green or almost white fleshy flowers.

Less common but florally attractive species were:

Epidendrum montigenum Ridl. This species is a close ally to *E. dendrobioides* but has very pretty pink flowers of a rather more open shape and thinner texture. It seems to be a rare plant, first found on Roraima but occasionally turning up on other tepuis.

Duckeella alticola C. Schweinf. This is a small, terrestrial species with attractive, relatively large, yellow flowers; it is not exactly rare but one never seems to find more than one plant in a day's searching.

Epidendrum secundum Jacq., a common species commonly called by this name but recently reidentified by Garay as *E. elongatum* Jacq. and remarkable for its variability both in color and in details of the lip. During this latest expedition normal flowers of this species were found in two places, but in addition a number of plants were found that were much smaller than normal. These small flowers showed a rather abnormal callus of the lip, outside the usual range of variations, and of a type that we had found during our much earlier explorations of Auyántepui. We had then listed the drawing (#782) of this variety as merely a depauperate version of the normal type, but during the present expedition it turned up with fair frequency in four different places and always with the same form of callus and the same somewhat unusual lobes to the lip. This unexpected invariability hints that these specimens, for some reason or other, are starting to leave the common herd to set themselves up as a separate species which meanwhile, for convenience, we refer to as "var. 782."

Maxillaria quelchii Rolfe. This rather small species with fair-sized flowers grows well, terrestrially, in very harsh conditions but can also be found occasionally as a larger and more flourishing epiphyte.

Cleistes rosea Lindl. This is a very common and widespread species but is also a very beautiful one. Like so many terrestrial orchids it is extremely difficult to transfer successfully from wherever it happens to be growing. It grows wild within yards of our Caracas home but every attempt to move it to our side of the fence has ended in failure so we no longer try.

Oncidium warmingii Reichb.f. One of the very few oncidiums in the Guayana tepui summits, it grows with widely spaced small pseudobulbs on a long rhizome and has suberect, lightly branching panicles of small but pretty white flowers with pink-spotted lips.

Zygosepalum angustilabium (Schltr.) Garay. This very handsome, epiphytic species has small plants with fair-sized flowers and was found in good quantity with flowers in half-withered condition with large, developing seed capsules. In Caracas the plants we brought back are responding surprisingly well — surprising because so many tepui-top orchids object strongly to being moved.

Epidendropsis violascens (Ridl.) Garay & Dunsterv. Small plants of this "two-pollinia epidendrum" were found growing lithophytically,

Eriopsis biloba

Zygosepalum angustilabium

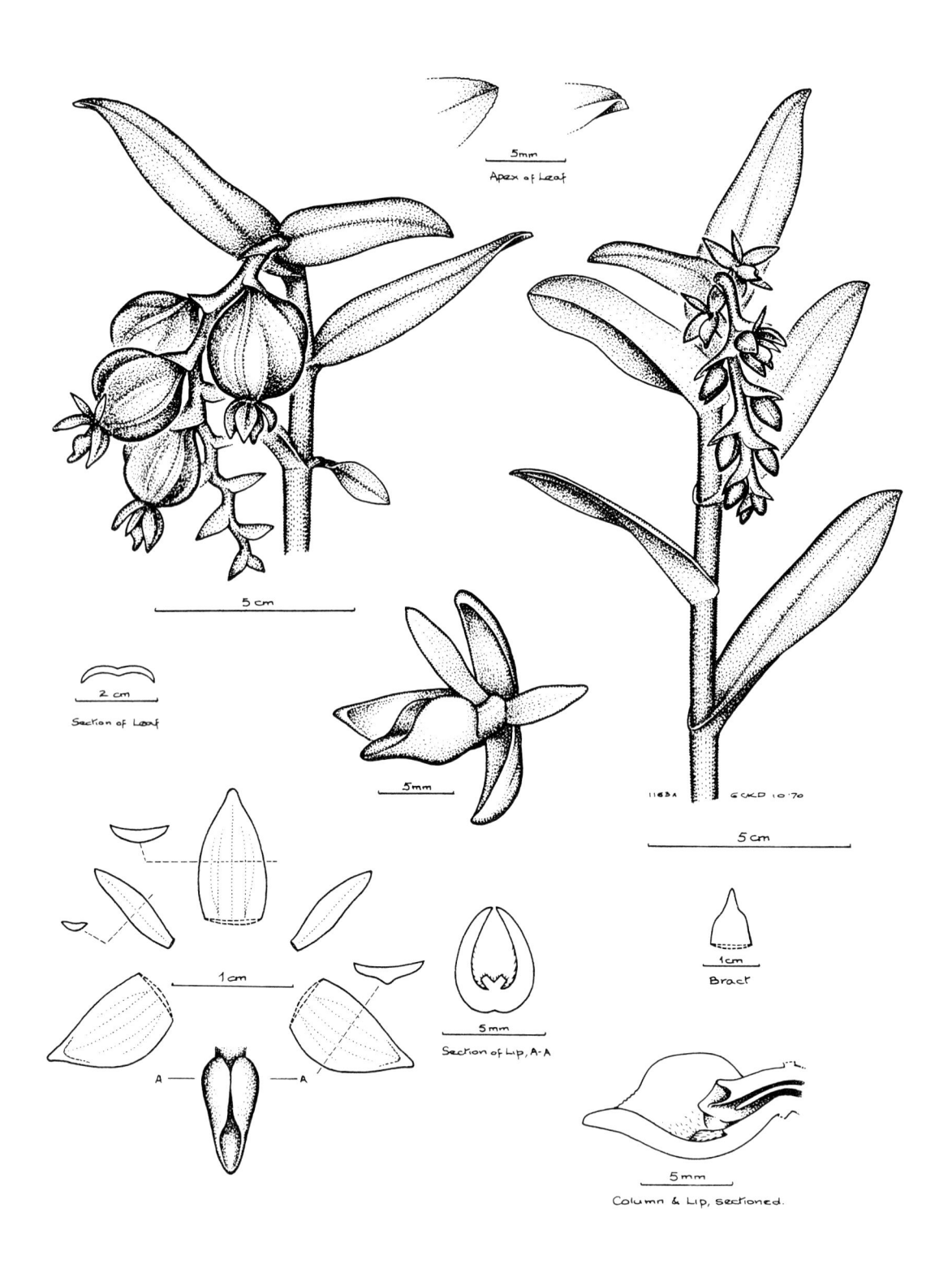

Epidendrum dendrobioides Thunb., Pl. Brasil. 2: 17, 1818. — E.E.

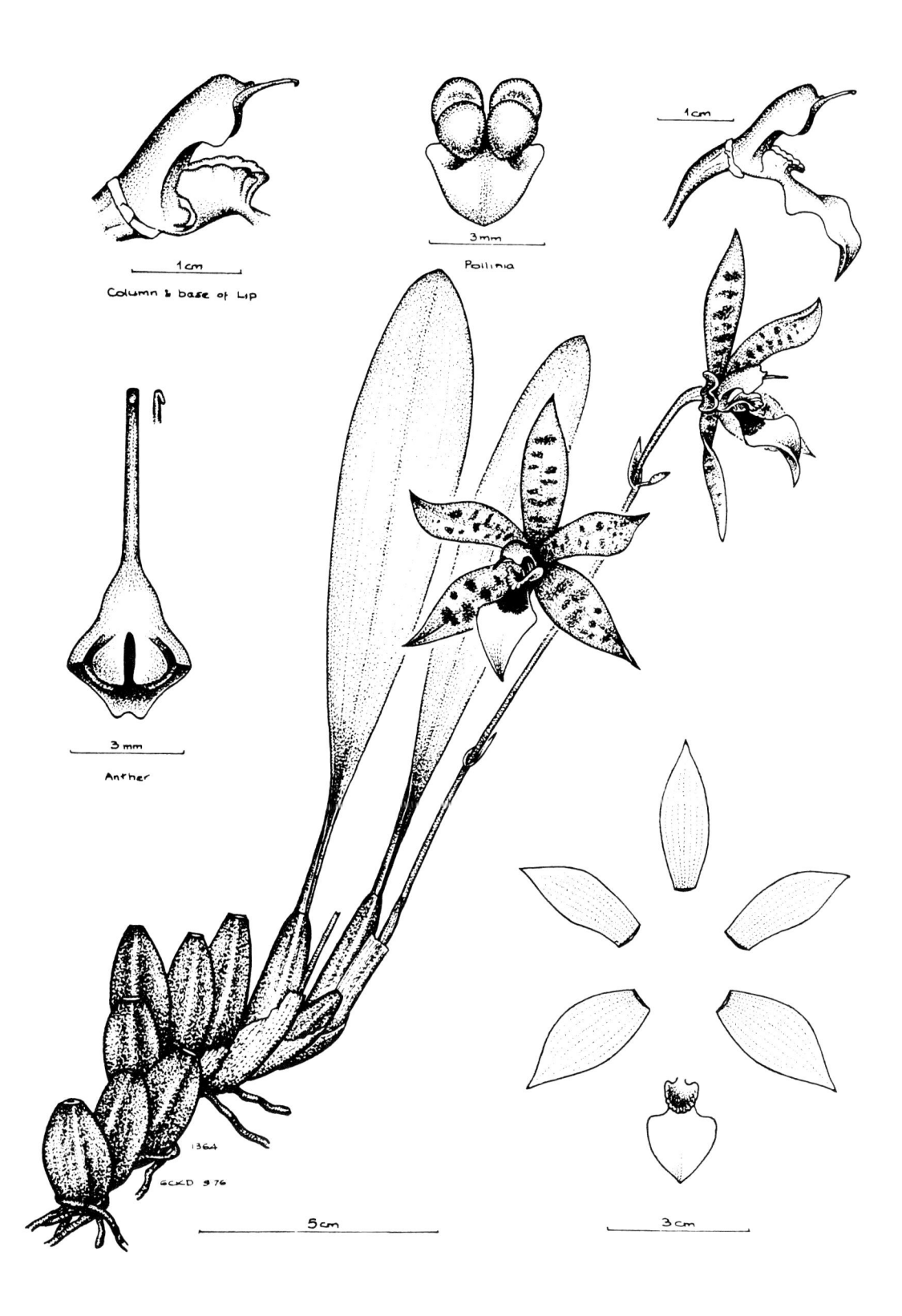

Zygosepalum angustilabium (C. Schweinf.) Garay in Orquideología 8: 34, 1973. — E.

usually with hard, dark purple leaves but occasionally (in identical conditions) with normal, green leaves. The erect, lightly branching inflorescences with very fine stems bear a number of pretty but very small flowers and the green-leaved plants seem to be taking well in Caracas.

Mention has been made at the beginning of this article to the presence on these summits of many endemic species of plants. The orchids, however, seem to be less exclusive. Of the total of 32 identifiable species found during this last expedition all are known to exist in countries outside Venezuela with the exception of four (*Duckeella alticola, Octomeria parvifolia, Stelis obovata,* and *Sobralia infundibuligera*) that are limited to this country but which occur elsewhere in the highlands of the State of Bolívar and the Federal Territory of Amazonas and two (*Elleanthus norae* and *Zygosepalum angustilabium*) that are limited to the Gran Sabana area of Bolívar State. None is endemic just to the tops of the tepuis we have just visited. It thus seems that despite the isolated and in many degrees "unique" nature of these summits they have not given rise to many endemic orchids; indeed, if new species of orchids do eventually turn up in such places, then we feel that it would be only a matter of time before other specimens of such species were found on other tepuis or elsewhere. Orchid species are born to be wanderers and obviously hate to be pinned to one single, small locality.

One final note may be mentioned. With tropical forests justifiably famous for their rich content of a great number of species, a total bag of some 40 orchids may seem a very meager result for a wide-ranging visit to a number of tepuis. But richness in species is very largely a function of the range of altitude covered during any botanical search, and our investigations were limited to what in effect were very thin slices of "altitude" and touched on habitats basically very similar. It is interesting to note, however, that the quite marked difference of roughly 600 m (2,000 ft) in altitude between the Auyán sites and the other tepui summits visited is not strongly reflected in the orchid species found. Discounting the sheltered habitat of the Auyán site D, there were only five species on the Auyán sites that were not represented in the other, much higher summits. This observation seems to show that the generally exposed, rock-slab character of all these places visited is of more influence than the 25% difference in altitude between the Auyán sites and the others. It remains true, nevertheless, that a slice of 1,000 m in altitude range in any of the forests covering the flanks of a tepui, even if severely limited in lateral scope, would produce far more species. But helicopters are not only very expensive to buy, maintain and operate, the operators would

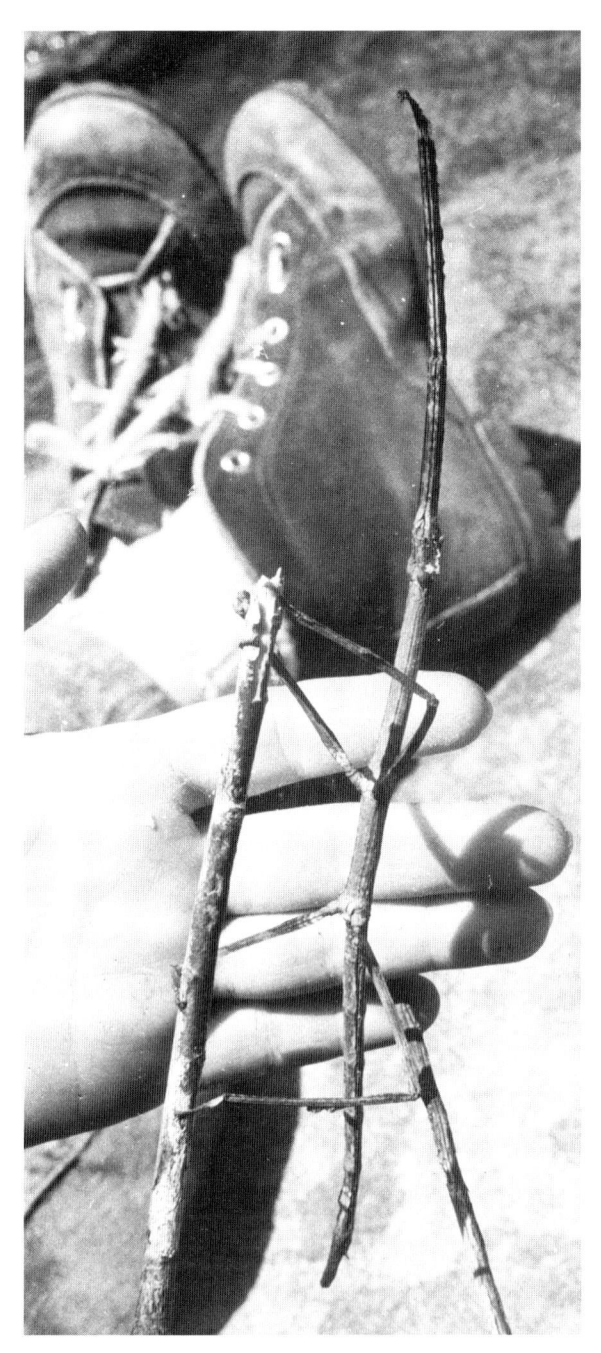

A Gran Sabana "stick insect"

not really be at all happy if asked to put one down on the steep and forested flank of a tepui. Where they, quite naturally, feel happiest about landing us is on firm, level, open ground devoid even of shrubs that could result in damage to the small, delicate, fast-revolving stabilizer propeller, set low at the end of the tail. Damage to this could leave one very uncomfortably stranded in a lonely spot for a long time before rescue arrived. So we are grateful not only to Charles and the Ministry for the opportunity to investigate these summits but also to the helicopter crews for getting us safely there and back.

100 Orchids (and 37 Snakes) Up the Orinoco[1]

IN A RECENT BULLETIN (see Chapter 4) article on tropical forests, we bemoaned the fact that what we consider a true rain forest — hot, flat, airless, largely non-seasonal and often flooded — is generally poor in variety and quantity of orchids. Regardless of where it is located, a large extent of flat forest is liable to be one of uniform habitat conditions, with diminished air movement in its interior, and a week's orchid hunting in better "aerated" sloping forest can bring far greater orchid rewards than a month in flat forest. Unfortunately, flat forest is typical of much of the low altitude parts of the Upper Orinoco region, but this is not to say that it is not worth looking for orchids there.

The *Lower* Orinoco is navigable for quite large vessels and ends at Puerto Ayacucho, the capital of Venezuela's Federal Amazonas Territory. The *Upper* Orinoco starts from 50 km above Puerto Ayacucho, separated from it by a series of very tough rapids, the two sections of the river being linked by a road from Puerto Ayacucho to a tiny rock-slab "port" named Sanariapo, above which all further river travel is by small craft such as launches and dugouts. In 1962 we had visited the Ventuari and Parucito tributaries at the lower end of the Upper Orinoco, starting from Sanariapo, and since then (though we found few exciting orchids) it had been our ambition to see what orchids could be found all along the Upper Orinoco itself. And at the end of 1965 a very good friend, Dr. Pablo Anduze, gave us and our daughter Hilary just this opportunity.

Pablo is a man of many talents with a Ph.D. in zoology. He has been Governor of the Territorio Amazonas, well loved and respected by the Indians living there and naturally with an intimate knowledge of their ways and customs. He owned a small house in Puerto Ayacucho, and more important for us also owned a small *embarcación* stationed at Sanariapo. There could be no better guide and mentor for an Orinoco trip, and we accepted with alacrity his invitation, when last in Caracas, to accompany him on a river trip up the Upper Orinoco to see what treasures he could find in the way of *animalitos* while we looked for orchids.

So we flew down from Caracas, and early December 1965 found us truck-borne from Puerto Ayacucho to Sanariapo together with Pablo, a pair of Indians and a hundred assorted packages. Pablo's craft, when we examined it, was revealed as a truly enormous *falca* of a very lordly type even if a bit old in the tooth. Its basis was a very wide dugout made from the trunk of a large and well-selected tree, increased in capacity in the standard manner, after gouging out a longitudinal groove, by stretching the wood laterally while heating it: a tricky operation that if not done very expertly can at any moment result in a loud crack and the trunk reduced to two long and completely useless pieces of wood. In the case of Pablo's *falca* it had resulted in a dugout which, with its sides further raised by the addition of planks along its upper margin, was some 50 feet long and wide enough to take camp beds cross-wise. All but the bow section was sheltered by a flat tin-sheathed wooden top supported on posts high enough for one to stand under and strong enough to be stood on, promising us liner-like comfort, at least until reaching some distance up a tributary, the Padamo, where we would have to change to a smaller and completely open dugout, or *curiara*.

This promise of comfort, unfortunately, came unstuck after only 20 minutes of travel when the main outboard motor of 75 horsepower blew some essential part, and the rest of the journey had to be made with the sole use of the small motor which had no more than a measly 20 horses inside it, and was intended solely for use with the open *curiara* in the Padamo. We were in no great hurry (whoever hopes to hurry in these parts dies young from ul-

[1] Originally appeared in *A.O.S. Bulletin*, Vol. 53, January 1984, pages 43-49

cers), but our speed now matched exactly the average cruising speed of clouds of very hungry sand-fly, black-fly, or other no-seeum villains, delighted to have captive prey at their mercy. Liberal use of repellent was of little avail as sweat washed it off as soon as it was on, but finally by enveloping hat and head in a globe of mosquito netting, using long sleeves, and covering hands in socks, life became more livable, even if making botanical drawings with socks on one's hands and a face enveloped in screening had certain disadvantages.

In this overclothed manner we spent day after day progressing very slowly up the river, stopping frequently to look for orchids (or zoological specimens) in the forested banks, and spending nights in mosquito-netted hammocks. Our orchid booty was not vast, but slowly we were adding to our list of species, some easily identifiable and others, of which we took live plants or bottled critical pieces, which would have to be dealt with after our return home. We stopped briefly at the largely deserted Mission of La Esmeralda, backed by the high cliffs of Cerro Duida, and eventually turned north up the Padamo. Later still we had to switch over to a long, narrow, open dugout which Pablo bought from some Indians, and into which we transferred the small outboard motor. By Christmas Day we were making our way for a few miles up the Cuntinamo, a tributary of the Padamo, in a yet smaller and very leaky dugout, apparently abandoned as useless by its original owner, and two days later began the long run home. On the way back we diverged for a while down the Casiquiare "canal," a natural stream that unnaturally splits away from the Orinoco to divert some of its waters southwest to link up eventually with the Río Negro and thus into Brazil and the Amazon — a freak of nature that thus provides a low-level water link between the two river systems.

By the time we were finally heading for home, we had collected bits and pieces, or whole plants, of some 100 species. No new species had rewarded our efforts, but we felt we now had a far better idea of the orchid content of this part of Venezuela. Most of the more showy species have been listed in our *A.O.S. Bulletin* article on rain forest, and their color portraits have appeared in the *A.O.S. Bulletin* at one time or another, so we shall mention here only a few of the Upper Orinoco orchids that have not been dealt with in the *A.O.S. Bulletin*. These orchids are:

Acacallis cyanea Lindl. — Alphabetically, and by special request of both of us, we give this species top ranking because it is always such a joy to see its bright flowers flaunting themselves from a plant that is apparently clinging for dear life to a small tree on the edge of a flooded river in full spate, with most of its scandent rhizome under water and

Acacallis cyanea

only one or two of its plicate leaves and the inflorescence itself in the clear. Far from being in danger, this seems to be the way this species enjoys life best, and on the few occasions we have tried to bring a specimen home to live a safeguarded life with us it has always expressed its extreme disgust by turning up its toes in a few years at most before expiring with a deep sigh of disappointment at the foolishness of humans who just do not understand its needs.

Photographically, its flowers are also rather disappointing because while they open decidedly blue to the eye (to match its *cyanea* epithet) the blueness rapidly takes on a tinge of pink, and this "redness," normally only moderately noticeable to the eye, dominates over the blue in the various color films we have tried out — as in the slide reproduced here.

Oncidium nanum Lindl. — This is a small but attractive epiphyte with fleshy leaves of the "mule-ear" type, fairly common in the Amazon part of Guyana, Brazil, Bolivia, Peru, and Venezuela, in which country it can often be found in the Upper Orinoco. We have collected it from a number of places on this river, such as the *Paso de Ganado* (Cattle Crossing) above San Fernando de Atabapo and the Caño Guaname two-thirds of the way from Puerto Ayacucho to the Mission of Tamatama and at the mouth of the Padamo itself, but although it must have been seen and probably collected here, or elsewhere in Venezuela, by many "aficionados" and botanists in the past, it has earned very scant mention in the *Flora de Venezuela;* it does, however, rate a picture in Rebecca Northen's *Miniature Orchids*, which is an honor by itself!

Rodriguezia leeana Reichb. f — As mentioned in an old "Dunsterville and Garay" article in *The Orchid Review*, when Reichenbach published this species in the *Gardener's Chronicle* for July 1883,

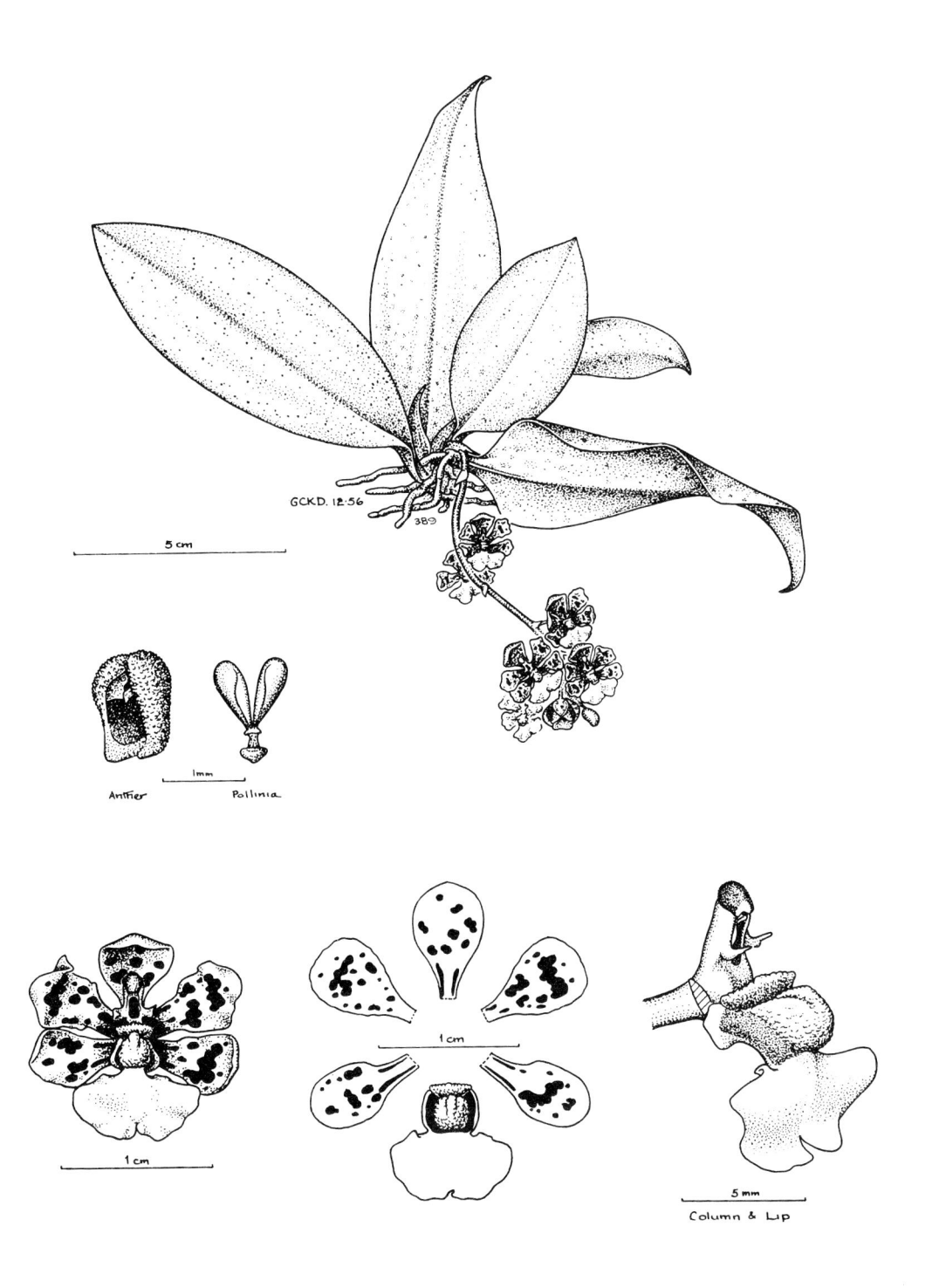

Oncidium nanum Lindl. in Bot. Reg. 28: Misc. p. 37, 1842. — D. E.

he referred to it in apparent "Americanese" as "A mighty curious novelty," leading one to envisage an orchid with some truly spectacular feature such as at least an enormous moustache — but when B. S. Williams described it in his 1885 *Orchid Grower's Manual* (under the generic name of *Burlingtonia)* he merely noted it as a "very distinct and beautiful species" which it certainly is, with its pendent sprays of white, or variably pinkish, flowers. While it is known from Brazil and the Amazonian parts of Guyana and Colombia it seems to be quite a rare species and does not figure in the 1970 *Flora de Venezuela,* so for all we know the only times it has been seen or collected are one record by Gaede from near the junction of the Río Mavaca with the Upper Orinoco, and our own two collections from near the Mission of La Esmeralda.

Maxillaria equitans (Schltr.) Garay — For a maxillaria, this species has a decidedly odd appearance as its fleshy and equitant, conduplicate leaves give it much more the stamp of a vanda than of a common-on-Orinoco maxillaria — which accounts for its earlier synonyms of *Camaridium vandiforme, Maxillaria vandiformis,* and *Marsupiera vandiformis.* It is fairly widespread in "Amazonas" territory from Guyana and Venezuela to Colombia and Peru, and our own specimens came from the Paso de Ganado site already mentioned as well as from quite close to Puerto Ayacucho itself; and we have seen thriving plants in San Fernando de Atabapo.

Sigmatostalix amazonica Schltr. and **Sigmatostalix huebneri** Mansf. — These delightful miniature orchids have slender racemes of tiny yellow flowers, and clumped growths of smooth, flattened and sharp-edged, unifoliate pseudobulbs. The flowers are characterized by prominently arched and very slender columns rising from a fleshy cup-shaped callus at the base of the lip, the shape of the column giving rise to the name of the genus because, as noted in Schultes and Pease's *Generic Names of Orchids,* the slender column is often so arcuate that it assumes the shape of a "C" (old Greek form of sigma). Our two plants came to light also from the Paso de Ganado, one from fairly low on a tree by the river bank and one farther back in the forest. The plant of *Sigmatostalix huebneri* was found by our friend G. Bergold much farther up the Orinoco at its junction with the Río Mavaca. As regards cultivation of these sweeties, we can best quote Hawkes' *Encyclopaedia of Cultivated Orchids,* where he says these little plants "are best kept in smallish well-drained pots, in a compost made up of chopped sphagnum moss and shredded tree-fern fibre."

But what of the bugs or *animalitos* that had fallen to Pablo's net or bottles while we were busy with our orchids? We never heard that he had made any great discoveries, but he was responsible for the trip we were making and equally responsible for the snakes of the title, and thus deserves a proper place in this tale.

The main stream of the Orinoco above Samariapo, showing our tin-roofed *curirara*

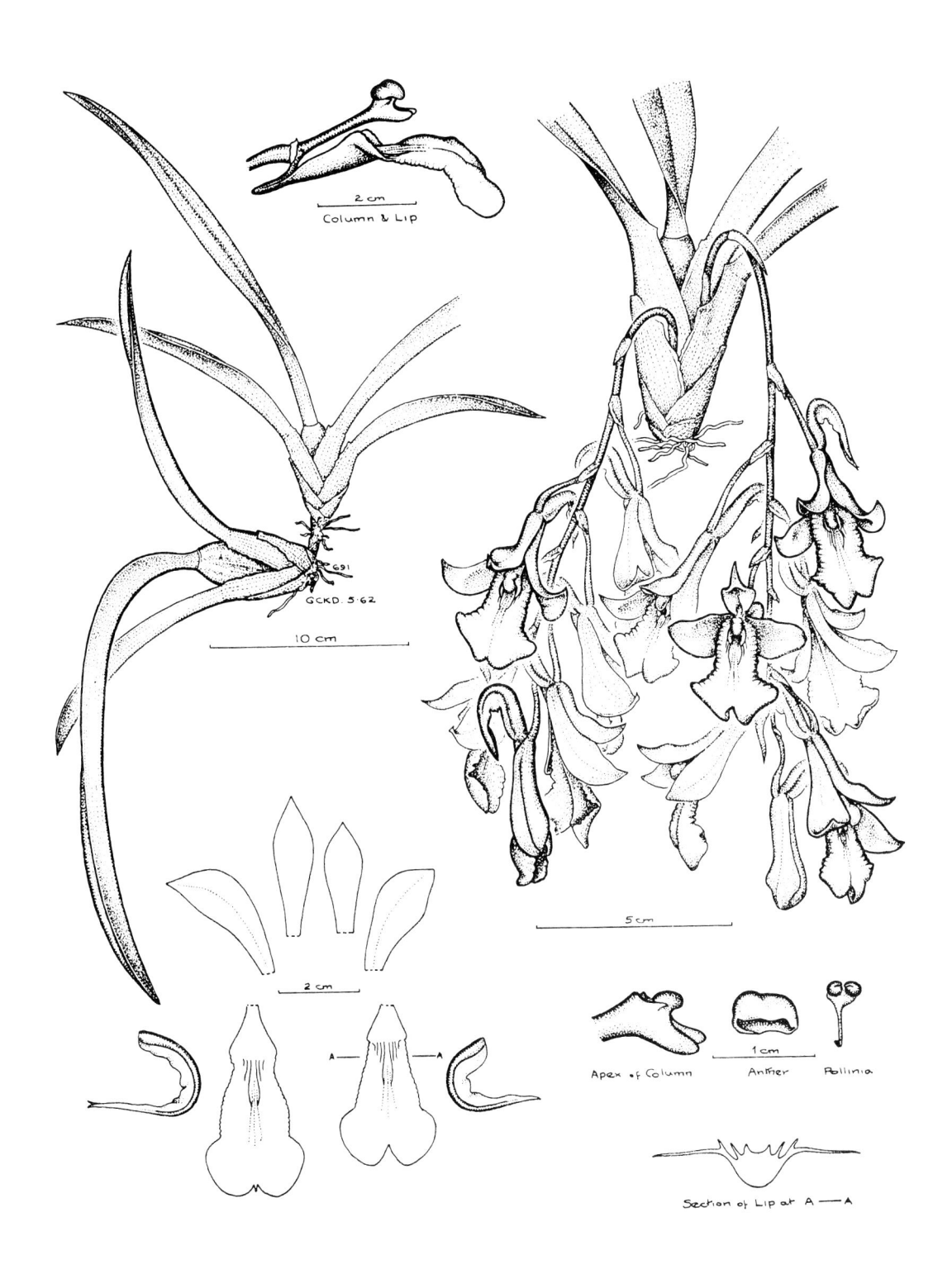

Rodriguezia leeana Reichb. f. in Gard. Chron. n.s. 20: 38, 1883. — D

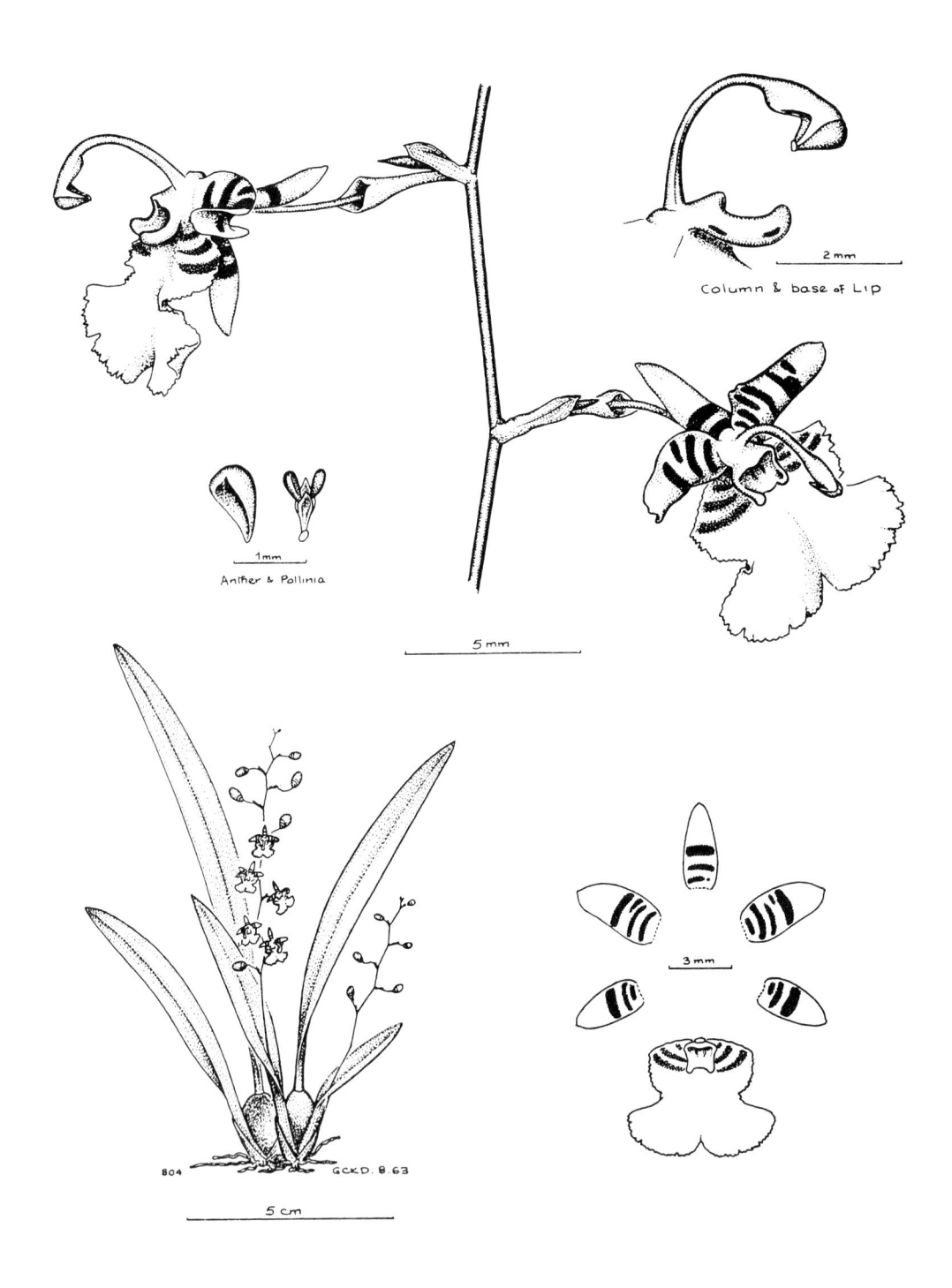

Sigmatostalix huebneri Mansf. in Fedde, Rep. 36: 62, 1934. — D.

The modern child is brought up on "fairy tales" peopled with batmen, supermen, and extraterrestrial heroes and villains, but in our young day these had not yet reached this planet and we had nothing more exotic to feed our minds on than old-fashioned, non-electronic giants and ogres. And among these simple tales there was one about a humble, timid, and very unheroic tailor who in a rare moment of valor managed to kill seven flies with one swat of a fly-swatter. Having achieved this unwitnessed triumph he then had the bright, unhumble, and rather dishonest idea of blowing his trumpet as one who had "killed seven at one blow!" leaving it to the listener's imagination to envisage armed giants as the victims. What happened to him as a result of this apparently successful bit of Madison Avenue flimflammery we have forgotten, but presumably he won the hand of a beautiful princess and lived happily ever after. The moral of this story would seem to fit modern ethics rather than the nursery ethics of childhood, but we do remember thinking even then that it must have been nice to live in fairy-princess times if such a bare-faced and obvious half-lie could gain credence among adults, whereas all our own best inventions were always disclosed in very short order for the wholehearted lies that they were. But at no time did it occur to us that we might ourselves some day be able to say that we had witnessed the death at one blow of 37 of the most dangerous snakes in South America.

The forest inhabitants where this act of valor took place should, we suppose, be thankful for it, and certainly those who otherwise might in due course have become victims of one or more of this band of 37 owe us a vote of thanks. But ecology is such an incalculable tangle of interdependencies that this act may have done far more harm than good. In which case we are sorry, but there is nothing to be done about it now and only Saint Peter will in due course be able to tell us if our share in this act rates as a plus or a minus in the Heavenly Books. At least we are not compounding a felony with a tailor's half-lie about the identity of the victims. These were all quite definitely *mapanares,* the most aggressive of Venezuela's pit-vipers, scientifically known as *Bothrops atrox,* a beastie that at the full height (or length) of his power carries enough venom to kill a half-dozen *Homo*s insufficiently *sapiens* to keep out of his way.

On our way up the Padamo, before changing to the small *curiara,* we had stopped fairly early in the morning to strike inland on foot at the base of a small hill to see what a short whiffle through the tulgy woods might produce, ourselves and Hilary armed with our usual machetes, Pablo armed with whatever he carries to bottle bugs and snakes in, and Joaquín the motor-man going ahead with a shotgun in case we should meet (or be met by) a hungry jaguar, and more importantly to see if he could shoot a wild turkey for the kitchen pot. At one spot in our wanderings we all converged to cross the horizontal trunk of a very large fallen tree which provided the easiest way to continue through the undergrowth-tangled forest, clambering up one side of the trunk and slipping recklessly down the other in direct contravention of one of the major laws of wise bush travel. Because of its inconvenience, this same trunk-crossing was used on our return route, with Hilary bringing up the rear some 30 yards back as she so often does — not because of laziness but from a reluctance even greater than ours to believe that no rare orchid is being left behind to laugh at us as we depart. Shortly after the rest of us had recrossed the trunk we heard a cry from Hilary: "Does Pablo want a snake?" Pablo yelled back "Yes — but wait until Joaquín gets back to you with his gun!" In due course Joaquín was summoned and we all trailed back to find Hilary keeping watch over a snake that had been hiding just where we had all been cheerfully scrambling over the trunk. The snake, most abnormally, was showing no haste to flee from all this fuss-and-bother, just staying put to stick its tongue out at us. Which was its undoing. Pablo said he wanted it as a specimen. Joaquín pulled the trigger, the headless body went into a sack, and that was that.

Back at the *falca* and freed of our other impedimenta, we had time to examine the snake at our leisure. That markings were definitely "*mapanare*" but, held up by the neck, the shape of the body was rather odd as it was much fatter in the lower part than at the top. Pablo quickly solved that problem by saying "pregnant" (which explained the snake's reluctance to move from its lair), and then went to work with professional skill to perform a post-mortem caesarian. Most snakes lay eggs, but a few, among them the *mapanares*, produce live babies, and to be true it did seem as if maybe a half-dozen progeny could be the cause of the bulgy lower end of the body. But what Pablo's knife produced seemed like magic: one by one, no less than 36 babies were revealed, each about eight inches long and each, naturally, dying or already dead. Seeing is believing, but if we did not have the photo taken on the spot we would by now be doubting if we had counted correctly.

Two other things were also of interest. Firstly, while the patterning on the snakes was very clear, there was so much variation from one to the next that no two seemed alike. Secondly, baby *mapanares* are reputed to be able to kill small prey as soon as they are born, and while these particular babies were premature they must surely have been within hours of seeing daylight when their mother's head was blown off. So it was a bit alarming to see Pablo prick himself by accident on an infantile fang, deeply enough to draw blood. He seemed little worried about this himself, but the rest of us watched anxiously for a long time to spot the first symptoms of his death pangs, before deciding that either "repute" was false, or Pablo was vastly more resistant than the baby mouse that might have been the snake's first meal.

We have many times since then made our boast of "37 at One Blow." Some have believed us; some have said "Oh, Yeah?" But for none of us, notably Joaquín, the principal actor in this drama, has there been sight, sound, or sweet scent of the beautiful princess as a reward. Or if there has, Joaquín has been very silent about it.

Hilary holds up her poisonous *mapanare* snake after its head had been blown off. It was still full of young live snakes.

Part II
The Flowering Seasons of Some Venezuelan Orchids[1]

ABOUT THREE YEARS AGO we received a request from Mr. L. F. Mezzera, of Atlas Fish Emulsion fame, asking us to check the flowering periods that he proposed to show on a small list of better-known orchid species being prepared for advertising purposes. Some of the dates agreed with our rather loose memory of what our own plants did, but others differed. Checking with friends, we found that in a number of cases their offhand memories by no means agreed with the list or with ourselves.

Clearly, memory would have to be backed by some proper fact-finding before we could offer any serious help, so we set to work to make a record of the flowering periods of the several hundred Venezuelan orchid species growing in or near our Caracas home, hoping (indeed, expecting) that clear-cut flowering seasons would be demonstrated by the study. Some of the results of this two-year study are set out in the tables at the end of this article. Many of the species listed are of purely botanical interest, unlikely to be in cultivation and thus of little individual importance. As part of a collective study, however, they set a pattern — or lack of pattern — that has caused us considerable surprise and that we feel may be of general interest.

The validity of the records is, in all but a very few cases, affected by the fact that the plants recorded have been moved from their natural habitat, in some cases by only a few yards but in others by several hundred miles in distance and several thousand feet in altitude. The flowering season of any given plant depends upon certain broad factors and certain narrow ones. The main broad factors are the general climate of the region (hours of daylight, dry and wet seasons, etc.), and the natural in-built "flowering instincts" of the species in question. The narrow factors, which are in many respects separate for each individual plant, are, first, the temperature, humidity, air movement, etc., making up the microclimate in which the plant grows — and secondly, the condition of health of the plant itself. Almost any movement of a plant, however short it may be, will affect its microclimate, and if moved far enough from its original habitat it may suffer from the considerable change in the general climate as well. Whether or not these changes affect its health, it is not surprising if a move results in the plant showing a flowering period differing in greater or less degree from its natural one. When we visit friends living not very far away, but at slightly higher or lower altitude, we very often find that there is quite a discrepancy between when their species flower and when ours do. It is evident that even small changes of temperatures, etc., without any change in daylength or overall general climate, may produce quite large changes in flowering period, and even varying techniques in cultivation may also have a considerable effect.

In brief, then, all that can be said about the records given here is that they apply to the special conditions surrounding the plants in the various orchid "houses" (most open air) around our home. Under other conditions it is probable that the very broad picture would hold good, but almost certain that the details would not.

In studying the records, the following facts should be borne in mind:

(A) — Where outright sickness, insect depredation, etc., was evident, the plant in question (with one exception) has been omitted from the record. Nevertheless, it is not always easy to say if a plant, without actually being sick, may perhaps be unhappy enough to flower less (or more) frequently than it otherwise would. The exception is *Platystele stenostachya,* a small pot of which, after two years or more of overflowing health and floriferousnes, suddenly — for no discernible reason — became moribund, and only after a lapse of 13 months

[1] Originally appeared in *A.O.S. Bulletin,* Vol. 36, Sept. 1967, pages 790-797

began flowering again. In this respect the record is abnormal but is included to show that when in health, this true miniature does have a very long flowering period.

(B) — For recording purposes, it was quite impractical to contemplate a day-to-day record, and a broad monthly basis was selected for the study. If the flowering period, however, were to be recorded as every calendar month during which any given species produced a flower, then a plant in flower for only a few days overlapping the end of one month and the start of the next would enter the records for both months and the record would thus give a highly exaggerated impression of the length of the flowering period. It was therefore decided to keep the records on the basis that a plant in flower in the first half of a month would not be recorded if it had already been recorded for the previous month. Thus a plant flowering, say, for the last two days in June and the first two days in July would rate only as "June." If the flowering period persisted beyond July 15th, it would then rate as "June and July." Under this scheme a flowering period of just over two weeks could still be recorded under two separate months and give an exaggerated impression of its length, but it at least prevented this impression being given by a flowering period of only three or four days.

(C) — The records cover the performance of *groups of plants* rather than of single plants. While in some cases single plants were available for study, in the great majority of cases the growths or pots contained far more than a single plant and it was quite impractical to try to study the behavior of individual plants. This applied to all miniatures and to the majority of the larger plants. The results tabulated thus indicate the periods when the species mentioned had one or more of a group of plants in flower. Thus, where a species such as *Pleurothallis barberiana,* for example, is shown as flowering continuously throughout the year, it does not necessarily mean that one single plant of this species will have such a nonstop record, although some individual plants might well come near to achieving this. *Scaphosepalum verrucosum,* another "year-'round" example, bears its intriguing insect-like flowers in succession on a continuously lengthening raceme. Many of these racemes reveal a history of 30 or more such flowers, and as each flower has a duration of a week or more, the flowering period of a single inflorescence can stretch to as much as eight months. It is no surprise, therefore, to find that a healthy caespitose clump is never without flowers.

Plants with racemes of the continuously lengthening type, such as is the case with the two species mentioned, are particularly well adapted for long flowering periods, but species with single-flower habits can also at times come up with very long total flowering periods. An example of this is *Stenia pallida*. While we have a number of plants of this species, and the records apply to them as a group, it so happens that several are quite separate single plants. These single plants show a flowering period almost as constant and long as that of the group as a whole, a new bud appearing on a new peduncle as the earlier flower dies off, and so on over most of the year — a very attractive feature of this rather rare species.

(D) — When we are away from Caracas, hunting for new orchids, records of what is going on at home are perforce neglected, and it is quite probable that in a number of cases plants with short flowering periods have gone unrecorded. Similarly, some of the many tiny-flowered species with infrequent flowering periods can escape notice, particularly in genera such as *Lepanthes,* where the flower has the bashful habit of hiding itself at the back of the leaf. Errors in the records due to these factors, however, can only be errors of omission, and the records remain valid if viewed as records of *minimum* flowering periods.

To formulate the study and carry it out over a period of two years has not been difficult. What is difficult is to see what pattern there is to the records or what conclusions can be drawn. There seems to be a tendency for the smaller species to have longer or more frequent flowering periods than the larger species, and to be more erratic in behavior. The cattleyas, for example, show (as expected) a fixed-season pattern, though occasional off-season freak flowerings may occur. But there are too many exceptions to allow this large-regular/small-irregular pattern to be considered in any way a rule. In fact, the record as a whole presents a picture of confusion, not of order, and any attempt at serious statistical analysis is defeated right at the start by the frequent discrepancy between the behavior of a species in the first 12 months of the test and its behavior in the second.

If the record of the 280 species listed in this article can be considered as representative of tropical orchids as a whole, and if the results are not invalidated by the fact that the majority of the plants are living in microclimates (and in a number of cases, general climate also) very different from their normal habitat, then perhaps the most interesting generalizations that can be drawn from the study are:

(1) — Relatively few orchids have short once-a-year flowering periods. The majority (about two-thirds in the test) flower for quite an appreciable length of time — in the case of the test plants, at least three "record" months, which means a minimum of two full calendar months. Ten per

cent show an average of at least eight months' flowering per year.

(2) — A very high proportion of species (about 40% in the test) show definite multi-season habits, or at least a strong tendency to flower in two or more periods during the year.

(3) — Surprisingly, few orchid species are creatures of habit. Many of them flower, as one would say in Caracas, *"cuando les da la gana."* If they feel happy, they flower; if they don't, they don't. Or, contrariwise, if they feel really unwell and threatened with extinction, they may make a final effort at perpetuation and flower once more, while if very comfortable, they may feel that flowering is a quite unnecessary exertion. Only one period is consistently shunned for flowering, and that seems to be the week of the orchid show.

	July	August	September	October	November	December	January	February	March	April	May	June	July	August	September	October	November	December	January	February	March	April	May	June
ACINETA superba		•								•	•		•										•	•
ASPASIA variegata	•									•	•												•	
BARBOSELLA cucullata					•			•	•	•												•	•	
BATEMANNIA colleyi				•						•					•							•		
BLETIA stenophylla		•	•								•	•												
BRASSAVOLA cucullata	•	•		•			•	•		•	•	•	•	•	•	•						•	•	•
martiana	•	•		•	•			•				•		•	•							•	•	
nodosa	•			•					•	•	•	•	•		•							•	•	•
BRASSIA bidens					•	•				•	•				•							•	•	•
caudata					•	•				•					•		•					•		
glumacea	•				•	•	•				•	•					•							
keiliana	•	•							•	•	•	•										•	•	•
wageneri		•		•										•									•	
CAMPYLOCENTRUM micranthum								•	•	•												•	•	•
CATASETUM barbatum		•	•	•		•			•				•			•						•		
callosum		•	•							•	•	•		•										
discolor				•				•	•				•									•		
macrocarpum		•	•																			•		
pileatum		•								•		•												•
planiceps		•				•				•		•												•
CATTLEYA gaskelliana										•				•								•		
lawrenceana					•		•	•	•	•									•	•	•	•		
lueddemanniana							•	•	•	•									•	•	•	•		
mossiae										•	•											•	•	
percivaliana	•	•	•	•	•		•						•	•	•	•	•							
violacea										•	•											•		•
CAULARTHRON bicornutum	•				•	•	•	•	•	•	•		•						•	•	•	•	•	•
CHAMELOPHYTON kegelii			•	•						•			•	•		•	•					•		
CLADOBIUM violaceum		•	•							•			•	•		•	•		•					
COMPARETTIA falcata		•	•	•	•	•	•							•	•	•		•						
DICHAEA morrisii	•									•														
muricata				•							•	•	•											•
picta	•						•							•	•	•								
DIPTERANTHUS planifolius	•	•	•	•	•	•	•	•			•	•	•	•	•	•	•	•	•	•		•	•	•
ENCYCLIA chacaoensis									•	•												•	•	
cochleata									•	•												•		•
cordigera					•	•	•	•	•	•							•	•				•	•	•
fragrans						•			•		•						•		•			•	•	•
EPIDENDRUM agathosmicum					•	•				•						•		•						•
attenuatum		•									•	•										•		
ciliare			•	•							•	•	•											
compressum				•												•	•							
coriifolium	•									•		•										•		
coronatum			•							•				•									•	•
cristatum	•					•	•		•			•	•			•						•		
difforme	•	•	•							•	•	•												•
diurnum	•									•	•		•	•	•							•	•	
elongatum	•	•	•			•	•		•		•	•	•		•	•	•						•	•
ferrugineum			•	•	•										•	•							•	
heterodoxum			•	•			•		•						•	•						•	•	

75

	July	August	September	October	November	December	January	February	March	April	May	June	July	August	September	October	November	December	January	February	March	April	May	June
huebneri					•	•	•	•										•	•					
ibaguense	•	•		•	•	•	•	•	•	•		•	•	•	•	•	•	•	•	•	•	•	•	•
leucochilum				•	•			•	•	•							•			•	•	•		
lindenii	•										•													•
moritzii			•						•										•	•	•			
nocturnum		•		•	•			•			•	•	•	•	•		•				•	•		
oncidioides										•													•	•
purum				•	•	•	•	•							•	•								
secundum	•	•	•	•	•	•	•	•	•	•	•	•	•	•	•	•	•	•	•	•	•	•	•	•
stamfordianum		•		•		•	•	•									•	•						
stenopetalum		•		•	•	•								•	•	•	•							
EULOPHIA *alta*		•												•	•									
EURYSTYLES *cotyledon*			•	•	•			•							•	•								
GALEANDRA *devoniana*				•					•			•				•		•						
stangeana			•	•		•	•		•						•	•	•	•						
GONGORA *quinquenervis*			•					•	•	•					•	•		•	•			•		
GOVENIA *superba*	•										•													
HABENARIA *alata*			•	•											•									
monorrhiza			•	•											•	•								
obtusa			•												•									
HEXADESMIA *dunstervillei*			•			•	•	•				•	•	•	•			•	•			•	•	
sessilis		•				•	•	•						•			•	•	•	•				
HUNTLEYA *lucida*	•	•	•							•	•	•		•										
IONOPSIS *satyrioides*	•		•			•	•	•	•		•	•	•			•	•			•	•	•	•	•
utricularioides	•	•	•			•	•			•			•	•	•							•	•	•
KEFERSTEINIA *graminea*	•						•		•	•			•									•		•
tolimensis	•	•	•		•								•	•	•									
KOELLENSTEINIA *graminea*		•	•	•	•					•	•	•	•	•	•	•	•	•						•
LANKESTERELLA *caespitosa*	•										•													
LEOCHILUS *labiatus*					•	•											•	•	•	•	•			
LEPANTHOPSIS *astrophora*	•	•	•		•	•			•		•	•	•	•	•			•				•		•
floripecten		•	•	•	•				•	•	•	•		•								•	•	
vinacea			•	•				•	•	•			•		•							•		•
LOCKHARTIA *acuta*	•	•			•	•					•	•		•					•	•		•		
imbricata	•		•	•		•	•				•		•	•		•	•		•	•	•	•		
longifolia			•					•	•						•						•			
LYCASTE *longipetala*			•					•							•						•			
macrophylla		•	•	•		•		•	•				•	•	•									•
MACRADENIA *lutescens*			•	•	•	•									•	•	•							
MALAXIS *caracasana*	•										•													
MASDEVALLIA *civilis*										•													•	
maculata	•	•	•							•		•	•											•
minuta		•	•	•					•						•		•	•	•					
picturata														•	•		•		•	•				
rechingeriana	•	•		•		•			•						•				•			•	•	•
striatella		•				•												•	•					
tovarensis		•	•	•			•											•	•	•				
triangularis	•	•		•	•			•		•	•	•	•	•	•	•	•	•				•		
wageneriana	•	•	•				•	•		•	•	•	•	•	•	•	•					•		
wendlandiana									•	•					•						•			
MAXILLARIA *alba*		•	•											•										
amazonica					•		•		•					•		•	•		•					•
arachnites			•						•	•				•	•							•		
bolivarensis				•							•	•										•		
brunnea	•				•						•						•							
caespitifica	•										•											•	•	•
camaridii	•	•									•	•	•										•	
conferta			•	•												•	•							
crassifolia		•									•					•								
discolor			•			•							•			•								

76

	July	August	September	October	November	December	January	February	March	April	May	June	July	August	September	October	November	December	January	February	March	April	May	June
histrionica			•				•							•										
jenischiana						•	•								•			•						
lasallei				•						•					•							•	•	
lawrenceana						•	•	•														•	•	
luteoalba										•												•	•	
macrura						•	•								•									•
mapiriensis	•							•	•	•				•		•		•	•		•			•
melina						•								•		•		•						
meridensis				•						•	•					•								•
miniata	•	•					•												•	•				
multicaulis							•								•									
nigrescens	•			•	•	•					•				•			•					•	
notylioglossa	•									•	•				•			•				•	•
parkeri	•	•		•				•				•								•				
quelchii						•									•									
ramosa			•							•				•									•	
ringens						•					•												•	
rufescens		•	•	•	•		•		•			•	•	•		•	•				•			
spilotantha	•		•							•	•	•		•		•		•			•			•
stenophylla		•	•							•	•	•												•
triloris					•	•		•							•				•					
uncata	•	•							•		•							•	•		•			
valenzuelana			•			•			•					•										•
violaceopunctata		•	•						•				•											•
xylobiiflora	•	•	•	•	•			•			•	•	•	•	•									
MORMODES *buccinator*					•	•								•	•				•					
NEOLEHMANNIA *porpax*	•	•		•	•	•	•	•		•	•		•	•	•	•	•	•				•	•	
NOTYLIA *bungerothii*						•		•									•		•					
incurva		•			•	•	•	•	•			•	•			•	•	•	•	•				
peruviana						•	•		•									•						
platyglossa							•	•												•				
rhombilabia							•	•														•	•	
sagittifera						•										•								
OCTOMERIA *deltoglossa*		•		•							•	•	•	•	•	•	•							
filifolia	•	•								•	•			•										•
integrilabia	•	•	•	•		•				•	•			•										•
taracuana								•	•				•	•							•			
ODONTOGLOSSUM *constrictum*		•	•	•									•	•	•									
naevium		•	•			•			•			•	•		•	•					•	•	
ONCIDIUM *ampliatum*					•	•	•			•				•	•	•	•	•	•	•	•		
baueri	•	•								•	•											•	•	
bicolor			•	•								•							•	•	•			
boothianum		•	•				•	•	•	•			•	•									•	•
carthaginense	•	•					•	•	•	•			•	•									•	•
cebolleta						•											•							
cimiciferum			•	•	•	•																	•	•
falcipetalum			•											•										
heteranthum	•	•	•	•							•		•	•										
lanceanum			•							•	•					•								•
luridum											•													•
murinum	•										•													
nigratum												•	•	•	•							•	•
nudum						•	•										•			•				
obryzatum			•	•	•					•	•			•	•							•	•
papilio	•	•	•	•	•	•			•	•	•	•	•	•	•					•			•
sphacelatum										•													•	•
volvox	•	•							•	•	•	•				•								•
zebrinum		•	•									•												
ORLEANESIA *maculata*						•															•			
ORNITHOCEPHALUS *bicornis*					•		•	•	•	•						•	•	•	•					

	July	August	September	October	November	December	January	February	March	April	May	June	July	August	September	October	November	December	January	February	March	April	May	June
PAPHINIA cristata							•	•			•				•	•								•
PHRAGMIPEDIUM lindleyanum						•	•	•	•	•	•					•	•	•	•	•	•	•	•	•
PHYSOSIPHON lansbergii								•	•												•			
PLATYSTELE lancilabris	•	•	•	•	•	•		•	•	•	•	•	•	•	•	•	•	•	•	•	•	•	•	•
ornata	•	•	•	•	•	•	•	•	•	•	•	•	•	•	•	•	•	•	•			•	•	•
stenostachya	•	•	•	•	•	•												•	•	•	•	•	•	
PLECTROPHORA cultrifolia	•		•	•	•				•	•	•	•	•	•		•		•			•	•		
PLEUROTHALLIS arbuscula							•	•	•												•			
archidiaconi			•			•				•	•		•	•							•			
barberiana[1]	•	•	•	•	•	•	•	•	•	•	•	•	•	•	•	•	•	•	•	•	•	•	•	•
barbulata	•		•	•	•		•	•	•	•	•	•	•	•	•		•	•		•	•	•	•	•
bivalvis	•		•	•	•	•		•		•	•	•	•		•	•	•	•	•	•		•		•
breviscapa	•	•	•	•	•	•	•	•	•			•	•	•	•	•		•	•		•	•		•
cabellensis	•		•	•	•		•		•		•	•	•	•	•	•	•	•	•			•	•	
cardiostola	•		•	•	•	•		•	•		•	•	•	•	•	•	•	•	•		•	•		
cardium		•		•	•	•	•		•		•	•			•	•	•	•	•			•		
ceratothallis[2]	•			•	•	•					•	•	•	•	•	•	•							•
chamensis		•	•									•												
ciliaris[3]	•		•							•	•			•			•		•			•	•	•
discoidea	•			•		•	•		•			•					•		•			•	•	•
endotrachys	•	•	•									•												
erinacea								•										•			•			
fimbriata	•											•												
flexuosa		•	•	•	•		•	•		•		•	•	•	•	•	•	•	•			•	•	
galeata		•							•		•	•	•				•					•	•	
grandiflora	•											•												
gratiosa	•	•			•						•	•	•	•	•	•	•	•	•					•
grobyi		•	•	•	•			•		•		•	•	•		•					•	•	•	
hemirrhoda			•	•	•					•			•	•	•							•	•	•
hitchcockii		•									•				•									
hystrix[4]					•											•	•							
ionantha							•	•									•	•		•				
lanceana		•	•	•	•	•								•	•					•				
lancipetala[5]	•	•	•	•			•	•	•	•	•	•	•	•	•	•	•				•	•		
loranthophylla	•			•	•					•		•	•	•	•									•
mentosa					•											•								
monocardia					•	•	•	•						•	•	•								
nephrocardia			•			•	•			•	•	•		•	•		•	•		•			•	•
obovata			•	•										•										
orbicularis[6]	•		•	•	•					•	•		•		•									•
peduncularis[7]					•					•								•						
pedunculata	•	•		•	•						•		•	•						•		•		
phalangifera							•		•	•											•			
pluriracemosa	•	•										•	•	•										
polygonoides		•														•					•			
pruinosa		•					•		•	•		•		•	•									
pubescens	•		•	•	•	•	•		•	•		•		•	•	•	•						•	•
reymondii[8]	•			•	•	•					•		•	•	•	•	•							
ruberrima		•								•		•		•								•		
rubroviridis				•	•	•	•		•	•			•		•	•	•	•	•					
ruscifolia							•					•					•							
sclerophylla		•			•			•		•			•			•		•			•	•		
secunda				•	•					•		•					•							•
semiscabra	•				•	•					•	•	•	•	•	•					•			
semperflorens		•									•		•											
sicaria	•		•		•		•				•		•		•		•			•				
subtilis	•										•					•								
talpinaria	•	•	•	•	•	•					•	•	•	•	•		•							
uncinata[9]	•			•	•	•								•		•						•	•	
velaticaulis			•							•		•									•			

	July	August	September	October	November	December	January	February	March	April	May	June	July	August	September	October	November	December	January	February	March	April	May	June
vittariifolia			•											•			•							
wageneriana				•	•				•		•				•		•	•				•		
xanthochlora				•													•							
POLYSTACHYA *concreta*			•											•	•									
foliosa			•		•	•	•			•				•	•		•			•	•		•	
PSYGMORCHIS *glossomystax*	•	•				•	•				•	•	•	•	•									
pusilla			•	•	•	•		•	•	•	•	•	•			•	•	•					•	
QUEKETTIA *pygmaea*							•															•	•	
RESTREPIA *elegans*	•	•	•	•	•	•	•	•	•	•		•	•	•	•	•	•	•	•	•	•	•		•
lansbergii	•				•			•					•		•			•				•	•	•
RESTREPIOPSIS *tubulosa*				•	•	•										•	•	•		•				
RODRIGUEZIA *secunda*			•	•				•		•				•	•							•	•	•
SCAPHOSEPALUM *verrucosum*	•	•	•	•	•		•	•	•	•	•	•	•		•	•	•	•	•	•	•		•	•
SCAPHYGLOTTIS *huebneri*					•										•	•								
SCELOCHILUS *ottonis*	•													•										
SCHOMBURGKIA *undulata*					•	•	•										•	•	•					
SOBRALIA *candida*		•	•											•	•									
fimbriata	•	•																					•	•
fragrans			•											•									•	•
suaveolens				•												•								
violacea				•																			•	
yauaperyensis		•		•										•		•								
STANHOPEA *eburnea*										•					•								•	
wardii		•	•											•	•									
STELIS *alata*	•									•				•										•
argentata	•	•	•	•	•	•	•	•	•		•	•	•	•			•						•	•
braccata										•	•											•	•	•
crassilabia						•				•	•							•						
cucullata										•	•													•
fendleri	•	•					•							•						•				
grossilabris			•				•								•	•				•	•			
guianensis			•							•		•	•	•						•			•	•
humilis	•					•				•						•								•
muscifera			•		•										•	•								
porpax	•			•	•	•					•	•				•	•							
tridentata			•													•								
STENIA *pallida*	•		•	•	•	•		•	•	•		•	•		•	•	•		•		•	•	•	•
TEUSCHERIA *wageneri*	•	•	•								•		•	•	•									
TRICHOCENTRUM *capistratum*	•	•	•	•	•	•				•	•		•	•	•	•	•					•	•	
TRICHOPILIA *fragrans*		•												•										
TRIGONIDIUM *acuminatum*					•	•				•					•	•		•			•			
obtusum					•	•								•			•	•			•	•		
TRIZEUXIS *falcata*					•	•	•	•									•	•	•	•				
XYLOBIUM *pallidiflorum*		•			•	•				•					•	•								•
variegatum		•	•	•	•		•			•		•	•			•					•	•		•
ZYGOSEPALUM *labiosum*			•											•										

[1] Now known as *Pleurothallis aristata*
[2] Now known as *Myoxanthus ceratothallis*
[3] Now known as *Trichosalpinx ciliaris*
[4] Now known as *Myoxanthus hystrix*
[5] Now known as *Myoxanthus lancipetalus*
[6] Now known as *Trichosalpinx orbicularis*
[7] Now known as *Myoxanthus parahybunensis*
[8] Now known as *Myoxanthus reymondii*
[9] Now known as *Myoxanthus uncinatus*

Finding Phragmipedium caudatum[1]

JULIAN STEYERMARK[2] and G. C. K. and E. DUNSTERVILLE

FINDING AN ORCHID that is at the same time rare, large, and beautiful is always an event to be remembered, even by the most blasé of plant hunters or field botanists. Among such orchids in the Western Hemisphere, there is no doubt that *Phragmipedium caudatum* ranks high, not only for its relative rarity and beauty, but also for the remarkable development of its petals. It is, however, an orchid with two very distinct varieties, so different that for a good many years one variety was botanically considered to be not just another species in the same genus but to belong to a separate genus altogether, created especially to accommodate it.

As with practically all the older species of the "slipper-lip" orchids known as the *Cypripedioideae*, *Phragmipedium caudatum* has been moved from genus to genus within this group. It started as *Cypripedium caudatum* when first described in 1840 by Lindley. It was then switched to *Paphiopedilum caudatum* by Pfitzer in 1894, and then by Rolfe into *Phragmipedium caudatum* in 1896. Various changes in the specific epithet need not concern us here, and it is safe to say that Rolfe's name is here to stay. This has not, however, prevented horticulturists, and even some botanists, from putting this species every now and then into the genus *Selenipedium,* just to keep the confusion active. Even as late as 1965, and in a publication as prestigious as the *A.O.S. Bulletin,* one finds a closely allied species, *Phragmipedium grande,* appearing as a selenipedium.

The normal form of the fine species we are dealing with here shared with other members of the *Cypripedioideae* the possession of the typical "slipper-lip," and a column where two of the six stamens fused into the column have developed externally into fertile anthers, as opposed to only one in nearly all other members of the orchid family. Above these two anthers, which lie one on each side of the column, extends a wing-like structure which is considered to be a staminode, i.e., an infertile external development of one of the buried stamens. The main distinction of this particular species rests on its petals; these are quite short when the flower opens, but rapidly increase in length, day after day, to hang down like two twisted strings to quite fantastic lengths — according to some authorities, as much as 75 cm. or "exceeding 30 inches." Many phragmipediums favor longish petals, for reasons best known to themselves, but *P. caudatum* outdoes them all.

According to Veitch (*Manual of Orchidaceous Plants,* 1890), herbarium specimens prove that this lovely species was first found by the famous pair of Spanish botanists, Ruíz and Pavón, who did extensive botanical explorations in Peru in the period 1778-89. At that time, however, the plant received neither name or fame, and the species languished in anonymity until Lindley, studying the old Ruíz and Pavón herbarium sheets from Lima, described the species and named it *Cypripedium caudatum* in 1840. Veitch's collector, William Lobb, worked the Andean area for orchids in the period 1842-47, bringing to Europe in 1847 the first live plants of this species. In subsequent years further specimens were discovered in other parts of Peru, and this is still the country where it is best known. In later years it has been found also in Colombia, Panama, and Guatemala, being by no means overly common in any of these. Louis O. Williams records it as by now largely exterminated in Panama, and in Guatemala it is so rare that to the best of our knowledge it has (at least until very recently) only been found there twice. The second of these discoveries was by the senior author of this note, one of whose most memorable experiences was the successful tracking down of this species in 1942. A good friend, Don Mariano Pacheco Herrarte, of Guatemala City, had told him about this rare

---

[1] Originally appeared in *A.O.S. Bulletin,* Vol. 39, June 1970, pages 484-491

[2] Deceased, October 15, 1988

Phragmipedium lindenii

orchid and asked him repeatedly to be on the lookout for it on his various expeditions in the country. At that time Don Mariano was Director General of Agriculture of Guatemala and a well-known orchid grower. He often mentioned this orchid, how rare it was in the wild state in Guatemala, and how only the famous collector, von Tuerckheim, has ever brought one back from any definite locality there, namely the region of Pansamalá in the Department of Alta Verapaz, in 1887. He stressed its beauty and unusual nature, describing with great enthusiasm how its petals reached extraordinary lengths.

In July 1942, the senior author, with his assistant Dr. Albert Vatter, Jr., had come to a remote sector of Guatemala in the northern part of the Department of Huehuetenango, north of the Cuchumatanes mountains, to make a general botanical collection for the *Flora of Guatemala,* a publication upon which Mr. Paul C. Standley and he were collaborating under the auspices of the Field Museum of Natural History of Chicago. The first expedition had covered the period of October 1939 to April 1940. Now this second expedition, started in December 1941, was in progress during 1942, covering sections of the country not previously botanized. Most of the traveling was by canoe, mules, and burros, or by long trips afoot with Indian guides and carriers for overland expeditions. A long and arduous walk north of Barillas had brought the party to wet virgin forest at about 1,400 m. to collect the rich flora of the area. With a return to base scheduled for the following day, there remained just this one day to explore the treasures of the area. It was a dense humid forest of tall trees rich in number of species. The terrain was hilly and dissected by numerous streams. A large diversified collection had already been assembled for the herbarium, and now the afternoon was drawing rapidly to a close. By about 4 p.m. the forest of tall trees, never prone to admit much light, was already beginning to spread an even dimmer somberness. It was at this time, while perusing the ground cover of the forest for possibilities of rare plants, that a large flower lying on the forest floor caught my eye. It was no ordinary flower. It was a rare treasure indeed — *Phragmipedium caudatum!* From where had the flower come? Careful search of the general vicinity showed no terrestrial plants from which the flower might have fallen — it must have dropped from one of the trees above. But from which tree? Trees surrounded us and many were laden with orchids, bromeliads, and other epiphytes. Under such circumstances, how could one judge accurately which was the one essential tree? It was most important to find the plant, bring it back alive, and prepare a permanent pressed specimen for a definite record of this orchid for Guatemala. We just *had* to find the elusive prize, but the late hour left us little time in which to do it. The trees here were inclined at different angles on the slopes of the ravine in which we were botanizing, and because of this it was most uncertain which of them could be harboring the prized orchid, assuming always that it was an epiphytic orchid that had dropped its flower. To com-

Phragmipedium caudatum

plicate the situation, there were other smaller trees between us and the taller ones, which made it difficult to see clearly.

By "educated guesswork" we picked out a tree some twenty meters tall as the most likely one. Cutting it down, we quickly checked all the orchids on it but could see none that might pass for a phragmipedium. The forest light was now truly dim, and prospects of success even dimmer still. In a last desperate attempt, a second prospective tree was cut down, falling with a crash across the trunk of the first one. Again we scurried over it and examined all the branches for orchid possibilities, but again our hurried search yielded nothing to indicate that our efforts had been rewarded. Sadly we gathered up all the orchids that had fallen from the two trees, stuffed them into the gunny sacks, and carried them away in the dim light of the forest.

It was dark when we reached the shelter where we were to pass the night. After a quick supper, we used candlelight to look over our catch of live orchid plants more carefully. The fallen flower of the phragmipedium, which had been pressed in the usual manner between folds of newspaper, could now be examined in detail, and showed a short dense pubescence at its very base, at the point where the sepals are joined to the apex of the ovary and flower stalk. Could this pubescent zone give us the clue we needed? The search now concentrated on seeing if there was an orchid plant in our collection that could tie in with this pubescent base of the flower. Finally, using up precious flashlight batteries as well as the candles, a plant was found with a fan-like cluster of narrow basal leaves, without a pseudobulb, from which rose a flower stem bearing a densely pubescent pedicellate ovary. Like the pieces of a puzzle, the pubescent base of the flower fitted onto the pubescent pedicel still attached to the living plant. What a magnificent stroke of luck! Color notes and measurements were taken on the parts of the flower, and the living plant eventually turned over to Don Mariano to grow at his nursery, where in later years it flowered again. So far as is known, this is the first record, subsequent to that of von Tuerckheim in 1847, of a specimen in the wild state from a definite locality in Guatemala, all the other recorded collections having been from purchased specimens in cultivation.

As mentioned earlier in this note, *P. caudatum* is distinguished by having a very distinct varietal form, and it is this that now concerns the second half of this note. This variety, which is illustrated here, is nowadays known as *P. caudatum* var. *lindenii,* but so odd is its form that Lindley originated created a new genus, *Uropedium,* to accommodate it, giving it the name of *U. lindeni* in 1846. The major visual distinction of this variety is that instead of the usual slipper-lip, it develops a third long, narrow, string-like petal that hangs down, as with the others, for as much as 50 cm. Less visually evident but also important is the fact that besides having the two fertile anthers and the staminodal wings described at the start of this note for the normal form, the "Uropedium" form has a third well-developed fertile anther springing from the base of the column, as shown in the accompanying illustration.

The French botanist Brongniart queried the idea that this oddity was anything justifying a new genus and suggested that it was no more than a very interesting and rather abnormal "peloric" form of the usual *Phragmipedium caudatum.* Peloria, an abnormal regularity in normally irregular flowers such as orchids (where the lip is a much-changed petal), is not uncommon, but generally occurs rather spasmodically, at times affecting only part of an inflorescence. This led the most famous orchid taxonomist of his day, Reichenbach filius, to reject the ideas of Brongniart because the two forms of this species were never found growing together and there was therefore nothing spasmodic about the occurrence of Brongniart's "peloric" form. This argument of Reichenbach's, however, was undermined by the occurrence of intermediate forms in cultivation, where a sort of bastard lip developed more or less halfway between the two types, and stronger evidence yet was produced when a cross of *P. longifolium* with the "Uropedium" produced exactly the same result as crossing *P. longifolium* with the normal *P. caudatum*. The peloria contention and the name *P. caudatum* var. *lindenii,* are now both fully accepted.

This strange form, which in the notes below we shall continue to call "Uropedium" for ease of reference only, is more scarce than the usual form and is known only from South America, i.e. Peru, Ecuador, Colombia, and Venezuela. In Venezuela, where the type specimen was found, it is definitely a rarity, and until the finds recorded here were made, the original collections of more than 100 years ago seem to have been the only ones made in that country. We had thus for long considered it as one of our main orchid targets in our frequent joint or separate visits to the Venezuelan Andes, where the original discovery was made.

Checking the early reports for guidance, it was noted that *Paxton's Flower Garden,* Vol. I, 1882, says that it was found wild by Linden, in flower in June 1843, "growing in the soil of little woods in the savannah which occurs in the high part of the Cordillera that looks down upon the vast forests of the Lake of Maracaybo...in the territory of the Chiguará Indians at 8,500 ft." Veitch's *Manual,* 1890, amplified this by stating, "growing among the underwood composed chiefly of *Weinmannia* and tall (tree?) ferns" and gave the altitude as 5,000 feet. The Chiguará Indians have long since gone, but

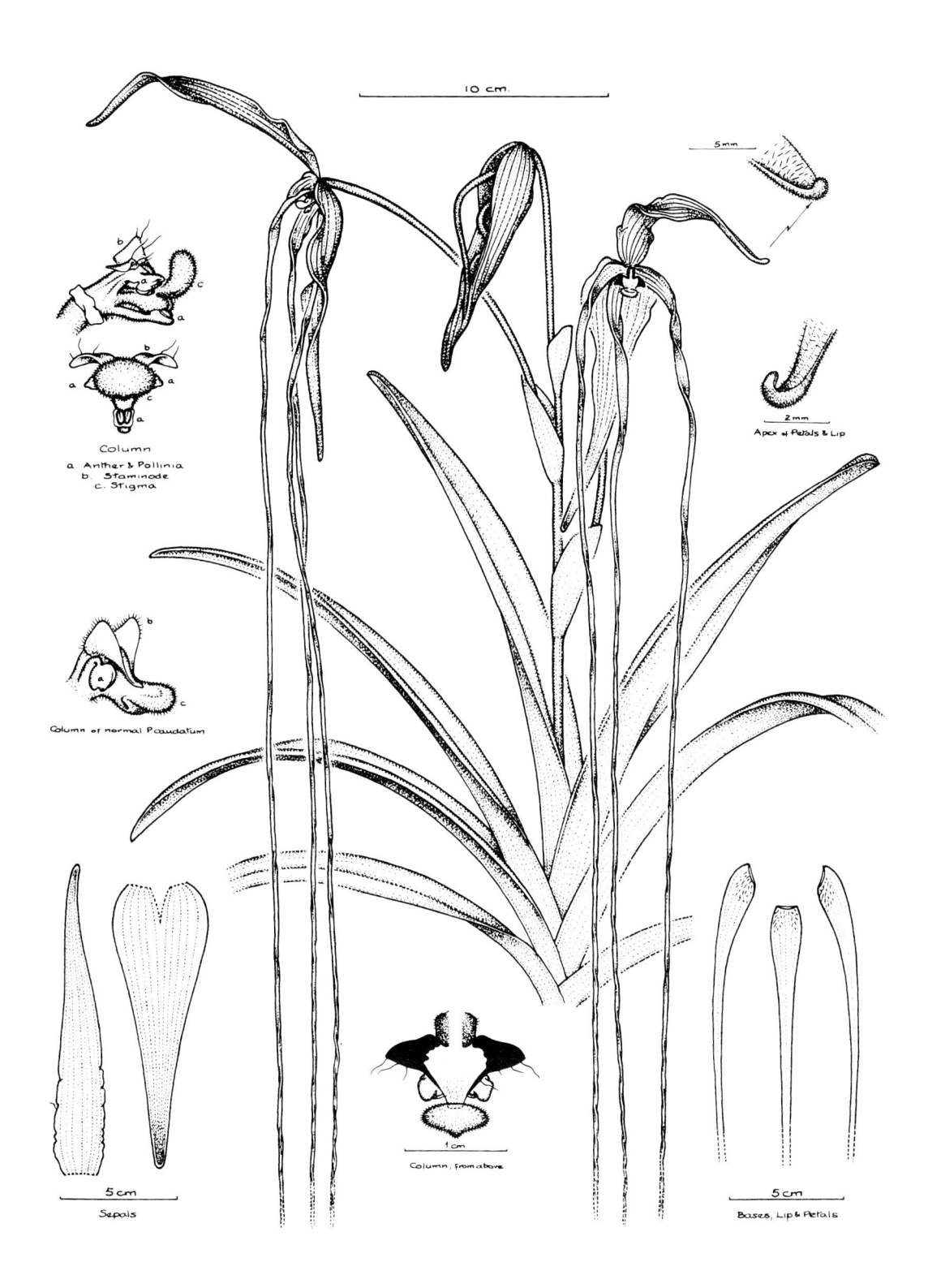

Phragmipedium lindenii (Linden) Dressler & N. Wms. in Taxon 24: 691, 1975. — A.

with the village of Chiguará near the city of Mérida as a signpost, the hunt was on. The general indication seemed to point to a terrestrial plant, but terrestrial or epiphyte, it soon seemed clear that altogether too much civilization had spread out in the immediate Chiguará area, whether overlooking Lake Maracaibo or not, to leave much prospect of locating it there — and who knew, anyway, what the original Indian "territory" covered? So it became a matter of keeping an eye carefully open for "fan-spread" orchids when searching forests almost anywhere in the Andes of the State of Mérida — a rather large target, admittedly, but there is little fun in botanizing unless one has a goodly base of optimism. And finally "V Day" arrived.

In the autumn of 1966, 23 after he began his Venezuelan botanizing, the senior author was joined for an Andean expedition by an orchid friend, Marvin Rabe, of Wilmington, Illinois, and *P. caudatum* was definitely in the eyes of the party as one of the main objectives. One afternoon at the end of August, just before getting ready to return to Caracas, the party was climbing steep-sided slopes of rich virgin cloud forest at an estimated 1,800-1,900 m. above sea level. Here grew many interesting terrestrial plants of different species of *Anthurium,* some with showy white spathes, others with spathes pink or rose-colored. *Acineta superba,* with pendent inflorescences from the base of the plant, was common, both as an epiphyte and even as a (presumably accidental) terrestrial. The handsome terrestrial *Peperomia maculosa* and the climbing and creeping *P. peltoidea,* together with ferns, *Begonia foliosa,* the dark-bracted *Heliconia schneeana* with erect inflorescences, and the acanthaceous *Beloperone flavidiflora* with large green bracts and showy salmon flowers, all abounded here in the rich forest of trees, shrubs, and epiphytes in great variety.

Fallen trees or large fallen branches are fine places for finding orchids and other epiphytes and naturally come in for very close attention. On one such branch at this locality two orchid plants, with fan-shaped sprays of fairly rigid leaves and no pseudobulbs, came to light, looking just like the plants from Guatemala. These just *had* to be the treasure we were looking for, but the prize would not be fully won until they had been cultivated and flowered. This was where the junior authors, or more properly Nora (E.) Dunsterville, came into the picture. One plant was given to Mr. Alfredo Blaumann, an expert orchid grower with a high-altitude site near Junquito, above Caracas, and the other was turned over to Nora to see what she could do with it in her home above Caracas at some 1,350 meters altitude. From 1966 to 1969 this latter plant grew, potted in well-drained, chopped tree-fern root and placed in semi-shade under slats. A new healthy growth developed, the original one died off, and finally an inflorescence started. In the last weeks of December 1969, to the joy of all participants, three fine "Uropedium" flowers opened up, the petals growing longer day by day until the final flower, three weeks after opening, had petals 50 cm. (20″) long, withering only after a full month had passed. While this excitement was going on, the junior authors were about to escape year-end festivities by undertaking an orchid hunt, and with this plant to inspire them, promptly headed for the Andes, determined to show that what the senior author had found, they also could track down, a task made immeasurably easier (though by no means certain) by knowledge of just where the flowering plant had been found. In dense, steeply sloping cloud forest on broken ground, "just where" is a somewhat vague term, and the junior authors set off more in a spirit of determination than with any real confidence in success. As luck would have it, however, they ran across a freshly fallen branch from high up a tall tree in the same general area, although perhaps not exactly where the original plant came from. The branch had fallen from a dying tree not only because of its rottenness, but also because of an enormous overload of orchid growths. (For those interested in knowing what other orchids were growing in association with the prize plants on the same branch, the following is a list: *Maxillaria triloris,* in enormous masses and in full flower; *M. lancifolia, M. miniata* [yellow-flowered variety]; *Maxillaria* sp., aff. *M. jenischiana; Pleurothallis undulata; Pleurothallis* sp., repent; *Oncidium globuliferum; Restrepia* sp.; *Trichopilia laxa.* Nearby were: *Spiranthes speciosa* [terrestrial]; *Ponera* sp. [probably *P. striata*]; *Acineta* sp. [probably *A. superba*]; *Pleurothallis ciliaris;* and various unidentifiable sterile plants of *Oncidium* or *Odontoglossum.)* Only after some minutes of investigation did a small fan-shaped spray of leaves show up amid the mass of common or forest orchids, but once it was spotted, its identity was clear enough — the junior authors could celebrate the opening of the new decade with a plant of their own. Several plants, in fact, as others turned up on this same dead branch, some with dead inflorescences, and two with developing seed capsules that have been sent abroad for cultivation. The stability of this abnormal peloric form of *Phragmipedium caudatum,* the characteristic that made Reichenbach doubt its validity, makes it a certainty that all these plants will turn out to be "Uropediums," but if by some million-to-one freak, one of them turns out to be the normal form, then Reichenbach from his grave will really have to give up the struggle for "Uropedium." We shall wait and see.

Oncidium meirax

ONCIDIUM MEIRAX is a well-known species that might normally be called a "pleasant little botanical," quite easy to find in Venezuela at elevations of 3,000 to 7,000 feet, in the Coastal Range and less commonly so in the Andes. It normally seems to shun a crowded life, preferring to grow in "singles" or at best in tiny clumps on the branches of its host tree. In cultivation, it can be induced to be somewhat more gregarious but, at least with us, never exuberantly so.

For this reason, when we first saw the clump shown in this slide, too high above us to see the exact floral details, we just could not believe it was "only another *meirax*" until we finally had it in our hands, so uncountably dense a mass of flowers that leaves and stems were quite invisible. The locality was in the remnants of once extensive cloud forest within 20 miles of San Cristóbal in the extreme west of Venezuela, at an altitude of about 3,000 feet. Should any reader wish to grow a similar clump, all he needs to do is to copy what Nature herself was doing at the spot, namely:

1. Surround his site with all the factors inherent in tropical cloud forest at 3,000 feet.

2. Grow himself a tree; probably one about 50 feet tall would suffice.

Oncidium meirax and Nora Dunsterville

[1] Originally appeared in *A.O.S. Bulletin*, Vol. 42, March 1973, pages 225-226

3. Allow the tree to die and its top to fall off, leaving a nice vertical stump about 25 feet tall, 12 inches thick.

4. Plant his seed near the top of the stump.

5. Allow the stump to rot slowly while the seed turns into pseudobulbs and leaves, more pseudobulbs, more leaves etc., etc.

6. When fully developed and the stump so rotted it will fall of its own accord within a month or two, collect the plant (as we did) and doll it up in a nice pot.

If he can achieve all this artificially, the reader will fully deserve the cultural award some kind judge will no doubt give him. In our case, neither we nor Sr. Roberto Mejía, the co-finder, can do more than thank Nature for one of her treats.

We are left wondering why, among all the hundreds of plants of *Oncidium meirax* we have seen in the forests, we have never before seen one luxuriating in the precarious conditions of rotting wood where it is condemned (as are so many catasetums — and as is Pride before its Fall) to come to ground with an almighty thump, just when life is at its most magnificent.

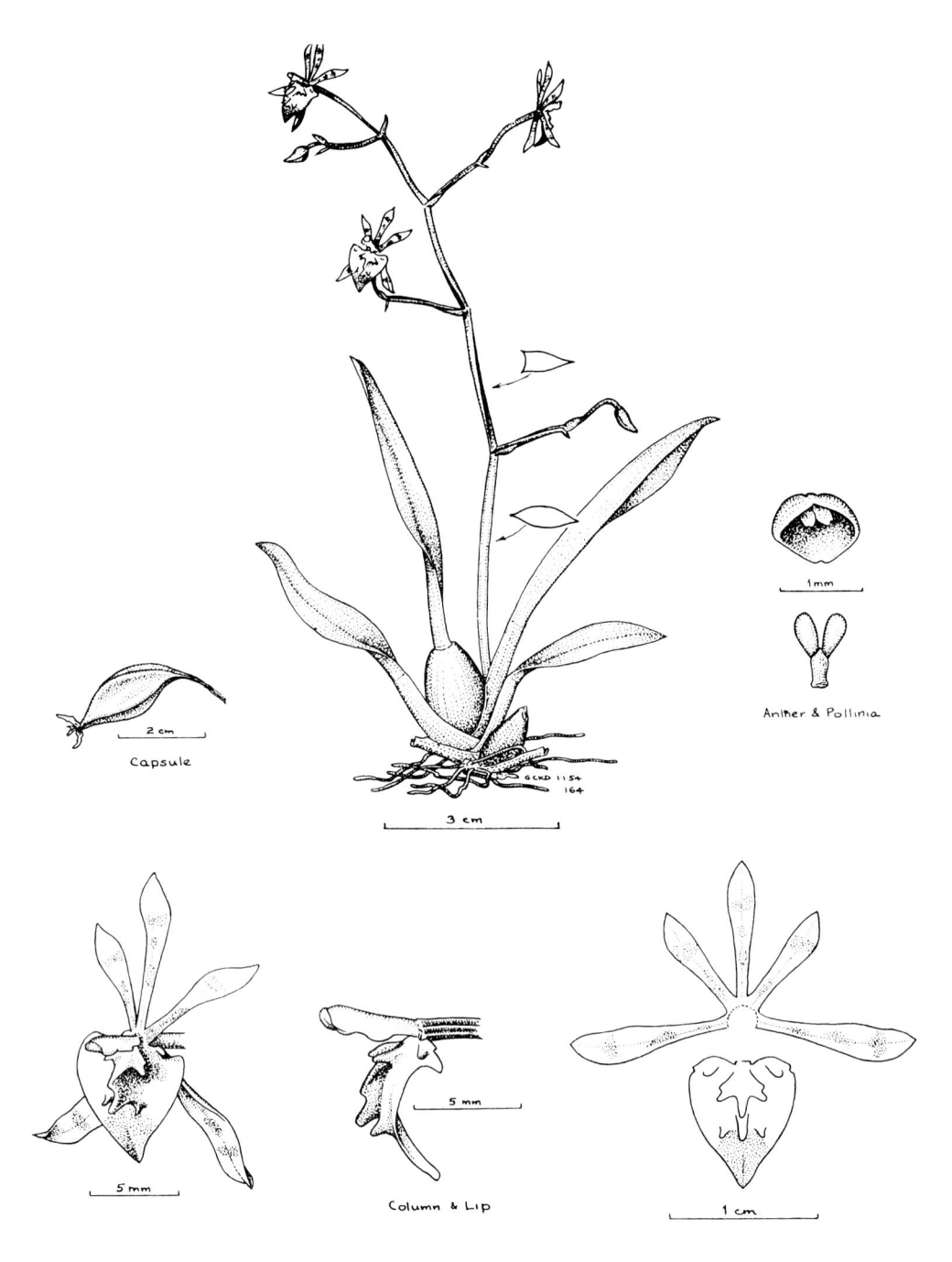

Oncidium meirax Reichb. f. in Bonpl. 2: 12, 1854. — A. B.

Some Maxillarias of Venezuela[1]

TO BOAST ABOUT THE HONESTY or good manners of one's children is a legitimate occupation indulged in by many parents, at least in those circles where honesty and manners are still appreciated. But to boast of their beauty has no basis unless the boaster can claim that he and his wife have control of their genes; if not, then the credit lies entirely with the Maker of those genes. In the same way, to boast that "my" country has more, or more beautiful, orchid species than "yours" is a negative reflection on the intelligence of the boaster rather than a positive reflection on the country he is boasting about. Moreover, it is in any case a difficult thing to boast about because, while "my" children cannot also be "yours," orchids do not respect national boundaries and many of "mine" may well be "yours" also. Nevertheless, as residents in, and lovers of, this beautiful country of Venezuela, it does give us a quite illogical pang to have to admit, for example, that Colombia not only has more orchid species than Venezuela but that in some genera, such as *Odontoglossum, Masdevallia,* and *Miltonia,* it can exhibit species more beautiful and striking than those of Venezuela. But Venezuela, with some 1,200 native species to draw upon, can still point with illogical pride to a very considerable number of most attractive orchids, both in these typically Colombian genera and in many others. Of these latter a goodly proportion lie in the genus *Maxillaria.*

The most prolific genus in Venezuela, in terms of species, is either *Epidendrum* or *Pleurothallis,* with approximately 150 species in each. The words "either/or" and "approximately" imply, correctly, a regrettable lack of precision, but no accurate count can be made so long as new, or new-for-Venezuela, species keep turning up, and so long as a really quite high proportion of species are subject to queries of misidentification or the always present problems of synonymy. The third Venezuela genus in terms of species is *Maxillaria,* with about 90, roughly equal to the combined *Oncidium-Odontoglossum* complex. *Epidendrum* species in this country tend to be not very eye-catching or are very large plants with panicles of many relatively small flowers that do not lend themselves kindly to home culture. *Pleurothallis* species, by contrast, are in almost all cases of sizes that would fit in anywhere, but while their flowers are often charming, they do tend very strongly to be small. So, except for the miniaturist or the unshakable cattleya fan, *Maxillaria* can probably be considered Venezuela's most attractive genus.

Not surprisingly for a genus represented by so many species, maxillarias are to be found throughout the country and in elevations from almost sea level to the tree line high in the Andes, so that wherever you find orchids, apart from the open *páramos* above the tree line, you are likely to find one or more *Maxillaria* species among them. A very few of these species have no pseudobulbs, or very rudimentary ones, but the genus as a whole has the great attraction of providing plants that are tough and accommodating, grand boosters for the owner's ego even when the plants succeed in spite of, more than because of, the treatment they get. In size, the plants may be attractive two-inch pot miniatures, such as *Maxillaria xylobiiflora* (with flowers that come singly, as with all self-respecting maxillarias, and to our eyes is neither "wooden" nor has any resemblance to any *Xylobium* we have yet seen) or *M. notylioglossa,* a rambling species with an intriguing V-shaped callus on its lip, made of a soft, chewing gum type of material. But more often a maxillaria in Venezuela is a plant of at least six-inch pot size and the more straggling or climbing types can take up quite a lot of space. The size of the flowers themselves, often by no means related to the size of the plant, is also very variable, ranging from the four-inch sepals of *Maxillaria*

[1] Originally appeared in *A.O.S. Bulletin,*
Vol. 43, November 1974, pages 960-966

Maxillaria triloris

Maxillaria luteoalba

Maxillaria setigera

Maxillaria nigrescens

macrura to the quarter-inch sepals of *M. purpurea* [now known as *M. conferta*] whose colorful name is, at least for us, belied by the fact that we have yet to find a plant with flowers other than plain white. In brief, for anyone living in Venezuela and crazy enough to specialize in growing local species of one single genus, a choice of *Maxillaria* would be a very happy one.

While personal tastes are variable, there is little doubt that an outstanding group of Venezuelan maxillarias is the one composed of what, for convenience, one might call the "Triloris Trio." The species in this trio are distinguishable from each other without much effort when dealing with flowers and plants that conform to the normal form, but the lips in particular are very similar and placing a flower in its right slot can be very difficult if it happens to stray from the typical shape. *Maxillaria triloris* itself is likely to come out at least very close to the top in any poll to select Venezuela's best maxillaria. It is a robust plant that, when well established, is prolific with fine flowers. The clumped pseudobulbs are lightly to moderately compressed, about three inches tall, and the strong leaves are up to 30 inches in length, so an exhibition plant will need plenty of room to develop. When it does, it may have over a dozen flowers of five-inch or even six-inch spread, standing erect and "open" on six-inch to eight-inch peduncles that arise laterally from the base of the pseudobulbs; as with the other members of the trio, the pseudobulbs are unifoliate and have no leaf-bearing sheaths. The sepals and petals are generally yellow in the apical part, red or red-flushed in the mid-section and white at the base; the normally fairly wide sepals are often more strongly red-flushed on the dorsal than the ventral surface. The lip is white, with strongly marked dark red or purple nerve lines on the lateral lobes. The texture is very firm, the flowers long-lasting, and as a final touch the flowers have a very pleasant scent, strong enough at times to perfume a very large room. It is native to the forests of Venezuela's Andes and Coastal Range, mainly from 5,000 to about 6,000 feet. On the whole it is rare, though where one does find it, it is sometimes present in quite large numbers. As it is a species with obvious horticultural merit and attractive to "strippers," we have no intention of pinpointing any of the places where we have found it.

The second member of this trio is *Maxillaria luteoalba,* with flowers not quite so large and the sepals and petals have an "embracing" attitude, being wide-spreading in their basal part before curving inward in the apical half, like a lover welcoming his beloved — or a spider welcoming the fly if your imagination is morbidly inclined. The sepals and petals are light yellow with white at the base and have little, if any, red flush, but specimens do turn up with wider than normal floral elements and quite a lot of red. Equally, we have found unusual types of *Maxillaria triloris* with much narrower elements than usual and with very little red flushing and only by a very careful consideration of all aspects, including form of pseudobulb and sheathing, petiolate base of leaf, etc. have reached conclusions as to which is what — and even then may be wrong. In both these confusing cases the plants were not growing (so far as we know) near those of the opposing species, so genuine variation, not natural hybridization, seemed responsible. The altitude range of *Maxillaria luteoalba* is larger than that of *M. triloris,* running from 8,000 feet down to as low as 500 feet. Perhaps because of this adaptability it is also geographically more widely spread. In Venezuela it grows "cool to cold" in the western Andes, "intermediate" in the Coastal Range, "warm to intermediate" in the Guayana, and "warm" in the Upper Orinoco, such as on the major tributary, the Río Ventuari. Outside Venezuela it ranges as far north as Costa Rica. By contrast, *M. triloris* was for a long time considered endemic to Venezuela and only recently has been found to extend into Colombia.

The third species in this often confusing trio is *Maxillaria setigera,* whose flowers are very similar indeed to *M. luteoalba* even in their typical form, being of the same size and general coloring. One floral aid distinction is the weak definition that the *setigera* petals and sepals are not so strongly curved inwards in the apical half; other aids are that the column has a fimbriate margin to the clinandrium and the anther has no pronounced median crest. There are also subtle and not very reliable differences in the lip. None of this is very positve so it is lucky that the pseudobulbs of this species can normally be easily distinguished from the others, being quite strongly compressed and tending to be circular in outline. As a species, it has the advantage of being frequently even more prolific with its flowers than either of its companions. Geographically, it spreads itself from Guyana to Colombia but was little known inside Venezuela until quite recently, despite the fact that the type specimen seems to have been collected here in about 1800. In the last few years, however, plants have begun to turn up from a number of places including the Venezuelan Guayana (Río Aonda) and the Venezuelan Amazonas (Río Extremo Sur), so it is already losing some of its aura as a local rarity. Its recorded altitude range is from about 500 feet in the Andean foothills near San Cristóbal to a reputed 5,000 feet near Caracas. This latter record, however, is a very old and possibly unreliable one and we have a distinct feeling that the species is basically a warm one even if, as with the others in this trio, it has no objection to cultivation in the 4,000 ft.-altitude climate of our home just outside Caracas.

Another fine Venezuelan maxillaria with large flowers is the white *Maxillaria ochroleuca;* the illustration of this species that appeared in the *A.O.S. Bulletin* for May 1972 shows a number of flowers from close up but does not show just how floriferous a compact plant of this species can be, with up to three flowers rising from each axil of the leaf-bearing sheaths on the newer growths. This species is becoming better known in Venezuela due to recent findings, but it is likely to remain rare in this country because of the remoteness of its known localities. One of these is far up the Río Caura in the western Guayana region; another is on the top of the unclimbable Cerro Autana and a third, where it has been found growing in profusion, is on the border with Brazil in the Venezuelan Amazonas, quite close to the headwaters of the Orinoco itself. In the first of these localities, at about 1,300 feet elevation, it was epiphytic and its relatively short peduncles (4") may reflect some dislike of such a low altitude. In the other places at about 4,000 feet it was found epiphytically and on the Brazilian border also terrestrially, with peduncles to 10 inches long. In the border site plants were also recovered that produce flowers of only half the size (with no intermediate sizes), and of this variety — if it is not later determined to be a separate species — some plants have been found in the Andes in the extreme west of Venezuela at about 5,000 feet.

High on the list of our personal favorites among Venezuelan orchids of any genus is *Maxillaria nigrescens,* a species that Venezuela shares with Colombia and (perhaps doubtfully) with Panama. The species here seems to be limited to the Andes, ranging from cool-intermediate forests at 5,000 feet to a preferred cool-to-cold habitat in the forests from 7,000 to 8,000 feet; but here again, the plants are very obliging and have settled happily into our 4,000-foot climate. The flowers appear generally two to six at a time on a five-inch-pot plant and have a spread of about three inches. The sepals and petals are red, varying from a rather dark tone in some flowers to a bright red in others. The lip, which is presumably the element that Lindley picked on when renaming the species in 1886, is a very dark red, so dark that in some cases it verges on what could loosely be called black. For us, what makes it such an outstanding species is the way it carries its lateral sepals in a wide, rather backward-stretching fashion; this combines with the forward curving petals to produce an aspect of swift and aggressive motion, suggestive, in a group of flowers, of a pack of red devils leaping hungrily for their victim.

All the maxillarias mentioned so far have fairly narrow sepals (though *Maxillaria triloris* sepals do have a fair width), which makes *M. parkeri* a pleasant contrast. This is an orchid of Venezuela's Guayana and Amazonas regions: outside Venezuela it occurs in Guayana (where the type was found) and in Brazil. Basically, it is a warm to hot plant, not too difficult to find (apart from general remoteness) in a number of places in the Upper Orinoco and its tributaries, at elevations from 200 to 300 feet, but is also occurs in the Guayana much higher, and even, perhaps freakishly, as high as 5,000 feet. It is probably unnecessary by now to add that at our 4,000-foot level the plants also do well. The flowers are rather smaller than the other species already mentioned, with a spread of no more than 2½ ", but the sepals are half as wide as their length so the flowers have a more solid appearance, particularly as the sepals are held in a wide attitude. The general color scheme is yellow, the lip having the usual, dark red nerve lines on its lateral lobes. The peduncles are normally about three inches tall, which is enough to raise the flowers above the level of the rather small pseudobulbs, but some cleaning up of the more ragged of the long and persistent sheaths in which the pseudobulbs are clothed may be needed if the plant is not to look excessively untidy.

Several otherwise very attractive maxillarias are handicapped by hiding their flowers at the extreme base of a mass of leaves, but although *Maxillaria violaceopunctata* suffers from this threat, its flowers are large enough and robust enough that the leaves cannot well conceal them. The strongly flattened, narrow pseudobulbs grow to six inches in height and are largely concealed by the wide leaf-bearing sheaths from the axils of which the flowers arise. Despite peduncles to seven inches tall, the flowers often only just get their heads high enough to put in an appearance; they are well visible. The widely spread sepals, up to 1½ " each in length, are of a very solid consistency, creamy yellow with a variable amount of pink overlay. The similarly colored petals lie forward alongside the column and allow full exposure of the very handsome, fleshy, mauve-spotted, creamy-yellow lip. This is also an orchid of the far Amazonas and Guayana regions, with a range that continues on into Guayana, Surinam, and Brazil; it is also recorded from near Iquitos in Peru. Basically a hot, or at least warm-climate plant, it has nevertheless been found as high as 5,000 feet in Venezuela's Guayana.

Maxillaria violaceopunctata is yet another species in this genus that seems easy to cultivate, and by now it is probably advisable to make it clear that while most of our native maxillarias do take remarkably kindly to being dragged from their normal habitat there are some that, at least in our experience, are by no means so docile. Outstanding in this is a pair of very similar species, *Maxillaria aggregata* and *M. sophronitis.* Both of these are mat-forming, epiphytic plants with thin but tough, creeping and much-branching rhizomes, with frequent small pseudobulbs and small leaves and very beautiful, half-inch, bright red flowers. A well-flowering specimen in nature, despite the smallness of the flowers, is a most attractive sight, but alas we have yet to see in our own captive plants any desire to enjoy our company for more than a year or two. In fact, so unsuccessful have we been with these two species that we would long ago have given up any wish to collect them, were it not for the fact that when we come upon a plant clothing a fallen branch on any floor of the forest, it is clear that it cannot survive in that manner either, so we may as well let it live out its days with us — and hope that some day we can solve the problem of why these species do not love us as much as we are prepared to love them. *Maxillaria aggregata,* though shared with Colombia, seems here to be the rarer of the two species, growing around 6,000 feet in the Andes, while *M. sophronitis,* endemic to Venezuela, is relatively common in cloud forest conditions of principally the Coastal Range at elevations of 2,500 to 5,000 feet. Certainly, for anyone who can solve (or perhaps has already solved) the problem of their cultivational needs, a foot-square mat in full flower would fully earn its space in any collection of species.

And finally we would like to put in a good word for *Maxillaria rufescens,* a species that we think tends to be underrated, partly because many plants have quite small flowers and partly, perhaps, because the species is so common (at least in Venezuela) that it suffers badly from the contempt bred by familiarity. Some, in fact many, plants are small and have flowers well under an inch in size that get rather lost at the base of the plant, but much finer varieties can be found, with leaves to 16 inches long and amply visible two-inch flowers. In Venezuela it accommodates itself to the climate at any altitude from almost sea level to 7,000 feet and is recorded from the Perijá Range in the far west to the Guayana and Amazonas in the far south and east, yet oddly enough it is not yet on the list for the Venezuelan Andes, though it must surely be there as well; outside Venezuela it extends from Guatemala to Brazil and Peru. The floral texture is firm and the basic color is pleasantly variable over a limited range of yellow, yellowy greens, browny yellows to white with pink flush, with red spots or splashes on the fleshy lip.

Some Venezuelan Sobralias[1]

NOT A FEW early botanical names for orchids appear to us nowadays to be almost laughably inaccurate. Anyone with any knowledge at all of orchids knows that dendrobiums and cymbidiums, for example, are Far Eastern plants, yet some 30 orchids native to Venezuela have, in days gone by, been placed in one or the other of these two genera. But before we start laughing, we have to remember that these are not taxonomic *errors,* but are the natural outcome of a general increase in knowledge and understanding of the orchid family that has led, over the years, to the splitting up of large and rather vaguely defined genera into more precisely defined, new genera. An originally widely-embracing genus such as *Dendrobium* thus ends up as a genus with much more clearly defined and restricted limits, and many species previously called dendrobiums are transferred to the other, more recently defined genera. This type of refinement in the classification of orchids is, in fact, still a very active feature in orchid taxonomy, and the switching of species from one genus to another is still quite common.

Many species in the genus of *Sobralia,* however, have been the victims of errors of judgment of a much less easily explainable type. This genus was established as far back as 1794 — nearly 200 — and now includes some 80 species of dominantly terrestrial, New World orchids. Botanically, these belong to a major group in the orchid family that is distinguished by having soft pollinia, a characteristic that sets them well apart from orchids with hard or cartilaginous pollinia. Basic characters of this type are indicative of lines of evolution, from which it follows that these two very distinct groups have been evolutionarily separated for a long way back, so far back, indeed, that it would seem incredible that there could have evolved a resemblance between the flowers of several species in one group and the flowers of some species in the other, strong enough to lead earlier taxonomists into confusing the two. Yet this confusion has occurred a number of times between species in the soft-pollinia genus of *Sobralia* and species in the hard-pollinia genus of *Cattleya.* There are nearly 20 species of *Sobralia* in Venezuela, and about a third of these have at some time in their botanical history been classified as cattleyas. That these mistakes were made well over a hundred years ago is, in this case, no real excuse as the genus *Cattleya* was not defined until 1824, by which time the genus *Sobralia* was well established and presumably should have been well known to all serious taxonomists; indeed, a number of species subjected to this "cattleya" error had actually been correctly given names as sobralias quite some time before being incorrectly named cattleyas. Even a minimal glance at the vegetative aspect of the sobralias involved in these errors is enough to show that they could not possibly be cattleyas. Sobralias have thin, often tall, reedy stems bearing thin, plicate (ribbed) leaves along much of their length, while most cattleyas have relatively short, thick, pseudobulbous stems and thick, smooth leaves that grow only at the apex of the stem. One is therefore led to conclude that the botanists concerned in these mistakes were in the first place working only from floral material, and in the second place, were too hurried or too lazy to check into details such as the type of pollinia or completely failed to recognize its significance — which sounds incredible. In any case, and for whatever reason, they allowed their judgment to be unduly influenced by the general aspect of the flowers which, in many cases, do most surprisingly have a strong resemblance to certain well-known cattleyas.

Blessed with flowers beautiful enough to have gate-crashed the occasional cattleya party, the sobralias are nevertheless not able to maintain this elevated status and plants are relatively seldom

---

[1] Originally appeared in *A.O.S. Bulletin,*
Vol. 44, March 1975, pages 193-199

short-lived flowers, and in this respect are better off than some other quite spectacular and popular orchids, such as stanhopeas, whose almost equally ephemeral flowers are produced at the rate of only one raceme per year.

Not all Venezuelan species in this genus have large and attractive flowers; some are quite small. But enough of them do to make *Sobralia* one of the most attractive smaller genera in this country when the plants are seen in their native haunts where their terrestrial habit, growing often in open ground, allows many of them to display their flowers to very full advantage. The following species are typical of their beauty.

Sobralia yauaperyensis is probably the best known by sight, if not by name, of all the Venezuelan sobralias. It is certainly one of the most beautiful, with large, well-formed flowers that are not bashful about displaying themselves to the passerby. It is a species that ranges geographically from the Andes to the far Guayana and on into Brazil. In the later months of the year it can be seen in large numbers on roadside cuttings or on the steep, grassy slopes near the cities of Mérida and Boconó, and in many other Andean places from about 3,000- to 6,000-ft. altitude. Thanks to its succession of flowers it can brighten the landscape in such places for several weeks despite the short life of each individual flower. Mostly, these flowers are of the "orchid" coloration shown in the illustration, with an intensity range from pale through to an occasional rare plant with a very deep and handsome tone indeed. The species also develops an equally beautiful white form, bright-

Sobralia fimbriata

Sobralia violacea

Sobralia infundibuligera

seen in cultivation — perhaps one sobralia plant to a thousand or more cattleya plants. This is due less to certain touchiness in cultivation than to the fact that, while blessed with lovely flowers, sobralias are cursed by their short duration. Many cattleya flowers will stay fresh and firm on the parent plant for a month or more; by contrast, many sobralia flowers last only one single day, and very few more than three days. However, while they are useless as a florist's orchid, as live plants they have the very useful character of developing a succession of their

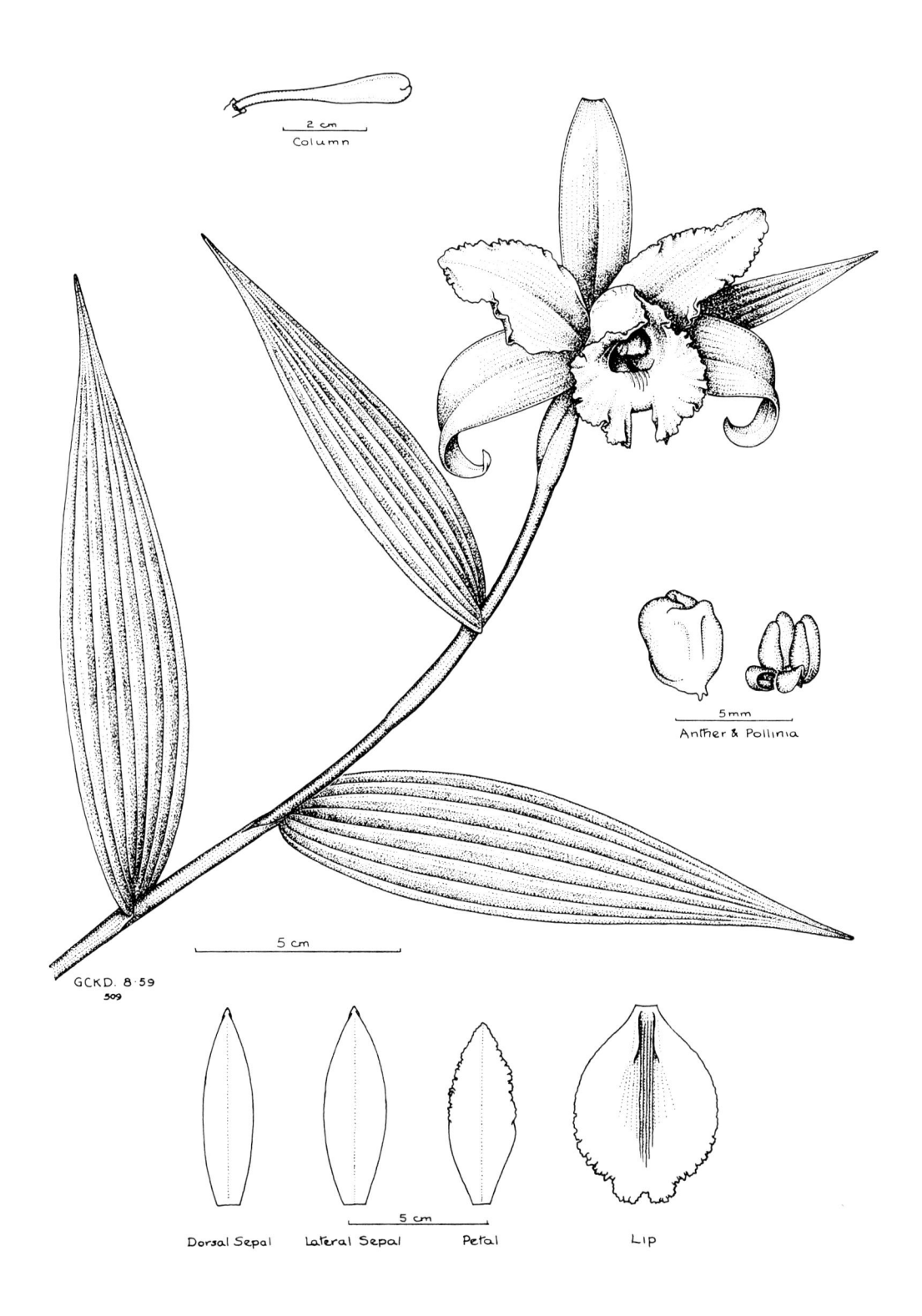

Sobralia yauaperyensis Barb. Rodr. in Vellozia ed. 2, 1: 131, 1891. — A. E.

ened by some yellow on the lip. This variety is sometimes seen in stands, sometimes mixed with the colored variety.

Sobralia cattleya (an oddly confusing name produced in 1877 by Reichenbach) is another basically Andean orchid, with a range that extends into Colombia. The flowers, of an unusual color, are not as large as those of *S. yauaperyensis,* but whereas the latter bears single flowers from the apex of the stem, *S. cattleya* bears its flowers in short, stout panicles that arise from leaf axils on the side of the stem and can carry up to a dozen flowers opening up two or three at a time. This species grows at altitudes around 5,000 to 7,000 ft., mainly in the state of Táchira that adjoins Colombia in the west of Venezuela. The robust, erect stems sometimes grow as tall as 15 feet, with leaves to a foot long, making it the largest sobralia plant in the country. It also makes it a difficult plant to display to advantage unless grown down the side of a steep bank so that the flowers come more closely to eye level! It also needs (as it gets when growing wild) some protection from surrounding vegetation to prevent occasional strong winds from flattening its tall, relatively slender stems, strong though they are.

Sobralia infundibuligera is an orchid that has so far been found only in the beautiful region of the cerros, tepuis, and "Gran Sabana" of the Bolívar state section of the Venezuelan Guayana — places with romantic names such as Aponguao, Uaiquinima, Auyántepui, Jaua, and Sarisariñama — where it can be found up to levels around 7,000 ft. Its stems are characterized by leaf-bearing sheaths that widen very noticeably in their upper part, giving them the flattened, funnel-like appearance that is the origin of this species' name. The flowers hang rather downwards, as shown in the illustration, but are by no means bashful as the stout stems carry them at anything up to seven feet from the ground, at which height the large and very striking lip is fully visible. This is the most recent of Venezuela's sobralias (and the only endemic one at present). Its discovery dates from 1965 when we found our first flowering specimens on Auyántepui. In this we were lucky because there is no doubt that plants had been seen and noted by exploring botanists such as Dr. J. A. Steyermark some years earlier, but as we were the first to find flowers, enabling Dr. L.A. Garay to declare it "new," we feel we can consider this very handsome species to be "ours." Since then, we have seen flowering plants in several other sites and now we have our own at home — though not yet seven feet tall.

Sobralia fimbriata is another species that grows in such distant places that it is very seldom seen in public. Those who have ever seen either of these orchids in flower must, in fact, be very few indeed. It was first published in 1901 and known initially only from a few places in Peru. Later it turned up in Brazil and finally in Venezuela when we found specimens at about 3,500-to 4,000-ft. elevation on the southern flanks of Auyántepui in 1963. Nothing more was heard of this obviously shy species here, until 1972, when the Joint Venezuelan-Brazilian Border Commission, led by George Pantchenko for the Venezuelan side, came across this species growing most prolifically at about 4,000 ft. right on the border with Brazil in the Sierra Parima range, somewhat north of the source of the Orinoco. It is one of the exclusively white sobralias (at least we have so far heard of no colored forms) and is characterized by the dense mat of yellow hairs or *fimbriae* on its lip and from which the species derives its name. Compared to other sobralias dealt with in this note, it is a small plant (those we have seen are seldom over three feet tall and often only half as much) but its flowers are of a good, three-inch size. In captivity, our plants flower well, and their relative smallness is an advantage, avoiding some of the problems connected with growing 15-foot monsters even if we do have outdoor space to accommodate the latter.

Sobralia violacea, the last in this note, can be found in most parts of Venezuela. It is in the Coastal Range at about 1,000 ft.; in the Andes at as high as 5,000 ft.; on the edge of the Llanos plains at around 1,200 ft.; west of Lake Maracaibo at 3,000 to 5,000 ft.; far up Orinoco tributaries in the Amazonas territory at 500 ft. to 1,500 ft. or near the base of Auyántepui in the heart of the Angel Falls paradise at 1,500 ft.; you name it, we have it. Yet despite such ubiquity (up to levels of around 5,000 ft.) it is not seen as often as one would expect as it tends to hide itself in the forest rather than display itself to the public gaze in the open like *S. yauaperyensis.* It is at times confused with this latter species but this resemblance is really only skin deep. The *S. violacea* plants are seldom as firmly erect as the general run of *S. yauaperyensis* plants; the sepals and petals have a more "forward" stance, with the lateral sepals usually being rather horizontal instead of angling downwards; and the lip is more tightly tubular. As a further clue to their identity, the extreme top of the stem (or rather the tubular leaf-bearing sheaths at the top of the stem) are distinctly rough, though this is a bit deceitful as once in a while this roughness is subdued. The color of the flowers is nearly always an almost uniform, very beautiful, and intense rose-purple. We say "nearly always" because we did once come across some rare plants near the top of the Siapa River in Amazonas that were very pale indeed: plain white we have not yet seen. In vegetative form, the species seems to enjoy looking different almost every time we see it, thus leaving us wondering about its identity until we can see a flower. Some

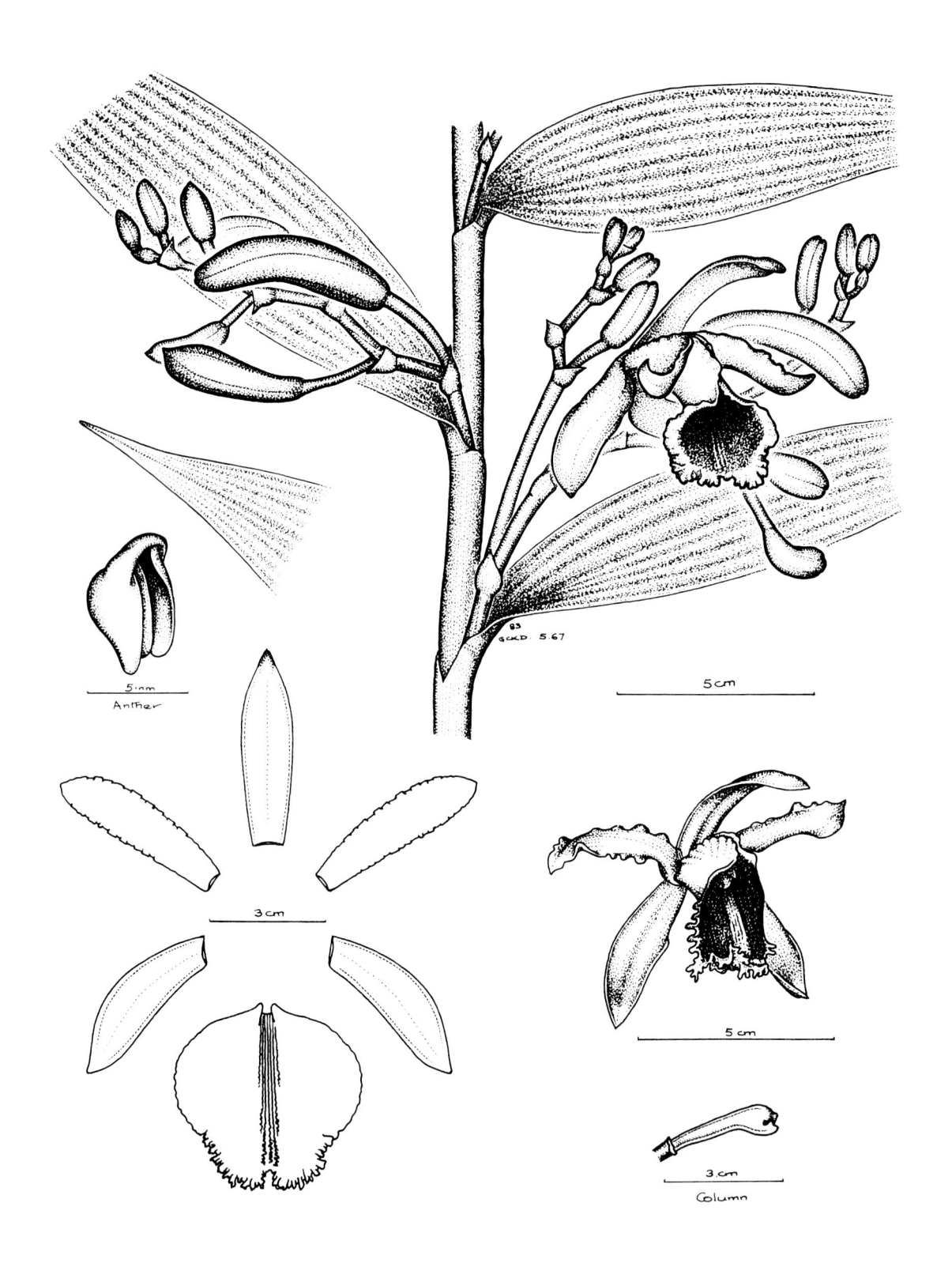

Sobralia cattleya Reichb. f. in Gard. Chron. n. s. 7: 72, 1877. — A.

plants have tough, almost rigidly erect stems, but there is every grade to be found between this and thinly-stemmed, wiry, and branching plants that droop all over the place. But whatever shape they take, and however annoying this variety can be to the collector who hopes he has found something possibly "new," they are all very beautiful, and a pleasure to have around.

From our records, the flowering seasons of these species are: *S. yauaperyensis,* August to November; *S. cattleya,* May and August; *S. infundibuligera,* February to May; *S. fimbriata,* April to July; *S. violacea,* January to May in most parts, but October-November for some places in the far interior, including the very pale Siapa plants.

Cultivation, insofar as it concerns growing plants in our near-Caracas home, does not seem to present major difficulties once a plant has become well established, but getting a forest plant started properly is by no means easy. The most critical part in the cultivation of any wild orchid taken from its home in field or forest is naturally in the transport stage, and this is particularly so with sobralias (and allied elleanthus plants) which are generally so resentful that they are frequently dead on arrival. Obviously, speed in transport is most important, and where delay is unavoidable much tender-loving-attention en route is essential. In the case of Coastal Range or Andean orchids accessible by fine paved roads, the transport problem is not great, but it is a very different matter with plants from far reaches of the Amazonas area or the region of the cerros and tepuis. These places can involve days of travel by dugout canoe or on Indians' backs (the orchids, not ourselves), and our catalogue of successes in such species only really began to look up when we were lucky enough to get in on some helicopter-aided excursions. For transporting these species, compactness is a help — even in a station wagon anything over five feet is troublesome — but fortunately any long stems can be whittled down without much harm and in any case are unlikely to reach home undamaged. Where special soil conditions appear to be involved, such as with the very acid soils in the tepui areas, it is very helpful to bring some back with the plant to help it get a good start, and a reasonably large root clump also helps. By one means or another, we have now got plants of all these sobralias growing happily, the only one about which we have perhaps some reservations left being the *S. infundibuligera.* Transport delays defeated our early efforts with this species, but our later ones, where helicopters or new roads have come to our help, seem to have taken good hold; plants have already flowered at home for a second time and will now hopefully prosper as confidently as the other.

The tall plants of *S. cattleya* have of necessity to be grown directly in the ground, but most of the other sobralias are grown in pots so as to enable a change of site to be made if we ever have reason to feel that something is going wrong.

Some Venezuelan 'Monospecific' Genera[1]

VENEZUELA gives a home to species from approximately 160 genera of orchids. These genera divide themselves statistically into a collection of about 100 genera with less than five Venezuelan species in each, a group of 55 genera with five to 30 species each, only one genus (*Lepanthes*) with more than 30 and less than 65 species, three genera (*Stelis, Oncidium,* and *Maxillaria*) with from 65 to 80 species, and two dominant genera, *Epidendrum* and *Pleurothallis*, each with 130 to 140 species, *Pleurothallis* probably leading by a small margin.

The first numerically large group of very small genera includes about 50 that are represented in Venezuela by one lone species each, and it is with this group of "monospecific" genera that the present notes are concerned, for no more logical reason than that it provides us with an opportunity to show *A. O. S. Bulletin* readers a number of very interesting orchids that are seldom illustrated and that may have escaped their attention. The word "monospecific," we must immediately confess, is bastard Greek-Latin and non-existent and has been invented purely for the present occasion to simplify reference to those genera that are represented in Venezuela by a single species, as distinct from really-truly monotypic genera which a glance at your *A. O. S. Orchidist's Glossary* will show you (should you not know it already) are genera that have only a single species anywhere. By no means are all these Venezuelan monospecifics of fabulous beauty — indeed many of them are strictly of botanical interest only — but out of the total of 50 there are more than enough of charm or of outstanding interest to make it difficult to select those that will illustrate these notes. Five of these monospecifics are also true monotypic genera of which two (*Solenidium* and *Polyotidium)* figure in these notes, and another is worth a passing note as its single species would be a contender in any competition for the smallest orchid with the longest name — *Hofmeisterella eumicroscopica.*

Ada

Ada is a genus with only three letters and two species to its name, and we have gone running to *Generic Names of Orchids* by Schultes and Pease to find out what Lindley's reasons might have been when he chose *Ada* as a name for the genus. *Generic Names of Orchids* tells us that Ada was "an historical character, sister of Artemisia, in Caria," which, to be honest, does not take us very far. So on behalf of A.O.S. readers and of our own ignorance we have extended our search into our old *Encyclopaedia Brittanica,* but have emerged no wiser as to the purpose of this name except for a sort of second-hand connection through Ada's sister who was a lady renowned principally for building a super-mausoleum for her dead husband in the third century B.C., but was also known as a botanist and medical researcher. We have said above that *Ada* is a two-species genus, but this needs a cautionary note because in a recent study of the *Brassia-Ada* complex, Norris Williams concludes that certain brassias should be classified as adas, a rather surprising conclusion that we understand has not yet by any means received general acceptance.

Basically, *Ada* is a strictly Colombian genus, but in recent years a number of such genera have been found to encroach at least a small distance into Venezuela, particularly in the border state of Táchira, and it was here that we found our specimens of *Ada aurantiaca* in 1968. Hiking up towards the Páramo de Judío above the small town of La Revancha, we passed some large boulders at about 6,500 feet in an expanse of meadow that had once clearly formed part of virgin forest, remnants of which were close by. The top of one of these boulders, about the size of a minibus, was a botanic garden of miscellaneous plants including several

[1] Originally appeared in *A.O.S. Bulletin,*
Vol. 45, July 1976, Pages 606-610

clumps of orchids, one of which turned out to be our first *Lycaste fulvescens* and the second delighted us in due course by proving to be not the probably ordinary brassia that it looked like, but Venezuela's first record of *Ada aurantiaca.*

The flower spikes of this species are produced quite freely from the axils of the leaves sheathing the base of the fairly small pseudobulbs but are nevertheless rather bashful in habit, the racemes adopting a shy, nodding attitude as if afraid to look you in the face; and the flowers themselves do not open at all wide. What draws the attention, however, and earns this species its place in a collection is the brilliant orange-red of the flowers. Two hybrid genera have been produced (*Adaglossa* with *Odontoglossum,* and *Adioda* with *Cochlioda*) in an effort to take advantage of this wonderful color, but the efforts have presumably not been very successful as one hears little about them. The plant we took from the boulder (had we known what the clump was we might have taken more) has done excellently and has been divided into several pieces, all growing happily in pots filled with tree-fern root and placed on the edge of a very well-ventilated slope with slightly more shade than our light-loving brassias.

Scuticaria steelei

Ada aurantiaca

Miltonia

Most of the "monospecific" genera dealt with in these notes are not particularly well-known. By contrast, *Miltonia* is a very famous New World genus, and, though it does not include a great many species, it does have a high proportion that are greatly appreciated, both on their own account and also for the fine hybrids formed from them. Miltonias are present all the way from Costa Rica to Peru and the Argentine, and form very roughly two groups: intermediate-to-warm species in Brazil and farther south; cooler-growing species elsewhere [now included in the genus *Miltoniopsis* — ed.]. With this geographical spread, it seems odd that no species of this showy genus had ever been located in Venezuela until 1960, when one plant finally came to light. Since then no further plants seem to have put in an appearance so it remains, for this country, a very rare genus indeed. The one plant in question, a *Miltonia spectabilis,* was found by a scientific friend, Carl Gaede, in a far part of the Upper Ventauri River, moderately close to the Brazilian border. Several scientists whose work takes them into such regions, usually in connection with research into Indian dicts or diseases, are also keen orchidists, and Gaede is no exception, but it was only some time after collecting his small plant, when it first flowered for him near Caracas, that he realized what a surprise package he had picked up and kindly brought it to us to examine.

Although *Miltonia spectabilis* is a Brazilian species, to the best of our knowledge no records exist of this species in the part of Brazil close to the Venezuelan find, but the amount of botanical exploration in these remote zones on both sides of the border is far from exhaustive so further plants may be awaiting discovery on both sides of the border. Alternatively, orchid geography is littered with a number of very odd, widely isolated occurrences, such as the case of the Venezuelan and Peruvian findings of *Chaubardiella tigrina* mentioned in our forthcoming note on the "Chondrorhyncha Alliance," and this miltonia find may be another such example.

Miltonia spectabilis had a number of beautiful color varieties, important enough to have received names. The Venezuelan variety is *Miltonia spectabilis* var. *moreliana,* and it makes a striking plant

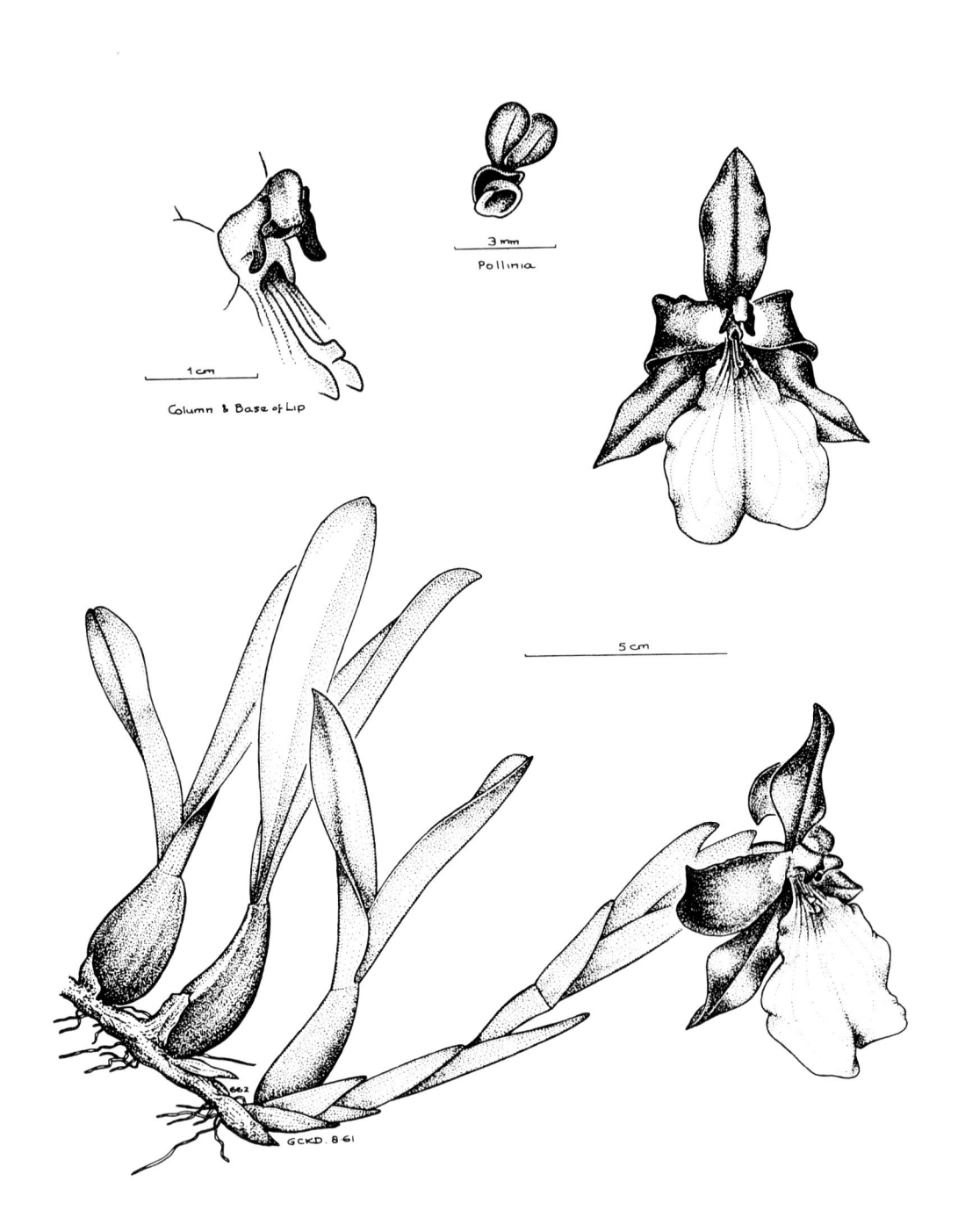

Miltonia spectabilis Lindl. in Bot. Reg. 23: sub. t. 1975, 1837. — D.

as its flowers are large (about 3½") while the plant itself is relatively small, three-inch pseudobulbs being spaced about an inch apart along the running rhizome, and bearing five-inch leaves that reach no higher than the flower itself.

Scuticaria

Scuticaria is a genus of five species that are known in the area from Colombia to northern Brazil, being represented in Venezuela only by *S. steelei,* illustrated here. Apart from its fine 2½" flowers, the most striking thing about this species is its extraordinarily long, thin, dangling terete leaves, characteristic of the genus. We saw our first plants some 20 years ago, when making our first (abortive) effort to get to the base of Angel Falls, and we almost failed to recognize it as an orchid. We had decided to camp on the sandy banks of an island in the Carrao River in the lee of some of the enormous cliffs that ring the great mesa of Auyántepui. The first "rationals" to visit this spot had drawn attention to its orchid qualities by naming it Orchid Island, and we were naturally anxious to see what it had to offer. But it was only after we had casually glanced at quite a few bunches of four- or five-foot, dangling, pencil-thin objects that we suddenly woke to the fact that these were not incipient lianas but were the leaves of an orchid we had never seen before, a conclusion confirmed when we noted the line of small, repent pseudobulbs at their base. Orchid Island is a natural camping site set in extraordinarily beautiful surroundings beside the clear red waters of the Carrao, and, since our first visit, has been used by practically every visitor to the area. A natural but sad consequence of this is that, while it is still a beautiful island, it is no longer an orchid island. When we were there last, some years ago, the scuticarias had almost disappeared; by now there are presumably none. Luckily, this species exists in a number of less visited places, not only in the Bolívar State section of the Venezuelan Guayana but also in the flooded-forest Amazonas Region.

Our very first plant did not get what it liked while we practiced the necessary fish-and-find-out tactics, but the next one has done well in our plastic-enclosed space, its long leaves dangling from the block of tree-fern root where the pseudobulbs have taken good hold. But a healthy plant does not necessarily mean a flowering one — sometimes even the opposite — and year after year we hoped in vain for another sight of its fine, large flowers. To keep the dangling leaves out of the way, and to give the plant plenty of warmth, it was kept fairly close under the plastic roof, and one day, as part of a slight reorganization, it was moved to an almost identical site but about three feet away; very soon after this, it developed buds and in due course produced some fine flowers. We still do not know what element in the move sparked off this gratifying response, or even if the plant would have burst into flower had we never moved it at all, but it is episodes like this that make orchid growing so fascinating, and which emphasize to us how much we still have to learn about what orchids do, or do not, like.

Teuscheria

Teuscheria is a genus that was published by L. A. Garay in the *A.O.S. Bulletin* for December 1968, based on an Ecuadorean plant, and named in honor of Henry Teuscher, then Curator of the Montreal Botanic Gardens and well-known for many years to *A.O.S. Bulletin* readers for his fine series of articles that are still appearing. There are three species of *Teuscheria* of which the Venezuelan one, by odd coincidence, was found by us just one month before the new genus was published. We found only the one plant in this original site at about 5,000 feet in the cloud forests of what is now the Henri Pittier National Park in the Coastal Range, and despite much searching never found another in that spot. Luckily, this first plant did well so we sent a piece to Montreal, which also thrived and allowed Teuscher to give a very full description of its unusual features in the Montreal Botanic Garden's *Memoirs* for December 1962. Briefly, the plant is characterized by small, onion-shaped pseudobulbs growing tightly up against each other along a very thin and completely hidden rhizome. The single leaves are plicate, long and narrow, with a long, thin, petiolate base. The pseudobulbs are clothed in a very distinctive, thin, very close-fitting and persistent inner sheath that extends as a tube quite a long way up the petiolate leaf base; outer sheaths are less persistent and break down into nerve shreds that give the base of the plant a rather untidy aspect. The inflorescence consists of slender, pendent peduncles, to 4" long, that rise (or rather fall) from the base of any but the newest pseudobulb and which bear terminal one-inch flowers that are "upside down," i.e., lip-uppermost or "non-resupinate." The lip has a small, basal spur projecting backwards beyond the point where the lip is attached to the column.

While we have never found more specimens of this species in the original area, we have found others rather closer to Caracas, in some remnant forest clothing an otherwise bare ridge at about 4,000 feet, and more recently still have come across plants several hundred miles away in the Bolívar State part of the Venezuelan Guayana, close to Guyana. It is thus a seemingly scarce but quite widespread species and its geographic limits may one day be found to be quite extensive. Meanwhile, further research by Garay unearthed *Bifrenaria wageneri,* a species described by Reichenbach in 1854, and as this appears to be the same as our plant

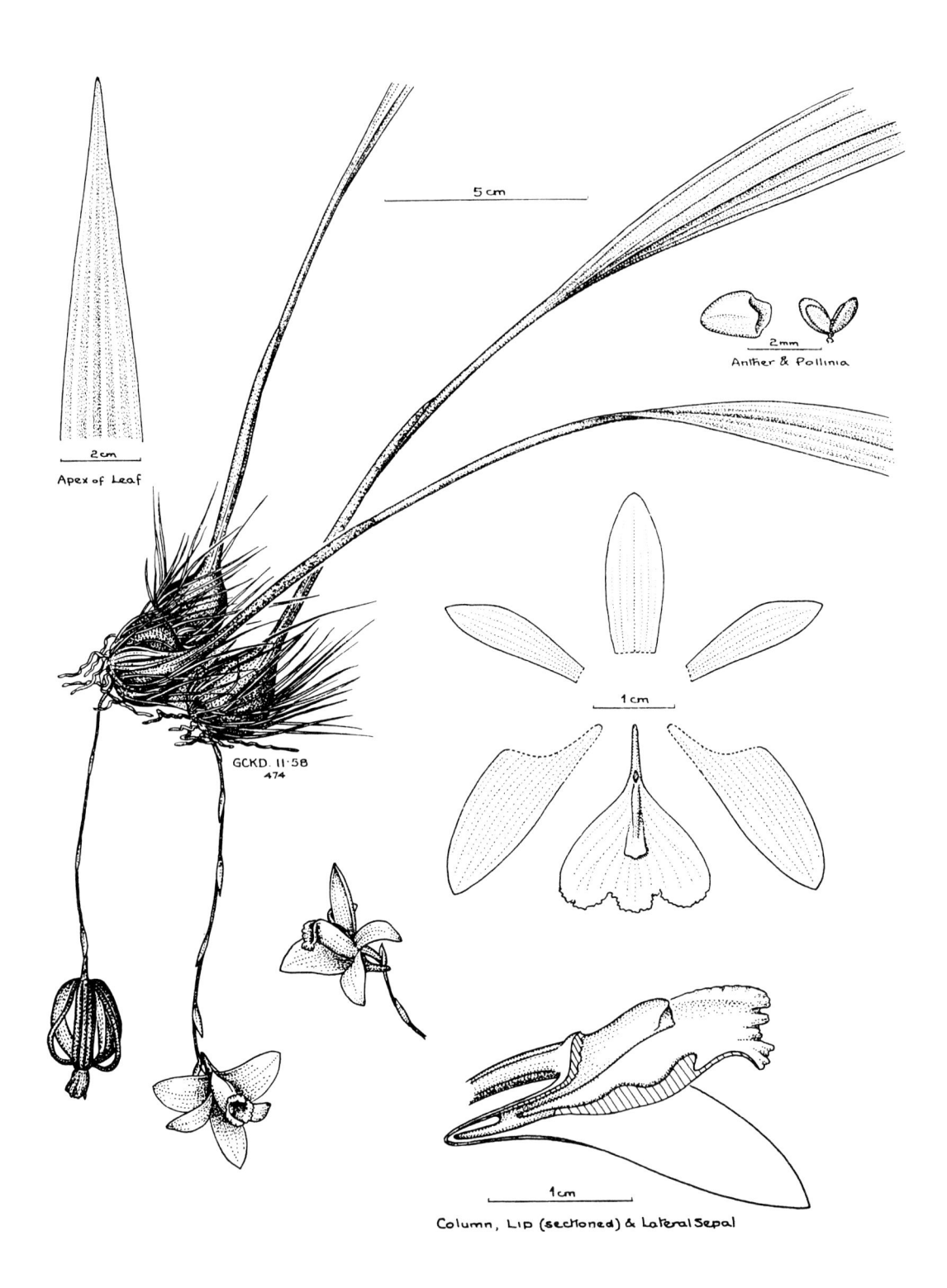

Teuscheria wageneri (Reichb. f.) Garay in Bot. Mus. Leafl. 21: 256, 1967. — B. E.

he renamed this species *Teuscheria wageneri* in 1967. Our "new-species" find was apparently more than a hundred years out of date when we made it!

This orchid is perhaps not wildly exciting to look at, but it does have the attraction of its unusual flowers and the ability to develop them, one or several at a time, with considerable freedom in any month or months from June to November. It takes kindly to captivity, growing on small, hanging blocks of tree fern to allow room for the pendent inflorescences to develop, and has the additional advantage of allowing itself to be propagated with fair ease by separation of backbulbs.

Working our way up the Río Carrao above Orchid Island

Bifrenaria maguirei, Zygosepalum tatei, and Otoglossum arminii — Three Fine Orchids Safe in Venezuela's Hinterland[1]

"THAT WHICH we call a rose, by any other name would smell as sweet," said Juliet to her Romeo, taking the words out of Shakespeare's mouth, and almost everyone since then has accepted this as a statement of fact. Which, of course, it is not, as the scent manufacturers very well know. Despite some odd but apparently successful names in the trade, such as *Russian Leather* or *Chanel No. 5,* it is doubtful if these scents would long command the market they do if their names were to be changed to *Sloppy-Joe's Stinkwater* or *Fischbein's Fischwasser.* Psychology as well as common sense enters strongly into the matter of names, and, in the plant world, probably no large group of flowering plants benefits — and suffers — as much from the psychological impact of its name as the orchid family. Due to the enormous glamour attached to this family when it first attracted public attention a hundred or more years ago, and to the publicity given ever since by florists to the more showy varieties, the word *orchid* has reached a point where, in the public mind, it is synonymous not only with exceptional beauty but also with great rarity and high value despite the general falsity of these latter characters. It is nice, of course, to have an impressive name such as Rockefeller, but, on the other hand, it is not so nice when this attracts thieves and scroungers. This is the position in which many wild flowers now find themselves. The plants threatened are beautiful, it is true, but not necessarily more so than many flowers in other families. It is the magic word *orchid* that has put many of them in danger — the thieves are breaking into the house of the Rockefellers and ignoring the just-as-rich Joneses alongside.

Collecting (i.e., buying) man-made hybrids, making your own crosses, or growing species from seed — all these are highly commendable and innocent hobbies. But the growing tendency of collectors to specialize in natural species is putting an increased and dangerous drain on plants taken from their natural habitat. This collecting is sometimes done commercially for sale to hobbyists in both tropical and temperate markets, and sometimes by amateur collectors living in the countries where the orchids have their existence. Both forms of this collecting can, when taken to extremes, definitely endanger the continued existence of the orchids concerned, particularly when to this attack is added the frequent widespread destruction of the fields and forests that are the normal home of these plants. In the case of some temperate climate terrestrial orchids it has been possible to pinpoint the damage being done and to take, or try to take, very specific measures to protect a specific orchid in a specific locality. But when dealing with plants from tropical areas, many such zones are so extensive, remote, and unpopulated that only a very small proportion of any given habitat is likely to have been adequately explored, and to say that any orchid growing there is in immediate danger of extinction is seldom possible. It is possible, however, to say that the chances for survival in the wild for certain species is clearly decreasing at a rapid rate and that the species is thus severely threatened.

In Venezuela it is only to be expected that the orchids most under attack should be those of the genus *Cattleya,* most of which unfortunately are either close to populated areas or at least moderately easily accessible, but other species of less notoriety are nevertheless in sufficient demand in orchid-horticultural circles that they are rapidly stripped out of each new locality where they are found. It is particularly unfortunate that any attempt to draw attention to the endangered status of such orchids carries with it the risk of making matters worse rather than better. Just the drawing of attention to an orchid can be of itself harmful, and to state in addition that it is endangered seems to inspire in certain types of orchidophiles and com-

[1] Originally appeared in *A.O.S. Bulletin,*
Vol. 45, September 1976, pages 783-787

mercial dealers a strong desire to grab what is left rather than any wish to conserve it.

The far interior of Venezuela is a fascinating and beautiful region that is fortunately still remote enough to offer a safe home to the orchids and other plants lucky enough to grow there, and particularly to those that live on the tops of its many mountains. The region falls inside the boundaries of two large political units, the State of Bolívar (Estado Bolívar — and do please pronounce it Bol*ee*var, not B*olli*var) and the Amazon Territory (Territorio Amazonas). The former contains all the land that drains north into the Lower Orinoco, or into Guyana via the river Cuyuní, while the Amazonas, separated geographically by a relatively low but important divide, drains either into the Upper Orinoco or into Brazil via the river Casiquiare. On geological grounds the whole of the southern part of these two entities can be referred to as the Venezuelan Guayana, but as there is no politically defined area of this name, and as the character of the low level parts of the two sections are in many ways distinct from each other, the Bolívar zone is frequently referred to as the "Guayana" to distinguish it from the Territorio Amazonas: this, not surprisingly, is frequently just called Amazonas, which can unfortunately give rise to confusion with similarly named parts of Brazil and Colombia.

Depending on their locality, the principal heights in the interior are called *cerros* or *tepuis,* and, as they are nearly all in the form of large table mountains, the word *meseta* is also used. Their height ranges from roughly 4,000 to 10,000 feet, and their sizes vary from tops measurable in acres as in the case of Cerro Autana (see Chapter 7) to hundreds of square miles in cases such as Auyántepui (see Chapter 6). A separate feature of Edo. Bolívar is the *Gran Sabana,* a large area at the headwaters of the Caroní River that lies at mostly 3,000 to 4,000 and consists of beautiful, open, rolling savannas with many streams and gallery forests. Taken as a unit, the relatively flat tops of all these *cerros* and *tepuis* of the interior form a very sizeable and unique plant habitat, a high proportion of whose plants are not to be found anywhere else in the world except where this "Roraima Sandstone" area extends a bit into neighboring countries; in some cases there are plants that are known solely inside the limits of a single summit. For botanists these heights are a never-ending source of extraordinarily interesting material, and it is indeed the botanical world that has in major degree led the efforts to explore them ever since the Schomburgk brothers, exploring between Guyana and Venezuela, put Roraima on the map about 130 years ago. Fortunately for the very specialized life on these summits, they are without exception difficult of access and broadly speaking only serious investigators have so far taken the trouble and effort needed to explore them. For the average man in the street, or even the commercial collector, they are still out of reach for physical and economic reasons, and only on rare occasions are they threatened by the other danger — fire. It is a pity in many ways that such a unique, beautiful, and extraordinarily interesting habitat should be so inaccessible to the general public, but it is nevertheless to be hoped that it will long stay that way, or at least until such time as some truly efficient way of protecting their plant and animal life has been developed. In any case, this problem will only arise when those who now fly small private planes are flying small private helicopters instead, or when enormous helicopter-buses for tourists are in the air. Until then, any exciting plant, orchid or otherwise, growing in this habitat can be happily considered safe, which is a particularly comforting thought in the case of the three orchids dealt with in this article as they would otherwise quickly join this country's cattleyas as persecuted species.

Apart from some difference in height above sea level, the special conditions in which these three species grow are basically very similar. On the tops of most of these highlands there are expanses, sometimes small but often very large, of open, savanna-like areas where the soil is peaty and, as they are frequently underlain at no great depth by solid sandstone, the drainage is poor and the conditions at least damp or more than downright boggy. In addition this soil is extremely acid, to the extent that the dense, generally calf- or knee-high vegetation that forms these savannas is highly specialized, botanically interesting, and largely endemic. All three orchid species grow mainly in these savannas where they live well-shaded by the taller surrounding vegetation but send up their inflorescences high enough to reach the open air, or at least to attain the higher degree of insolation that they need to develop their buds and eventually open their flowers where they can attract the necessary insect for fertilization.

The first of this trio, *Bifrenaria maguirei,* has already been touched upon and illustrated in our article in the *A. O. S. Bulletin.* It is by far the most restricted in geographical range of the trio and has yet to be recorded outside the limits of the *cerros* of Amazonas. In a recent expedition to the *macizo* of Jaua-Sarisariñama which lies almost on the hinge between Amazonas and Bolívar, we kept a sharp look-out in the hopes of spotting it, but although the altitude of 4,000 feet on the Sarisariñama section was right and, in some places the general habitat also seemed entirely suitable, no sign of it could be seen, a further indication that this species may indeed not exist outside the confines of the Territorio Amazonas. The restriction of habitat

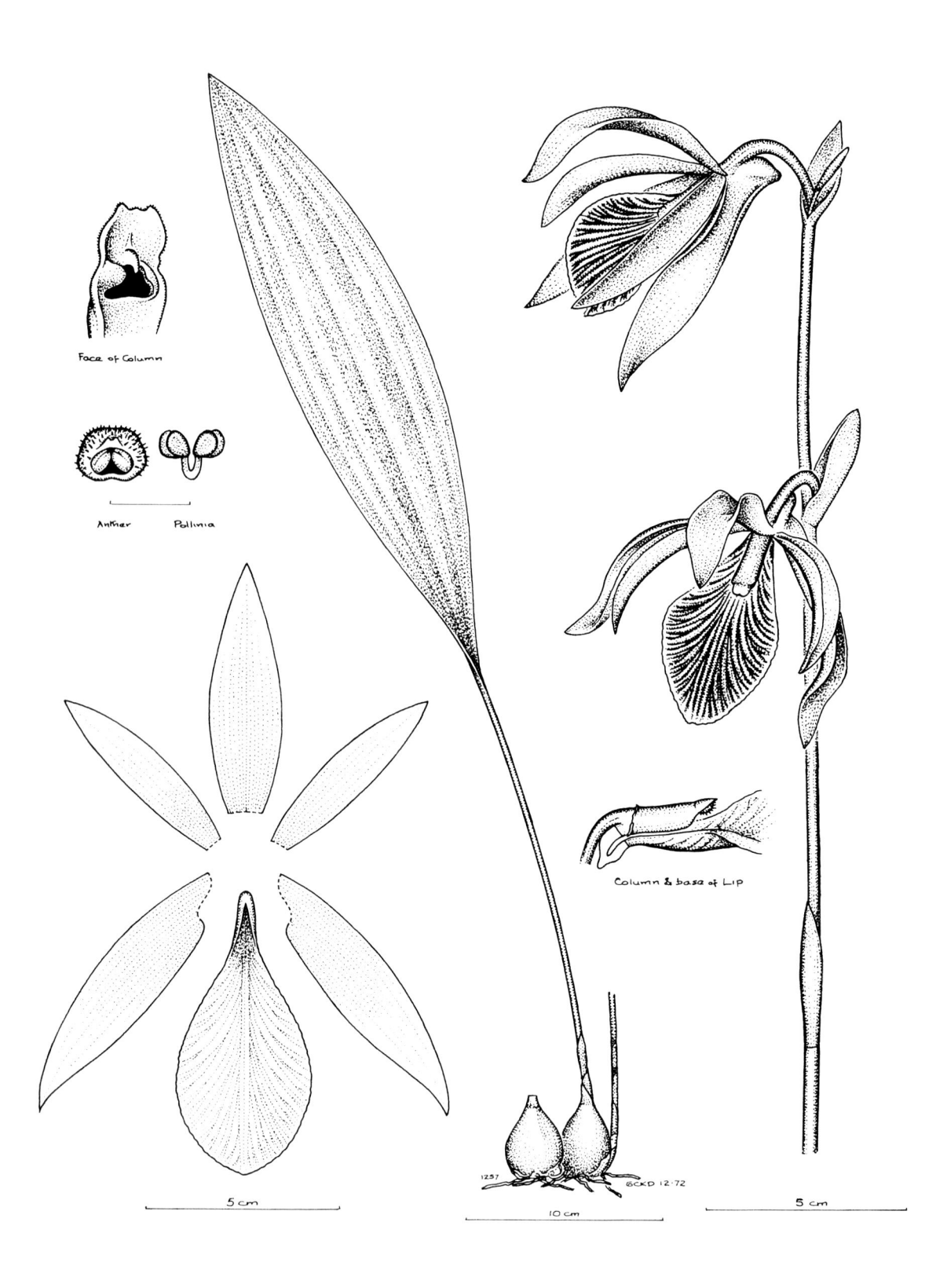

Bifrenaria maguirei C. Schweinf. in Amer. Orch. Soc. Bull. 28: 199, 1959. — D.

presumably plays its part in the fact that this orchid is the "youngest" of the trio, having been found by Steyermark in 1944, although not published by Schweinfurth until 1959. In its native home it can be found in a variety of conditions including dry and exposed terrestrial sites, and even epiphytic ones, in addition to the more highly favored damp and boggy locations where its leaves can develop to two feet long or more. Its yard-high, erect inflorescences are the tallest among this trio of orchids and, although they bear no more than three flowers at a time (and usually only two), these are of a good size, and the lip in particular, with its dark purple nerve lines on a white base, is very striking. If it was in any way an "accessible" orchid there is no doubt that commercial hands would be snatching for it with great eagerness.

Zygosepalum tatei, the second of our trio, was discovered by Tate on Cerro Duida in Amazonas in 1928. It started life as *Zygopetalum tatei* but was switched to the genus *Zygosepalum* by Garay in 1972 (*Venezuelan Orchids Illustrated,* Vol. 5, page 318) as part of a complete and much needed revision of the whole *Zygopetalum* complex that was published by him in 1973 (*Orquideología,* Vol. VIII). By contrast with the *Bifrenaria*, this *Zygosepalum* species exists not only in Amazonas but also in the highlands of Bolívar where it has been found on Auyántepui and on the *meseta* of Jaua: as it is also known in Guyana farther yet to the east, these Bolívar records are not unexpected. More recently it has been added to the list of Brazilian orchids when it was found at 6,000 to 8,000 feet on both sides of the Venezuelan-Brazilian border where this cuts across the top of the very large Cerro de la Neblina in the extreme south of Venezuela. It thus grows higher and cooler than the bifrenaria but like it, while basically a terrestrial species, it can occasionally be seen growing in fairly dry conditions as an epiphyte or lithophyte. Its usual form is that of a series of fairly small, slender, bifoliate pseudobulbs clustered so tightly along the rhizome that they conceal it. The leaves are tough, narrow and seldom over six inches long, and in epiphytic conditions it shows a fairly strong scandent tendency. It is certainly not as pretty an orchid as the quite striking *Zygosepalum lindeniae* which inhabits much lower levels in Amazonas and Bolívar, but its erect inflorescences of flowers with brown-marked, yellow brown sepals and petals and pure white, pink-crested lips are definitely attractive. The brown markings are very variable from fairly pale to a very dark browny puce.

Otoglossum arminii (=Odontoglossum arminii), the third of this trio of "safe" orchids, is by contrast a fairly antique species that dates from 1855 when it was first found in Colombia and much later found also in Venezuela. Its record in Venezuela is obscured by the confusion between this species and the very similar *Odontoglossum brevifolium-chiriquense-coronatum* group, so it is only safe to say that it has been found on Cerro de la Neblina in Amazonas at 6,500 to 8,000 feet, and on the *meseta* of Jaua at about 6,000 feet (more or less as for the *Zygosepalum tatei*). Its tough, creeping rhizome bears smallish, well-separated, unifoliate pseudobulbs at regular intervals of two to six inches, the leaf small, oval and tough. Its manner of growth is variable as with the other members of this trio: we have found it growing very occasionally as an epiphyte (though never very far up its host tree) in some fairly tall forest on Jaua as well as in semi-depauperate form on exposed rocks in the same locality, but both here and on Neblina it seems to prefer damp conditions where it is almost, but not quite, a terrestrial. In such places it behaves like a timorous maiden at the seaside who likes to paddle but fears to get her feet too wet, so it grows with its roots in contact with the wet, acid soil but seldom actually in it, getting its support by twining itself among the basal part of the terrestrial plants surrounding it. Once a rhizome gets going well, it can grow to considerable lengths as (in its native habitat) the older pseudobulbs seem reluctant to rot away. One rhizome we picked up on Jaua had a length of over six feet forming a string of more than 20 pseudobulbs of which most of the early ones were devoid of leaf but by no means devoid of vigor. The flowers of this species are borne in a fairly close raceme at the top of an erect stem that varies from quite short to over 18 inches tall; the individual flowers are about two inches in diameter and have a wide, circular form that shows off their yellow and red-brown color to full advantage. The brown and white lip is relatively small, but a spike with five or more flowers can nevertheless be quite showy, and we consider this species among the best of the genus in Venezuela.

All three of this trio of beauties should be fine plants to grow in captivity and to propagate for wider distribution, but unfortunately our experience to date has been that they are all difficult to cultivate despite their obvious toughness in their natural habitat as shown by their ability to accept epiphytic and even lithophytic conditions on occasion. The peaty soil is extremely acid and retains much moisture, the air is absolutely clean and at these altitudes presumably ultraviolet radiation is strong. Temperatures recorded on our visits to this highlands ranged from minima of 43°F on Neblina at 8,000 feet in October to 44°F on Jaua at 6,000 feet in February to 58°F on Avispa at 5,000 feet in December. In our home above Caracas at about 4,000 feet we are still far enough from the smog of

Caracas Valley to offer our plants good clean air and our temperatures, though a bit warmer, are not drastically so. Some of the plants are even growing in soil taken from their natural home. What may well be our main trouble in making these plants enjoy life is the non-acidity of the water they get from natural rain or from the city water supply, so we may yet have to try a daily sprinkle of vinegar.

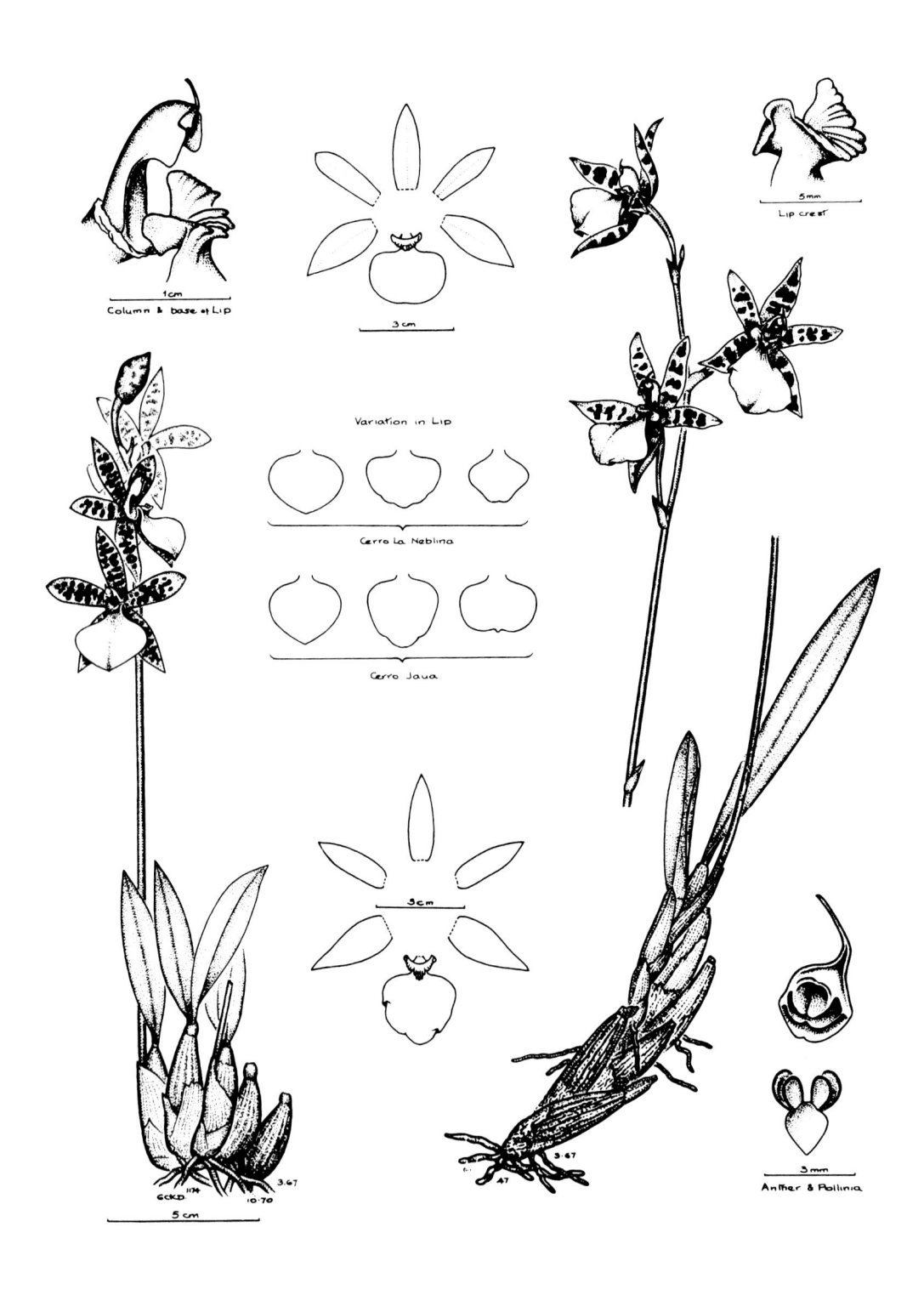

Zygosepalum tatei (Ames & Schweinf.) Garay & Dunsterv., Venez. Orch. Ill. 5: 318, 1972. — D. E.

The Chondrorhyncha Alliance in Venezuela[1]

CHONDRORHYNCHA is a small genus of orchids whose attractive appearance belies the rather awesome name produced by Lindley when he published the genus in 1846. A glance at the very useful A.O.S. *Orchidist's Glossary* reveals that this name refers to the beak-like rostellum characteristic of the genus; unfortunately, beak-like rostella are not so very uncommon, and this character alone is not sufficient to identify a plant as a chondrorhyncha. In fact, there are several closely allied species, with or without beak-like rostella, in a group of once poorly defined and understood genera, and, as a result, these have for many years suffered from much taxonomic confusion, species being allocated to one genus by one expert, switched to another genus by the next, to a third genus by yet another taxonomist, and so on. Vegetatively, the plants in these species are very similar. All have more or less fan-shaped sprays of leaves, and, with the sole exception of those in the genus *Chaubardia*, are without pseudobulbs. Even then, the chaubardias are scarcely a visual exception as the pseudobulbs are really quite inconspicuous, and one has to poke around in the base of the leaves to uncover them, an exercise to which the owner of the plant might strongly object.

All these related genera, a total of nine, constitute the *Chondrorhyncha* alliance, which has been the subject of an important critical study by Dr. L. A. Garay, published in the November 1969 issue of *Orquideología*. In this, he sorts out and clearly defines the genera concerned (largely on the basis of somewhat hidden but critical details of columns and lips), transfers a few species from one genus to another, adds a new genus to accommodate several "misfits," and finally cleans it all up by providing an invaluable key to facilitate distinguishing one genus from another. All orchid fans seriously interested in species are, one assumes, also interested in some degree in their botanical as well as their horticultural aspects (it is a sad picture if this is not the case), so perhaps this is a good moment to remark that anyone wanting a very readable, botanically oriented orchid publication to supplement the excellent general coverage provided by the *A. O. S. Bulletin*, is well advised to subscribe to *Orquideología*, a well-illustrated, bilingual quarterly put out in Medellin, Colombia, by the Colombian Orchidological Society.

As eight of these nine *Chondrorhyncha* alliance genera are inhabitants of Venezuela, it seems not out of place to provide this note on the group as part of the series of miscellaneous articles about Venezuelan orchids on which we have embarked.

Cribbing liberally from Garay's Key, and taking the genera in the same order, the first to be treated here is the genus **Chaubardia**. This is a three-species genus which, as already mentioned, is distinguished from the other genera in the alliance by having pseudobulbs, albeit small ones. In Venezuela it is represented by only one of its three species, *C. surinamensis*, an orchid that lives in the distant and scantily populated areas of Bolívar state, south of the Lower Orinoco, where it is found (infrequently) at elevations of around 1,000 feet near the banks of the Paragua River in Eastern Bolívar, and the Erebato River in the west of that state. In common with all the orchids in the alliance, the flowers appear singly (i.e. never in racemes), and, as in the case of *C. surinamensis*, they are small (about ¾ ") and the pale green coloring with a white lip is rather unexciting. The species is by way of being a very humble member of the group, with an interest that is basically limited to botanical specialists.

If, having thus spurned the poor *surinamensis*, the next member of the group you study has no pseudobulbs, and the lip is firmly attached to, and continuous with, the foot of the column, then it is either a *Stenia* or a *Bollea* species and certainly

[1] Originally appeared in *A.O.S. Bulletin*, Vol. 45, December 1976, pages 1079-1087

Bollea hemixantha

worth a place in your collection. Confusion between these two genera is most unlikely as all stenias have fairly slender, "normal-looking" columns, while the bolleas have completely different, very wide, hood-like columns. Both are small genera, and, in each, Venezuela has only one species.

Venezuela's sole representative of the genus *Stenia* is *Stenia pallida,* a species that this country shares with Peru as well as its more direct neighbors of Trinidad, Guyana, and Brazil. In Venezuela itself the species is widespread, mainly as a not uncommon epiphytic inhabitant of the Coastal Range, including places quite close to Caracas, and its eastern limit approaches Trinidad; its Venezuelan coastal range is thus something over 400 miles long with a vertical range from roughly 1,000 to 5,000 ft. In the extreme west of the country it is found in the Perijá Range that forms Venezuela's border with Colombia west of Lake Maracaibo. In addition, it has been found on the Paragua River in the far southeast of the country, and also in the Upper Orinoco or Territorio Amazonas region. The somewhat pendent peduncles bear very attractive, white, creamy white or yellow-cream, widely open flowers of almost two-inch spread, with a lip of most unusual pinched-apex form rather like what one imagines an early Christian pottery oil lamp looked like, pale yellowy green in color and with purple spots inside the bright yellow lateral lobes. While no single plant seems to flower constantly, the species does flower many times a year, and with apparently no fixed season, so that a small collection of plants could be said to be in flower virtually throughout the year. The only month none of our plants has flowered is February, and this may well be because we have just not been around to record a February flowering.

Bollea is also a small genus — indeed all the alliance genera are small — and here again Venezuela is honored by the presence of only one species, *B. hemixantha.* Its habitat here is exclusively in the distant, uninhabited parts of the "interior," places such as the most extraordinary, low-lying Casiquiare River that splits away from the main stream of the Orinoco not very far from its source to flow southwest into the Río Negro and thus into the Amazon, while the main flow of the Orinoco continues northwest, then north and finally east to reach the sea south of Trinidad. The Casiquiare is by no means an unknown river as its link between the two great river basins is of great interest and considerable importance but its high concentration of pestiferous biting insects, mainly mosquitoes and "no-seeums," makes it a painful area for travelers and unpopular even with orchid hunters. Luckily, there are much more pleasant surroundings in which this bollea can be found, at about 1,400 ft., such as in the upper reaches of the Erebato (a major tributary of the Río Caura, itself a tributary of the Lower Orinoco) or in the very beautiful country of the far southeast of Venezuela more or less bordering on Brazil at about 1,500-2,500 ft. or somewhat higher in the Parima Range that forms the border with Brazil in the Territorio Amazonas. The flowers of this species appear on rather short peduncles at the base of the fan-shaped spray of leaves. They are about three inches in diameter and hold themselves nicely wide open. The sepals and petals are of firm consistency and the hood-like column and prominent lip are very fleshy indeed. The color of the sepals and petals is normally white or almost white, but some have a definite yellow tone and others, rarely, a bluish tinge that may reflect its close affinity to *B. violacea.* The lips are pale yellow with a large, yellow callus with radiating ribs. The flowers are quite long-lived, though ours unfortunately have a powerful attraction for tiny black beetles that enjoy making a meal out of the apex of the lip. The plants flower quite freely, but somewhat erratically, our records showing they favor the months of March, June, August, and September.

If your "alliance" species is not a chaubardia, a stenia, or a bollea, but does have a very widely spread, indeed almost flat, flower, then it belongs to the horticulturally well-known genus of **Huntleya,** an allocation you can further check by looking at its two-part lip, the basal section of which should have a many-pointed, erect crest. This time, this is a genus of which Venezuela has two species, *H. lucida* and *H. meleagris.* The latter is the type species for the genus and the extremely handsome

Colombian form of it is well known to many orchid fans. The Venezuelan form of this famous species, which J. A. Fowlie, in a finely illustrated issue of the *Orchid Digest* for May 1974, treats as a separate species, *H. sessiliflora,* is less brilliantly colored than the Colombian type and has little of the pronounced "quilting" pattern that is so characteristic of the sepals and petals of the latter, but with its 3½" diameter flowers it is still a very striking and handsome plant. Like the *Bollea hemixantha,* and at times growing close to it, it is a shy inhabitant of distant places south of the Orinoco, and hopefully will retain its ability to hide from the public gaze as otherwise it might quickly succumb to the greedy fingers of overenthusiastic aficionados or commercial dealers. In cultivation, after an initial failure, it has proven to be a willing flowerer in conditions outlined at the end of this note. In addition, the flowers have the advantage of lasting as long as six weeks on the plant. We cannot vouch for its flowering season in the wild, never having found a plant in flower, but there seems no reason to expect it to differ much from the habits of our few captive plants which have shown flowers in all the months from August to March, and once also in June. As with *Stenia pallida,* this does not mean that a given plant will be flowering all this time, but that it might produce flowers at any time during those months.

Following down the Garay key, we find that all the remaining genera have flowers that are not flat like the huntleyas, but are "ringent" or gaping in form, i.e. while the apices may be fairly wide open, the bases of sepals and petals at least start in a forward direction. If, in such a specimen, you find the callus on the lip is a high, massive, horseshoe-shaped ridge (to quote directly from the key) then your plant is in the genus **Pescatorea.** At first glance, these flowers are very like the bolleas because of the strong similarity between their prominent lips, but a glance at their slender columns shows that they are by no means the same genus. *Pescatorea* is a genus of much horticultural favor, particularly the type species, *P. cerina,* and, regrettably, is the one genus in the *Chondrorhyncha* alliance that is not, as far as we know, represented in Venezuela. At one moment we thought it might be, as a friend produced a plant of *P. coronaria,* believing it to be Venezuelan. Unfortunately, he later hedged on this, so, with no real assurance that it is to be found here, we must reluctantly consider it a foreigner while hoping that some day it will nevertheless be found growing wild in this country. However, in view of its rumored existence, and to complete the nine genera of the alliance, a portrait of this most striking species is included in this series. Apart from the fact that it

Pescatorea coronaria

was flowering in June, we can give no information on either its habitat or its habits.

Still following the Garay key, matters now become a little more involved. Assuming your plant does not fit with any of the genera already mentioned, the details of the column now become critical. If the column is cylindrical and does not form a pronounced mentum or chin where it joins with the lip, and the rostellum is long and narrow, then it is in the genus **Chaubardiella.** This is a completely new genus, published by Garay at the same time as his study of the alliance, to accommodate one new species and four earlier ones that would no longer fit into the latest conceptions of the genera to which they were formerly allocated, such as *Stenia, Keferstenia, Chondrorhyncha,* and *Chaubardia.* The species selected by Garay to represent the type for this new genus is Venezuela's sole representative, *C. tigrina.* This is the most elusive of all the Venezuelan orchids we have ever met. We came across it on a trip to the base of Angel Falls in 1958, and, when Garay expressed great interest in it, we naturally hoped to find him more specimens, the more so since our first and only plant did not like the treatment we tried out on it and lasted only a couple of years — today we believe we could do much better. Angel Falls is a wonderful place to visit, but even now, 16 years later, it is not the sort of trip one can make at the drop of a hat; moreover, in common with similar river trips to tricky spots in the interior, it is quite expensive. Nevertheless, we have been lucky enough to have passed close to the spot where we found this species, four more times, each time with our eyes very wide open for another plant. But our hopes have always been disappointed, and our one-and-only finding of this species* remains, as far as we know, the one-and-only time it has ever been seen in this country by anyone. As it has escaped not only our own searches in its original site, and many other searches by ourselves and others in the same general region of the Venezuelan Guyana (and elsewhere for that matter), it must at least be counted an extremely rare species. Yet, to show the surprises always lurking in the world of orchid species, a good many years after our discovery another plant turned up in Peru, 1,500 miles away from Angel Falls! The flower of our plant, of which we were lucky enough to get a photo before it passed away, is about 1½" in spread, and the sepals, petals, and lip are all characterized by the strong tiger-striping that gives it its name. If P. C. Hutchison & J. K. Wright, collectors of the Peruvian specimen, have managed to keep a plant alive and well, we would greatly welcome news of the treatment they give it so that we can do better with our next specimen when (and if!) they find it.

Moving further yet down the key, if the rostellum of an alliance plant in a genus we have not yet touched on is tripartite, and the column not only forms a mentum at the base but in addition is keeled or ridged down its inner face, then (allowing for two aberrant species) we are dealing with the genus **Kefersteinia**. Species in this genus are also distinguished by having a lip the apical half of which is sharply folded downwards. Three of the 10 or so species in this genus are to be found in Venezuela, namely *K. sanguinolenta, K. tolimensis,* and *K. graminea,* the last-mentioned being the species selected by Reichenbach in 1852 as the type for this genus. While these species all have quite small flowers, their floriferousness (particularly of *K. sanguinolenta* and *K. graminea),* combined with the attractiveness of the flowers themselves, make them very nice additions to any collection of small orchids. To illustrate this note, we have selected *K. graminea,* with flowers about an inch in size. The coloring is variable in intensity, some being quite heavily red-spotted (particularly the apex of the lip) while others are much more lightly spotted. Even a small plant can produce 20 of these flowers at a time. Its flowering months are more or less anywhere in the period from January to September, and if an old collection doubtfully attributed to the Andes is discounted, it is to be found in Venezuela only in a quite limited area of the Coastal Range from Caracas to the west. In line with the past confusion afflicting nearly all the older species in this alliance, it has also been known as a zygopetalum and a huntleya despite what seem to us nowadays enormous differences between these genera and *Kefersteinia.*

Having at this point dealt with seven alliance genera, we are left with only two more, **Chondrorhyncha** (which gives its name to the alliance) and **Cochleanthes.** Neither of these have a keel down the face of the column and their lips are concave or "cochleate," very different from the "replicate" lip of the kefersteinias. These two final genera can be distinguished from each other by the fact that the chondrorhynchas have a prominent foot to the column, forming a sharp mentum, while the cochleanthes flowers have a short-footed column that produces only an obtuse mentum. In addition, the *Chondrorhyncha* lip has a fleshy callus in the center while the *Cochleanthes* lip has a semicircular, transverse callus near the base. In Venezuela, the genus *Chondrorhyncha* is represented only by *C. rosea* and *C. flaveola,* both very nice orchids. *Chondrorhyncha flaveola* has been discussed and illustrated in our article "Some Orchids of the Sierra de Perijá" (see Chapter 9), so we are illustrating here *C. rosea* which comes from the Andes of Mérida and Táchira states, at levels around 6,000 ft. Although it is present also in Colombia, it is here quite a rare plant, with only three findings recorded to date as far as we know. The first of these, not very far from the city of Mérida, was by Linden many years ago; the second, closer yet to the city, was by a friend of ours Carlos Garcia E.; and the third find was by ourselves, in company with another orchid friend, Roberto Mejía C., in some forest remnants near the town of Las Delicias in Táchira state.

We now reach the final genus, *Cochleanthes,* represented in Venezuela by three species. One of these, *C. marginata,* has already been discussed and illustrated in the *A. O. S. Bulletin* in the above-mentioned note on Perijá orchids. The second species, *C. flabelliformis,* is quite uncommon here, with only one official record outside the central part of the Coastal Range, where it grows, or grew, within easy reach of Caracas. The other record is from a quite distant spot in the Venezuelan Guyana (Bolívar State), so sooner or later one can expect its known habitat in this country to be extended quite a bit in that direction — which would be natural enough seeing that it is also on record for Brazil. The third Venezuelan *Cochleanthes* species is illustrated here. This is *C. discolor,* a very handsome representative of the genus that ranges from here northwards to Honduras and over to Cuba. In Venezuela it is again an uncommon orchid with one official record from around 6,000 ft. near Caracas and another from the Perijá region some 450 miles to the west. It undoubtedly exists in a number of places in between and we hope some day to see it ourselves in its natural state while, in the meantime enjoying our one-and-only plant, donated to us some years ago by a friend who found it in the "near Caracas" locality many years after the original official record from there.

Cultivation

In all the above discussion, we have avoided mention of how we grow our own plants in this alliance group so as not to get too repetitive, our treatment of many of them being the same. As mentioned in our note on Perijá orchids, the *Cochleanthes* and *Chondrorhyncha* plants are grown in pots filled with well compacted, chopped tree-fern root. With the exception of one small plastic-enclosed space, all our orchid-growing areas are open and uncontrollable: if it rains heavily, everything gets soaked; air- or rain-borne fungus spores are ever-present visitors; new supplies of insects hop, crawl, or fly happily in from the forest whenever our bug-killing efforts achieve some success. Only by providing shade and doing some watering with chlorinated town water during the dry season can we really provide any effective modification of what nature provides, helped by "plant concentrations" here and there that maintain their own special fairly humid microclimates. As our first *Cochleanthes* plants had been found fairly low and dry, we felt it best to keep them in the main "open" part of our establishment where they would (we hoped) enjoy the dry season, but they never did at all well. When we found the Perijá plants in cool and damp conditions, we decided to risk the rather higher temperature of our small plastic house as its humidifier helps to maintain a higher humidity in the very dry months. To our joy (and surprise) they have responded very well to these conditions. Our first *Chondrorhyncha* plant, donated by a friend, had also been kept outside, but, following our cochleanthes experience, our Perijá plants of this species also went into the plastic house. But here, to show their independence, these plants, though coming from close to the same spot as the cochleanthes, expressed their displeasure, and although one plant is still doing moderately well in the plastic house the rest looked weak and, after moving them outside, they have done much better.

Some stenias and kefersteinias grow in pots of tree-fern root, but on account of the rather pendent nature of their flowers (particularly the kefersteinias) they are better grown on small chunks of tree-fern root. Some of these are partly under a rain-leaky, glass-louvered roof which allows quite a lot of overhead light; the remainder also do quite well about five feet high just inside our piece of light forest. The *Chaubardia* and *Chaubardiella* plants are among our early failures and we never did own the *Pescatorea*, which leaves only the bolleas and huntleyas to be discussed. Both of these species we

Cochleanthes discolor

found growing low in the forest, and in apparently heavy shade, so we have done what we can to duplicate this by hanging them about three feet below a rather low, corrugated fiberglass roof, now so dirty and deteriorated that its light transmission hopefully corresponds to forest conditions. Side light is also limited, so the plants can be considered as growing in permanent, moderately deep shade. The bolleas are hung in open plastic baskets filled with tree-fern root, and the huntleyas, to accommodate their more decided tendency to climb, are on the sides of long, hanging slabs of tree fern root. Watering and general humidity maintenance are done by a daily sprinkle from a hose, but, when we are out of town, this may or may not be maintained by those we leave in charge. The most drastic change from the plants' natural habitat, however, results from the considerable mid-day radiant heat projected from the low plastic roof, but far from being fatal (and far from being any carefully-planned idea of our own) this new factor seems to be just what the plants need to offset the many other factors of microclimate we have unwillingly and unwittingly changed for them. In other words, for the first time in our experience of these rather touchy species, the plants have responded well. Unfortunately, we fear that this note on our experience is likely to be of little use to anyone else, and to try and copy it might, for all we know, prove fatal. All it really shows is that orchids are tough but also touchy, and there is no real substitute (outside highly controlled, commercial-type houses) for the time-tried system of fish-and-find-out, backed perhaps by some vague instincts for doing the right thing, borne of past failures and successes. Liberal quantities of plain good luck, particularly if there are very few plants with which to experiment, is also a *sine qua non*.

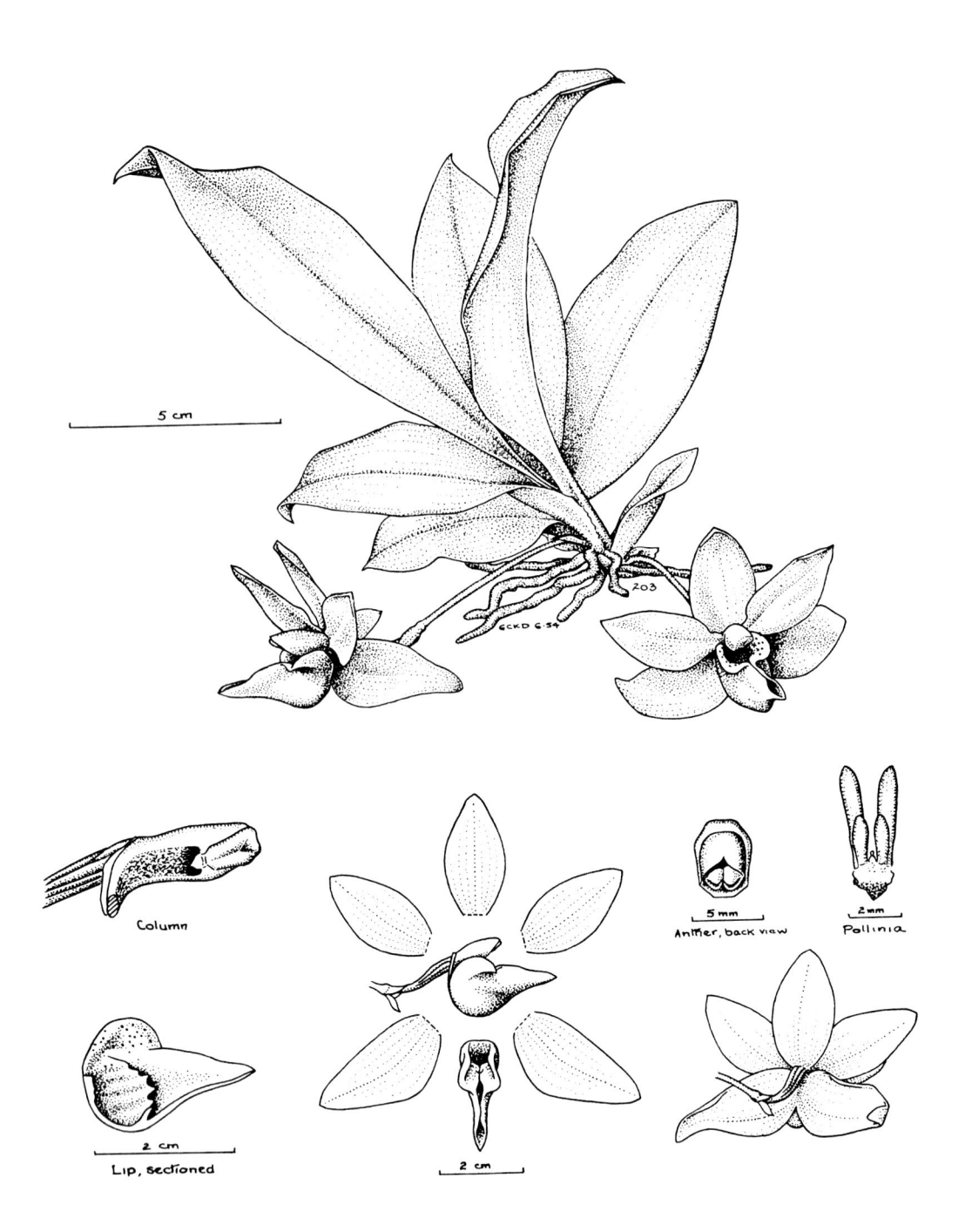

Stenia pallida Lindl. in Bot. Reg. 23: sub. t. 1991, 1837. — A. B. E.

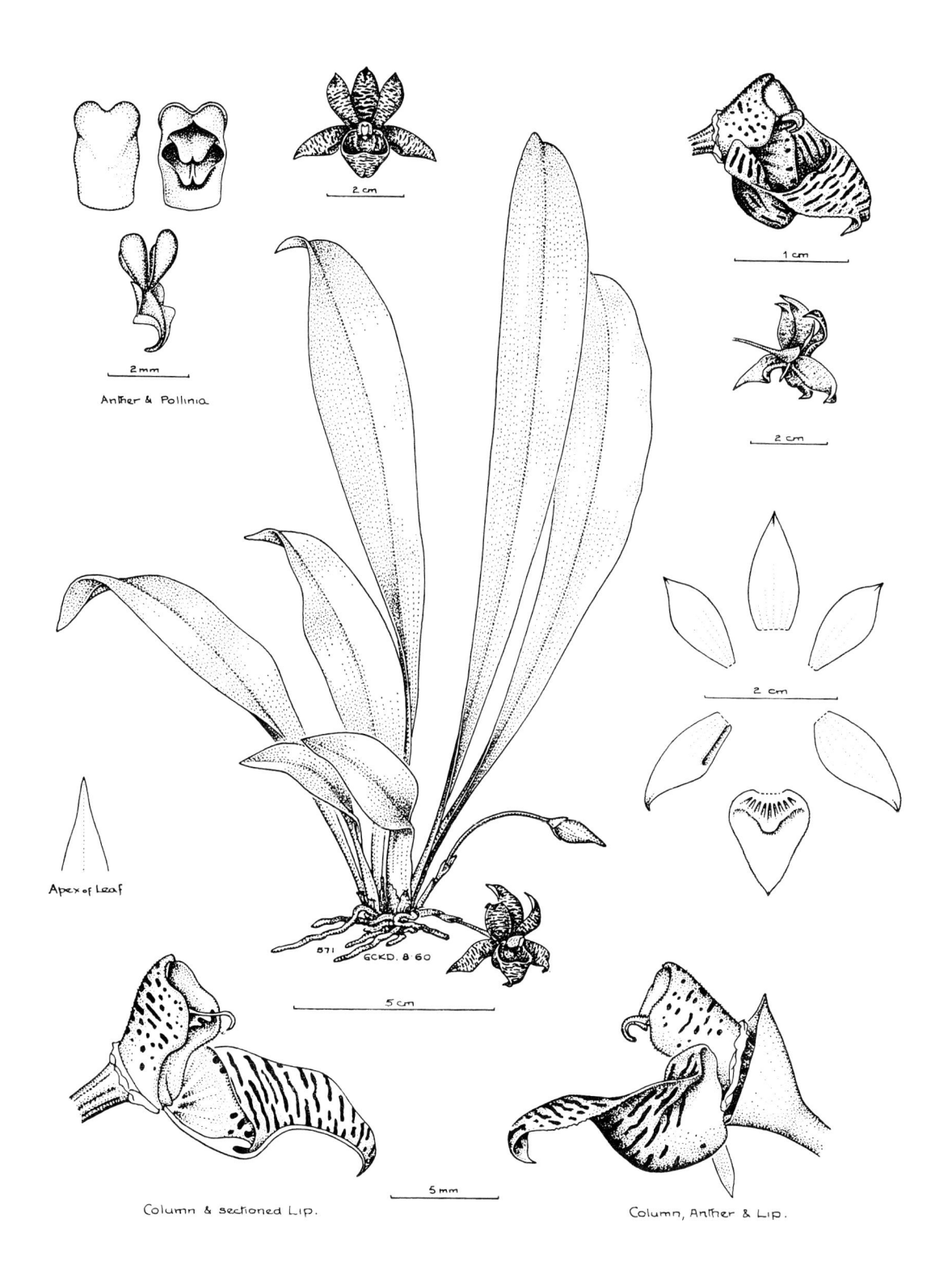

Chaubardiella tigrina (Garay & Dunsterv.) Garay in Orquideologia 4: 149, 1969. — E.

Kefersteinia graminea (Lindl.) Reichb. f. in Bot. Zeit. 10: 634, 1852. — B.

Some Small Venezuelan Orchids — I[1]

HOW BIG is big — how small is small? Does an orchid with quarter-inch flowers rate as small if the plant is a yard high? If the flowers are bigger than silver dollars (remember them?) but the plant itself is smaller, is it a small orchid or not? We doubt if anyone could define "small" in terms of orchids without at least half his audience disagreeing with them, and, in any case, any effort to produce precise definitions smacks of scientific research and tape measures, which by no means agrees with the aesthetic pleasure the small orchid gives to its many admirers. For the purpose of this series of notes, therefore, we prefer to avoid any attempt to define "small" and have worked instead on what is our own personal taste and feeling in the matter.

Everywhere where orchid species abound in nature, Venezuela included, the number of small orchid species far outnumbers the large, and the species available to us illustrate this article, though limited by the need to have adequate photos, is still very large. In making our selection we have therefore tried to choose as widely different small orchids as possible. Some of the orchids thus selected are very clearly in the miniature or even mini-miniature class, about whose smallness there will be little dispute, and we have excluded any species with small flowers if the plant itself is large. We have, however, included one species (*Oncidium globuliferum*) with really quite large flowers but whose plant is small, at least small enough to provide the excuse to show its portrait as it is a species of which we are very fond.

We suspect that there are very few orchid lovers who sneer at all reasonably small orchids, however beautiful the flowers, but a taste for the miniature and mini-miniature orchid is perhaps rather restricted. Once acquired, however, it can quickly grow on one, at least as far as the miniatures are concerned. For the mini-miniature orchid the picture is rather different because to appreciate the beauty of what we rate as mini-miniatures a hand lens is really not enough — only a low power microscope can reveal their quite extraordinary beauty, not only in color but also, frequently, in their glowing, glass-like, cellular textures that are completely absent in the world of macro-orchids. Unfortunately, we have never been able to take (or get experts to take) good photos of these tiny orchid flowers on a scale large enough to show their true beauty, and for all we know, a microscope's depth of focus problems may make a satisfactory photo in any case impossible. Even if your camera can be stopped down to f/128, it still cannot give you definition in those parts that are out of focus to the microscope itself. The eye can follow through a series of changes of focus and memory can combine these into a very satisfactory whole, but this is something that a still camera cannot achieve in a single photo.

Altensteinia rostrata

Altensteinia rostrata is among the world's highest growing orchids and can be found in Venezuela at over 14,000 feet, not far below the permanent snow that crowns the Andes in the state of Mérida. The tropics provide a favored home for epiphytic orchids, but when the tree line is reached (in Venezuela at about 10,000 feet) such orchids are obviously out of business and have to give way to a variety of interesting terrestrial orchids. Among the highest-growing of these are several species of *Altensteinia,* a genus that may be better known to some by the very odd name of *Aa* that Reichenbach invented when he split off a number of *Altensteinia* species to form a new genus. Apparently he left no record of his reasons for this odd name, but the possible reason that has most appeal is that it was a joking (or serious?) error to ensure that a Reichenbach genus would forever be at the top of any alphabetical list of genera, not only in the orchid

[1] Originally appeared in *A.O.S. Bulletin,*
Vol. 46, May 1977, pages 406-414

family but among all plants in the world. If this is true, the only flaw in his scheme is that taxonomists have not accepted his new genus as valid, and his aas (looks silly, doesn't it!) have reverted to being altensteinias.

We knew for some time of these high Andean species but had little idea just where to find them, until on a short visit, Dr. L. A. Garay outlined the sort of place to look. We knew where to find a habitat of that type and when we went there with him, there they were, albeit not in flower. Without that expert guidance we might still be looking for them as these particular plants grow almost invisibly amid the short greenery of narrow, alpine meadows alongside small streams, with only an occasional, old flower spike sticking up an inch or two to show where they are when not in flower.

Trying to cultivate at 4,000 feet a terrestrial from 14,000 feet needs more skill and optimism than we possess, so it was only by repeated visits to the same spot that we eventually managed to catch the plants in flower. Two species were concerned, of which the more attractive is *Altensteinia rostrata*. This produces a thick spike of spirally arranged flowers, rising some two inches above ground level, with a spray of small leaves alongside. The visible part of each flower consists of a tiny "head" about a seventh of an inch across, which is white with a yellow center and is nicely adorned with the fringe of its upright, cup-shaped lip.

We wondered at the time how these flower spikes survived the constant browsing activities of the cattle often kept on these meadows by the peasants. The answer was revealed when we pushed our fingers into the cold, damp soil to pick an entire plant and found ourselves the victim of the quite strong prickles of the other plants among which *Altensteinia rostrata* has chosen to grow and which would presumably be a fine deterrent to any cattle whose tender muzzle came in contact with it.

Brachionidium brevicaudatum

Brachionidium is a small genus of basically cloud-forest epiphytic orchids having its maximum development in Venezuela where there are seven species, three of which are endemic. Five of these seven species are inhabitants of the Andes and of the remaining two, one comes from the Amazonas territory far up the Orinoco and the other, *Brachionidium brevicaudatum* illustrated here, comes from quite close to the Guyana border in the far southeast. This species has not only been found on Roraima, the famous "Lost World" table mountain that is shared between Venezuela, Guyana, and Brazil, but it has also been found in other places in Guyana. We are therefore happy, but not greatly surprised, when we came across it not over 10 miles from the Guyana border, in a spot at about 4,500 feet elevation where an old and decaying log lay across a very small creek cutting deeply through fairly dense cloud forest. The fallen trunk was in very shaded and damp conditions, and the plants on it were obviously trying to survive in a micro-climate very different from their original situation on the live tree. Their condition was not very happy, and some healthier and larger plants were found nearby where a more or less lithophytic existence, but with more light and air, clearly suited these fallen plants better than life on the rotting trunk. Despite some initial success in cultivation, we had no real idea of what conditions the plants required and we eventually failed with all the bits we brought home: hopefully, the rest of the lithophytic ones we left behind will manage to continue spreading seed despite their lowly position, and there may, of course, be more plants growing high up on healthy trees in the same locality.

Forming an erect plant some three to four inches tall, and bearing a series of narrow, one-inch leaves up its rather root-entwined, slender rhizome, *Brachionidium brevicaudatum* can be accommodated easily in a very small pot; as its flowers are no more than three-quarters of an inch in size it must surely qualify for the "small orchid" category and may even fit many people's idea of miniature. The flowers, which are non-resupinate (i.e., grow lip-uppermost) are distinguished by the lateral sepals uniting to form a single lamina very similar indeed to the dorsal sepal, so that the flower could be turned top-to-bottom without the change being noted. Far from being shy, the flower displays itself proudly at the end of a thin peduncle which is long enough to reach beyond the tip of the leaf from whose base it rises, and, as the peduncle is persistent several years after the flower has fallen, the plant develops a quickly recognizable spiky appearance.

Quoting Schultes and Pease's *Generic Names of Orchids,* the name *Brachionidium* selected by Lindley for this genus refers to "two short arms on the column that are not stigmatiferous." This is indeed the case with, for example, Venezuela's *Brachionidium floribundum* but it quite definitely is not the case with our *B. brevicaudatum* plants, so if these "columnar arms" are critical in the definition of the genus (and if our plants are not freaks) someone, someday, may decide that this species should belong in some other genus despite the close floral similarity to other brachionidiums in other respects.

Bulbophyllum exaltatum

Bulbophyllum is by way of being an all-embracing genus, so much so that some authorities include it in so many once-separate genera that it becomes by far the largest genus in the orchid family

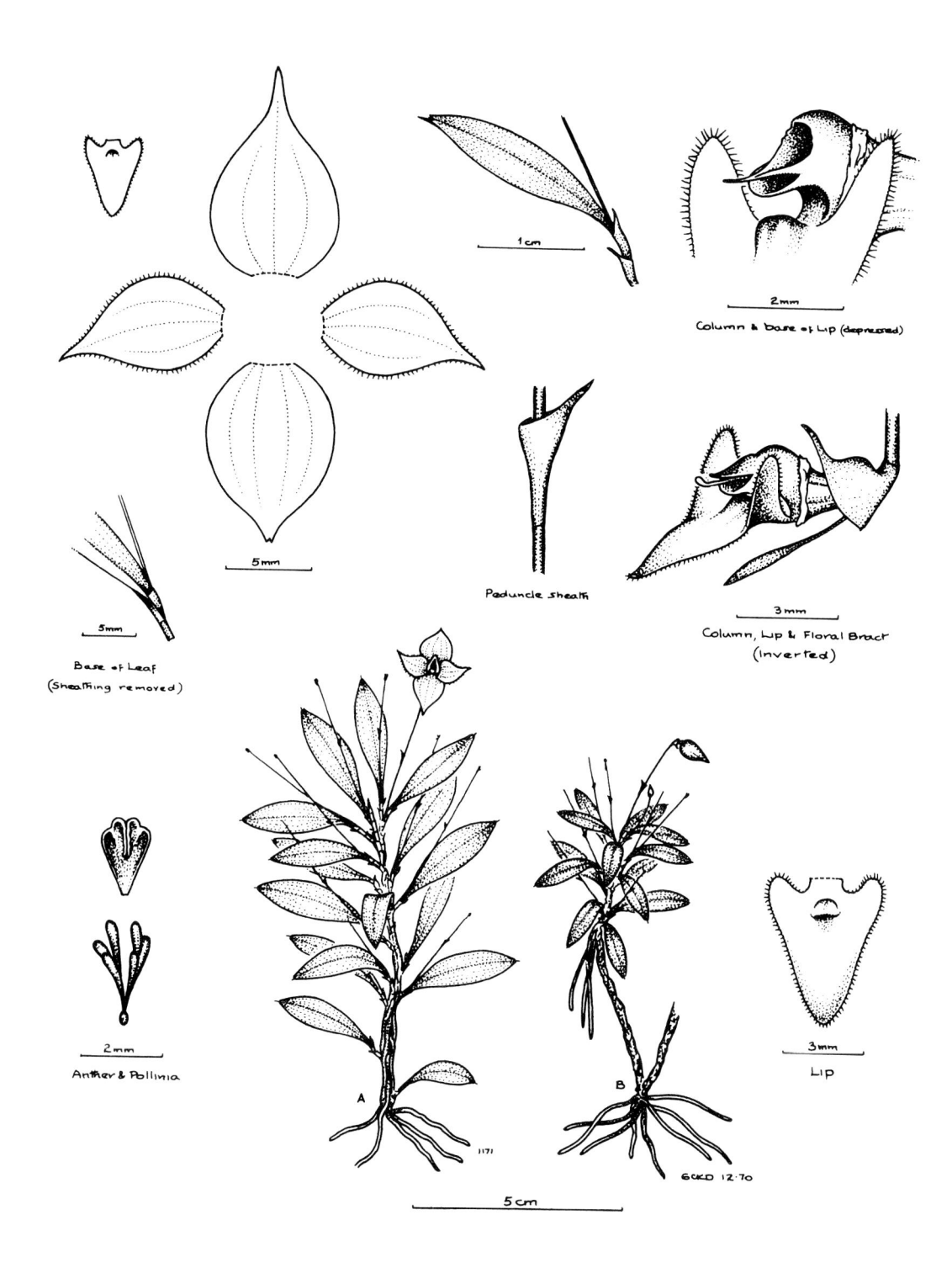

Brachionidium brevicaudatum Rolfe in Trans. Linn. Soc. Bot. ser. 2, 6:59, 1901. — E.

Bulbophyllum exaltatum

Notylia mirabilis

— or maybe in any plant family — with a count of something like 2,000 species. Other views of the scope of the genus cut it back to as few as 500 species, but whichever way you look at it it is a large genus. It belongs predominantly to the Old World or Far East, where all the really striking species occur, but it is adequately represented in the New World. In Venezuela it is present in the form of over a dozen small or even miniature species, one of which, *Bulbophyllum exaltatum,* is illustrated here. This species consists of a string of small, hard pseudobulbs with erect, slender peduncles curving up from the base to a height of about 10, rarely 20, inches. Typical of almost all Venezuelan bulbophyllums, the pseudobulbs of this species are noticeably "quadrate" or four-edged. The flowers are about a half-inch in spread and very pretty, the deep red markings on the lip being offset by the yellow of the sepals and petals.

Venezuelan bulbophyllums are in a group characterized by columns that have outstretched "arms" at the apex. In *Bulbophyllum exaltatum* these are particularly long, and, if you have a fancy for anthropomorphic resemblances, these arms give the column, with its anther in position to act as a head, the appearance of a priest leaning forward to bless whatever lies on the altar before him, the altar in question being formed by the thick, fleshy mound that makes up most of the basal half of the lip. The back of this altar, facing the priest, is provided with a nice, secret cubbyhole where the priest can keep the holy wine — or would it be the sacrificial hatchet? Orchids abound in anthropomorphic resemblances, and though it is much to be frowned upon to stress such flippant things, they do nevertheless add a special touch of spice to the study of this wonderful family.

The type specimen of this species came from Guyana well over a hundred years ago, and its Venezuelan sisters can be found in both the Amazonas and Bolívar parts of the Venezuelan Guayana. The plants that provided us with the illustration shown here came from the headwaters of the Aponguao, a river that starts right on the border with Guyana, runs southwards paralleling the border until approaching Brazil, then joins the top of the Caroní River to swing west, then north again until it reaches the Orinoco. Here its waters flow east until they meet the sea south of Trinidad. Had the Aponguao started a mile or two farther north than its actual source it would have saved itself many long miles by flowing north right away and reaching the sea via the Cuyuní River and Guyana. Near its source, the Aponguao, at 4,000 to 5,000 feet elevation, is a delightful, red-water stream lined with orchid-rich gallery forest and flowing through mostly open savanna, with flat-topped tepuis like Roraima lining the horizon.

Bulbophyllum exaltatum is a tough-growing species of epiphytic habit, and our plant has settled kindly to a home in our garden, mounted on a vertical block of hard tree-fern root and hung in a moderately exposed position.

Dipteranthus obliquus

This enchanting species is a true miniature, and, although we grow ours in two-inch pots or on very small chunks of tree-fern root, a very satisfactory plant could equally well be grown in a one-inch "thumb pot." It is a species that Venezuela can claim as exclusively its own. We have, it is true, found a specimen growing not far from Guyana, so some day that country may also claim it, but basically it is an orchid of Venezuela's Coastal Range and of the extreme east end of the Andes. In these places, it grows epiphytically in cloud forests at elevations of around 4,000 to 6,000 feet. The plant has tiny, almost globular pseudobulbs, very occasionally a quarter-inch in size but more usually around one-eighth and in any case tending to be completely hidden at the base of the small, narrow, fleshy leaves: these latter seldom exceed two inches in length and often, even on a well-developed plant, are not much over an inch. From the base of these leaves rise many-flowered racemes. The yellow flowers are less than a quarter-inch in size, but in a nice plant are in such profusion that the leaves are almost lost to sight, an effect aided by the fact that the racemes do not much mind which way they grow — up, sideways or down — and thus spread out in all directions. The species is also rewarding to grow because, unlike many miniatures, *Dipteranthus obliquus* takes quite willingly to captivity, and we have a number of small plants scattered around that have been with us for a good many years.

It is among a number of small species here that, unlike most large-flowered orchids, seem to have no fixed or limited flowering season, and we have had plants in flower in one or other of all the months in the year.

Campylocentrum schneeanum

Campylocentrum schneeanum is a member of a very interesting genus of small, monopodial orchids with a distribution of Florida to Brazil, some of whose members have the unusual feature of being plants that have roots all the time, flowers sometimes, and leaves never. In the wild, such plants are oddly enough not so very difficult to spot as even when the floral part is represented by nothing more than a few, tiny, dried-up "sticks," there is usually a radiating mass of white roots, large enough to give it away once one knows that such root-only orchid plants do exist. One such plant, brought to us by a friend a dozen years ago, had nothing visible but the roots, a few old, half-inch, pin-like, flowerless spikes, and one three-quarter-inch tall raceme of flowers, the largest of which was about a tenth of an inch in size. It proved to be a new species, *Campylocentrum tyridion*. By contrast, other *Campylocentrum* species can be relatively normal-looking plants, with leaves up to five inches long.

Campylocentrum schneeanum is between these two extremes of form and size: it does have leaves, but as a plant is definitely in the miniature or even mini-miniature category. The white flowers are a tenth of an inch, the leaves about half an inch, and a single, mature growth perhaps two inches in height. Yet a multiple growth forms a plant fully worthy of a place in the miniaturist's collection, where it can be admired by those who feel such tiny botanicals unworthy of the effort of growing them, but nevertheless worthy of being looked at with (perhaps concealed) pleasure when cultivated by someone with the "time to waste" on such sillinesses. This tiny orchid is endemic to Venezuela where it grows in various places in the Coastal Range as an epiphyte, in mainly cloud forest, at 4,000 to 6,000 feet altitude, and (a very recent find) in very cold, dwarf forest at about 10,000 feet in the Andes. Our Coastal Range plant is doing nicely, growing on the side of a small piece of tree-fern root where most of its roots can hang out in the open and receive the very quick drainage that campylocentrums seem to prefer, to judge by the bare and exposed way the roots of most local species grow in nature.

Hexisea bidentata

This small orchid may already be known to a number of A.O.S. readers as it is not only widely spread from Mexico to Guyana and Peru but has already been illustrated in the *A.O.S. Bulletin*. The original author of 1959, although including it in an article on "Fascinating Botanicals," seemed to us to be very subdued indeed in his appreciation of the worthiness of this species, ending his note with the remark that "it will please the grower when it flowers, even though it may not receive the plaudits of the general visitor..." on which we can only comment that *our* general visitors seem to be of a far more appreciative type than those of which he apparently had experience. The flowers illustrated are about an inch in size, which is adequately visible even to one who spends his days among cattleyas, so how could anyone be so hardhearted as to deny it at least a couple of plaudits, if not a loud cry of joy?

This brilliant red species is to be seen in many places in Venezuela's "interior," generally about 1,000 feet to 3,000 feet altitude and sometimes as high as 5,000 feet, but it is also on record from as low as 500 feet in the flooded-forest Amazonas territory. Mostly it is to be found not far from the banks of the many beautiful streams that abound in the Bolívar section of the Venezuelan Guayana; in some places it clings to low shrubs that at times are swept by flood waters, but more often can be seen growing epiphytically, well above flood level, on trees lining, or not far from, the river banks. This apparent liking for proximity to water does not, however, keep the species from thriving quite a long way from flowing water, usually at the higher altitudes.

It is the kind of plant that immediately catches the eye when in flower, and it is fortunate that it grows in so many places as it is in considerable danger of being over-collected in tourist-frequented localities. The plant itself is quite small, the proliferating, pseudobulbous, noded stems growing in clumps that are not normally over eight inches tall, through specimens to 18 inches can be found. Our plants are cultivated on smallish slabs of tree-fern root where their roots can either hide inside the material or preferably climb around on the outside to get the exposure most of these plants seem to enjoy in their natural habitat. The flowering season with us is anywhere from January to June.

Lepanthopsis vinacea

Lepanthopsis vinacea is a fine representative of a small genus of mostly very small species, with tiny but often prettily colored flowers. Some of these species are further characterized by having racemes with many flowers lined up, neatly and closely, in a double rank, like well-trained soldiers on parade, but with one rank facing forward and the other facing to the rear, back to back. *Lepanthopsis floripecten,* an orchid of Venezuela and many other countries, is a fine example of this "military" form, and *L. vinacea* is another. On the official records, *Lepanthopsis vinacea* is a purely Venezuelan species, but as we have found it very close to the Guyana border, where indeed it seems to have its maximum development, it will almost certainly have to be shared with that country when botanical exploration of Guyana nears the present Venezuelan habitat.

The leaves of this species are about three quarters of an inch to one inch in length and are borne like paddles on slender stems, generally one inch to two inches tall, that are clothed in the narrow, tubular, *Lepanthes*-like sheaths that give the genus its name...a resemblance that does not extend to the flowers which are not at all *Lepanthes*-like in their columns and lips. The inflorescences rise from the base of the leaf blade, the slender peduncles bearing racemes one inch to one and one-half inch in length, very occasionally as much as two inches. The total height of a plant is thus not often more than some three inches, including the inflorescences, but we have had one or two whose total height exceeded five inches. The plant illustrated here has inflorescences about one and one-half inches long, each with some 20 flowers whose wine-red color is enhanced by the gleaming nature of the surface of the sepals and petals, and by the golden "pearl" in the center of each flower, which pearl, with a hand lens, can be seen to be the minute anther.

Mostly we grow this miniature species on slabs of tree-fern root, with the grain more or less vertical for quick drainage, but also have a few growing in very small pots, or even small, plastic, ice-cube freezers (with holes punched for drainage), stuffed with chips of tree-fern root. Kept in fairly high general humidity but with plenty of air around, they seem to enjoy life, and one or more plants are likely to be in flower some time or other in the period from June to November.

Notylia mirabilis

There must be very few people by now who have not heard of the *Guinness Book of Records,* even if they have not yet read it. Reputedly put together originally as an argument-settler for use in English pubs, where Guinness is a much-consumed liquid product, it is a "you name it, we have it" opus, a fascinating catalog of man's most noble, and even more of his most idiotic, achievements, from the most accurate clock to the most expensive watch, from the fastest airplane to the fastest threading of a needle, from the longest overdue library book or the longest sermon ever preached to the longest chemical name or the longest distance ever spat. The book equally records Nature's efforts, from record-breaking earthquakes to the heaviest domestic cat, the longest animal or the shortest snake, the tallest tree, and the smallest orchid — which final item explains at last how the *Guinness Book of Records* happens to get into this series of notes on Venezuelan orchids. The prize for the smallest orchid *flower* is awarded by Guinness to an Australian bulbophyllum, but the prize for the smallest orchid *plant* goes to Venezuela's *Notylia norae,* which is now considered a synonym of *N. mirabilis.* Whether or not this claim can be surpassed by some other orchid species, there is no doubt that, as the illustration shows, this little orchid can indeed produce mature inflorescences from no more than a tiny spray of tiny leaves, producing a plant of which half a dozen could be cultivated in a normal lady's thimble like the one in the photograph. The thin, erect peduncle, on the other hand, is relatively tall, and the two-flowered raceme bears delicate flowers that, while decidedly small, are by no means the smallest of Venezuelan orchid flowers.

We first found this orchid in 1956, in the region of the headwaters of the Caroní River, a diamond-rich area of beautiful, small, red-water streams close to the Brazilian border. Since then we have found further specimens at about 1,500 to 2,500 elevation in this same general area, and also at about 500 feet in trees on the banks of the whitewater Upper Orinoco in Venezuela's Amazonas Territory.

Cultivationally, these tiny plants have not proved very accommodating. Luckily, in most places where we have found them they have been present in fair quantity, mostly on twiggy, upper branches of fallen trees, a situation where they would in any case be unlikely to survive very long, so we do not feel that our failures have materially diminished the natural crop. Mainly we have collected them, and subsequently kept them, still attached to their tiny twigs, and in this manner have kept a few plants going well enough to flower once in a while even if obviously not as happy as they once were in the forest.

Some Small Venezuelan Orchids — 2[1]

THOUGH SMALL to one man may be unacceptably large to another, we feel that the orchids chosen for this two-part article all possess certain qualities shared by all miniature orchids — small vegetative growth with small to large flowers. The quantity of orchids fitting such a loose description is extremely extensive from which we could select but a few.

Oncidium globuliferum

It has been almost axiomatic, in our orchid hunting experience, that a species that is elusive, or hard to reach, once found, thereafter becomes visible and accessible on every side. If, in desperation, you cut a tree down to get at some tempting attraction in its upper branches, it is highly probable that before long your path will lead you to some naturally-fallen forest giant spreading the same orchid in quantities at your feet. Actually, from a spirit of conservation heavily reinforced by the difficulty of felling more than a sapling when a machete is one's sole weapon, we have managed to get along very well without artificially felled trees on our many orchid hunts, though always willing to take advantage of those that botanist friends may legitimately fell for their own purposes. For us, the supreme example of this character of initial elusiveness and subsequent abundance is *Oncidium globuliferum,* illustrated here.

A recent synopsis of the genus *Oncidium* published in *Bradea* (Volume 1, Number 40) by Dr. L. A. Garay, provides a key to the many sections into which this large genus can be divided, and shows that *O. globuliferum* has only two companions (*O. serpens* and *O. sancti-pauli*) in the very distinctive section *Serpentina*, a trio of species characterized by pseudobulbs very widely spaced along a long, slender, wiry, and twining rhizome. In the case of *Oncidium globuliferum,* this unusual habit is enhanced by flowers frequently quite enormous compared to the smallness of the pseudobulbs and leaves.

For many early years of our orchid-hunting hobby, we knew of the existence of this desirable species and had proof of its existence on the occasions when we came across fallen flowers with large, bright yellow lips lying at our feet. But the plants from which these flowers came were always invisible, hidden far above us in the crown of a forest giant, and there seemed no way to get closer contact. Then one day, looking down onto the cloud forest of the Coastal Range from a high vantage point, we saw below us the crown of a large tree almost covered with bright yellow flowers, and, with the aid of field glasses, realized that we were looking at a splendid development of this elusive species. Normally, a sight such as this from above is no more than an extra frustration as, once on the forest floor, there is little chance of ever knowing which is the tree involved, but this time we were lucky: a slight clearing showed the base of the tree to be right on a corner of the winding mountain road below us, a location that could be clearly pinpointed. But knowing which tree held the treasure was one thing, reaching it was another, since we neither wished, nor were able, to fell the tree. Eventually, after careful preparations followed by a complicated use of stone-weighted string and light block-and-tackle equipped with a horse's cinch, followed in turn by the application of hammer and large nails, the female half of the present authorship was successful in reaching the target. That the female rather than the male half was dispatched on this task was due to the male member's valid (?) excuse that muscle would have to do the hauling, and light-weight would have to do the climbing. The result in any case was a complete success, but from that day on we have seldom made a trip in the cloud forests of any part of this country without finding quantities of this most at-

[1] Originally appeared in *A.O.S. Bulletin,* Vol. 46, September 1977, pages 792-797

Oncidium globuliferum

Platystele stenostachya

tractive species laid at our feet on fallen trees or branches.

The dominant feature of the flower of this species is its very large, bright yellow lip, which on a good specimen can measure a full two inches wide — possibly one of the largest lips in the whole genus outside the section *Glanduligera* represented by *Oncidium papilio* — yet the pseudobulbs are frequently under an inch in size and the leaves less than two inches. Our first plants did not do too well, probably because we gave them too much shade, but a number of later plants are growing well in fairly exposed positions with lots of air movement. But growing well and flowering well are two very distinct things, and while we do get the occasional (and very fine) flower we are far from reproducing the magnificent display presented *in situ* by our very first specimens of this species. For that, we would presumably have to produce fully exposed, yet cloud-forest conditions, and that we cannot achieve.

Ornithocephalus bicornis

Ornithocephalus is a genus of some 20 species of miniature orchids ranging from Mexico to Brazil, with a maximum concentration in the latter country. Venezuela gives a home to six species including *Ornithocephalus bicornis,* illustrated here. This species is native to Central America as well as Venezuela, and in the latter country is to be found both in the "civilized" Coastal Range area as well as in the "uncivilized" parts of the Venezuelan Guayana. The genus derives its "bird's head" name from the exceptionally long, narrow rostellum of the column producing a form not unlike a bird's head with a long, narrow beak. If the pollination of the Peruvian species *Ornithocephalus avicula* by *Paratetrapedia testacea,* as recorded by Dodson in his fascinating work on the pollination and evolution of orchid flowers, is in any way typical of the pollination of other species in the genus, then there is some very special relationship between the shape and actions of these tiny bees, or similar ones, and the unusual shape of the column apex, anther, and pollinarium, enabling the pollinia to be extracted from one flower and in due course reinserted in another by more or less long-distance action, without the bee having to get very close to the stigmatic surface itself.

The densely many-flowered racemes of these species often have a definitely jewel-like aspect, and *Ornithocephalus bicornis,* illustrated here, is no exception: to reproduce it as a brooch in gold and small pearls would be a task worthy of the most highly skilled jeweler. All *Ornithocephalus* species have fan-shaped sprays of flat, conduplicate leaves, from the axils of which the racemes arise, and in some cases the plants seem equally happy growing right way up or upside down. *Ornithocephalus bicornis* is one of these, but most of the fully mature plants we have seen favor the upside down form, where the inflorescences can develop straight down instead of having to curl over into a pendent attitude from an erect start. The cultivation of this little enchanter, on small blocks of tree-fern root, is apparently not difficult, or at least is not so in our climate, but rather than let the plants take entirely what nature provides we keep ours under a plastic roof so that the degree of watering and humidity can at least in some degree be controlled.

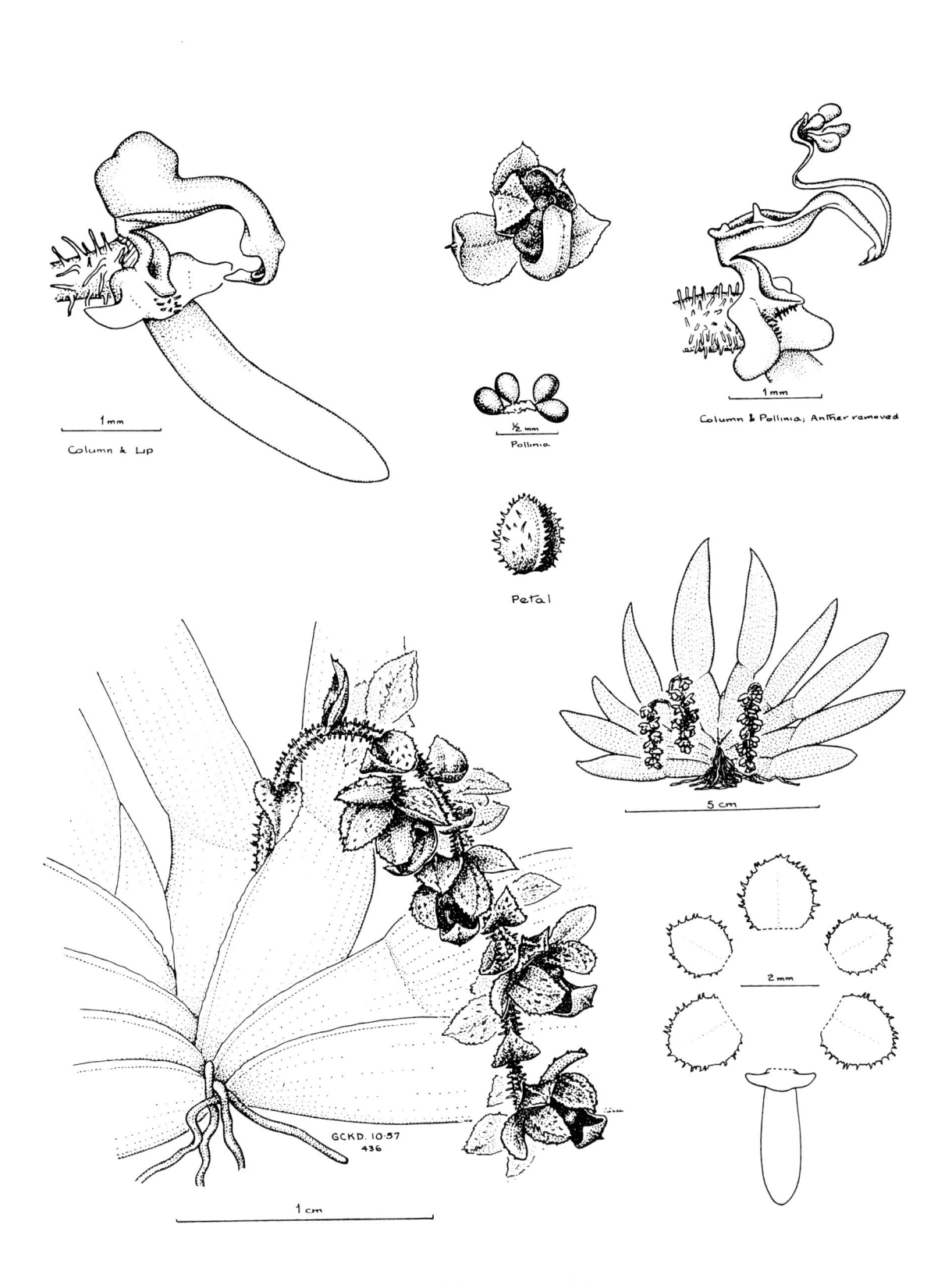

Ornithocephalus bicornis Lindl. in Bot. Voy. Sulphur 172, 1843. — B.

Pityphyllum amesianum

Rudolf Schlechter, an orchidologist as famous as any in that field in the early part of this century, spent his life studying orchids and published hundreds of new species. One can thus believe that only an extremely unusual orchid species could have produced a letter from him to Oakes Ames of Harvard saying, "The evolution of this plant beats anything that was ever known until now amongst the orchids." There is no denying that this little orchid that he named *Pityphyllum amesianum* is truly something most unusual. The original plant came from Colombia in 1924, but the first Venezuelan specimen came to light only some 10 years ago during a trip that we made with Julian Steyermark to the Andes of Táchira state. The species is a true miniature as its tiny pseudobulbs are only a third of an inch long and the most extraordinary radiating, pine-needle-like leaves that crown the pseudobulb (and give the genus its name) are only half an inch long, and frequently much less. The only thing that keeps it out of the mini-miniature class is that it grows by means of fairly long rhizomes along which the tiny pseudobulbs are spread, and with a branching habit it can form mats of quite considerable extent. The most-unorchidy aspect of such a mat is well shown in the illustration here. The flowers are about a fifth of an inch in size and can quite correctly be called insignificant, but the oddness of the plant itself well justifies its place in this series of notes.

The first plant that came to hand was on a large forest tree at about 8,000 feet close to the edge of some of the extensive forest clearing by local peasants, a distressing characteristic of this isolated area at the headwaters of the Quinimari River, not very far from the Colombian border. When this small piece flowered for us in Caracas we were able to get it identified by Dr. Garay and thus add a new genus and species to the list of Venezuelan orchids. Julian, ourselves, and such hired help as we had with us tried hard to find more of this species on this original trip but without success, so it was a very pleasant surprise, on a second visit to this region only two years ago, to come across more of it, growing in dense mats in a small piece of remnant forest at about 7,000 feet. As the deforestation has long since passed this spot, there is perhaps some hope that this tiny remnant will now be allowed to live out what life is left to it in peace.

This second find enabled us to send a piece to the Royal Botanic Garden in Kew, England, where its arrival almost came unstuck when the mycologist who inspects imported orchids took it at first for some unwanted moss used as packing material. It escaped this hazard and we heard in May 1974 that it was "settling in very well indeed," so we hope that in due course it will be able to be shown to the public and provoke the expected remark — "Don't tell me *that's* an orchid!"

Platystele stenostachya

In the introduction to these notes we mentioned that the true beauty of some of the mini-miniature orchid flowers can be appreciated only under the lens of a microscope, and some of the species of the genus *Platystele* illustrate this very well indeed. This *Pleurothallis*-like genus is distinguished not only by the smallness of its flowers but botanically by the thin, winged, hook-like form of its tiny, footless column, and Venezuela is fortunate in being the home of five of the rather less than 30 species in this genus. *Platystele ornata,* with lovely, purple flowers truly pinhead in size, is the smallest of these Venezuelan species, while *P. johnstonii* has the largest flowers by virtue of its quite extraordinarily long, narrow, dorsal sepal, three times the length of the lateral sepals and petals and sticking up like a mast above the creeping leaves that are only half its length. The flowers of all these tiny species are extremely difficult to photograph in a manner that shows more than a fraction of their beauty, and the present illustration of *Platystele stenostachya,* while showing a full plant, does little to show what a microscope can reveal. Its flowers, a pinhead-and-a-half in size, are characterized by golden yellow sepals and petals and a red lip, all nicely spread to view. There is also a yellow-lipped variety. As seen under the microscope, these flowers could have been ideal subjects for modeling by the famous Blaschka brothers who made Harvard's celebrated "Glass Flower" collection. The cellular structure of the floral elements, and very particularly of the lip, is relatively coarse and "inflated" with clear, internal fluid, creating an effect of brilliantly reflecting glass bubbles. On the lip, these cells become tiny glass-like stumpy "hairs." The color, the gleaming effect, and perhaps some scent are the elements that presumably attract whatever insect the plant needs for fertilization, but one assumes that perception of beauty as we know it is not in an insect's make-up, and what strikes us, as two of the few people who have had the thrill of seeing these flowers properly lighted under a microscope, is a feeling of regret that this pleasure has been enjoyed by perhaps no more than one ten-millionth of the world's inhabitants.

The flowers come in ones and twos at the apex of slender, erect peduncles, rather shorter than the narrow, one-inch leaves, and, as the illustration shows, even a small plant can be extremely floriferous. The flowering season seems to be truly every day of the year for a plant of the size illustrated, and we have yet to find ourselves without a flower

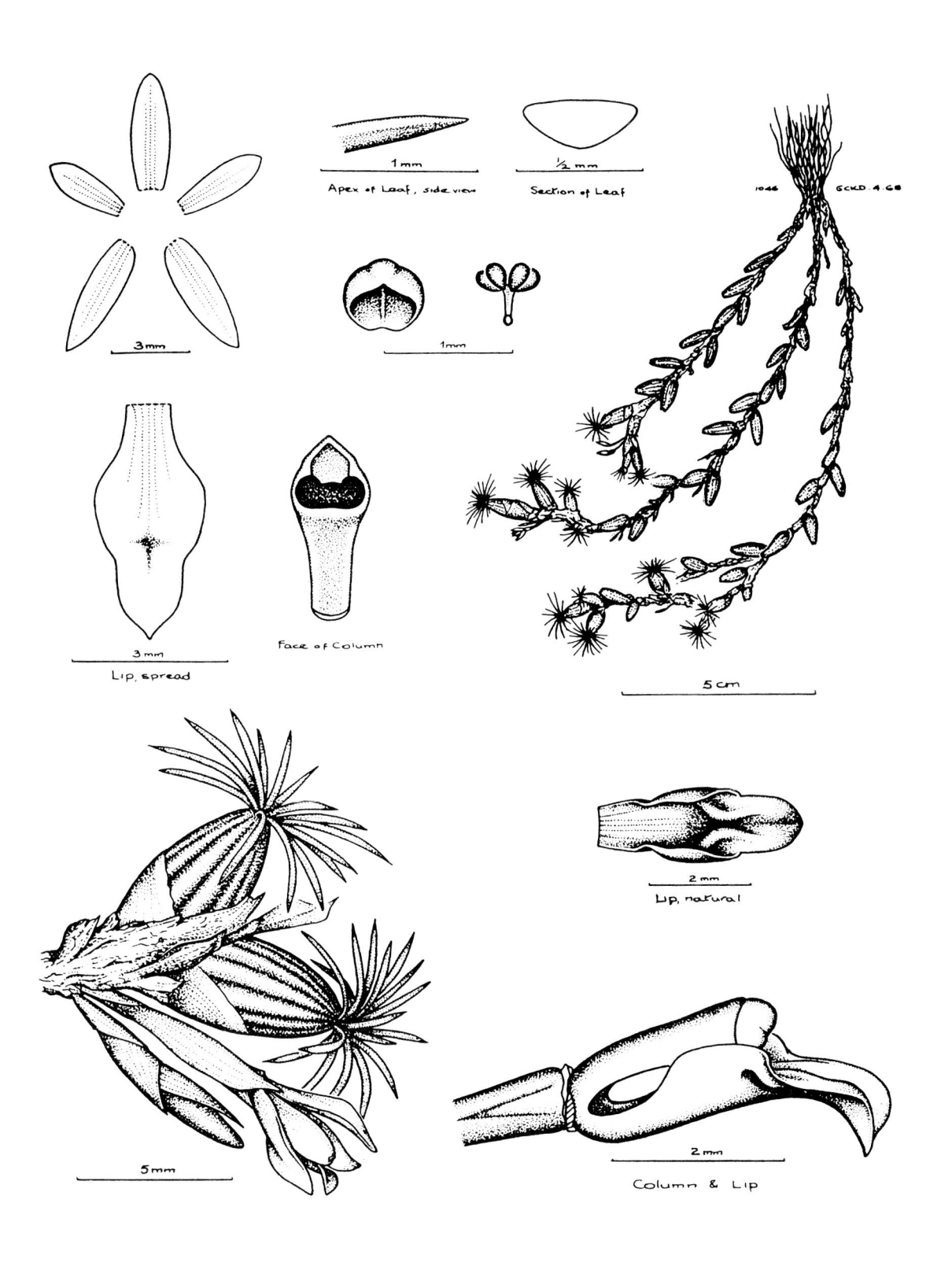

Pityphyllum amesianum Schltr. in Fedde, Rep. Beih. 27: 86, 1924. — A.

to put under the microscope to delight a visitor. The species ranges from Venezuela to Mexico, and in Venezuela, though not overly common, has been found in both the extreme west and extreme east of the Coastal Range, at altitudes varying from about 1,500 to 4,000 feet. In cultivation with us, while one or two plants seemingly flowered themselves to death in a few years, other small plants are continuing very happily, mounted on the usual vertically-hung, small blocks of tree-fern root.

Telipogon croesus

Telipogon is a genus of over 50 species, of which Colombia seems to have the greatest number, leaving Venezuela to get along on only a short half dozen, but these luckily include some very pretty ones. In our experience, telipogons are all very frustrating plants when it comes to trying to cultivate them. This is in large part, no doubt, due to the fact that most of them come from much higher altitudes than our 4,000 feet, but their reluctance to thrive with us must also be blamed on what seems to us to be an abnormal sensitivity to being moved, and in our failure to know what we can do to help them to at least tolerate life with us even if true enjoyment is not possible. After a number of failures we now no longer touch any species of this genus unless it is already "condemned" by being on a fallen tree — which is not often, as many in any case prefer a terrestrial or lithophytic life.

The prettiest of all our local species, and the one that has the largest flowers, is *Telipogon croesus*. The plants we have found have all been epiphytic or lithophytic and have come from altitudes of 8,000 to 10,000 feet in the extreme west of the Venezuelan Andes. This is a zone that is somewhat divorced from the main run of the Venezuelan Andes and is more properly to be considered as a small Venezuelan corner of the otherwise Colombian Andes. The plants run to some four inches tall, with leaves to about two inches long or slightly more. By contrast with the smallness of the plant, the flowers, borne in erect two- or three-flowered racemes, can be as much as almost two inches in diameter. The sepals are small and hidden, but the petals and lip are large and have a very showy coloring of pink at the base, grading through white to yellow at the apex and margins, with green or reddish nervation. Whereas most *Telipogon* columns (as implied by the name of the genus) are distinguished in truly modern style by dense and rather untidy masses of long hairs, the *T. croesus* column is an unashamed "square," clean shaven except for a fine covering of very short hairs on the back of its neck. Croesus, living some 2,500 years before shipping magnates and oil sheiks had been invented, was reputedly the richest man on earth, and it is presumably the connection between riches, gold (not oil), and the color of this orchid flower that induced Reichenbach to give it this name when publishing it almost a hundred years ago.

Epidendrum nocturnum, a Schizoid Species[1]

OUR OLD TYPEWRITER has just coped with addressing a letter to our Caracas ear doctor who works in a "Clinica Otorrinolaringológica," so it should not balk at typing a 19-letter word when we write about orchids. The fact it that it is almost impossible to avoid the crime of writing anthropocentrically when discussing the eccentricities of Nature. The dictionary says that anthropocentric means "interpreting natural processes in terms of the human mind," and scientists, we are sure, should not (and we hope never do) talk about Nature being wise, or clever, or foolish, or even doing things just to annoy us. We are told that everything in the universe is made of nothing but waves of probability and that, scientifically speaking, everything since the Big Bang has just "growed like Topsy" without purpose or plan. Nature is what it is, and that is that. But to say that Nature should not be talked about in an anthropocentric manner will not stop us from talking as if it did have a mind of its own.

Many eons ago, Nature invented genes and gender so that the qualities of parents could be mixed and could be passed to their heirs in a form very close to but never identical with the original. It then allowed evolution, helped maybe with occasional mutations of the genes themselves, to continue this game and to develop ever widening differences that, given the right circumstances, could result in what we call "different species." By this means, Nature sometimes, in fact quite often in the plant world, produces a series of individuals that leave us most unsure as to whether they should all be considered a single species or should be grouped into two or more species. Nature wisely does not enter into such discussions and leaves it up to us to disentangle things as best we can. Taxonomy, as a result, is a very lively discipline with much scope for discussion of the classification of plants in their major groupings and possibly even more discussion relative to species, subspecies, and varieties.

Among puzzles that Nature likes to tease us with is that of plants that have what one may call a "standard form" of flower, so that one can immediately say "This is species X," yet at the same time have such variable features in all other respects that, if it were not for the flowers, one could say with equal confidence "These can *not* all be of species X." In such cases one assumes that the genes governing floral form pass relatively unchanged from one generation to another, while the genes that govern the other features can act in a much freer and easier fashion and frequently produce variations of a widely different character. With luck, some of these may be improvements or changes that will help the plant to adapt to some change in the *ambiente* where the plants grow. One superb example of this is provided by the orchid species, *Epidendrum nocturnum,* which is well known to most of our readers in at least one of its many forms.

This species inhabits a range from southern Florida to Mexico and Brazil and from the West Indies to Peru and Bolivia. In the 200 years since it was first published by Jacquin it has acquired about a dozen different names apart from varietal names or changes of generic name. It can be found in Venezuela from practically sea level to 2,300 m (7,500 ft.) with preference for altitudes not much above 1,500 m (5,000 ft.). It occurs as an epiphyte but grows just as happily in the ground or at times on almost bare rock. In other words it is blessed with genes that produce variable progeny that in one form or another can adapt to a wide variety of conditions, and it has taken full advantage of this birthright to become one of the most widespread and common orchids of the New World tropics. Its near-white flowers have narrow, widely spreading sepals and petals, and a very characteristic lip that is united to the base of the column almost up to the apex of the

---

[1] Originally appeared in *A.O.S. Bulletin,*
Vol. 46, October 1977, pages 888-893

latter, the free part having two large, white wings with entire margins, two calli at the base, and a very long and narrow mid-lobe. The size of the flower is very variable, from dwarf forms with a spread of two cm (less than one inch) to fine flowers with a spread of 16 cm (over six inches), sepals to 8.5 cm (3½ inches) long, and lips whose mid-lobes alone can be six cm (2¼ inches) long. But regardless of these extreme variations in the size of the flower, it is a case of once-seen-never-forgotten, and (with one exception to be mentioned later) there need be no hesitation in identifying it.

The trouble starts when one finds a plant that is not in flower. The vegetative appearance can then be so confusing that until one has accumulated a large fund of experience covering all types of this species one may well be deceived occasionally into believing that one has found something new and exciting, only to find later that it is "just another *nocturnum*." Basically the plant is a simple collection of generally erect stems arising in a closely spaced (approximate) manner from a tough rhizome provided with thick roots. The stems are terete at the base and grade to compressed in the upper part, or sometimes almost from the base. The leaves are borne sometimes almost the entire length of the stem (particularly in younger growth) but more generally appear only in the upper half. It is when one comes to questions of gross plant size, leaf size, leaf shape, leaf quality and width, and rigidity of stem that it becomes impossible to find words to describe this species briefly in any meaningful manner. To illustrate the varietal range would be an enormous task and end up by being so confusing it would be of very little help at all. So for the purposes of this article we have limited ourselves to illustrating only some of the extreme types.

Figure A-1 shows a miniature form that we found on the Aonda River near Angel Falls at about 600 m (2,000 ft.) altitude. This is a recognized variety appropriately named *minus* by Cogniaux in 1907. Our plant is no more than 6 cm (2¼ inches) in total height and has slender stems with narrow, very thick, fleshy leaves about 4 × 0.5 cm (1½ × ⅕ inches) in size. As an example of the variation in size to which this species normally grows, several plants of this (epiphytic) variety could grow happily on a single leaf from a large plant, such as the 17 × 7.5 cm (7 inches × 3½ inches) leaf of a terrestrial (sublithophytic) plant from about 2,000 m (6,500 ft.), shown (in outline only) as Figure A-2. Our expedition to the top of this tepui was made about 13 years ago, at which time it unfortunately did not occur to us to make detailed notes or sketches of complete plants of a number of fine specimens growing there, so we cannot be sure just what type of plant this leaf came from (all we can state now is that the form and size of the leaf did go down in our notes.) The probability is that it was one of a number of plants with stems approaching one m (three ft.) and with flowers to at least eight cm (more than three inches) spread, but otherwise "normal *nocturnum*" in appearance — if there is such a thing as a normal form. Almost certainly it was not of the shorter few-leaved type of Figure C which has extremely wide and sharp-edged leaf-bases which would have made a lasting impression on us at that time.

The most flexible we have found so far, Figure B, were growing terrestrially in a forest at about 700 m (2,500 ft.) on Cerro Guaiquinima on the Paragua River of southeastern Venezuela. Though normally erect, just the weight of the leaves and small flower is at times sufficient to bend the slender 25-cm (10-inch) stem right over. At its base this stem is no more than 1 mm (1/25 inch) thick and only slightly wider at its lightly compressed apex. The very narrow leaves and the slender stem gives this plant an aspect very different from other types, yet the flowers, though small, are completely typical. Also from Guaiquinima is the plant, with a large but unfortunately withered flower, shown in Figure A-3. This also has thin and narrow leaves but with dimensions of 13 × 2.5 cm (5 inches × 1 inch). These are by no means as narrow as the variety "B" above; moreover, the stem is six mm (¼ inch) wide, strongly compressed and well able to stand erect. The general appearance of the plant is very different from that of Figure B, as well as from any other variety we have met. It grows to about 50 cm (20 inches) tall.

In Figure A-4 is shown a variety with very fine large flowers that we found at about 1,800 m (6,000 ft.) on the summit of the large mesa of Cerro Jaua at the southern end of the Caura River, not far from the Brazilian border. By contrast with all the other varieties so far mentioned, this type has a very tall, erect, highly compressed and extremely robust, ancipitous (sharp-edged) stem bearing relatively small, very rigid "half-closed" leaves with a strongly marked, suberect manner of growth. Many plants of this variety were over 150 cm (six ft.) tall, and one that caught our particular attention was crowned with a large capsule so high up that "GCKD" could just touch it with the tip of his machete extended at arm's length above his head. Admittedly we use only small machetes on our trips but by subsequent measurement at home this added up to a plant 245 cm (eight ft.) tall. Naturally a plant of this size, however strong its stem, could only survive strong winds if growing terrestrially and well protected by surrounding vegetation also of considerable height, such as the undergrowth where this plant was found.

And to end this series of illustrations Figure C

Epidendrum nocturnum *(Figure A 1-5)*

shows a plant with a large and quite typical flower but with very wide, fairly thin and flatly-spread leaves to about 15 × 8 cm (6 inches × 3¼ inches). The few-leaved stems are only about 50 cm (20 inches) tall and are wide and very strongly compressed in the upper part where they are concealed in extremely wide (two cm) and very ancipitous, leaf-bearing sheaths. A greater contrast with Figures A-4 or B it would be hard to imagine. The actual plant illustrated came from about 1,300 m (4,000 ft.) in the coastal range not very far west of Caracas, where we found it growing epiphytically in typical cloud forest conditions but we have, since then, found specimens in the Gran Sabana National Park and have seen similar wide-leaved but flowerless plants in other parts of southeast Venezuela including Guaiquinima. Thus, it is by no means a rarity.

Forgetting the flowers, and just looking at the various plants ranging from three inches to eight feet tall, with leaves that are long and very narrow or short and very wide, thin or very rigid, and with stems that are very thin and flexible or wide and strongly erect, one could be forgiven for failing to credit that all these belong to a single species. Indeed, despite the many intervening forms that one comes across, one cannot escape the feeling that several distinct species must be involved in this group. It is thus most encouraging to note that some five years ago, Dr. Leslie A. Garay took a bold step and promoted Lindley's *Epidendrum nocturnum* var. *latifolium* (Figure C in this article) to full species status as *Epidendrum latifolium* (Lindl.) Garay & Sweet. We trust that all other taxonomists are accepting this so that everyone will use this concise and meaningful name when talking about this plant. Apart from having very distinctive leaves and a widely ancipitous stem, the very large flowers appear singly, as distinct from the shortly racemose types of certain *E. nocturnum* plants that can be seen frequently. However, the inflorescence of the very large-flowered *Epidendrum nocturnum* varieties shown in Figures A-3 and A-4 also show no signs of being other than single-flowered, so it is possible that, when more specimens become available for study, these types also may some day be found to justify their promotion to the status of distinct species.

Apart from the *Epidendrum latifolium* from the coastal range, all the plants shown in this article come from the Venezuelan "Guyana" region south of the Orinoco River. This does not mean that *Epidendrum nocturnum* is absent from the Andes or other parts north of the Orinoco but does indicate that, at least in our experience, the outstanding varieties (and possible new species?) come from the south.

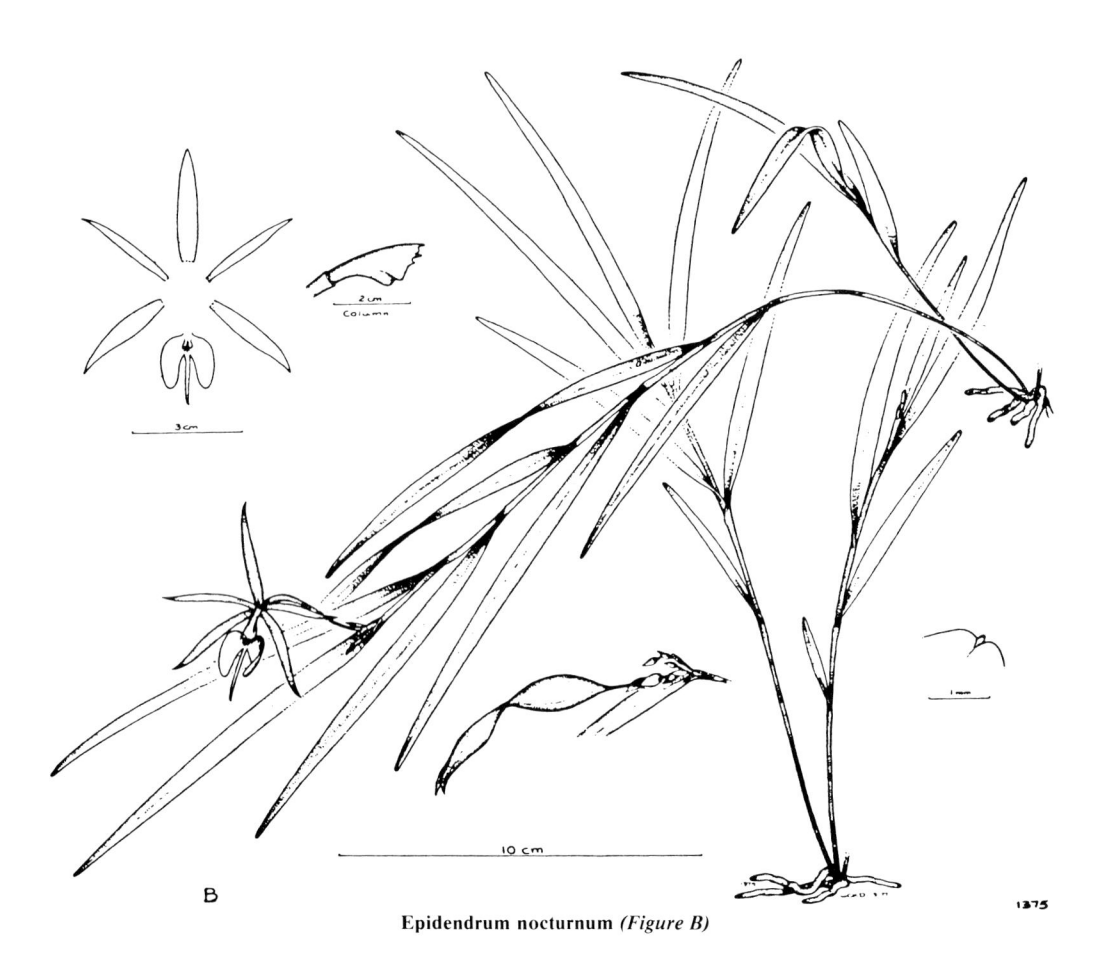

Epidendrum nocturnum *(Figure B)*

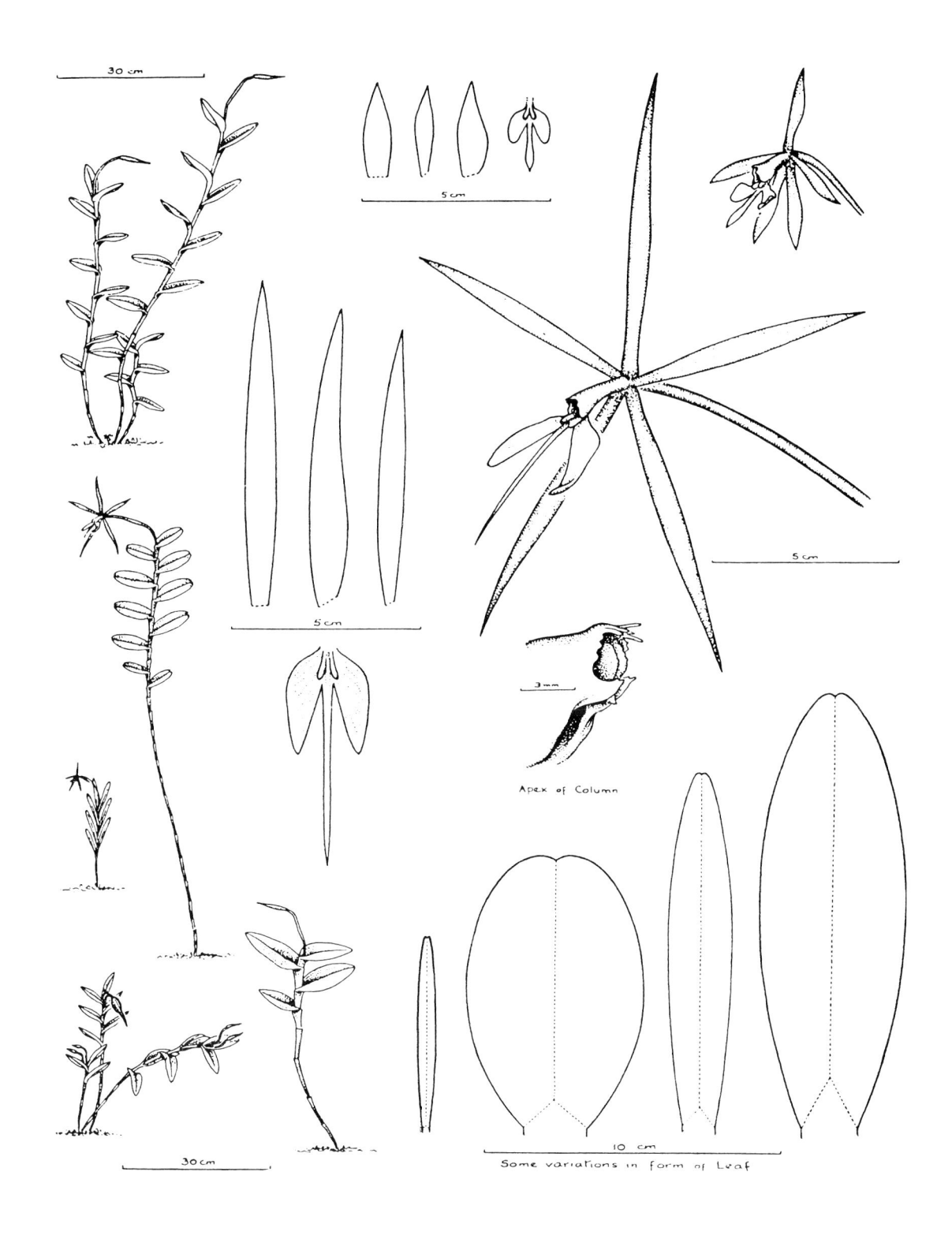

Epidendrum latifolium (Lindley) Garay & Sweet *(Figure C)*

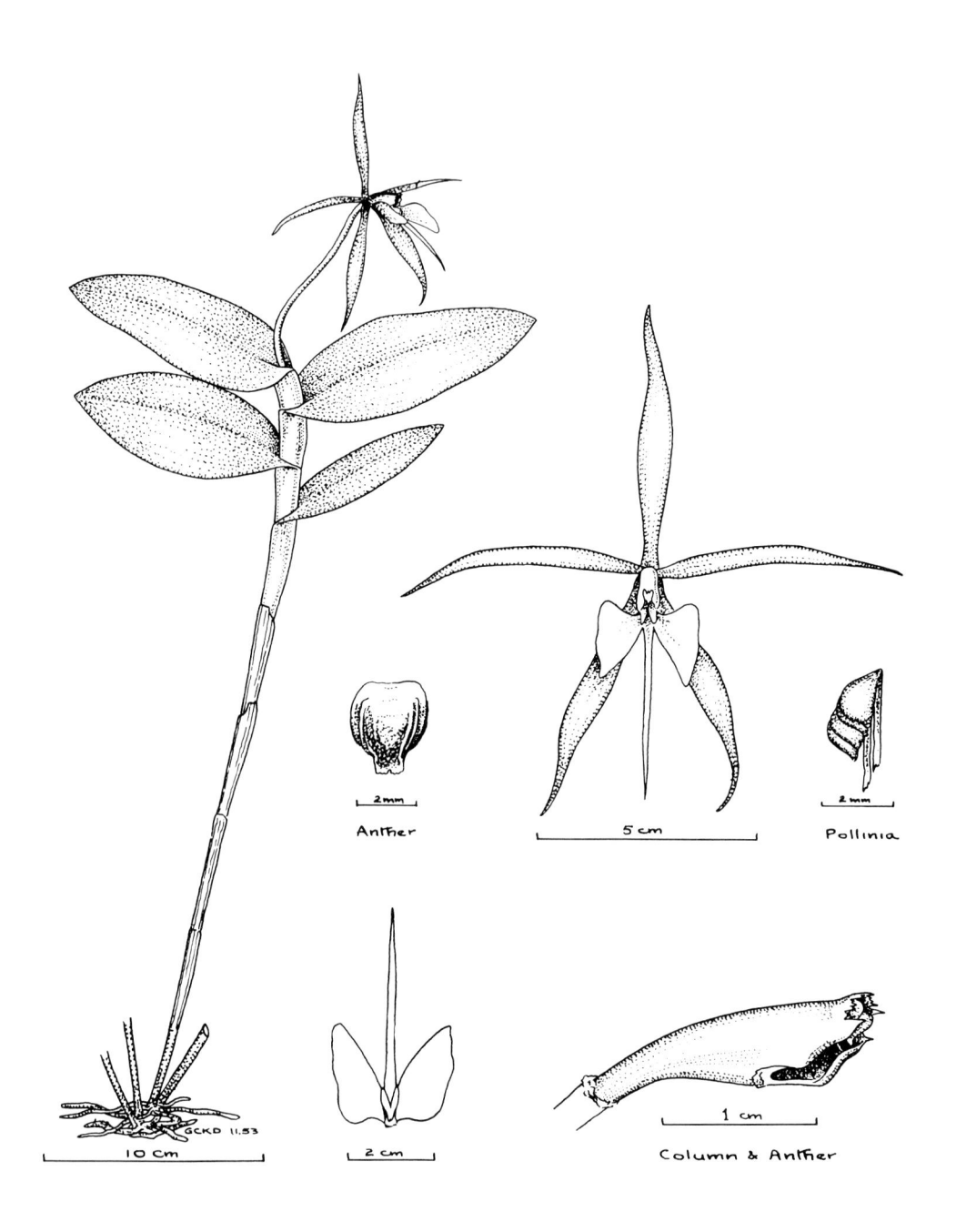

Epidendrum nocturnum Jacq., Enum. Pl. Carib. 29, 1760. — A. B. D. E.

Some Venezuelan Endemic Orchids[1]

BUBONIC PLAGUE is still endemic in a certain small area that we call the Tiara Forest, not far from Caracas, at least to the extent that the disease is still carried by the local rodent parasites. The area is consequently forbidden to any intending residents and not exactly recommended for frequent use by such transients as orchid hunters. But "endemic" in this medical sense has a much looser meaning than the very restrictive sense in which it is used by biologists and botanists. Bubonic Plague is medically endemic in the Tiara Forest but is also to be found in a number of places a long way away from there: by contrast, if any orchid species living in the Tiara Forest can also be found anywhere else, then no botanist could call it endemic to Tiara. In other words, endemic in the botanical world means "to be found in a given area and nowhere else." Proving that a plant is endemic to a given zone or a specific country thus becomes tied in with the notorious difficulty of proving a negative: to show that a species does grow in a certain area is easy; to prove that it does not grow anywhere else is almost impossible. As a result, anyone (including ourselves) who says that a species is endemic to any zone is implicitly, if not explicitly, prefacing this by saying "To the best of my belief" and is offering no proof.

The tendency of any plant species to endemicity will depend on the interplay of a number of factors, and the tendency of any plant family to incorporate a high proportion of endemic-prone species will depend on the degree to which endemicity-favoring factors are shared by most of its species. Species that produce very few seeds or that drop their seeds heavily at their feet, that attract or make use of few seed-transporting agents, that need very complicated or specialized aids to fertilization or germination, that cannot tolerate varied climatic or soil conditions or are poor competitors with other plants — all such species, if they survive at all, are likely to find themselves restricted to very limited areas and are thus highly prone to endemicity. In practice, very few plants incorporate many pro-endemic factors without balancing these off with other anti-endemic factors, and the orchid family is quite normal in this respect. A great number of its (quite successful) species have developed what might be considered as dangerously endemic-prone characters, such as highly specialized requirements in the insect or bird vectors capable of effecting the necessary removal of the pollinia from one flower and their reinsertion in another. On top of this, unlike most other plants, orchid seed carries no "food" to start it off in life and, in nature, can only germinate and get going where it meets up with the special mycorrhiza (fungal root mycelium) capable of feeding it. These conditions set up a strong handicap against the seed being able to germinate anywhere strange or "far from home." But again these factors strongly favoring endemicity, the orchid can set three anti-endemic factors. The first is that it produces quite fantastic quantities of seed, in many cases literally in the millions, for each individual plant. Secondly, this seed, extra-minute in the first place, is normally enclosed in a minute but fairly loose jacket of fine net-like consistency, so that the resulting seed-in-jacket is ideally suited to being airborne for great distances. And thirdly, at least insofar as concerns the majority of tropical species, their adoption of an epiphytic way of life brings them the advantage of relative freedom from adverse soil conditions or intense competition with terrestrial plants, and opens up to the air-floating seed a whole variety of microclimates on the host-tree where the seed may land. On balance, this combination of plus and minus factors can be said to leave the tropical orchids in the ranks of the plants with above average ability to spread themselves and thus less than average proneness to endemicity.

[1] Originally appeared in *A.O.S. Bulletin*, Vol. 47, February 1978, pages 103-111

This statement might seem to be contradicted by the fact that known records indicate that some 20% of Venezuelan orchids are endemic to this country, but this is certain to prove a factitious figure when adjoining areas of Colombia, Guyana, and Brazil have been intensely explored botanically. Moreover, quite a high proportion of orchids on the present endemic list have only recently been found. The fact that all such new species are almost by definition endemic at the start to the spot where they have been discovered by no means indicates that matters will stay that way. Such initial endemicity frequently proves to be a purely temporary condition, as exemplified by *Epidendrum rostratum,* new to science when found by us in the Tiara Forest in 1957 yet almost simultaneously picked up in Colombia; or *Epidendrum pachyphyton,* found in Colombia and published in December 1973 and found by Steyermark and ourselves two months later on the Venezuelan Meseta de Jaua a thousand kilometers away. Plants are no respecters of political boundaries, and the physical breaks between Venezuela and its land neighbors are not strong. The border with Guyana is in many places extremely "weak," as we know ourselves from having unwittingly strayed from Venezuela into Guyana on an orchid hunt. The watershed delimiting the border with Brazil is in many parts a fairly low and gentle range and, in some other parts, just a flat, swampy forest stretching from one country into the other: the border with Colombia is equally weak in the *llanos* and not overly strong elsewhere except for the stretch of the Perijá Range west of Lake Maracaibo. Thus the only major section of Venezuela conducive to endemicity, and where indeed the majority of its endemic species are located, is in the long, northern, coastal stretch where a hilly and mountainous region is trapped between the low plains to the south and the sea to the north. Special zones of local endemicity also occur inside this major zone, such as the small, limestone region behind the city of Coro and on the peninsula of Paraguaná.

As regards individual genera, only one sizable genus, *Lepanthes,* seems to show a quite disproportionate tendency to endemism. Of 34 species listed in the official *Flora de Venezuela,* 21 are shown as endemic. That this is likely to prove a purely temporary condition is indicated by the fact that 15 of these endemics are species that have been found in very recent years, mostly thanks to a burst of botanical exploration in the Andean levels where this genus seems to have its Venezuelan epicenter; similar activity in the adjoining parts of Colombia could well rapidly diminish the present list of these endemics. It is true, however, that the extraordinary number of different *Lepanthes* species that are turning up in this relatively limited area (many more have been found since the publication of the *Flora*) indicates that "something odd" is going on, and if this means that a number of these species are for some obscure reason fairly new "evolutions," they may not yet have had time to extend far from this epicenter and thus still may be true endemics.

While the world in general may need reminding that by no means all orchid plants have large and showy flowers, it will be no surprise to *A. O. S. Bulletin* readers to know that the majority of Venezuelan endemic species (indeed the majority of orchid species anywhere) are true "botanicals," i.e. orchids that even the orchid fraternity would not, on the whole, consider worth looking at. But there still remain enough endemic species with very attractive flowers — small, medium, or large — to have made it quite difficult for us to select the following group to illustrate this article, as follows.

Cattleya lueddemanniana

Obviously at the head of any list of Venezuelan endemic orchids must come our native *Cattleya* species, if those who prefer to call these subspecies or even mere varieties of *C. labiata* will allow us to treat them more "specifically" for the present purposes. Among the eight *Cattleya* species to be found in this country, those endemic to Venezuela are all in the northern half of the country. In the central part there is *C. lueddemanniana* (more commonly known here as *C. speciosissima*) which ranges from near sea level to about 1,500 feet, and *C. mossiae* (the National Flower) at cooler levels from around 3,000 to 5,000 feet. In the east there is *C. gaskelliana* ranging more or less from 2,000 to 3,000 feet, and in the west there is *C. percivaliana,* the highest growing of our cattleyas with a range up to about 6,000 feet where it is largely lithophytic. All these endemic cattleyas have distinctive varieties, including alba or semi-alba forms, and it is a matter of personal taste to decide which of these many beauties should be chosen to illustrate this note. In the end, we have decided to stick to the "ordinary" color varieties, and our choice has fallen on *C. lueddemanniana* because, while all the others have very fine forms, in our experience this species is by far the most consistent in producing flowers of excellent shape. Fine forms of *C. mossiae,* for example, naturally do exist, but the average run of unselected plants is by no means as well formed as the average run of *C. lueddemanniana,* the former suffering from the well-known tendency for its dorsal sepal to fall backwards and the petals to droop, a bad-mannered behavior almost unknown among *C. lueddemanniana.* When it comes to forming hybrids, using carefully

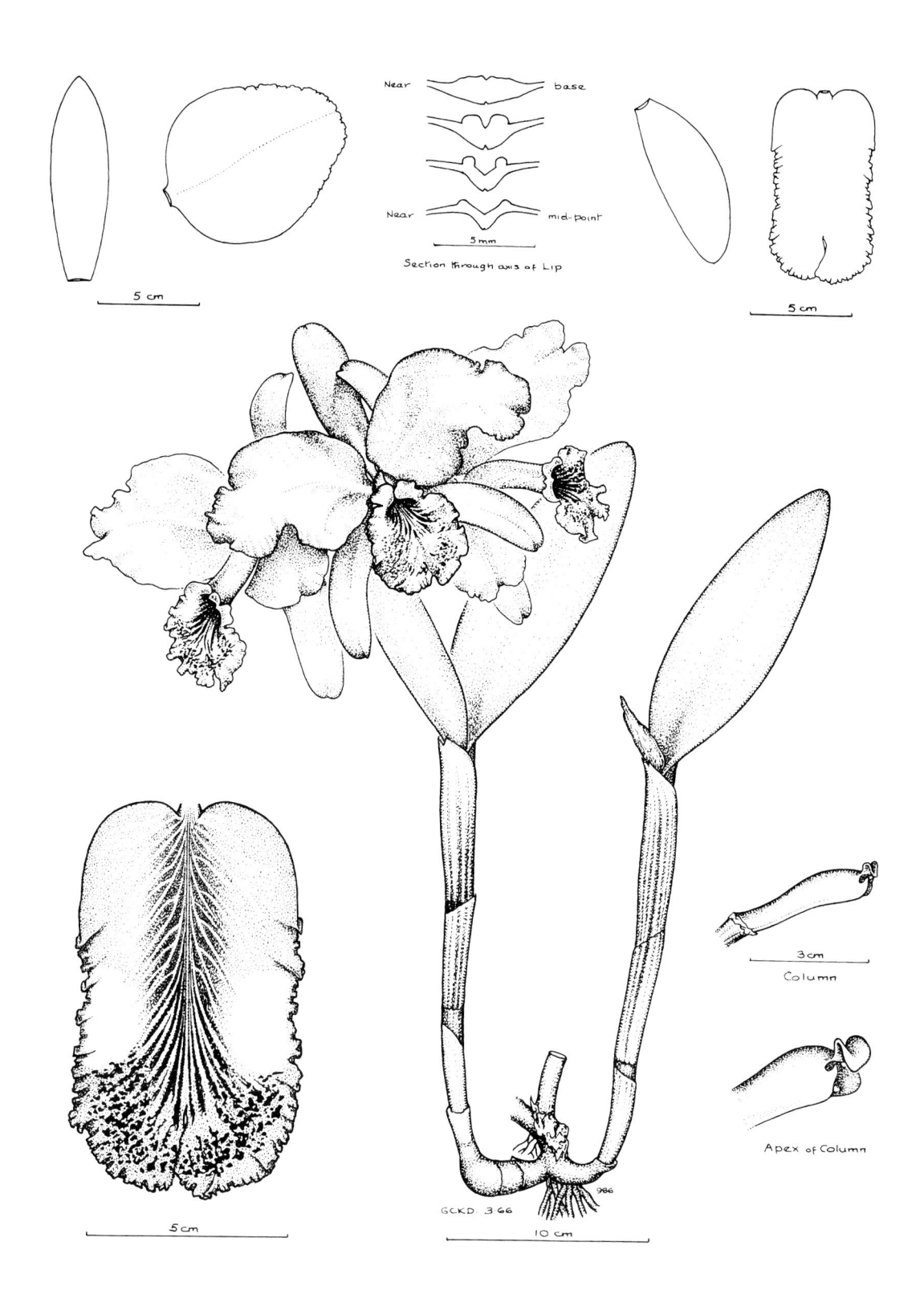

Cattleya lueddemanniana Reichb. f., Xenia Orch. 1: 29, 1854. — B.

selected clones, then *C. mossiae* comes into its own, which is another example of the fact that while the patricians may as a group look better and behave better than the plebs, true genius more often springs from the latter. The normal flowering period with us is anywhere from January to April.

Acineta alticola

So far recorded only from Venezuela, this species grows on the summits of distant sandstone heights, a number of which are close to the Brazilian or Guyanan border, and, in some cases, such as Roraima and Cerro de la Neblina, are even shared with Venezuela's neighbors. It thus seems likely that it is only a matter of time before this species is also found on non-Venezuelan territory, which is perhaps a good excuse to include it here while it still retains its endemic status. Mostly found on the tepuis of Bolívar State (frequently referred to by the rather vague and undefined term of "Venezuelan Guayana"), this species has also been found in the Parima range bordering on Brazil, in the Venezuelan Amazonas territory. Its altitude tolerance is quite considerable, ranging from as low as 1,800 feet to as high as 8,000 feet. Acinetas have been designed by nature to be exclusively epiphytic plants, with long inflorescences of heavy-textured flowers developing in a fully pendent form from close to the base of the tough pseudobulbs. So strong is this yen to go straight down that in most *Acineta* species the inflorescence, as it develops, is armed with a quite hard, sharp apex whose penetrating ability is extraordinary: one plant of *A. superba* in our collection forced its way unharmed right through a 2½" block of quite hard tree-fern root. More surprising still is that these plants seem able to sense whether or not open air exists below them and thus judge if it is worth trying to break through or not. We say this because on a number of occasions we have found *Acineta* plants, including many of *A. alticola,* growing terrestrially in areas where their original epiphytic supports have been eliminated by fire or other cause, and in these conditions the spike seems at a fairly early stage to abandon any effort to continue vertically into the soil, switching instead to the hopeless task of trying to get back to the surface and ending as a more or less horizontal inflorescence buried fairly shallowly in the soil and naturally failing to develop proper flowers. As mentioned in the "On the Record" section of the *A.O.S. Bulletin* for December 1972, this terrestrial, non-flowering existence does nothing to dampen the ardor of such plants and in fact seems to suit them better than the epiphytic life, if growing fat rather than producing seed is taken as the criterion for health.

In its general aspect, *A. alticola* is similar to the yellow-flowered *A. erythroxantha* of the Venezuelan and Colombian Andes, but botanically can easily be distinguished as it has a simple, uncomplicated, fleshy callus in the lip, quite distinct from the complicated callus of *A. erythroxantha* which has fleshy projections both fore and aft of the midpoint. For cultivation, the standard "acineta" treatment is adequate, hanging the plants in baskets or open-bottom pots, or growing them on the side of blocks of tree-fern root.

Epidendrum garcianum

Among the Venezuelan endemics most likely to resist removal from this list by being found outside Venezuela is *Epidendrum garcianum* (named for its discoverer, Carlos Garcia Esquival, a Caracas species enthusiast) which grows in the limestone area near Coro, mentioned at the beginning of this note as a special endemic enclave inside the broader endemic zone of the northern edge of Venezuela. Inland from the city of Coro, on the coast, is the Sierra de San Luis, some 4,000 feet high and covered with cloud forest mainly on its seaward slopes. It is a range with many caves and sinkholes, so hollow that springs at its base will disgorge berries and other plant remnants from the summit within hours of a heavy rainfall on top, and its crest and upper flanks form a very distinct habitat with naturally a very distinct flora. In this zone, *E. garcianum,* if not common, is by no means rare, and the species also appears on the small Sta. Ana range in the heart of the very dry Paraguaná peninsula some 50 miles to the northwest, yet it seems completely absent anywhere else. The flowers are about two inches wide, with intensity of color varying from plant to plant, and, in some lesser degree, depending on the degree of isolation. They usually appear in the form of two-flowered racemes and in reasonable quantity during six or seven months in the year, making a nicely growing plant a welcome addition to the orchid house. It is among the minority of orchids that favor a non-resupinate attitude for their flowers, the fleshy white lip bending right over to shelter the small column from the midday sun (or whatever). As a landing ground for an insect bent on removing or placing pollinia, this attitude would seem to be useless, but without knowing how its fertilization is effected we cannot criticize it for acting foolishly. In cultivation, we originally had quite a bit of trouble getting our plants to do well. Having found them in rather damp and shaded positions at about the same altitude as our house, we naturally placed them in as nearly the same conditions as we could — and naturally, since in the process we must inevitably have changed a number of climatic factors that the species likes besides shaded dampness, the plants demonstrated considerable disapproval of our well-meaning efforts. By the usual process of

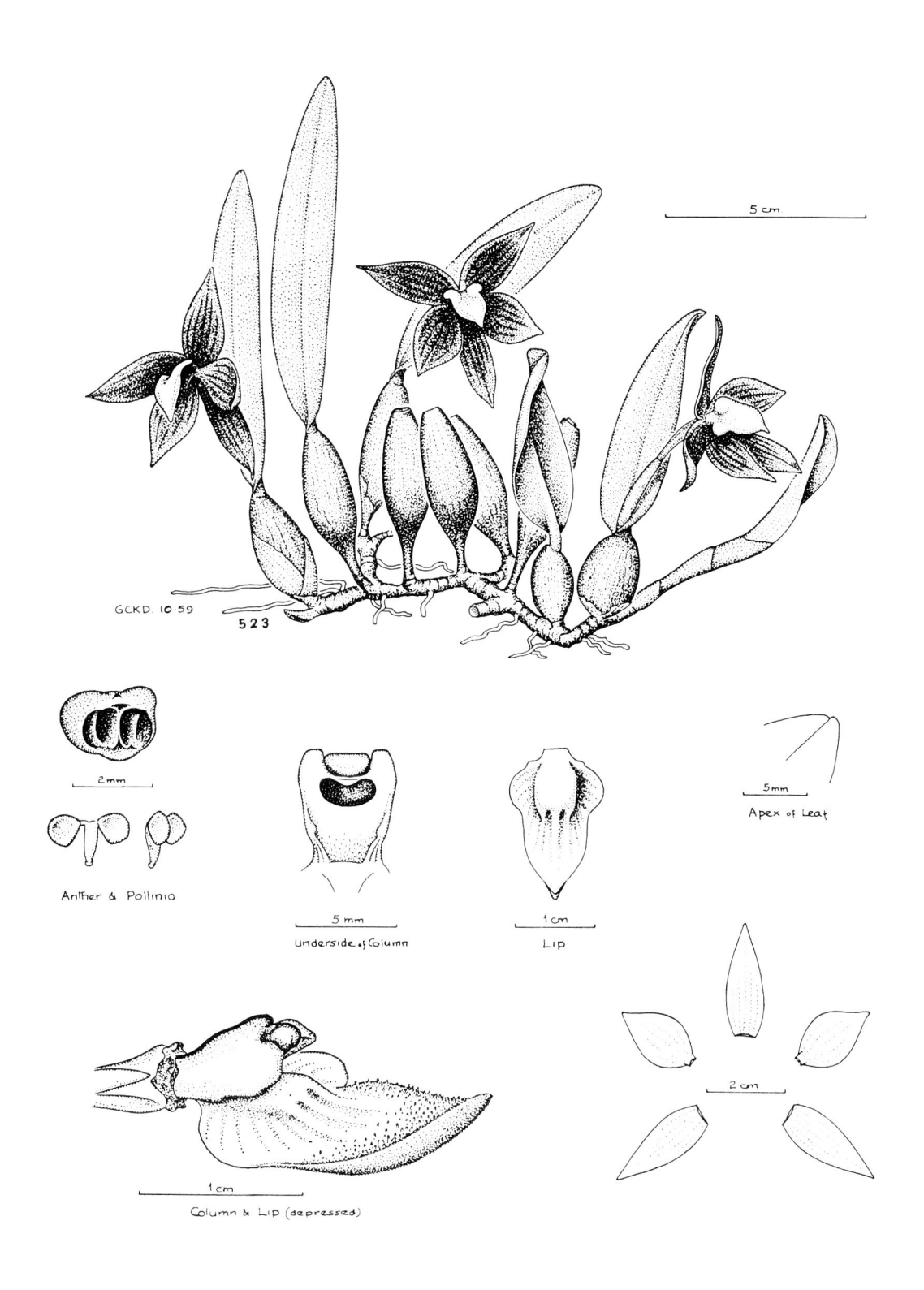

Epidendrum garcianum Garay & Dunsterv., Venez. Orch. Ill. 2: 122, 1961. — B.

Acineta alticola

"fish-and-find-out" we now have them growing very happily in shallow baskets (actually plastic bread baskets) filled with tree-fern root, hung in well-aired positions with only moderate shade (but with little direct sunshine) and apart from natural rainfall they get only touches with the hose.

Cyrtopodium glutiniferum

Venezuela has a very pretty representative of the genus *Cyrtopodium,* in the form of *C. glutiniferum*. This fairly rare, or at least seldom-collected species, has been found recently by a friend of ours, R. A. Crebbs, in the eastern part of Venezuela, north of the Orinoco, but the species otherwise seems to favor the area south of the Orinoco, mainly in the iron mines area from which another friend, Elizabeth ten Houten, produced the first plants we ever saw; or even farther south where we later found our own specimens. Some of these latter were not far from the Brazilian border, so here again this species may someday lose its Venezuelan endemicity although it does not appear in the fairly extensive treatment given this genus in the *Flora Brasilica*. Cyrtopodiums are occasionally epiphytic but far more often are terrestrial, as is the case with *C. glutiniferum,* and many of them form impressive plants not well adapted to the small orchid house. The normally erect pseudobulbs often bear painfully spike-tipped, close-fitting sheaths, and can be found in some species more than three feet tall. *Cyrtopodium glutiniferum* is not in this giant class, but, with pseudobulbs to around two feet tall and a total height, with inflorescence, to about five feet, is not precisely in the dwarf category. Many species in this genus tend to be difficult to distinguish botanically without careful and critical study of the details of the lip. From this point of view it is fortunate that Venezuela has but a half-dozen *Cyrtopodium* species in total, and among these *C. glutiniferum* stands out because of the general lack of marks and spots on its basically yellow and yellow-brown flowers.

Masdevallia wageneriana

Venezuela's best known masdevallia is *Masdevallia tovarensis*, a species with fairly small but most attractive white flowers with short tails to the sepals. This species is endemic to Venezuela but, as it is fairly well known, we have preferred to include in this endemic series *Masdevallia wageneriana,* a lesser-known and rather smaller species that grows in roughly the same area and is equally a "safe" endemic. *Masdevallia tovarensis* dates from 1854 and is to be found in several localities more or less throughout the Coastal Range at a 5,000- to 7,000-foot altitude. In its near-Caracas habitat it is facing extinction from the depredations of collectors who supply it in large quantities to street-corner vendors during its flowering season of December to March, a trade that is financed by the hundreds of unthinking members of the public who buy them, knowing little about orchid culture and unaware than even the most expert of growers would be hard put to keep them alive in the climate of Caracas. *Masdevallia wageneriana* dates from 1853 and has the good fortune to be less spectacular; it also enjoys a habitat that includes a spot as far west as the Sierra de San Luis near Coro and its future is hopefully less threatened. As distinct from *M. tovarensis, Masdevallia wageneriana*

Cyrtopodium glutiniferum

belongs in the category of masdevallias with long, slender tails or *caudae* to the sepals. The heart of the flower is only some 5/16" in diameter, but the rather wildly waving tails extend this by a further 1½" in three directions. The leaves are fleshy, dark green with almost black, petiolate bases, and normally only about 2" in total length, so that both plant and flower fit into the category usually classed as "miniature," which often means that in terms of pleasure rendered per square inch of orchid house space, they rate very high indeed. Its habitat range includes places rather lower than that of *M. tovarensis* and this is reflected in the fact that, while even at 4,000 feet the latter only just enjoys life, *M. wageneriana* feels rather more comfortable, growing on a small block of tree-fern root in airy shade. As distinct from the fairly regular flowering season of its mate, *M. wageneriana* has at one time or another flowered for us in March, June, August, September, and October.

Trichopilia oicophylax

This pretty species is basically an inhabitant of the Coastal Range, a zone with good prospects for the development of endemic species, and the fact that it also occurs in the extreme eastern end of the main Andean range (Yacambú National Park in the State of Lara) does little to endanger its future endemicity as this is still a very long way from any international boundary. There exists, however, a record for this species from the Venezuelan Guayana, and if this is not some freak occurrence or a confusion with *Trichopilia fragrans,* then a leak in the endemic shield might exist in that direction. Searching through R. W. Brown's most useful *Composition of Scientific Words,* we find that *oicophylax* means "house guardian" or "house

Masdevallia wageneriana

Trichopilia oicophylax

watcher," but this, we fear, leaves us no nearer to understanding the real meaning of this orchid's name than before undertaking this piece of important research, and until someone with access to Reichenbach's early records can supply us with the answer (as we hope will happen) it must remain a rather annoying teaser.

In its main center, i.e., the Coastal Range, this species has shown its pretty face for us in various sites in the large Henri Pittier National Park, a well-known zone that includes the Rancho Grande research center made famous by Walter Beebe. It is easily accessible by two roads leading from the city of Maracay, south of the main part of the Coastal Range, over the top and down to the coast in the north, and its National Park status provides very necessary protection to the fine cloud forest lining the ridge itself from 3,000 to 6,000 feet and spreading a considerable way down towards the sea. We have also found this species in the small remnant forest of "bubonic plague" renown lining a ridge at about 4,000 feet near the small town of Tiara. Although this Tiara location is the only Coastal Range reference in the official *Flora of Venezuela* we somehow feel that it is by no means as rare as this would indicate, and it could be that the explanation for this is that very few collectors of orchids bother to check their finds with the Caracas Botanical Institute herbarium. The normal form of the inflorescence is an arching, three-flowered raceme, with the flowers bending over rather below the horizontal. Our plants are doing well in pots tightly filled with chopped tree-fern root and placed in an airy position with fairly constant but light shade, alongside plants of *T. fragrans.* Its flowering season seems erratic, and we have had flowers in March, August, and October.

Hexadesmia dunstervillei

This endemic Venezuelan orchid comes from very near to Caracas, and has been selected as an example of how *un*intensively most tropical forests have yet been explored, even when easily accessible. This is largely due to the great difficulty of achieving thorough exploration in such forests where the dense foliage hides far more plants from a searcher than he ever manages to see. From accompanying our botanical friend, Julian Steyermark, on a number of plant-hunting expeditions, we have gained the impression that so little are Venezuela's forests yet known that if you enter them and pick at random 200 different plants in flower (which with keen eyesight would not take you terribly long) you are likely to have found at least one new species in some family or other, and as about 10% of all the species you pick will probably be in the orchid family, the chances of a frequent visitor to the forests finding a number of new orchid species is quite reasonably high, a fact that experience has borne out. Nevertheless, there is something very special about one's very first, new species discovery, and finding the species illustrated here, almost 20 years ago, gave an enormous boost to our then neophytic, indeed larval enthusiasm for orchid hunting when Dr. L. A. Garay declared it "new" and kindly named it *Hexadesmia dunstervillei*. The plant was found on a large, fallen tree in the fine forest area of Guatopo (now a National Park) within very easy reach of Caracas, and while it still seems strange that the species had not been discovered much earlier it is true that, despite our many visits to this forest, we have found no more specimens and it really does seem to be a distinct rarity in this accessible zone. On the other hand, we have subsequently found other plants of this species, in at least mild abundance, in the Guyana region very far away from its original discovery site. Here again, the proximity of this location to Guyana puts the endemicity of this orchid in danger, though we can say that a fairly thorough search (insofar as any such search can ever be thorough) of the immediately adjoining Guyanese territory did not reveal its presence there.

Apart from its fairly large (for the genus) and attractive flower, the plants themselves are easily distinguished by their pretty leaves of glossy green with small, transverse, purplish flecks. The narrow, dark, almost cylindric pseudobulbs are strongly stipitate, i.e., have long thin stems, and the plants often proliferate by developing new stems from the base of an existing leaf. The altitude at which this species grows varies from about 1,500 feet in the site near Caracas to about 4,000 feet maximum in the Guyana zone. Grown in small pots, the original Guatopo plant failed to survive more than a few years, but the later Guyana ones are thriving happily in airy shade and have suffered only when our absence from home has meant a deficiency in more or less regular daily sprinkling in dry weather.

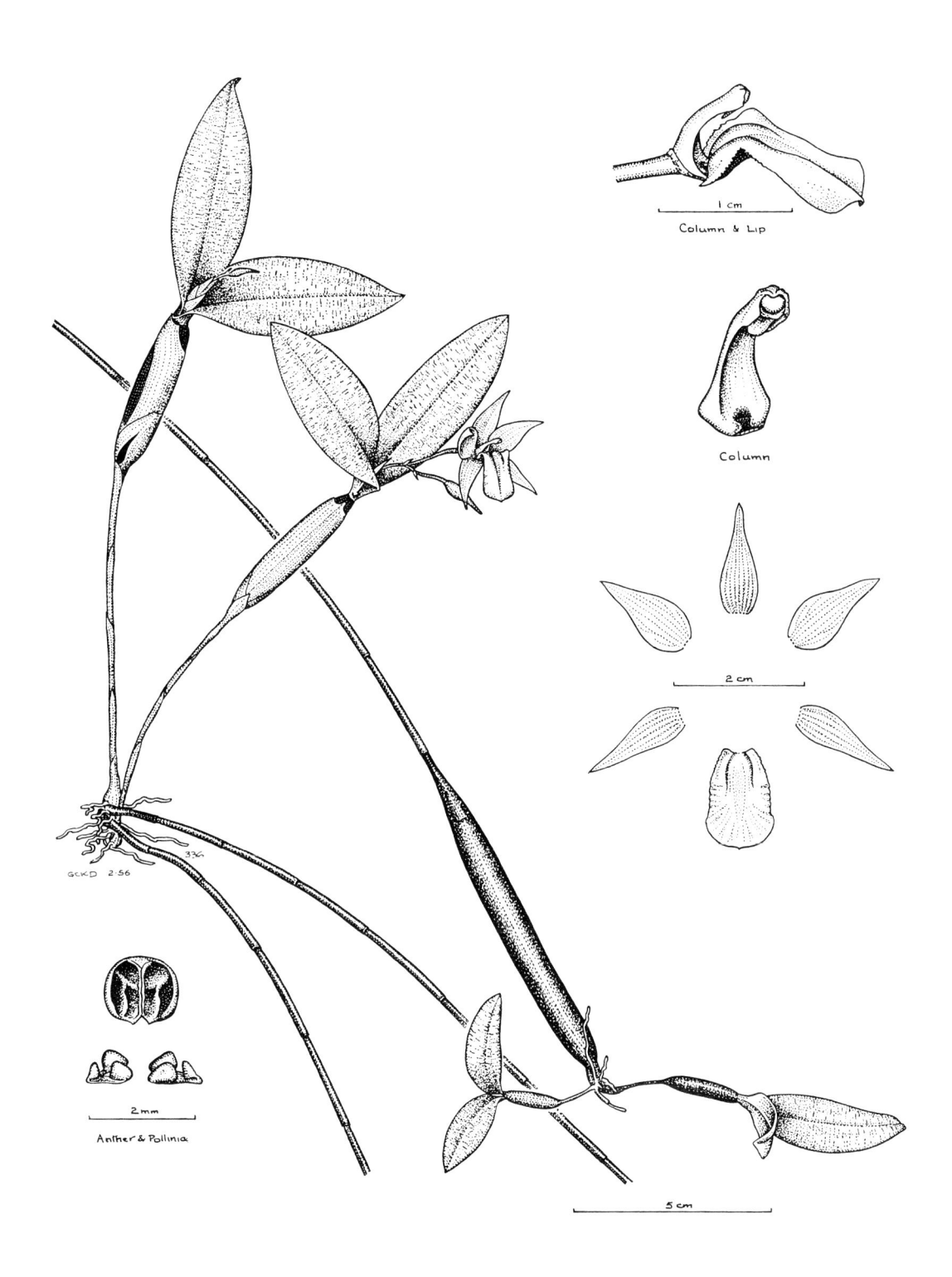

Hexadesmia dunstervillei Garay in Bot. Mus. Leafl. 18: 203, 1958. — B.E.

Octomeria steyermarkii[1]

WITHOUT DRAWING ON the world of truly weird orchid flowers, of which there are many, there are still lots of species with flowers odd enough to draw cries of surprise or even ugh! from those who have not seen them before. *Pleurothallis reymondii,* for exam- looks just like a dangerous insect daring you to touch it. Another species with possibly ugh-making flowers is *Octomeria steyermarkii,* the subject of this short note. The genus *Octomeria* is fairly large, with species that might be described as "pleuro- thallises whose petals and sepals are almost equal in size and shape and which have eight instead of the regulation two pollinia." All these octomerias are attractive, even if not overly exciting, because of the more or less standardized form of their flowers, but *Octomeria steyermarkii* is a remark- able exception to this generalization. It is one of our favorite miniature orchids, but in this we may be a bit exceptional in that we quite like spiders, or at least do not flee from them in horror. However, we fully admit that others might indeed be repelled by the resemblance of the flowers of this species to five-legged spiders with inordinately long and thin legs — not the sort of thing an average person would be overjoyed to find creeping up the back of his or her neck.

This species has several things to recommend it that place it high on our list of favorites among our miniature species, quite apart from its oddness.

Firstly, it is an orchid that, when we found it, turned out to be a new species. This is seldom the sort of event that enables one immediately to cry "Eureka!" and frequently it is only after a lapse of months or even years that a qualified taxonomist publishes it as "new." In the case of this particular orchid, while we were "sure as sure can be" that nobody had even (at least consciously) seen it before, we could not feel legally entitled to a trium- phant dance even if the steep terrain would have allowed it. But early or late, it is nice to be able to count yet another new species to one's credit.

Secondly, this orchid is also "ours" to the extent that it is endemic to a very small area of the Venezuelan Guayana and a tiny bit of Guyana that adjoins it, and very few people will have seen it in its native haunt. It must be admitted, of course, that claims for endemicity are at no time more than statements that the plant in question, be it orchid or anything else, has not yet been found elsewhere, and, in the case of *O. steyermarkii*, it would not surprise us to find plants turning up some day very far away from Venezuela because similar and equally suitable montane cloud forest conditions must be present over a quite large proportion of tropical South America.

Thirdly, with Dr. Garay's kind agreement, this orchid appeared eventually in *Venezuelan Orchids Illustrated* (Volume 3), named for our "favoritest" company on botanical field trips into very out-of-the-way corners of this country, namely Dr. Julian Steyermark, Venezuela's most outstanding field botanist, whose reputation is worldwide. It was a great pleasure to be able to add yet another "steyermarkii" to the list of hundreds of such "steyermarkii" species that already exist in many and varied plant families and genera.

And fourthly, *Octomeria steyermarkii* is a species that has shown itself quite remarkably will- ing to adapt itself to our particular climate outside Caracas, which, on an open slope at about 4,000 feet, is in many ways quite different to the heavily shaded, still-air conditions of the orchid's natural home at 3,500 feet. Adaptability is by no means al- ways a feature of small orchids, and we (and we hope Julian) are in its debt for its willingness to ac- cept the new home we have been giving it for these past 14 years.

Where we first found this species was on the steep-sided, densely forested west flank of the

---

[1] Originally appeared in *A.O.S. Bulletin,* Vol. 47, April 1978, pages 312-314

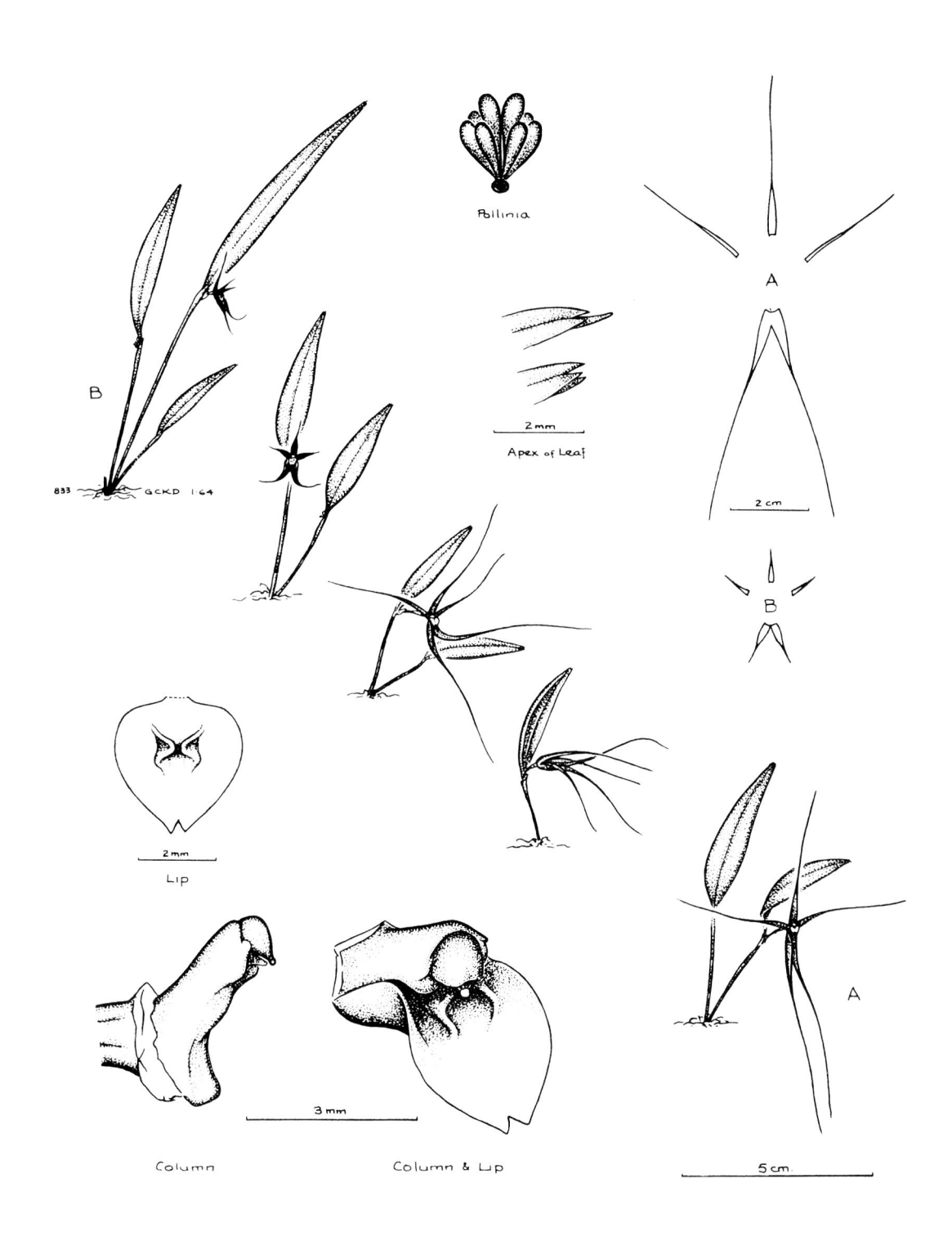

Octomeria steyermarkii Garay & Dunsterv., Venez. Orch. Ill. 3: 204, 1965. — E.

valley of the small Venamo River that forms the boundary with Guyana for some distance along Venezuela's easternmost margin, about 320 kilometers (200 miles) south of the mouth of the Orinoco. This small boundary river has its source on the northern edge of the beautiful Gran Sabana section of southeast Venezuela and flows north until it joins the large Cuyuní River which, in its turn, continues as the boundary until it crosses the border and becomes a 100% Guyanan stream. Working our way down to the Venamo River (along with Julian, of course) we found ourselves frequently clutching for support at the trunks of not-large trees. Although not as exaggerated as in some higher-level "mossy cloud forests" that we know, where an apparently six-inch thick trunk can turn out to be no more than an inch when stripped of its covering of moss, the trunks of these trees were nevertheless well equipped with a very thick coat of moss, and we suddenly noticed the tips of a couple of "pleurothallis-type" leaves peeping out through this coating, at eye level, on one of the trees. We looked for more, found more, and finally found a plant in flower that was not so deeply buried. Since then we have found this species to be not uncommon but within a strictly limited area that includes at least a small encroachment into Guyana itself. Some of these nearby localities bearing plants of this species had less tall forest where the trees were not so mossy, but in this original site the thick covering of moss appeared to act, not as an additive to the dampness, but as a protection against it for the orchids: after stripping away this mossy covering to extract the small orchid plants largely hidden in its depths we noticed that the inside of this moss, up against the bark of the tree, was often definitely on the dry side. Thus, while the moss itself obviously favors a very damp ambience, it serves to shed water and provides the orchid with a microclimate that, if scientifically analyzed, would surely prove to be very different indeed from the general surroundings. Our own plants, that so kindly thrive with us, grow moss-less in small pots tightly filled with chopped-up, rather hard, tree-fern root, well ventilated and well drained, where they get shade and no direct sunshine.

Normally this species grows fairly low on the trunks of small trees, in relatively solitary, caespitose clumps of only a few leaves. The leaves (with their secondary stems) vary from suberect to arcuate and occasionally subpendent attitudes. The leaves themselves are dull-surfaced and quite variable from a slim 6 × 0.6 cm size, to shorter, wider (1 cm) forms, but all are fairly thick and rigid. The slender secondary stems are up to 4.5 cm long. The flowers are normally white or pink, but occasionally dark wine, and tend to hide themselves rather shyly under the overhang of the leaf. They make no claim to beauty, being content to leave their fame to their oddness. The largest flower we have yet measured had a dorsal sepal 35 mm long and lateral sepals 50 mm, giving the flower a diameter of around 75 mm (3 inches) which is quite large enough for a "miniature" species! It is interesting to note, however, that some plants produce flowers that are vastly smaller in length of sepals and petals, though the insignificant lips remain about the same size as in the larger flowers. As these very small-flowered varieties are usually the dark-colored ones and grow in among the paler, larger ones, the initial impression is that one is dealing with an entirely different species, but study of the lips shows them all to be a single species. One plant of the small-flowered type (though with pale coloring) was also very exceptional in that, instead of having only three or four leaves, it was a clump of not less than 60 very narrow (40 × 4 mm) leaves.

Some Venezuelan 'Monospecific' Genera — II[1]

IN JULY, 1976, on pages 606-610 of the *A.O.S. Bulletin*, we published the first section of this article on the "monospecific" genera of Venezuela, hoping readers would be intrigued by these lovely species whose claim to our made-up term of "monospecific" lies in their being, as far as we can tell, the only representatives of their genus in Venezuela. More than 50 such monospecifics exist and we hope that readers, if not exactly startled by their beauty, will at least appreciate the charm of those few pictured here.

Chysis

The pronunciation of orchid names has always presented problems, and the A.O.S., in publishing the *Orchidist's Glossary* has made a noble effort to help a large part of the orchid community in this difficulty. Unfortunately, and inevitably, it cannot provide a final and universally "correct" solution because there is no such thing as a correct way, and what one wants to know is what is the customary way to pronounce these names, and what is customary depends on where you are — it is as unwelcome in English to say "Don Kee*ho*tay" or "Trafal*gar*" as it is in Spain to say "Don *Quick*sote" or "Tra*fal*gar." Even when personal names are involved, attention is by no means always paid to how the original persons concerned pronounced their names. Josef Warscewicz, a Polish friend tells me, would have spelled his name Wars*z*ewich and pronounced it Var-*shay*-vich, but finds his orchid progeny in many places (including the A.O.S. *Glossary*) coming out as War-se-wik-zella, which apart from turning the V sounds into W sounds, commits the impossible crime of splitting the cz into two, like splitting the P from the s in Psyche, or pronouncing Hughes *Hew-jes*. But in the United States the right way, i.e., the accepted customary way, to pronounce this orchid genus is the way the *Glossary* puts it. Custom overrides logic.

But even when one has trained oneself to be ready for any kind of pronounciation in such a polyglot country as Venezuela, and takes Wa-*hen*nery in one's stride as a pronunciation of *Wageneri,* there are unthinking moments when one can get caught out. One of these moments was when we were on an orchid hunt with a friend, and in the process Nora (the "E.D." of our matrimonial orchid team) found a clutch of plants of *Chysis aurea,* some of which she collected. In line with the A.O.S. *Glossary,* we call this genus *Kye-siss,* but have become accustomed to the local *Cheese-is*, since few people here realize that the ch in such words is hard. But when the friend sidled up to the male half of the team in a confidential manner on the way home, to ask *sotto voce* if there would be any objection to his asking Nora for some of her "kisses" it took more than a double take before the required permission was given with pleasure.

Chysis is a two-species genus of which *C. aurea* has a range from Mexico to Peru and Venezuela. In Venezuela it seems to be decidedly on the rare side, and we have met it only once (on the above-mentioned occasion) when we found it in the fine Guatopo forest not far from Caracas at about 2,500-feet elevation. The plants we found were growing in typical fashion for this species, namely subpendent, fusiform, branching pseudobulbs hanging from the side of the trunk of a forest tree. The pseudobulbs are leafy in their terminal sections, their racemes of up to a dozen two-inch, fleshy flowers originating near the end of the pseudobulbs. As to how to grow these plants, we fear we have no advice to give as our own efforts have not been successful.

Cyrtidium

Cyrtidium is a four-species genus of Colombian, Ecuadorean, and Venezuelan orchids that has been the subject of a most useful and well-illustrated

---

[1] Originally appeared in *A.O.S. Bulletin*, Vol. 47, May 1978, pages 438-442

analysis by Garay, published in *Orquideología* in April 1969. Venezuela's sole representative in this genus is *Cyrtidium rhomboglossum,* a species that was discovered in Colombia in 1899 but remained unknown in Venezuela until, on a trip with Julian Steyermark to the border state of Táchira in 1968, we found some plants growing on coffee shade trees in hilly country at about 5,800 feet. Not long after this discovery, another friend, Carlos García, brought us a "strange orchid" that he had picked up much farther east in Trujillo State and which proved to be another specimen of *Cyrtidium rhomboglossum.* Quite recently, Julian has found another specimen in Lara State yet farther east, so this curious species is now firmly on the records as one of Venezuela's Andean orchids.

Our guess on first seeing this (then flowerless) plant was that it must be one of those maxillarias that start with a clump of pseudobulbs and then send out long stems that develop leaves and flowers near the end, but as soon as the first flowers appeared we saw that we had found something much more interesting. These flowers arise on short peduncles from the axils of the leaves quite some distance short of the apex of the branching stems (actually rhizomes) and not a few flowers appeared from old sheaths quite low on the leafless part of the stem until the whole stem developed a continuous series of flowers over a period of two or three months. The most interesting part of the flower, apart from its rather unusual shape, is the rather flat but fleshy lip. The upper surface of this, while not brilliant, is furnished with a sheeny coat of brown and maroon hairs that produce a pattern and texture very reminiscent of certain finely hairy bees or flies, and one supposes that this is in fact meant to attract some such insect for fertilization.

In cultivation it has proved reluctant to take proper hold, and, although to our eye the position we have allocated it on one of our trees is very like where it came from, to the orchid's eye it must be very different; and if we do not soon find out what is wrong, we shall end up without a plant.

Diothonaea

Diothonaea is a genus very closely related to *Epidendrum,* so closely that it is one of those genera, like *Encyclia,* that are recognized by some authorities and not by others. In the *Encyclia/Epidendrum* case, this has the unfortunate result that a number of fairly common plants are known to some by one name and to others by another name. Luckily the genus *Diothonaea* is a very small (in Venezuela just one representative) and the species are not often encountered, so the confusion is not important. The distinction between *Diothonaea* and *Epidendrum* is basically that the column of the former has fairly well-pronounced margins which in their basal part join with the margin of the lip to produce a sort of hollow space. This structure is nicely described by the name Hooker chose for this genus when he established it in 1884. Quoting from *Generic Names of Orchids,* by Schultes and Pease, *Diothonaea* derives from Greek words meaning "two-fold" and "sail," alluding to "the two membranes stretched from the column to the lip like jibs from the foremast and the bowsprit of a ship."

The Venezuelan species, *Diothonaea megalospatha,* was originally described as an *Epidendrum* by Reichenbach in 1877, but was transferred to *Diothonaea* when it was included in *Venezuelan Orchids Illustrated* in 1965. It is an epiphytic inhabitant of Colombia and Ecuador and of a number of localities in the Venezuelan Andes, where it has a vertical range from around 5,000 feet to as high as almost 9,000 feet. Its general habit is in the form of subpendent, occasionally branching, leafy stems to about a foot long, the stems being clothed for most or all of their length in persistent, fleshy, flatly spread, distichous leaves and bearing a short terminal, few-flowered raceme with flowers about an inch in size. The color is somewhat variable, the most attractive type having green sepals and petals that serve nicely to set off the purple-red lip (with a spot of yellow at the base) which is the dominant feature of the flower.

All the plants we have found have been in more or less cloud-forest conditions and have shown considerable dislike of our best efforts to keep them happy in our drier surroundings at 4,000 feet, to the extent that we have long since given up collecting any plants that are not in any case "condemned" by being on a fallen tree or branch.

Lueddemannia

In recent years we have given up exhibiting species orchids at local shows or accepting invitations to help with species judging. This is because experience at earlier shows revealed the degree to which enthusiastic but unscrupulous *aficionados,* scorning rules requiring plants to be well-established, were obviously combing the countryside for immediately showable plants and in the process doing the countryside no good. It is not feasible for judges to tear a prettily exhibited plant apart to judge how long it had been in captivity and prizes would frequently go to individuals where only Nature should have been so honored. In other words, the lust for prizes was proving a damaging incentive and we want no part in any exhibition in any way encouraging this, however innocent the motives behind the prize-giving. However, while this is our present attitude, there was a time when we enjoyed showing a species plant or two; and, when a "sort of acineta" of ours, collected some

Sievekingia jenmanii

Cyrtidium rhomboglossum

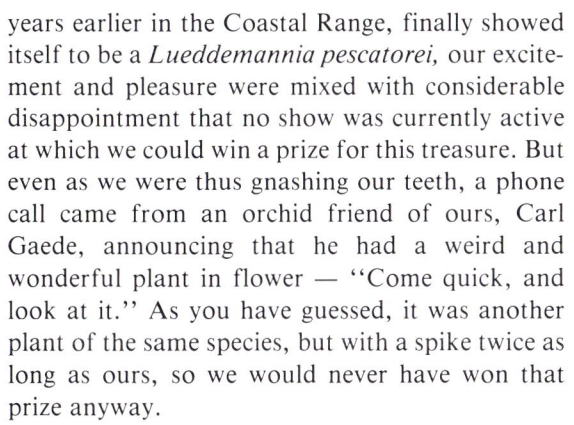

years earlier in the Coastal Range, finally showed itself to be a *Lueddemannia pescatorei,* our excitement and pleasure were mixed with considerable disappointment that no show was currently active at which we could win a prize for this treasure. But even as we were thus gnashing our teeth, a phone call came from an orchid friend of ours, Carl Gaede, announcing that he had a weird and wonderful plant in flower — ''Come quick, and look at it.'' As you have guessed, it was another plant of the same species, but with a spike twice as long as ours, so we would never have won that prize anyway.

This coincidence is made doubly remarkable by the fact that the species had never been recorded before for Venezuela and the plants, although both from the Coastal Range, had been found a very considerable distance apart. The rarity of the species in this country was emphasized when the publication of the official *Orchid Flora* in 1970 showed these two specimens still to be the only recorded plants, but since then another plant has been unearthed (or rather, de-treed) by Roberto Mejía C., an indefatigable orchid hunter living in the western Andes of Táchira State where he came across his plant. Perhaps it is more common in Colombia, Ecuador, or Peru, where it also exists, but one feels that only a high degree of true rarity in Venezuela can have kept it hidden so long and so well.

The fully pendent, *Acineta*-type spike is up to two feet long, all but the fairly short peduncle bearing brightly colored, one-inch, fleshy flowers. Coming from 4,000- to 5,000-feet altitude we were optimistic that our plant would do well in our 4,000-foot high home where *Acineta* plants thrive, but, alas, our one-and-only plant did not like our *Acineta*-type treatment and did not survive very long. Such an early death for such a rare plant is a tragedy, but we are at least somewhat comforted by the fact that we found the plant on a large fallen tree (high in a live tree and without flowers we would not have seen it, or have said ''just another acineta'' if we had), so even in its natural habitat this particular plant would not have survived any longer, nor have been able effectively to produce and disperse any seed.

Sievekingia

Sievekingia jenmanii is Venezuela's only species in this small genus, and as far as we know the only Venezuelan specimen on record is the plant we found growing very close to the Guyana border

Lueddemannia pescatorei

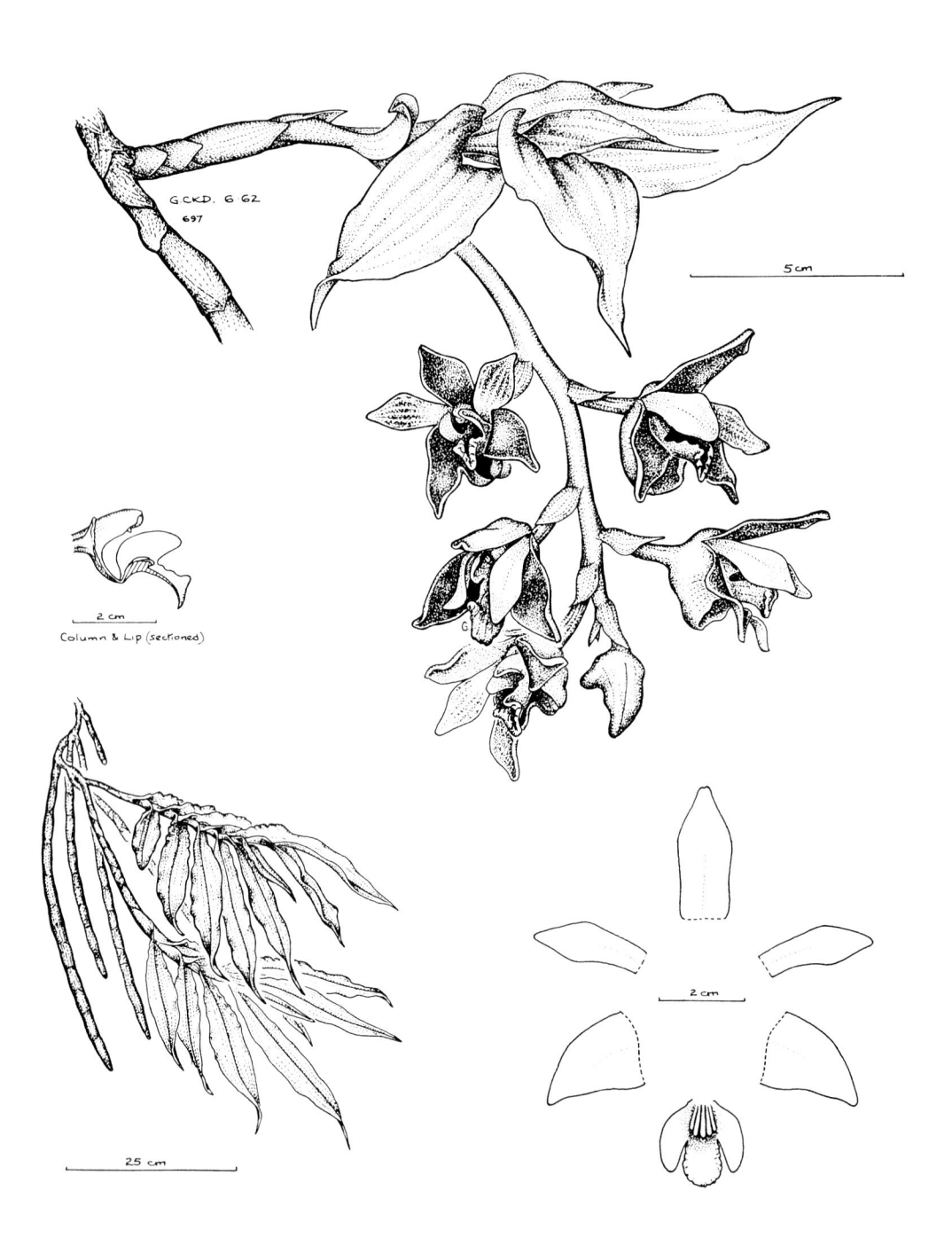

Chysis aurea Lindl. in Bot. Reg. 23:t. 1937, 1837. — B

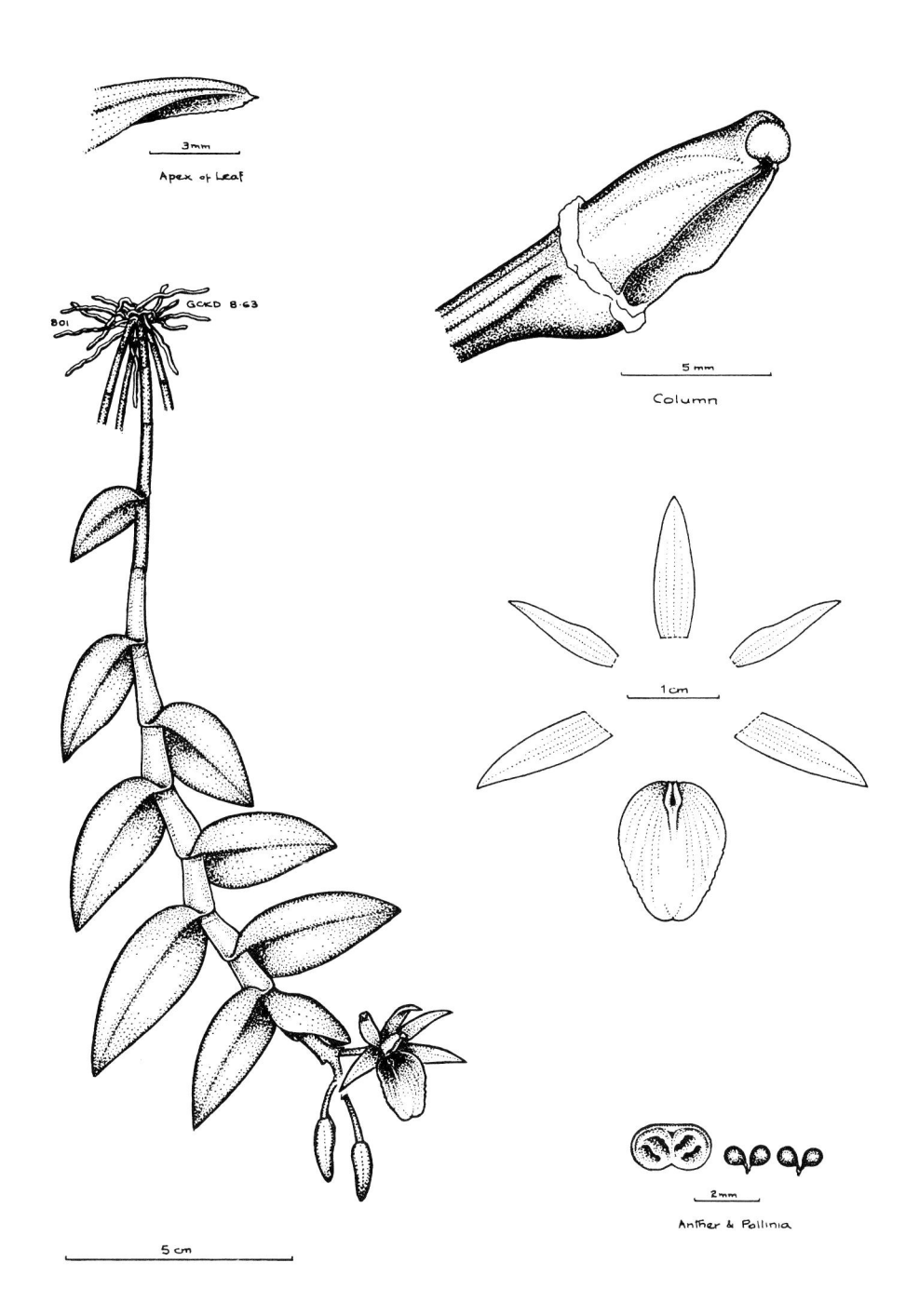

Diothonaea megalospatha (Reichb. f.) Garay & Dunsterv., Venez. Orch. Ill. 3: 74, 1965. — A.

when exploring an area of southeastern Venezuela with our botanical friend, Julian Steyermark, in the Christmas season of 1963. Ever since the early 1950s, spasmodic activity had been pushing a road slowly through fascinating forest and savanna in this region in an effort to connect the isolated community of Sta. Elena de Uairén on the Brazilian border with the main body of Venezuela. By 1963 progress had made little headway beyond about 90 miles south of the penal settlement of El Dorado, but this fine section opened up some splendid virgin forest up to a height of about 4,000 feet, provided one was equipped with four-wheel-drive transport, and for a number of years this road-in-the-making had been a favorite place for us to visit whenever we could afford time for the thousand-mile round trip. At a point on the road that used to be known as Km. 125 (later confusingly altered to Km. 117) there is a small elevation called Cerro Wei that faces the much larger Cerro Venamo whose base is only a mile away but which lies entirely inside Guyana. While we explored both cerros, it was luckily on Cerro Wei at 4,200 feet that we came across the small, flowerless collection of pseudobulbs, growing low on a small tree, that later proved itself to be the plant illustrated here. Had it been found on Cerro Venamo we could not truly claim it as Venezuelan, but it is already known as a Guyanan species so that country need not regret this close miss.

Certain differences between our plant and the recorded form of *Sievekingia jenmanii* encouraged the author of the official *Venezuelan Orchid Flora,* published in 1970, to consider it a new species and name it *S. dunstervilleorum,* but Garay, with a wealth of experience and material to draw on, concluded that it was no more than a variety of *S. jenmanii* so "our" species fell back into what is called "synonymy" — which in no way diminishes our fondness for this very delightful and unusual orchid. This plant, our only one, still grows on a small tree-fern slab in our plastic-lined house where we can more easily maintain humidity during the dry season, but it is now accompanied by a similar-looking plant from another spot in the Venezuelan Guayana which we hope (but scarcely expect) will turn out to be another specimen of the same species.

The flowers of *Sievekingia jenmanii* are characterized by sepals and petals of a very delicate membranaceous, almost transparent texture. While this adds considerably to the luster and attraction of the flowers it unfortunately also means that they are far from robust and need careful handling.

Two and a Half Paphinias of Venezuela[1]

WORDS AND GRAMMAR were invented so that, by combining them intelligently, man (or must we now say "persons"?) could express ideas with clarity. For us, as certainly for many others, isolated words themselves can be a lot of fun if you start delving into their origins. We were brought up in families where a good etymological dictionary (if not the entire *Encyclopedia Britannica*) beside the soup plate was as common a sight on the dining table as the sight of the soup itself slowly congealing while the dictionary was in use. As an example, just look at the exciting soup-congealing time you can have when you look up the word *Paphinia,* which will take you far beyond its strict meaning as a genus of orchids. Schultes and Pease's *Generic Names of Orchids* starts you on your travels by referring you to Paphia, the name of Aphrodite of Cyprus, and that moves you on to "Lemprière's Classical Dictionary" which tells you that Paphos was an ancient city of 1,000 B.C. "where Aphrodite, goddess of beauty, was worshipped and where all male animals were offered on her many altars which daily smoked with the profusion of African incense. The inhabitants were very lascivious and the young virgins were permitted by law to get a dowry by prostitution." This information describes a modern city with all the "modern" conveniences of smoke, stink, and sexual license, and it shows the type of garden path that etymology can lead you down in providing an opening paragraph to an orchid article!

While we cannot really claim true "goddess of beauty" category for our two and a half paphinias,

Paphinia cristata "½"

Habitat of Paphinia "½"
(leaves discernible to immediate left of N. Dunsterville)

[1] Originally appeared in *A.O.S. Bulletin*, Vol. 48, January 1979, pages 33-37

there is no doubting their claims to be eye-catching and attractive. As a genus *Paphinia* is very small, with only a couple of species in addition to the 2½ to be found in Venezuela. In Hawkes's *Encyclopaedia of Cultivated Orchids* it rates as "rare and seldom encountered, occasionally found in particularly choice collections." What a nice compliment that is for our own collection of miscellaneous species from the Venezuelan countryside, and it is so different from the compliments we generally get from non-orchid-species visitors viewing our collection; our plants are admittedly mostly in the florally insignificant class and the normal remark we get is more along the lines of "Good Lord, I thought that was a weed!"

In line with all paphinias except ½, the genus consists of epiphytic plants with characteristically pendulous, racemose inflorescences; the pseudobulbs are fairly small and bear two or three plicate leaves not over 30 cm. long.

Paphinia lindeniana, the first illustrated here, has a range from Venezuela eastward to Guyana and south to Brazil, and in this country seems so far to exist only in the "Amazonas" part of the Upper Orinoco. Even here, in line with its reputation of "seldom encountered," it has so far limited its appearance, so far as we know, to the original type-specimen from an unspecified spot "on the Upper Orinoco" and to three other cases. The first of these was at an elevation of some 100 m at the base of Cerro Yapacana, near the Orinoco not far upstream from the junction of that river with its major tributary, the Río Ventuari. The second locality was at about 600 m on the Río Putacó, a small tributary far up the main stream, fairly close to its source. The third locality was where we found our own plant in light woods on a small island just below the point where the wide, slow-flowing Lower Siapa River (a very "buggy" tributary of the Río Casiquiare which eventually drops its waters into the Amazon basin via the Río Negro) comes to an end in a steep uphill gash through a small range of hills that in its turn leads to the (much less buggy) Upper Siapa. The apparent scarcity of this species indicates that it either occurs very infrequently or at least manages to hide its flowers well from eager collectors. Despite the single record at about 600 m altitude (which after all is scarcely in cool climate) it seems likely that it rates basically as a hot-climate orchid, which may account for its reluctance to stay more than a few years with us at over 1,300 m.

The raceme produced by our specimen held five rather crowded flowers, with an old rachis showing an original number of seven, which we believe may put it in the list of "most floriferous" of the *Paphinia* species. The flowers, true to the genus, are non-resupinate; i.e., they carry the lip above the column instead of the more normal orchid habit with the lip below. The sepals and petals, about five cm long, open wide from a somewhat closed base, and give the flower a natural spread of seven to eight cm. The coloration is white, almost completely overlaid by a very dark wine-red in the petals and somewhat less so in the sepals which thus have strongly contrasted, rather erratic, longitudinal stripes of dark red and white. The upside-down lip is remarkable for its white mid-lobe which bears a tough, erect fringe of long, white hairs; the base of the lip is dark red and the column is light green. The effect of all this is more dramatic or striking than truly beautiful.

Paphinia cristata is our second species illustrated here. The growth habit, both of plant and of inflorescence, is similar to *Paphinia lindeniana* but it seldom has more than three flowers, frequently only one, on its pendulous inflorescence, although it can certainly rate as being beautiful as well as striking. The flowers are rather larger than those of *Paphinia lindeniana,* opening wider, and the basically similar color pattern is a much brighter red. The lip has conspicuous, erect, flat, and pointed lateral lobes that are red, while the equally red mid-lobe has a loose fringe of long, white hairs to serve as a signpost for the bee to home in on his way to the upside-down column. While this is also a rather rare orchid, our impression is that it is much less so than *Paphinia lindeniana,* and that it has a greater vertical range. In such matters it is difficult to be dogmatic as so much depends on what one personally happens to have found or to know about, and so little is known of what really does exist in so many miles and miles of forest. All we can really say is that it covers a wider territory, as our first specimen came from the Coastal Range and our later ones from the State of Bolívar, with the final ½ coming from Amazonas. The coastal specimen was found at about 600 m altitude in the large and heavily-forested National Park of Guatopo where its sister plants enjoy a high degree of protection as this park is adequately maintained and protected; the plants here seem to prefer the margins of small streams to the deeper shade of the forest, or perhaps it would be more correct to say that at the stream edges they are more visible.

Where we have seen more specimens, which is what give us the impression that *Paphinia cristata* is more common, is in the great State of Bolívar, which together with the Amazonas Territory takes in virtually all the country south of the Río Orinoco. In the western extreme of Bolívar State we have seen it growing in the upper section of the Caura River, where a part of its habitat is threatened by plans for a hydroelectric dam at about 200 m altitude, and a long way farther up towards the Brazilian border on the flanks of Cerro Sarisariñama at perhaps 500 m. But it is not an orchid exclusively of low and generally hot country, as we have found it on Cerro Venamo on the Guyana border at some 800 m and in several places in the Gran Sabana region of the eastern corner of the State, including the flanks of Auyántepui at slightly over 1,000 m. In most of these places it grows well protected inside the forest and not necessarily on the edge of streams or rivers.

This brings us finally to the mysterious "Half Paphinia" of the title of this article. It is half a *Paphinia cristata* to the extent that this is presumably the name that the serious taxonomist would give it, but at the same time it is not a *P. cristata* that any self-respecting member of that clan would care to acknowledge. After all, a clan member and all his progeny who spend their lives standing more or less on their heads in a manner never seen before in the world of paphinias must surely rate as only partly paphinia whatever other true paphinia attributes they may have. This is in fact the case with this freak group of plants that we came across, far up the Río Autana. This is a sidestream in a flooded section of the Amazonas forests, not far from the foot of Cerro Autana, forever famous as the provider of the *A.O.S. Bulletin*'s first (and so far only) *National Geographic* cover on the May 1973 issue.

There are times when these forests are transitable and times when they are definitely not so. On this occasion (1969) we seemed to be between seasons and had hopes of reaching a small but intriguing little cerro near the base of Cerro Autana itself. The Indian with us said it was called Cerro Karíwa but we can guarantee no certainty of this, as each Indian you meet in this area is likely to give different names each time you ask. Direct access to this small hill, a kilometer or so back from the river bank, quickly proved impossible either by foot due to excess water or by canoe for its lack. Traveling a few kilometers farther upstream, there were indications of a slight ridge of treadable land leading back towards Karíwa. With an Indian to help, we started off but very shortly lost all sense of direction as the semi-dry ridge wound an intricate way through the forest which blocked the view. The sun was invisible through the dense canopy of leaves above and a compass would have been of no use on such a tortuous track. By virtue of hard work on the part of the Indian (not us) who made frequent ascents of tall palm or similar branchless trees to look around and keep us roughly heading for Karíwa, and returning each night to camp by the river, we made slow but sure progress and on the third day found ourselves at last at the foot of Karíwa. As a change from the expected annoyance of biting insects, we suffered instead from occasional terrifying attacks by a strange species of fly whose ambition is not to bite (nor to burrow into one's hair like the pestiferous but non-stinging "pegon" bees) but to dig itself into every crack and cranny of clothing or body it can find. With a dozen of these pests determined to make a home in one's ears or up one's nostrils, while one's hands are fully occupied with goods and chattels or maintaining balance by grabbing trees or bushes, only the strongest will can avert a panic flight certain to end with feet permanently entangled in roots and face buried deep in mud.

Rising gently up the lowest slopes of Karía and in the process quickly removing us from the flooded part of the forest, the vegetation changed in a short distance to rather low woods on a dry-looking soil made of 99% sand and then higher up (but by only a few meters in actual elevation) to tall forest again. Here there was a large, circular clearing where some forest giant had fallen and rotted away many many years before and this was where we met our extensive colony of freak paphinias. At first we were sure we had found a new species altogether but later concluded that we could only rate it as a half. The flowers of these plants all had the normal paphinia "upside-down" attitude and the pseudobulbs and leaves were also pure paphinia, but instead of being epiphytes with slender, laxly-hanging racemes, they all had strongly erect, quite thick peduncles that under no circumstances would bend over. The flowers, up to five (and with signs of six) to each peduncle, were of the same coloration as the normal *Paphinia cristata,* the red perhaps a bit darker than our normal plants, but lost some attraction by the fact that while their sepals and petals were quite a bit longer (seven cm) they were at the same time narrower than the usual, giving the flowers a rather untidy aspect. In any case, only a worm on the ground could look up into them and appreciate what internal beauty they had. How this colony of freaks, presumably derived from once-happy epiphytic ancestors, had managed to survive and breed sufficiently through enough generations to allow for gene changes adequate to alter it so significantly, is a mystery to which we can see no answer.

The plants we brought back have, not surprisingly, failed in our cool Caracas climate, so different from the hot and humid forest of their native "ambiente," and a plant we sent to a grower in the United States has presumably also died as we have heard no more about it in the intervening years. The last time we touched the foot of Karíwa on a hurried pass-by a few years back, we failed to find the exact spot and may well not try again. While it is most interesting as a plant, it is hardly likely ever to be a horticultural success. The many plants we left there are no doubt still thriving, and we wish them and their future progeny many years of peace, quiet, and solitude.

Paphinia lindeniana

Paphinia cristata

Anguloas of Venezuela[1]

ANGULOA is a small genus of about a dozen species at most, all with cup-shaped or tulip-like flowers, well known because all its members are attractive enough to find a place in orchid catalogs and exhibitions; some have also served in hybridizing. There is still considerable uncertainty as to which are proper species and which are mere varieties, and there are even claims that all could be reduced to only three species: *Anguloa ruckeri, Anguloa clowesii*, and *Anguloa uniflora.* But even this does not clarify matters as *Anguloa ruckeri* and *Anguloa clowesii* are considered to be conspecific by some other taxonomists. The fact is that there is great variety in color in many of them, and no very great differentiation in form so that it is difficult to be very positive in resolving problems of identification. Venezuela has only three recognized species within its borders, these being the above-mentioned *Anguloa ruckeri, A. clowesii*, and *A. uniflora,* and all of these are well worth providing space for in any collection, not only for their impressive appearance but also because, as noted by Veitch almost a hundred years ago, "they are among the most tractable of orchids to cultivate, exacting no extra care or vigilance at the cultivator's hands." How nice it would be if we could say this of all our orchids!

Our first acquisition in this small group was a

Anguloa clowesii

Anguloa ruckeri

[1] Originally appeared in *A.O.S. Bulletin,*
Vol. 48, February 1979, pages 116-120

plant of *Anguloa ruckeri,* which in our early orchid days we foolishly purchased on the roadside near its main center of growth at Caripe in Eastern Venezuela; we later learned that this species was suffering badly from stripping by the local campesinos for sale to visitors to the region, in particular to the locally famous *Guacharo* ("oil-bird") caves. This is exceptionally serious as this species is found in very few other sites in this country, and we have long since learned not only to remain silent about such sites that we do know of but also to do our best to discourage others from buying roadside plants. In this we fear our efforts have little effect as it is easy for a buyer to justify his action when it concerns a plant already taken from its native ground — "If I don't buy it, someone else will" is a difficult argument to counter.

Although *Anguloa ruckeri* has at times been put into synonymy with other *Anguloa* species, it seems at no time to have had more than the name it now bears, which was given to it by Lindley in 1846. It is a robust species with large, clustered pseudobulbs to about 15 cm tall, bearing two or three apical, plicate leaves and one or two smaller, leaf-bearing sheaths around the base. The single flowers (on freak occasions two at a time) are borne on very stout, erect peduncles to some 30 cm tall which develop from the base of the pseudobulb more or less concurrently with the new growth. A considerable number of inflorescences can develop simultaneously from around a single pseudobulb and thus provide quite an impressive display despite the fact that the external coloring of the flowers is a rather unexciting, dull pink or a greenish-brown. In this, the flowers do not do themselves justice as, for reasons best known to themselves but obscure to us, they hide their real glory inside. This was made very evident to us one day when, passing the site where most of these plants are on sale by the roadside, a peasant held up an orchid plant with a magnificent red flower of a form we had never seen before. This brought us to a rapid halt, but when we examined the flower, which was being offered to us as something new and priceless, we realized that the peasant had, with great skill, managed to turn the thick and rigid sepals and petals inside out, so that instead of seeing a rather dull-colored "tulip" we were seeing a highly colored flower with widespread tepals. Opening up these flowers without breaking the sepals takes, as we found out, much skill and patience, but we did eventually succeed in opening out at least the lateral sepals of one of our flowers. As shown in the illustration here, an opened-up flower well merits its name of var. *sanguinea* and could win a prize in any show if only the plant could be trained to do this trick on its own, and even more prized if the dorsal sepal and the petals could be similarly educated. The heavy lip of this species is lightly attached to the column-foot and is delicately balanced in a vertical position. In an artificially opened flower, the lip can fall forward, as in the illustration here, to show its bright red anterior. But in a flower that has not been tampered with, the lip has only a very limited scope for movement and, when tilted gently towards the column, its relatively massive weight could easily, even if only momentarily, trap a large bee sufficiently for the orchid's fertilization purposes. Speaking of fertilization of anguloas reminds me of an embarrassing mistake I made some 10 years ago when I gave the *A.O.S. Bulletin* a short, tongue-in-cheek note describing how I had been surprised, when photographing a "ruckeri" flower, to find that I was taking a portrait of a minute froglet peeping out from inside it. In a careless moment I got my zoology mixed up and referred to this as a possible reptilian fertilizing vector when I should have said batrachian. Many A.O.S. readers, it seemed, knew quite enough about the difference between creepy snakes and jumpy frogs to write and point out the error of my ways, and I have since been careful not to insult our frogs by relating them to snakes. Not that I dislike snakes either, provided the poisonous ones keep out of my way, but frogs are charming and much more *simpático*.

Such reference books as I have are not very clear about whether *Anguloa ruckeri* can be rated as more than just occasionally epiphytic in habit. As we have never found one ourselves, we have no personal guide on this matter, but, while it is in some books referred to as "terrestrial or epiphytic," the consensus of general opinions coming our way seems to be that it is, as with anguloas in general, basically terrestrial. The local campesinos could no doubt give a valid decision but are unlikely to reveal the exact situations where they have found the plants.

Anguloa clowesii is the second species we have in our garden. Our original plant was given us by a friend who may well have bought it in the market of Mérida City in the west of Venezuela where it grows. In full flower with half a dozen scapes it is a most impressive sight and it is surprising that any plants of such an eye-catching species are still left in the wild. Hoping to find a plant ourselves, we had previously described it in emphatic detail to a *campesino* we had met tilling his field far from city streets and markets, stressing the large pseudobulbs and the ball-shaped, bright yellow flowers borne singly on tall upright stems. "Sí, Sí, como no!" he said. He would have a plant for us by the next noon if we passed by. With some difficulty we

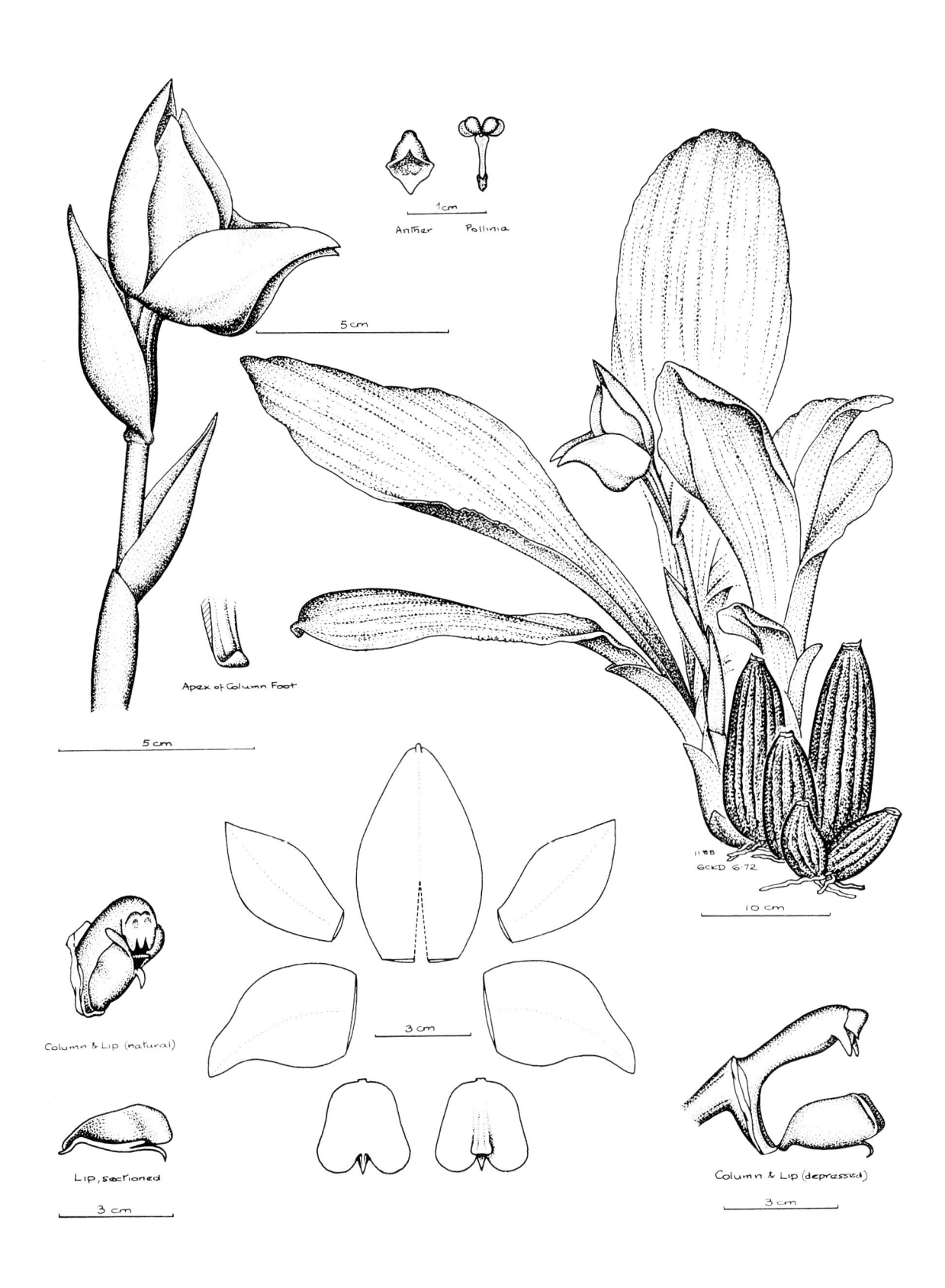

Anguloa uniflora Ruíz & Pav., Syst. Veg. 1:228, 1798. — A

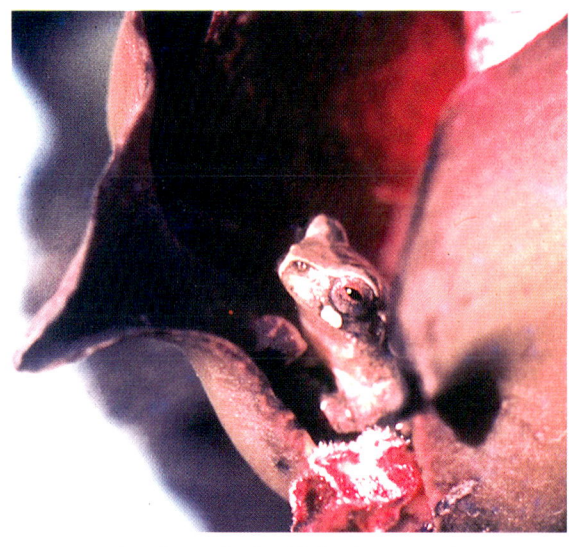

Anguloa ruckeri, with froglet companion

Anguloa ruckeri (spread open flower)

did pass by the next day, and he showed us in triumph a stanhopea in full glory of its many-flowered, pendent inflorescences. Which is not because our Spanish is poor but because the overly polite *campesino* mind works on providing the customer with something to keep him happy, and if it is not a single flower on an erect stem, then clearly more flowers yet on a dangling stem should be equally good! We later found our plants at a much higher altitude than Mérida City, in a place where not many people go, so we have never been tempted to buy a roadside plant and in any case, genuine "home-grown" plants are now available from responsible commercial growers. Where we did find our plants was where they were growing terrestrially at about 2,000 m altitude in the soil of a cleared piece of once-was cloud forest not very far from the Colombian border in the State of Táchira. Here we found them growing in association with some extraordinarily healthy *Acineta* plants with enormous pseudobulbs, plants that were born to be most decidedly epiphytic but which had had no option but to adapt to an unnatural life on the ground when their host trees had all been felled. It could be, of course, that the *Anguloa* plants were also growing in the soil for this same reason and would have preferred to be epiphytic, but we rather doubt this.

The appearance of *Anguloa clowesii* plants is very similar to that of *A. ruckeri* plants (the leaves perhaps generally wider for their length) and the form of the flower differs little, to the extent that some taxonomists have treated the two as synonymous. The striking difference in color, however, reinforces some difference in the finer details of the lip and supports the view that these two are truly distinct species.

Anguloa uniflora is the species on which the genus was founded by Ruíz & Pavón in 1798, and is the third on our present title list of Venezuelan anguloas. It has also been known as *Anguloa eburnea* and *Anguloa turneri,* and even as a variety "eburnea" of *Anguloa clowesii.* It has, however, an appreciably smaller flower than the latter, the extreme "tip" of the lip is completely different, and the color also is distinct, being (in the case of our plants at least) a pure white. If you open up the flower (we hope with the owner's permission) to check on the form of this lip-apex, you can also see that there are tiny, red spots on the inside of the flower. This species does not have the immediate and somewhat blatant attraction of the yellow *Anguloa clowesii* but instead has a quiet purity that is also very attractive. The flowers are less globose in form than those of the former two species, and the lateral sepals project a bit more as if to allow easier access to an even larger type of bee. Scent is understood to be the bee-attracting element in this genus, and the insects are unlikely to be dismayed by this scent being referred to in the *Orchid Journal* of February 1953 as "rather objectionably candy-scented." It was a very pleasant surprise when we came upon our first plants of this species in exactly the same spot where we had found our plants of *Anguloa clowesii,* and the same remarks about the doubtful possibility of their having been epiphytes apply.

As already mentioned, anguloas are easy to grow, and in our intermediate climate our plants need no more than well-drained pots filled with home-made compost and placed in open light (but not direct sun), the pots being moved to a more shaded place and given some (but only occasional) watering during the dry season.

Cattleya jenmanii — Late to the Party, Early to Leave?[1]

VENEZUELA was for long well known as the home of five fine unifoliate cattleyas of the "labiata" group, *Cattleya gaskelliana, C. lawrenceana, C. lueddemanniana, C. mossiae*, and *C. percivaliana,* so it was a surprise when, some 15 years ago or more, a "new" cattleya was rumored to exist in a far corner of the beautiful Gran Sabana section of Bolívar State, near the small town of Santa Elena de Uairén, about 4° north of the equator and right on the Brazilian border. The Gran Sabana is a broad expanse of gently rolling country, sloping from about 1,400 m altitude in its northern extreme to about 500 m in the south, a distance of nearly 200 km overall, and is the home of the justly famous enormous sandstone table mountains variously known as cerros or as tepuis, or as in the case of the small but most famous one of all, just "Roraima."

When these rumors of a new cattleya first began to be heard, there was no road link with Santa Elena, only a scheduled flight once or twice a week and occasional flights by small private planes. A road, beginning in the north at El Dorado, had been started in about 1958 and, as it slowly ate its way south through initially splendid forest in the headwater region of the Cuyuní River, it became for us an enchanted and favorite place to visit for camping and for orchids. Progress on the road was very slow, partly because of "political" holdups and partly because of the very difficult terrain in the first section, climbing from 100 m to the Gran Sabana at 1,400 m. Even then progress continued slowly because of the poor (90% sand) type of terrain in the Sabana itself and the many streams and rivers that had to be crossed. The new cattleya, if indeed it was not an interloper illegally straying onto Venezuelan soil from Brazil, thus arrived very hesitantly at the "party," and all sorts of questions were raised as to the identity of this visitor, so like, yet not so like, *Cattleya labiata* from Brazil. Once it became certain that it was truly indigenous, the problem of its identity became more important, until finally, in about 1970, it was pinned down by Garay as *C. jenmanii,* a little-known species native to Guyana. But the problems of road access remained as a defense for this newcomer against eager hands anxious to welcome it. The road was by now close to completion but it was not yet a journey to be undertaken lightly. There was no gasoline available anywhere along the 300 km stretch from El Dorado to Santa Elena. At the El Dorado end only the poorest quality was available, if at all, and at Santa Elena, if and when it was available, it was also bottom quality, five times the normal price and out of drums containing almost as much water as gasoline. When we went that way, we always traveled with half a dozen jerricans of extra gasoline and two spare wheels; on one trip we had four flats and lost not only the exhaust pipe and silencer but also the connecting pipe to the exhaust manifold, completing the ride to Caracas making a noise like all the sons of Beelzebub and risking immediate arrest at every town or village we passed.

As the road improved, more visitors went that way, but only the hardier ones persisted until finally, by the end of 1973, no real obstacle remained except one ferry of irregular performance and one utterly terrifying pontoon bridge across the Kukenán River. The first section of this bridge was missing, or more correctly was anchored 50 yards away as if refusing to join the other floating sections because of a fit of the sulks. So we started in our aged Willys station wagon with an initial diving act into water of unknown depth and then had to climb onto the remaining part which was so flexible and unfloating that we could only progress by dint of creating a bow-wave of pontoon sections ahead of us. During our crossing we were urged on by shouts of encouragement from truck drivers waiting, we thought, for their turn, foremost among them being one

[1] Originally appeared in *A.O.S. Bulletin,* Vol. 48, June 1979, pages 593-597

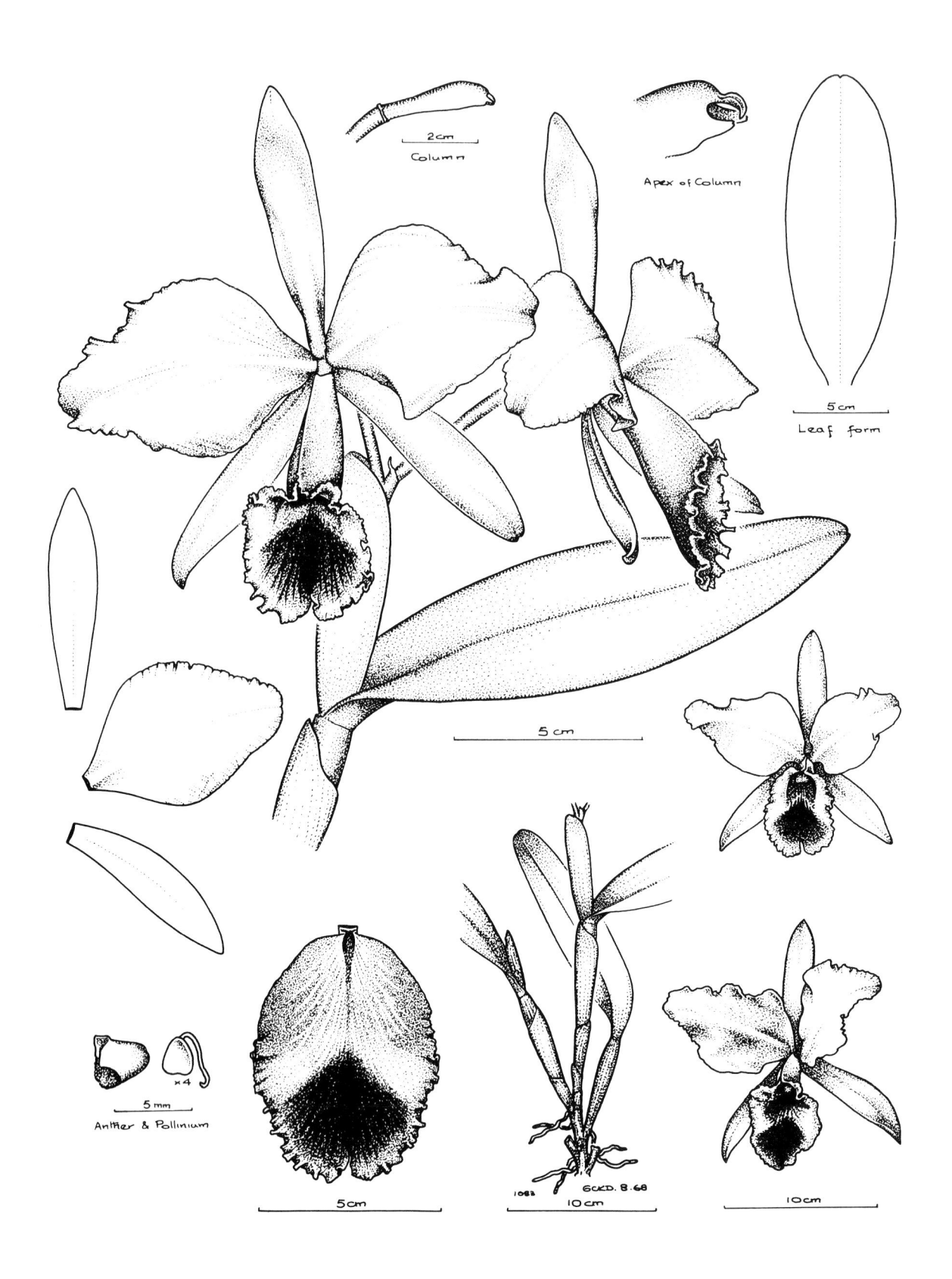

Cattleya jenmanii Rolfe in Kew Bull. 85, 1906. — E.

Cattleya jenmanii 'Bergold'

whose T-shirt was proudly emblazoned with the words "Sex Instructor." When no trucks prepared to follow us, we asked the sexman why. "We," he said, "are waiting for the river level to drop so the pontoons will rest on bottom!"

Finally the road was through and was officially opened with joint ribbon-cutting by the Presidents of Venezuela and Brazil, and the orchids were not at the mercy of all and sundry. For the next three years or so, hotel accommodation in Santa Elena remained limited to a couple of not exactly sanitary places, with rooms that had only head-high partitions between them, no lockable doors and no toilets (or what are here politely called *baños*) other than small cubicles well away from the rooms. Trade was now starting to boom, with truckloads of timber heading north from Boa Vista in Brazil and tankerloads of gasoline heading south to Boa Vista from Venezuela, with Santa Elena itself bursting at the seams with visitors and travelers from both countries. In late 1976 a fine new hotel was born, with clean rooms-with-bath and a tolerable dining room. But by then it was already well known that the new orchids were coming principally from an Indian group settled by the Government just west of the town (and outside the limits of the vast Gran Sabana National Park), where the Indians had been clearing forest for their cultivations and had soon found that they had a remarkable product growing on the trees they were felling — and on others yet to be felled. Fortunately for them but less fortunately for the orchids, the new hotel thought it would be a fine idea to celebrate its opening with a grand display of *Cattleya jenmanii* plants, which the Indians supplied by the truckload. These were planted in earth in the many large, concrete plant-coffins artistically lining the large patios, and draped up all the many columns supporting the roof. A year later all had gone; dead, stolen or otherwise disposed of, a tragic start for a fine species "new" to Venezuela. Many more plants, of course, have left this area besides those used for the hotel, and many more plants must surely remain in hiding in the locality, but, with apparently no control being exercised, the future for *C. jenmanii* in this corner of the Gran Sabana does not look overly bright. Easy come, easy go! One small bright spot remains; among my photos taken when *C. jenmanii* was just starting to appear on the scene is one of a plant reputed to have come from another part of Bolívar State quite some distance away, namely the Río Caura. Whereabouts on the Caura it was collected I have no information but, if it really did come from there, then there is every reason to hope that this other colony is still safe. And in any case, a good number of plants from Santa Elena must have found their way into experienced commercial hands and with luck are being propagated. Like all of the "labiata" group, this species shows the expectable wide variation between poor and good specimens, with wide variation also in matters of color and form, so there should be a good pool of genes for hybrid experimentation.

The climate around Santa Elena is typical for the southern end of the Gran Sabana at about 800 m elevation and the scenery is one of patches of forest dotting otherwise open, grassy savanna based on a sandy soil that is of poor value for intensive cultivation or cattle raising. There is the usual dry season from December to June and wet season from July to November, both quite variable in duration and in intensity. We are growing our plants on the usual suspended slabs of tree-fern in about 60% shade and with plenty of fresh air (but no nasty winds) and they are doing well, with flowering times mainly around July but also anywhere from then on to November.

Some Venezuelan Elleanthus Species[1]

PLANT NAMES TEND TO BE DULL when based on the botanical characters of the plant or the names of persons associated with the plants but, when ancient Greek history or mythology is involved in the names, as in the case of *Paphinia* (See Chapter 27) or *Elleanthus* as in the present note, things can liven up immensely. Greek mythology is full of thoroughly immoral and unscrupulous people (perhaps reflecting on the character of the Greeks themselves in those days?) and their ability to wave magic wands around to get others into trouble or themselves out of it seems to have kept all of them permanently in a wildly exciting state of flux. The generic name *Elleanthus* owes its origin to Helle, daughter of Athemas, King of Thebes. When Athemas got tired of Helle's mother Nephele, because she was going crazy (he said), he married again, but the new wife Ino grew envious that Helle and her brother would still have priority over her own children, so she planned to have Nephele's brood eliminated. Nephele heard about this and arranged with Neptune for a golden ram (no cheap ordinary rams for ex-wives of kings) to carry the children away to safety through the air, golden rams in those days being equipped with whatever was needed to make flight easy. This particular ram, besides being golden, was a very special one-off job that had resulted from Neptune having at some earlier date changed his financée Theopane into a sheep to protect her from lascivious suitors and then going to bed with her himself. Unfortunately, Neptune, in producing the ram, had forgotten to fit it with seat belts, so Helle fell off into the sea at a spot that later became called the Hellespont, and, as the Hellespont does actually exist, you can be quite sure this tale is true, however complicated it may seem! Subsequent to this sad event, the Goddess Juno got into the act and in revenge arranged for Athemas to become so mad at Ino that he thought she was a lioness and killed one of her sons as he didn't like baby lions. So she ran away and jumped off a high rock to become a sea deity called Leucothoe. Whatever else it was, life among the elite in those days was never dull, and apparently never very safe either, but if it hadn't been for Helle we would never have had any nice *Elleanthus* species to adorn our collections!

The genus *Elleanthus* covers some 70 species spread throughout the New World tropics and is represented in Venezuela by almost 20 species. Hawkes's *Encyclopaedia of Cultivated Orchids* lists the genus as "primarily epiphytic, rarely terrestrial" but, in our experience, about four or five of the Venezuelan species seem equally happy with either way of life and of the remainder twice as many show a decided preference for the terrestrial mode of existence as those that vote for the opposition. The latter, with their predilection for life in the trees, naturally tend to be among the smaller species while the larger ones prefer the ground, and very large plants, such as those six feet tall, would indeed look out of place as epiphytes. However, and speaking very broadly, one gets the impression that the genus as a whole maintains a very open mind about where to make its home.

The plants are characterized by having generally (but not always) erect stems that bear plicate leaves in at least the apical portion, and in this respect are often very difficult to distinguish from *Sobralia* plants when no inflorescence is yet visible. But once this appears the difference between the two genera becomes easily apparent as the *Sobralia* produces relatively few (or even single) large flowers while the *Elleanthus* has many-flowered racemes of very small flowers. Horticulturally there is no doubt that, despite the ephemeral nature of their flowers, sobralias are much the more desirable, but *Elleanthus* species have the advantage of considerably longer flower life and

[1] Originally appeared in *A.O.S. Bulletin*, Vol. 48, July 1979, pages 665-671

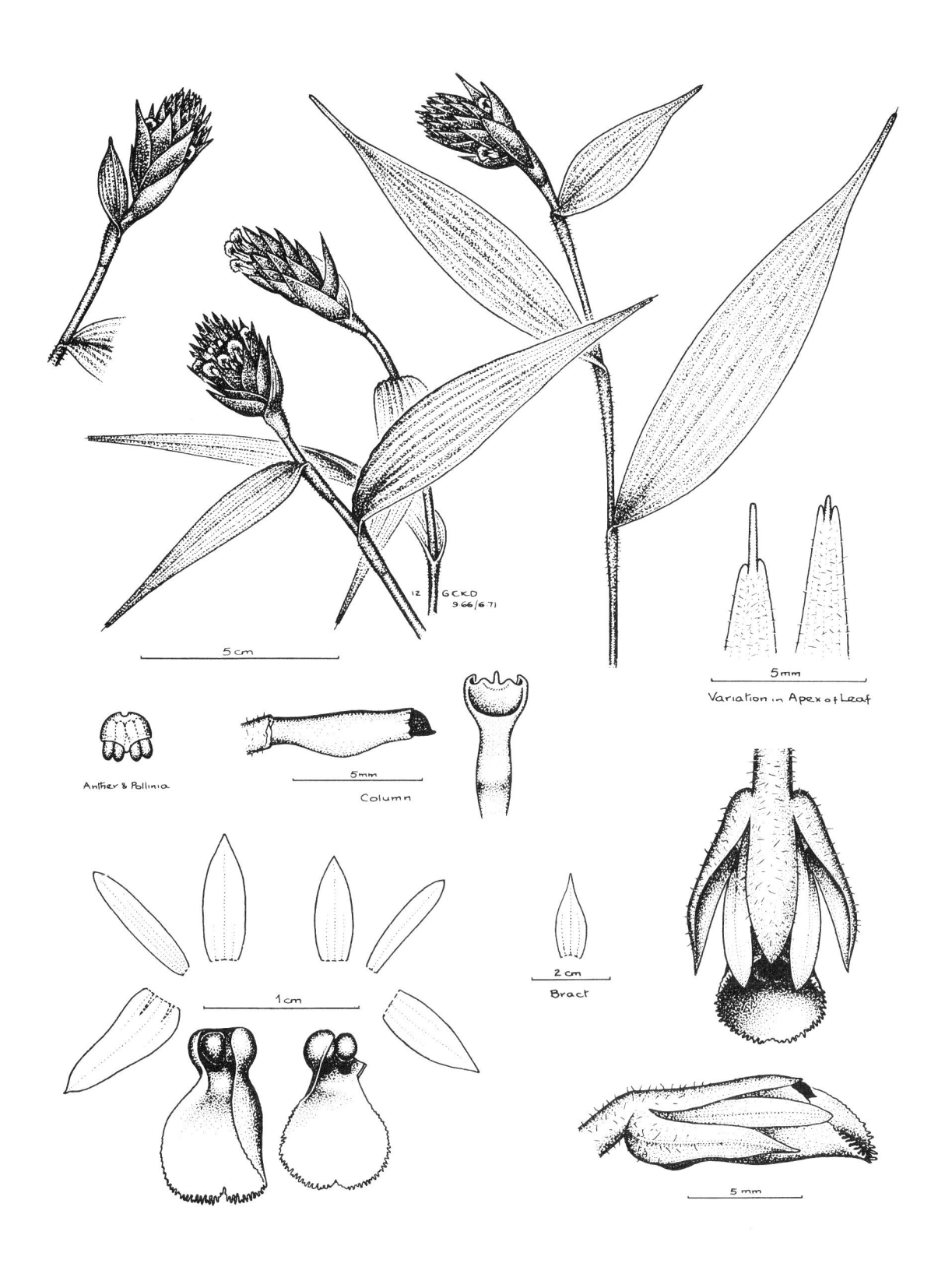

Elleanthus caravata (Aubl.) Reichb.f., Otia Bot. pt. 2 : 62, 1881. — E.

some of them, such as *E. caravata* shown here, could well merit a place in a general collection that is not overly squeezed for space. Larger species, such as *E. wageneri,* are unlikely to be seen except in collections of the botanical-garden type that have ample space available.

The following notes cover seven Venezuelan *Elleanthus* species, ranging over large and small sizes and terrestrial-growing, epiphytic, or intermediate types.

Elleanthus sphaerocephalus has recently been the subject of some rapid changes of name. It was fairly well known here (erroneously, it seems) under its 1962 name of *E. capitatus,* but this was corrected to *E. cephalotus* by Garay & Sweet in 1972, and this in turn has now given way to *E. sphaerocephalus,* a name given it by Schlechter in 1924. The other names formerly applied to this species are still "alive" but belong to different species as outlined in a very recent study by Sweet in which he sorts out the confusing and confused *Cephaleleyna* section of the genus, a section characterized by the tightly packed, almost globose racemes of the 10 species concerned. This "ball-head" character shows well in the illustration given in the *A.O.S. Bulletin* for May 1973 (where it is entitled *E. capitatus*) but it is mentioned here because it is by way of being a rather spectacular species and this seems to be a good place to stress this change of name yet again. The species is known from Colombia, Venezuela, and over to Bolivia, and is here known from the Andes and the Venezuelan "Guayana;" there is even a very old reference to it as coming from near Caracas. Nevertheless the actual records are very few, but it could be that as it flowers principally in the wet season months of July to October it has escaped the attention of those who prefer to do their botanizing in more comfortable months. In conclusion it is worth mentioning that all the plants we know of were terrestrial (or lithophytic) in habit, but the species is also recorded as being epiphytic.

Elleanthus arpophyllostachys is a pretty species with a rather awe-inspiring name which seems to mean "with sickle-shaped leaves like an ear of corn," presumably referring to the thin, rather curved and generally imbricate bracts of the rather untidy raceme. It is a species with some close similarities to *E. columnaris* which is wide-ranging in this country but which has rose-colored flowers, whereas the only plants we ourselves have found here of *E. arpophyllostachys* have had pretty orange flowers; it seems possible that some records of this latter species really refer to the former. The only places where we have found *E. arpophyllostachys,* which is endemic to Venezuela (and as far as we are concerned always terrestrial), have been in the central part of the Coastal Range at some 1,300 m altitude, and the type specimen is also recorded from the Caracas area. The stems are around 1.4 m tall, leafy in the upper part and fairly slender, the plicate leaves shiny green and with a long attenuate apex.

Elleanthus amethystinus, known also from Colombia, is a species of convenient size for collectors; we have not found plants taller than some 30 cm. It is fairly widespread. We have known it since 1967, so it must surely by now have been found by others in Venezuela. The only records we know of are our own findings in the Andes of Táchira State at about 1,900 m, in Zulia State at about 1,600 m where the Perijá Range separates Venezuela from Colombia, and in the Central Range not overly far from Caracas at around 1,500 to 2,000 m. *Elleanthus amethystinus* has pretty racemes of small, rose-violet flowers that all open more or less simultaneously and last a week or more. The individual flowers are characterized by fairly wide-open, prominent lips with nicely frilled or lacerate margins; there is a patch of brown near the base of the throat and the anthers have dark purple margins that show up clearly in the illustration.

Elleanthus oeconomicus is another fairly small species, epiphytic in our experience, with a sub-caespitose habit suitable for a collection. As implied by its name, however, the terete stems are very slender (not much over one mm in diameter) so that when they reach a length of 40 to 50 cm they tend to bend right over and look rather untidy. The narrow leaves, to 10 cm or less, have tapering apices. The flowers seem to be quite variable in color from white to rose-pink and the short racemes vary also from fairly dense to fairly open so that some plants may not be much to look at while others can be decidedly attractive if a number of stems are in flower at the same time. While the species is on record from 1,900 m in the Venezuelan Guayana (Bolívar State), it seems to be, as understandable with a species known also from Colombia, more properly an inhabitant of the quite high Andes. Our own plants came from around 2,750 m in the State of Táchira. With us it flowers in the April-May-June season.

Elleanthus norae is a plant endemic to Venezuela and is unlikely yet to be found in any normal collection as it grows, terrestrially, only in remote places in the highlands of Amazonas and of Bolívar State. In the latter area we have collected it on Auyántepui at about 1,700 m altitude and on Amurí-tepui at 2,450 m. A friend has found it at some 1,300 m near the border with Brazil in Amazonas where there is no sharp break between the two countries, so its endemicity to Venezuela alone is likely to be valid only until the Parima range that forms the border has been botanically explored on both sides of the line. The plants are

Elleanthus wageneri

Elleanthus amethystinus

characterized by compressed, sharp-edged, funnel-shaped leaf bases that sheathe the stem rather loosely and have an appearance rather similar to that of another orchid inhabitant of this area, *Sobralia infundibuligera* (see Chapter 17), so that when not in flower these two species from different genera could easily be mistaken for each other. Normally *E. norae* grows in caespitose clumps which in the open are not more than some five feet tall, but, growing in forest shade, the stems can reach to almost 12 feet, with leaves of 10 inches — not exactly a plant for a small orchid house. The inflorescence is typically "elleanthus" in that it is a rather dense raceme of small rose-pink flowers (sometimes pink-flushed cream) with green or lavender floral bracts, and, as with a number of *Elleanthus* species, the racemes seem to have a definite tendency to angle away from the direct line of the stem itself. The "norae" epithet was produced in recognition of "E. Dunsterville's" part in the finding of this plant as a new species on Auyán-tepui a good many years ago. This name may sound confusing unless one knows that the E. stands for Ellinor while the only name she is every known by in practice is Nora. Apart from being the "owner" of what may well be the world's tallest elleanthus, she also has the pleasure of being able to claim what may be the world's smallest restrepiella, *R. norae*, an inch-and-a-half tall plant with minute flowers from western Venezuela.

Elleanthus caravata is a fairly small, "orchid-house size," caespitose species known from Guyana and French Guiana as well as Venezuela and has the honor of being one of the only two species of *Elleanthus* to rate a mention in Schlechter's famous 1927 opus, *Die Orchideen*. In Venezuela it is known only from the Bolívar State part of the Venezuelan Guayana, one record being from as low as 300 m on the Paragua River. It does not seem to be very common and we ourselves have found it in only two places, one at about 1,200 m from the same forested, north-facing slopes of the Cuyuní Basin mentioned under *E. wageneri* above, and the other at about 500 m altitude near where the run-off stream under the base of Angel Falls joins the river Churún. It is a distinctly hairy species; the stems are clothed in the hairy sheathing bases of the leaves and the backs of the leaves (and sometimes part of the leaf face as well) are hairy, with at times an almost woolly feel. The plicate leaves are quite strongly, if finely pleated, all of which go to make *E. caravata* a fairly easy species to spot even when not in flower. When the flowers show themselves, one can see that the pedicels and the outside of the sepals are also hairy. The inflorescence is in the form of a dense, subcapitate, rather ball-like raceme and the pretty yellow

Elleanthus arpophyllostachys

flowers show up quite well. Our plant flowers in the range of June to September and is still growing satisfactorily after several years' residence with us, potted in chopped tree-fern mixed with the "rubbish" from the top layer of its native forest soil. Similar treatment applies to all our other *Elleanthus* plants that are small enough to be kept in "potted" form, the others being planted directly in our local earth.

Elleanthus wageneri is another robust species endemic to Venezuela, normally but apparently not always terrestrial. It grows mainly in clumps to some six feet tall, with leaves to 10 inches long, and is thus also not well fitted for a small collection! The terminal racemes are about four inches long and also have a tendency to angle away from the line of the stem. Before the flowers open, the cylindrical racemes, neatly and smoothly clothed in their overlapping red or magenta bracts, are very impressive but do not fully live up to their promise. As the flowers open in slow succession from the base upwards, the paler lips and petals begin to dominate the color scheme, but unfortunately the lower flowers tend to deteriorate long before the whole raceme is open and this rather destroys the initial impressions. It remains, however, a nice example of the genus. *Elleanthus wageneri* is basically a species of the Venezuelan Andes (although surprisingly not yet recorded from Colombia) where it can be found up to 2,800 m altitude. We have also found it on the edge of the far distant Gran Sabana area of Bolívar State as low as 1,360 m in the fine, forested, northern slopes draining to the Cuyuní River. The most impressive display we have seen was near the city of Mérida during September where great clumps almost six feet tall were growing in full flower.

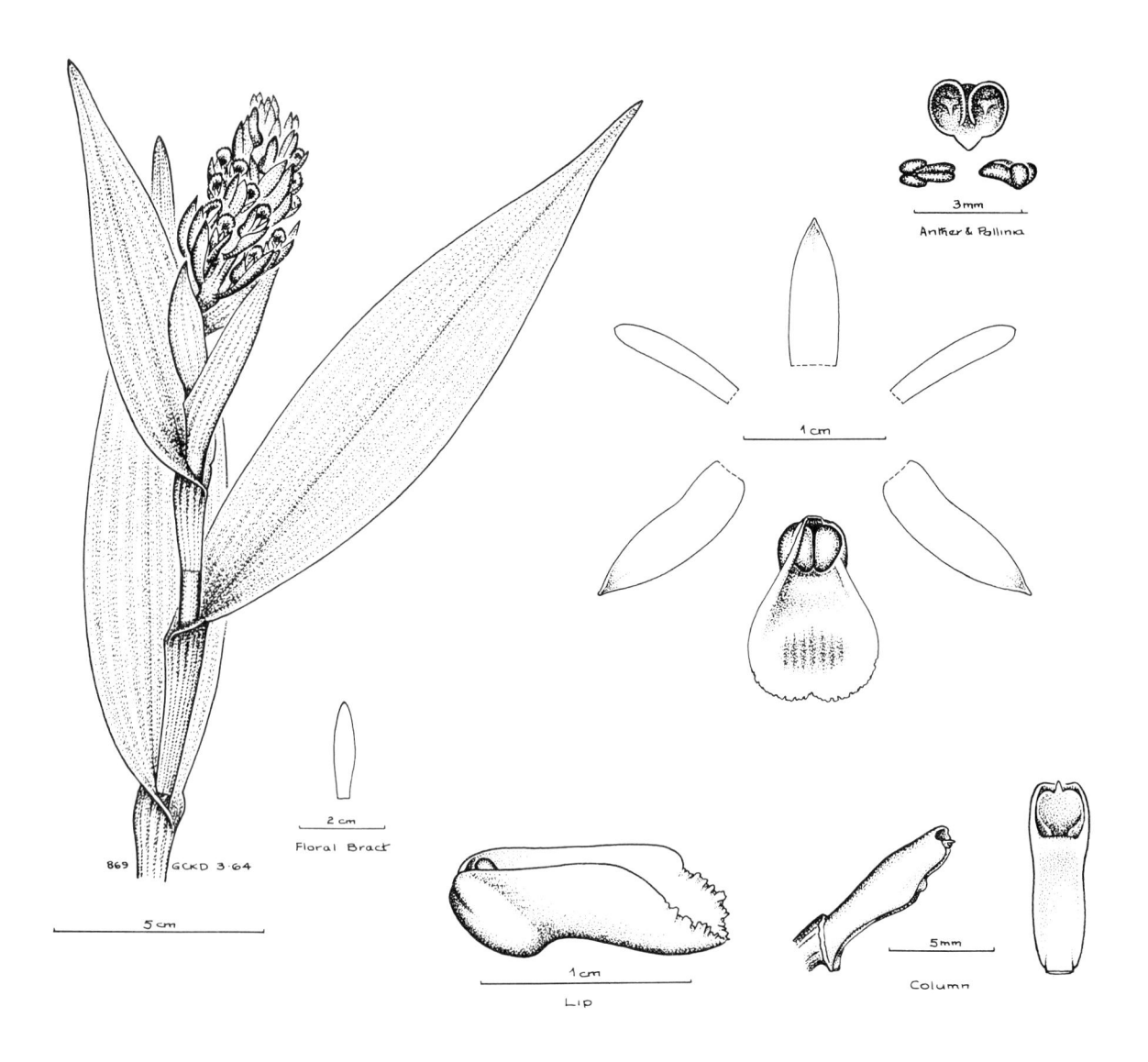

Elleanthus norae Garay & Dunsterv., Venez. Orch. Ill. 6:110, 1976. — D.E.

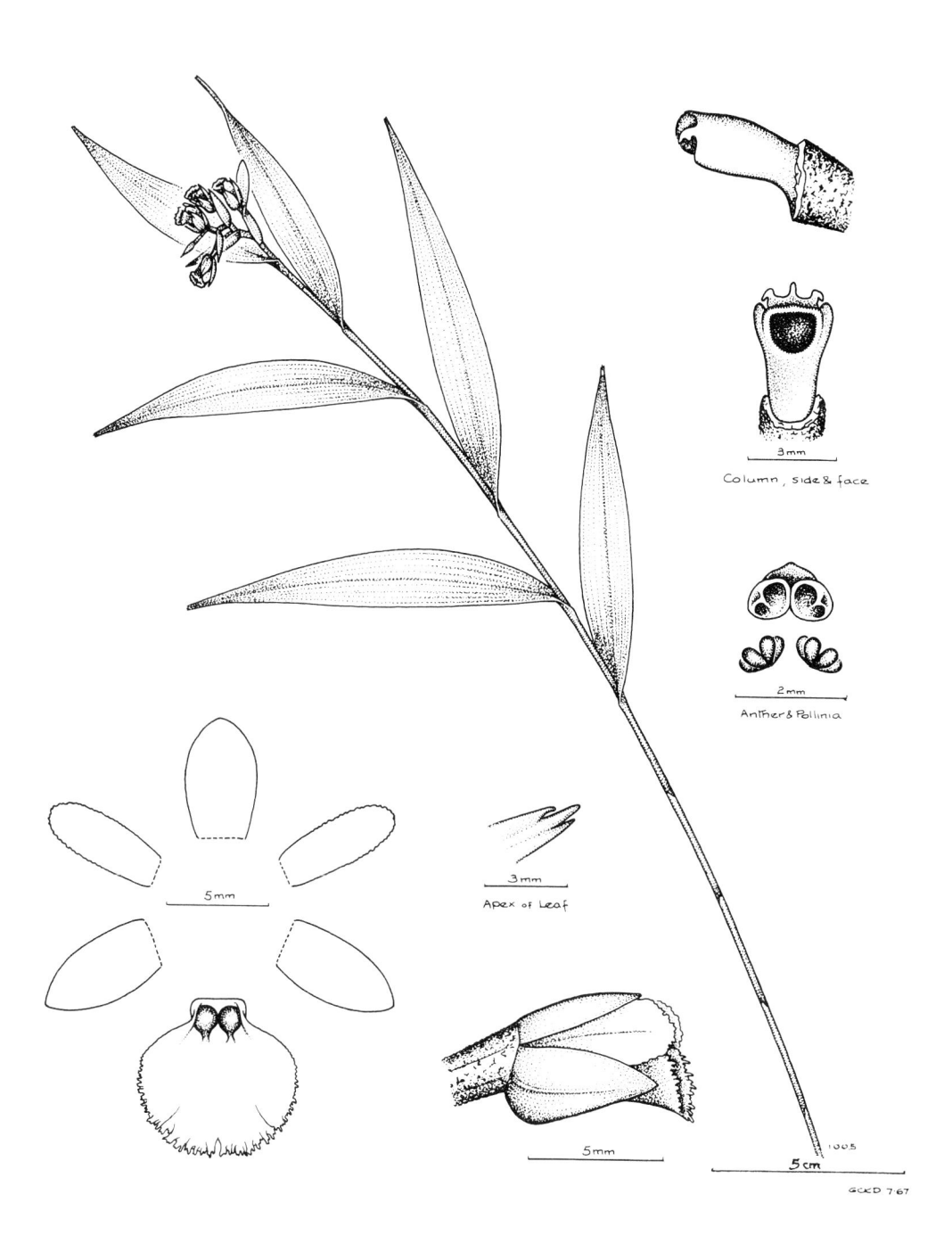

Elleanthus oeconomicus (Reichb.f. & Warsc.) Garay & Dunsterv., comb.nov. — A. Basionym: **Evelyna oeconomica** Reichb.f. & Warsc. in Bonpl. 2: 113, 1854.

Zygosepalums of Venezuela[1]

THE ZYGOSEPALUM SPECIES to be found in Venezuela have all, at one time or another in the past, been called *Zygopetalum,* and are still quite often erroneously called by this name. This confusion rests not only on the simple resemblance between these two names but is also the result of frequent uncertainty in the past as to what is the real distinction between these two closely allied genera. However, if anyone still wonders if a plant he has collected, or has acquired for his collection, is a Venezuelan "SEPalum" or a Venezuelan "PETalum," the answer is simple — it must be a *Zygosepalum* because under the latest definitions of these genera no zygopetalums are known to exist in Venezuela. The taxonomy of these two genera, and of several other closely allied genera, has been dealt with in recent years very clearly and concisely by Dr. Leslie A. Garay in articles published in the Colombian magazine *Orquideología* but, reducing this particular problem to simplest terms the clue to differentiate a zygosepalum from a zygopetalum rests in the anther. In zygosepalums the anther bears a very prominent long beak that projects well beyond the apex of the column like a dagger; the anther of a zygopetalum does not have this beak. As the flowers of species in these genera are fully "visible" in size, and their columns are prominent, only a casual glance is needed to see if a flower is a zygosepalum or not.

All four of the zygosepalums in Venezuela are attractive orchids, but not many people have actually seen them in their native habitats as these are all in parts of Venezuela far from the Coastal Range or the Andes where most of the country's activities are concentrated and where travel is easy. The first of these orchids we ever saw, *Zygosepalum labiosum,* was a species published almost 200 years ago as *Epidendrum labiosum* by the botanist L. C. Richard and its subsequent taxonomical history has been given in detail by Teuscher in the *A. O. S. Bulletin* for April 1972. Briefly, about 150 years ago, when the genus *Epidendrum* became better understood, this species found itself switched to *Zygopetalum* by Hooker, and later still, in 1836, to the genus *Menadenium* by Rafinesque. In 1859 it was transferred back to *Zygopetalum* (as *Z. rostratum)* by Reichenbach f., and in 1902 it found itself once more called *Menadenium labiosum* by Cogniaux. Finally this namegame seems to have come to an end, following the reworking of a whole group of related genera by Garay which has firmly placed it as *Z. labiosum* (L. C. Rich.) Garay. This species, not illustrated here, is a epiphytic inhabitant of the State of Bolívar, of the Orinoco Delta, and of the Federal Territory of Amazonas, the last named being virtually synonymous with the Venezuelan part of the Upper Orinoco basin. We ourselves first found it 25 years ago quite close to what is now the crowded tourist resort of Canaima in Bolívar State, where it grows (or used to grow) in a deep shade, low in light forest at the sometimes flooded margin of the Carrao River. The elevation here is about 400 m, and this seems to be about the highest it likes to grow.

We have also found it near the magnificent Las Pavas Falls which are part of the major "Para" break dividing the Upper from the Lower Caura River in the extreme west of Bolívar State, at some 200 m altitude. These falls are now under study with a thought of damming the river above them and using the energy stored in their drop of some 130 m for hydroelectric purposes. This may well be most desirable economically, but it will inevitably result in the destruction of many square miles of magnificent and so far untouched forest. Many more square miles of this forest will remain, however, so there is reason to hope that plants of this species will continue to thrive there. Plans for the dam are still only in their early stages, but there

---

[1] Originally appeared in *A. O. S. Bulletin,* Vol. 48, August 1979, pages 779-783

seems to be a toss-up between eventually stripping the forest and using its wood before closing a dam and flooding the area, or the alternative of just damming the water into a vast lake and letting the affected forest drown and rot away. There are technical pros and cons to both sides of this question but it is much to be hoped that at a suitable moment botanists and people such as orchidists will be invited to harvest the condemned plants before they all disappear.

As at Canaima, the *Zygosepalum* plants here grow also fairly low, often quite low, near the margin of the river, and some of them may well be flooded for short intervals at high water times. This also applies to plants that we have found in the tall wet forest at the edge of the Paragua River where it winds its way past the great, cliff-protected, sandstone massif of Cerro Quaiquinima, a mountain that seems to create its own wet and stormy climate around its flanks. In the Amazonas territory there are but few records of this species, and we ourselves have never seen it there. Its normal manner of growth is as a repent, climbing and sometimes branching rhizome (generally on a vertical trunk rather than on a branch) with pseudobulbs at intervals of some three to six cm, each pseudobulb having two or three plicate leaves; the short inflorescences rise from the axil of one of the leaves sheathing the base of the pseudobulb and bear one to three flowers. The white expanse of the projecting and often rather convex lip, marked with a few, subdued, purple nerves and with a purple crest at its base, helps one to spot the otherwise bashful plants in the shade of the forest. We have seen plants in flower in May and in September-October. In cultivation our experience has naturally been limited to its behavior in the relative cool of our Caracas home, and we have not succeeded in maintaining plants for more than a few years. If we find more, we shall not try again as it is clearly not a species to tolerate abnormal conditions.

The second *Zygosepalum* species that we found was **Zygosepalum tatei**, published originally as *Zygopetalum tatei* by Ames & Schweinfurth in 1931, based on plants found at about 1,800 m on Cerro Duida in the Amazonas Upper-Orinoco area. (Its portrait and a note on its habitat was given in the *A.O.S. Bulletin* for July, 1974 (see Chapter 8), but, for those many new readers without access to this publication, we offer supplementary notes at this time.) For many years this species seemed to be limited to this region, occurring as a terrestrial species in the cool conditions of a number of cerros, and we eventually found our own plants on Cerro de la Neblina, the highest of all these sandstone mountains. Neblina lies on the border with Brazil and is split between the two countries, the highest peak (just over 3,000 m) ly-

Zygosepalum lindeniae

ing in the Brazilian section. Our specimens were found on both sides of the border at levels of 2,000 and 2,400 m, and subsequent plants were found at 1,800 m on Cerro Jaua in the extreme southwest of Bolívar State. Our friend, Julian Steyermark, found other plants higher up at about 2,200 m. In these places this species likes to grow well hidden among the short, usually dense vegetation of damp or even boggy situations, and its erect, 30- to 50-cm inflorescences, bearing four to six flowers, are only just tall enough in most cases to allow its buds to reach the better light conditions where they can open. Of the four species covered by this article, this is the least colorful; the brownish green sepals and petals bear very dark purple-brown marks and the white lip has only a touch of purple at the base to liven it up. The very damp and highly acid soil conditions to which these plants are accustomed in nature makes them difficult to keep happy for more than a year or two in captivity, though in their native habitat they grow very freely. We have known plants to be in flower in February/March and in October.

Zygosepalum lindeniae is the third species of this genus that we have managed to find, and it appears to be limited to the Amazonas territory. Like *Z. labiosum,* it is a low-level, hot-country species that likes the shade of epiphytic positions low down on the trunks of trees near the water's edge. This species began its career as *Zygosepalum lindeniae* in 1890 and was then switched by its original author, R. A. Rolfe, to the genus *Menadenium* in 1902; it has finally settled down as *Zygosepalum lindeniae* (Rolfe) Garay & Dunsterv. after Garay transferred it to this genus in 1965, following his revision of this complex. Its growth habit is very similar to *Z. labiosum* mentioned above, and at first glance the two species could easily be confused.

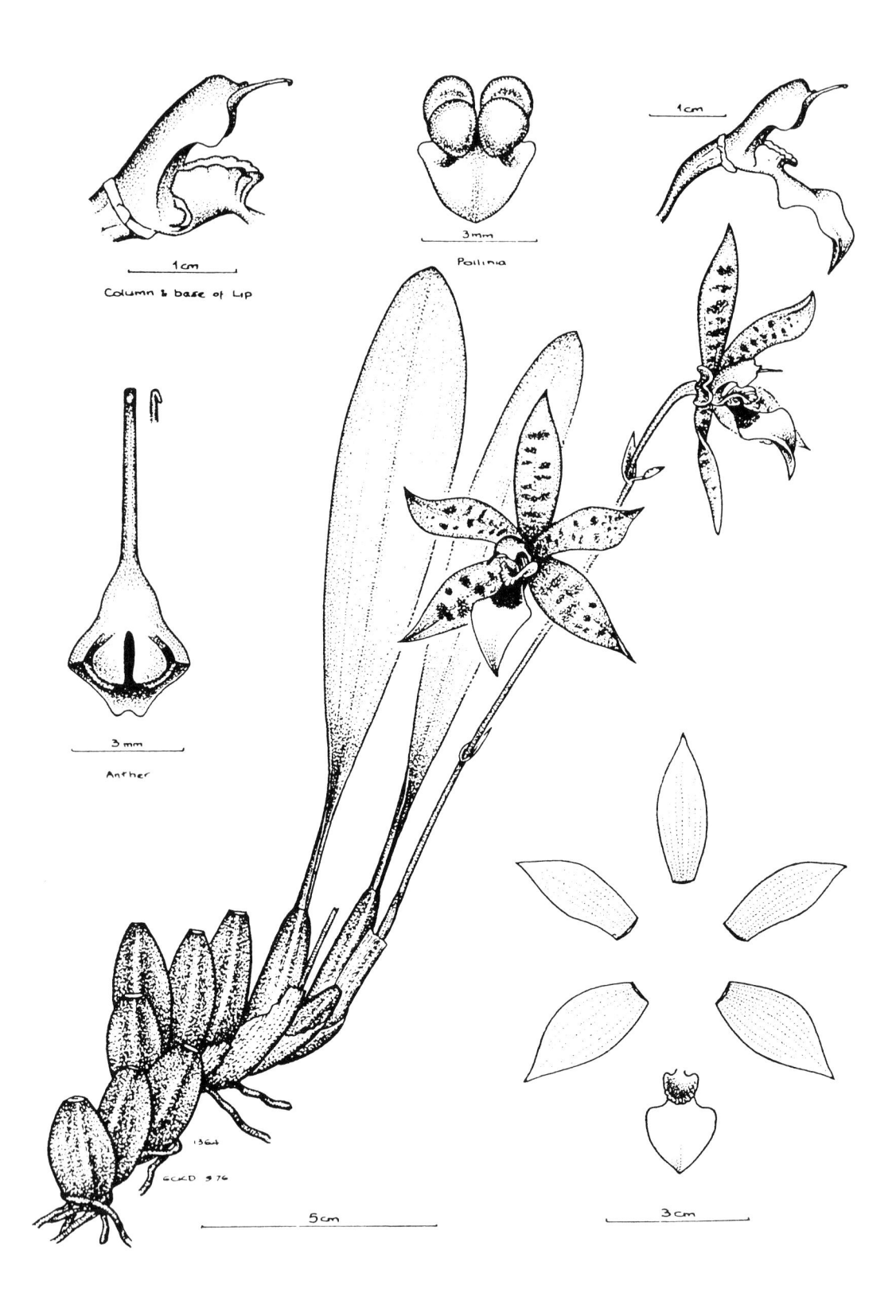

Zygosepalum angustilabium (C. Schweinf.) Garay in Orquideologia 8: 34, 1973. — E.

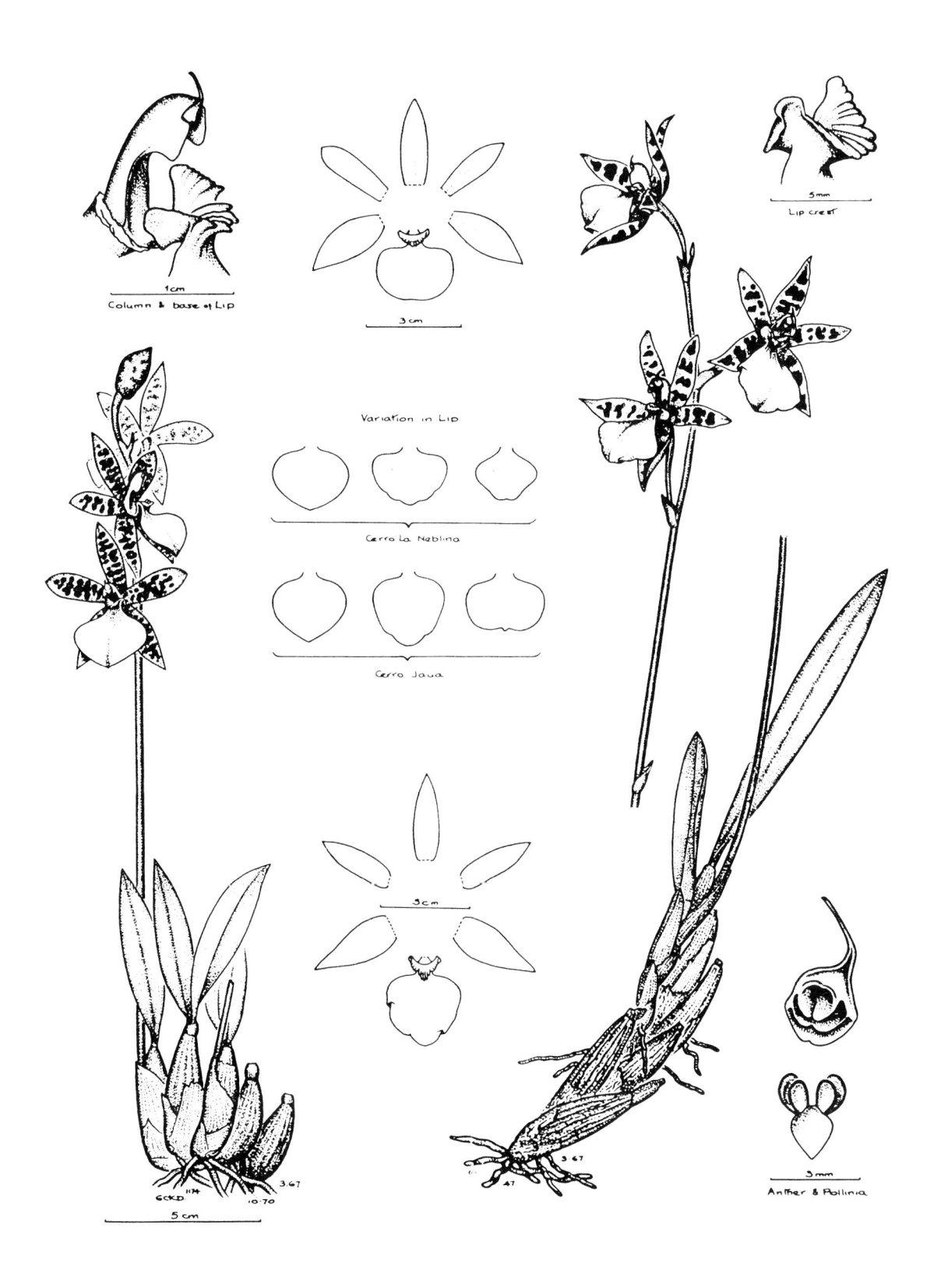

Zygosepalum tatei (Ames & Schweinf.) Garay & Dunsterv., Venez. Orch. Ill. 5: 318, 1972. — D.E.

The eight-cm flowers of *Z. lindeniae,* however, bear large, well-marked, red-purple nerve lines over most of the white lip, offsetting the pale-bordered, reddish brown sepals and petals. As with *Z. labiosum* the floral elements hold themselves nicely wide and the beak of the anther is easy to spot. We have found plants at several places along the main stream on the Upper Orinoco as far up as its tributary, the Río Padamo, near Cerro Duida. We have received plants from the Río Casiquiare that joins the Upper Orinoco, near Río Padamo, with the basically Brazilian stream of the Río Negro, and have collected our own plants from the banks of the Río Siapa at the break between the Upper and Lower Siapa, one of the most pestiferous and painfully "buggy" places we have ever camped in for orchid hunting. All these zygosepalums were growing low on trees by the water and all have failed to survive more than a few years. They flowered April/May and October/December, and they served us well as botanical study material, but it would be pointless to try growing more plants even if they come our way.

Our fourth and final *Zygosepalum* species is **Zygosepalum angustilabium.** This is quite a "recent" orchid, starting life humbly as merely a "named" variety when Schweinfurth of Harvard University published it in 1951 as *Zygopetalum tatei* var. *angustilabium,* based on specimens brought back by the famous Venezuelan topographer, Felix Cardona, on his first ascent of Auyán-tepui in 1937. These plants were at an altitude of 2,000 to 2,200 m and higher plants were later found by Steyermark on Carrao-tepui at 2,500 m. Our own plants, which we have found only recently, came at first from less than 300 m on the northern slope of the Gran Sabana in Bolívar State, and have been reinforced by later plants found on Auyántepui at levels of around 1,800 to 2,000 m. In the Gran Sabana site they were growing epiphytically in dense, tangled, very wet dwarf forest with poor light conditions. We first found two "oncidium-like" plants that greatly intrigued us by their appearance, obviously very different from any of the many other orchids we had found in this richly forested area, and on every subsequent visit we tried to find one with an inflorescence, finally succeeding in September 1976 when on our way back from Roraima. With great care we carried it home and when its buds opened in October we could see it was clearly a zygosepalum, but of a species we did not recognize, as at that time we had never seen a live flower of Schweinfurth's "variety *angustilabium.*" When Garay not only identified it but told us he had raised this variety to full "species" status as *Z. angustilabium* (Schweinf.) Garay, we were delighted. This promotion seems fully deserved as apart from being an epiphyte, as distinct from the terrestrial *Z. tatei,* it is an altogether prettier orchid with, as its name indicates, a narrow and pointed lip quite different from the "tateis" we had found before on Neblina. Later still, early in 1978, when on an expedition to other and previously unvisited parts of the top of Auyántepui (see Chapter 6) we found a number of rather larger specimens of this species, also growing epiphytically, in dwarf but more open and not so drippingly-wet forest at 1,800 to some 2,000 m.

These *Zygosepalum* plants are small, with dark, rough-surfaced pseudobulbs growing in "approximate" manner along, and largely hiding, the repent rhizome. They usually carry a pair of small, rather hard, terminal leaves (sometimes only one) about eight cm long, and the inflorescences rise from the axil of sheaths or leaf-bearing sheath at the base of the pseudobulbs. They carry two to four two-inch flowers and are very variable in attitude, seldom erect and seldom subpendent, but mostly in a variety of in-between forms. The sepals and petals of the flowers are shiny green with dark markings and the lip bears a bright violet crest with a fairly large patch of similar color at the base of the lip. The prominent beak of the anther, which is the trademark of the genus, shows up well in the illustration here.

Unlike our other epiphytic zygosepalums, which come from hot country, these plants come from cool or even cold climate, and as distinct from the cold-climate *Zygosepalum tatei,* which is terrestrial in habit, *Zygosepalum angustilabium* grows divorced from direct contact with the very acid soil enjoyed by the former. We thus had high hopes of future success when bringing back some small plants still undisturbed on small pieces of branchlets (as an additional note, we might mention the advantage of carrying with one on all plant-hunting trips some small but efficient clippers for cutting small branches without disturbing the occupants, a thing that is very difficult to do with a knife or a machete.) These we hung in shaded spots at home and they flowered (in August) about three months later. We are now optimistic about getting them properly established and hope that some day (the clutching hands of Fish-and-Wildlife notwithstanding) this very attractive species will become well established in collections also.

Some Venezuelan Notylias[1]

WHEN ONE SEES a tiny-flowered orchid such as *Jacquiniella globosa* (which must be also one of the commonist orchids in these parts) advertised in a commercial catalog in the United States for $10 a plant, then it really must be true that the very small-flowered, small-plant orchid is reaching some degree of popularity in the world of the orchid-species enthusiast. Not that, to be quite honest, I can myself work up any great enthusiasm for this species, which is perhaps the most uninspiring of all our miniature orchids, but there are other miniatures here, not in the genus *Jacquiniella*, that are well worth more than just a quick and casual look. The genus *Notylia*, for example, is unlikely to run away with many prizes in the normal orchid show, but, if and when you get tired of oohing and ahing over those gorgeous, great *Cattleya* or *Vanda* or *Phalaenopsis* or *Odontoglossum* flowers, or whatever your lady's corsage is likely to be made of, I can highly recommend a few minutes in a quiet corner with some nice examples of *Notylia* as an antidote, just as a plain glass of clear, sparkling, spring water is a nice refresher after too many hours spent in the company of the Widow Cliquot.

Notylia is a small, Neotropical genus of some 40 species of epiphytic orchids, and, just in case anyone is interested, takes its name from Greek words meaning, roughly, hump-backed, with reference to the quite noticeable dorsal bump near the apex of the finger-like column, where the stigma lies. Most notylias have pendent, many-flowered racemes of small, usually white-lipped, cream, green, or yellowish flowers borne on pedicels that spring from all around the rachis. The flowers themselves have in most cases a "standard" form that has given the genus a well justified reputation for being a bit of an Esso Bee (or should I say Exxon Bee?) when it comes to separating the species, since the demarcation between a number of them is anything but clear-cut. But, if you don't have to worry about taxonomy, then you can just enjoy them as enchanting miniatures, many of which only need the art of an expert jeweler to turn them into adornments fit to grace the most sophisticated and beautiful of women. In fact, if I were a jeweler, I would find it hard to resist trying my hand at modeling a gold, *Notylia* inflorescence for a necklace or bracelet, though I must admit that it would be an uneconomically slow and difficult process; and the result would probably be much too scratchy in the wearing to achieve its object of luring the young lady to one's bosom. In any case, as I have neither the skill nor the time to make such jewels, we must content ourselves with studying Nature's products and writing about them.

A typical, white, arrow-head lip shows up well in the central flower of *Notylia incurva* and in the lowermost flower of *Notylia platyglossa*, though in the latter case the shaft of the arrow is much shorter. Actually, both these "arrow heads" are too wide to serve any reasonable needs of a serious archer and could be put to better use as arrows to point the way on a street sign, but there are other species with very narrow and much more convincingly arrow-headed lips. When it comes to matters of identification, the form of *Notylia* plants is sometimes as good a guide, or better, than the flower itself. *Notylia peruviana*, for example, has narrow, thin-textured leaves; *Notylia rhombilabia* has narrow but coriaceous leaves; *Notylia platyglossa*, whose lip is very like that of *Notylia rhombilabia*, has quite wide leaves; *Notylia incurva* has fairly wide but generally rather folded leaves; and *Notylia yauaperyensis* is a much smaller plant with very variable leaves even on a single plant. Probably the species in Venezuela with the largest leaves is *Notylia sagittifera* which has widely oval leaves to some 18 × 5 cm, which completely dwarf (and usually hide) the very small pseudobulbs. Although first

[1] Originally appeared in *A.O.S. Bulletin*, Vol. 48, September 1979, pages 899-902

recorded many years ago as coming from near Caracas (or perhaps just explored from there?) all the plants of this species we have found come from the State of Bolívar south of the Orinoco where it occurs in forests from 100 to 800 m levels. This species, only part of the raceme of which is illustrated here, is the species that would most raise my enthusiasm as a jeweler because of its obvious usefulness as a model for a part of a bracelet.

Thus far I have dealt with the "standard" form of *Notylia* plants and flowers, which make up most of Venezuela's species in this genus; but there are two other species that are quite distinct from these in the form of their leaves and of their inflorescences. These two species, one very small and the other minute, have equitant leaves, i.e., leaves whose sides are flatly folded together along the mid-nerve and so closely appressed that, like the leaves of iris plant, they fuse together, separating only enough at the base to enclose the preceding leaf. The first of this pair, *Notylia mirabilis,* is a true mini-miniature orchid species that was honored with a color portrait in the *A.O.S. Bulletin* for March 1977. The second, though not so extremely small, is still tiny and rather overswamped by its very large name of *Notylia wullschlaegeliana*. Like *N. sagittifera,* it comes from the State of Bolívar at an altitude of about 600 m, but it is also one of those intriguing Venezuelan species that have jumped the wide barrier of the eastern Llanos

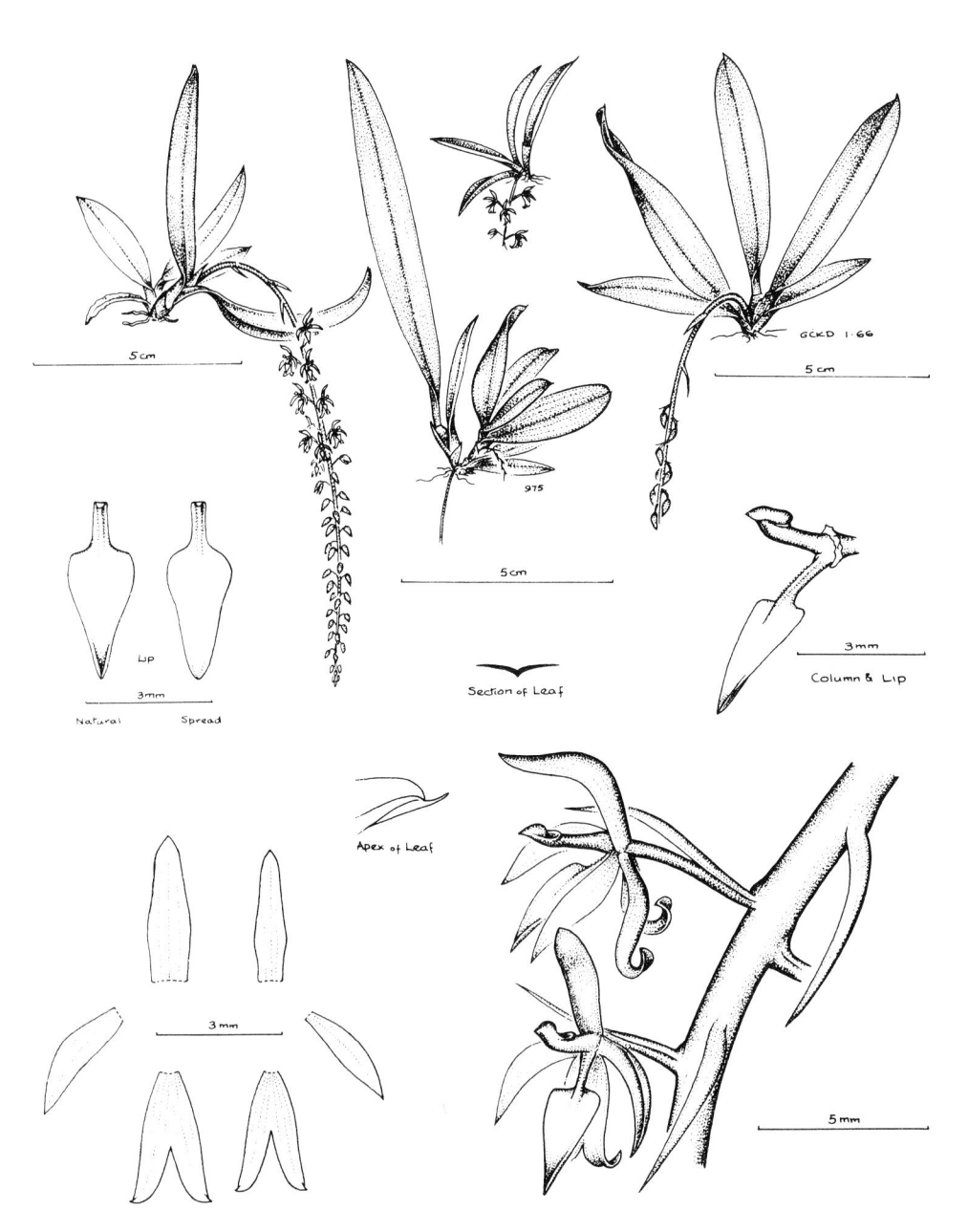

Notylia yauaperyensis Barb. Rodr. in Vellosia ed. 2, 1: 131, 1891. — D.

Notylia platyglossa

Notylia sagittifera

to set up home also in the cloud forests of the Coastal Range in the far northeastern extreme, also at some 600 m elevation. Its equitant leaves, somewhat fan-shaped in arrangement, are seldom much over an inch in length and its pseudobulbs only about an eight of an inch; the inflorescence, instead of being a many-flowered, pendent raceme, is a very short, almost umbel-like, few-flowered raceme of radiating flowers distinguished by their relatively very long and slender (one cm) pedicels and the quite extraordinarily long and slender column that juts far out from the flower.

This pair of very small notylias has proven to be not nearly as easy to cultivate away from their native home as the normal notylias that do not have equitant leaves. The latter have taken quite kindly to life in our Caracas home, fastened to suspended blocks of tree-fern root, but the two miniatures eventually gave up trying and expired, even the few we were nursing along still growing on the original twigs from the trees where we found them. If some day we come across more on a fallen tree, we shall take the opportunity of trying again; otherwise we will leave them where they are.

Notylia incurva

Notylia wullschlaegeliana

Some Pleurothallis Species from Venezuela's Western Andes[1]

CARACAS is excellently located for orchid searches in the Coastal Range, but, while it is also as centrally placed as one could wish with respect to the country as a whole, it is fairly remote from a number of fine Venezuelan orchid spots both in the "Interior" and in the western part of the Venezuelan Andes. The main Venezuelan Andes range starts just east of the city of San Cristóbal, quite close to the Colombian border, and from there runs some 400 km to the northeast to a gap near the city of Barquisimeto that marks the end of what we commonly refer to as the Andes and the start of the Coastal Range. On a number of occasions we had searched this Andean section with considerable profit, taking full advantage of its fine and fairly extensive road system. But, for many years, we had had it in mind to see what could be offered by the tiny wedge of true Colombian Andes that exists, beyond the main road system, between San Cristóbal and the border. To make a serious search in this zone was not something just for a weekend, nor to be done without planning for some hiking and camping.

The fact that this small, western tag-end of the country seemed to be very little known, and access to its forests by road doubtful, added to its attraction as a good, untouched site for possibly new-to-Venezuela orchid species. But it was not until nearly mid-1967 that we finally got moving on a joint trip with our botanical friend, Julian Steyermark. May 16 found us parking our station wagons in the small Andean township of Las Delicias, at the end of the road, slap on the border, some 40 km southeast of San Cristóbal. Here we quickly found that among the "delights" boasted by the town was a small hotel whose dining room provided the most inedibly tough meat we have ever come across (even the dog under the table retired defeated) and a small church that provided the most distorted and powerful church-bell amplifiers we never hope to hear again, calculated to summon the faithful from many miles around and scare away untold legions of evil spirits. When it first burst into full voice just over our heads in the small plaza, we really did think the end of the world had come.

Nowadays one can get on four wheels a very long way up towards the top edge of the cleared land at around 2,500 m where the dense forest starts and continues up to the edge of the páramo at about 3,000 m. But in 1967, Las Delicias was for all practical purposes the end for wheels and we had to spend a day or two organizing *bestias* and *muleteros* to carry our equipment further. I have never felt happy on four-footed transport that has neither steering wheel nor brakes, so opted personally to continue on foot, figuring correctly that with neither mules nor their owners in a hurry to get to the top, it would not be too great a struggle to keep up with them. The first night on the trail found us sleeping on the bare floor of an empty barn in a small village, and the next day we were camping at about 2,500 m on a fairly flat, open meadow on the edge of the untouched forest which from there reached unbroken up to the páramo of Tamá. Up to this camping point (referred to below as our Tamá site) virtually all the original forest had long since been cleared for simple, peasant agriculture or as pasture for their cattle and sheep. It was a true border zone, so isolated that the peasants seemed uncertain whether they were in Colombia or Venezuela and where they lived lives of maximum simplicity and at least apparent tranquility. They grew their own food and wove their own clothes and saw few visitors except the inevitable *maletero* toting his *maleta* or suitcase full of a contraband from "poor" Colombia to "rich" Venezuela. Rather like gold miners, a *maletero* would be staked to a full suitcase by someone in Colombia, to repay his staker his share on return — a tough and probably not very profitable way of

[1] Originally appeared in *A.O.S. Bulletin*, Vol. 48, October 1979, pages 996-1002

life even if the authorities seemed to be paying little attention to its illegal nature. Our trail, heading south, followed close to the east bank of the small, fast-flowing stream of the Río Táchira which here forms the border and, at one point, where the river was crossed by a small, rickety foot bridge, we saw convincing evidence of this local smuggling industry. Winding steeply down the Colombian hillside to the bridge was a well-maintained dirt road obviously much used by trucks. At the bridge the road came to an abrupt stop. Beyond it, only well-worn mule tracks led on into Venezuela.

Our excursion had been left until dangerously late in the season so we did not avoid some wet moments during the days, and in our tents at night, with temperatures falling to a minimum of 44° F., we were very glad to have the help of good sleeping bags on top of our air mattresses. But we got in a lot of most productive hunting between our camp and the top of the páramo at about 3,300 m, with a satisfactory haul of species new to Venezuela and quite a few altogether new. A rather surprising feature of the forest here was the quantity of orchid species growing terrestrially where one might have expected to see many more in the trees. Many of these "terrestrials" were in the large genus *Pleurothallis,* and among these probably the most prolific of them all was the first species to be discussed here.

We had first met **Pleurothallis phalangifera** in the main body of the Venezuelan Andes, not far from the city of Mérida, where it was growing "here and there" but mainly in the trees. Here, however, the plants were all on the ground, where they formed dense masses over quite large patches of steeply sloping forest floor at levels from 2,500 to 2,700 m. The species is, for a pleurothallis, quite large, with leaves some 20 × 10 cm on secondary stems to 40 cm. The racemes, on thin and arching peduncles, are as long as 30 cm, each with up to a dozen large but rather spindly flowers. The dorsal sepal of these flowers measures a very respectable five cm and the lateral sepals are connate to form a single "synsepal" of almost exactly the same size and shape as the dorsal sepal. The forward-reaching petals are rather shorter and very narrow. The color of the flowers of this species is moderately variable, ranging from a light creamy green or a brownish white to a proper green and finally to a brownish pink, with a tendency for the color to get darker and more intense at higher altitudes. The lip itself is small and inconspicuously brown or pinkish brown, but the total effect of a floriferous plant is quite eye-catching even if the long, thin flowers give it a rather untidy aspect.

Pleurothallis secunda is a very common epiphytic orchid in the Coastal Range and Andes of Venezuela, and has a very surprising range of color variety. The inflorescences are in the form of pendent racemes with very thin rachises that dangle down from the base of the leaves (if not actually supported by the blade of the leaf), the leaves themselves being borne on normally erect (but sometimes arching) secondary stems. The flowers themselves are carried in a non-resupinate attitude, with the deeply concave cup of the united, lateral sepals arching like an umbrella over the column as if to make sure it stays dry during the frequent rains — and indeed this may be nature's purpose. One color form, the prettiest, is one in which all the floral elements are an almost pure yellow with only very faint indications of nerves. Another form, also illustrated here, is a rather translucent pale brown with well-marked, wide nerve-stripes of purple-brown, and a clear yellow lip. The size of plants and flowers of this species is every bit as variable as the color, but the giant of them all in this corner of the Venezuelan Andes was a plant that we found growing terrestrially at about 2,800 m altitude, where the normal cloud forest was starting to change slowly to the dwarf and mossy type of forest that is typical of the highest forest at the tree line. This plant had leaves 28 cm long by 11 cm wide, which is a large leaf by any pleurothallis standards, carried on stout secondary stems to 80-cm-tall, thus making a formidable plant about one m tall. To match with the size of the plant, the combined spread of the sepals of the flower was only just short of four cm, but, to compensate for this gigantism, the racemes carried only five flowers. The flowers were of yet a third variety of color, illustrated here, that is more striking than beautiful, and appears to be the most common type of all, with intense, sharply delineated, wide nerves of dark purple (almost black) on a base of pale translucent brown. We did not bring back the giant plant, though tempted to do so. It was "nothing new" as a species and we were already carrying more exciting material. But other plants of *Pleurothallis secunda* have done reasonably well with us above Caracas, and one plant in particular was a standout. Potted in chopped tree-fern root it produced some 60 leaves with two to four racemes per leaf, each with three to six flowers per raceme, giving an estimated total (we did not make an accurate count!) of perhaps a thousand flowers. Since we had not grown this plant from its "childhood," unaided Nature must get the full credit for this, but at least we claim credit for not having obstructed Nature in producing it.

Pleurothallis dunstervillei is a rarity that, to the best of our knowledge, is endemic to the cloud forests on this border with Colombia. Endemic sounds exciting but really means nothing more than that to date this species has been found only here but, as we found plants rather widely sep-

Pleurothallis dunstervillei

Pleurothallis ruscifolia

arated in altitude, it seems very likely that it will eventually turn up in places quite distant from these original finds. The first plant we found was growing as a terrestrial on the cloud forest floor at about 2,700 m altitude, not very far above our Tamá camp site. Though not as enormous as the freak *Pleurothallis secunda* mentioned above, it was nevertheless definitely on the large size for a pleurothallis, with stout, erect stems half a meter tall and rigid leaves of 16×9 cm. When we found it, it bore no flowers, but not long afterwards in Caracas rewarded us with a bunch of about eight flowers growing in fasciculate fashion from the base of the leaf, all maturing at the same moment. The flowers, carried in a rather downfacing attitude, each on its own slender pedicel about 3.5 cm tall, have narrow dorsal sepals about 1.5 cm long, almost exactly matched in shape and in size by "synsepal" into which the lateral sepals are united. The colors are definitely attractive, the pink bases of the sepals grading into yellow, with some fine, red spotting internally. The lip, hidden inside, is relatively small, round, and rather fleshy. It is white with a red basal half and bears a fringe of white hairs.

About five years later, on a return visit to the area around Las Delicias (when we found the belfry low-fi as violent as ever and a new hotel dog no better off than his predecessor), we found some much smaller, terrestrial-growing plants of this species. This time, the locality was appreciably lower (1,900 m) and a bit to the north of Las Delicias instead of to the south, and, instead of growing in deep forest, the plants were quite in the open, shaded only by low, surrounding vegetation. Our original 1967 plant had been planted in the cool shade of our own little patch of cloud forest, where we hoped it would thrive in conditions that

seemed to us as close as we could get to matching its original home, but the drop of some 3,000 feet proved too much and within a couple of years it went into a decline. The newer plants were treated very differently by being potted in chopped treefern root and placed on the flat, exposed top of our dog kennel, with very little shade for half the day or more, and here they are bearing up quite well despite being almost 2,000 feet lower than where they began life.

Pleurothallis ruscifolia is another pleurothallis with fasciculate flowers. These flowers are not at all impressive individually but collectively can make quite a display. Unlike the aristocratic *P. dunstervillei,* which seems to prefer a generally solitary and aloof life, *Pleurothallis ruscifolia* is a member of a very plebeian and gregarious species that is known over a large area of Central and South American tropics, occurring in Venezuela from the Andes to Bolívar State in the "Interior," at elevations from 400 to 1,000 m. The cream or greenish yellow flowers frequently come so tightly packed together, like a rather whiskery powder puff, that it is hard to see the individual flowers at all, and it was only many years after our first acquaintance with the species that we became aware that instead of being a fasciculate bunch of single flowers, they were made mainly of fasciculate, two-flowered racemes with extremely short peduncles, which explains the denseness of many of the inflorescences. The very similar species, *Pleurothallis peduncularis,* does not seem to have this habit, which may explain why the latter's inflorescences generally look more loose and ragged. Under the microscope, of course, one can quickly see that the lips of these two species are quite distinct.*

Pleurothallis stenosepala*, whose name most justifiably means narrow sepals, ranges from Co-

---

* *Pleurothallis peduncularis* has now been placed in the genus *Myoxanthus* by Carlyle A. Luer — ed.

lombia into Venezuela. That, vice versa, it can be said to range from Venezuela into Colombia seems unlikely as it has so far put in an appearance in Venezuela only in this far western corner where the high country belongs geographically much more to the Colombian Andes than to the Venezuelan. Here it grows epiphytically at about 2,600 m. It was first identified locally as a new species and given the name of *Pleurothallis tamaense* but was then correctly identified by Garay as a fairly old species named *Pleurothallis stenosepala* by Rolfe in 1892. The slender secondary stems and elongate leaves, to about 45 cm long in total, are very variable in attitude, sometimes almost erect but in others (and perhaps more frequently) almost pendent. The flowers appear singly and in succession from the base of the leaf and immediately catch the eye by being so very long and so very narrow, the flowers often reaching seven cm in length. This is yet another pleurothallis with lateral sepals connate into a single "synsepal" but, instead of the narrow petals being swept forward as in *Pleurothallis phalangifera,* the petals of *Pleurothallis stenosepala* are swept backwards. The sepals and petals are a pale greenish or brownish yellow; the lip is red and very like that of *Pleurothallis lansbergii* (until recently incorrectly known as *Pleurothallis linguifera)* but is longer and narrower.

Pleurothallis secunda

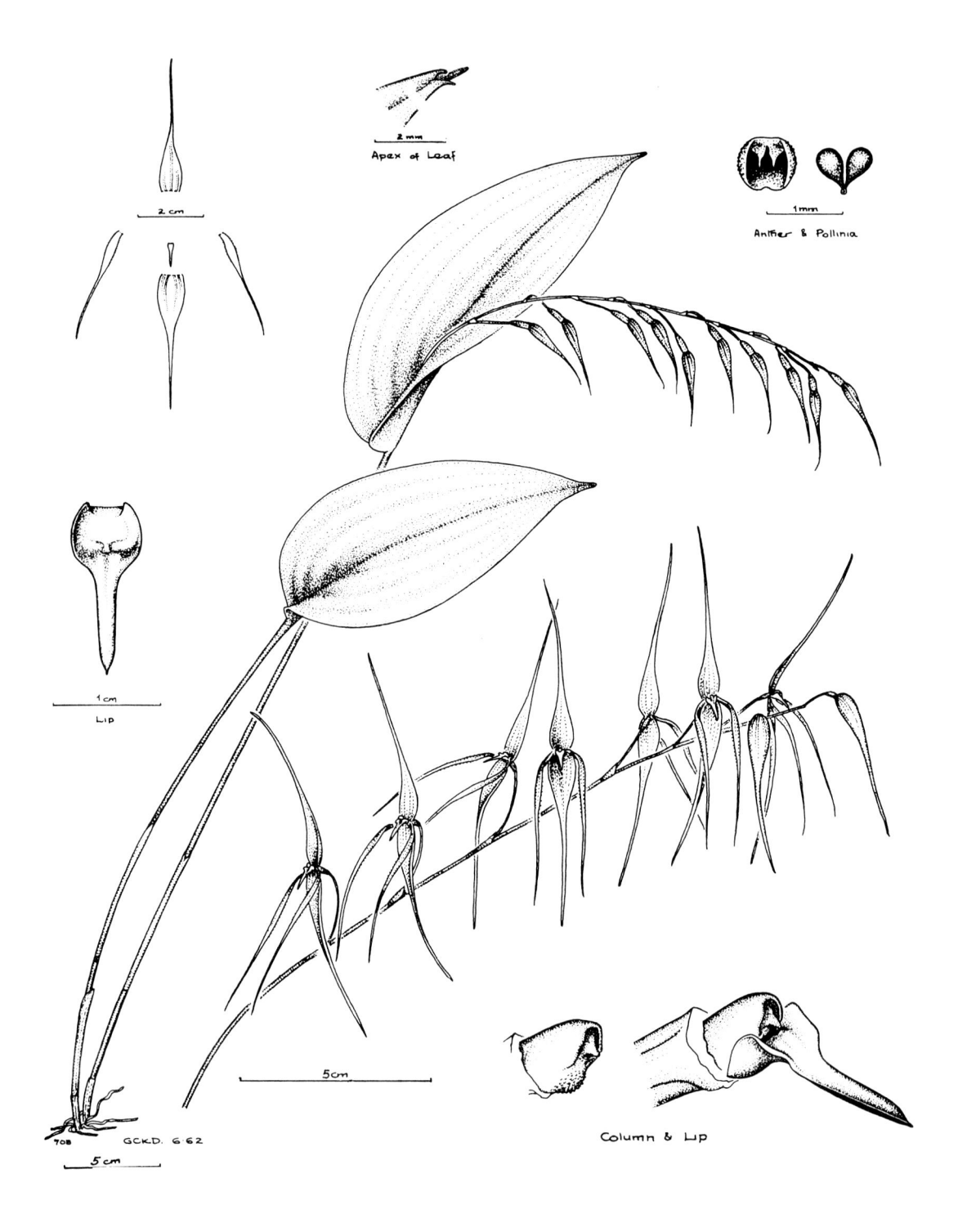

Pleurothallis phalangifera (Presl) Reichb.f. in Walp., Ann. 6: 168, 1861. — A.

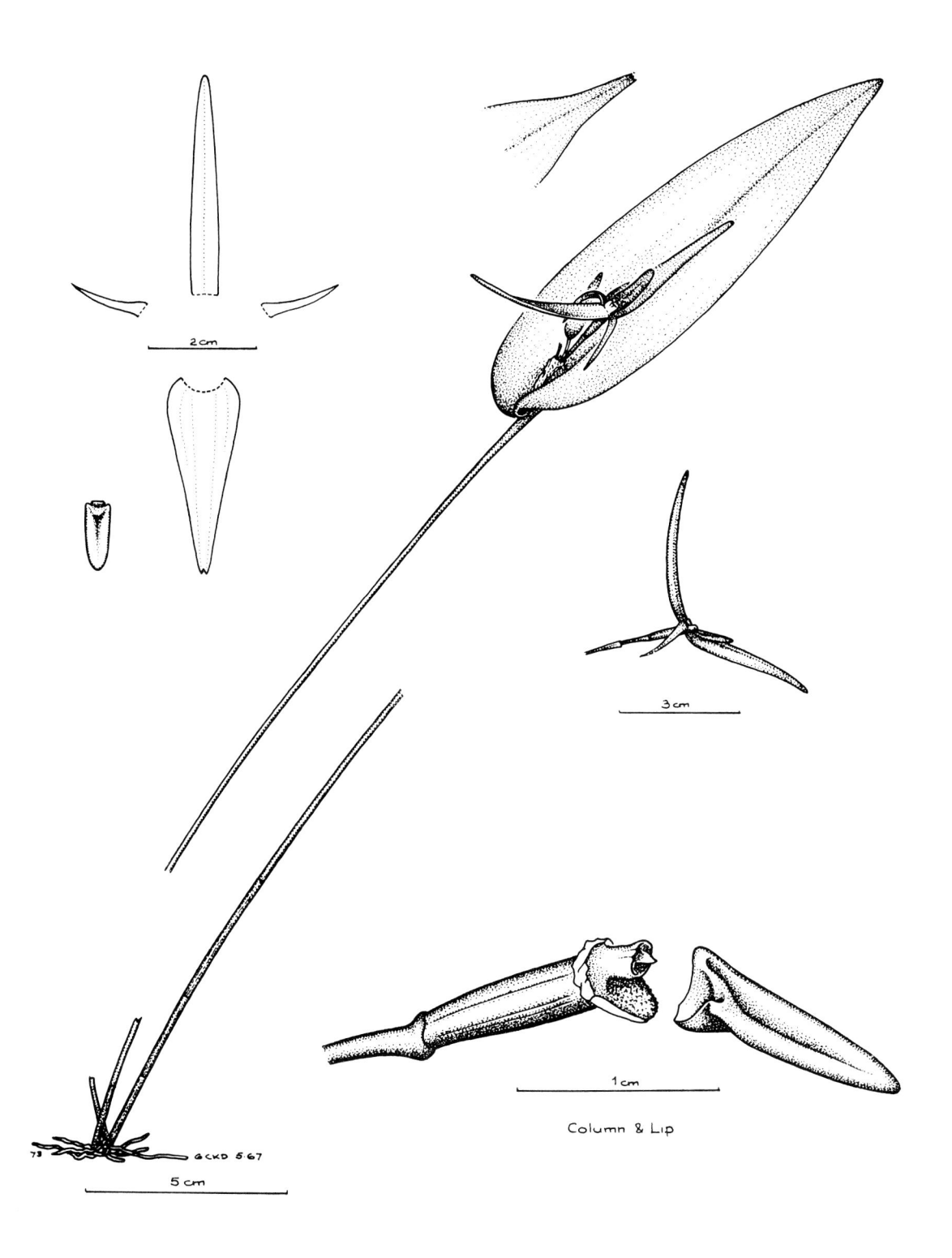

Pleurothallis stenosepala Rolfe in Kew Bull. 208, 1892. — A.

Galeottia into Mendoncella[1]

MOST PLANT LOVERS naturally dislike, and usually strongly resist, changes in names they have gotten used to; and they tend to blame taxonomists for disturbing their peace. Kipling said that "East is East and West is West and never the twain shall meet," and it often seems that the same idea applies to horticulture and taxonomy. But matters are not as daggers-drawn as they once were and there is hope for the future. "What goes up must come down" was once a self-evident "fact," but we now realize (despite Skylab) that many things go up and will never come down again. So perhaps some day (with Einsteinian help?) East may yet meet West and the taxonomical Lion lie down with the horticultural Sheep — or should that be put the other way 'round? In the meantime, we have to live with the fact that names are not static and new names for old is a way of life. Though not a New Yorker, I am slowly accepting Kennedy Airport as a modern version of Idlewild and, if I live long enough, will no doubt some day be dragged kicking and screaming from Sixth Avenue to the Avenue of the Americas.

Most changes in the names of orchids, as of other plants, result from revisions of botanical classification. Thus what was a *Catasetum eburneum* the day before yesterday, yesterday became a *Catasetum dilectum* and today finds itself with an entirely new generic name as *Dressleria dilecta*. The trouble is that Nature forgot to put names on the plants it developed, leaving humans (with their inbuilt urge for classification) to puzzle out the correct arrangement and apply their own name tags; inevitably, as we improve our understanding of Nature's arrangement, new and different tags are continually being called for. This is, of course, a pain in the you-know-what, but much of "progress" is painful and we have to put up with it or we shall never get beyond Pluto, let alone get our plant labels right.

Some name changes, however, are not produced, like the *Catasetum/Dressleria* case above, by changes of botanical classification, but by the need to correct mistakes made by people who name plants but fail to follow the rules. With heaven knows how many plant names (even excluding man-made hybrids) already current, and more coming along all the time, very strict plant-naming rules are necessary or chaos would quickly ensue. Today these rules are embodied in the International Code of Botanical Nomenclature. Basically, the Code is simple, but in detail so many openings for error, misunderstanding, and ambiguity have had to be plugged by the rules that in effect they are not at all simple to follow and only an experienced taxonomist is fully competent to understand and apply them correctly. And if not applied properly, then name changes will later result when the errors are corrected.

One excellent example of this starts with the genus *Galeottia* and ends with the genus *Mendoncella*. *Galeottia* was published by Achille Richard in 1845, in ignorance of the fact that a genus of grasses had been published with this name by Ruprecht just one year earlier. It is very sensibly "illegal" to give a genus of plants a name that is already in use for another genus of plants, whether in the same family or not, and Richard was quite wrong in using *Galeottia* as a name for an orchid genus. That such a mistake is easy to make, however, is shown by the fact that another botanist, Nees, pulled the same boner two years later when he gave the name of *Galeottia* to a genus in the Acanthaceae, following a popular urge around that time to honor the name of Henri Galeotti, a famous plant collector in Mexico and Central America who had found the plant that became the type species for the genus, *Galeottia grandiflora*. Nees was smart enough to see his error and rename his genus *Glockeria*, but Richard never noticed his

[1] Originally appeared in *A.O.S. Bulletin*, Vol. 48, Dec. 1979, pages 1220-1223

Mendoncella fimbriata

Mendoncella burkei

own mistake. Ignorance is no excuse before the law. Richard's *Galeottia* was illegitimate and the species that eventually held that name were all outside the law. Nobody in those days, however, spotted Richard's mistake, and nobody told the *Galeottia* children about the flaw in their birth certificates until one day, more than a hundred years after the genus was published, Alex Hawkes happened to notice the existence of the 1844 grassy genus of *Galeottia*. This had clear priority over the orchid genus and Hawkes had the sad (or happy?) task of breaking the news to the children (fairly old ones by then) that their names were invalid.

Hawkes saw there was a chance to legitimize these galeottias by producing a new generic name, and this he did (or tried to do) by naming it in honor of Dr. Luys de Mendonça e Silva, long the

Mendoncella jorisiana

editor of the well-known Brazilian publication *Orquídea*. The most obvious name for this purpose was *Mendoncia*, but Hawkes was too wise to fall into that trap, knowing that the name *Mendoncia* was already in use for a genus in another family of plants. The Code does not allow the use of the letter "ç" but gives authors discretion to use "s" or "c" instead, so Hawkes eventually picked on "s" and decided to publish the new genus as *Mendonsella*, no doubt figuring that that would be an end of the matter. But it wasn't. Neither Hawkes nor Mendonça himself are alive today to tell us just what happened, but it is known that Mendonça did not like the proposed spelling (too reminiscent of *donzella* = damsel?) and, when the new genus was published in *Orquídea* in 1964, it appeared as *Mendoncella*. Hawkes may well have been annoyed, but the Code says, "The original spelling of a name must be retained, except for corrrection of typographic or orthographic errors." Both "c" and "s" were permissible orthographic alternatives for "ç" and there was no typographic error involved, so *Mendoncella* was legal and *Mendoncella* it remains, despite Hawke's use of *Mendonsella* in his own *Encyclopaedia of Cultivated Orchids*.

The species that had once been galeottias were *Galeottia grandiflora* (1845), *G. beaumontii* (1952), *G. fimbriata* (1854), *G. jorisiana* (1919), and *G. nigrensis* (1925). These have all become mendoncellas with the same specific epithets (except for *G. beaumontii* which has fallen into synonymy with *Mendoncella ciliata*) and are living in harmony with seven other mendoncellas that never were galeottias at any point in their rather checkered careers. But the uniting of these orchids into one coherent group in the genus *Mendoncella*, which was achieved by Garay in *Orquideología* for April 1973, has not come about without a lot of shuffling with genera other than *Galeottia*, and the mendoncellas now include species that at one time or another were known as *Zygopetalum* (six different species), *Batemannia* (four different species), and even *Stenia* (one sole species, *S. beaumontii*) — a fine merry-go-round. The only unblemished mendoncella in the lot is *Mendoncella colombiana* which (one assumes) is the species that sparked this study by Garay as it is incorporated and published therein as a new species.

Of all these mendoncellas, only three have been found in Venezuela, which is a pity as we could do with more of them.

Mendoncella jorisiana was the first to show itself to us, an epiphytic species that we first met some 20 years ago when it was known as *Galeottia jorisiana*, to which illegitimate rank it had been promoted in 1919 from its previous status as a zygopetalum. Around that time, the Venezuelan government was starting to make a road that was planned to cross the Gran Sabana from the village and penal settlement of El Dorado in the southeast of the country, to reach the Brazilian border at Santa Elena de Uairén, still farther to the south — a matter of something over 300 km across mainly untouched territory. The first part of this road consists of about 80 km of hot lowland forest with rather limited orchid content, after which comes about 55 km of steeply rising country that lifts one to the edge of the Gran Sabana at about 1,400 m elevation. All this steep part passes through superb cloud forest in what was then virgin territory, and, with thousands of trees being felled to make the clearing for the road (and many more for later-abandoned trial sections while looking for the best route), it became a treasure house for orchid enthusiasts, and indeed for botanists of every taste from algae to giant trees. The trunks and branches of the felled trees remained unrotted for a number of years by the roadside and formed a constant invitation to return year after year to see what exciting epiphytes they might still contain that we had missed on former visits. By now, of course, these original trees have fallen apart and dense second growth is making orchids no longer as easy to come by as before, but it remains one of the best regions for cloud-forest botany in Venezuela. *Mendoncella jorisiana* grows here at around 1,100 to 1,400 m altitude, and we have also found it on the summits of Auyántepui and Cerro Guaiquinima, and on the flanks of C. Kukenán. It is a very worthy species, with pseudobulbs to 10 cm long, leaves as much as 25 cm, and inflorescences bearing up to five quite large flowers (about six cm spread) that are of good consistency and last well on the plant.

Mendoncella burkei is, by contrast, a terrestrial species. It started life as *Zygopetalum burkei* and it was under this name that we first met it on the flanks and summit of Auyántepui in 1963-64. Later we have come across it in a number of other places in the Venezuelan Guayana and Amazonas area, such as C. Jaua, C. Guaiquinima, and C. Avispa, all localities with very acid and often almost boggy soils. Well grown, it is quite a striking plant, with narrow pseudobulbs bearing two or three erect and tough leaves 30 to 45 cm long, and the inflorescence, with its raceme of up to six large fleshy flowers, rises to 60 cm tall. The flowers are rather variable in intensity of color, green with heavy brown marks on sepals and petals, very similar to *M. jorisiana*, and like that species it has a prominent white lip with some red-purple on its heavy, many pointed, basal crest.

Mendoncella fimbriata, the last in this list, is an Andean, not Guayanan species that has only recently shown its face in Venezuela, having been found not far from the border of Colombia by Sr. R. Mejía of San Cristóbal at about 900 m altitude. The species is epiphytic and its eight-cm flowers have striking dark-nerved sepals and petals, and a very hairy white lip with dark nerves and a basal crest of many keels.

Mendoncella jorisiana seems to thrive best in decidedly damp (but for epiphytes adequately drained) conditions typical of cloud forest; *Mendoncella burkei* is a terrestrial from acid soil and has not done well with us; *Mendoncella fimbriata*, unfortunately, is a plant we have never owned, and is thus outside our direct experience for cultivation, but could be expected to like cloud-forest conditions also.

Some Venezuelan Catasetum Species[1]

MOST ORCHIDS have bisexual flowers with both male and female elements in each flower. By contrast, *Catasetum* is one of the relatively few orchid genera with plants capable of bearing separate (and frequently different-looking) male and female flowers on one and the same plant, or even on a single raceme. Most catasetums are also renowned for their rather alarming pollinia-spitting abilities, a truly fascinating mechanism triggered by a touch on their sensitive, usually antenna-like arms that project from the sides of the column. Some catasetums, however, do not have these sensitive arms, and in August 1975, Dodson published in *Selbyana* a proposal to restrict the genus exclusively to those species that do have such arm-based trigger mechanisms, placing the remainder in either the old (1843) Lindley genus of *Clowesia*, or in a new genus that in the same proposal Dodson names *Dressleria*. The clowesias and dresslerias all have bisexual flowers; the catasetums are usually unisexual. Clowesias, as distinct from dresslerias, eject their pollinia when pressure is applied to the stipe that joins the pollinia to the viscid disc; the dresslerias eject theirs when the tip of the anther cap is lifted; and the true catasetums, as now defined by Dodson, eject theirs when a sensitive arm or antenna on the column is touched, as mentioned above.

These Dodson proposals have received general acceptance in the taxonomic world but have not had a great effect on the list of Venezuelan *Catasetum* species as a whole as it has resulted in only two species being removed from the previous catasetum list and transferred to the genus *Clowesia* (viz. *C. russelliana* and *C. warczewitzii*). Venezuela also gives a home to a species known earlier from Colombia as *Catasetum dilectum*, but its discovery in the Venezuelan State of Táchira by Sr. Roberto Mejía of San Cristóbal came just a bit too late for its visa to be marked "Catasetum" and it entered the Venezuelan lists right away as *Dressleria dilecta*. These minor deductions from the list of Venezuelan catasetums still leave this country with over 20 species, a number not to be compared with the 60 or more to be found in Brazil but still enough to make their study rewarding. Some of these are very beautiful, and most of the others, if not beauty-prize winners, are at least extremely interesting, not only because of their dimorphic character, with male flowers quite different from the female ones, but because they are often polymorphic and show a whole range of hermaphroditic forms between true male and true female. Six typical catasetums are dealt with in this article.

Catasetum pileatum is an orchid of the hot forests of Venezuela, Trinidad, and the Amazonas region of Brazil, Colombia, and Ecuador. It was published in 1886 by Reichenbach and since then has accumulated a mass of varietal names, or names of natural hybrids in which it is reputedly involved. In Hoehne's *Flora Brasilica* there is mention of seven named varieties, all of which he considers to be natural. In the form shown here, it is the best known and one of the most prized of Venezuela's catasetums, and was once officially adopted as Venezuela's National Flower under the popular name of *Flor de Nacar* (Mother-of-pearl Flower), a name that confirms that this white or pale cream type, with its very real resemblance to mother-of-pearl, was in the minds of those who chose this name. This variety is, indeed, the commonest form of this species and may well be legitimately considered the truest type, unblemished by contamination with possible hybridization. Its female flowers are larger than most female catasetums but otherwise very similar in form and unlikely to inspire lust in a beauty competition. But the males of *Catasetum pileatum* are generally well to the fore in any orchid show where they are exhib-

[1] Originally appeared in *A.O.S. Bulletin*, Vol. 49, January 1980, pages 5-12

ited, a well-grown inflorescence of a dozen or more three-inch, waxy-lustered flowers being a certain eyecatcher.

As for *Catasetum pileatum* hybrids: "O wad some Pow'r the giftie gie us, to see oursels as others see us! It wad frae mony a blunder free us, and foolish notion." I am not sure that Robert Burns's idea of being able to see ourselves in this manner is really a good one as it would inevitably be disastrously ego-deflating. But if we had the giftie of seeing what species had gone into the making of a natural hybrid, there are times when it might well free us from blunders and foolish notions. It is certainly a felt want in the case of some of the spectacular hybrids (if indeed they are hybrids) commonly attributed to *C. pileatum* and *C. macrocarpum*. If the normal (?) *C. pileatum* is one parent and the normal *C. macrocarpum* the other, then two plus one is making four — which may not be a blunder but verges on the foolish notion. In any case, where a good normal *C. pileatum* may be no more than a contender in a show, some of these superb, mainly red hybrids are certain prizewinners. Several of them were splendidly illustrated in an article by Pierre Couret in the *A.O.S. Bulletin* for March 1977 which must have had many readers gasping with lust. Unfortunately, winning beauty prizes often results in more misery than pleasure for the winner, and the spectacular forms shown in that article have subsequently (and expectedly) been largely stripped from their home in the western Llanos of Venezuela.

Catasetum splendens, published by Cogniaux in 1894, is another native of the Amazonas region and was also from the start considered by Cogniaux to be a probable hybrid between *C. pileatum* and *C. macrocarpum*. A foolish notion? Or not? I do not feel competent to judge. It seems to be a very variable orchid, being listed in Hoehne with at least 20 named varieties, not counting the many artificial hybrids that have been produced. It cannot compete in dramatic impact with the red hybrids mentioned above, but is still (in the form shown here) a potential prizewinner. *Catasetum splendens* has a less widely open (more cup-shaped) lip than the "normal" *C. pileatum*, a shape that presumably reflects its connection with *C. macrocarpum* if, indeed, this is one of its parents, but its color shows little of such relationship. The plant illustrated came from the Venezuelan Amazonas and, as can be seen, had a robust inflorescence of some 15 flowers whose size can be appreciated by comparison with the four-inch spread of the *Cattleya violacea* flowers beside it. Had meristem techniques been well known when we owned the plant we might have been able to spread some progeny around, or with better foresight have made a number of propagations; as it was, our then-embryonic skills were inadequate to offset the cool airs of our Caracas home-in-the-clouds and the plant did not survive.

Having said so much about the role ***Catasetum macrocarpum*** may have played in creating a great number of most striking hybrids with *C. pileatum*, it is only fair that its portrait should appear here. By comparison with such exciting orchids, *Catasetum macrocarpum* may seem rather ordinary, the more so as it is fairly common from Trinidad through Guyana and Venezuela and on into part of Brazil. But this does not mean it cannot earn its keep in a general collection. The color of its sepals and petals varies from clear green to a darkish maroon externally, and from pale with red spots to a heavily blotched maroon internally. But there is little variation in the yellow or yellow-green, helmet-shaped lip, and, as the flowers are non-resupinate, with the lip uppermost, the outside of the lip provides a dominant color feature. In this, *Catasetum macrocarpum* is distinct from the resupinate lips of *C. pileatum, C. splendens*, etc., so if it really is one of the parents in the natural hybrids mentioned, it seems to have failed to transmit the "resupine" character.

At the start of this article, it was mentioned that an essential feature of Dodson's *Catasetum* definition is that a catasetum should have a pollinia-ejecting mechanism based on sensitive projections from the side of the column. These are commonly in the form of slender, antenna-like things, so placed that they guard the entrance to the hollow part of the base of the lip. A division of the genus has been proposed based on whether these antennae are bashfully crossed (or one even curled up behind the other) or run parallel to each other (or even lightly spread apart). The bashful ones form the section *Anisoceras*, the others the section *Isoceras*. The orchids previously dealt with in this note are all anisoceras, if one may coin such a word. ***Catasetum sanguineum*** and the following species, *Catasetum costatum*, are isoceras. The moderately rare *Catasetum sanguineum* is to be found in the east or east central part of the northern section of the country, and also in the extreme west where it lives in the low country between Lake Maracaibo and the Perijá range that here forms the border with Colombia. From here it ranges farther north to Costa Rica and west to Ecuador. The inflorescences vary from suberect to arching, and bear a dense, generally rather few-flowered raceme at the end of a 10-inch peduncle. In line with its sanguine name, the two-inch flowers of *Catasetum sanguineum* are mainly red, and are characterized by a very interesting and complicated lip with a deeply cup-shaped base overhung by fimbriate, lateral lobes and ending in a very thick, apical lobe which is sometimes wide and spade-like, and in other

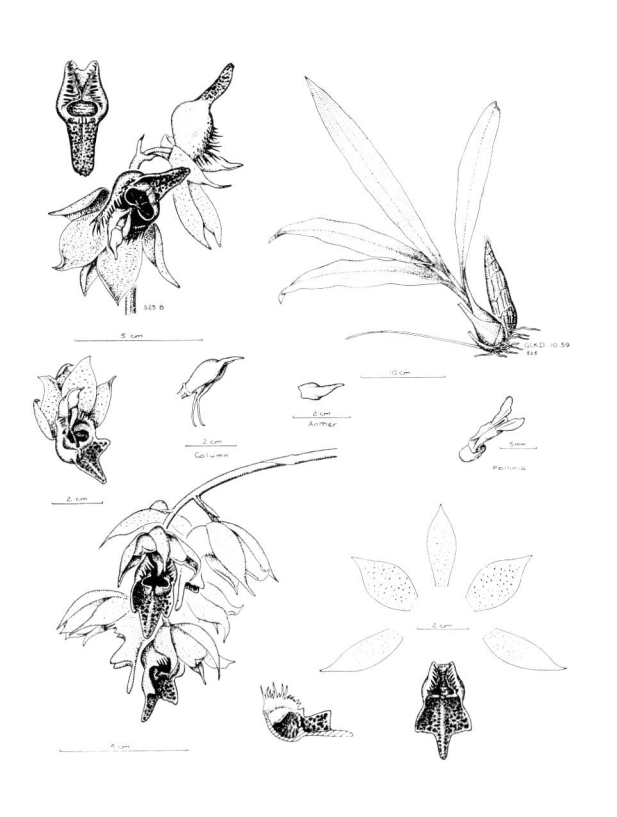

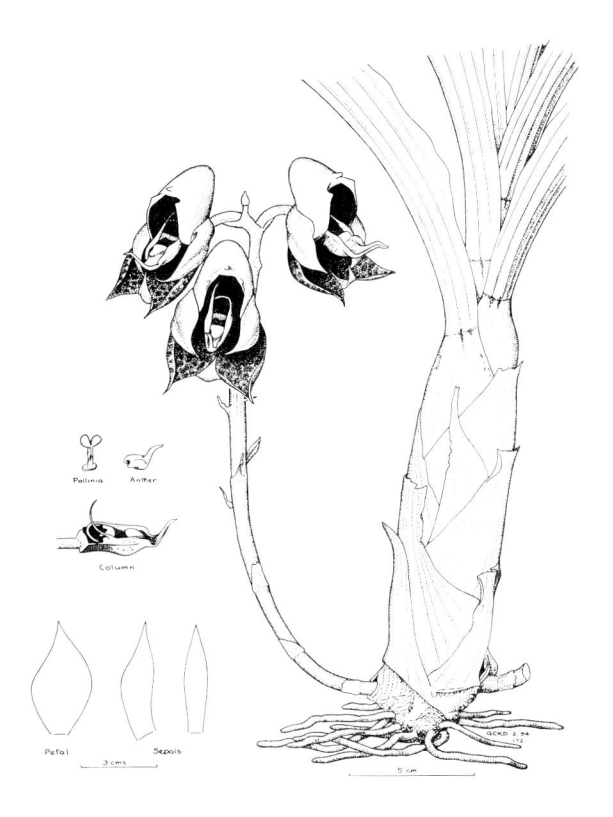

Catasetum sanguineum Lindl. in
Paxt.Fl. Gard. 2: 168, 1852. — A.

Catasetum macrocarpum L.C. Rich. ex Kunth,
Syn. Pl. Aequin. 1: 331, 1822. — B.

Catasetum pileatum Reichb.f. in
Gard.Chron. n.s. 17: 492, 1882. — D.

Catasetum longifolium Lindl. in
Bot. Reg. 25: Misc. p.94, 1839. — E.

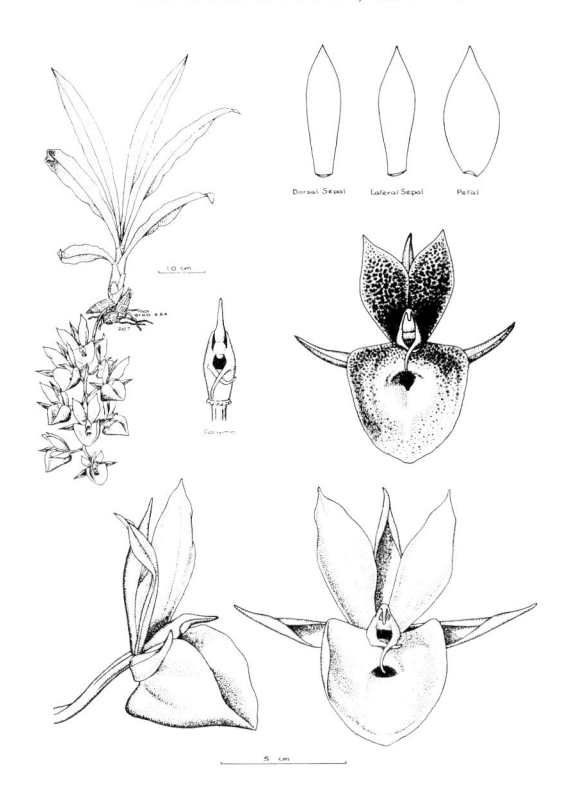

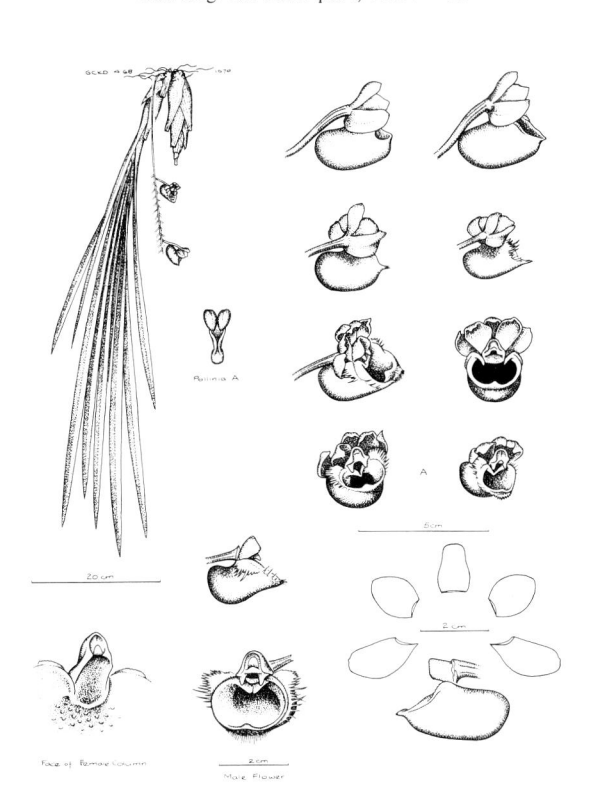

flowers may be narrow and pointed.

Catasetum costatum is the second *Isoceras* species in this article, a rather rare (in Venezuela very rare) Amazonas orchid of the upper reaches of the Orinoco and Amazon Rivers. The only plant we have ever seen is one that was found by Ing. Pantchenko of the Venezuelan-Brazilian Border Commission who found it at about 100 m elevation in the Parima Range of hills that forms an important part of the border with Brazil. The smooth, white-bordered, pinkish-red lip is visually quite distinctive and apparently has the characteristic of developing raised nerves when dried and pressed, which is why Reichenbach gave it its name of *costata*, meaning "ribbed."

Catasetum longifolium, while a true catasetum by virtue of possessing sensitive elements on the side of the column, does not have the typical antenna-like triggers of most catasetums. Instead it relies on two very small and almost inconspicuous, tooth-like projections, a structure that implies reliance on a very different type of insect from the usual, small bee to activate it — something much heavier or perhaps able to clasp or pinch the two teeth together to some degree. The species is not mentioned in Dodson's invaluable work on the pollination and evolution of orchids, so this is mere speculation.

This most interesting species has a range from Venezuela south and east into Guyana, Surinam, and Brazil. It does not aim to compete in beauty or magnificence with such well-known species as *C. pileatum*, but *Catasetum longifolium* has quite striking colors and is a splendid example of the polymorphism to be found in a number of species in the genus. More interesting still is its habit of growth. Due to its unusual (one is tempted to say unnatural) predilection for growing totally upside down, a number of early references to it failed to recognize this idiosyncracy, and this led to some of the early illustrations showing the plant upright, like any well-behaved catasetum should, for example, the original illustration accompanying the publication of this species (under the name of *Monacanthus longifolius*) in 1840, or the very fine and very convincing painting by Miss Drake published in color in 1840 by Putnam as part of Lindley's *Sertum Orchidaceum, a wreath of the most beautiful Orchidaceous Flowers*. As these illustrations were made by competent botanical artists, it seems probable that they were made from wrongly mounted specimens, the sort of error that can easily arise whenever a plant of grossly "unnatural" habit is concerned, such as the much more recent but equally inverted drawing of the well-known species, *Maxillaria camaridii*, in Schweinfurth's *Orchids of Peru*.

But mounters of herbarium specimens cannot always be blamed. We are the lucky owners of a set of very beautiful Spode china plates and cups decorated with late nineteenth-century, colored portraits of a dozen orchid species, realistically painted and with the proper scientific names inscribed on the back. One of these shows *Cattleya citrina*, perhaps the best known of all "upside-down" orchids, growing wrong way up, as indicated by the flowers themselves and by the placing of the artist's name (J. Frost) on the painting. We wrote to Spode to ask how this could have come about and received a very courteous reply to the effect that "the designs were all made on the spot by the artist when visiting the orchid houses of the nobility: if the paintings are wrong in any respect then the artist himself must have made a mistake or been misinformed by the owner or his gardener." In this particular case one is left to assume that, having finished several paintings in a row, the artist forgot to mark this one with a large arrow to remind himself which side was up before adding his signature.

But getting back to *Catasetum longifolium*, there seems little doubt that the correct habit of this species was known a good many years ago, despite some incorrect illustrations at the start. At Kew, for example, there is a colored sketch made in 1886 by the botanical artist John Day, which shows a plant growing in a completely upside down manner, with an appended note by Day himself saying, "The bulbs were growing on a block hanging down, which I think must be the natural habit;" and it is nowadays accepted that this really is a truly upside-down orchid.

Its habitat seems to be restricted to Guyana, Surinam, and Venezuela, but as *Catasetum longifolium* is found in Venezuela's Gran Sabana quite close to the Brazilian border, here marked by no more than a low and quite inconspicuous watershed, it would not be surprising if it turns up one day in that country also. In Venezuela the species is to be found growing at the very top of the clean part of the trunks of *moriche* palm trees, *Mauritia flexuosa*, right at the base of the crown of palm leaves. The plants are usually lightly hidden among the lowest leaves, but occasionally have their 10-inch pendent pseudobulbs and dangling (sometimes yard long) narrow leaves quite well exposed. It would be safer for them to grow deep among the leaves, where their flowers would be better concealed from the public eye, but, not anticipating the perfidy of human beings, they have developed in this more eye-catching manner, presumably to expose their flowers better to insect pollinators. While this habit of growth puts them decidedly at risk from clutching hands, they are not entirely defenseless as they can count on a quite efficient ally in their present fight for existence. This ally is the nature of the *morichales* in which they grow. Many a moriche palm stands within scant yards of the highway, or is at least clearly visible therefrom, and the intervening grassy savanna looks easy to cross. But appearances can be deceptive, and it takes more than a modicum of enthusiasm to keep an orchid hound wading ever deeper into the virtual swamp of a morichal to reach his target. Unless a flowering plant is in full view, discretion may soon prove stronger than valor and the hound will go sniffing for easier prey elsewhere.

The 10-inch to 15-inch pendent racemes of *Catasetum longifolium* can bear 20 or more resupinate flowers of an attractive, if often rather dark, mixture of red or golden brown, with yellow or orange inside the cup of the lip; and they sometimes have a complete range of flowers that grade from male at the base (i.e., the physical top) of the raceme to female at the apex, passing through intermediate hermaphroditic forms on the way. As already mentioned, the male flower has only a pair of small and not at all conspicuous "teeth" to trigger the pollinial mechanism, and has a relatively short, pot-shaped lip with a fringed border. As the flowers grade towards full femininity, the margin of the lip becomes smoother and the lip itself more elongate, and the final female flower has a quite smooth rim to its by then rather bag-shaped lip.

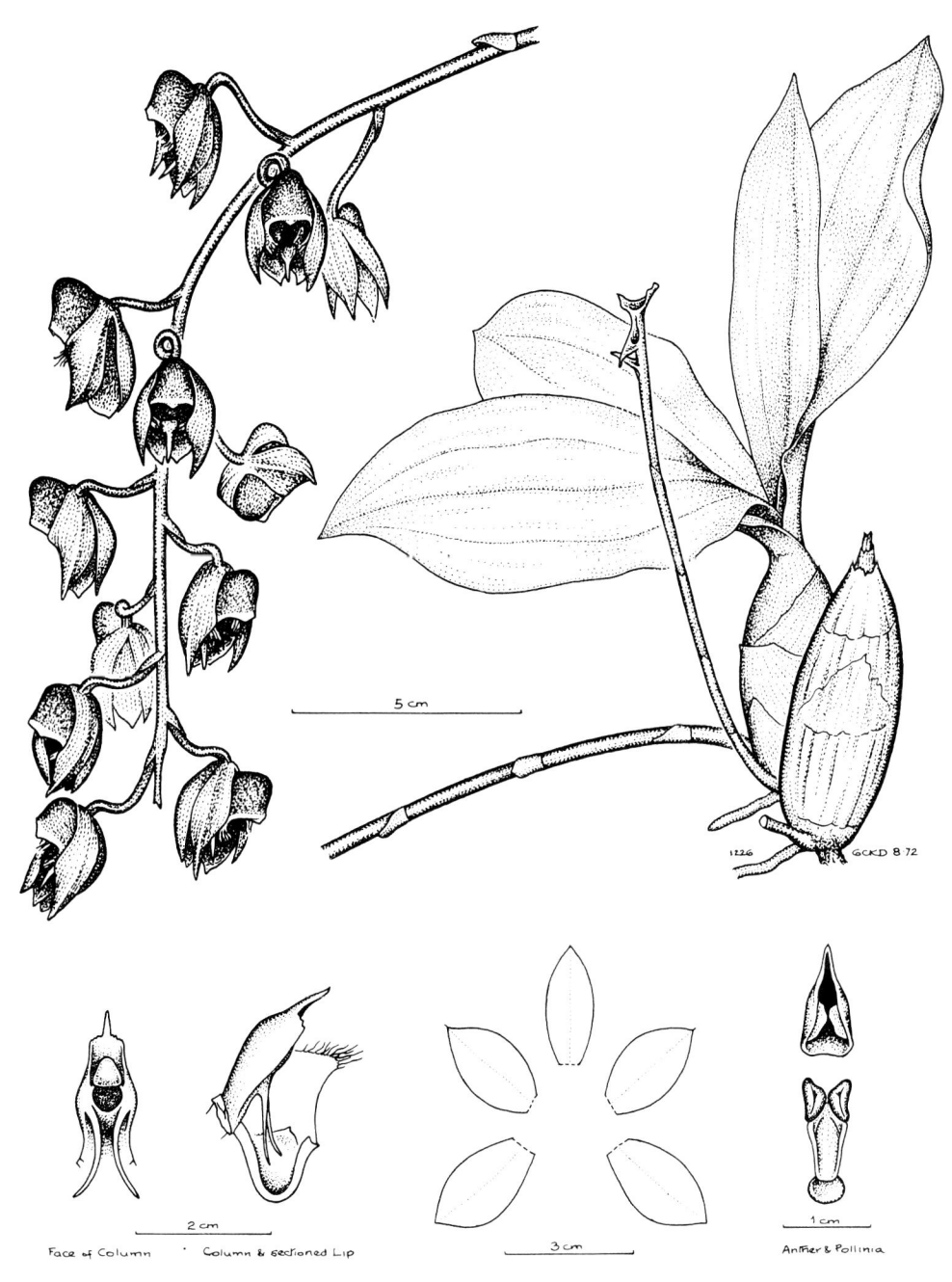

Catasetum costatum Reichb.f. in Gard.Chron. ser.3, 1: 72, 1887. — E.

Altensteinia, Bifrenaria, Chrysocycnis, and Dichaea of Venezuela[1]

ALTENSTEINIA FIMBRIATA was named in 1815 in honor of an enthusiastic, botanically minded Prussian minister bearing the imposing name of Baron Karl Stein zum Altenstein. *Altensteinia* is a fairly small genus of mainly high-altitude, terrestrial orchids, many of them quite small in size though some are quite appreciably tall. One of the smallest species of this genus, *A. rostrata*, was described and illustrated in the *A.O.S. Bulletin* of May 1977 and is definitely "alpine" in character as it grows around 4,000 m altitude. By contrast, *Altensteinia fimbriata*, shown here, grows in the State of Táchira at the less alpine, but still appreciable height of somewhat under 2,000 m to at least 2,800 m, and is far from being a miniature. The plants we found were up to 75 cm tall, but these must rate as insignificant beside the height of 1.80 m, or say six feet, noted for this species in Peru where some records show it growing as high up as 3,600 m. Here in Venezuela the favorite habitat of *A. fimbriata* seems to be open meadows or steep, grassy slopes or even roadside cuttings where they receive maximum protection from storms. The stout flower stem rises from a basal rosette of leaves and bears at its apex a dense raceme, to 20 cm long, of pretty white or pale, yellow-brown flowers that have the kind habit of displaying their relatively large, round, fimbriate-margined lips in a neat pattern all around the raceme. The plants of *A. fimbriata* we saw were in flower in January, but they almost certainly die back later and become much less conspicuous, which may account for the fact that this orchid does not seem to have appeared on any local lists until about 1970. Our general lack of success with high-altitude terrestrials was repeated with the plant of *Altensteinia fimbriata* we brought back and we do not plan to try again.

Bifrenaria aurantiaca is a very attractive epiphytic orchid inhabiting the region that extends from Colombia through Venezuela and on down to Brazil. In Venezuela it seems to be absent in the western part, which is basically Andean in nature, but occurs in the south and east, both in Bolívar State, and in Venezuela's Amazonas territory. *Bifrenaria aurantiaca* is obviously an orchid that likes to be warm, as we have found it in low-altitude forests of the Río Padamo and Río Siapa of the far end of the white water Upper Orinoco and also on the Río Ciutana which is a basically black water tributary of the Río Sipapo that reaches the upper Orinoco in its lower section. In the great expanse of Bolívar State we know of this species in the hot climate of the Río Paragua, but we have also found it in less hot sites near Auyántepui, on the flanks of the Sarisariñama (the table mountain famous for its vast holes — (see Chapter 10) and cooler yet at 1,000 m on the flank of the Auyántepui itself. This latter site seems to represent this orchid's upper limit, because, although we have cultivated plants with adequate success many years ago in the Valley of Caracas at 900 m, now, on the hilly outskirts of the city 400 m higher, our plants do not thrive, though all are not yet dead.

As a plant, *Bifrenaria aurantiaca* is fairly easily recognizable, having single, plicate leaves on its round, dollar-sized, flattish pseudobulbs that grow closely spaced, even superposed along the rhizome, and often appressed to the branch of its host tree. The pseudobulbs moreover are characteristically lightly and smoothly ribbed and their hard, shiny green surface bears fine, dark spots. The inflorescence of *B. aurantiaca* is a raceme borne by a peduncle that starts from the side of the pseudobulb at its base; one of its attractions is its habit of adopting all sorts of unconventional and twisted attitudes between "straight up" and "straight down." The main attraction, of course, lies in the flowers themselves which sit up and face the public nicely to display their color or orangey-red with

[1] Originally appeared in *A.O.S. Bulletin*, Vol. 49, February 1980, pages 144-148

Dichaea histrio

Chrysocycnis schlimii — side view

strong red markings. In an adequately warm climate this species should make a welcome addition to any collection of epiphytes, preferably fastened to hanging blocks of tree-fern to enable the inflorescences to develop in whatever direction they wish. March through May seems to be the preferred flowering period of *Bifrenaria aurantiaca*.

Chrysocycnis schlimii: *Chrysocycnis* is mentioned in Hawke's *Encyclopaedia of Cultivated Orchids* as being a genus of "Strange plants of unique vegetative habit, excessively rare and little known epiphytes native to the high Andes of Colombia." While my hackles always rise at the use of the word "excessively" when "exceedingly" is meant (how can one have an orchid that is *too* rare?), there is no doubt that it is a seldom seen genus with odd-looking flowers. This genus of orchids was dealt with in more sober scientific detail by Sweet in an article in *Orquideología*, in April 1971, but even there acknowledgment is paid to the unusual nature of these orchids which are referred to as members of a group of genera with "bizarre floral morphology." The genus was published by Linden & Reichb.f. in 1854 and the name they gave it means "Golden Swan." While *Chrysocycnis schlimii* does not quite live up to the expectations of magnificence promised by this name, it does at least have a very unusual and attractive flower with

Bifrenaria aurantiaca Lindl. in
Bot. Reg. 22: t. 1875, 1836. — D. E.

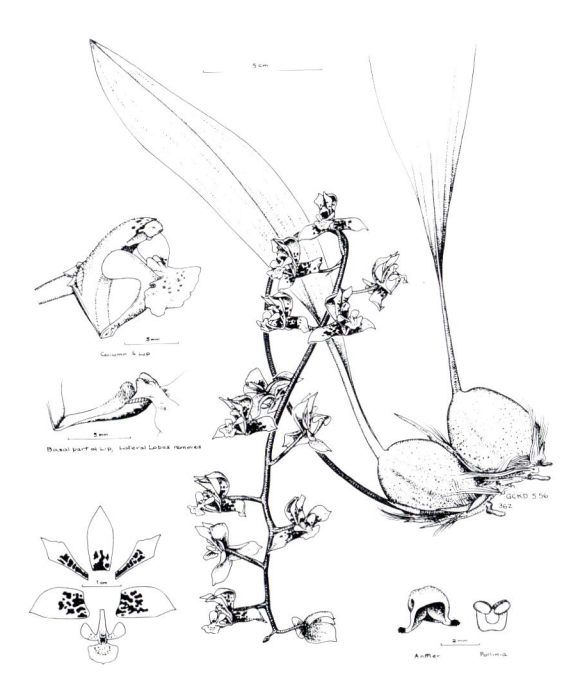

Altensteinia fimbriata H. B. K.
Nov. Gen. et Sp. Pl. 1:333, 1816. — A.

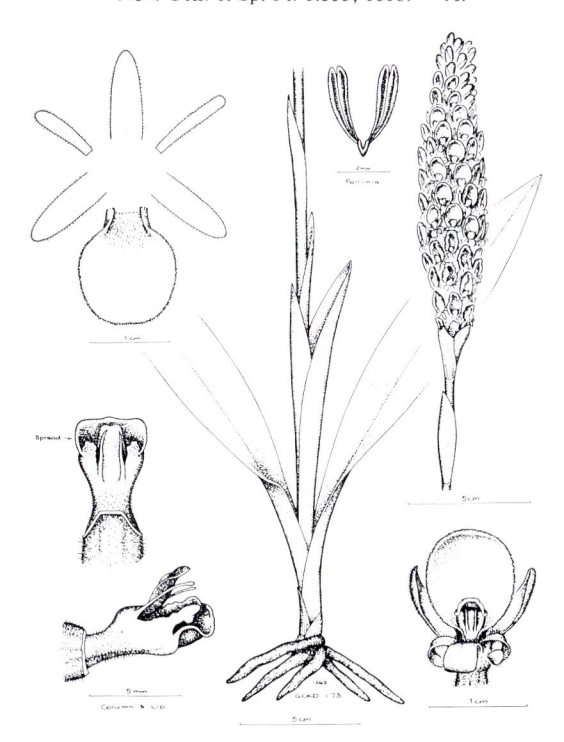

a "golden" column bent like a swan's neck. The genus *Chrysocycnis* often had five species attributed to it but these eventually boiled down to only two, one of which, *C. schlimii*, has had the good taste to present itself in Venezuela as a subject for this article — even if only by the skin of its rhizome, as its penetration appears to be limited to a part of Táchira State that borders right on Colombia.

We owe our introduction of *Chrysocycnis schlimii* to Sr. Roberto Mejía of San Cristóbal, the capital city of Táchira. It is one of a number of species from that state whose presence in Volume 6 of *Venezuelan Orchids Illustrated* is due to Sr. Mejía and his *campesino* assistant known to us as *Ojo-del-Aguila* (eye of the eagle) because of his extremely sharp eye in spotting orchids. With them as guides we visited the home of this rare species, growing in half-cleared cloud forest at about 2,000 m altitude, and were able to get a specimen for cultivation and study. This plant of *C. schlimii*, now some seven years old, has done well with us and has provided the illustration given here. The plant is typically epiphytic but at its base may reach down to the soil, and take hold there also. This species has a long, climbing, and occasionally branching rhizome bearing pseudobulbs at irregular intervals of up to some 20 cm, with new roots appearing at the base of each (unifoliate) pseudobulb. The smooth, green leaves are also very variable in size and form, some reaching the very impressive size of 45 cm long and over 10 mm wide. The inflorescence of *Chrysocycnis schlimii* is in the form of single flowers on suberect peduncles that rise from the rhizome itself just below the pseudobulb. The resupinate flowers have spotted, brownish-yellow sepals and petals with a considerable overlay of red tinge, and they stand up nicely to be admired. The lip is a smallish, hairy, beelike thing of dark coloration. Just how tall a plant of *C. schlimii* might grow I have no idea; though branching here and there, it is mainly a straight-up-the-tree climber and as such could perhaps grow as tall as its host tree, with new "handholds" at each pseudobulb to keep it on course. Our original plant seems quite happy with us, though its home in Táchira was far higher. The single stem with which we started has over the years been broken into several pieces and each piece restarted from the base of a six-foot-tall piece of very hard tree-fern core with its natural coating of fibrous material. This seems a more logical way to grow the orchid rather than to let it continue straight up a tree — and then have to borrow a fireman's ladder every once in a while to see if it is still flowering nicely. While the leaves of our plant of *Chrysocycnis schlimii* do not even start to compete with the 18-inch leaves of the plant we saw in Táchira, they are a quite respectable 10 inches in size. We cannot show visitors a flower any time they ask to see one, but it has produced flowers at one time or another in all months of the year except March, and we think a bud may now be forming to complete the calendar.

Dichaea histrio: *Dichaea* is a genus of about 40 species, none of which has large flowers but many of which have an attraction of their own due to the normally pendent habit of their long stems which bear closely-spaced "distichous" or two-ranked leaves which sometimes look like a dangling type of fern. *Dichaea swartzii* is one such species with stems reaching down to some 60 cm, looking rather like a comb with three-cm teeth. Another is *D. muricata* with stems of the same length but with smaller, often quite roundish leaves, very impressive by virtue of their neatly regular appearance. Between these two *Dichaea* species in general appearance lie *D. kegelii* and *D. histrio*, the former with more closely-spaced leaves than the latter. As both these species have flowers whose lips are strongly marked with violet, they are not too easy to distinguish with certainty; but the *D. kegelii* lip has pointed lobes while the lobes of *D. histrio* are subdued. Both make attractive species for a small collection.

Dichaea histrio seems to be a rather rare species in Venezuela, and even outside the country has a limited range, being known only from Surinam and Guyana. It must surely have been collected in Venezuela by others, but when the Foldats opus on Venezuelan orchids appeared in 1970 as part of the official *Flora de Venezuela,* this *Dichaea* species was noted as having been found only in one unspecified locality by a specified person (v. Lansberge), and in a specified locality (Caracas area) by an unspecified person. We have ourselves found *Dichaea histrio* at 1,800 m only in the Andes of Táchira State, near Colombia, but another plant was found by a friend in Amazonas territory near the Brazilian border at about 1,200 m. Obviously this is a species that gets around but is bashful about being seen. *Dichaea histrio* flowers for us at any time during May to August. Our plant is still alive after some 10 years, though it is not doing more than holding its own, pegged at its base (i.e., the top of the plant) to a vertically-hung slab of tree-fern in a shady but airy place.

New Names for Old[1]

IT HAS BEEN INEVITABLE that during the few years that we have written miscellaneous articles for the *A.O.S. Bulletin* a number of changes should have occurred in the names of the orchids illustrated. Whatever has been the reason behind each change, it is important that the new or corrected name should receive proper, and if possible repeated, attention in the hopes that it will be remembered, and the old one fade away. Now that this more regular series of notes on Venezuelan orchids has been properly launched, it seems appropriate to look back and note the names that these species should now be bearing. When a change is needed in the name of an orchid that has already appeared in the *A.O.S. Bulletin*, it is very difficult to give the change a publicity equal to the impact made originally, particularly if its first appearance was illustrated. A picture and its title stays in the memory, which is fine if the title is correct but is unfortunate if the title is wrong or is "out of date." By contrast a mere written reference makes less impact and a subsequent correction of name has a better chance of eliminating the former name. For this reason, while some changes are also needed in old articles that bore no illustrations, this present note refers only to changes in those that did. Although the small publicity provided by this present article will not solve the problem right away, one can hope that in due course the correct names will take hold and the previous ones will be forgotten.

The name changes to which I now wish to give some publicity are:

(Dates refer to their appearance in *A.O.S. Bulletin*)

Name Used	Proper Name
June 1970, p. 489	
Phragmipedium caudatum var. *lindenii*	*P. lindenii*
May 1973, p. 394	
Maxillaria ochroleuca	*M. splendens*
May 1973, p. 420	
Elleanthus capitatus	*E. sphaerocephalus*
December 1975, p. 1077	
Maxillaria spilotantha	*M. guareimensis*
December 1975, p. 1077	
Odontoglossum hastilabium	*Oncidium hastilabium*
September 1976, p. 785	
Odontoglossum arminii	*Otoglossum arminii*
September 1977, p. 792	
Oncidium globuliferum	*O. scansor*
February 1978, p. 107	
Cyrtopodium engelii	*C. glutiniferum*

To fix these changes in the mind it would be nice to re-reproduce the original illustrations, but this would certainly exhaust the Editor's budget as well as his patience. However, in two cases I have managed to twist his arm enough to allow the inclusion of some new pictures. These are:

Phragmipedium lindenii: In 1970 this was illustrated, in black and white only, under the name of *P. caudatum* var. *lindenii*, but it was mentioned that it has started out as *Uropedium lindenii* some 50 years earlier. The taxonomic status of this very extraordinary orchid was the subject of botanical dispute for many years until it was finally elevated to the rank of species by Dressler & N. Williams. This name now seems to have general approval. In the meantime, however, the name *Phragmipedium* had gotten itself onto the list of Venezuelan orchids with no clear reference as to which of these now separate species it was referring. But as we have not found the "proper" *P. caudatum* in our searches here, nor have heard of anyone else who has, I think it is very probable that only *Phragmipedium lindenii* is truly a Venezuelan species. Unfortunately, while *P. lindenii* is an exceptionally interesting plant for the botanist with its normal "slipper-lip" replaced with a third petal, there is no denying that horticulturally and visually *P. caudatum* is by far the more desirable. Our plants of this *lindenii* species, all progeny by division of the original plant acquired from Sanders some 20 years ago, do not compete in length of petals with the *giganteum* variety il-

[1] Originally appeared in *A.O.S. Bulletin*, Vol. 49, March 1980, pages 223-227

Cyrtopodium glutiniferum

lustrated in the *A.O.S. Bulletin* for September 1978 (p. 816); but at times they can run to three fine, large flowers on a single inflorescence.

In cultivation here we have found *Phragmipedium lindenii* a most amenable plant when potted (as befits an epiphytic species) in chopped tree-fern root and placed in an airy situation where, for about half the day until noon, it is in open shade and, for at least the first part of the afternoon is in full sun. The plants divide easily for propagation and they bear capsules freely, but as far as we can see the seed is never fertile and the capsules "wither on the vine" without fully maturing. Our original plant of *P. caudatum*, bought in the United Kingdom some 20 years ago, still goes strong and by division has also provided its share of offspring. It is potted as the *P. lindenii*, but by trial and error has settled best in a situation with rather less than direct sunlight. The flowering seasons for these two *Phragmipedium* species here can be anything from December to July and may very likely depend more on what the weather was doing before the inflorescence was born than what it does later. Right now, in mid-February as I write, one plant of *P. caudatum* is in full flower and one plant of *P. lindenii* is in early bud — and at 8:00 a.m. we are in our usual mountaintop cloud (or wet mist) while El Hatillo itself below us is probably in bright sun. I am wearing a good, wool cardigan as the temperature is a miserable 15° C, or 60° F if that is the way you look at temperatures as I still do myself because of a youth spent in the Fahrenheit camp. In an hour or two I expect to be sweating in blazing sun, down to my short sleeves. And if it is any guide to anything, I can mention that alongside the *Phragmipedium caudatum* a plant of *P. lindleyanum* is also in flower, as well as a large plant of *Vanda* (*dearei* X *tatzeri*) which always does well here, though, when acquired 10 years ago, we thought it was supposed to be a "warm" hybrid.

Cyrtopodium glutiniferum, previously erroneously called *C. engelii*, is a most attractive species of the far eastern part of Venezuela and deserves more attention than it seems to have attracted so far. Though it was honored with a color illustration in the *A.O.S. Bulletin* for February 1978,

Cyrtopodium glutiniferum inflorescenses, collected in the wild, dwarf this 5'6" man.

Phragmipedium lindenii

other references to it are scarce. When published in the *A.O.S. Bulletin* it was already known that its identification was wrong, but it takes time for such changes to filter through to the printed page. This present article gives me a chance to apologize to this cyrtopodium (and to the *A.O.S. Bulletin* readers) for the misnaming and to take advantage of this to flatter its ego with two more pretty pictures. One of these shows a couple of inflorescences of *Cyrtopodium glutiniferum* held by a 5′6″ Indian for scale; the other is a close-up of part of a panicle. The first photo was taken *in situ* at a spot on the Río Chicanan (tributary of the Río Cuyuni that later flows into Guyana) at something less than 100 m altitude. In this hot climate location, with only occasional shade, fine clumps of this orchid were growing in sandy savanna on the edge of some light woods and were in full flower in late November. The second photo, showing part of an inflorescence, was taken in April some 17 months later when a plant we brought back had already settled in at our 1,300 m altitude. Despite the considerable difference in climate this cyrtopodium appears to be enjoying itself. The specimen of *Cyrtopodium glutiniferum* is no doubt greatly helped by being planted (in ordinary garden soil) in a place of maximum sunshine. The color of the flowers seems to be darker than the plant we photographed *in situ*, which might reflect some change in the soil that it now lives in.

Cleistes rosea[1]

IN THE *A.O.S. Bulletin* for January 1978, Henry Teuscher gave us a very concise and clear exposé of the closely allied genera of *Pogonia, Nervilia, Cleistes, Isotria,* and *Triphora* in which, from the horticultural point of view, he rated all except *Nervilia* as hardly worth the attention they would require in cultivation. This remark prompted an article in the December issue of that year by Warren Stoutamire in which he said that, in his experience, some species of *Pogonia* and *Cleistes* do deserve a place in his "winter-cold" greenhouse in (I presume) Akron, Ohio. Having no experience in winter-cold greenhouse culture (nor, to be honest, any desire to live where such culture is needed) I can express no valid opinion in this matter, but in our experience with tropical *Cleistes* species there is at least one that certainly deserves cultivation here in Venezuela.

As Teuscher makes clear, there has been much confusion in the past between *Pogonia* and *Cleistes;* all four of the *Cleistes* species in Venezuela with which I am acquainted have at one time or another been listed as *Pogonia*. Certainly two of these are not likely to arouse much lust in the mind of the orchidist. *Cleistes stricta* is a tall (to 85-cm), very slender-stemmed species that seems only to consist of an erect stem bearing a number of very small, fleshy and bract-like leaves, and a few flowers on separate, up-trending branches. The flowers are about an inch in size, bronze-gold in color with a white lip marked by a blue midline. Rare in Venezuela, this cleistes is an orchid of high, remote places in our Guayana-Amazonas region. There I found our one-and-only plant at about 2,000 m altitude on Cerro de la Neblina, growing in boggy soil on the very edge of Brazil.

Cleistes tenuis, as its name implies, is another slender species. Growing to about 40 cm tall, this cleistes has larger (but still bract-like) leaves than *C. stricta* and a terminal raceme of a few, somewhat larger flowers that are pale green or white, with some purple marks at the base of the lips. As distinct from *C. stricta, Cleistes tenuis* is an orchid of low areas in Amazonas, Venezuela. We have also found this species in Bolívar State at about 840 m altitude, again right on the border with Brazil, but this time near Roraima.

Cleistes moritzii grows to 60 cm tall, with fleshy, erect leaves about six cm long. The flowers have elements around three cm long, the sepals being peach-colored on the face, pink at the back; the petals are rose-purple, and the lip also, but with a yellow callus down the axis. We have met this *Cleistes* species on Auyántepui at about 1,800 m and it is also on record from Roraima where the type specimen was found a good few years ago by our friend, Julian Steyermark. But most extraordinary, *C. moritzii* has recently been found by another friend, Gernot Bergold, growing on open slopes on the outskirts of Caracas. It is inconceivable that these latter plants could have been artificially introduced to this locality, but I have seen its flowers and, despite a doubting-Thomas attitude, must agree that they are indeed *C. moritzii.* Nature has many surprises up its sleeve when it comes to orchid distribution!

I can understand no ordinary collector bothering with either *Cleistes stricta* or *C. tenuis*, but *Cleistes moritzii* might have some attraction for an enthusiast, although, in common with the prevous pair, the flowers do not open wide enough to show their full merits. But when one comes to **Cleistes rosea** things are very different indeed. This species has stout, erect stems to 85 cm tall; the erect, pointed leaves are 10 cm long. The inflorescence consists of two (rarely three) large flowers that open in succession. The six-cm sepals of *C. rosea* are pale green inside, dorsally flushed with pink, and hold themselves beautifully wide. The petals are dark pink and the lip mainly white with strong purple veining

[1] Originally appeared in *A.O.S. Bulletin*, Vol. 49, April 1980, pages 358-359[1]

in the exposed, apical part. Although the petals do not spread like the sepals but remain closed up alongside the lip, the whole effect is nevertheless highly attractive. Perhaps the widest spread of all showy terrestrials in Venezuela, *Cleistes rosea* is on record for all major division of the country, from about 1,000 m to 2,000 m. We have found it in easily accessible spots such as on the northern end of the Gran Sabana Road to Sta. Elena de Uairén, and in hard-to-reach sites such as the summit of Auyántepui or Cerro Jaua. We even have *C. rosea* growing wild just outside our garden fence above Caracas!

I have remarked above that this fine *Cleistes* species should be in cultivation; I did not say that it was, and I rather doubt if it is. As it is not a rare species, we feel we have done no harm in trying to grow *C. rosea* in our own garden, but after a number of failures we have given up trying any more. Moved only a matter of yards and taken with a complete bucketload of the soil in which it grows here, we have failed to keep a plant of *C. rosea* alive for more than a year. The climate is identical, the soil seems to be identical, the air and light seem to be identical. The only reason we can see to explain our failure is that the plants fall in love with the many and varied other plants they grew up and went to school with, and die of heartbreak when parted. Perhaps if we could find a plant of *C. rosea* in extremely young status it might accept a transplant, but in all the grassy undergrowth where we find them, it would be most difficult to see it, and it

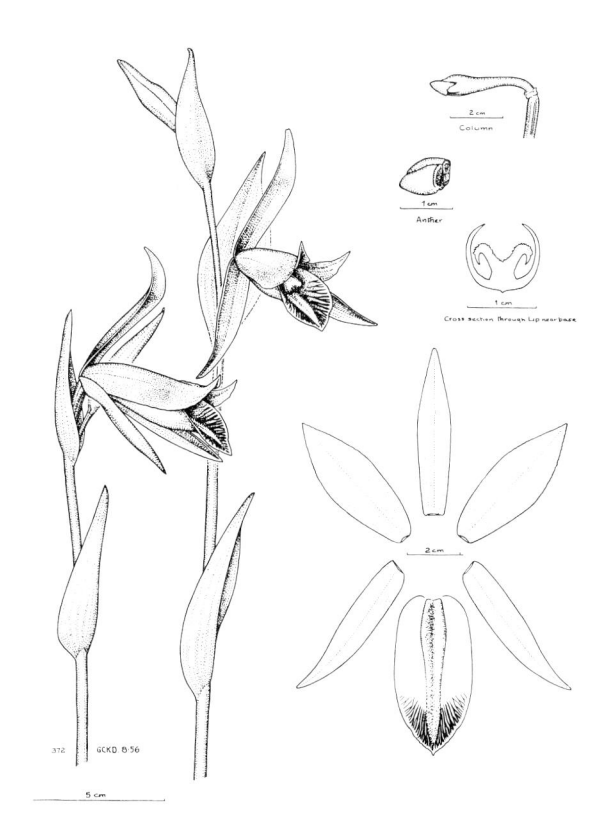

Cleistes rosea Lindl., Gen. and Sp. Orch. Pl. 410, 1840. — B. D. E.

is likely to remain the most disappointing, showy terrestrial in this respect that we have ever laid gentle or violent hands on. But left to itself, *Cleistes rosea* is wonderful.

Sobralia sessilis — An Orchid Hunt in an Orchid Herbarium[1]

SOME YEARS AGO I wrote a long account for *The Orchid Review*, describing a frustrating search for a small package of orchids in the depths of our parcels and customs offices in Caracas, Venezuela. This present account deals with a long but eventually very rewarding search for an orchid in the inexhaustible depths of the Orchid Herbarium of Oakes Ames at Harvard University, Cambridge, Massachusetts.

A few months ago I had occasion to visit this herbarium to discuss with its curator, Leslie Garay, a number of problems related to our plans for a jointly-authored *Illustrated Field Guide* to the orchids of Venezuela, taking with me Nora to help with a lot of anticipated mechanical-type chores associated with putting titles and page numbers in their right places. Several of these problems concerned matters of identification of a number of orchid drawings that at that time had not been published. One of these was a drawing I made in 1969 of a purple-flowered sobralia that we had found in the cloud forests of the upper end of the Aonda Valley, a cliff-sided, fairly wide gash that almost completely separates the small, northern end of the great massif of Auyántepui from the major, southern section that is the home of Angel Falls. The sobralia plant had a resemblance to *Sobralia violacea*, but only vaguely so as its flexible and branching habit was quite uncharacteristic of that fairly common species. We took a piece home, grew it, and in due course it thanked us by flowering. These flowers, from their color, still suggested an affinity with *S. violacea*, but other differences continued to make us doubt this provisional diagnosis. As always in such cases I took a photo of it, made a drawing of it, and sent the result to Leslie Garay at the Herbarium. Leslie also agreed that it was "odd," but many other and more important chores intervened, and it was not until mid-1979, when we got together to finalize the material for the *Illustrated Field Guide*, that he had the time to go properly into this problem.

The result of this work achieved four things. Firstly, it produced a very convincing answer to the identity of the Aonda sobralia; secondly, it completely upset the identification of another sobralia that was on the verge of going into our book under an erroneous name; thirdly, it gave us a ringside view of how a taxonomist goes about solving a tricky identification problem; and finally, it convinced us of the impracticality, indeed impossibility, for anyone, however expert, to determine with certainty the identity of a doubtful plant in a family as large as the Orchidaceae unless the work can be done in a herbarium with very ample resources indeed, not only in actual herbarium specimens but also in photos of specimens (and particularly of type-specimens) in other herbaria, copies of old records, old books, and old drawings or paintings, all pulled together with a very complete indexing system without which many essential references would be unfindable when wanted. An essential personal asset for all taxonomists to possess is also a computer-like memory, so when at first Leslie was not able to put a name to our sobralia (a genus of "only" some 80 species), I expected to hear him suggest that it must be a new species. But he still felt sure that somewhere he had seen something that linked it to some known orchid species, so the search had to be intensified.

Unfortunately the *ambiente* in the herbarium was not at all conclusive to intensive searching, or even any searching at all. Along with some other outlying sections of the main Harvard Botanical Museum, the Orchid Herbarium was at that moment involved in a major physical reconstruction, part of which required messing around with the air-conditioning system. Being thoroughly modern, these sections of the otherwise rather antique Botanical Museum were fully air-conditioned, and

[1] Originally appeared in *A.O.S. Bulletin*, Vol. 49, May 1980, pages 486-488

in line with modern techniques had been built with unopenable windows. Being advised of our imminent arrival, some mastermind had decided that it would be a suitable moment to put the air-conditioning equipment out of order, with the heat control immovably at maximum. In midwinter this might have been accepted as no great disaster, but we were now close on midsummer and the herbarium climate was rivaling Death Valley. Nobody knew (or admitted to knowing) how to get the air circulation under control, or how to get the temperature regulation back to normal, and only the most dedicated of herbarium occupants could stand it for more than brief spells at a time. Emergency fans of great power, and of equally great ability to blow workpapers into complete disorder, were plugged in, and similar fans in the corridors blew hot air from corner to corner. Working conditions hovered on the intolerable; Nora at times had to go and lie down in the shade outside; and, for a while, the herbarium was more or less closed down. But Leslie was not going to let this defeat him, and as co-author of the book that was the cause of my presence there I also had to suffer, even if there was little of real value that I could contribute to solving the sobralia problem.

With my drawing as a starting point, Leslie first began by checking all his reference cards on sobralias that were not yet thoroughly identified, but, although card after card, photo after photo, emerged from his own files in addition to specimens from the herbarium, nothing came to light that matched the Aonda specimen with any degree of certainty. When these were exhausted without yielding an answer, the search switched from unidentified material to material that already had a name attached, and here at last the bell was rung. A photo of Lindley's type-specimen of *Sobralia sessilis* showed an unusual feature, in that it had small branches, gracefully arched and with a knob or swelling at their base. A photo of the duplicate of this type in the Reichenbach Herbarium showed identical characters. This just had to be our Aonda species, a certainty that was made triply sure when Leslie compared it with a watercolor painting, made in 1846 by Loddiges, of a plant originally introduced by Loddiges himself, showing a purple flower.

But the name *Sobralia sessilis* is commonly applied to a white-flowered species well known in Venezuela and elsewhere. We had found it ourselves in a number of places in the Venezuelan Guayana, and had even shown its picture in the May 1973 *A.O.S. Bulletin*, but none of these plants were purple or had ever shown a growth habit like our Aonda plant. If our plant was indeed Lindley's *S. sessilis*, then something had been radically wrong for many years with the generally

Sobralia sessilis

accepted identification of this latter species. While we continued mopping brows and watching like a pair of Watsons, Leslie continued his Sherlocking task to find out the how, the when, and the wherefore of this new complication. Eventually he traced the responsibility for this to the erroneous use of the name *Sobralia sessilis* on an illustration of a quite distinct species in the very prestigious *Botanical Magazine* for March 1851, a misnaming that was repeated in another illustration in an 1894 issue of the same publication. These had led to the perpetuation of this error for more than a century and a quarter, with hundreds of plants and specimens in many herbaria being wrongly labeled in the meantime. With yet more searching, Leslie found that the misnamed illustrations in the *Botanical Magazine* represented *Sobralia decora*, a Central American species not native to Venezuela.

This, of course, was not yet the end of this tale. At this point we had convincing arguments that the name of our Aonda species was *Sobralia sessilis* but were left with the question of what should be the name of the white sobralia that until now had been commonly called by that name. More cards were shuffled, more references consulted, and finally Leslie had it pinned down as *Sobralia valida*. We cried "Eureka" and Leslie could at last relax. We had got a name, *Sobralia sessilis*, for our new-to-Venezuela *Sobralia* species from the Aonda River. We had got a new-to-Venezuela name, *Sobralia valida*, for the many sobralia plants previously known as *S. sessilis*. And some drawings wrongly attributed to *S. sessilis* had been re-attributed correctly to a non-Venezuelan species, *Sobralia decora*. The Sherlock behind these successes was still at least moderately fresh. The Watsons who had sat on the sidelines and watched were exhausted.

We wholeheartedly agree with the saying that a good illustration is worth a thousand words, but the corollary to this is that a wrongly-labeled illustration can equally result in a thousand misnamings. Our sympathy goes to those who will now have to change a lot of herbarium labels, or, like us, make corrections in their books; or more specifically at least mentally correct that illustration in the May 1973 *A.O.S. Bulletin* to read *Sobralia valida*. And we sincerely hope that the ghost of the original misnamer of the 1841 *Botanical Magazine* illustration will remain forever in a suspended state of extreme distress!

Four Odd P(eas) from Venezuela[1]

PORROGLOSSUM ECHIDNUM is the first of the "Four Odd P(eas)" to be dealt with here. It comes from the headwaters of the Río Quinimarí, very close to the isolated, high-altitude, border area of the Río Táchira described in "Some Pleurothallis Species from Venezuela's Western Andes" in the *A.O.S. Bulletin* for October 1979 (see Chapter 33). But despite the closeness to that river, the topography (and presumably the soil) is very different, and when we followed our 1967 Táchira trip with a 1968 Quinimarí trip, the route to our planned camping site, at about 2,500 m altitude, was also different. This time (again traveling with Julian Steyermark) we left our vehicles at a village with the long name of San Vicente de la Revancha. Bargaining for the necessary mules started on the wrong foot when Julian mentioned that we were botanizing on behalf of a Ministry. This immediately led the locals to assume that we were yet one more Government *Comisión* to whom money would be no object, and we had to talk loud and long to convince them that we were more or less penniless travelers. When we were finally ready to move off the next day, I unwisely allowed myself to be coaxed onto the back of a mule. It was a very nice, well-behaved, and gentle beast, but when, within the first mile, the trail suddenly dived over what looked to me to be a minor cliff, my diving technique was not as expert as that of the mule. I landed on my chest on a very large, very hard, and very uncomfortable rock. Thanks to the intervention of the special *angelito* that guards us on our travels, no bones were broken, but I decided once more that it would be safer, and in the long run no slower, to continue on foot.

The critical part played by the topography in this corner is demonstrated by the fact that while the headwaters of the Táchira and Quinimarí Rivers are kissing-close, and both start by aiming north for Lake Maracaibo, only the former makes it. The Quinimarí quickly forgets where it is supposed to go, twists itself around to flow east, then south to join the Orinoco and eventually drops its waters into the Atlantic about 1,200 km to the east. The topography at our Tamá site had been one of a steady, gentle slope up to the páramo. Our Quinimarí site, by contrast, was one of high cliffs, with the camp itself on the edge of the forest at about 2,500 m, close to the Las Copas bluffs, and with direct access to the top of the páramo hindered by the long line of the Judio cliffs in the background.

At our Quinimarí camp we enjoyed (?) cold nights, with temperatures dropping to 40° F, but, as we were only in mid-January, we found the days to be consistently fine, and the "pickings" were even more rewarding than they had been at Tamá. Unlike the latter site, where the forest had been cleared years before and not much more clearing was in progress, the clearing here was recent and still active, so that, besides untouched forest above us, masses of trees were laid out alongside and just below us for us to examine at our leisure. Not that checking through several acres of recently felled forest is unalloyed leisure pleasure. To "walk" from the edge of a clearing to a spot 50 yards away in the middle of it can be, and nearly always is, an extremely slow and even dangerous operation. If I had to train a squad of embryo paratroopers I would give them a full hour to cover 100 yards by night and confine the lot to barracks when they failed to make it.

Not far from our camp the clearing ended at the edge of a small stream filled with forest and boulders, and it was here that we found our normally epiphytic porroglossum growing in fairly thin soil as a "lithophytic terrestrial" on top of a large rock. It is a small plant with erect, extremely hairy peduncles, considerably taller than the rough-surfaced leaves. The peduncles bear one

[1] Originally appeared in *A.O.S. Bulletin*, Vol. 49, June 1980, Pages 601-606

(perhaps two or three in slow succession?) pretty, but not large, *Masdevallia*-like flowers, and the excitingly odd thing about them, and the aspect that has brought them fame, is the mechanism that operates their mobile and "muscular" lips. The lip hangs invitingly out in a lax position from the end of the long, curved column-foot, but the moment a hump at the base of the lip is touched, the claw by which the lip is attached to the column-foot contracts and raises the lip up against the column, much as one's arm might raise one's hand if a sensitive biceps were tickled. If an insect of the right size is responsible for triggering this action, then the chances are that it would be momentarily trapped between column and petals and, in escaping, brush against the column and go off with the pollinia, or deposit pollinia as the case may be. This action has been studied and written about by experts (and by nonexperts such as right now) but it is always a fascinating thing to watch. When we checked our own flowers, we found that the lip closed completely in rather less than a second and was fully open again about half an hour later, and could be activated not only by touch but also by shaking the flower or by the action of direct sunlight (or sun warmth). This sun factor was also a nuisance when it came to photographing the flower in a relaxed-lip attitude. With direct sun on the flower for good lighting, the lip would close up just as the picture was ready to take and, as mentioned, a half hour would be needed for it to relax again.

In a study by Herman Sweet published in the June 1972 *A.O.S. Bulletin*, he notes that the lip gradually closes after sundown and opens again before sunrise. This seems to reverse the reaction to sunshine or heat noted above, but, as Sweet also says, it is a mechanism that still needs much study before it can properly be understood. In fact, even the studying must present some complications, not least of which might be the possibility of the poor flower getting worn out by having to raise and lower its lip too frequently at the touch-command of an investigator. Perhaps those who believe in the direct intelligence of plants should encourage a porroglossum union to demand time-and-a-half for overtime — before it is too late!

Polyotidium is a genus of great rarity, but its one-and-only species, **Polyotidium huebneri**, the second "P(ea)" of this note, is also an oddity for other reasons. Starting its taxonomic career in 1934 as a member of the genus *Hybochilus* (named by Mansfield for their "humpbacked" lips), its column showed such unusual features that, when critically re-studied by Garay in 1958, it emerged as a "founding member" of a new genus that Garay named *Polyotidium*, meaning "many-eared." Some orchid columns have ears or flaps extending beyond the apex of the clinandrium in which the anther lies, but *Polyotidium* goes beyond this in having two pairs of lobes, one pair shielding the anther and another pair joining to form a sort of cup below the stigmatic surfaces. This is fully described in Garay's article establishing the genus in 1958 (Botanical Museum of Harvard University Leaflets) but, as odd as all this column-flap business is, this is not the oddness that gains *Polyotidium* its place in this note. What does make it an "Odd P(ea)" is its bright orange-red color, or not so much the color as the fact that the color suffuses the whole raceme of flowers — the peduncle is red from the point where it leaves the base of the leaf, and by the time it reaches the flowers everything is orange; rachis, floral bracts, pedicellate ovaries, sepals, petals, lip, and all. Even the anther is a yellowish orange, and only the two small, hard pollinia are white.

The plant itself is fairly small, with small (1.5 cm), slender pseudobulbs each with its 10- to 20-cm, dark green, and almost terete leaf. The inflorescence rises from the base of the leaf and is just about as long. A fully open flower is only about one cm in size — no giant, but definitely attractive. Plants have been found in the Colombian Amazonas area and a friend found a plant in the Venezuelan Amazonas not far from San Carlos on the Río Negro which eventually runs into the Amazon itself. Our own plants were also found in the Venezuelan "Amazonas" territory, but quite a long way from the Río Negro. In the *A.O.S. Bulletin* for January 1979 (see Chapter 27), we described the spot where we came across a most extraordinary terrestrial form of the normally epiphytic *Paphinia cristata* and mentioned that nearby was a short stretch of very sandy soil just high enough to stand out above the flooded floor of the forest. On this there was a light scattering of low trees bearing quite a number of orchid species and among these we found our polyotidium. At the time it had no mature inflorescences and only later, at home, could we appreciate eventually its very odd, all-pervading coloration. Such a feature is rare but not unique among orchids (we have an imported repent *Coelogyne* species that shows a similar tendency although in not nearly so pronounced a manner), but we have seen it in no other Venezuelan orchid. Both Venezuelan specimens of *Polyotidium huebneri* come from a very low, hot, and damp climate. The Colombian ones are recorded as from rather higher ground (900 ft), but the climate is unlikely to have been other than still stickily hot. Our own plant survived to produce flowers for study but not surprisingly decided that life at over 3,000 ft was not to its liking, so one day, like Lewis Carroll's Baker when it found the Boojum, it softly and suddenly vanished away.

Of the "Four Odd P(eas)" covered in this article,

Porroglossum echidnum — closed lip

Porroglossum echidnum — open lip

Pleurothallis immersa is probably the one that is most familiar to enthusiasts of small, New World, tropical orchid species, certainly in Venezuela where one sees it in a number of private collections. Species of the enormous genus *Pleurothallis* typically produce their inflorescences, be they single flowers, racemes, or fasciculate "bundles" of single flowers, from the base of the leaf (or the top of the secondary stem). One species, *Pleurothallis lappiformis*, however, is quite exceptional in producing its flowers directly from the rhizome at the very base of the secondary stem, and it remains a puzzlement to us why no taxonomist has yet picked on this extraordinary feature to set it apart in some entirely new genus. We have in some degree a vested interest in this idea because we have such a plant, found by our friend, Charles Brewer-Carias, at the bottom of one of the enormous holes in the top of Sarisariñama mentioned in the *A.O.S. Bulletin* for April 1976 (see Chapter 10). This weird plant seems to thrive well and each year produces new growths and inflorescences, clearly with ambitions to become also another "Odd P(ea)". Unfortunately each year the new bud rots away before maturing, so we still do not know for certain whether it is a *Pleurothallis lappiformis* or some quite new species with a similar way of producing the inflorescence.

Pleurothallis immersa, illustrated here, seems at first glance to be another pleurothallis whose inflorescence disobeys the "base-of-the-leaf" rule as its racemes first appear a long way up the leaf towards its apex. On careful examination, however, one can see that this is a falsification of the evidence. The peduncle actually starts in the normal way from the base of the leaf but hides itself in a deep groove, with overlapping sides, along the mid-nerve of the leaf until it finally surfaces to develop its raceme. Bending the sides of the leaf backwards, the groove can be opened to reveal the peduncle. The racemes themselves are attractive, erect or sometimes arching, and sticking up at

Platystele johnstonii

Pleurothallis immersa

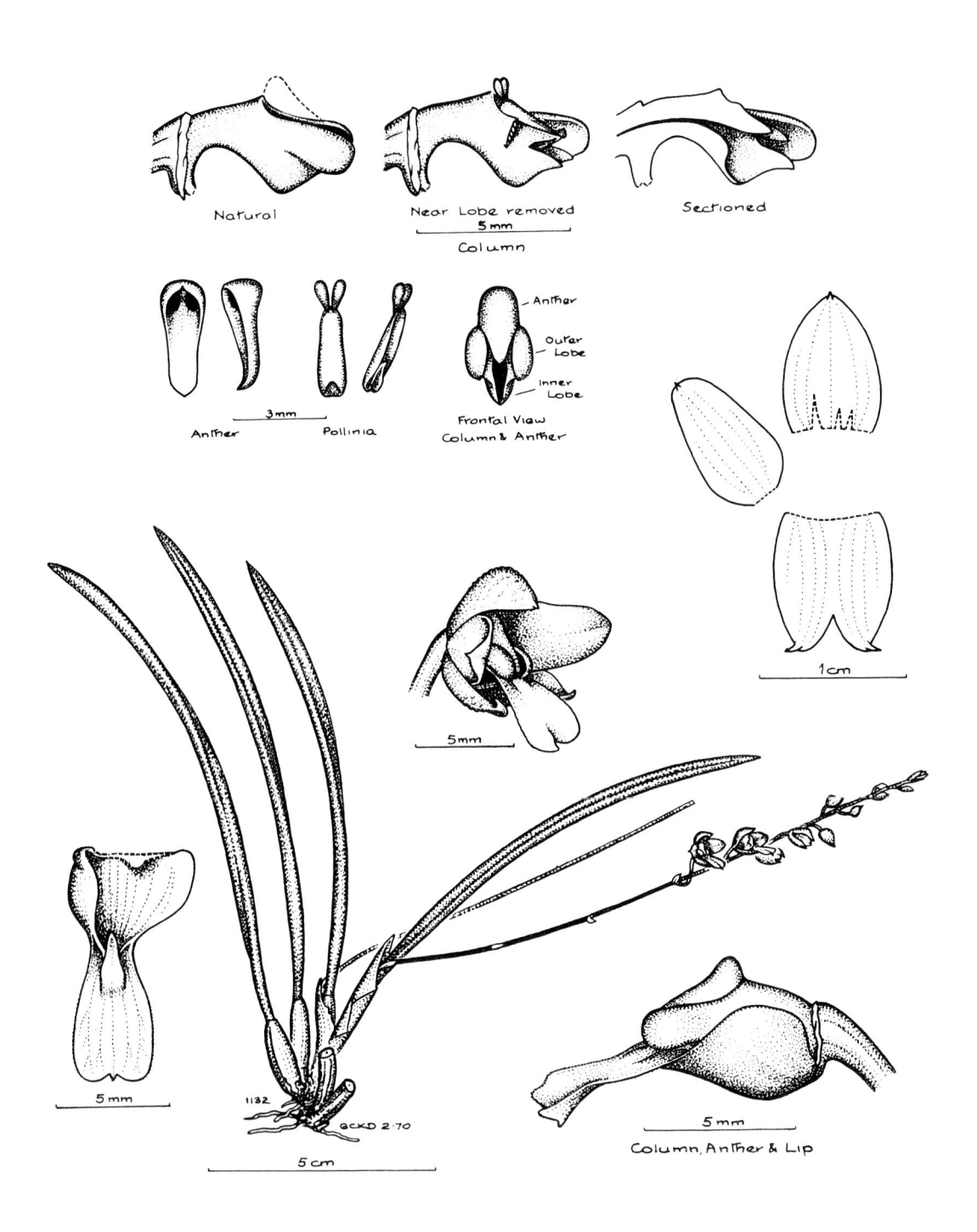

Polyotidium huebneri (Mansf.) Garay in Bot. Mus. Leafl. 18:105, 1958 — D.

times as much as 35 cm beyond the part of the peduncle hidden in the leaf. The color of the flowers varies from plant to plant, from plain yellow to golden yellow and on down to quite a dark yellowish brown.

As a species it is spread from Mexico to Venezuela, and in this country seems to reach its geographical limit with a (dubious?) record close to Caracas at about 1,500 m. Elsewhere here it is known no farther east than near the village of La Soledad, at about 1,800 m, in the Andes of the State of Barinas, and in the Andes of the State of Lara in the National Park of Yacambú at about 1,700 m. We have also found it at about 1,600 m in the cloud forests of the Sierra de Perijá, the range that forms the border with Colombia east of Lake Maracaibo, a habitat that shares many species with the Andes. Back in Caracas, *Pleurothallis immersa* has shown itself to be a nicely behaved plant, flowering with fair frequency in a number of miscellaneous months on its vertically-hung piece of tree-fern root in a shaded and well-ventilated spot, away from direct air currents.

Platystele johnstonii is the final "Odd P(ea)" of this note, and it only takes a quick glance at its picture here to see why it qualifies for this honor. *Platystele* is a genus of species that make up for their mini-ness by being quite enchanting — that is, unless the viewer believes that size is indispensable for enchantment. Venezuela is happy to provide a home for five of these species — *Platystele ornata* with dense racemes of gleaming, purple "bubble-glass" flowers each no bigger than a pin's head, incredibly beautiful under a microscope; *P. stenostachya* with flowers far smaller than its name and with red or yellow lips against yellow sepals and petals; *P. ovalifolia* with single, two-mm, pale cream flowers and minute leaves; *P. lancilabris* with sometimes considerably larger flowers appearing in succession; and *P. johnstonii*. Other plants can also be found here very like *Platystele lancilabris* but somewhat larger and sometimes with yellow flowers, all of which may prove to be distinct species although the differentiation is not very clear.

Platystele johnstonii, as you can see from the illustration here with a normal household pin for scale, has tiny leaves on a creeping and branching rhizome, forming a sort of mat on the bark of the host tree; from this rise the flowers on short, slender peduncles bearing short, one-flower-at-a-time racemes of perhaps eventually some three flowers in total. The flower is translucent creamy white with an orange lip and is dominated by the most extraordinary dorsal sepal. The petals and the other sepals are only about four mm long or less, but the dorsal sepal is as much as one cm tall and sticks way up above the plant like someone in a crowd waving his hand in the air to say, "Here I am. Can't you see me?" Which indeed one can.

Once again one is left wondering what trick of nature has resulted in such an odd exaggeration of just one sepal, and, if in one species, why not in others? Has it resulted from a sudden accidental but heritable mutation of a gene that proved to be of advantage by producing this dorsal sepal as a signpost for wandering insects, or did it result as a slow development from the intermingling of genes, encouraged by improved success in life as longer and longer sepals developed?

This lovely little oddity has so far been recorded in Venezuela from the lush forests of the Guatopo National Park just east of Caracas, at about 700 m, and is also on record from the close-offshore island of Margarita where it was found at 600 m by the person whose name it bears. While it does not seem to be known elsewhere in Venezuela it must certainly be hiding in a number of other places as it is on record also from Colombia and Ecuador. In our rather cooler climate above Caracas, *Platystele johnstonii* did well for some years in our plastic-roofed-and-sided "house" where we hope to avoid too much contact with the cool night air, but it has lately gone off its oats. The responsibility for this, we feel, may well lie in the quality of available corrugated fiberglass plastic sheet. This slowly rots and darkens as the plastic "evaporates" and leaves the rough fibers exposed to catch the dirt, making cleaning fruitless. There is no doubt that the light value inside this "house" is now dangerously low for most of the plants. Re-roofing is urgent but by now will no doubt cost at least five times what it first cost us. Yet we hate the idea of being limited only to plants that will grow fully exposed to our weather.

Epidendrum tigrinum and Epidendrum pamplonense — Old Species Restored to Life[1]

EVERY LARGE GENUS OF ORCHIDS contains at least a fair number of plants that leave one uncertain if one is dealing with two or more separate species or with merely two or more varieties of a single species. Some Neotropical genera, such as *Pleurothallis*, are kind enough to produce only relatively few troublesome species of this type, but other genera seem to delight in producing many. The genus *Epidendrum* is an example of the latter — a mixture of species some of which are easy to fix, such as *E. sceptrum* or *E. leucochilum*, but the majority of which belong to groups that are full of cases where even the taxonomist, let alone the *aficionado* untrained in taxonomy, finds it difficult to give a positive answer to the question "Is this a variety of species X or is it a species distinct from X?" Certainly, when one comes across a species that has been blessed (or cursed?) with a large number of named varieties, or has accumulated over the years a number of specific names that have later been relegated to synonymy, one can be sure that this is one of those annoyingly "ambiguous" species, so variable that few taxonomists have been ready to battle to the death in defense of either "lumping" or "splitting" the various types, with "lumping" probably being favored in most cases as providing the easiest way out of a seemingly insoluble problem. One has only to think of *Epidendrum vespa* (or *Encyclia vespa* for those who prefer to keep *Epidendrum* and *Encyclia* separate taxonomically) to appreciate this headache, as it is a species (or group of species and varieties) that includes in its checkered history the following epithets besides *vespa: variegatum, coriaceum, crassilabium, tigrinum, pamplonese, pachysepalum, christi, longipes, leopardinum, feddeanum, saccharatum, rhabdobulbon, rhopalobulbon,* and *variegatum* var. *virens,* var. *crassilabium,* var. *coriaceum,* var. *leopardinum,* and var. *lineatum!*

Taxonomic "splitters" tend to be very unpopular with orchidists, who naturally dislike changes in well-known names. It certainly removes the problem if one considers *Epidendrum vespa* to be no more than a single, albeit very variable, species, and the existence of so many names is proof in itself that in most, even if perhaps not all, cases it would be very difficult to maintain a rigid separation. But it also remains a fact that in a number of cases very obvious differences do exist between extreme forms of these epidendrums, even if marginally they may merge into each other. Certainly, from one's own personal point of view, there is no law against playing favorites, and, if one has the luck to have close contact with many specimens of a variable orchid of this type, one may eventually become convinced that some splitting of these into separate species is justified, even if only in one's own mind. And if later this splitting happens to coincide with some recent splitting by a proper taxonomist, then one can enjoy a feeling of having guessed right for once.

It was thus a happy moment when, for example, Dr. Garay in 1973 confirmed *Zygosepalum angustilabium* as a separate species in its own right, because from the moment we first saw this pretty orchid we felt it deserved a better fate than to be merely a variety of *Z. tatei,* as originally classified by Schweinfurth in 1951; or similarly with the less conspicuous but very attractive miniature species *Pleurothallis picta* of Lindley, long hidden behind synonymy with Bateman's *Pleurothallis grobyi* but honored in our personal records of 1961 with a separate drawing because of what we felt were constant differences from the typical *P. grobyi.* Here again, *Pleurothallis picta* was restored to life by Garay when he agreed to its inclusion in our recent *Illustrated Field Guide* to Venezuelan orchids.

Now it is the turn of *Epidendrum vespa,* well known in Venezuela and in most of the New World

[1] Originally appeared in *A.O.S. Bulletin,* Vol. 49, July 1980, pages 716-720

tropics, to receive a welcome cure from at least part of its past lumping troubles and come back from the hospital after a successful treatment by splitting. This species began its career in 1883, and, as already mentioned, went through a long series of named varieties and separate specific names, all of which eventually became lumped, in general taxonomic acceptance, into the one variable species of *Epidendrum vespa*. (Two of the many names produced for this orchid, *E. rhabdobulbon* (Schlechter 1920) and *E. baculibulbon* (Schlechter 1923), are worth special mention. Our botanical dictionary gives *rhabdo-* as derived from the Latin *baculum* meaning "stick, rod, staff," and it would be interesting to know why, in producing these two names, Schlechter failed to let his Greek left hand know what his Latin right hand was doing. Most of the "vespa" plants that we originally collected were puzzling by reason of the variability of their vegetative characteristics rather than their floral aspects: the pseudobulbs sometimes small, oval or suborbicular types and sometimes quite long and slender, but in all cases bearing fairly dense, erect racemes of small, easily recognizable flowers with irregularly shaped, dark green or brown spots. Not having flowers large enough or colorful enough to gain much favorable comment, they are typically the sort of orchid that earns the disparaging comment of "Oh, just another vespa" as one passes by.

But after a while, as we found more and more "vespas," we began to wonder if some plants with exceptionally tall and slender pseudobulbs, and with decidedly larger flowers than the usual "vespa" might not have differences constant enough to justify treatment as representing one of the old "species" that had passed into synonymy with *Epidendrum vespa*. The first tentative choice for this seemed to us to be *Epidendrum tigrinum*, an 1846 species of Linden, and at least mentally we began referring to such plants as "tigrinums" as an easy way to distinguish them verbally from the smaller "vespas," stressing this name in a note (with drawing) on *E. vespa* var. *tigrinum* in *Orchid Digest* for March 1972. These tall "tigrinums" started to figure in our collecting bag as far back as the early 1960s when we were looking for orchids in the fine, virgin cloud forests being penetrated by the new road under construction from El Dorado to the Gran Sabana and eventually on into Brazil. Looking for floral features to back up our feeling that the "tigrinums" were truly distinct from the "vespas," we eventually found what seemed to be not one but two types of tall "tigrinums," the difference between which was by no means obvious, but intriguing enough to call for critical study. Both types were visually separable from the normal "vespas" not only because of the very tall pseudobulbs and far larger flowers, but by the

Epidendrum pamplonense

character of the spotting on the flowers — the "vespas" having, as mentioned, irregular-shaped marks while the "tigrinums" had relatively round spots. The callus on the lip of the "tigrinums" differed from that of the "vespas" by having an open, not closed, apex to the callus, and differed quite strikingly by the callus itself being placed well back from the apex of the lip while that of the "vespas" lies well in the center of the exposed part of the lip. The calli of the "tigrinums" and the basal part of the lip bear short stumpy hairs while the "vespa" lips we have studied are glabrous.

But we did also note that there seemed to be two types of "tigrinums," one with a rounded form to the free part of the lip and the other quadrate (when flattened), and with a squarer, more boxlike form to its callus. And finally, the apical part of the lip beyond the callus bore several thickened, converging nerves in the quadrate type. These are all "finicky" details but in total did seem to us to add up to important differences.

Some very tall plants of the "round-lip" type of "tigrinum" were also found in the Andes, above La Grita, but our real prize was an albino form of the quadrate type that we found in light forest on the rocky top of Auyántepui in 1978. This plant was not as tall as most "tigrinums" but had even larger flowers of pure, unspotted yellow, with a red apex to the lip. The inflorescence, which developed in Caracas after our return from the tepui, bore only four flowers, but if we have not permanently upset the plant by selfing it to get seed, we have hopes of eventually obtaining plants with tall racemes of many more flowers, which would be quite spectacular. The plant was illustrated in color in the *A.O.S. Bulletin* for March 1978, and in that issue was referred to as *Epidendrum vespa*. Subsequently, when Garay was studying all our orchid material prior to the publication of the *Illustrated Field Guide*, we had the great pleasure of hearing him decide that the round-lip form of "tigrinum" should indeed regain full specific status as *Epidendrum tigrinum* Linden ex Lindl. (1846), and that the quadrate-lip type (and the yellow specimen) should once more wear the label of *Epidendrum pamplonense* given it by Reichenbach in 1850.

Epidendrum tigrinum, as now reborn, is illustrated in the *Illustrated Field Guide* of Venezuelan orchids, but in selecting the drawings for the *Guide* it slipped our minds that an improved form of this drawing had already been published in the above-mentioned *Orchid Digest* article on *Epidendrum vespa* var. *tigrinum*. The drawing in *Orchid Digest* shows also a close view of the inflorescence, made before "tigrinum" and "pamplonense" had officially parted company. This drawing of the inflorescence has been transferred to the *Illustrated Field Guide* where it correctly represents *Epidendrum pamplonese*. For the purposes of this present note a new drawing of this latter species has been made, showing not only the inflorescence of the normal form but also a full plant of the albino form from Auyántepui, together with side sketches to illustrate the difference in the lips of *Epidendrum vespa*, *E. tigrinum*, and *E. pamplonense*.

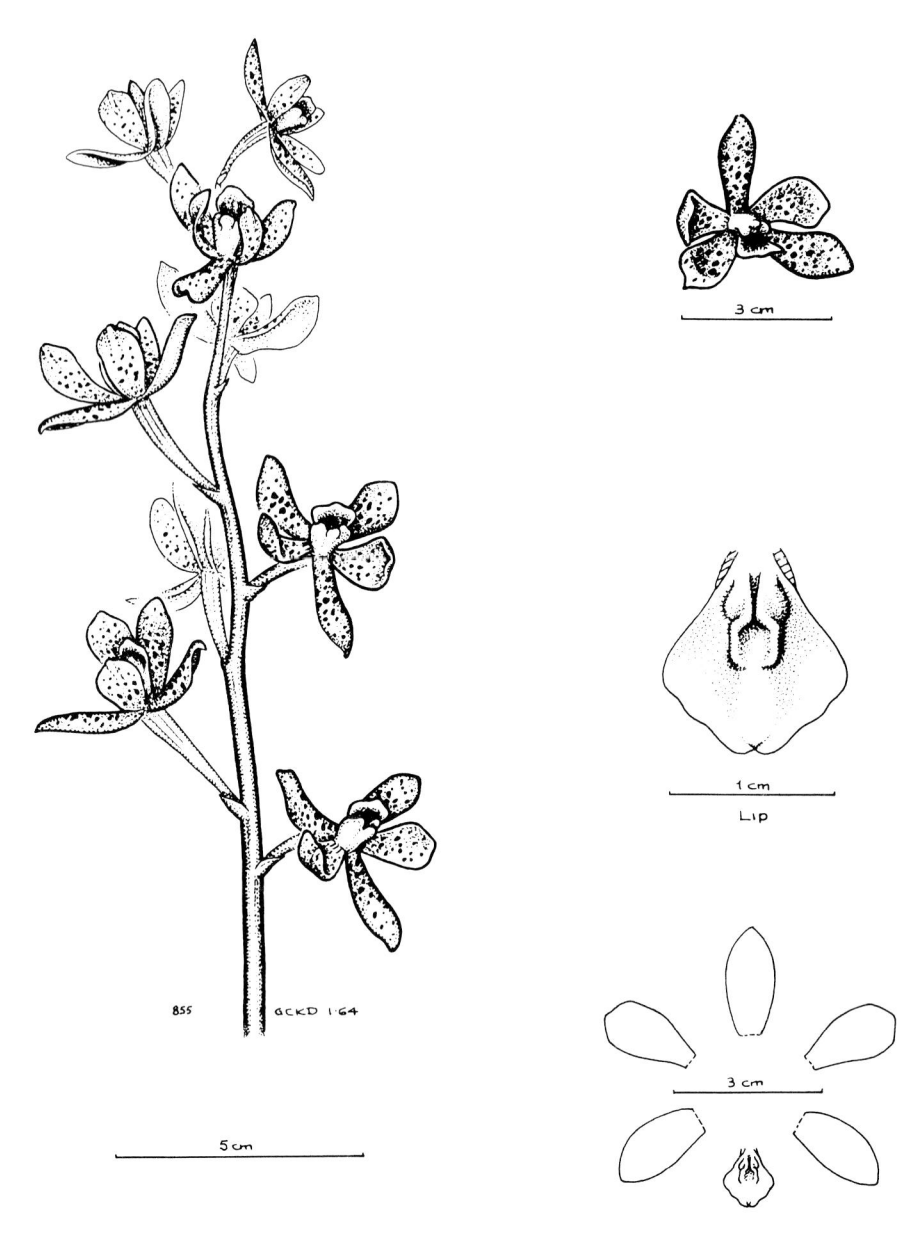

Epidendrum pamplonense Reichb. f. in Linnaea 22: 837, 1850. — E.

Epidendrum leucochilum[1]

IT IS SAD BUT TRUE that an appreciable proportion of the articles we write about Venezuelan orchid species seem to end on a downbeat note that records our failure to keep some new acquisition from the forests alive for more than a few years. This must in some degree be due to an unfortunate choice of plants to write about; otherwise, if this phenomenon were common to most of our plants, there would be very few old plants left in our garden, and not the hundreds that there are. But in any case it is nice for once to be able to write about a fine orchid that year after year rewards us with lots of flowers. This is *Epidendrum leucochilum*, an old species first found in Colombia in 1843 but also an inhabitant of Venezuela.

To judge by the paucity of official records, and the relatively few places where we have found it ourselves, *Epidendrum leucochilum* appears to be rather rare in Venezuela, but is not infrequently seen in private gardens here where there is adequate coolness and space for it to develop. For exhibitions, its size could be a drawback, but this has not prevented at least one plant (*E. leucochilum* "Christine") from gaining an A.O.S. Certificate of Botanical Merit. In the wild the species can sometimes be found growing epiphytically, but in our experience it is more commonly seen as a terrestrial, with tangled masses of thick *Sobralia*-like roots giving rise to large clumps of tough, erect or suberect, leafy stems about four feet tall. The stem itself is about one cm thick, basally terete, and usually thickening appreciably at the extreme base. In the leafy upper half the stem is concealed by the compressed and rather sharp-edged (ancipitous) sheathing bases of the leaves. The blade of the leaf itself is shiny green, with finely revolute, sharp margins, and an apex that is finely and shortly reflexed, almost "hooked." In size the leaf can be up to 30 cm long by about six cm wide, on occasion as much as 10 cm wide.

When nicely developed, the inflorescence of *Epidendrum leucochilum* is in the form of a large, many-flowered raceme, the individual flowers being borne on a relatively short, and generally arcuate peduncle that rises from a very large and prominent, compressed spathe, commonly 15 cm long and to three cm wide. The shortness of the peduncle, combined with the very long (12 cm) pedicellate ovaries, results in a clustered, almost ball-like head of up to 50 flowers, the cluster itself being as much as an impressive 25 cm in diameter. The drawing of this species that is shown in the Dunsterville & Garay *Field Guide to Orchids of Venezuela* was unfortunately made some 25 years ago on the basis of a rather poor specimen. The photograph shown in the present note is far more typical, and even larger flower heads can sometimes be found. The individual flowers of *E. leucochilum* have a spread of five to six cm, with pale green sepals to four cm long, and are dominated by the strongly trilobate white lip and prominent white column. Many people are surprised to find that orchids often have a strong and pleasant perfume to back up their beauty. *Epidendrum leucochilum* is one of these.

A well-grown plant of *Epidendrum leucochilum* with several flower heads makes an impressive display, but such plants are seldom exhibited because they are cumbersome to transport. The species is not widely cultivated outside the tropics because of the large amount of valuable space it would occupy in a glass house. Hybrids of *E. leuchochilum* with a smaller and more compact habit, however, should have a very promising future ahead of them, as indicated by the very fine hybrid, *Epicattleya* Alfredo Blaumann "Oripoto," bred in Caracas by Señor Blaumannn himself and given a Certificate of Merit by the local Orchid Society of the State of Miranda.

Epidendrum leucochilum is found in the forests

---

[1] Originally appeared in *A.O.S. Bulletin*, Vol. 49, Oct. 1980, pages 1095-1097

Epidendrum leucochilum

of the Central Range of Venezuela at about 1,500 to 2,000 m altitude, including both flanks of the Avila Range that separates the valley of Caracas from the sea. We have found it in the eastern part of the Venezuelan Andes at about 1,700 m and in the heart of the western part, above the City of Mérida. Other sites are on record in the States of Mérida and Trujillo, as high as 2,500 m. The most recent place we have found the species was at about 1,700 m, growing epiphytically on a large tree in the forested slopes of the Perijá Range that forms the border between Venezuela and Colombia. The most luxurious growth of any specimen we have seen was in the above-mentioned locality above Mérida City where *E. leucochilum* was thriving in soil on the top of a large boulder in a narrow, mountain torrent. Its natural habitat can thus be said to be that of typical montane forest zones, with ample wetness much of the year, though less constantly damp than typical cloud forest.

Our own efforts at cultivation of *Epidendrum leucochilum* in our home 500 m above Caracas have been made at much lower altitudes than most of the natural sites mentioned above, but our plants have behaved very well, even if not achieving the very large clumps seen in nature. Our garden is on the edge of a small patch of true cloud forest, so for much of the year our problems are those of excessive moisture and lack of sunshine rather than too much dryness (though we do have very dry spells also). We have found that certain plants, such as *E. leucochilum,* do best on the edge of a steep, open slope, with a wide view to the northeast (for five months of the year the sun here passes through the north, not south). Here there is nothing to block the cool breezes coming our way. The shade received by our plants varies greatly with the age and seasonal development of the surrounding trees and shrubs, so there are distinct advantages in growing plants in "portable" form instead of our original system of plants firmly rooted in the soil. We now grow *E. leucochilum* mainly in earthenware pots filled with a mixture of local earth, leaf-moldy soil from the forest, and chopped tree-fern root. A local, expert commercial grower is growing his plant of *E. leucochilum* in a similar pot, using 30% forest soil, 50% tree-fern root, and 20% styrofoam. Our plants are mostly placed where, during our heavily clouded "wet" months, they get perhaps too much, rather than too little shade, particularly from some banana "trees" whose voluminous and rapid growth is, as always, a jump ahead of the pruning machete. But we aim for a mixture providing plenty of light without very much direct sun. This may well be fairly close to what they would get in their natural habitat.

On the upper edge of the city of Caracas, where we lived many years ago, we had plants of *Epidendrum leucochilum* growing reasonably well, with cool air sliding down on us from the high slopes of the Avila Range. But with the Caracas Valley now filled to overflowing with high-rise buildings, an incalculable mass of traffic, and an atmosphere that is heavily polluted, the average temperature in the city must by now be far above its old-times figure, and we doubt if this species would be happy there, outside, perhaps, of some extra-large private garden. But while we would hesitate to recommend *E. leucochilum* nowadays as a suitable plant for Caracas, there are still gardens on the higher outskirts where it could be, and probably still is, quite commonly cultivated by true orchid lovers.

From the point of view of conservation, the main protection of *Epidendrum leucochilum* from over-eager collectors would seem to rest on the size and voluminousness of its terrestrial clumps, which would hinder removal of an entire clump, while allowing the relatively harmless removal of marginal younger growths. And if, as is to be hoped, the present start of breeding new intergeneric hybrids based on this species catches on, which implies cultivation from seed, this may further reduce temptations to bring in plants from the forest.

Selenipedium steyermarkii — A 'Commodious' Orchid[1]

D R. JULIAN STEYERMARK has long been recognized as one of the most outstanding field botanists in Latin America. This is not the place to record the many botanical works he has published, but it should certainly be noted that there are seven Venezuelan "Steyermark" species named for him in the genera of *Bifrenaria, Bulbophyllum, Lepanthes, Lepanthopsis, Maxillaria, Octomeria,* and finally *Selenipedium*, one species in the last-mentioned genus being the one that is covered by this present note. It is not given even to Julian to have a number of magnificent "corsage" orchids named for him, such as *Cattleya* or *Vanda* species. Almost all such spectacular orchids were found and named long before Julian came on the scene. But at least he has the distinction that two of the most "odd" flowers in the world of orchids now bear his name.

The first of these, *Octomeria steyermarkii*, looks like an anemic spider with five long, thread-like legs, and was illustrated in the *A.O.S. Bulletin* for April 1978 (see Chapter 25). The second, the "slipper-lipped" *Selenipedium steyermarkii*, is the subject (or object?) dealt with in this present note. But don't ask me why orchids of the Cypripedioideae subfamily, which includes the genus *Selenipedium,* should be commonly referred to as "slipper" orchids. Slipper, my foot! *My* foot may not be the most beautiful one in the world, but it is at least human in shape, whereas the lip of a member of the Cypripedioideae could only have been designed for a clubfooted mini-elephant. This is not to decry the great beauty of the species in this subfamily, but, when it came to naming it, Linnaeus must have been taking drugs. Schultes (*Generic Names of Orchids*) records it as meaning "Venus's Sandal." Correll (*Native Orchids of North America*) has it down as "Aphrodite's Shoe," but what kind of thanks other than a slipper in the kisser would you expect to get from this

Selenipedium steyermarkii

double-named lady if you offered her the lip of one of these orchids as a gift and asked her to try it on! One expects plant-namers to use some imagination, but there ought to be a law against such distortions. However, in the absence of any such law, there is naught we can do about it, so I had better get off this slippery subject and get back to more serious aspects of the matter!

Selenipediums, with their plicate leaves, are easily distinguishable at a glance from species of the slipper-lipped genera of *Paphiopedilum* and *Phragmipedium* with their smooth, conduplicate leaves, but are by no means as easy to separate visually from the remaining slipper-lip genus of *Cypripedium*, which has plicate leaves. In the wild, any South American, plicate-leaved orchid with a slipper lip is virtually certain to be a selenipedium, as cypripediums are unknown there, though this

[1] Originally appeared in *A.O.S. Bulletin*, Vol. 49, November 1980, pages 1225-1229

[2] Some information contained within this article has already appeared in G.C.K. Dunsterville's and L. Garay's article on "Venezuelan Orchids — Selenipedium steyermarkii" in *The Orchid Review*, December 1963, pages 384-387 and 410; and G.C.K. and E. Dunsterville's article on "Selenipedium steyermarkii Foldats" in *The Orchid Digest*, March 1971, pages 50-52.

does not mean that the name *Cypripedium* does not figure widely in older lists of South American orchids. It is not so long ago that great confusion existed among "slipper" orchids, to the extent that most "paphs" were "cyps," and very few slipper species of any type escaped bearing a dog's breakfast of synonyms derived from other genera in the Cypripedioideae. But while the aspect of the leaves enables one to distinguish a selenipedium immediately from a paph or a phrag, and the location of their natural habitat separates out the selenipediums from the cypripediums, such an offhand separation is not easy to make in a collection of home-cultivated orchids; so if you are not well acquainted with all the species concerned, the only really safe way to make sure is to snitch a flower when the owner is not looking, and then cut open the developing ovary (or the capsule itself) to see how it is divided up internally. In cross-section, the ovary of the cypripedium shows ovules (or seeds) that develop from the walls of the ovary towards the center, which a reference to the A.O.S. publication, *An Orchidist's Glossary,* will show is known as "parietal placentation." Ovules that develop from the central axis towards the walls, giving the capsule a three-walled structure, as with the genus *Selenipedium,* are the result of "axile placentation."

Selenipedium is a very small genus of rare and "primitive" orchids, and has only two representatives in Venezuela. *Selenipedium palmifolium*, which was found as far back as 1840, has only one synonym, and it is no surprise to know that this is *Cypripedium palmifolium*. The species is also known from Trinidad, the Guayanas, and Brazil, where it grows in hot climate. *Selenipedium steyermarkii* is a recent (1960) discovery that was lucky enough to appear on the scene after the mix-up of genera in the Cypripedioideae had been straightened out. This species, as a result, has a virginal name not polluted with any synonyms at all. It was first published in 1961 by Foldats of the Caracas Botanical Institute who named it for its discoverer. *Selenipedium steyermarkii* is known only from Venezuela, though may well also exist close by in Guyana. In Venezuela it is, so far, known only from the State of Bolívar, but as this state occupies a quarter of the entire national territory (and by itself has an area rather larger than Kansas), it is worth adding that so far this species seems to be restricted to no more than a very small section of that state on its eastern edge. It may, of course, be found later to be more widespread, but at present it remains a rarely-seen plant, so rare that few orchidists, even among those living in Venezuela, have seen it in flower, or even consciously seen the plant at all. This invisibility is no doubt largely due to the un-orchid-like appearance of the plant, whose narrow, suberect leaves blend easily into the background formed by the tall, grass-like plants in the habitat it most favors. Even when one knows what one is looking for, and from past experience knows that in that spot there *should* be plants, it is seldom easy to spot. This protective ability to disappear into the background is aided by the flowers which are of a fully "visible" size but are of a sort of sunburnt-red color not brilliant enough to catch the eye.

We found our first plants of *Selenipedium steyermarkii* at about 1,500 m altitude during an ascent of Auyántepui in 1963 (see the Chapter 6), and, although it was in flower, we might well have missed it had we not found ourselves almost treading on the poor thing. Compared to 10-foot plants we found later elsewhere, these Auyántepui specimens were quite small, only some four feet tall, and were in sandy soil among rocks and fairly-open, scrubby trees on a steep slope. One of the flowers had an erect dorsal sepal but the others, though apparently quite fresh, all had fully depressed dorsal sepals closing over the lip. This open-or-closed feature we later noted in all the specimens of this species that we found elsewhere, and it seems to be characteristic of the species.

On later occasions, knowing by then what to look for, we found plants of *Selenipedium steyermarkii* in places much more accessible than the flanks of Auyántepui, mainly at around 1,300-1,400 m elevation on the northern edge of Venezuela's Gran Sabana, and from there down to about 1,100 m on the steep and densely-forested slopes that dip northwards to form the headwaters of the Cuyuní Basin. Some of these sites are very close to the road that now links El Dorado to the Gran Sabana, and this easy accessibility may well eventually sound the death knell for many of these plants. However, this forest is not easy to wander around in, and there must be many relatively inaccessible places where this species will be in no danger. And even when in full view of the public it is remarkable how efficiently *S. steyermarkii* is protected by its natural camouflage. We know of several spots (and one in particular) where, within hand-reach of the passing public, there are plants with stems as tall as six feet visible to the experienced eye, but otherwise hidden among the other tall, leafy growths of other plants that give support to its slender stems. Some plants that we first saw at least 10 years ago are still there.

But this article was sparked by the oddity of the flowers of this species of *Selenipedium*, not by its fortunate ability to hide itself from the public gaze. Cypripediums have bloated slipper-lips very similar to those of selenipediums — lips that, to my mind, as I have already remarked, do not really have any resemblance at all to a "human" slipper.

But many of these lips do have a close resemblance to certain utensils used in hospitals for bedridden patients who cannot reach more private accommodation. The flower of *Selenipedium steyermarkii*, however, goes beyond this and achieves a truly "commodious" appearance by virtue of its clean symmetry, and even more so by having a dorsal sepal that, while sometimes open, more often is realistically closed over the "bowl" to form a well-fitting lid. Nature seems to be using this action as a means for limiting access by the fertilizing insect to certain hours controlled by factors (unknown to us) such as insolation, temperature, etc., or possibly as the result of direct action by an insect. In any case, the result, for those with coarse minds, is certainly indelicate in its suggestion. Which is why I am not sure that Julian can be altogether happy to be the "owner" of this otherwise most-desirable species.

When it comes to matters of cultivation, we can report no permanent success at growing *Selenipedium steyermarkii*. Though our observations of climate are based only on spot visits over a number of years, the climate where these terrestrial plants grow is clearly composed of a longish spell of typical cloud forest weather (i.e., lots of rain or wet mist) and a generally shorter spell, at the start of the year, of fairly fine weather; at a guess, about four to five months dry, eight to seven months wet — in other words, very similar to the climate of our own small patch of cloud forest above Caracas, though probably with a much higher total rainfall. It is very noticeable that the climate in the Gran Sabana itself is very different from that of this forest zone on its edge. The moment one reaches the top of this forest at 1,400 m and continues on into the open savanna beyond, the weather almost always seems to change from low clouds and general wetness to high clouds, blue skies, and general dryness. It is thus highly probable that the habitat suitable for Julian's selenipedium does not penetrate far into the Gran Sabana itself. But while there is a climatic similarity to that of our above-Caracas home, the acid and very sandy soil of the selenipediums' home is very different, and our few experiments with cultivation have therefore all been made by bringing back with the plants as great an amount of the original soil as we could conveniently transport. At the start we thought we had solved the problem when we kept a plant alive for well over two years and saw it in flower; but the third year it weakened, and within four years it was dead. It could be that our major handicap with such terrestrials from the Gran Sabana region lie with the water that we use when the clouds do not provide it. Our garden water supply shows a pH of 6.5 to 7.0, which is not likely to please plants that thrive in acid soils.

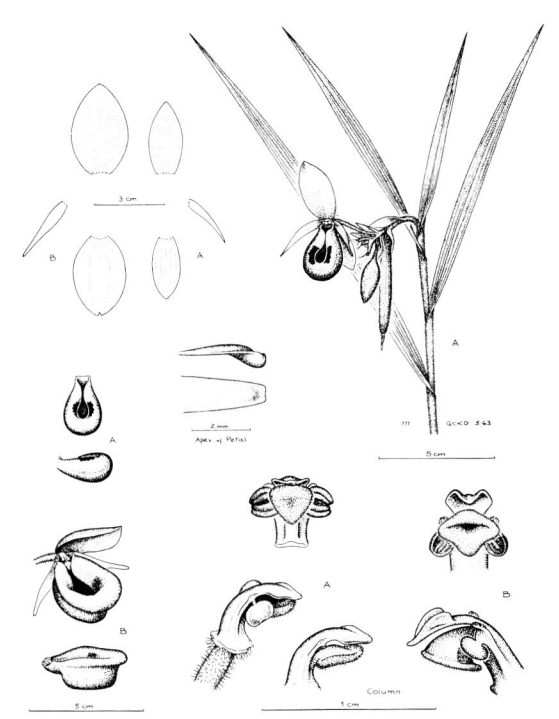

Selenipedium steyermarkii Foldats in Bol. Soc. Venez. 22: 253, 1961. — E.

Shady Business with Maxillaria callichroma[1]

THERE ARE OCCASIONS when we envy orchid growers in temperate climates who have enclosed houses where the climate can be controlled within fairly close limits, whereas in our open-air conditions there is very little indeed that we can do to control anything, be it climate, stick insects, scorpions, or coral snakes — though let us remark right away that while we have felt or seen the ill effects of the first three of these (and have several times seen the fourth) we have luckily not yet put a finger into the mouth of a coral snake hiding in one of our plants! But our spasms of envy for folks "up north" fade quickly when we hear about the climatic vagaries they have to cope with, their disasters when the power supply fails in midwinter, and their perhaps even greater disasters when their fuel bills are presented! So whatever our problems here, we accept them with meekly-bowed heads, and forbear to complain, though we do reserve the right to "comment unfavorably." Right now we seem to be suffering one of the wettest Julys we can remember, or at least the most sunless one, and this has highlighted our problems with shade. The Spanish for summer is *verano* and for winter is *invierno,* but here in Venezuela *verano* signifies the dry season, which is normally around December to April, and regardless of the fact that I write this in July, "winter" is what we now have.

When we started our garden 20 years ago we had fine cloud forest on one steep flank of our ridge, but the rest was open to all the winds of heaven with no more than some scrappy pineapple plants growing on such soil as had been left by the builders' bulldozers. The open view to the sea 50 miles to the southeast was something to boast about to visitors, but our minds were more set on growing the orchids we hoped to find in the Venezuelan backwoods during our coming retirement, and we knew that the creation of natural shade was urgent; we had no wish to surround ourselves with

Maxillaria callichroma

a lot of unsightly Saran-covered sheds just for orchids. So we started a crash program to fill our open grounds with trees or shrubs, and, in this winterless land of constant and rapid growth, got quick results.

To provide shade for the upper part of our grounds, where most of our orchid growing is concentrated, we started with seedlings or seeds of various, locally successful trees, and went beyond that by planting a sapling of a saman tree (*Samanea saman*), which in lower and warmer regions produces a very large and most handsome shade tree with a flat crown of very wide-spreading branches on a short, stout trunk. At the start, pessimistic experts, or expert pessimists, told us that a saman would never flourish at our relatively high altitude. So much for experts. Though still a youngster, this tree now spreads its shade over a circle some 60 feet in diameter, and is still getting wider. For more rapid and concentrated shade we planted a lot of garbanzillo (*Duranta* sp.) shrubs which are not only useful for shade purposes but also can form dense shiny hedges to keep "undesir-

[1] Originally appeared in *A.O.S. Bulletin,*
Vol. 49, December 1980, pages 1355-1358

ables" out, and are very decorative with their bright purple-blue flowers and massive festoons of orange berries. These plants have the ability to spread rapidly, and when 10 feet tall or more their slender overarching branches and stems form excellent umbrella-like shade. These garbanzillos were placed mainly on the upper (northern) side of the house, or to the east, leaving a south-facing open garden on the lower side of the house, given over mainly to sloping "lawns" of coarse Saint Augustine grass, which right now is growing four to six inches every week, much faster than the mower can cope. A few orchids are grown here, but not enough to make shading them difficult. But what was urgently needed for shade on this lower side of the house was protection for the second-story workroom where much time is spent in two-finger banging of an aged typewriter to produce orchid articles for the American Orchid Society, and similar activity.

We have seen in the Andes, at about 7,000 feet, a splendid forest of very tall, redwood-type trees that bear up nobly under the weight of their scientific name of *Podocarpus rospigliostii*. In the forest these trees have large, dense crowns topping tall trunks that are branchless for half their height or more, and we brought back a seedling to plant in front of the workroom window in the hopes that it would soon be shading the room from the morning sun.

All these shade-producing efforts quickly gave results, but enough finally ends in more than enough, and, as with so many tropical plants, initial successes have now become problems. The podocarpus is now four stories high (or would be if we had four stories to measure it by), with a trunk 30 inches thick and dense foliage from the ground up, so that even on the brightest day artificial light is needed to make the workroom usable. If it ever gets its roots well under the house it will be goodbye to the workroom, but that moment has not yet arrived so it remains as an impressive and immovable object. The saman has spread its canopy of shade over a large proportion of the main orchid house, which is immovably carved out of a steep bank and "roofed" with saran. The saman is equally immovable, so the saran is being taken off so as to leave the orchids open to the sky — or such sky as can be seen through the leaves of the saman. Thus the only really movable (or removable) things are minor trees, separate orchid plants, or the individual orchid shelves standing here and there, or the garbanzillos that shelter them and by now almost hide them. No doubt, when the dry season begins again and we start begging for cloud and rain, we shall regret the steps we now feel forced to take to rescue our plants from their days of darkness, but the saran has had to be removed and the machete has been fully occupied with drastic pruning or even elimination of many garbanzillo plants. In some cases altogether new sites have been sought for once healthy, but now weakening plants.

One of these is *Maxillaria callichroma*, an admirable species with abundant, quite large flowers, rather like those of *M. triloris*, but not by any means as big as the latter, which are among the largest of all *Maxillaria* flowers here. We found this species at about 1,300 m elevation in the higher part of some cloud forest a three hours' drive from Caracas. This species is shared with Colombia and was named by Reichenbach in 1854. Later it spent many years disguised under the synonym of *Maxillaria setigera* var. *angustifolia* bestowed on it by Klinge in 1898, only coming to light again when our specimen was examined by Garay in about 1975 and restored by him "back to from whence." Apart from the characteristics of leaf shape, midlobe of the lip, and the short, erose clinandrium of the column, designated by Garay as distinguishing features, the plants we found struck us immediately as something visually quite different from *Maxillaria setigera*, because they lacked the highly compressed and orbiculate pseudobulbs of the plants of *M. setigera* that we had gotten to know earlier, and, even more strikingly, had large sheaths, both to the pseudobulbs and to the floral peduncles, that were densely and darkly "lepidote" which, to quote the A.O.S. publication, *An Orchidist's Glossary*, means "covered with small scurfy scales." Moreover, the plentiful sheathing of the pseudobulbs seems to break down rapidly into separate nerves, giving the base of the plant a very ragged appearance. The flowers have generally curving sepals and petals, white at their bases, and the lip is white with dark red nerves. Dorsally the sepals are sometimes heavily over-flushed with dark red, leaving a bright yellow margin. The flowering season seems to be March and April.

The site where we found plants of *Maxillaria callichroma* in 1973 has since been messed up by road-making activities, and when we revisited the spot only two months ago we saw no more plants. But our failure may have been due less to the absence of plants and more to the presence of a failure of one of the lockable front-wheel hubs of our old front-wheel-drive Willys, leaving us stranded for many hours in deep mud on a steep and isolated rustic track, and in no mood for chasing maxillarias! So it is quite probable that more plants are surviving there, bulldozers notwithstanding. We had one plant of *M. callichroma* inseparably united into a clump with *Elleanthus arpophyllostachys* in just the way it came from the forest; this we hung in a wire basket. Another plant we mounted on a vertically hung block of tree-fern root. Now that we have thinned the garbanzillo shade the latter plant should be quite happy, but the wire basket has had to be moved, not to get more light but because, as a result of our pruning activities, there was nothing left for it to hang from! We hope it will harbor no resentment and will now flourish in its new location.

On final note remains to be said on the subject of unwanted shade, and that is to beware of using corrugated "fiberglass" sheets for roofing, or at least sheets of some unknown make that we bought here under the general name of "plastividrio." We roofed one small house with this some eight years ago so as to be able to control the degree of water received by the orchids by eliminating adventitious rain and substituting a hose and a humidifier. Since then these sheets have gotten darker and darker as the external layers of "plasti" evaporate under our strongly ultraviolet sunshine, and when the "vidrio" fibers of glass (or is it asbestos?) become exposed, every possible atom of dirt gets caught, and the corrugated sheets cannot be cleaned. Finally the roof has now reached such a stage of midnight obscurity that we have had to strip off the sheets. Replacing them with new sheets would nowadays be terribly expensive, and again probably last only a short while, so at least for the moment, while we ponder this problem the "house" has been re-roofed with saran cloth. This lets in the rain, of course, but does at least allow plenty of light without excessive direct sunshine. Our various cats used to enjoy scampering about on the plastic roof, but if they try this now either they or we (or both) will be in for some sad surprises!

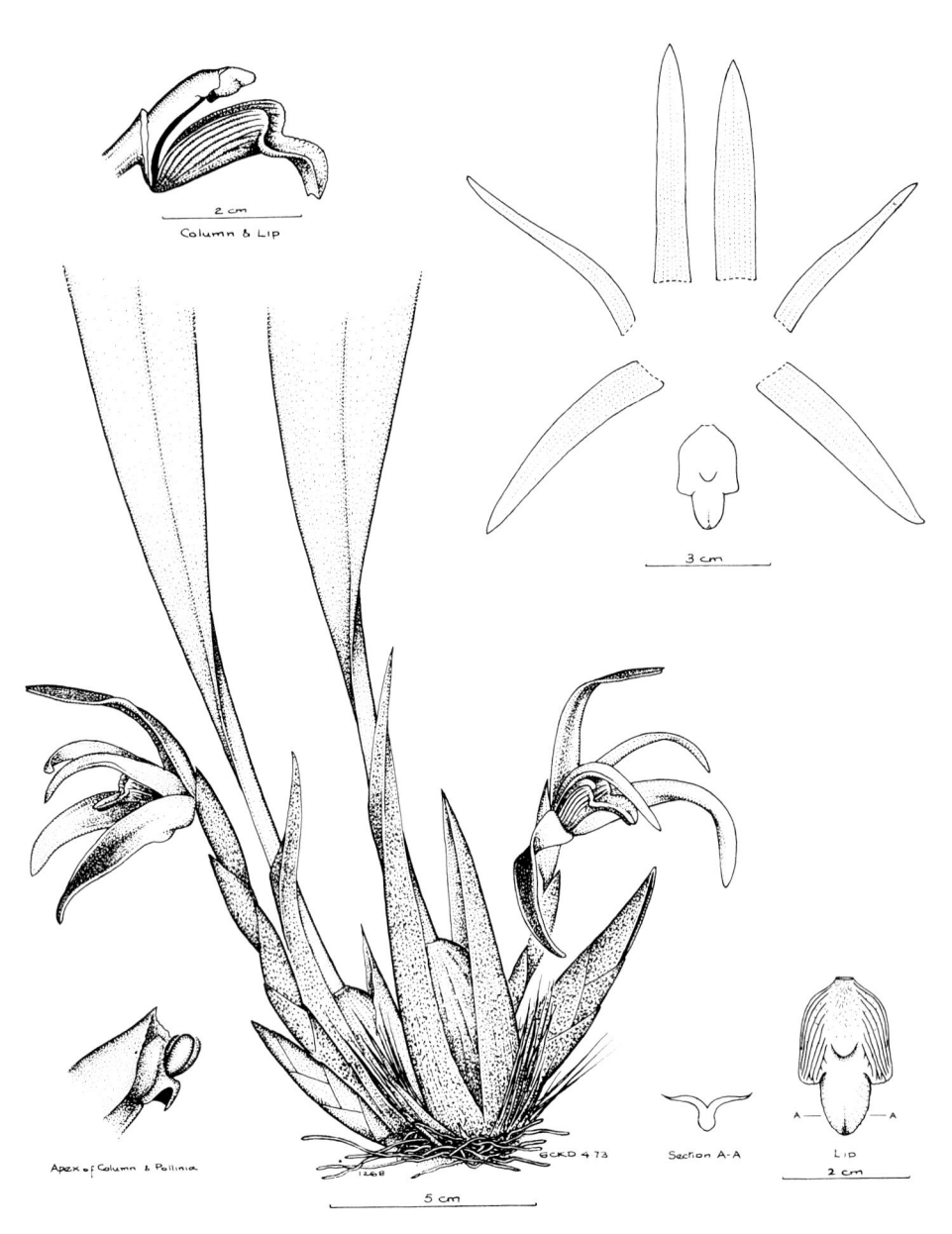

Maxillaria callichroma Reichb. f. in Bonpl. 2: 16, 1854. — B.

Brassia bidens from 'Dumpleen Camp'[1]

AVAILING OURSELVES of our rights as "Senior Citizens" (ugh!) to look back with nostalgia to the by-no-means-dim but nevertheless rather distant past, there was a time, no more than 30 years ago, when the active body of the north half of Venezuela was about as divorced from its inactive, southeast "Gran Sabana" as the extreme ends of the long extinct "whatsit" from the age of reptiles that reputedly had to have a separate brain near the farther end to be able to make its tail behave properly. This forgotten Gran Sabana corner was, of course, accessible for many years before, but only if, like early "immigrants," you cared to spend weeks pushing your way up some six or seven hundred kilometers of twisting rivers. You could also reach Gran Sabana by light plane if you didn't mind the risks of landing on unattended airstrips laid out on savannas dotted with lumpy booby-traps formed by white ant nests, or by foot if you enjoyed the thought of backpacking several hundred kilometers across largely unmapped and bridgeless country crisscrossed with small rivers.

But until about 1972 there was no crossing by road from El Dorado, of Penal Settlement fame, in the north to Sta. Elena some 320 km to the south, near the Brazilian border. When, in 1956, we got our first chance to put foot on the southern edge of the Gran Sabana, we went there by light plane to Icabarú, then a diamond prospectors' village with an airstrip so humpbacked that only the most skilled pilot could stay on the ground after landing and avoid being airborne seconds later. While there, looking for orchids but secretly hoping to find at least a 30-carat diamond, we heard "firm rumors" that work had already started on what we later grew to call "The Road" that was going to cross from El Dorado to Sta. Elena and thus at least incorporate that far-off corner of Venezuela into the national life. To check this out we took off by light plane from Urimán, about 200 km downstream from Icabarú on the River Caroní, and headed for El Dorado some 250 km to the northeast. The pilot started by losing his way, and we had to set down first at the small airstrip of Guasipati. After asking the way, we then had to fly another 100 km to the southeast before landing happily and in one piece at the savanna airstrip of El Dorado.

In Venezuela much can be achieved if you are lucky enough to "know someone" or, at least, to know someone who knows someone. We were armed with general letters of recommendation supplied by a friend in Caracas who knew just about everybody, so on arrival in El Dorado we presented our credentials to the local military boss and asked him if he could help us visit this wonderful new road we were hearing so much about. "With great pleasure," he replied, and promptly ordered the local office of the main road-building contractor to help us out. After stocking up with provisions for a trip of a few days, we were on our way in a front-wheel-drive jeep trucklet manned by a large, black driver known as Joe. Crossing the River Cuyuní by a small barge soon after leaving El Dorado (the permanent steel bridge that now exists had not then been started), we found the rumors to be true. A wide, dirt road, with alarmingly washed-away shoulders on the many cuts, already stretched some 80 km to the west across low-level but very switch-backy terrain densely covered with tall, hot forest at an average of 100 m elevation or lower. At about 88 km from El Dorado the road ended at a large camp set up by the contractor; a collection of fairly solidly made, wooden houses that served as dormitories, offices, mess hall, etc., plus a proper guest house with proper *baño* and all. This camp later formed the nucleus of a permanent village with the name of San Isidro; but even today, 23 years or more later, it is still commonly referred to as "Km

[1] Originally appeared in *A.O.S. Bulletin*, Vol. 50, Jan. 1981, pages 17-20

Brassia bidens

88." Here we were put up at the guest house and obtained our first sight of a homemade, anti-bug flame thrower: ingenious, unpatented, and incredibly dangerous to use in any building, let alone a wooden one. But effective! It consisted of an old flit-gun, loaded with kerosene, and with a lighted candle somehow fastened some distance in front of the spout. One good shot from this awesome weapon produced a magnificent flame that spelled immediate death to the thousands of flies and other *animalitos* thickly clustered against the wire mosquito-screening of the unglazed windows. In a matter of a few puffs these screens were wiped clear; in an hour they were once more covered with flies. It would be hard to imagine a weapon that so completely combined simplicity, cheapness, and (temporary) efficiency with so small a chance of ever winning the U.S. Underwriters' certificate of safety!

The next morning Joe and the jeep took us up the next (and most difficult) stage in the construction of the road. Apparently no real maps of the terrain to be traversed had ever been made, so survey parties headed off in the general direction desired to scout out the most feasible route. Clearing parties followed on their heels and these were later followed by gangs who turned the track (with much use of dynamite) into a "road" just wide enough and good enough for use by jeep-type vehicles. By the time we arrived on the scene, the road had advanced to about Km 119, though some years later this would rate only as Km 112 when a change was made in the official starting point for mileage measurements. Kilometer 88 became (in theory only, not in name) Km 81, and all other "mile posts" changing similarly up to Km 140 and beyond — a proceeding most annoying to orchidists trying to keep accurate records of their findings.

The first part of the "road" started by forcing its way up steep, rocky scarps where much blasting had been needed. Our progress up this was violently uncomfortable and incredibly slow, but did give us the excuse to get out and look for orchids while Joe flogged the jeep up the trail, and in due course we reached the makeshift contractor's camp marking the then-limit of the road: a forested spot at Km 119, 1,100 m above sea level. We got to the camp just after the small work force had finished their midday meal, but the cook willingly set to work again to feed the newcomers, and was soon frying up some lumps of what looked like things that back home we would have called dumplings. They smelled good and they tasted good, so hoping to add a useful, new Spanish word to our kitchen vocabulary, we asked "cookie" what they were called. "Dumpleens," he replied! Our arrival with a lady in the party rather upset the normal routine, but the introduction we had gotten from the El Dorado military continued to wave its magic wand. The camp boss flung a number of hammocks out of one end of the workmen's "dormitory" and hung bits of tarpaulin here and there to provide a more or less private space for our own hammocks. When night came we settled in for the first of many camping nights we have since spent on this fascinating "road." Two days later our holiday was over and duty demanded our return to Caracas, but in the meantime we had taken advantage of the surveyors' advance trail to look for more orchids, and had thus obtained our first plants of *Brassia bidens*.

This terrestrial species does not match some of the non-Venezuelan giants of the genus, such as *Brassia verrucosa*, but in our view is nevertheless one of the most attractive, not so much because of its quite appreciable size, with sepals to three inches long, but because of its pleasing habit of producing fine, erect inflorescences, some well over four feet (1.3 m) tall and with a dozen large flowers nicely spread up the uppermost third. Venezuela can count on 13 *Brassia* species, all handsome except the rather uninspiring (to us) *B. glumacea;* but of these all except *B. bidens* are epiphytes and develop their inflorescences rather bashfully as horizontal, subpendent or flatly arching racemes so that their flowers are often rather poorly displayed. By contrast, *Brassia bidens*, with its terrestrial habit, has inflorescences that quite brazenly catch the eye. The first plants of this species that we found in the "Dumpleen Camp" area had quite non-typical calli on their lips, consisting of only a pair of parallel keels. This scarcely corresponded to the name *bidens*, but that was the way we found them, so that was the way they were drawn in 1957, and that was the way they were depicted in Volume 2 of *Venezuelan Orchids Illustrated*. Later, specimens turned up that had the normal, bidentate callus, with a separate tooth lying beyond each keel, and this gave us an opportunity to substitute a sketch of the "proper" callus when the *Illustrated Field Guide to Orchids of Venezuela* was published in 1979.

This fine orchid was first recorded from Brazil, and is also known from Peru and the Guayanas. In Venezuela it was for long considered to be limited to the State of Bolívar, mainly from the area of "The Road" where the road climbs through fine forest from Km 88 to the Gran Sabana, also from the flanks of Auyántepui, and from the Altiplanicie de Nuria some 100 km to the north of El Dorado, all being localities at elevations of around 600 to 1,200 m. But more recently we have found this *Brassia* species living quite happily in much lower and warmer conditions at some 200 m elevation in the upper reaches of the Autana River in the Federal Territory of Amazonas. Some of the plants of *B. bidens* we have found were growing on almost bare (but frequently wet) rock slabs. Others were in what appeared to be quite deep soil, and as this soil also seemed to be (and was) quite different from the cloud forest soil of our Caracas home, we had doubts about our ability to cultivate this species. But brought back with a fair amount of their own soil, and placed in an earthenware pot in a relatively open and unshaded spot, these plants have survived. They are at roughly the same elevation as their original home, and the climate is roughly identical, so it is only natural to expect them to have accepted the change of home, without protest; but orchids, particularly terrestrial-growing ones, have strong minds of their own and are not averse to protesting any sort of move by turning up their toes and dying, so we are thankful for the cooperation of *Brassia bidens* in staying alive and showing us its flowers every year.

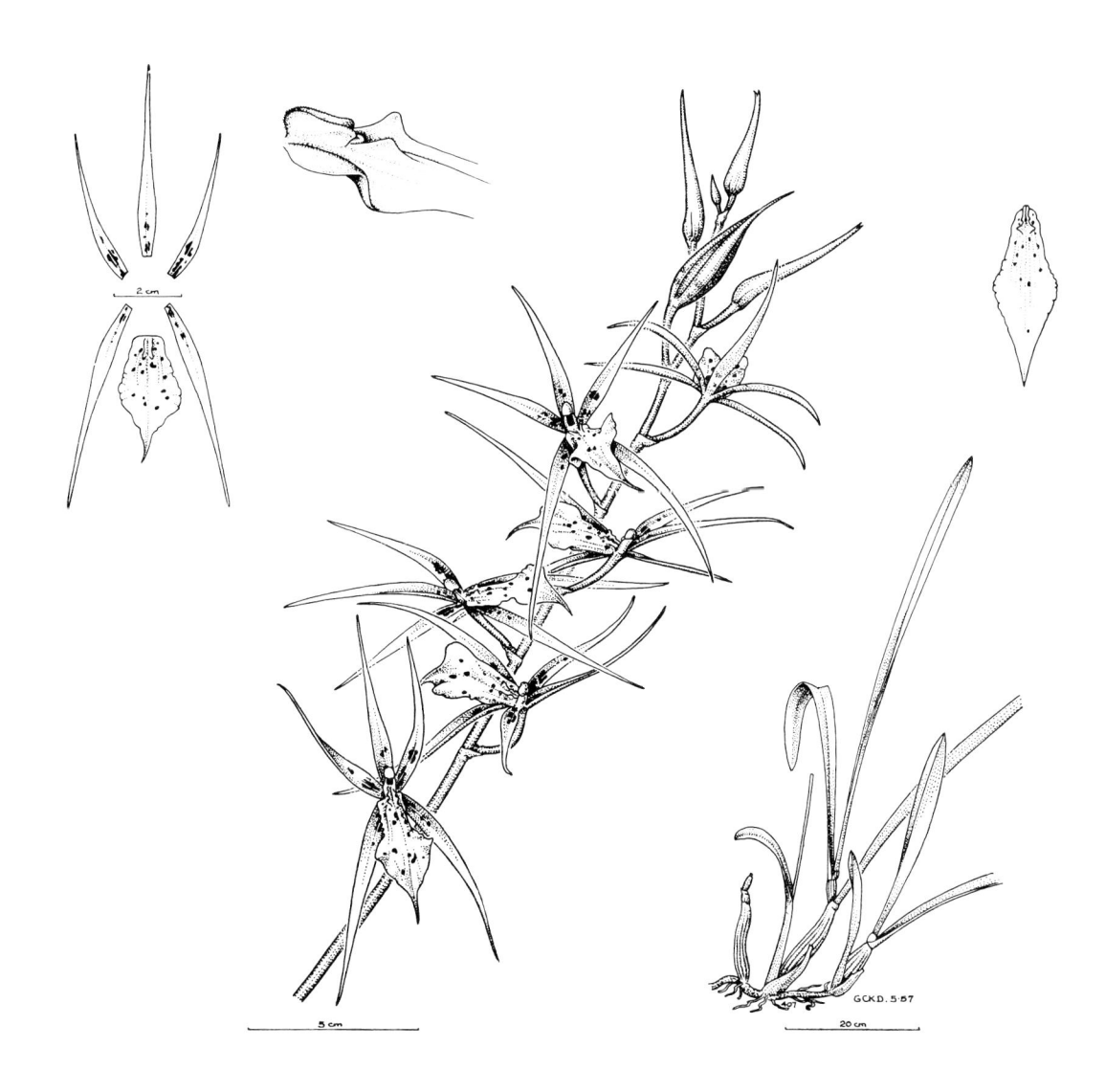

Brassia bidens Lindl. in Bot. Reg. 30: Misc. p. 6, 1844. — D. E.

Sobralia ruckeri — A Jinx-afflicted Beauty Queen[1]

ONE PROBLEM with writing articles on Venezuelan orchids with moderate frequency over a number of years for various publications is that it is very hard to avoid confusion over what has been said about what and in what and when; so one risks occasionally boring readers (or editors) with repetitions, or far worse, contradicting oneself. With our not very reliable filing system as a backup to weakening memory, straight repetition is an ever-present risk which we hope editors will help to guard us against; or, if we repeat in Spanish what has been said (at least in similar terms) in English, or vice versa, we hope that bilingual readers will forgive. To contradict ourselves would be unforgivable and we hope this has not yet occurred and never will — but the day may come!

In an article that we wrote for the March 1975 issue of *A.O.S. Bulletin* (see Chapter 17) on the subject of Venezuelan sobralias, we made no mention of *Sobralia ruckeri* for the very good reason that until 1976 we had never seen a plant in full and vigorous flower despite having actually found it, as a species new to Venezuela, in 1972. In an article published in 1978 in the *Bulletin of the Orchid Committee of the Venezuelan Natural Sciences Society*, we wrote up this very fine sobralia, but, as the readership of this Caracas publication and that of the *A.O.S. Bulletin* are not likely to overlap in major degree, we feel it would be a shame not to give some English-language publicity to what is in our view quite the finest of Venezuela's sobralias.

Strictly speaking, one should call this a Colombian species because it was previously endemic to that country and its encroachment onto Venezuelan soil seems to be very decidedly limited. Yet the border where *Sobralia ruckeri* grows is very clearly defined by nature (as distinct from some other boundaries elsewhere) and the presence of this species in Venezuelan soil is undeniable. This well-defined border is the summit of the mountainous ridge of the Sierra de Perijá (say "Perry-ha" if in any doubt) that separates Venezuela from Colombia just west of Lake Maracaibo, a ridge that topographically can be considered as a small branch of the Venezuelan Andes, running NNE from the Andes proper. Its flora, though having many unique items, is basically Andean in its composition.

The Sierra de Perijá itself was until very recently largely *terra incognita*, defended by the most inhospitable Motilone Indians who decided they wanted nothing to do with the white man's civilization and managed to get rid of a number of invaders by skillful use of bow and arrow. But "progress" cannot be held at bay indefinitely, and the time came when, very recently, the Motilones gave up the struggle. They are now "pacified" and have learned to tolerate the white invader. It was, however, not without some remaining misgivings that we decided in 1972 to fall in with a suggestion of Julian Steyermark to make a joint investigation of a part of this Sierra de Perijá. In the end, it turned out that the area we selected lies just to the north of Motilone territory. This was perhaps a pity as the Motilones now have a reputation for reliability, whereas (as mentioned in an article in *The Orchid Review* in 1973) the porters we ended by using were Yupa Indians who were most unreliable. But the hidden dangers of the trip, as we realized afterwards, came not from wild Indians or unreliable ones, nor from snakes, jaguars, or mountain lions that are known in this area, but from white *delincuentes* who roam the Perijá area to prey on misguided travelers trying to sneak into "rich" Venezuela from "poor" Colombia along the many hidden trails, or *caminos verdes* as they are called, through the intervening forests.

Lacking a helicopter to help us, we had no option but to go as far as we could by car and then, with Yupa Indian porters, to hike to the border,

---
[1] Originally appeared in *A.O.S. Bulletin*, Vol. 50, February 1981, pp 176-180

and finally after a stay of some two weeks, to hike out again with our plants. The vehicles were left at the bottom with the Mission at Tocuco, situated near a small but sometimes rather violent little river whose narrow, twisting valley forms the main access to the border through Yupa territory, an access that when the river is in full spate could be blocked for perhaps as much as two months. With the wet season imminent, we would have to watch the weather carefully, or we could end up immobilized, with nothing to do but learn Yupa-talk, which, for the men, seems to consist of sheep-like maa-ing and baa-ing and, for the women, a high falsetto imitation of a child's voice, neither of which would be of much use to us in Caracas orchid society.

Looking for plants on the way up, we made a final camp in cloud forest at about 1,500 m and then used this as a base for checking the vegetation from there up to the border at about 2,000 m. Here, beside a little-used trail, we found some gigantic clumps of a very robust *Sobralia ruckeri*, growing within rock-throwing distance of the edge of a ridge from which we could look down over Colombian territory. These plants were up to three meters tall, the stems to 1.5 cm thick at the base, and the plicate leaves in some cases as large as 35 × 12 cm, not counting their wide, compressed, tubular sheathing bases which concealed the upper half of the stem. The inflorescences were only in early bud, but they gave promise of being something quite out of the ordinary as the several-flowered rachis was 20 cm long, a shiny dark-purple in color, and at its base a full one cm thick. We opened a bud or two to see if there was any particular clue that would help in identification but the buds were too immature for this. We clearly could not take back home a full clump as we were several days distant on foot from our cars at the Tocuco Mission. So when the time came to break base camp and head for home, we took only a small piece of a clump plus, of course, many smaller plants of other species. Selecting six young Indians to carry our bulky (but not heavy) loads, we abandoned Julian to return the way we had come up, and then set off ourselves along a different and less-traveled route in the hopes of finding more orchids yet.

By now it was late March and the weather was increasingly wet and threatening. The streams were rising, producing a moment of anxiety when the distaff side of "G. C. K. & E. D." almost got swept away in fast-flowing, knee-deep waters. But that we might now, on our narrow, deep-forest trails, be in really dangerous territory did not occur to us until we came upon a gruesome reminder of the activities of the aforementioned *delincuentes*. This reminder was in the form of a couple of piles of female clothing and a single, quite fresh-looking but fleshless human lower jaw bone. Our suspicions of foul play were more than confirmed months later when, back in Caracas, we saw a report in our least sensational paper, *El Universal,* of August 17, 1972, to the effect that some murderous malefactors had been arrested in this area, and had confessed to killing women on these *caminos verdes* and then boiling and eating their heads. When we remind ourselves that the Press always exaggerates, we also think back to the jaw bone and wonder if they always do?

Back home in safety, we realized that our small clump of this sobralia could not possibly reach maturity and flower for us in less than four years, even if it survived in the rather different conditions of our Caracas home. In any case, it was never to get this chance. Planted in our soil *Sobralia ruckeri* began well, with a healthy new growth developing nicely, but one day a large and clumsy dog (our own, of course) broke off the new growth, and the plant soon after this took to looking reproachfully at us, and finally died.

We thought seriously of a return to the Colombian border to see if we could at least find a plant in full flower and thus get it identified, but we decided this would be impracticable in the wet season, the time the species presumably flowers. It was thus a great pleasure when a fresh plant and some lightly-pressed flowers were brought to Caracas by Steven Tillett, a botanist from the Caracas Central University, following a helicopter-based exploration of Perijá territory organized by the Venezuelan Boundary Commission. Despite some withering suffered by the flowers, it was clear that they had been very fine specimens and were soon identified by Leslie Garay at Harvard University as *Sobralia ruckeri*. (Rücker is a common name in German and one is tempted to jump to the conclusion that this species should more correctly be called *S. reuckeri,* but in this case [as also with *Anguloa ruckeri*] the gentleman in question was English, so *S. ruckeri* is correct.) The plant we received in this manner took well to a shady part of our garden and in April 1976 finally produced the first new inflorescence we had ever seen. It was truly magnificent, and in our opinion quite the best sobralia we have yet had in (brief) cultivation. The flowers had four important factors that contributed to this. Firstly, they had an exceptionally firm texture; secondly, they were developed on an erect raceme of up to six flowers; thirdly, each flower lasted up to a week before falling away, so that the complete inflorescence lasted about three weeks, most of the time with two flowers in bloom at the same time; and, finally, the flowers themselves were very beautifully colored and of good size. The sepals, 85 × 5 mm in size, were dorsally a

Sobralia ruckeri

very dark, lustrous magenta-purple, ventrally a fine rose-purple with a paler line down the axis. The equally long petals, over three cm in width, were spread wide to show the lip to full advantage and were also rose-purple with a pale midline. The lip, to 8 × 6 cm when spread, graded dorsally from rose-purple to dark wine-purple at the apex. Ventrally it was light rose-purple at the base and throat, changing abruptly to a very dark wine-purple at the widely-displayed apex and margin, beautifully offset by a large splash of bright yellow down the axis. Certain deep colors in the purple-red range have always defeated our color-photo efforts, our pictures failing to reproduce the intensity of the darker purple elements. While this is again the case with the illustration accompanying this article, it does at least show what a fine specimen *Sobralia ruckeri* is.

In our 1978 article for the Venezuelan *SVNC Bulletin* mentioned above, we reported that our plant was still in good health, with a new stem nearly five feet tall and with smaller growths at the base. It looked all set for a long and happy life, but alas, this was not to be. In an evil moment a branch fell from the shade tree above and squashed it flat. We nursed it with the best of TLC, but it had lost all desire to live where it had received such a brutal and unprovoked attack, and never recovered. A clumsy dog had put an end to our first plant, a fallen branch had killed the second. Perhaps some day we may go back to Yupa-land and get a third, but we fear that if we did some other disaster would fall upon our new *Sobralia ruckeri* and this time perhaps upon us as well. There is clearly a jinx at work somewhere!

Polycycnis vittata, Polycycnis ornata, and a Night with the Virgin[1]

THE ANDES IN VENEZUELA, with its fine system of roads and its vertical range from zero to heights with eternal snows, is not only spectacular but, although almost barren in many parts, is also in other parts rich in orchid species. We have made no statistical study, but offhand it would not surprise us to learn that we have found considerably more species in the Andean States of Táchira, Mérida, Trujillo, and Lara than we have ever found in the State of Bolívar far away to the southeast, despite the fact that the latter state has four times the area of these Andean States put together and, though not reaching to the snows, does at least go as high as 2,800 m. Acre for acre, Andean orchid hunting has probably, almost certainly, been more productive in species than in Bolívar; the same applies to hours spent in hunting. Moreover, the farther parts of the Venezuelan Andes are no farther from Caracas than the farther parts of Estado Bolívar.

Yet when we start itching to go hunting, our first thoughts go to Edo. Bolívar rather than to the Andes. Why this should be so we do not know for sure, but at least it must be rooted in part in the fact that the Andes is "civilized," with hotels and motels, and has gas pumps and places to fix your flats or your mechanical troubles; whereas, once away from the "iron mines" fringe along the Orinoco in the State of Bolívar, these facilities, and the roads themselves, are much fewer and farther between. Once south of El Dorado in Edo. Bolívar one can drive a day or more and see no gas pump and no repair shop, and much of this part of the state has no roads at all. In the Andes, if you park your car by the roadside to sleep in it, you are liable to be disturbed all night by offers of help from other vehicles passing by, usually truck drivers who are helpful and friendly folk, not hurrying by too fast to see you. In the open, Gran Sabana part of Bolívar State, in contrast, the truck drivers are mainly transporting lumber from Brazil (or returning empty) and are just as likely to be helpful if you clearly need help, but they quite often speak only Portuguese and will otherwise leave you in peace. In other words, in the Andes one is always conscious of the presence of others, while in the Gran Sabana or equivalent parts of the State of Bolívar one feels a sense of freedom from the cares of this world — at least until one finds that one has mistakenly emptied the spare container of water into the gas tank, or one of those wonderful automatic or "improved" gadgets on today's cars fails a hundred miles from any spare-part store!

In a recent note for the *A.O.S. Bulletin* on *Brassia bidens* (see Chapter 45), we outlined the early history of the construction of the road (to us "The Road") across the Gran Sabana and on into Brazil. What with physical troubles in building the road over extremely unstable terrain of pure sand or loose rock, fiscal troubles in getting the costs ap-

Polycycnis vittata

[1] Originally appeared in *A.O.S. Bulletin*, Vol. 50, March 1981, pages 262-265

proved, and political troubles arising from changes in government policy, when do-it alternated with stop-it and back to do-it again, the road was years longer in the making than necessary and we had many opportunities to check its orchid content as it progressed, opportunities greatly enhanced by the felling of trees in the first section where it traversed excellent cloud forest. And it was in 1957, when the road was still more or less in its infancy, and not long after our first *Brassis bidens* appeared, that we came across our first plants of *Polycycnis vittata*. This is a species from Brazil across to Colombia, and in Venezuela is known from the warm to hot, low-altitude parts of the Venezuelan Amazon Territory and from the southern half of the State of Bolívar.

The genus *Polycycnis* contains less than 10 species, the characteristic ones having long, pendulous, *Gongora*-like inflorescences that leave one in no doubt that the genus is closely related to that better-known genus. But *Polycycnis vittata* has erect racemes of a very different aspect. We have found large and robust plants of this species, with plicate leaves to 70 cm long, thriving in the hot and intolerably buggy climate of the Lower Siapa River in the Venezuelan "Amazonas" (see Chapter 8), but the plants we found on "The Road" 17 years earlier, in 1957, were more moderate in size, though with inflorescences almost as large. These plants were growing at an elevation of some 300 m not far from the village of San Isidro, or more correctly, at that time the road-contractor's camp at Km 88. Here the "bugs" were no great problem.

The flowers of *Polycycnis vittata* are fairly densely packed around the rachis of the erect, many-flowered raceme and produce a somewhat jumbled effect that rather detracts from the interest of the individual flower. These flowers have dark red nerves that almost cover the yellow of the sepals and petals but leave a fine and well-marked margin of yellow on the sepals. The lip is glabrous and is typically composed of a lobed hypochile at the base and an epichile in the form of a rhombic blade, all pale green with strongly marked, purple nerves. The slender, pale green, arching column is typical of the genus but does not dominate the flower as much as it does in other species.

Four years later we were back again at "The Road" and found that not only had it progressed, as a track, a long way farther up towards the Gran Sabana (only to retreat later in a period of abandonment), but that the contractor had moved his main camp up the road also, and the remnants of the Km 88 camp had become the nucleus of a small but fairly active "village" that was beginning to be known as San Isidro. The village had a sell-everything store whose stock included Guinness Stout in bottles at some incredibly expensive figure, awaiting purchase by some incredibly unlikely customer, but as yet there was no sign of the gasoline pump that many years later appeared on the scene. Gasoline was available, however, dished out in five-gallon kerosene cans or by hand-pump from drums standing at the roadside, both systems delivering to the unwary customer a rich mixture of water and gasoline. Holding the suction well clear of the bottom of the drum, or discarding the last half pint of each can-load helped to hold the water content to no more than the occasional spit-and-hiccup on the subsequent take off, but as this was the last place to fill up before heading south into the unknown, nobody complained.

We had arrived too late to press on and make a possibly wet camp by the roadside, so we asked at the store if there was anywhere with a roof where we could hang our hammocks for the night, and were referred to a Señora Rosa who "owns the hotel." We located the Sra. Rosa, large and jolly, who welcomed us with the statement that she did indeed own the hotel. When I asked what the charges would be she told me that to sleep in a room would cost three *bolívares* (roughly 75 U.S. cents), but to sleep with the virgin would be only two *bolívares*! While greatly tempted to jump at such a bargain, ignorance of local customs in these matters called for caution. The presence of a wife at my side was a further handicap to prompt action, so a preliminary inspection of the accommodation was demanded before deciding whether the reduction in price was due to generosity on the part of Sra. Rosa, or to the extreme age or lack of beauty of the virgin. We were led 100 yards or so to a rather barn-like structure with three furniture-less, board-floored rooms fronted by a long, covered veranda. "The room is three bolos," said Rosa, "But if you prefer to hang hammocks on the veranda, it is only two bolos," she continued, pointing at the same time to the usual image of the Virgin Mary hanging on the wall with a lighted candle below it. We had quite forgotten that we were in a predominantly Catholic country, where Jesus is a commonly used Christian name and the Virgin is spelled with a capital V. We did, in the end, economize by sleeping with the Virgin, and spent a quiet night, protected by the screening of our jungle hammocks.

The next day we continued up The Road, or rather the road-in-the-making, and at about 1,000 m altitude, exploring a forested gully, we came across our second polycycnis, *Polycycnis ornata*. By contrast with *Polycycnis vittata* from lower down, this plant was a typical *Gongora*-type plant, with heavily ribbed, bifoliate pseudobulbs with plicate leaves to about 40 cm long, bearing from its base a 50 cm-long, pendulous raceme of a dozen or more pretty and delicate flowers, quite distinct from the stoutly erect inflorescence of *P. vittata*. These flowers, though having the long and slender, arched columns that give the genus its name of "many swans," rather failed (in our specimen at least) to live properly up to its swanny name because its spotted but basically red sepals were distinctly droopy, and at best the flowers looked like very exhausted and disappointed swans — which is not to say that they were neither interesting nor attractive. The lip of *Polycycnis ornata* consists of a long, very narrow, dagger-like, almost white epichile (very different from that of *P. vittata*) which, far from being glabrous, bears long, white hairs on its lower margins and shorter hairs on its lobed and rather complicated hypochile. A nicely-grown plant, which we have never seen, but which surely must exist, must make a quite impressive sight. Unfortunately our Caracas climate, or the treatment we gave our plant, was not to its liking, and far from ever turning into an impressive sight, it soon became "invisible." As for the *Polycycnis vittata*, having learned from our first experience that this hot country species just doesn't thrive in our cool, cloud-forest climate above Caracas, we made no further trials and left the Siapa plant to continue enjoying its bug-laden life where we found it.

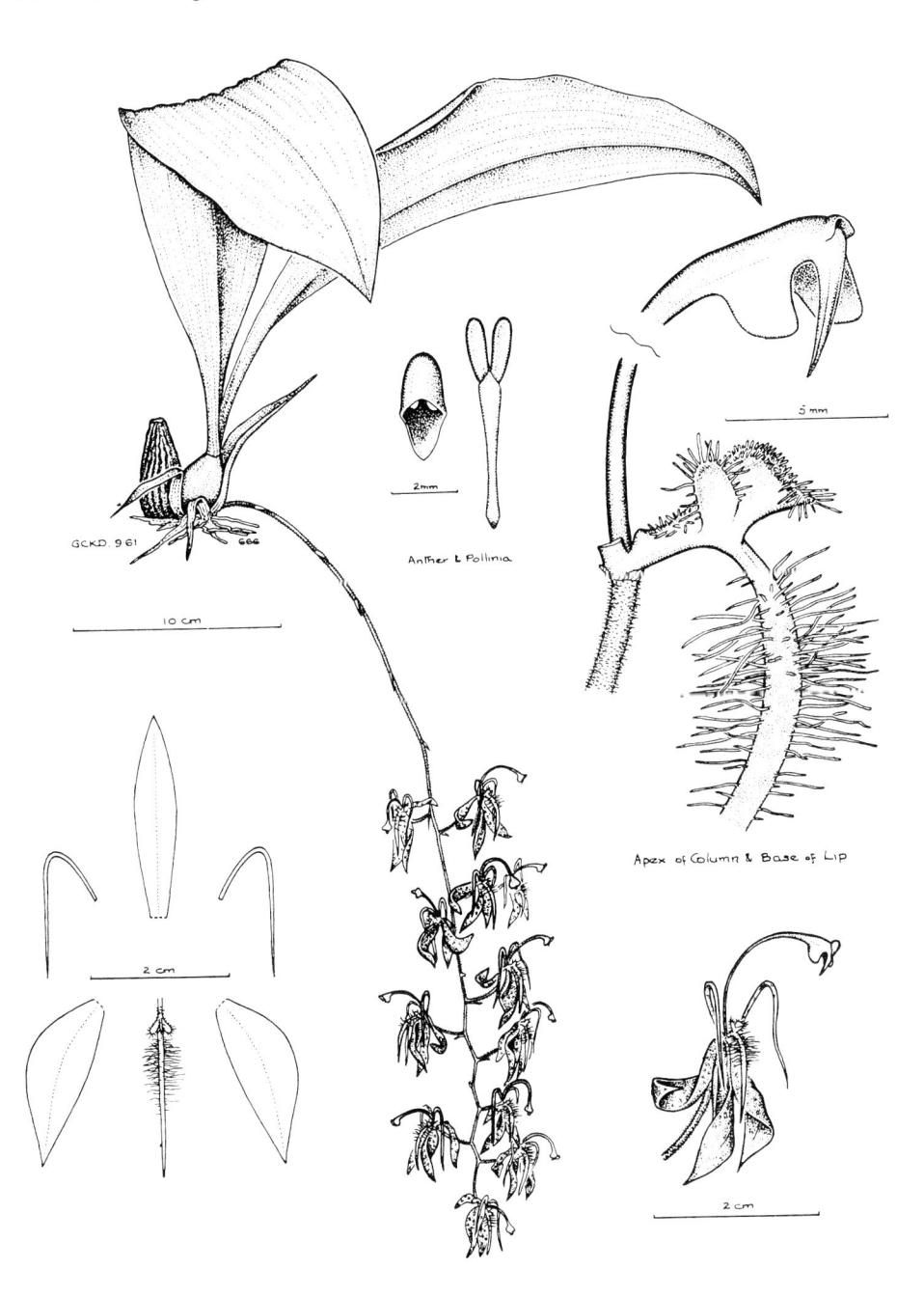

Polycycnis ornata Garay in Can. Journ. Bot. 34: 256, 1956. — E.

Masdevallia sprucei

SO MANY SPECIES of *Masdevallia* come from fairly cool forests of the South American tropics that one tends to forget that warmer- or even hot-growing masdevallias do exist. In Venezuela, for example, only five out of some 35 species come from hot areas of the Amazonas Territory or from the State of Bolívar which lies south of the Lower Orinoco; all the others are cooler-growing species mainly from the Andes or the Coastal Range. Moreover, the cooler-growing species tend to have larger and more exciting flowers, and this adds to the impression that all masdevallias are cool-growing by nature. Venezuela cannot, unfortunately, boast of such splendid and well-known species as *Masdevallia coccinea* or *Masdevallia veitchiana,* but it has some that it can display without any sense of inferiority, such as *M. tovarensis, M. triangularis*, or *M. mooreana,* which are all cool-growing plants. Venezuela's hot- or warm-growing masdevallias from the Amazonas-Bolívar "interior," such as *M.* (now *Trisetella*) *huebneri, M. peruviana*, or *M. wendlandiana*, are nice to have in a collection of miniatures (and what orchid is not?) but are nothing to write home about. But there is one hot-to-warm-growing miniature masdevallia here that in our opinion deserves an honored place in any collection of the smaller masdevallias. This is *Masdevallia sprucei* Reichb. f.

Masdevallia sprucei is a native of Colombia, Ecuador, and Brazil, and most particularly of Venezuela — "most particularly" because not only have we found it here ourselves, but much more importantly because the type specimen was found in Venezuela by the explorer Spruce after whom it was named by Reichenbach in 1878. At that time it was presumably considered to be a Brazilian discovery as it appears in Martius' *Flora Brasiliensis*, but this same record also says it was found "in forests of the stream Uaianaka, a tributary of the River Pacimoni," and the Pasimoni (to give it its

Masdevallia sprucei

modern spelling) drains north to the Venezuelan Casiquiare; only later does its water flow with the Casiquiare into the Río Negro and eventually into Brazil. The latest map of this part of Venezuela shows several tributaries to the Pasimoni, none of which has the name of Uaianaka; but this is of no significance as in the process of map-making in Indian territory many names are subject to much uncertainty both as to the Indian name itself and equally as to the geographic feature to which it refers. This is a map-making complication of which we have several times had direct experience, a given mountain or river being called "X" by one local Indian and "Y" by the next Indian living 10 miles away. And even worse than that, we have been with official map-makers when they ask an Indian questions such as "What is this stream called?" get a reply of, say, *Kakarapata,* and then under our eyes write into the field-book *Patarakata.* But even

[1] Originally appeared in *A.O.S. Bulletin*, Vol. 50, April 1981, pages 382-384

if there is now no way of knowing exactly where the Uaianaka stream is, it just has to be in Venezuela if it is a tributary of the Pasimoni. This river drains a large, low-lying area to the west and northwest of Cerro de la Neblina, the highest (10,000 ft.) of all the sandstone massifs (often known as "tepuis") that are characteristic of the "wild lands" of south and southeast Venezuela.

We found our own first specimen of *Masdevallia sprucei* on the Río Castaño, to the northeast of Neblina, where the international border with Brazil, after crossing the highest part of Neblina, turns northeast along the axis of the Sierra de Parima to head for the very top end of the Upper Orinoco River. In so doing, it enters territory every bit as unknown only a few years back as the Pasimoni was in Spruce's day — or perhaps even less so as Spruce at least knew of the Pasimoni by name, whereas the details of this area behind Neblina have only very recently come properly to the light of day and been given names that (one hopes) will be fixed forever. And it is in this very remote and inaccessible part of Venezuela that we found our *Masdevallia sprucei.* This is certainly not the sort of place to which one could run sight-seeing or even orchid-hunting tours. If any participant shunned Venezuelan air travel, he would find his simplest (if not necessarily the shortest) route from Caracas would take him firstly 600 km to the southeast by road to Ciudad Bolívar on the Lower Orinoco, then some 700 km west-and-south by boat on the Lower Orinoco stream to Puerto Ayacucho where long rapids end all Lower Orinoco navigation, then 50 km by road to the start of Upper Orinoco navigation at the landing of Sanariapo, then almost 500 km to where the Río Casiquiare splits away from the main Orinoco stream to head southwest toward Brazil. After about 150 km on the Casiquiare the route turns southeast up the Lower Siapa River, and after some 100 km more comes to an end where further navigation is stopped by a series of falls in a narrow, steep gap joining the Upper and Lower Siapa. At this point the tour would come to an end and the tourist would be stuck, suffering the tortures of the damned from the clouds of mosquitoes, "no-seeums" and other biting pests that are here sensibly called *la plaga,* until he turned tail and ran!

With normal air travel, of course, this roundabout route could be cut a lot by flying straight to San Carlos on the Río Negro and then finding a boat to take you up to the top of the Lower Siapa, but again only to get stuck there and have to run home pursued by *la plaga.* The only civilized way to reach our *Masdevallia sprucei* is the way that we went, which was by helicopter — in our case due to the most generous help of the Venezuelan government entities of CODESUR and the Border Commission. Traveling all the way by helicopter, with various stops en route for refueling, we arrived at a base camp at the top of the Lower Siapa (see Chapter 8, "Helicoptering for Orchids"). From this base, jumping the gap between the two parts of the Siapa took a matter of minutes only before we were flying over forests untrod by civilized feet until CODESUR and the Commission came along. The preliminary work done by these bodies had, by means of an aerial radar survey, disclosed an unsuspected but very important feature in the boundary. Instead of the Parima Ridge running fairly steadily northeast, they had found a stream about 100 km long flowing into Venezuela from a salient in the Parima Ridge, a salient that extended so far south into Brazil that it had become the most southerly point in all Venezuela, almost touching the equator itself. This stream has already been unofficially named the "Río Extremo Sur" (i.e., the Southernmost River) by the Commission members, and it figures under this name in our records for *Masdevallia sprucei.* But when the official map appeared in 1975 it showed the stream under the name of Río Castaña; moreover, what we were calling the Upper Siapa was marked with the quite new name of Río Matapire, even though its connection with the Lower Siapa was not in doubt. So if we get confused over names when we have all modern techniques to aid us, there is every excuse for Spruce to have been uncertain whether he was in Brazil or in Venezuela when he first found his masdevallia, the more so as the border at the head of the Río Pasimoni is flat and flooded, and has virtually no visible watershed.

From our camp at the junction of the Alto Siapa and the Extremo Sur (sorry, Matapire and Castaño Rivers) we went some distance up the latter in an inflatable craft with a small outboard motor, but most certainly did not go 100 km up its course, so we cannot claim our *Masdevallia sprucei* was more southerly than Spruce's. It was, however, from higher country, as we have our find logged at 520 m altitude whereas Spruce's was probably not much over 150 m. On another occasion, without helicopter aid, we found a second specimen of our own of this species some 500 km to the north of Extremo Sur, where the Río Paragua winds it way round the enormous bulk of Cerro Guaiquinima itself, at a riverside elevation of 300 m; and a final plant came to light later still, at about 800 m, on the southern edge of Venezuela's Gran Sabana, very close to Brazil but about 500 km northeast of the Extremo Sur. It is thus evident that this *Masdevallia* species has quite an extensive habitat in the interior of this country, and climatically ranges from hot to quite a lot cooler, if not actually cool. We have a very flourishing clump of rather dull-colored *Masdevallia guttulata* also from the

800 m site, and a less-flourishing plant from the Extremo Sur, so while the eventual failure of our *M. sprucei* plants to survive their moves might otherwise be blamed on our much cooler climate above Caracas, we can see no reason why they should die when our *M. guttulata* plants enjoy life with us. Orchids, as so often is the case, "are a puzzlement!"

As a miniature orchid, *Masdevallia sprucei* is a very delightful species, with leaves to about seven cm tall (on almost invisibly short secondary stems). The relatively large flowers, almost an inch in diameter, are borne one by one on slender, suberect peduncles almost as tall as the leaf. The sepals, which have rather short caudae, are yellow, and, once free of the short basal section, hold themselves wide open to look you proudly in the face, and display the dark red, clearly-defined patches at the base of the lateral sepals. The species is mentioned in Rebecca Northen's book, *Miniature Orchids,* so there is a good chance that someone "up north", if not right here in Venezuela, has it in his collection. If the owner of *Masdevallia sprucei* has worked it up to a fair-sized clump with numerous flowers, it must be a greatly prized member of the "Miniature Orchid Club."

Barbosella cucullata and Barbosella orbicularis — Chalk and Cheese[1]

THERE WAS A TIME, not long ago, when a number of botanical authors, such as C. Schweinfurth in his *Orchids of Peru* of 1956, or A. Hawkes in his *Encyclopaedia of Cultivated Orchids* of 1965, considered Schlechter's 1918 "four-pollinia" genus of *Barbosella* to be no more than a section of the very large, "two-pollinia" genus of *Pleurothallis*. But since then it has been more clearly acknowledged that the number of pollinia in an orchid's make-up is a basic taxonomic element which cannot be ignored in establishing generic criteria. To quote Garay (*Orquideología* VI (3), 1969): "Generic distinctions are primarily in the organization and structure of the column and its related organs... such details are the cornerstones upon which generic boundaries are built." *Barbosella* plants must therefore be maintained in a separate genus from *Pleurothallis*, despite their very close relationship to that genus.

Our first acquaintance with *Barbosella* was in the form of *Barbosella cucullata*, an attractive "miniature" orchid that is not uncommon in Venezuela. This species is characterized by fairly thin but narrow leaves rising from a slender, branching, and generally mat-forming rhizome. The unifoliate secondary stems are very short in comparison with the leaves, which in exceptional plants can attain a length of eight cm but are usually much less. The single flowers are borne on slender, suberect peduncles, mostly not more than some five cm tall, but we have found specimens in the Andes with peduncles 15 cm tall, and lengths of 18 cm are on record. The cream-colored flowers are distinguished by the extreme slimness of their outline. The erect dorsal sepal, which is linear in form, combines with the very narrow form of the connate, lateral sepals to produce flowers that, in a large specimen, can reach a spread of almost eight cm — such a flower on a 15-cm peduncle would, for us, no longer rate as a miniature, even if the more normal-sized specimens would. The petals of this species are shorter than the sepals and also very narrow, so these "skinny" flowers, rising usually well above the leaves, result in an orchid that is quickly recognizable. But despite this skinniness, a well-grown plant with dozens of flowers, grown all around a hanging block of tree-fern root, can be quite impressive, as can be seen from the illustration here, although the flowers, with only a four cm spread, are no more than half of what the species can do when it tries.

Barbosella cucullata is known from Colombia, Ecuador, and Peru, and in Venezuela is to be found in the Coastal Range and the Andes, mostly from 1,000 to above 2,000 m. The largest plants we have found came from 2,400 m in the far west state of Táchira. We collected our first plants as far back as 1954, and for many years thought this species was the only representative of the genus in this country. The only other barbosella we know of was *Barbosella fuscata* of Colombia, which has also very skinny flowers, so in our ignorance we thought that if further *Barbosella* species were to come to light in Venezuela they would at least be roughly of the same form so we could point to them and right away claim them learnedly as barbosellas. But when we did eventually find another species in this genus, it was so utterly different from what we figured a well-behaved barbosella should look like that for long it remained a puzzlement — and in some degree still remains so.

Our one-and-only specimen of what we now know to be *Barbosella orbicularis* was one of the very few new-to-us orchids that we found at about 1,400 m altitude on the top of Cerro Sarisariñama in the State of Bolívar, during a multidisciplinary expedition organized by Dr. Charles Brewer-Carías (later Venezuelan Minister for Youth) in February 1974. The most exciting feature of the expedition,

[1] Originally appeared in *A.O.S. Bulletin*, Vol. 50, June 1981, pages 661-664

Barbosella orbicularis

Barbosella cucullata

and one of its main objectives, was the exploration of some truly enormous holes in the relatively flat summit of this cerro (see Chapter 10); holes 1,500 feet wide and with vertical or overhanging walls as much as 1,000 feet high, their boulder-filled bases covered with tall forest. It would be nice to report that "G.C.K. & E.D.", following Charles and Jimmy Brewer, and David Nott, rappelled in one heroic drop to the bottom of the largest hole, to jumar their way back up loaded with rare orchids. But it is not given to everyone to be alpinists like this trio, so we, and all the other members of the expedition, stayed firmly on top, having decided that discretion, and the demands of our various objectives — orchids, plants, birds, bats, snakes (there weren't any!), frogs, lizards, and rocks — overrode our burning desire to see the insides of these holes.

Among the orchids sent up by Charles from below by hand-winch was a very strange pleurothallis, possibly *Pleurothallis lappiformis,* with an inflorescence arising from the rhizome itself instead of from a secondary stem; but the plant had only an old capsule to give a clue to its identity. With loving care we kept it alive for five more years at home, but it never did produce a flower and finally expired from disappointment. But on the top of the cerro, not far from our camp site, we came across a tall, hardwood shrub (or small tree), one branch of which bore a coating of a tiny, mat-forming orchid plant with confetti-like leaves not more than five mm in diameter, clinging flatly to the thin bark of the branch. This orchid was very similar to *Pleurothallis nanifolia,* which we know from Venezuela's Amazonas territory, but with enough difference to make us doubt it was that particular species. This tiny plant came home with us, still adhering to the piece of branch that we had cut from the host tree, and today, some eight years later, it is still alive and apparently happy on this same twig. We hung it just as it was in our main open-air house (all our houses are open-topped, but this one has walls to protect the plants from rapid drying out due to excessive air movement). Trying to relate Sarisariñama conditions to those of our garden, even though at a comparable altitude, is at best a matter of inspired guesswork, with all of its risks of early and fatal consequences for the plant concerned, and we were not at all optimistic that we would achieve more success than to see a single flower before the end came. But our luck held. At this very first trial we hit on just the right spot and it is still going strong, showing us flowers every year during July and September, when the rainy season has become well established.

We now had flowers to study and could see that it could not be a pleurothallis, as it had four pollinia. But knowing this did not help us to decide what it was. A pleurothallid with four pollinia should be either a restrepiella (most unlikely), or a restrepia (no! no!), a dresslerella (impossible) — or a barbosella! Could this tiny plant, creeping around with its minute, flat, cling-to-the bark confetti leaves and equally small, rather bell-shaped flowers on extremely short peduncles, be a barbosella? Perish the thought! We certainly had an orchid that must be a new species, and perhaps even a new genus. But this is a lesson in not getting ensnared in preconceived ideas. In *Selbyana,* Volume 3, 1976 (a publication we did not see until quite a bit later), there was our orchid, illustrated as *Barbosella orbicularis* Luer, already known in Panama, so it was not even a new species. Even so, "Chalk and Cheese" is what we put at the head of this article, and chalk and cheese it is. There must be something screwy in Denmark if two such disparate forms as *Barbosella cucullata* and *Barbosella orbicularis* belong in a single genus, and a taxonomic Hamlet needs to be born to set it right!

Pleurothallis perijaënsis Dunsterv.[1]

IT IS SAID that fools step in where angels fear to tread, but it has never been clear to me as to whether this is meant as a warning to fools, or as a hint that sometimes a fool can hit the jackpot by risking an irresponsible act. Or is it just a straightforward statement with no bias either toward the angels or the fools? In any case, when it comes to the taxonomy of orchids and the publication of new species, there is no doubt (as has many times been said before) that irresponsible actions are not wanted; fools should stay away, and the identification and naming of plants should be left to the professionals. Even so, this warning has not prevented some redoubtable professionals from once in a while tripping over their own feet and later suffering the ignominy of fathering illegitimate offspring because of failure to follow the rules!

Obviously the most important initial step in naming a plant is for the namer to be quite sure that the plant has not been published before, and for this it is necessary that the namer should not only have the proper taxonomic knowledge but also have access to adequate herbarium and library resources. Even with a very small genus of only half a dozen species to be checked, it is not really safe for even the most expert of amateurs to reach a firm conclusion that his plant is truly a new species, because the publication of new species is so frequent an occurrence that someone else may have "gotten there first" and have published it recently in some place that the newcomer has not yet seen. When it comes to genera with 100 or even 1,000, it is 100 or 1,000 times more difficult. Despite the appearance of many "Garay & Dunsterv." orchids that have appeared in Dunsterville & Garay publications, the "Dunsterv." is there because Garay is a kind and courteous man and feels it proper that it should appear thus in a jointly-authored book, even if "Dunsterv." is quite unqualified as either taxonomist or botanist. So how has it happened

Pleurothallis perijaënsis

that a new species of orchid has finally been identified and published by "Dunsterv." all on his own, as *Pleurothallis perijaënsis* Dunsterv.?

The fact is that in 1978 "Dunsterv." succumbed to temptation and broke his own rule. Finding new orchid species in the tropics is neither difficult nor unusual, and anyone who spends much time looking for orchids finds "unusual" plants with fair frequency. Sooner or later, one of these will be identified as "known" and its name will be forthcoming (which is always welcome news), or it may turn out to be truly new and be properly published by an expert (which is better news, still). But with some plants this intervening period of "Is it or isn't it?" seems, like watched pots, to be terribly slow in coming to the boil, and the fact that no preexisting name has in the meantime been produced increases one's certainty that the plant just *has* to be new. In the case of *Pleurothallis perijaënsis*, this species came to light in 1972 when Nora and I made a very interesting (and rather tough) excursion with Julian Steyermark and a bunch of very sloppy Yupa Indians into the little-explored Perijá Range

[1] Originally appeared in *A.O.S. Bulletin*, Vol. 50, July 1981, pages 805-807

that separates Venezuela from Colombia, just west of Lake Maracaibo. In this area we found a lot of interesting orchids, mostly (as expected) with Andean connections, and one of these was a pleurothallis from cloud forest at about 1,550 m. This plant kindly survived the trip back to Caracas, and when it flowered it struck us as definitely in the "probably new" class, and certainly new to Venezuela. Its portrait and description went into our collection as "No. 1212" to await identification by Harvard.

Two years later, when visiting the World Orchid Conference in Medellin, Colombia, we were with our friend Becky Northen when she (and we) found a pleurothallis vegetatively very like ours. When our plant of this pleurothallis flowered we could see that there was indeed a strong resemblance to our "1212," but that at the same time there were equally strong differences. When Becky's plant flowered in Florida she sent it to the Marie Selby Botanical Gardens where it was identified as new, and was published under the name of *Pleurothallis northenae* Luer in the *A.O.S. Bulletin* for March 1976. Eventually both Harvard and Selby expressed their views that "1212" was most likely a new species, but both were very busy at the time and unable to provide a positive answer. There are over 1,000 species of *Pleurothallis,* and to check the "newness" of yet another is not a task to be done quickly. Nevertheless, to have an unidentified "1212" running around loose in the forest, so close to Colombia and so more-or-less close in appearance to *P. northenae,* seemed to cry out for positive action to make sure the two would never be confused. So, while fully recognizing a complete lack of qualifications for making a valid decision on the uniqueness of "1212," the decision was made to publish it as a new species, based on the original "Steyermark and Dunsterville" specimen lodged in the Caracas Botanical Institute. Text and drawing were sent to Selby, and in *Selbyana,* Volume 2 it finally appeared as *Pleurothallis perijaënsis* Dunsterv. Nobody has yet come up with any prior name to knock it back into synonymy, so we hope it will retain this name forever and aye!

Vegetatively, *Pleurothallis perijaënsis* is caespitose and develops pendulous leaves on its slender but strong, suberect petioles, and has the interesting (but not unique) character of forming leaves that when young, though almost full size, have attenuate bases quite distinct from the strongly cordate base of the adult leaf. The flowers are rather smaller than those of *Pleurothallis northenae,* though of much the same color, and differ by having an almost flat lip with a markedly rugose surface, as compared to the lip of *P. northenae* which is smooth and strongly folded in the apical half. The flowers of our *P. perijaënsis* vary much in their attitude, but those of *P. northenae* (at least those on our own plant of this species) seem to be incurably bashful, all of them turning to face the leaf and presenting their backsides to the public. Neither *Pleurothallis* species can, in our view, rate as beautiful, but both are quite striking. Our plant of *P. northenae* has taken well to its new home and has flowered frequently; our plant of *P. perijaënsis* has been less enthusiastic, but still survives.

Octomeria flaviflora[1]

OCTOMERIA is a genus of "pleurothallid" orchids that are similar to those of *Restrepiella/Restrepiopsis,* but can usually be distinguished by having sepals and petals all of about the same size and shape, and by having, as the name implies, eight pollinia, as distinct from the four pollinia of *Restrepiella,* or the two of the true *Pleurothallis.* There are rather more than 20 species of *Octomeria* in Venezuela, but most have flowers too small to appeal to anyone other than the true miniaturist, though *O. steyermarkii,* described in the *A.O.S. Bulletin* for April 1978 (see Chapter 25), can be weird enough to attract more than a mere miniaturist's attention. But a good plant of *Octomeria flaviflora* is not to be lightly brushed aside, as a healthy specimen can produce fasciculate clusters of as many as a dozen very pretty, half-inch, yellow flowers from the base of a single leaf.

Octomeria flaviflora is endemic, or almost endemic, to the highlands of the Venezuelan Guayana region, where it is not uncommon on the dramatic sandstone table mountains characteristic of these parts. It seems to thrive best in fairly tough conditions, as the finest specimens we have found, with strong, erect secondary stems 50 cm tall and topped with 15 cm leaves, were thriving in almost lithophytic conditions on the very inhospitable summit of Roraima at over 8,000 feet. This is the most celebrated of all these cliff-encircled "tepuis," but is actually one of the smallest, having a summit area of only about 45 square kilometers, as compared with such giants as Auyán-tepui with over 700 square km. Its renown comes from the fact that it was the first of these tepuis ever to be reliably reported to the outer world, in 1838. Roraima was first climbed in 1885, and later served as the inspiration for Conan Doyle's famous "Lost World" story. But it also gained fame as the meeting point of the boundaries of Venezuela, Brazil, and Guyana (then British Guiana) when it was noted that the waters from its summit were feeding the headwaters of three distinct rivers, one Venezuelan, one Brazilian, and one Guyanan. Somewhere on its "flat" top there had to be the critical point where these three rivers began, and in a magnificent (and almost unpublicized) effort, a Brazilian expedition, climbing from the Venezuelan side some 50 years ago, reached this point, surveyed it, and erected there a permanent three-sided "monument" some six feet tall as a marker.

The only access by foot to the top of Roraima, other than for alpinists, remains still from the Venezuelan side where a hike of a day or two from the nearest vehicular track leads to the foot of the southwest line of cliffs, whence a slanting trail leads to the edge of the not-so-flat summit — an increasingly popular there-and-back hike of some four days for the young and energetic. But the reward is likely to be a sample of Roraima's hate for visitors, whether orchidists or not, in the form of paralyzing mists or violent rainstorms of the type that over the ages have carved the summit into a vast expanse of fantastic rock-formations largely devoid of soil and trees. The monument lies far away to the northeast from the access point and, apart from a very few survey parties and the inevitable botanists, virtually nobody has seen the monument from the day it was erected until quite recently, when it was realized that the old-fashioned survey methods using astronomic observations through erratic cloud cover might have resulted in equally astronomic errors, compared to the extremely precise results now obtainable through observation of fast-moving satellites by electronic means unaffected by clouds.

That we ourselves, however, have visited the monument is not due to our muscular perseverance but to the fact that we have been lucky enough to

[1] Originally appeared in *A.O.S. Bulletin,* Vol. 50, Aug. 1981, pages 942-944

Octomeria flaviflora

have been lifted to the top by helicopter to search for orchids, as somewhat unofficial invitees of the Venezuelan-Brazilian Boundary Commission and of Dr. Charles Brewer-Carías, later Venezuelan Minister for Youth. The Commission was about to set up a camp close to the monument, with the necessary equipment and personnel to make the required satellite observations, and it was the idea that the survey party would start the camp, radio communication and all, and that we would follow, with botanist Julian Steyermark, when all of the initial fuss had died down. But something upset these plans, and the three of us found ourselves dumped alone on the top, in the late afternoon, equipped only with our sleeping material, two machetes, two flashlights, a radio we had no idea how to use, and two peg-type tents.

Valuable time was lost looking for terrain that was neither already under water nor bare, hard rock where no tent pegs could hold and where no loose rocks were visible to act as substitute pegs. But at least, though it had evidently been raining shortly before, it was not raining then. Finally, right under the lee of a giant mass of the weirdest rocks we had ever seen, we found a slight hollow filled with enough sand to hold a tent peg, and got settled in by flashlight — with neither skill nor will to try for radio communication with the operational base on the Brazilian border, some 90 km away, to report our safe arrival.

The next morning the rest of the party arrived, selected good, hard-rock sites for their self-supporting tents, and removed the radio from our useless hands. As we can seldom understand a word of the usual radio gobbledygook, however intelligible it is to the initiated, it is unlikely that our instructions to use the radio would have borne fruit even if we had got the machine (and its generator) to work. The new day was fine, and we started looking around for orchids without worrying about finding any better spot for our tents than the one we had already selected — which was a bad mistake. It only needed the arrival of these extra humans to stir up the wrath of Roraima. That night thunder, lightning, winds, and rain, and a temperature drop (by the feel of it) to freezing fell upon us. Our tent held up under this onslaught, but we soon realized that we had placed it in the middle of a growing lake, that, largely (but not entirely) missing Julian, now showed itself as the bed of a stream. We sat there shivering on our camp stools while the water rose, with our essential clothing bundled onto the now-floating rafts of our air mattresses, until the water reached the tops of our calf-high rubber boots, at which point we decided to abandon the ship before it sank or we froze. One forgotten camera remained sunk below the waves.

Charles Brewer-Carías, an expert in alpine and other rescue work, saved us from complete disaster by setting up a temporary, ground-hugging, tarpaulin shelter on sloping, non-flooded rock while Julian crowded into Charles's tent. We shared our tarp with another (Indian) refugee from the storm until the next morning when the storm abated and we could start to find a new tent site. It had not been a very comfortable night, not improved by the fact that the only exit for GCKD for nocturnal bladder relief, while pinned between tarpaulin and rock, with a wife on one side and an Indian on the other, was to slide feet first down the sloping rock, fall off a steeper slope at the bottom, and then to reverse the process to regain shelter. But thanks to Charles's efforts, without which we would have been in truly parlous condition, we were able to take full advantage of the occasional dry spells during the remaining days to devote ourselves to serious orchid hunting while Charles devoted his time to serious photography and the survey crew did their serious satellite-watching with complicated electronic instruments connected to an antenna at the top of the monument. We later heard that by this means the location of this monumental top, relative to the rest of the world, had been determined with an accuracy of less than half a meter "up, down and to all sides."

By the time we were lifted off for the return trip, during a sudden clear moment five nights and days after our arrival, our orchid findings had unfortunately not amounted to anything like the exciting load we had expected. The general barrenness of the rocky landscape was not conducive to much epiphytic life, nor even extensive terrestrial orchid life. Apart from a few small patches of scrubby trees, the principal vegetation was in a wide but crack-like valley leading to the edge of the main cliff and which we named Crystal Valley, as its floor was covered with a mass of quartz crystals varying in size from six-inchers to layers of microcrystals. Here we found a very pretty pink or red *Epidendrum montigenum* (illustrated in the *A.O.S. Bulletin* for March 1979) and a variety of *E. elongatum* with exceptionally fine flowers (illustrated in the *A.O.S. Bulletin* for May 1979). Otherwise our finds were limited to items not exciting enough to warrant mention here, apart from the giant specimens of *Octomeria flaviflora* mentioned at the start of this article, specimens which acquired extra emphasis by growing close to clumps of almost black, weather-beaten plants of the very small *O. parviflora* with their practically invisible, tiny, white flowers.

In brief, while the visit to Roraima proved to be every bit as exciting and impressive as we had anticipated, the orchid results were disappointing. We came back with armfuls of memories that will last us our remaining years, but no more than fistfuls of orchids, which may well last no more than a few years, as our restful cloud forest climate above Caracas is so utterly different from the much higher and vastly more violent *ambiente* of Roraima.

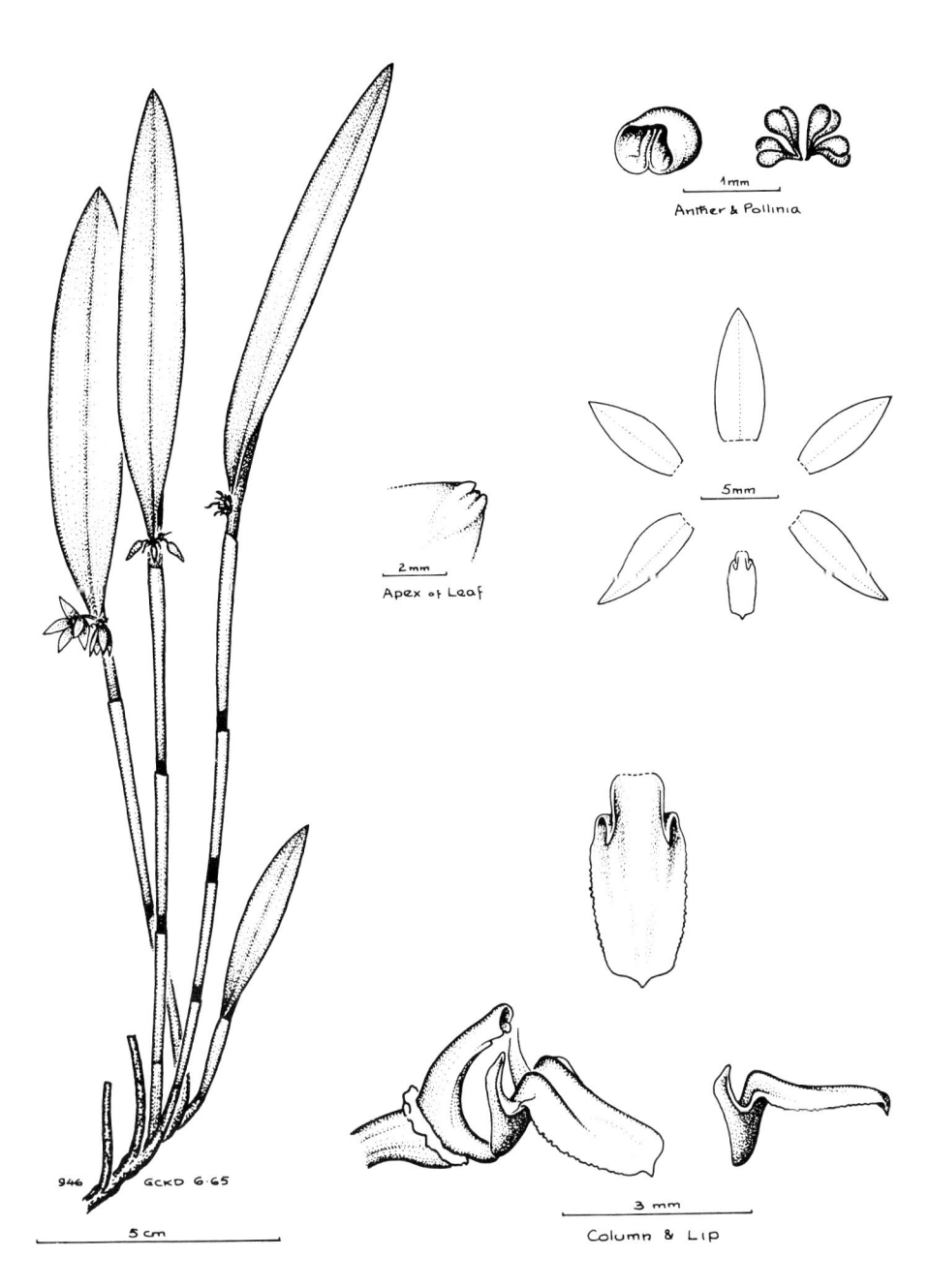

Octomeria flaviflora C. Schweinf. in Bot. Mus. Leafl. 19: 207, 1961. — E.

Apatostelis garayi — A Thank-you Orchid[1]

LIKE OIL, GOLD, AND DIAMONDS, orchids are where you find them; but looking for them is no guarantee they will be found. What is certain, however, is that if you don't look you will most certainly never find, and we always welcome a chance to explore any previously unsearched corner of orchid potential in Venezuela. At the end of 1980 our choice fell on a part of the headwaters of the River Cuyuní that we had heard about but had never gotten around to visiting.

There are two main outlets for rain falling on Venezuela. One is by short, steep rivers flowing straight to the Caribbean in the north from the coastal ranges and the northern slopes of the Andes. A second, and larger one, takes the waters flowing off the southern slopes into the Lower Orinoco, where it blends with water collected by the Upper Orinoco that has come from the far south of Venezuela on its borders with Brazil. A third very small outlet starts close to the very top end of the Orinoco where a small portion of the stream gets diverted by a freak of topography into the Casiquiare "canal" and thus into the Río Negro and then via the Amazon into the Atlantic just north of Belém. And yet a fourth outlet is via the top end of the River Cuyuní (not to be confused with the Caroní) which starts in the far east of the country and continues through Guyana to reach the Atlantic at Georgetown. These headwaters of the Cuyuní provide an outlet for all the water draining to the north from the northern edge of Venezuela's Gran Sabana through cloud forests that have provided many species, old and new, and even one new genus, to add to our collections. This drainage is mostly short and steep, but the Cuyuní also takes waters draining from a quite extensive area of low ground west and northwest of the point where it breaks eastward through the border of Guyana, not far from the village of El Dorado.

On previous occasions we had tried our luck looking for orchids, with mild success, up the small piece of the Cuyuní itself and some very short streams flowing into it from the Gran Sabana, but we had not tried the longer streams flowing mainly through hot, flat country and which together drain about 3,000 square miles of Venezuelan territory. Most of this area is "civilized" terrain, mainly cattle country, with limited scope for orchids apart from the low Sierra de Imataca and the equally low Altiplanicie de Nuria which has yielded us some treasures in the past, including an intriguing and not yet identified epidendrum. But the extreme west of this low altitude part lies in hills far from normal civilization, and its forests would be virgin territory for us. Forests generally hold few accessible or even visible orchids in their depths, but where rivers cut through them to allow more light and air movement there is always a chance of finding something interesting.

To judge from our not-very-detailed maps, the target area we selected lay near the top end of the River Yuruan which flows over an 80-mile course to join the Cuyuní right at El Dorado. El Dorado would then be the obvious starting point for a trip that would of necessity have to be entirely by river. El Dorado is a village lying on the main stream of the Cuyuní not far from the Guyana border, and, despite its romantic name, is nowadays best known as the site of a penal colony for persistent vagabonds. Its sole connection with its golden past is the occasional presence of a prospector buying cans of food or the trade it receives from a small ore-crushing and gold-extracting mill in the neighborhood. But its moribund condition has recently been relieved by the presence of a young Englishman, Sidney Coles, who has set up a clean riverside "camp" where paying visitors can spend the night or hang their hammocks, and who owns a *curiara* or dugout, with outboard motor, obviously waiting to transport us up the Yuruan to where naviga-

[1] Originally appeared in *A.O.S. Bulletin*, Vol. 50, Sept. 1981, pages 1072-1076

tion stops at a little-known falls (actually a cataract) called the Salto Paravan.

Starting the day after Christmas, we picked up Savas, a local Indian who was supposed to know all the tricky parts of the rapids-filled river we were aiming to explore. We very shortly had passed the mouth of the large tributary of the Yuruan known as the Yuruari, flowing in the north. (What with the Yururan, the Yuruari and, in the neighboring Gran Sabana, the Yuruani — plus the Cuyuní and the Caroní, Guyana and Guayana, visitors may be excused if at times they get lost!) The first day's travel was uneventful until we made camp on a small forested island to hang hammocks for the night. Jungle neophytes are frequently pictured as falling out of the far side of their hammocks as soon as they get in from the near side, or cutting their legs off with sharp machetes while clearing a site for a camp. We no longer fall out of our very comfortable hammocks nor are we apt to sever our limbs, so it was most distressing when, slashing at a high-overhead piece of vegetation, I let my machete slip out of my outstretched hand and put my other hand in the way of the falling blade, calling for help when a fountain of blood came streaming out of a largely severed vein. In the end it proved to be much more dramatic and sympathy-attracting than mortal, though it did interfere a bit with subsequent activities and definitely lost me the respect due a bush-experienced orchid hunter.

The next day we entered more complicated river conditions amid many rapids and small islands which caused us much tricky and at times dangerous zigzagging back and forth across the river. It finally came out that Savas had not only never seen this part of the river before but, in addition, was blind in one eye with a cataract — and it did not help that his knowledge of English was far from being extensive! But, surviving some moments of crisis when all hands bent to the task to avoid being swept crosswise down the current while obeying conflicting orders to pull right or push left, hand on or let go, we finally, two days after Christmas, reached the "end of the road" where the Salto Paravan blocks all further river transport unless one is prepared to walk the rest of the way with an Indian bark-canoe on one's shoulder and a can of beans in one's pocket.

For two days we searched for orchids, but, inside the forest, we were frustrated, as usual, by the fact that such orchids as there were were high up and invisible. At the very edge of the river, however, some exposed tree bases were densely coated with mats of tiny *Pleurothallis spiculifera*, and hither and yon we came across some old friends such as *Batemannia colleyi, Trigonidium obtusum, Brassavola martiana,* various maxillarias, and a truly splendid *Scuticaria steelei* in full bloom, far up the trunk of a tall tree. We have failed before to keep this species alive at home, and the plant was far out of reach, so muttering "sour grapes" we left it in peace to shed seed for future generations. But at the river edge, just below the base of the cataract, where the water was covered with a thick, almost solid coating of orange-colored, meringue-like and long-lasting foam and where the trees were damp with orange-colored spray from the orange-colored waters of the Yuruan, we came across a fallen tree bearing a few common looking stelis or pleurothallis plants and some rather unhappy encyclia-type plants. Eureka! One of these latter bore a single flower rather like *Epidendrum halatum,* but with enough differences in its flower to allow ourselves, with a modicum of optimism, to hope that it might some day be declared a new species by some enthusiastic *Encyclia*-minded taxonomist. Anyway, this was all we had to show for our trip and, as (based on our luck the previous two Christmas outings) we would need to find at least one new thing to keep our record clean, this plant would have to serve. With our plants carefully packed for the return journey we set off back downstream, finding it even slower going down than it had been coming up. Savas lacked confidence to run all but the simplest of rapids so we crawled down by lowering the *curiara* from point to point by rope, or waited long minutes while he scouted the route ahead. On the very last day of

Apatostelis garayi Dunsterv.

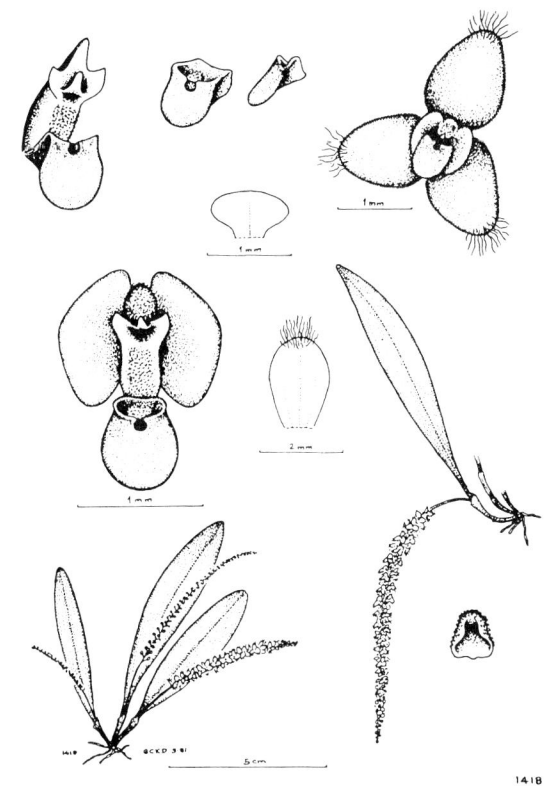

1980 we were back in Sidney's camp and after a couple of days spent looking for orchids up the road towards the Gran Sabana, headed for home in our aged Willys wagon.

Once back home our orchid duties diverge, with myself doing the paper work while Nora, having first checked that no major disasters had smitten our plants at home during our absence, set to work to clean up, pot up, or mount up the plants we had brought back. Apart from the "possibly new" epidendrum, all were S.O.S. (same-old-stuff) things, but nevertheless useful replacements for gaps in our collection, plus a few unidentified plants which could be confidently expected in due course to reveal themselves also as S.O.S. Among these, the "possible stelis," after a month or so, began to show signs of new inflorescences, and from then on it was not long before Nora was able, excitedly, to draw my attention to something odd developing — and within a few more days was proudly showing me the start of a raceme of pink *Stelis* flowers that were quite new to us. As soon as a flower was fully ripe it went under the microscope to reveal most unusual tufts of white hairs at the end of each pink sepal. A further quick look under the microscope showed it to have a single stigma (or two stigmas united into one), and, as we had quite recently been studying Leslie A. Garay's most useful *Systematics of the Genus Stelis Sw.* (*Botanical Museum Leaflets,* 1979, Vol. 27, No. 7-9) it did not take us more than a second to understand that our new plant was one of a group that, because of the single stigma, had been separated out by Garay into a newly-named genus of *Apatostelis.* And it did not take much further checking before we were sure, from detailed information in the monograph, that what we had was either *S. leinigii* (of which we had no detailed description) or something new. A letter and sketch went off right away to Garay and right away came back the answer that it was a new species. Finding the plant had been sheer luck — because of its ordinary appearance we had almost failed to pack it in with the other Paravan plants — but its appearance at home in full and very pretty flower could only be credited to Nora's T.L.C. and skill in attending to its unspoken needs.

Garay has with great kindness put our name to a number of new orchids that we have discovered, and it has always seemed unfair to us that the taxonomist who puts names to other people's plants should, by custom, if not by law, be barred from ever putting his own name to one. But here at last was a chance to return the compliment. For the non-professional orchidist one of Leslie A. Garay's most useful contributions to taxonomy is the detailed analyses he has published over the years, in *Orquideología* and elsewhere, on various "complexes" or groups of allied species and genera. This monograph on *Stelis* was typical of such things and had been the key to our having been almost on our own able to identify our plant as positively new. In gratitude for this and for years of past help in our jointly authored works on Venezuelan orchids, this new species is being published as *Apatostelis garayi,* an "honor" that, knowing Garay, he would in the normal way of things almost certainly decline, but in this case we have been able to "bring pressure to bear!" It is at least one public way to say "Thank you!"

Pleurothallis sclerophylla[1]

"**V**ARIETY'S the very spice of life" said the poet Cowper a good many years ago. It is most unlikely that he had orchids in mind when he said it, but there is no doubt that, in addition to its many other attractions, the orchid family can boast of plenty of life-spicing variety, both in genera and in species. Indeed, when it comes to variety within a single species, it even seems at times to overdo the spicing, leaving the owner of plants collected from their natural habitats very puzzled as to whether among them he has gotten a new species or merely another form of a well-known one. *Epidendrum elongatum*, for example, has flowers so variable that over the years since it was first published in 1763, it has accumulated 36 specific or varietal names, all of which are now, by general accord, relegated to the list of synonyms; and one has to admit that none of these forms show signs in the field of enjoying the "reproductive isolation" that is the clue to the establishment of separate species. Unfortunately, proving the existence of such isolation is seldom feasible, and one can then only infer its existence by relying on visible features revealing a constant character or group of characters setting them clearly apart from others. Such a method for determining if a plant does indeed constitute a new species is clearly insufficient to prove that it is, but it can become accepted *faute de mieux* if enough expert taxonomic weight supports it. The accumulation of synonyms, however, is not always a one-way street and, once in a while, a many-hued orchid will shed some synonyms when expert weight supports the re-birth as a full species of a form that had previously been listed only as a synonym. Thus *Epidendrum vespa* recently lost two of its 16 synonyms when *Epidendrum tigrinum* and *E. pamplonense* were revived (see Chapter 41) and *E. nocturnum* lost one out of a similar number of synonyms when *E. latifolium* was restored to species status (see Chapter 23). We now look forward to the day when some other forms of this "nocturnum" complex get full recognition, such as the very tiny *Epidendrum minus*, the slender-leaved *E. longicolle* and the robustly tall *E. strictum* (*A.O.S. Bulletin*, October 1977.)

The small epiphytic species, *Pleurothallis sclerophylla*, the main subject of this present note, is another species that has highly variable flowers (much more so than *Epidendrum elongatum*) but unlike *Epidendrum nocturnum* shows relatively little variety in size and form of the plant itself. It has a very extensive geographical range, and in Venezuela can be found in most of the cooler parts of the country, having a vertical range from about 1,000 m to 2,500 m, and a predilection for cloud forest conditions. The inflorescences are in the form of fairly densely flowered racemes of white, cream, or light yellow flowers, produced from the base of oval, fleshy, coriaceous leaves borne by stout, suberect secondary stems so closely packed along (and hiding) the repent rhizomes that the appearance of a plant is often caespitose. The variety that spices this species rests in the flowers themselves and can best be demonstrated by the accompanying drawing. The constant features are few: short petals with a single, raised mid-nerve and a rounded apex, and a keeled lip that is unspreadably arcuate and ventrally rough (tuberculate) in the apical half. The variable features are the lobes of the lip, the length, proportion, and attitude of the sepals, and the presence or absence of a small, sharp chin at the base of the lateral sepals. But most probably the most significantly variable feature is the column. Columns tend to be invariable, but the column of this species sometimes has no more than a fairly short, hooded clinandrium with a rather irregular apical margin (Type A), and in other cases a very long, narrow, sharply pointed apex (Type C), or even with the point bent down and back into a sharply reflexed hook (Type B).

[1] Originally appeared in *A.O.S. Bulletin*, Vol. 50, Oct. 1981, pages 1182-1184

The most recent plant of this species that we have found came from some 2,500 m altitude in forests above Boconó in the Andes of Trujillo State. This type has a very pronounced apical hook in flowers similar to, but larger than Type B, and shows yet another striking variation from the normal in that the sepals are entirely glabrous, whereas in all other specimens we have heard of or come across they are ventrally pubescent.

For the record it may be mentioned that Type A came from 1,300 m altitude in Bolívar State on the road from El Dorado to the Gran Sabana; Type B from 1,500 m in the Coastal Range, not far to the west of Caracas; and Type C from 2,500 m in the western State of Táchira below the Páramo de Tamá. And yet another type, which we shall call Type X, came from a zone we shall also call "X" because some time ago the label on the plant, in the manner of so many labels, decided to fall off and disappear. We think this plant came from somewhere in the western Andes but we cannot be sure. The column of this type is very interesting in that the apex of the clinandrium is elongate but instead of being pointed or hooked is bifurcately notched. The presence of a hook in Type B and in the Boconó specimen seems to imply some special function of critical importance to the plant, and the absence of this hook in Type C, and more importantly in Types A and X, is very remarkable. It is nevertheless an oddity that is confirmed by Schweinfurth's *Orchids of Peru* where the column of this species (listed under its synonym of *Pleurothallis stenopetala*) is described as "terminating in a prominent, triangular, concave wing." Yet again, in *Selbyana* 1975, Volume 1, Number 3, where this species is listed as having a very wide distribution from Mexico to Brazil, no direct reference is made to the clinandrium but it is shown in the illustration as having a very short and simple peak, unlike any of the types mentioned above. All these are one single species. Or are they?

But to break away from this rather dry discussion of the details of the variations in this species, what about it as an orchid? The Scots have a saying that "A wheen o' mickles mak's a muckle", and while this is surely meant to apply to bawbees rather than to orchids it can also be very aptly applied to a number of generally insignificant, "bo-

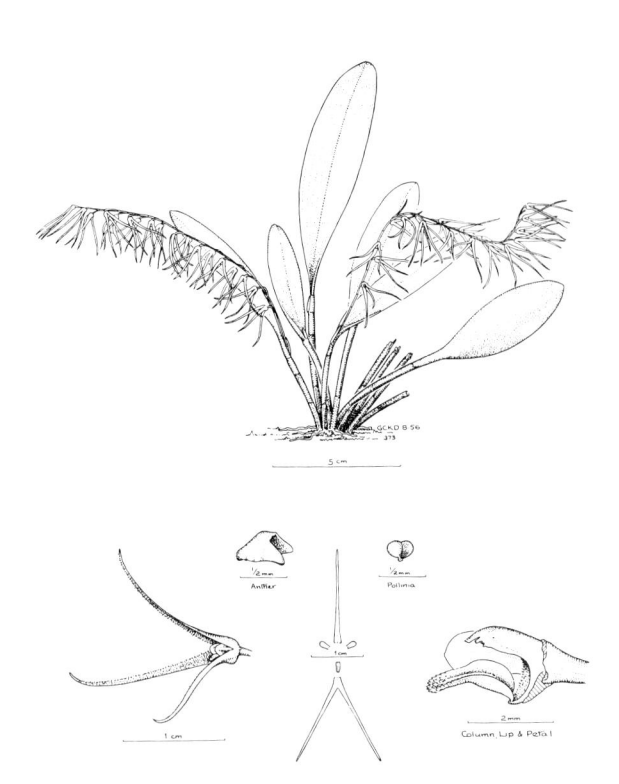

Pleurothallis sclerophylla Lindl. in Bot. Reg. 21: sub t. 1797, 1835. — A. B. D. E.

tanical" species which are normally unexciting but which, when the mood is on them (which is usually when there is no "show" on and nobody is looking) can put on quite a spectacular show of their own, such as *Barbosella cucullata* illustrated in the *A.O.S. Bulletin* for June 1981 (see Chapter 49). *Pleurothallis sclerophylla* is definitely a species of this type, with many a mickle making a very considerable muckle. A single inflorescence is unexciting, but a well developed clump is something else again. It is not tolerant of neglect (few orchids are) but is not unduly sensitive. Mounted on the usual piece of tree-fern "root" and hung in 50-50 sun and shade, with a daily sprinkle of city water from the hose (and rather more in the heart of the dry season) it has responded well, as have all our other pieces of this species. But what mysterious factor produces a "special" plant, such as the one shown here, is something else again; orchids are so often a law unto themselves.

Maxillaria lepidota Lindl. — or How Silly Can an Orchid Name Be?[1]

MANY, in fact most orchid names give one no clue at all as to what the plant or its flower looks like. *Maxillaria meridensis*, for example, tells you only that it was presumably found originally in Mérida. *Maxillaria parkeri* tells you it was found by, or is otherwise associated with, a Mr. Parker, but gives no more clue to the beauty, size, hairiness, or other character of the flower or plant than it does of the beauty, size, or hairiness of the late Mr. Parker himself. As this species was named in 1827, the chances are that Mr. Parker was heavily bearded, but this is, in any case, beside the point.

But a number of orchids do get named to indicate some character of the plant that has struck the namer as important and the name is therefore a clue as to what the plant or flower looks like. *Maxillaria grandiflora*, for example, is likely to be an orchid with reasonably large flowers — which it is, even if the flowers grow upside down and thus form an even more striking characteristic. *Maxillaria violaceopunctata* implies a flower that shows some violet spotting, and indeed it does. And so on. But even names of this type are not always reliable guides to what the orchid should look like, and at times can even be rather misleading. *Kefersteinia graminea* (originally *Zygopetalum gramineum*) has a name that implies that the namer, Lindley, considered it to be "grassy" in appearance. We have naturally never seen the original "type" specimen of this species, but the plants we have found here are not, to our eyes, in any way grassy or "grass-like," and this name would hinder rather than help anyone who went looking for it in the wild.

Perhaps the most confusing orchid name that we have yet met is that of the species that has inspired this article, *Maxillaria lepidota*. One of our botanical reference books says that "lepidote" means "covered with small scurfy scales." Another says

Maxillaria lepidota

with maximum brevity that it means "scaly." Another says "covered with small scales," and our large Spanish botanical dictionary says, in translation, "Scaly, or covered with squamous trichomes," which sounds to us rather like an unnecessarily erudite way of saying "scaly." All in all, there seems no way to escape the obvious conclusion that a "lepidote" orchid should by all rights be scaly, and scaly is just what *Maxillaria lepidota* is not!

Though fairly widespread, this species is known more from Colombia and Ecuador than from Venezuela, where the only plant we have ourselves found (and perhaps still the only one yet on record for this country) came to light in 1973 in a patch of cloud forest at 1,400 m in an accessible but little-known corner of the State of Táchira in the farthermost corner of the Venezuelan Andes. When it flowered at home in Caracas, it was clearly something new to us. The flower was not exactly

---

[1] Originally appeared in *A.O.S. Bulletin*, Vol. 51, January 1982, pages 4-6

beautiful in terms of corsage quality, but it was of an appreciable size (sepals seven cm long) and prettily colored yellow with a touch of red at the base of sepals and petals; most certainly in the striking category and a very welcome addition to any species collection. As can be seen from the illustration, it is one of a group of maxillarias that have long, very narrow sepals and petals, typical of which is *Maxillaria arachnites* whose name means "spider-like" and which was among the very first species we found, in 1956, at the start of our orchid career.

At much the same time we also found another maxillaria, this time in the State of Carabobo not far from Caracas and at about the same altitude as the Táchira plant. In the usual manner, we submitted the flowers of these two orchids to Dr. Leslie A. Garay at Harvard University for identification under their drawing numbers of 1267 for the Táchira plant and 1268 for the Carabobo one. When in due course Garay came up with *Maxillaria lepidota* for #1267 and *M. callichroma* for the Carabobo plant, it was clear that somewhere along the line the specimens or their numbering had got crossed over. By no means, and under no stretch of imagination, could the Táchira plant be considered scaly or scurfy, being perfectly smooth and unblemished throughout. By contrast, the Carabobo plant, with large flowers somewhat like the handsome *Maxillaria triloris* was very decidedly scaly, with dark scales covering the sheaths at the base of the leaves, and generally scurfy in appearance due to the shredding to mere nerve-remnants of most of the sheathing of the pseudobulbs. Had we ever gone looking for a "lepidote" orchid, this Carabobo plant would have caught our immediate attention, the Táchira one never.

We could scarcely tell Garay that he just had to be mistaken somewhere because of the proximity of the numbers of the plants, but we did write back and hint this very strongly. Nevertheless, the reply came back that the names he had provided for 1267 and 1268 were indeed correct — and since then the names of *Maxillaria lepidota* for #1267 and *M. callichroma* for #1268 have appeared in our joint publications, and an article on *Maxillaria callichroma* has appeared in the *A.O.S. Bulletin* for December 1980 (see Chapter 44).

All the same, this naming problem remained always at the back of our minds as a teaser with no apparent solution, until one day we decided that,

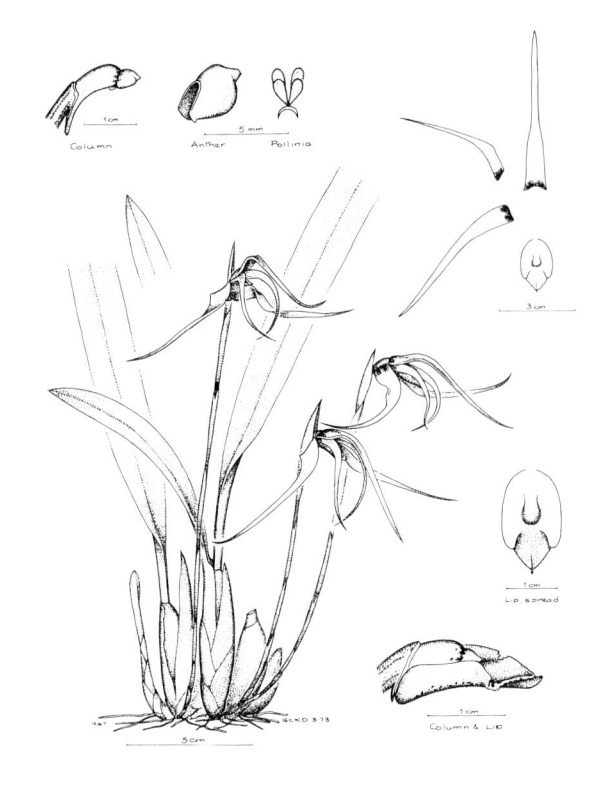

Maxillaria lepidota Lindl. in Ann. & Mag. Nat. Hist. 15: 38, 1845. — A.

as *Maxillaria lepidota* itself is worth a picture in the *A.O.S. Bulletin*, an article on the subject of how silly can an orchid name be might be of interest to *A.O.S. Bulletin* readers. And in doing this we believe we have, quite by accident — and with the aid of the A.O.S. itself — come across the answer. While scanning our reference books once again for any definitions of lepidote that might conceivably not be associated with scaliness, we were making due note of the definition in the A.O.S. *Orchidist's Glossary* of 1974, which (reading "covered with small scurfy scales") merely repeated what we had already gleaned from our other references, when our eyes lit on the next line immediately below:

"*lepidus, -a, -um* (LEP-id-us). Neat, pretty, pleasing; graceful; elegant." Indeed an apt description of our orchid!

If only Lindley, as it now seems, had paid better attention to the difference between *lepidotus* and *lepidus* our orchid would have been born as *Maxillaria lepida* — and we would probably never have written this article!

The 'Ochroleuca Group' of Venezuelan Maxillarias

WE ARE VERY GRATEFUL to Nature when she supplies us with orchid species that are nicely distinct, and we are inclined to grumble when she comes up with a number of similar-but-dissimilar plants, forming groups that cause us much annoyance before some kind-hearted taxonomist sorts them out into separate, permanent (we hope) and recognizable species. In the past, for example, we have referred in the *A.O.S. Bulletin* to the *Epidendrum vespa* group which caused us much trouble until *E. tigrinum* and *E. pamplonense* were confirmed as separate species. Similarly, the *Epidendrum nocturnum* group, once a real headache, has begun to soften up with *E. latifolium* and *E. minus* separating out, and we hope it will not be long before this group is extended by *E. longicolle* and others that are vegetatively very distinct from the normal form of *E. nocturnum*. Another small group that has given us trouble in the past is one to which we have quite unofficially given the name of the *Maxillaria ochroleuca* group as much because of the confusion in its names as because of certain basic similarities in its flowers. Despite the implication of the name *ochroleuca*, derived from one of its members, that the flowers should have at least a clearly yellow aspect, all ours are dominantly white, with no more than a yellowish or greenish tone in the apical part of the sepals. The lips, it is true, do have some yellow or even orange in their composition, but they are too small by comparison with the sepals to justify any yellowness in the name.

Our interest in this group began in 1964 at a remote airstrip of Kanarakuni in the State of Bolívar, at the far headwaters of the Río Caura and not far from the border of Brazil. Kanarakuni lies under the lee of Cerro Sarisariñama, and we are not likely to forget the somewhat unusual circumstances that were the background to our finding there the very first plant of our "*ochroleuca* group" species, namely *Maxillaria splendens*. When we visited Kanarakuni it was (and we understand still is) an area thinly populated by Indians, mainly of the fairly primitive Waika or Shirishana tribes, at that time suffering greatly from measles, malaria, and other blessings passed to them by the outside world and against which they have little resistance. In an effort to improve their health, a medical mission was being set up, run by a religious order, and this in its turn was relying fairly heavily on spontaneous help from the Venezuelan Air Force to bring in medical supplies and general hospital furnishings. Through the influence of kind friends or friends of friends, we were offered a ride to Kanarakuni, with the prospect of staying long enough between one flight and the next to reach the top of Sarisariñama and explore it for orchids. This offer was naturally most gratefully accepted, though we did not at that time anticipate the odd manner by which it would lead us, if not to the top of the cerro, at least to lay hands on our *Maxillaria splendens*.

The almost invisible airstrip at Kanarakuni is fairly short even for a DC3, and is accessible only by careful maneuvering around the corner of a hill that cuts off a full view of the runway until quite a late moment during the run-in. After we had successfully landed, and offloaded not only ourselves but also a mountain of hospital beds and similar impedimenta that had cramped us during the flight from Caracas, the plane left again to fetch a load of lightweight plastic piping for the mission's water supply project. When it came back the next day the touchdown was made a bit too late, brakes were applied too violently in the effort to avoid overrunning the airstrip, and the plane dug its nose into the ground, crumpling it badly and causing one large rotary engine to break loose with all its pipes and connections. The pilot found his foot entangled in bent levers and, if the plane had burst into flame

---

[1] Originally appeared in *A.O.S. Bulletin*, Vol. 51, April 1982, pages 363-366

Maxillaria ochroleuca var. longipes

from all the gasoline spread around, it is unlikely that he would have escaped alive. As it was, he suffered no more than a bad bruise on his leg and an even worse blot on his copybook.

As no physical damage had resulted to anyone, and blotted copybooks were not our responsibility, we were able to view with disinterested amusement the lighthearted help given by the almost naked Indians in clearing the damaged plane and its motor off the runway so that a follow-up rescue plane could land. In a fine mixture of primitive and modern techniques, very small Indians in little more than G-strings contributed their very effective push-or-pull manpower, laughing their heads off each time a tow-rope failed to hold and all the pullers fell flat on their fannies. The audience included not only elderly Indian men, but a group of almost equally naked women, most of whom were happily smoking cigarettes in flagrant disregard of the Surgeon General's determination that cigarette smoking is dangerous to their health. One doting mother was even sharing hers with her naked, two-year-old infant who grabbed hold of it with great eagerness, inhaling the smoke and blowing it out through its nostrils in a completely adult manner.

All these excitements were fascinating to watch but had obviously ruined our hopes to search for orchids on the summit of the cerro. The airstrip lies at about a 400 m altitude and the top of the mountain looked to be no more than roughly 800 m higher, but with no certainty as to when the rescue plane would arrive, and complete certainty that when it did it would be "all aboard" in a hurry as the next chance might be weeks later, the most we could hope to do would be to make short excursions each day with one eye scanning the countryside for orchids and the other scanning the horizon for rescue planes. It was not surprising that under these conditions we found the pickings to be very small, with no obviously exciting finds. The padre who ran the mission had described for us a "slipper-lipped" orchid that might be a rare phragmipedium, but when we found the spot he had indicated with great accuracy the orchid turned out to be nothing more exciting than a "slipper-lipped" female *Catasetum* flower! But among some epiphytic plants growing on fair-sized forest trees near the base of the cerro was a sterile maxillaria. It did not strike us as anything very exciting but we took it along just in case, and only much later, when it flowered at home, could we see that it was new to us and destined to enter our files at first as an unidentified species, No. 948 on our list, later to be classified as *Maxillaria ochroleuca* and later still to be corrected to the name it still bears today of *Maxillaria splendens*. This species is undoubtedly the queen of our "*ochroleuca* group," with a name that is very appropriate in its original "splendid" meaning of "bright" or "shining", even if less appropriate in its later connotation of splendid in the sense of something gorgeous or highly colored, like a movie-queen's latest ballgown. Its sepals and petals are white and do not spread widely open, but this "defect" is amply compensated by their large (seven cm) size and by the way a nice plant will develop flowers in considerable numbers.

The next time we met this fine species was equally in rather unusual circumstances, namely as the result of an "airlift" by helicopter to camp on the very top of the dramatic, tower-like Cerro Autana in Venezuela's Amazonas Territory. It was in the account of this trip given in the *A.O.S. Bulletin* for May 1973 (see Chapter 7).

Maxillaria chlorantha was the next member of this group to show us its pretty face. This time, while also growing at an altitude of about 1,400 m, it came from a very different part of the country, namely the Andes of the State of Táchira, very close to the border of Colombia. *Maxillaria chlorantha* has the same type of flower as *M. splendens* and a lip of very much the same form, but the flowers are less than half the size, and the only plant we found was not prolific enough with its flowers to make it visually very exciting, though finding any species new to us is always a red-letter event.

The third species in this group, a variety of *Maxillaria ochroleuca* (this time with its proper name) came from roughly the same altitude in Amazonas Territory as the *M. splendens* from Cerro Autana, but from a more remote part of the Territory, namely the Sierra Parima that forms the boundary with Brazil for many miles in the southeast of Venezuela. Later still, yet another plant of this species, from about 1,300 m altitude, welcomed us on a visit to the flanks of Cerro Duida, which in 1928 was the first of the great sandstone massifs of Amazonas to be extensively explored. Like *Maxil-*

laria chlorantha, the flowers of this species have relatively small sepals and petals (and similar lips) but make up for this by a very free-flowering habit. It is mainly distinguished by the tall slender peduncles that carry the flowers some 15 cm or more above the base of the large, flat, and sharp-edged pseudobulbs and make its flowers fully visible. This variety of *Maxillaria ochroleuca,* because of these very long peduncles, bears the official name of *longipes,* given it by Sander in 1901. This is the species illustrated here. It is admittedly rather "untidy" to look at but is nevertheless quite a striking plant.

At the start of this note we mentioned that the similarity in form between the flowers of the members of this "*ochroleuca* group" has originally given us some troubles in separating out the constituent members, but there is another feature besides the floral one that clearly distinguishes *Maxillaria splendens* from the others. This lies in the fact that the pseudobulbs of *Maxillaria splendens* terminate in short but quite distinct, highly compressed "collars" that are firmly part of the pseudobulb and not part of the base of the leaf. When the leaf falls, the collar remains. This clue is what has led us to place the name of *Maxillaria splendens* against our Kanarakuni plant despite the fact that it is vegetatively different from the properly identified plant from Cerro Autana. It is much shorter and stouter, with relatively short, wide leaves, short peduncles, and wide collars to the pseudobulbs, and if you look for differences rather than similarities, the lips are far from being identical. But such things can well be the effect of geography as the two sites are about 400 km apart and there is an altitude difference of some 800 m.

All that now remains is for us to tell our readers how best to care for these plants. Alas, alas, they are no more, and all we can tell our readers is how not to treat them. We have lived and learned, and it is a tragedy that so often, in the process of learning, we have done the wrong thing to a plant so that while we have lived the plant has died. In the years since we first found these orchids we have learned that these plants like, indeed seem to need, close company, and if left alone for too long just do not thrive. Hoping to do the poor things a good turn when they began to look a bit crowded in their pots, we repotted them with more growing space. When they showed us that they were unhappy, we thought of everything we might have done wrong except to think they might be suffering from extreme loneliness. Only after they had gone did we realize that, as certain other maxillarias have since shown us, they are plants that thrive best, and perhaps even exclusively, in cramped quarters.

Trichocentrum cornucopiae[1]

WE HAVE OFTEN BEEN ASKED if the thought of snakes does not interfere with our enjoyment of orchid hunting in Venezuela, to which we can reply that we have had the good fortune to have grown up without the instinctive (or inculcated) fear of snakes and similar crawlies that afflicts many otherwise quite courageous people. We avoid as far as possible moving about in snakey places at night, make plenty of heavy movements (snakes are deaf but very sensitive to vibrations) and, if we see one, we approach it with due caution until we are sure that it is not a poisonous one. If it is, then we get no closer to it than we can help; if we are sure it is "innocent," then we try to prevent others from killing it because most such snakes are useful vermin exterminators (some even killers of poisonous snakes) and at times are even kept as pets for that very reason.

But what does worry us is the fear of bumping into a nest of really nasty wasps or bees in the middle of a forest where the insects can fly so much faster than human feet can flee through tangled undergrowth. This did happen to us once and it was definitely panic-making even though the wasps were small, their stings not violent, and they did not follow us very far. At least the crashings of our exit must have fully convinced any snakes within reach that elephants were stampeding so better get out of the way! There is, however, one further fear that lurks in the back of our minds. This is a fear of finding ourselves in a treeless expanse confronting an irate member of the *Bovidae* while collecting a terrestrial orchid — a fear that is best avoided by never entering a treeless savanna without first checking for bulls, or, worse still, cows. We all know that a *toreador* can bluff a bull into diverting its charge by waving a rag under its nose, but a cow is said to keep its eye firmly on the target. In any case it is preferable not to have to put either idea to the test in person. Luckily, treeless expanses in Venezuela are not generally very promising orchid territory, and it was only by carelessness that, when we found our first plant of *Trichocentrum cornucopiae*, we also found ourselves in bovine danger.

Trichocentrum is a small genus whose numbers have been further reduced in recent years by the relegation of many of them to synonymy; thus *Trichocentrum brenesii* and *T. panamense* have been absorbed by *T. capistratum,* and *Trichocentrum longicalcaratum, T. maculatum*, and *T. verruciferum* by *T. pulchrum*. The plants are epiphytic, small or even miniature, fleshy-leaved and compact, and a number of them have relatively large and quite pretty flowers, often borne in fair quantity. Moreover, they are generally not difficult to cultivate. So all in all, they are well worth space in any general collection, even one with limited accommodation. Six species are mentioned in Rebecca Northen's most useful book, *Miniature Orchids,* where two are illustrated.

The genus was "founded" in 1858 by a German-Hungarian team of two botanists of repute, Poeppig and Endlicher (for simplicity, often referred to just as "P&E") and the name *Trichocentrum* that they gave to this genus is derived from Greek words meaning "hair" and "spur." Veitch, in his 1887-1894 *Manual of Orchidaceous Plants,* states that this derivation is "Probably in reference to the slender spur of several of the species, but as Dr. Lindley remarked, the applicability of the generic name is not apparent." To us, this latter remark seems inexplicable, as the type species on which the genus was founded, *Trichocentrum pulchrum,* has a slender spur that can be as much as six cm long. While this is not exactly "hair-like," it fully excuses the reference to such a character in the naming of the genus, and is not invalidated by the existence of some subsequently discovered species that have very short, stubby spurs.

[1] Originally appeared in *A. O. S. Bulletin*, Vol. 51, May 1982, pages 475-478

Venezuela gives a home to only five species of this genus, or perhaps even fewer because one of them, *Trichocentrum orthoplectron,* is only dubiously on record here and seems more securely based in distant Costa Rica or even Mexico. Moreover, although another species, *Trichocentrum hartii,* seems to be endemic here, it is based on a single finding (or identification) by Rolfe in 1894 and there is no mention of just where this plant was found. It is therefore probably safer to say that Venezuela contains only three and not five species. Of these, *Trichocentrum capistratum* is a plant from western Venezuela, and, as found by us and identified by Garay for *Venezuelan Orchids Illustrated,* has smallish flowers, no bright colors, and an insignificant spur — in general more of purely botanical interest than a type to get excited about. This description does not match with the illustration of this species in *A.O.S. Bulletin* for May 1961, but as this genus has been afflicted with so many synonyms it could be that different species are involved. Of the remaining two, *Trichocentrum pulchrum,* also from the west, is a very pretty species, and is closely matched by *Trichocentrum cornucopiae* which is found here only in the far southeast "Guayana" section of Venezuela.

Anyone who has read a number of the "G.C.K. & E.D." articles in the *A.O.S. Bulletin* must long ago have realized that besides orchids as plants another thing that intrigues us about them is the why and wherefore of their names. This has nothing to do with orchidology and is just a late echo of the urge, common to all children, to ask "Why?" In our extreme youth we accepted the answer "Because!" only when it clearly meant "Shut up!" This thirst for generally useless information was happily not discouraged, even if at times it must have driven our parents at least half way up the wall. And it is an extension of this inquisitiveness into adulthood that now has us inquiring into the origin of the name *cornucopiae.* On the face of it, this epithet has a very obvious meaning as the lip, with its spur, is horn-shaped, and even if we have never seen nor can hope to see a cornucopia, we all know that it is a horn-like object, the so-called "Horn of Plenty," filled with an inexhaustible supply of goodies for Christmas and other occasions. But what we did not know, until our curiosity-itch urged us to investigate further, was that the name represents a shocking lack of sympathy for animals on the part of the ancient Greeks. According to Brewer's well-known *Dictionary of Phrase and Fable,* Amalthea, daughter of the King of Greece, fed the infant Zeus with milk from a goat. Zeus, destined to be top-man in Greek mythology, was even at that tender age a tough little lad. He broke off one of the goat's horns and gave it to Amalthea as a reward, promis-

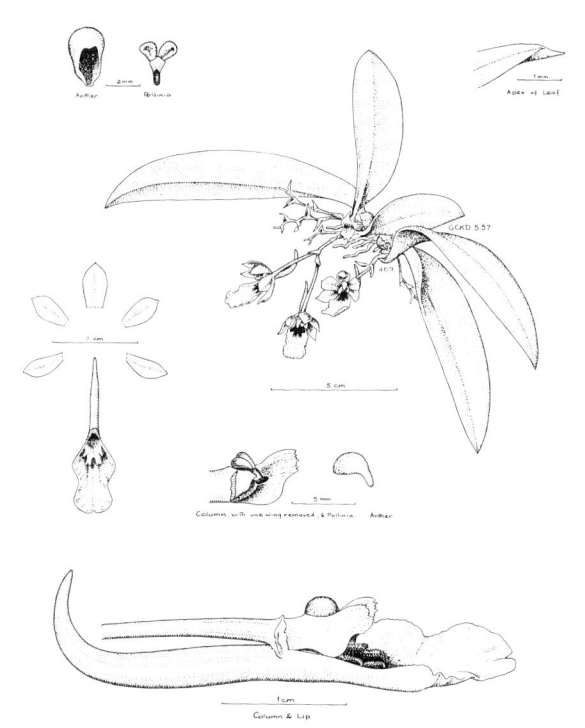

Trichocentrum cornucopiae Linden & Reichb. f. in Gard. Chron. 266, 1866. — E.

ing that the possessor would always have in abundance everything desired — which was splendid for Amalthea, but not so splendid for the poor goat.

Classical mythology, however, is seldom straightforward, and our other classical dictionary gives a very different picture of what went on. It first states that Amalthea was rewarded by being placed in heaven as a constellation of stars — which may sound good for prestige, but who wants to be stuck up there forever with nobody to talk to? The wonderful Horn of Plenty, which Amalthea would surely have preferred, went instead to a bunch of nymphs who had taken care of the infant Zeus. Nymphs, according to the book, are somewhat second-rate deities, stated by Plutarch to live for the rather odd figure of "at least 9,720 years," and are represented as being young and beautiful virgins, veiled up to the middle. Although it was deemed "unfortunate to see them naked," there were clearly advantages to living in those distant days as Hesiod, an 8th century poet who obviously had inside knowledge, says that there were more than 3,000 of them flitting about. The idea of just one nearly 3,000-year-old virgin, let along thousands of them, is a mind-boggling thought, and leaves little room for sympathy for the poor cornucopial goat that started all this business in the first place.

Trichocentrum as a genus does not seem to have had much publicity. Apart from the reference in Rebecca Tyson Northen's book, there is a nicely illustrated article by Henry Teuscher in the *A.O.S.*

Bulletin for May 1961 and another, by John Beckner, in the *A.O.S. Bulletin* for March 1963, but there seems to have been no further mention of the genus other than two very short A.O.S. notes, with no illustrations, referring to *T. pfavii* in June 1970 and *T. tigrinum* in November 1971. This is a remarkable gap to find in a genus of such visible attractions and perhaps our Editor could induce some knowledgeable person to work up a well-illustrated article devoted to a complete revision of the genus. Color illustrations would, of course, be desirable, but in view of budgetary considerations we are sure readers would forgive the use of black-and-white. As the genus itself is somewhat bashful of publicity, it is not surprising to find that *Trichocentrum cornucopiae* has inherited this character also. In the official *Flora de Venezuela* of 1969, it earns only a single mention. This is based on a plant that we found ourselves just south of what is now the small town of Tumeremo in the State of Bolívar in 1957, though we have also found it later just north of the town and again (also in Bolívar State) in the neighborhood of Angel Falls. The first specimen was in fairly dry, open country at about 300 m altitude, the second one in the damp cloud forest of the Altiplanicie de Nuria at 600 m, and the final one in rather less damp riverine forest on the Río Carrao.

It is, we think, a common experience among orchid hunters that each new find is likely to leave a lasting memory of the "where and how" of the event, unless the species proves later to be so common that the memory gets wiped out by sheer volume of similar events. *Trichocentrum cornucopiae* is one of these "firsts," the memory of which remains clear because it is associated with the only moment of "bovine danger" that we have yet run into here.

In the very early days of the construction of the road which now links El Dorado in Venezuela with Boa Vista in Brazil, we had the temporary use of a vehicle loaned us by the road-construction contractor. Near the end of our visit, when the plane that was to take us back to Caracas was delayed by a day, we decided to drive north 100 miles or so to see what orchid possibilities there might be in the low and rather unpromising country to the north of El Dorado, limiting ourselves mainly to the occasional stretches of trees along small streams. We spent a night in an extremely primitive "hotel" (just one large room with head-high partitions to provide a vague impression of privacy) in the then definitely one-horse village of Tumeremo, and then stopped a few miles outside the village on the way back, to have a last-chance look at a small copse some distance from the road across an expanse of dry grass and scrub. Crossing a barbed-wire fence that we failed to realize indicated the presence of cattle, we headed for the copse and were well out in the open when we noticed that we were the object of scrutiny by a large and clearly inimical animal advancing towards us, even more clearly equipped with a pair of long and well-pointed horns. Another pair of horns now faced us, those of the dilemma as to whether we should beat it for the road or the copse. Fear of being lofted over the fence by a painful prod from behind struck us as the more serious danger, so we continued towards the copse at what we hoped was a well-judged balance between a provocative panic and an unnecessary slowness. Our judgment proved sound as we achieved the shelter of the copse in safety and our valor was rewarded by finding, on the largest tree, our first plant of *Trichocentrum cornucopiae*, and, as a bonus, a nice specimen of *Oncidium lanceanum*. While we examined these treasures, our opponent lost interest in us, if indeed it ever had designs on us other than curiosity or a wish to make friends, and disappeared around to the other side of the copse, whereupon we managed a dignified but hasty retreat to the car. Altogether it was a silly and ignominious episode, but one that, as already mentioned, has fixed the locale of this species very firmly in our minds.

As regards cultivation, in Teuscher's article he states that pot culture is not very suitable as the plants are conditioned to long dry periods and are easily harmed by overwatering. In the Montreal Botanical Gardens the plants there did best on suspended slabs of cork bark. In the case of our three Venezuelan species we have only very limited experience with very few plants, and our climate can be damp in some years even in the dry season and in other years be dry for several months. In general, though, Teuscher's recommendations seem suitable for us also although we use suspended pieces of hard tree-fern root instead of cork bark. In any case, it seems probable that the species would do equally well if placed on a well-ventilated shelf and mounted on any sort of solid non-rotting material. The illustration of *Trichocentrum tigrinum* in *Miniature Orchids* shows a happy and nicely flowering plant growing on the outside of an inverted half-coconut, and there are few woods as hard and rot-proof as coconut shell.

Houlletia tigrina and Serendipity[1]

MOST of our orchid hunting in Venezuela has been completely general in character because, to misquote Gertrude Stein, "An orchid is an orchid is an orchid" wherever you may find it. But once in a while some particular species, not yet seen but suspected to exist here, becomes the target of a special search. And if, after a long period it remains unseen, one can be excused for concluding that either it never did exist here or that it has long since disappeared. And if, again, after the search has been abandoned, it then suddenly and surprisingly *does* appear, it is tempting to believe that at least a touch of serendipity has been responsible and that for a short while one has become the sort of person who, like the original fairy tale Prince of Serendip, makes discoveries by accident of things not looked for; such as, in an extreme case, finding a large diamond among the roots of a terrestrial orchid in Venezuela's Gran Sabana area, a felicitous event that we have often hoped would come our way but which, alas, has so far eluded us, although it is not impossible that one day it might! After all, it is not so very long ago that a diamond of over 100 carats in size was found in the Gran Sabana by a prospector who couldn't tell an *Aa* from an *Ada,* so why shouldn't well-educated orchidists have equal luck?

In any case, we feel that some degree of serendipity was responsible for our first finding of *Houlletia tigrina.* Our searches for this rare species had their origin in 1966, when an article by Jack Fowlie appeared in *The Orchid Digest,* indicating that both this species and *Houlletia lansbergii* should be findable in Venezuela, and we later received a strong hint from J.F. himself that we had better get busy and find them! — Or "it!" With a history confused by lack of herbarium specimens and by misidentification of illustrations, these two species might well be synonymous. *Houlletia lansbergii* was recorded vaguely as coming from "near

Houlletia tigrina

Cumaná" in eastern Venezuela, and no locality at all was given for *Houlletia tigrina,* other than that the collector who found it had been working in Venezuela; slim clues indeed on which to base an orchid hunt more than 100 years after the event.

After failing to get even a whiff of these *Houlletia* species in our searches hither and yon, some real encouragement finally came our way when about 1970 our botanical friend Julian Steyermark showed us a plant that he had collected from a high part of the ridge that forms the Paria Peninsula in the far northeast corner of Venezuela. The plant had no flowers but did look like a houlletia, and as at that time *Houlletia tigrina* and *H. lansbergii* were the only species expectable, if at all, in this part of the country (*Houlletia odoratissima* and *H. roraimensis* coming from much farther south in the Guayana and Amazonas regions), it seemed that we were on the verge of success. All we had to do now was to visit Julian's new area and find plants in flower. From the condition of his plant and the date when he had found it, it was likely that the propitious moment to look for more

---

[1] Originally appeared in *A.O.S. Bulletin,*
Vol. 51, June 1982, pages 589-592

would be some time "bang" in the middle of the wet season, an unfortunate moment to go orchid hunting there, not only because of the general discomfort but because, for people who wear glasses, vision becomes regrettably blurred when rain falls on them. But needs must, so we started planning. The usual succession of "other things" interrupted, but July 1972 finally saw us climbing the last miles up the south flank of the Paria Ridge, our hammocks, plastic tarps, and food borne on the backs of three minute burros, and all of us, including our local peasant help, sliding madly about on the steep and now-muddy slopes in the anticipated tropical *palo de agua* rain storm. But once we had reached a good campsite and the tarps had been slung between the trees, the camp itself was not too messy, the night quiet, and we enjoyed our campfire meal of large and very tasty spiny-haired forest rats which the hired help had shot with their more-or-less homemade .22 guns. The next day was rather less wet and we continued without the burros to an altitude of about 5,000 feet where we at last came across some small trees, amid the very large ones, that bore in the lower part of their trunks a number of *Houlletia*-like plants. Success was imminent!

But our rejoicing was quickly dampened when we found more plants that had inflorescences, in bud, that were erect, a habit that no self-respecting *Houlletia tigrina* and *H. lansbergii* could tolerate. When we got back to Caracas we could not resist the temptation to accelerate matters by opening up the largest bud. As we feared, it was quite definitely not what we were looking for, and quite definitely was *Houlletia odoratissima*. For what it was worth, it looked as if this find had at least extended the known habitat of this latter species a long and important jump to the north, but we had not got what we had come for and must now continue searching elsewhere, preferably nearer to Oumaná, 100 miles or so farther west.

But before we could organize this, Julian again interrupted things. He had come up with another *Houlletia*-type specimen, this time in the Coastal Range west of Caracas, and this now clearly warranted top priority. In due course, other things as usual intervening, we visited this site in late 1972 and did indeed find quite a colony of such plants, growing terrestrially. But again, when we finally found one with an inflorescence it was not only small and withered but also quite definitely erect. Obviously all the houlletias in the north of Venezuela were *Houlletia odoratissima* and our chances of finding the very nebulous *H. tigrina* or *H. lansbergii* were nil. The latter probably did not even exist here any more and the former was perhaps entirely mistaken in its attribution to Venezuela. So we abandoned the idea of making further searches for these two elusive species. However, we still had a few days on our hands for general orchid hunting before being due back home, so we decided to move a bit farther west along the spine of the Coastal Range in these parts, to where the damp air currents rising from the coast supported a fine growth of cloud forest on the northern slopes in which other interesting orchids might exist.

Above a small village to the west of the city of Valencia a steeply winding road, little more than a track at that time, led to the crest of the ridge at about 4,000 feet, at which point the almost treeless, south-facing slopes changed abruptly to dense cloud forest on the northern side. At the very top of the ridge the road ceased to exist and became a steeply descending track which the sharp hoofs of generations of burro traffic had converted into a narrow, 10-foot-deep gulley with earthen sides. Bulldozers had recently been engaged in sidetracking the gulley to follow a wider and more usable trail to one side, but, hoping to find a shortcut to the lower forests, we continued down the gulley itself. In doing this we had no thought of finding orchids in the bare and almost vertical banks, but suddenly found ourselves face-to-face with some terrestrial-growing plants of an obviously *Houlletia* type. One of these even showed the start of a two-bud raceme of a pendent nature, but this lax habit might have been due to discouragement at finding itself in such a dark and airless situation, so it did not greatly raise our hopes. Later, as the inflorescence continued to develop in Caracas, we allowed ourselves to feel more optimistic, and its progress was watched with great care to make sure no malevolent insects could harm it. Finally came the exciting day when its buds opened up. It was clearly *Houlletia tigrina* — or could it be *Houlletia lansbergii*? We quickly sent a note to Jack Fowlie for *The Orchid Digest*, since he had inspired our search in the first place, and followed this up by sending full details to Leslie Garay, our orchid mentor in Harvard, in which we posed the double query: was this indeed *Houlletia tigrina*, and, if so, were *H. tigrina* and *Houlletia lansbergii* one and the same thing? When Garay's answer came back that it was indeed *Houlletia tigrina* and that *Houlletia lansbergii* was a later synonym, our search was at an end. *Houlletia tigrina-cum-lansbergii* had finally come back to Venezuela in fully tangible form after its rather intangible start more than 100 years before! When we had looked for it, it has failed to show up; when we had stopped looking for it, it appeared; so we feel we can honestly claim that the find was due to some degree of serendipity.

It had struck us as strange, however, that this species should grow as a terrestrial because, except when situated on a very steep bank, as our plants were, the flowers would be touching or even lying on the ground; and thinking back we remembered having seen a couple of small, epiphytic plants in the forest near the gulley. These might very well be "tigrinas" also, so when an opportunity arose in October 1980, we revisited the site with the specific intention of looking for more epiphytic, not terrestrial, plants. By then, the gulley had largely disappeared under the onslaught of bulldozers continuing the road downhill to the north, leaving only some short and orchidless sections behind, but, as we had hoped, we did find some adult, epiphytic plants growing fairly low on trees inside the forest edge. While the light here was rather dim, as it always is inside a forest, there seemed to be plenty of air. But it surprised us to note that these plants were on the trunks of large tree-ferns rather than on normal trees because, while the lower parts of tree-fern trunks or "roots" make fine material on which to grow orchids in captivity, we have seen very few orchids growing on them in the forests. Our own plants have been fairly happy in Caracas, but while our climate must be very similar to that of their original home, we seem to lack some important ingredient, as they have so far failed to produce any flowers. We had been careful to take for ourselves only two plants, leaving others to ensure continuation of the species well away from the new road, taking one plant precisely because it had a developing seed-capsule. This we later sent to our friend, H. Phillips Jesup, in Connecticut in the hopes that he, or some other expert, could develop green-pod seeds and continue the species in captivity. The results of this we do not yet know.

As can be seen in the illustrations to this article, *Houlletia tigrina* is a most interesting species with quite large (six cm) flowers, but it is not likely to win any prizes for beauty. Due to the pendent habit of the raceme and its pedicels, the flowers show only their rather unexciting "backs" to the public, and the impressive red coloration of their "insides" is visible only to snakes, worms, or observers lying on their backs — or to the camera. The narrow pseudobulbs, clustered along the rhizome close enough to hide it, are fully clothed when young in long, gray sheathes that quickly fall away, and the single, lightly plicate leaves have relatively long, sub-terete bases. The flowers are of fleshy consistency, and are characterized by a large, white, broad-bladed epichile borne at the end of a red-flecked hypochile with narrow, erect, sharp-pointed, lateral lobes.

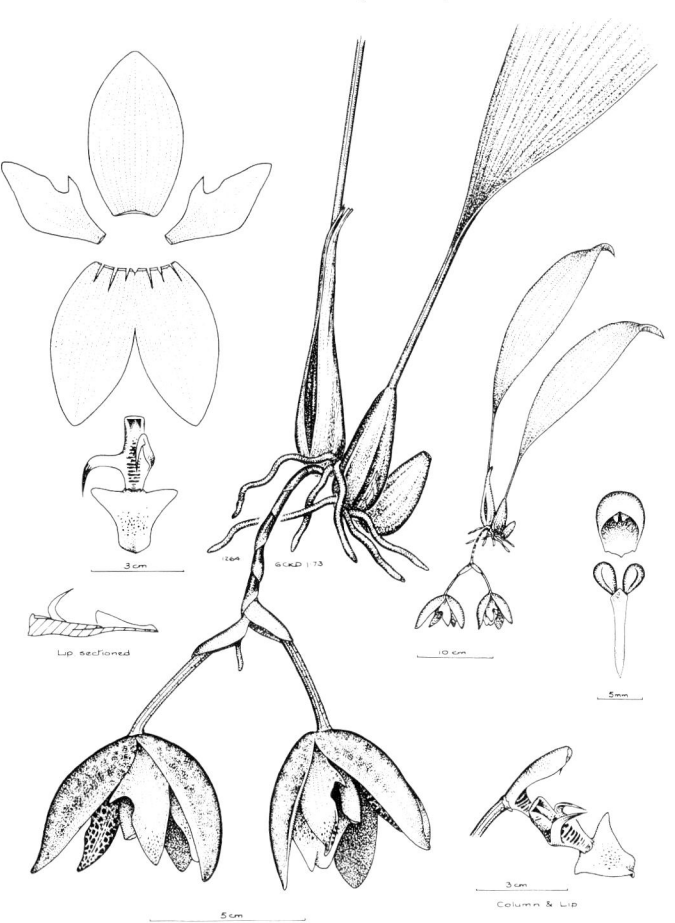

Houlletia tigrina Linden ex Lindl. in Paxt., Fl. Gard. 3: 172, 1853. — B.

Hunting Phragmipedium klotzscheanum — An Agony in Eight Fits[1]

KNOWING where an orchid should be is not the same thing as finding it — a simple fact of life but one that sometimes has to be learned the hard way, as we found out a long time ago when we first heard of *Phragmipedium klotzscheanum* and thought it would be nice to have one in our collection where we could study it at our leisure. First found in the mid-nineteenth century in the region where the famous sandstone table mountain of Roraima shares a common border with Venezuela, Brazil, and Guyana (then British Guiana), this species did not begin to appear in Venezuelan records until quite recent years and then only very sparingly. This rareness was naturally a major spur to our determination to find a plant.

In the late 1950s we made our first contact with the fascinating southeast corner of Venezuela, at that time only little explored, known as the Gran Sabana, the home of Roraima and a number of other mesas or "tepuis," several of them far larger than Roraima. We not only fell in love with it immediately but from then on made frequent visits to it, following up on the new road-in-construction as it penetrated slowly and ever deeper across the Sabana towards the Brazilian border. Especially in the cloud forests clothing its northern extreme, there were many distracting orchid species new to us but, from the very start, we kept a sharp eye open not only for *Phragmipedium klotzscheanum* but also for *Sobralia stenophylla*, the latter a much larger and more "visible" species that we had been told was frequently found growing in company with the phragmipedium and should thus be a useful indicator. On successive visits, however, no success crowned our efforts, and we began to wonder if this species really did exist where it was supposed to exist.

In early 1963 we had an opportunity to visit the great sandstone massif of Auyántepui. We felt sure

Phragmipedium klotzscheanum

that here, at last, we would find at least one plant of the phragmipedium as a friend had told us exactly where he had found a plant not long before, at about 1,200 m (ca. 4,000 foot) altitude on the south flank of this tepui. There were no detailed maps of this mountain available, nor even maps with any details at all, on which this phragmipedium site could be marked, but we went with great expectations as there is only one main trail up the mountain. At about the right altitude we found, as described, a stream flowing through lightly wooded country. We even found a plant or two of *Sobralia stenophylla*. Our spirits rose. We searched. We searched. We searched. But neither there nor anywhere else on this flank of the mountain, nor later

[1] Originally appeared in *A.O.S. Bulletin*, Vol. 51, July 1982, pages 709-712

Phragmipedium klotzscheanum *in situ* along a riverbank in Venezuela's Gran Sabana

on its top, did we find a plant of *Phragmipedium klotzscheanum*. By now we were feeling like a couple from the wildly crazy group of characters hunting for the elusive Snark in Lewis Carroll's *Agony in Eight Fits,* who "sought their quarry with thimbles, and sought it with care" — like them we had, as it were, "pursued it with forks and with hope," and were fully ready, if we ever caught a glimpse of our own particular quarry, to "threaten its life with a railway share or charm it with smiles and soap."

Luck finally came our way before we needed either railway shares, of which we had none (the $500 worth of Argentine Cordoba Central Railway shares that we once had owned many years ago had been disposed of in 1939 when their total value fell to 12½¢), or soap, which like all sensible bush travelers we did have. Not long after our Auyán venture, we made a joint expedition with our botanical friend, Julian Steyermark, to explore the small, not very impressive, but botanically very interesting sandstone mountain called Cerro Venamo, lying right on the border with Guyana, and made a camp at about 1,000 m at the side of the small stream of the Río Venamo itself. The next morning, always with the phragmipedium in mind, we were doing our usual searching along the river bank when E.D. saw some spots of color among a mass of "grass" right at the water's edge. After what must have been our eighth searching fit, here at last we had before us, not the Snark but far more importantly, *Phragmipedium klotzscheanum*! But had it not been for the fact that the plants were in flower we might have, in fact, we almost certainly would have, passed it by, so excellent was its grass-like camouflage.

Now that we had seen and touched this most interesting orchid, and knew not only that it really did exist in the Gran Sabana but also what it looked like in the wild, we had little difficulty on later trips in finding many more places in the Gran Sabana. These were almost always between some 1,200 and 1,400 meters in altitude, the plants growing quite often not only close to the water of a stream or small river, but even on boulders in the stream bed itself where they would be frequently completely submerged in the rushing water, if not for long periods at least for several days. When a number of flowers are in bloom, *Phragmipedium klotzscheanum* makes quite a display and can catch the eye of even a non-orchidist, but when not in flower, it still takes a good look from a knowing eye to spot that these plants really are orchids. In recent years, however, since access to the Gran Sabana has become so easy that hundreds of families visit it on major holiday seasons, there has undoubtedly been a mass attack on the species that cannot have failed to deplete their numbers. However, the area is large and, with many streams and only few visitors bothering to walk far from their cars, it is doubtful if this lovely orchid is anywhere near to being placed on the list of threatened species, and even less risk that it will become extinct, provided that recently published plans for hydroelectric installations involving the flooding of hundreds of square miles of the Gran Sabana remain only as plans. If they are ever put into effect then not only the phragmipediums and other orchids will be blotted out, but uncounted other plants and animal life will disappear with them.

The illustrations accompanying this article show the main features of the flower of *Phragmipedium klotzscheanum* and need only the addition of the main dimensions to make them complete. These are: dorsal sepal to 35 × 10 mm; lateral sepals, connate into a single lamina, to 30 × 20 mm; petals to

Nora at work on Cerro Venamo

Nora crosses the Río Venamo.

80 cm long, 10 mm wide at the base, narrowing to three mm at the apex; lip to 35 × 15 mm.

As for cultivation of this species, our initial group of plants began well but did not last more than about three years. These plants were put in an earthenware pot filled with the natural soil from the Gran Sabana, and placed where they would receive mixed shade and some, but not much, sun. They were watered frequently. Two things may have caused their downfall. Firstly, lack of watering at some point during our dry season. *Phragmipedium klotzscheanum* is sensitive to dryness and, when we are out of Caracas looking for orchids elsewhere, those left in charge of watering chores may have failed to do that which they "did ought to have done." A wet pot presented as evidence when one gets back home is no proof that the pot was kept wet all the time. Secondly, the alkaline quality of our city tap water is most unlikely to please the palate of terrestrial plants from the Gran Sabana where the sandy soil is mostly very acid. So when the chance came to collect a few more plants, we changed our tactics. These new plants were put into a yet larger pot with greater moisture-retaining capacity, and placed at the very edge of our small lily-cum-goldfish pond, with a view to making sure that nobody would forget to water the plants, dipping water from the pond for the purpose. Though the plants now live in the fairly deep shade of a large fir-tree-like podocarpus, and do not get more than late afternoon sun, it seems that the change has been decidedly to their liking because for several years now they have remained fresh, with shining green leaves, and not infrequently show us flowers.

Apart from the obvious benefits of more constant watering, the plants are no doubt greatly benefiting from the change in quality of the water they receive. Our city water is an alkaline pH7 +, and the pond water contains many luscious ingredients that the city fathers do not incorporate into the water they supply us for our taps — such as "fish manure" from the 30 or so goldfish in the pond, the rotting remains of a constant intake of vegetable matter in the form of dead leaflets from the podocarpus, ripe "nuts" from the podocarpus (which happens to be a female tree), and dead leaves from the water lilies. The effect of all this is to produce a pond water that is still far from the very high acidity of Gran Sabana soil but, with a pH of 5.5 is also a great improvement, from the point of view of a phragmipedium, on what comes out of a tap. It also shows that our intentions are for the best, and the mere proximity of a body of water, small though it is, may be providing a further and critical boost to the morale of *Phragmipedium klotzscheanum*.

Psychopsis and Psychopsiella — One Old and One New Genus[1]

WE SINCERELY HOPE that the sight of this title, implying the need to learn yet more strange orchid names, will not lead readers into any psychotic reactions! Instead, we hope that curiosity will overcome any such tendencies and lead them to wonder what it is all about. Briefly, it is about a number of *Oncidium* species whose history is anything but simple and thus, unfortunately, not susceptible to being dealt with briefly. An outline of the background is essential, and for this it is best to refer to a technical article, "Analysis of the Genus *Oncidium*", by Leslie Garay and John Stacy in *Bradea* (September 1974), and to a more popular and magnificently illustrated article on the section *Glanduligera* of this genus by the late George C. Kennedy in *The Orchid Digest* for July-August 1977. In both of these works there appears, among the synonyms used, the rather obscure name of *Psychopsis*.

As outlined in these works, the section *Glanduligera* was established by Lindley in 1855 to accommodate three *Oncidium* species: *O. papilio*, *O. limminghei*, and *O. kramerianum*, the last of these being at the time considered by Lindley as no more than a synonym of *Oncidium papilio*. In 1922, when Kränzlin produced a new name (*Poikilophylla*) for this section he added *Oncidium sanderae* and *Oncidium versteegianum*. With regard to all these species, Kennedy, in the article cited above, makes the following comments:

Oncidium papilio is readily distinguished by the apical portion of the flower stem being flattened. Moreover, two small knobs mark the two upper fimbriae of the column wings. (These "knobs" are what are known as "glands," defined in our *Botanical Dictionary* as "multi-cellular secretory structures" and which presumably give rise to the *Glanduligera* name for this section. Such a gland is shown in the sketch accompanying this present note.)

Oncidium kramerianum, which in many respects is very similar to *O. papilio*, is equally distinguished from this species by virtue of its terete stem with swollen nodes. The glandular fimbriae of the column wings of this species show up very clearly in Kennedy's photograph.

Oncidium sanderae is characterized by pectinate (comb-like) column wings, of which Kennedy also shows a very clear photograph. It is, he says, locally abundant from Moyobamba in Peru, and is identical with *Oncidium versteegianum*: "My *sanderae* plants differ from the type specimen in Kew mainly in that the lateral sepals hang about half an inch below the apex of the lip." He makes no reference to "glands," but C. Schweinfurth in *Orchids of Peru* says of this species, "Column wings long pectinate, with glandular tips."

Oncidium versteegianum ". . . is a mystery plant from Surinam," according to Kennedy. The essential type specimen was destroyed during World War II, and the one-and-only other specimen, in Kew, is "a bit battered." Kennedy notes that the description of this species (in *Rec. Trav. Bot. Neerl.*, 1909) agrees with the description of *Oncidium sanderae* and his Moyobamba plants.

Oncidium limminghei, originally assigned by Lindley to the *Glanduligera* section, was moved by Garay and Stacy to the section *Plurituberculata* in 1974, but Kennedy remarks that after seeing fresh material Garay agreed that the original assignment to *Glanduligera* was correct.

Psychopsis

The genus name *Psychopsis* (listed by Kennedy among the synonyms for *Oncidium*) have been used for members of the section *Glanduligera*, but the name is unlikely to be familiar to any orchidist reader of this note unless he was active some 150 years ago when Rafinesque gave the name of *Psychopsis* to these species because ". . . psyche means 'butterfly', and the flowers strikingly resemble certain tropical butterflies." Similarly, the name

---

[1] Originally appeared in *A.O.S. Bulletin*, Vol. 51, September 1982, pages 942-947.

Psychopsiella, which also appears in the title to this note, is equally unlikely to be familiar to non-taxonomic readers unless they can read German and subscribe to the well-known German periodical *Die Orchidee.* We ourselves, though not exactly juvenile, were not personally acquainted with Rafinesque; and unfortunately we are by no means able to read German with sufficient ease to make it worth our while to subscribe to *Die Orchidee,* excellent though that periodical is. So while these generic names are no doubt well enough known in the world of taxonomy, it is a matter of luck that they have now been brought firmly to our attention. And in the belief that what interests us may also interest other readers, we have embarked on the present note as a way of attracting attention to the existence of these rather esoteric orchid names, and expect that more will be heard of them in future if only because one of them, *Oncidium (Psychopsis) papilio,* is one of Venezuela's most striking species.

The "luck" in this matter rests in the thoughtfulness of Messrs. Emil Lückel and Guido J. Braem (hereinafter, as the lawyers might say, referred to as L&B) who sent us a copy of the extensive and well-illustrated article they had recently published in *Die Orchidee* (for January 1982). The article is headed by an English-language summary which clearly explains that its purpose is firstly to reinstate Rafinesque's 1838 genus, *Psychopsis,* pointing out the technical error that had made his name for *Oncidium papilio* "illegitimate" under modern nomenclature rules, and secondly to propose a completely new genus, *Psychopsiella,* to accommodate *Oncidium limminghei* "because of its outstanding characteristics." This old-new genus of *Psychopsis* is thus left to include the previous species of *Oncidium papilio, O. kramerianum, O. sanderae,* and *O. versteegianum.*

While this English summary puts the matter in a very useful nutshell, the article itself is quite long and obviously contains much information necessary to a proper understanding of what *Psychopsis* and *Psychopsiella* are all about. We can understand bits and pieces of the German text, but we can by no means understand it all, and for this present note we are greatly indebted to Michael Sinn for a translation into Spanish of a part of it, and to Ursula Ploch for a quite indispensable and many-paged translation of the rest of it into English. Only a small part of this valuable preliminary work is incorporated into this present note, but, without an understanding of the whole of L&B's article, it would have been impossible for us to determine just which parts were essential for limited needs.

As explained by L&B, the original description of the genus *Oncidium* by Swartz in 1800 was so indefinite that there was nothing to prevent the subsequent inclusion of a great many heterogeneous species which subsequent taxonomists have divided into sections, totaling 14 in the days of John Lindley (1855) and 26 in 1974 as classified by Leslie Garay. To simplify matters, a number of new genera have recently been created to cover a number of former oncidiums; for example, *Psygmorchis* by Dodson and Dressler in 1972, *Jamaiciella* by J. Braem in 1980, and three others with only one species each, namely *Antillanorchis* by Garay in 1974, *Mexicoa* by Garay also in 1974, and *Hispaniella* by Braem in 1980. And now, continuing this trend, L&B have proposed the reinstatement of the old genus of *Psychopsis* to cover *Oncidium papilio, O. kramerianum,* and *O. sanderae,* plus a new genus, *Psychopsiella,* to accommodate *Oncidium limminghei.*

The old *Psychopsis* genus, as revealed in the L&B article, certainly began its life in a very muddled manner. *Oncidium papilio,* which Rafinesque used to typify it in 1836, suffered from a series of bad and confusing illustrations, and in his Latin description he says it has "bilabiate petals, three outer ones equal in size, linear in form and erect, and two inner ones, falcately recurved and undulate." In fact, it has one erect linear dorsal sepal, two falcate and undulate lateral sepals (quite obviously pretending to be petals!) and two erect, linear petals looking just like the dorsal sepal. He also says that there are four pollinia, whereas there are only two, as with all oncidiums. And to top this all off, there is the fact that Rafinesque could not foresee the future sufficiently to realize that his species epithet was going to be considered illegitimate under later nomenclature rules because he had not transferred the *papilio* epithet to the type species. This latter species should (nowadays) properly be called *Psychopsis papilio,* not, as Rafinesque named it, *Psychopsis picta.* L&B point out that, in modern taxonomy, characteristics such as chromosome number ($2n = 38$ for *Psychopsis*), chromosome configuration, etc. should be taken into consideration, in addition to morphological ones.

The history of each species making up this reinstated genus is given by L&B in some detail, but there is only room here for the following references from their article in the January 1982 issue of *Die Orchidee* which serve to illustrate some of the complexities:

Oncidium (Psychopsis) papilio — "Only one variety deserves a name. This is var. *latourae,* with pure white and yellow flowers, described by Broadway in 1927; var. *limbatum,* with red-brown lip margins, can be regarded as taxonomically unimportant, as can var. *majus,* var. *pictum* and var. *eckhardtii.*" L&B also refer to a number of albino forms, such as var. *albiflorum* with "white flowers which according to Rchb.f. has been found around Caracas." (In this respect it is worth mentioning that in his July-August 1977 *Orchid Digest* article, Kennedy shows a photograph of a large, orange-yellow variety, remarking, "When *Oncidium* species are subjected to isolation of a small number of individuals and consequent long in-breeding, the anthocyanin pigment-producing ability is impaired, as in this example. However, due to coloration by yellow-to-orange anthoxanthin pigments, yellow-to-orange flowers result instead of white flowers as in other genera."

Oncidium (Psychopsis) kramerianum — In 1874 Morren proposed the name of *Oncidium nodosum* for a purportedly new species with very thick nodes, but the plant was already known as *Oncidium kramerianum*. He then proposed a new generic name of *Papiliopsis* but this was superfluous as *Psychopsis* already existed! Regel described an *Oncidium papilioniforme* in 1879, "a form midway between *O. papilio* and *O. kramerianum*, possibly a natural hybrid, but drawings and description are inadequate to confirm this as a species," according to L&B. In 1888 there is also mention of a var. *resplendens*.

Oncidium (Psychopsis) sanderae — L&B call this "the papilio from Peru." Sanders received some plants from Moyobamba in Peru and when one flowered it was described by Rolfe as a new species "closely related to *O. papilio* but with very strong slits in the column wings and with fimbriate extensions ending in glandular points."

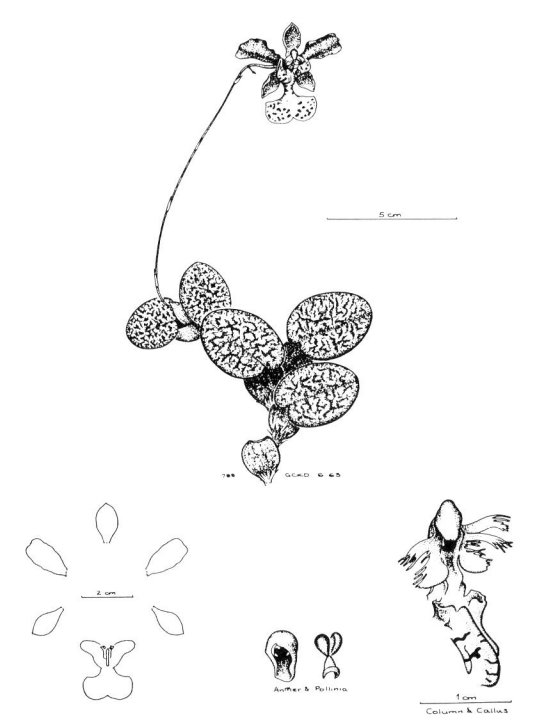

Oncidium limminghei Morren ex Lindl., Folia Orch. Oncid. 56, 1855. — B.

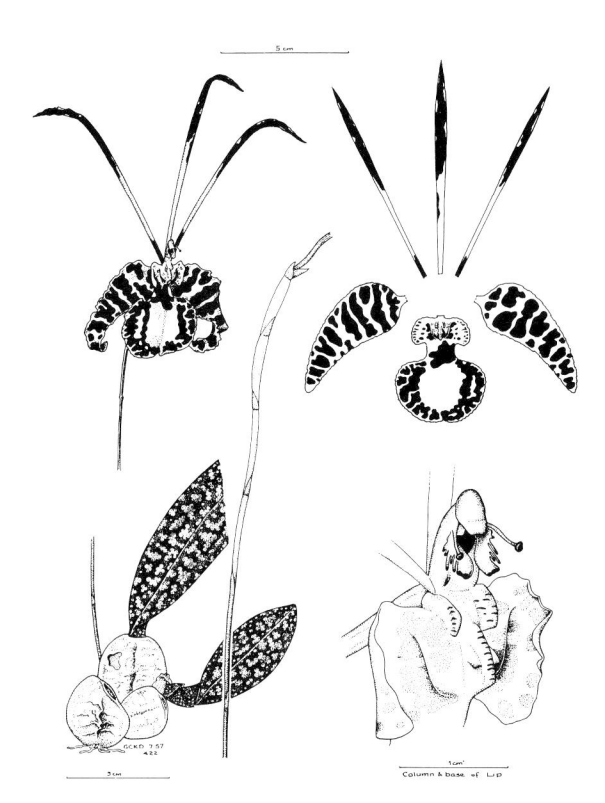

Oncidium papilio Lindl. in Bot. Reg. 11: t. 910, 1825. — B. E.

Oncidium (Psychopsis) versteegianum — L&B call this "the lost relative from Surinam." As mentioned by Kennedy, only one rather battered specimen now exists. It was described by Pulle as having finely slit column wings with hair-like extensions that do not have glandular points. L&B state that there is no basis for Kennedy's assumption that this may have been a plant of *Oncidium sanderae*.

Psychopsiella

Having dealt with *Psychopsis*, L&B then turn their attention to *Oncidium limminghei,* which Lindley had called a "papilio on a very small scale." This species they separate out from the others of the section *Glanduligera* (no "glands" appear in its description) and treat it as the sole representative of a new genus which they publish in their *Die Orchidee* article under the name of *Psychopsiella,* based on the single species *Psychopsiella limminghei*. The generic description, which naturally follows that of the species, contains no single key feature to distinguish it from *Psychopsis*. Instead, as stated by L&B, they base it on a "unique combination of characters," none of which individually would be conclusive but which, together, do result in a form quite different from other *Psychopsis* species. In particular, the sepals do not show the striking dissimilarity between dorsal and lateral sepals so characteristic of *Oncidium (Psychopsis) papilio* and its allies — a comparison which is made clear in the sketch accompanying this note. For the layman, at least, it is easy to see why L&B wish to put this species into a separate genus, and *Psychopsiella*, though a long name, is not, after all, a very hard one either to remember or to pronounce!

What is less easy is to believe that because the "type" specimen of *Oncidium* (*Psychopsiella*) *limminghei* is credited with coming from Caracas, this species really is Venezuelan. The plant was sent from Caracas to Europe by the Brazilian consul in Caracas, but even Morren, who named the plant, doubted that Caracas was truly its origin. In the days before air travel, it is unlikely that the plant had traveled from Brazil to Caracas by sea or land from the very restricted locality in Brazil where, as stated by Kennedy, it is known to grow in highly endemic form, halfway between Río de Janeiro and the Brazilian coast, but it does seem quite possible that, as Kennedy also remarks, "...some error was made in the assignment of locality to the type sheet." Kennedy overstresses some sentences we once wrote to him when he says in his *Orchid Digest* article that we are "firmly convinced" that the species is not Venezuelan, but trying to prove a negative is seldom a profitable pastime, and published records cannot be dismissed just by saying they might be wrong. The safest solution is to continue to list *Oncidium* (*Psychopsiella*) *limminghei* as a Venezuelan species — and who knows but that some day a new plant will be found here and all the "negatives" will be confounded!

Comparettia falcata and Psygmorchis glossomystax — Miniature Orchids for a Very Large Christmas Tree[1]

"HE FLEW THROUGH the air with the greatest of ease, that daring young man on the flying trapeze." So what? That's what he is paid to do, but our orchid seeds do it free, gratis, and for nothing. Besides which, one can see the trapeze man when he flies, but our orchid seeds manage to do it in completely invisible secrecy. Nevertheless, there is no denying that seeds do get from "A" to "B" even if we have yet to see one in the act, and we now have a very nice example of this in our own backyard.

The Christmas tree habit is not native to the tropics, but in Venezuela it has become a standard and highly commercialized practice for every household to have its own tree when Christmas comes, the sidewalks of Caracas tending to become clogged with imported cut-trees for sale, all condemned a few days later to become unwelcome fodder for the trash men to clear up. But when, in 1960, we were about to celebrate our first Christmas in our brand-new house high above Caracas Valley, we felt that only a live and growable tree would be suitable for the occasion, and someone suggested buying a *Pino Suizo* (Swiss pine). This, after further inquiry, proved to be the local name for the Norfolk Island Pine, a species of *Araucaria* (*A. excelsa*) native to the island of that name far to the east of Australia! Checking this in our *Bailey's Encyclopedia,* we read that araucarias "are probably the most prized pot evergreens in cultivation, much in use for house decoration, particularly at Christmas time. *A. excelsa*, a most beautiful pot plant, is commonly seen in residences and is grown in many nurseries for decoration as window or table plants. It keeps well in a cool room near a window." A potted plant of *Araucaria excelsa* was obviously what we needed. In short order we had bought one, and found that when placed near our sitting room window, where the hummingbirds outside could look through and admire it, it did indeed fulfill to perfection its role as a Christmas tree. Its almost horizontal branches stood out in neat whorls of six, ideal for hanging small presents or doodads to shelter the larger presents spread at its base. It clearly needed the finishing touch of a decorative star at the top, and this was provided.

The next year our plant of *Araucaria excelsa* did its duty again — in fact even better, as it had meanwhile grown two more whorls of branches, and this time a minor stepladder was needed to place the star at its top. When the third year arrived it was clear that more drastic measures were needed, so it was taken out and planted in a carefully chosen site *outside* the window. Here for one more year it bore its star at the top, though this time a full-size stepladder was needed to put it in place. Since then, there has been no holding it back, and it has long ceased to function as a Christmas tree. In its early years, it produced two whorls of branches each year, later only one. Now it is about 60 feet tall, with 27 whorls, and the tips of the lower branches are pushing against the side of the house while its top reaches skywards another yard each year.

When we built our house, the ridge on which the *Araucaria excelsa* stands was bare of all but grass, and our view stretched 50 miles to the sea, east of the gap where the Coastal Range turns to the southeast. We could have placed our tree anywhere we wished, but with Christmas in mind we set it firmly in the ground less then 20 feet from the house. Since then we have grown trees of many sorts and sizes around the house, and in the process have totally lost our view, but have gained instead some badly needed shade and shelter. The house is now invisible amid its cloak of green, but our one-time Christmas tree still stands out like a beacon to mark where the house lies. We realize now how foolish we were not to have studied the rest of Bailey's wise words before planting the tree so close to the house. These words are, "In its native

[1] Originally appeared in *A.O.S. Bulletin,*
Vol. 51, December 1982, pages 1236-1239

wilds *var. robusta* reaches a height of over 200 ft.," which scarcely agrees with his earlier remark that it can serve as a pot plant on a table!

While our house is far distant from the Pacific Ocean, it is clear that our climate and our soil are very much to its taste, and that our tree should have been planted at least 100 feet away from the house. But it is too late to dig it up now and move it elsewhere, and vastly too expensive to move the house, so we must learn to live with it and rely on insurance to rebuild the house or pay the hospital bills if the tree ever reaches 200 feet and then collapses on top of us — or, "ye Gods and little fishes," at least pay for a fancy tombstone reading "Crushed by their own prized pot evergreen" and signed, "Bailey"!

Having now graduated from trapezes to tombstones via a dissertation on giant araucarias, it is time to bring these disparate ends together or our readers will lose interest in what it is we are trying to say! This, to put it briefly at last, is to place on record that our Christmas tree has, in the last few years, decided to become a home for two small orchid species that have taken hold from seeds that have quite clearly flown through the air with consummate ease while we were not looking, and which have taken up residence on its lower branches, but which do not seem to flourish on any of our other non-araucaria trees. These species are:

Comparettia falcata — This pretty little species, with sprays of rose-pink flowers, is quite common in many parts of Venezuela and in other countries as well, but is always a welcome visitor. In the edge of the cloud forest on the far side of the house it grows fairly happily (though not as happily as it once did) and seems to enjoy life in untidy tangles on small twigs, or when hanging precariously in mid-air, supported only by one or two roots attached to a branch of a liana. We have tried to move such plants the few yards from where they grow to the orchid section of our garden, but never with lasting success. A fair number of these comparettias have not put in an appearance on our "Christmas tree." Some are still embryonic, as befits late arrivals, but quite a few are now mature enough to have flowered *in situ* and add more yet to our supplies.

Psygmorchis glossomystax — *Psygmorchis* is a genus published in 1972 by Dodson & Dressler to cover a group of jewel-like, miniature orchids with fan-shaped sprays of equitant leaves, previously included in the genus *Oncidium,* and in our opinion *P. glossomystax* is the prettiest of the lot. Like the comparettias mentioned above, it is native to many tropical areas from Mexico to Brazil, and in Venezuela can be found not only in the Coastal Range and the Andes, but also in the "Amazonas" and "Guayana" regions of this country. Where we first came across it was near Caracas when in 1956 we were searching for a suitable site to build a house far enough from the main body of the city to ensure some peace and quiet, and high enough above the city to provide a reasonably cool climate. In these weekend wanderings we came across a small copse of *guamo* trees (*Inga* species) on which we spied a number of these tiny beauties in full bloom. It was unfenced, so we took the liberty of removing a few plants to grow in Caracas. Not unnaturally, perhaps, they objected to the move and did not survive long. On our next visit to the copse it had been fenced all around so we got no more specimens, and soon after forgot all about these orchids in the complications of house building.

Many years later, however, when well settled in our new home, we saw more of these treasures growing happily in a mango tree not far outside our fence. Once more we took a few plants, but again with the same negative result, even when transferred on the twigs on which they were growing. The construction of an illegal shack by the mango, and a small bush fire on this spot, then put an end to all the remaining plants, at which point we lost all hope of seeing any more. But very recently, to our great delight, among the *Comparettia* plants that have taken root on our "Christmas tree," there has appeared a single tiny plant of this much-coveted species. Where the seed has come from we have no idea, but whatever its source it is greatly welcome.

We are now interested to know why, having

Psygmorchis glossomystax (Reichb. f.) Dodson & Dressler in Phytologia 24:289, 1972. — B.D.E.

Comparettia falcata

Psygmorchis glossomystax on Araucaria excelsa

hopped across our house, these two species have chosen to make their home on our "foreign" Christmas tree and not on the many other, equally accessible trees native to this country that now decorate the one-time barren spaces of our garden. It is noticeable that the bark of our tree bears a lot of white lichen, which is an excellent sign that our air is uncontaminated (trees in the semi-smog of Caracas being free of lichen), and this may have something to do with it, although these orchids have not yet appeared on our other trees with an equal load of lichen. But whatever the answer may be, we are grateful indeed to find ourselves giving a natural home to them after failing so often to provide an unnatural home that they would accept among our captive species elsewhere in the garden.

Unfortunately, while our "Christmas tree" seems good for a long, long life, we cannot be sure of an equally long life for its precious *Psygmorchis* burden. In her book, *Miniature Orchids,* Rebecca Tyson Northen says that *Psygmorchis glossomystax* "may have a short life span, especially in cultivation," and, while our baby is definitely not being "cultivated," it has decided to start life on one of the small, closely-spaced branchlets that develop on the main branches of our Christmas tree, and these branchlets, as opposed to the branches themselves, die off with fair frequency, to be replaced with fresh, green ones with no orchids on board. The comparettias can survive fairly easily, as there are now so many of them they can be expected to produce more children faster than branchlets fall off; but at the moment, with only a single plant of *P. glossomystax* at bat, it will be a struggle for survival between seed production on the one hand versus branchlet-fall on the other.

There is, however, one feature of *Psygmorchis glossomystax* that encourages us to some degree of optimism for its future, and this is the rapidity with which this species seems to develop from seed to maturity and then to seed again. Many of the plants we have collected in the past have been found as fully mature "singles," with no apparent connection with others, which we take to be an indication that its slowness in rhizome production is more than offset by its speed in maturing to seed-bearing adulthood. In this, it is possible that its known tendency to autogamous self-fertilization (as noted by van der Pijl and Dodson in their book, *Orchid Flowers: Their Pollination and Evolution*) plays a part, the plants having no need to await a visit from an insect before getting down to the business of reproduction. But whatever the answer may be, we wish our baby a long and very happy life and "Many Happy Returns," if not in its present form then at least in the form of future progeny.

Aa, Aha, Aha ha — and What Next?[1]

HUMBOLDT, Bonpland & Kunth's 1815 genus of *Altensteinia,* and Reichenbach's genera of *Myrosmodes* and *Aa* of 1854, have been the cause of much confusion in the past, producing headaches quite out of proportion to the generally very small size of the orchids concerned, with species being switched from one genus to the other and back with alarming frequency. Taking into account only the three Venezuelan species involved, we find *Altensteinia cochleare, A. leucantha, A. nubigena, A. palacea,* and *A. rhynchocarpa; Myrosmodes cochleare* and *M. nubigenum;* and *Aa brevis, Aa hartwegii, Aa leucantha, Aa maderoi, Aa nigrescens, Aa paludosa, Aa rostrada,* and *Aa rhynchocarpa,* all listed in one place or another.

In an article published in *The Orchid Review* for August 1970, I ventured the remark that the genus *Aa* had failed to "take hold" and that the species that were once allocated to this genus were back to being altensteinias. This is now not fully correct as in the *Orchids of Venezuela Field Guide* of 1979 Garay has maintained at least one aa, namely *Aa hartwegii.* This species, whose portrait is shown here, is a rather rare terrestrial species native to the high Andes of Venezuela, where it grows near the extreme limit of plant life at around 13,000 ft. (4,000 m) altitude. Horticulturally it is insignificant, but in common with some 10 sibling species of the Andean regions of Ecuador and Colombia it does have the distinction of being a member of the truly unique genus of *Aa.*

Various reasons have been put forward to explain why the famous orchid taxonomist H. G. Reichenbach invented and published this very odd name of *Aa* in 1854, but the one that appeals to me most is that he did it to ensure that a Reichenbach genus would for all eternity stand at the head of any alphabetical list of genera — not only of orchids or even of plants, but of anything that was living, had lived, or some day might live on the face of this globe or outside it. Which is quite an achievement to attain by the mere publication of a two-lettered name for a taxonomic group!

It is rumored that Reichenbach was by way of being a cantankerous character, often at loggerheads with other taxonomists, and if this is true one can visualize him saying, as he signed his name to *Aa,* "That will fix those !!!'s!" But whatever its true origin, I feel that *Aa* does provide a break with the humdrum — a break that is to be welcomed provided it is not overdone. Actually, according to information that has recently come to my attention (see note at end of this article), the possibility of overdoing a good thing does seem to loom more closely than I could ever have imagined a few months ago.

Taxonomy, described in my dictionary as "The science of classification of animals and plants according to their natural relationships," is often considered by those not close to the world of taxonomy as one of the driest and least humorous of disciplines — and most decidedly without any humor at all if an orchid name produced by a taxonomist should conflict with a well-known name previously used by the orchid's owner.

But it has long been evident, even if seldom publicized, that at least some taxonomists do possess a rather whimsical, or even at times somewhat pornographic, sense of humor when it comes to inventing and publishing names for their newly-devised taxa. After all, the word *orchid* itself, which goes back to the first-century A.D. herbalist Dioscorides, refers to the testicle-like tumeroids at the base of the stem of some terrestrial species. Similarly, in the days when taxonomy was just becoming a science, the first binomial (genus-*cum*-species) name ever to be used for a fossil dinosaur was *Scrotum humanum,* produced as far back as 1763 by Brookes.

[1] Originally appeared in *A.O.S. Bulletin,* Vol. 52, January 1983, pages 53-55

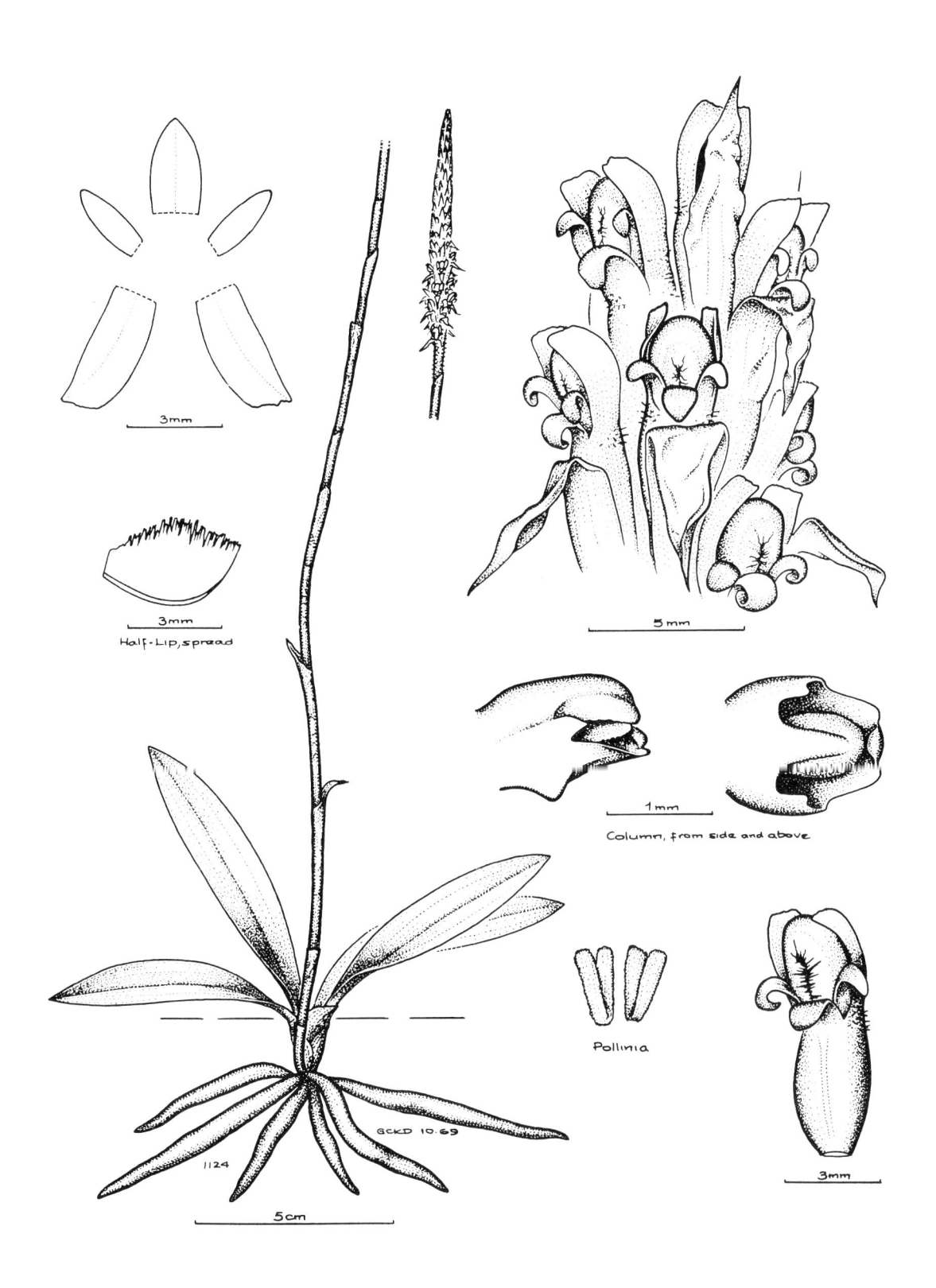

Aa hartwegii Garay in Fl. Ecuador, Orch. 9: 161, 1979. — A

On equally "porno" lines there are quite a number of examples (fortunately, for the morals of the very young, clothed in Latin or Greek) such as the indecently exposed fungus, *Phallus impudicus,* or the doggy fungus, *Mutinus caninus,* names which your editor may, or may not, decide to translate into English. [We dare not! — *Editor*] Certainly in Victorian days it must have taken courage to publish such names which, even in Latin, were presumably spoken only in whispers.

Leaving porno on one side, and moving to less blush-making names, there is the example of the taxonomist (for whom I have neither name nor date) who was obviously inspired by the example of Reichenbach and came up with the name of *Zyzzyx* for a genus of wasps, to ensure that his genus would always be *last* on any list; a rather vulnerable position as he might yet be displaced if another author comes up with *Zzyx* for (who knows?) another genus of wasps. Which is not so unlikely as one might think when bearing in mind that there seems to be something about wasps that brings out the best (or worst) instincts in taxonomical whimsyists. Like, for instance, a certain Dybowski who in 1926, with obviously clairvoyant talents, produced a name for a genus of wasps that was surely designed as a candidate for the "longest name" category in the yet-to-be-thought-of *Guinness Book of Records*; and it is not unlikely that by now the *G.B.R.* has taken note of it and has already set it up for their 1983 edition. In full it reads (in capital letters to make it more imposing yet):

CANCELLOIDOKYTODERMOGAMMARUS
(LOVENINUSKYTODERMAGAMMARUS)
LOVENI

Practice saying this a time or two in secrecy and at your next dinner party you will be able to surprise your guests with your erudition, just as when, at age six, I was taught to astound my father's visitors by rattling off long botanical names like *Lonicera quinquelocularis.* Had papa waited a while, he might have been able to train me on such orchid items as *Warczewiczella flabelliformis* which would one day be part of my daily diet.

Wasps, as mentioned above, seem to dominate this world of taxonomic whimsy as there is a genus of wasps named *Lala,* which obviously leads to a species called *Lala palusa.* And yet again, there is another genus of wasps with the name of *Aha,* with its equally inevitable species *Aha ha* (and one can be quite sure that if the rules of nomenclature would allow it, it would have been written "*Aha ha!*").

But all is not wasp in the world of whimsy. There is a clam genus with the name of *Abra,* with a species — you guessed it — called *Abra cadabara.* Even snails, not to be outdone, have given birth, as it were, to *Trivia* and *Anticlimax,* while sea urchins have produced *Disaster.* And every Tom, Dick, and Harry will be delighted to see himself enshrined taxonomically among the oysters with the names of *Ptomaspis, Dikenaspis,* and *Ariaspis.*

A final word of reassurance is perhaps needed. Readers may be inclined to think I have dreamed up all this just for the fun of it, but I can assure them I have proof of it all in print. *Aa* is to be found in any full list of orchid genera, and as for *Aha, Aha ha, Lala palusa,* and all the rest, these are to be found in the columns of *New Scientist* (UK), where they are quoted by Milton Love in the issue for May 13, 1982, and by Patrick McClellan in the issue for July 15. My thanks to all of these for the information on which this note is based, and I hope some day to hear of more cases of whimsy in botanical nomenclature from the past. It would spoil things, however, if the idea should now lead to too much whimsy for the sake of whimsy in taxonomic nomenclature in the future!

Kefersteinia Species in Venezuela[1]

WE ARE OF A GENERATION far too antique to wax enthusiastic about computers. In our very young days we suffered the agony of classes in mental arithmetic where the teacher would say "Joe — add four and eight and fifteen, take away three, double, add twelve, divide by four — what's the answer? Nowadays, one is expected to do these calculations on tiny pocket machines capable also of such domestically useless tasks as producing square roots, and with keys so minute that one makes mistake after mistake by pressing two keys simultaneously with a single finger, or so sensitive that at the lightest touch they add another million to the total. So, in due course, one ends up by adding everything up in one's head or on a piece of paper anyway!

Which is not to deny that computers have their uses, even for humble folk with no space-travel ambitions. It is, for instance, a decided advantage at the local bank to be able to get an immediate answer as to how much money there is in one's account. Computers cannot lie, and if the answer comes up negative when one is sure that it should be positive, then that is just too bad. But otherwise, the savings in time at the bank is greatly appreciated, and there are even times when we hope to see yet more computers come into use, provided they are limited to doing things useful for us and to heck with the moon or outer space.

These computeristic thoughts have been inspired by the sight of one of our *Kefersteinia* plants bursting with flowers, which in its turn has inspired us to produce this short note on Venezuelan kefersteinias for the *A.O.S. Bulletin*.

We have long cherished our plants of the three species known in Venezuela — *Kefersteinia graminea, K. sanguinolenta*, and *K. tolimensis* — for their general attractiveness as miniature but by no means invisible orchids, their convenient size, their ease of cultivation (at least in our locality),

Kefersteinia tolimensis

and their at times most rewarding floriferousness. But before putting typewriter to paper it is clearly necessary to find out what has already been written about these plants, or better still about the whole *Kefersteinia* genus. This has not been an easy task. How wonderful it would be if, by merely punching a button, all the articles ever written about these orchids could be regurgitated from the miniscule memory of a central computer and passed by satellite radio to the display screen of our (presently non-existent) home computer to be studied at our leisure. Or better still (?), now that computers that can think like humans are understood to be just a short jump away, and could have word processors to help them, we need perhaps do no more than suggest a subject to the *A.O.S. Bulletin* Editor and his computer will do the rest without any live authors being needed at all, thus putting G.C.D. & E.D. permanently out of business! This rather alarming idea, however, must surely be at least a couple of years off in the future, so that we can, in

[1] Originally appeared in *A.O.S. Bulletin*, Vol. 52, June 1983, pages 583-589

the meantime, cheer the Editor with an article for which we have undertaken our own tedious searching through our very moderate orchid library.

This library consists of the *A.O.S. Bulletin* since 1952, the *Orchid Review* since 1956, *Orquideología* since 1969, and the *Orchid Digest* since 1966 — plus a few old standard reference books such as Veitch's *Manual of Orchidaceous Plants* of 1887-1893, Schlechter's *Die Orchideen* of 1927, and Hawkes' *Encyclopaedia of Cultivated Orchids* of 1965.

In doing this searching we may well have missed something important due to synonymy, the genus *Kefersteinia* having had a very mixed history with many name changes; but the total bag remains definitely skimpy. In effect it boils down to a very useful article by Leslie A. Garay in *Orquideología* for November 1969, in which he gives a critical analysis of the *Chondrorhyncha* alliance (including the genus *Kefersteinia*), the *Orchid Digest* for May 1970 which gives fine individual portraits of the flowers of six *Kefersteinia* species, and a short article on *Kefersteinia sanguinolenta* by Henry Teuscher in the *A.O.S. Bulletin* for January 1974. Rebecca Northen's *Miniature Orchids* also has a short but useful note on *Kefersteinia* which covers the three Venezuelan species and *Kefersteinia lojae* from Peru.

For our own part, we can refer to a short note on *Kefersteinia graminea* (with color photo) in our "Introduction to the World of Orchids" of 1962, and a note on our three *Kefersteinia* species in the *A.O.S. Bulletin* for December 1976 (see Chapter 20). This latter gives a color shot of *K. graminea* but is otherwise mainly an extract from Garay's article in *Orquideología*. For a genus of such promise, this is not a very rich reward.

By now, the Editor must be wondering if we are ever going to write anything useful about our *Kefersteinia* species, so we must get to work. Starting with the genus as a whole, the first question to be answered is just what is a kefersteinia? This question has been fully dealt with in Garay's key to the *Chondrorhyncha* alliance already referred to, but, as it is 100 to one against any reader being able to remember offhand just what this key says, and most will be reluctant to hunt up the reference unless it is very easily accessible to them, it will be simpler for everyone if we repeat the essence of it here. Condensed to a bare minimum, this alliance is a group of closely related, pseudobulb-less plants growing in clumps, and includes the well-known but seldom seen genera of *Bollea, Chaubardia, Chaubardiella, Cochleanthes, Huntleya, Kefersteinia, Pescatorea, Stenia*, and, of course, *Chondrorhyncha*. In Venezuela this genus is usually pronounced with the Ch as in cheese, but correctly, as given in the A.O.S. *Orchidist's Glossary,* it should be pronounced as a K, being derived from the Greek. (So why should one not pronounce *Chaubardia* also with a K? Because M. Chaubard, after whom the genus was named, was not a Greek!)

Out of this group of genera, *Kefersteinia* species can be distinguished by the following characters: The flowers are borne singly on the peduncle and are ringent or gaping, i.e. neither with flatly spread elements nor, by contrast, arranged into a close tubular form. The lip is hinged to the foot of the column, has no distinct divisions, is strongly folded down-and-back in its outer half, and its base bears a conspicuous bidentate callus (never a continuous, horseshoe-shaped one); the column is semiterete, with a foot developed into a conspicuous chin, and has a keel running down its face from below the stigma — a keel that is probably the most critical feature of the genus. The callus on the lip is difficult to describe but its form is generally a clue for separating one species from another.

In Venezuela, our three species are epiphytic inhabitants of the cloud forests (or montane forests) of the Coastal Range and the Andes. There is a tendency to refer to any and all tropical forests as "rain forest," and, to be true, it would be difficult to find a really satisfactory definition of these two types of forest however clear the distinction might be, in most cases, for those who have experience of them. Ten experts would almost certainly come up with at least five different definitions, but for us the main difference is that rain forest is a lowland, hot-country phenomenon distinguished by many tall trees, limited undergrowth, and very heavy rainfall; whereas cloud forest, as its name implies, is a zone of less total rainfall but much more constant humidity in the form of light rains, fogs, or mists, and is usually found below an altitude of some 500 m (much higher up it may grade into dwarf or mossy forest).

One would expect our Venezuelan, cloud-forest, *Kefersteinia* species to be easy to find as their habitats are seldom far from civilization and often close to one of the many good roads to be found in the northern half of the country. Yet they have scanty notice in the official *Flora of Venezuela.*

Kefersteinia tolimensis is probably the least known of the three Venezuelan species as it seems to be absent from the Coastal Range, limiting itself to the western Andes at altitudes of 1,800 to 2,000 m. It also appears in the Perijá Range near the Colombian border at around 1,400 m. Our plant of this species has leaves to about 25 × 3 cm, characterized by sharply carinate midnerves that end in fine, fairly long mucros. It is the least floriferous of our three species, at times producing no more than two slender, suberect or subpendent, eight-cm-long peduncles bearing single flowers. The flowers themselves are relatively large, being about four cm wide, but too dark to be very eye-catching. The cream-colored sepals and petals are marked with red-brown spotting and the lip with dense spotting all over except near the margin, which is finely lacerate-dentate. The callus is also spotted with red-brown marks.

Kefersteinia sanguinolenta is recorded in the *Flora of Venezuela* as occurring in the Coastal Range at altitudes up to 2,100 m (which sounds exceptionally high) but is also recorded from much lower just north of Caracas, and we have found it ourselves in the small patch of cloud forest adjoining our home above Caracas at about 1,400 m. Farther afield, friends have found plants at about 1,500 m near La Florida in Táchira State in the western Andes, and (as with *K. tolimensis*) plants also occur in the Perijá Range adjoining Colombia at about 1,600 m.

As compared to our other species, *Kefersteinia sanguinolenta* tends to have narrower leaves, generally to about 20 × 1.5 cm, and in fact is much more grass-like in appearance than the "grassy-named" *K. graminea*. If it were not for the fact that *K. sanguinolenta* was named some eight years after *K. graminea* received its baptism, one might be tempted to believe that Reichenbach had got his names mixed!

The peduncles of this species are relatively short (three cm) and of variable attitude, and the flowers are markedly smaller than those of our other two species, with a width of little more than two cm. They make up for this, however, with much lighter and more eye-catching colors, the sepals and petals being very pale greenish cream (almost white) with fairly fine purple spotting at the base. The white lip bears irregular, dark red spots over most of its exposed face which also bears some fine, short hairs that give it a velvety appearance. Like *K. tolimensis*, the margin of the lip of *Kefersteinia sanguinolenta* is finely lacerate-dentate, and the callus is a rather narrow, square-edged process that is bifurcate only at its extreme apex. When in full bloom, with some 20 flowers open around the base of the plant, this species makes a very impressive miniature.

Kefersteinia graminea is known also from Colombia and Peru, but, if one disregards an old and rather dubious record by Moritz quoting a specimen from near Mérida in the western Andes, it seems to be limited in Venezuela to a very restricted area around Caracas. Our own findings have certainly been exclusively from close to Caracas and began in January 1958 with a plant from the small, remnant forest that still exists at around 1,400 m above the village of Tiara, less than 50 km by direct pigeon flight southwest of the heart of Caracas. Later, in 1970, we found a specimen on the slopes above Caracas at about 1,800 m, and another plant came from the now well-known village of Colonia Tovar, the home of *Masdevallia tovarensis*. Colonia Tovar is also no more than 50 km to the west of Caracas and is close to the coast. As its name implies, it was founded many years ago by a colony of Black Forest peasants from Germany who settled in what was then an extremely isolated locality at about 1,800 m altitude, in the hopes of being able to make a living with horticulture on the unforested, south-facing slopes. It is no longer the Germanic village that we first knew about 30 years ago, but is now accessible by paved road from Caracas, and, as a result, has become a popular weekend "breathing space" for the overcrowded city, a tourist trap filled with fake souvenirs made in Peru or Taiwan. *Sic transit gloria*?

The forested slopes between the village and the sea to the north, however, though by now well worked-over for orchids, still retain their cloud-forest character, and, in May 1961, provided us with the material for our very first article for the *A.O.S. Bulletin*, describing how a single fallen tree near the Colonia had proven to be the home of almost 50 species of orchids. Yet despite this super-abundance it did not hold a single plant of *Kefersteinia*, and it was not until some 10 years later that we found our first Tovar plant of *Kefersteinia graminea* in the forest, at nearly 2,000 m, part way between the Colonia and another small village known as Junquito.

Our plants of this species have leaves with sharply carinate midnerves, to around 25 × 3 cm, but are on record as reaching as long as 36 cm. The flowers are borne on slender peduncles that vary from erect to subpendent, with flowers about 4.0 cm in width. The sepals and petals are pale green with maroon spots marking the nerve lines, the spots being heaviest along the axis and near the base. The lip when spread is some 24 mm long and 20 mm wide, pale green like the petals and with red-maroon marks mainly concentrated on the axis and near the base.

In full flower, *Kefersteinia graminea* is a quite impressive species. Our very best plant, now some 10 years old, last year developed some 50 flowers and buds, but unfortunately the peduncles were rather short and semipendent so that while it was very impressive to a moving eye, the overhanging leaves tended to hide its full glory from the eye of a static camera. Our plant also had the distressing habit of failing to flower at show time, or we could have hoped for a nice blue ribbon to place at its base. Perhaps next year we will be luckier and will then be able to exhibit it on a small pedestal where the flowers and the ribbon will show up nicely!

As for the cultivation of our three *Kefersteinia* species, this has proved to be a fairly simple and satisfactory process — a pleasant contrast to some

Kefersteinia graminea

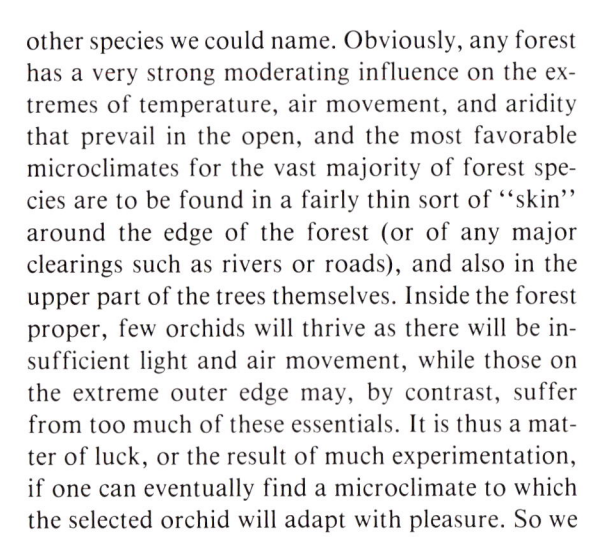

Kefersteinia sanguinolenta

other species we could name. Obviously, any forest has a very strong moderating influence on the extremes of temperature, air movement, and aridity that prevail in the open, and the most favorable microclimates for the vast majority of forest species are to be found in a fairly thin sort of "skin" around the edge of the forest (or of any major clearings such as rivers or roads), and also in the upper part of the trees themselves. Inside the forest proper, few orchids will thrive as there will be insufficient light and air movement, while those on the extreme outer edge may, by contrast, suffer from too much of these essentials. It is thus a matter of luck, or the result of much experimentation, if one can eventually find a microclimate to which the selected orchid will adapt with pleasure. So we must confess that it is mainly by accident (or can we claim some intelligent inspiration?) that at a very early date we found that our kefersteinias do very nicely in small pots or on tree-fern slabs, hung some five feet above the sloping forest floor and 15 feet or so inside the edge of our own little piece of cloud forest where, bless them, they flourish with little attention, or even for long periods with no attention at all. They get minimal direct insolation, an adequacy of gentle air movement, and whatever nature gives them in the way of the frequent night and early morning mists that cover us for most of the year, interspersed with occasional short, but sometimes quite heavy, wet-season rainstorms that serve to maintain the health and humidity of the forest as a whole.

Solenidium racemosum — The Return of a Prodigal Son[1]

SOME EPIPHYTIC ORCHIDS can be found growing very happily in odd places such as on tiny shrubs, small leaves, or cacti, but most of them, as we all know, prefer to grow in trees — trees of all sizes and shapes, and in all types of "communities" from single trees to small copses or light woods, or finally to the massed agglomerations that we call forests. It is in the forests of the tropics that we find most of our rare, epiphytic orchid species, and it is depressing and alarming to read in so many serious publications that (thanks? to the hand of man) the virgin tropical forest is a dying phenomenon.

Jokes at funerals, even those of forests, are in very bad taste, but perhaps some exemption from this may be claimed for jokes that pop up like unexpected jack-in-the-boxes in otherwise very serious and useful but generally very dry places such as the definition in our *Chamber's Dictionary* of éclair as "A cake, long in shape but short in duration," or the schoolboy howler, "The epistles were the wives of the apostles," which popped out at us from R. W. Brown's most serious and useful work of 1954, *The Composition of Scientific Words* — jokes that by themselves may not be particularly remarkable but which become so when set amid entries such as "*Keleusma,* -tos, n: *Keleusmos,* m. order, command, call; *Keleustes,* m. signaller," and so on. It thus gave us exceptional joy when, again in Brown's book, we found virgin forests defined as "Forests in which the hand of man has not yet set foot."

But to get back to our muttons, the type specimen of *Solenidium racemosum,* according to the records, was found in 1842 by Lindley in forests near Pamplona in Colombia, at about 8,500 feet altitude, and was published as a species (and simultaneously as the type for the new genus of *Solenidium*) in 1846. Shortly thereafter, in 1847, Lindley's plant collectors, Funck & Schlim, found more plants in the same locality, after which it escaped collection for over 100 years before, in 1973, it was found again, this time in Venezuela. We cannot claim to have been present in Pamplona when it was first discovered there, nor do we have any specific information as to the type of forest where it was growing, but the betting is heavy that as far back as that it was montane cloud forest and typically "virgin." Which makes it all the more extraordinary that its rediscovery near San Cristóbal in Táchira State, not far from the border with Colombia, should have been not only in non-virgin forest but not even in a forest at all.

After such a long absence from the orchid world, it is not surprising that the return of this prodigal should have been the occasion for great rejoicing. Though we were very closely associated as midwives with this rebirth, it is not a discovery for which we can claim any credit. This credit goes entirely to Sr. Roberto Mejía of San Cristóbal and to his *campesino* assistant known to us as "Ojo del Aguila" for his eagle-eyed ability to spot orchids. Together with El Ojo, Roberto, a very keen orchid enthusiast, had already made many exciting discoveries in Táchira and we had helped in getting some of these identified through the kindness of Dr. Leslie Garay at the Orchid Herbarium of Oakes Ames, Harvard University. So it was natural that we should suggest to Roberto that he should send a specimen to Harvard, though at that time we had no expectation that it would turn out to be anything wildly exciting.

But this casual attitude changed dramatically when we got a letter from Garay in April 1973, saying "A very interesting orchid, *Solenidium racemosum,* because in the herbaria of the whole world I have seen but two collections, the 'type' and one of Schlim, both collections over 100 years old. By all means get a whole plant and prepare a drawing. This is indeed an exciting find."

---

[1] Originally appeared in *A.O.S. Bulletin,* Vol. 52, November 1983, pages 1157-1160

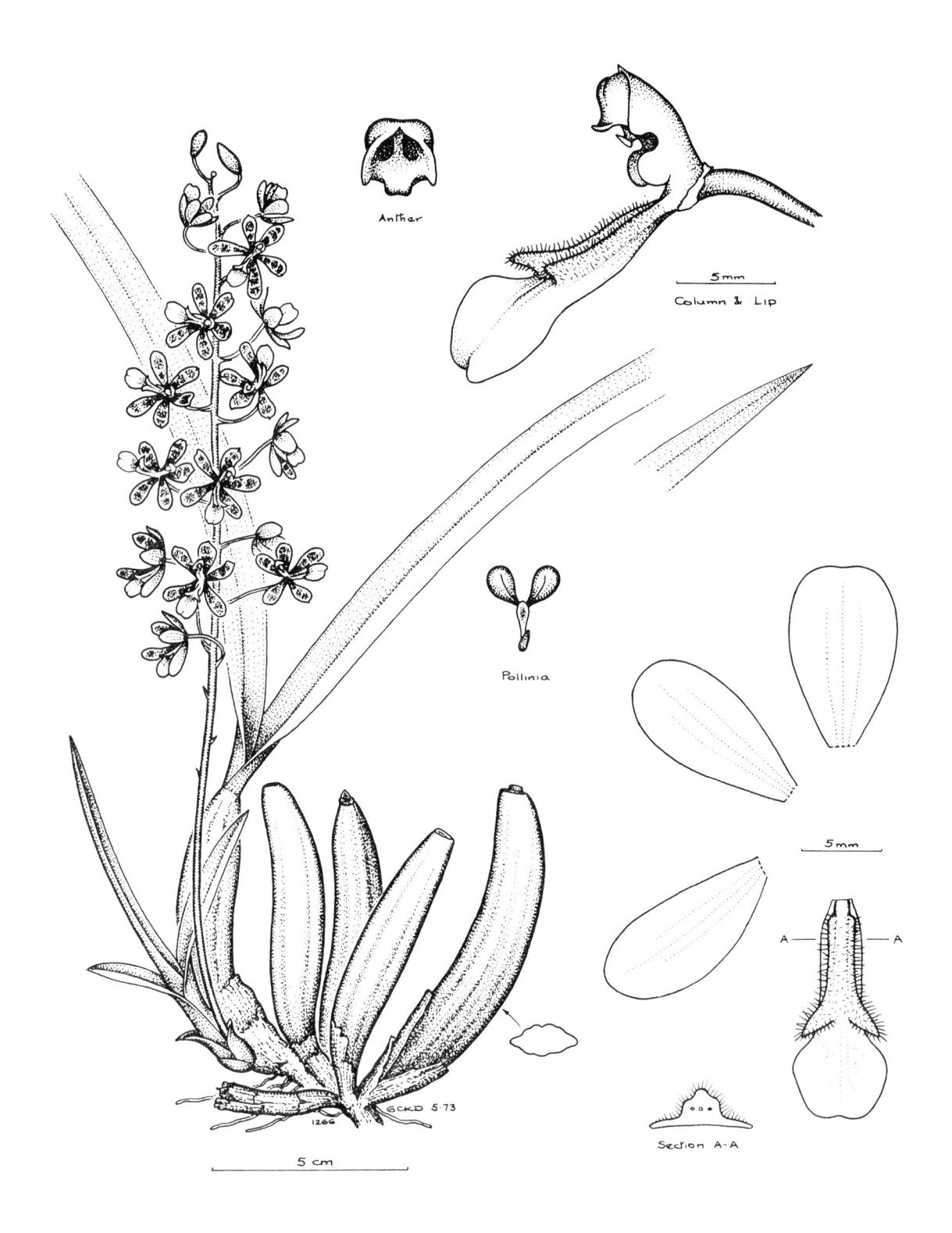

Solenidium racemosum Lindl., Orch. Linden. 15, 1846. — A.

So back we went to Roberto to ask him to show us where we could get more material for Garay (and to beg a piece for Kew to grow in London), and to see at first hand just how and where the plants were growing. These tasks proved easy to carry out. We returned to Caracas with the required plants, still in flower, made the necessary drawing (which went later into our Volume 6 of *Venezuelan Orchids Illustrated*), and had been able to appreciate the decidedly non-virgin character of the habitat (at about 1,600 feet altitude) in which this species was growing. A country lane at this spot runs close to a small stream by no means far from "civilization," but which, in the interests of conservation, will remain nameless even if, by now, it must surely be known to many. Quite small, non-foresty trees lined the high bank of the stream, and on two of these several plants of the solenidium were growing, low enough that El Ojo had little trouble in picking off two adequate samples, and with these we headed for home.

News of such orchid finds gets around fairly fast, and it was not long before another active orchid enthusiast, Carlos García of Caracas (whose name is already on the orchid map as the finder of the excellent species *Epidendrum garcianum*) came up with a superlatively fine plant with hundreds of flowers on a dozen or more erect racemes, which he loaned to us to be photographed; this is the plant illustrated here.

This rediscovered species was the subject of a detailed article by Dr. Herman Sweet in the Colombian magazine *Orquideología* for September 1973, and of another very useful article by Dr. Phillip Cribb of Kew in *Curtis's Botanical Magazine* in 1976, the latter accompanied by a fine colored plate by Margaret Stone, made direct from the plant we had sent to Kew. In his note, Cribb mentions that the forests of Pamplona are only 40 miles from San Cristóbal, or say 50 miles from where the plants have been found. In view of the considerable climatic difference between the Pamplona forests at 8,500 feet and the 1,600-foot altitude of the Venezuelan site, it is unlikely that this could have been made in a single jump in nature, and it is highly probable that many intervening plants exist — and indeed at least one such plant was later found at about 3,000 feet altitude by Roberto.

This species was at one time considered by Reichenbach to belong to the genus *Oncidium* but, as Cribb mentions in his article, Lindley noted that it differed from *Oncidium* in a number of minute but important floral features. For those without microscopes, the relatively visible features are the "earless" column, and more particularly the base of the lip which is in the form of a long, narrow "claw" adorned with what Lindley calls "long feathery plates which stand up considerably above the lip itself, and being free at the end look like a pair of shaggy ears." This can be seen in the drawing accompanying this article, though we would prefer to call the ears "hairy" rather than feathery. The drawing also shows the typical growth habit of the plant, with narrow pseudobulbs growing in "approximate" form from the rhizome and looking rather like a collection of small bananas. The pseudobulbs are bifoliate and the leaves narrow, somewhat keeled dorsally and with a long, tapering apex.

Lindley's "long feathery plates" (or keels) form a sort of channel and give the genus its name. To quote R. W. Brown again, but this time in a serious mood, *solen* is a Greek word meaning "pipe or channel," and in Schultes's *Generic Names of Orchids* is stated to refer to the long, canaliculate claw of the lip — which is indeed a clear and distinctive feature. Sweet, in his *Orquideología* article, takes into account additional differences beyond those noted by Lindley, and concludes that only *Solenidium racemosum* completely fills the bill, and that the other species should be excluded, thus leaving it as a monotypic genus. But it was later felt that it would be simpler to apply less strict criteria and the genus *Solenidium* is now generally accepted as covering *S. racemosum, S. lunatum, S. endresii,* and *S. peruvianum,* the first pair having their home in Venezuela and figuring in the *Orchids of Venezuela: An Illustrated Field Guide.*

As for cultural notes, we cannot improve on those given by Cribb in his article, where he says that the plant in Kew is "grown on a suspended bark-block, the minimum night temperature 13-15°C, and during the day reaching 24°C. Moderately moist conditions are maintained for most of the year but in winter atmospheric and root moisture are somewhat reduced. Shade and ventilation are provided in summer."

Kew's horticultural skills are obviously much superior to ours as our one-and-only plant has not survived the intervening years and we do not plan to look for a replacement.

One final remark to this article may be necessary, just in case (as with our article "Aa, Aha, Aha ha — And What Next?" in the January 1983 *A.O.S. Bulletin*, Chapter 61) some readers may think that the quoted "jokes" were all invented by us. May we reassure readers that none of these are home-grown, and in support of this we will end with the "hand-on-the-bible," whole truth oath as adapted by R. W. Brown for use by dentists: "We promise to pull the tooth, the whole tooth, and nothing but the tooth."

Afterword

Conservation in an Overpopulated World[1]

I HAVE BEEN ASKED to write a few notes on "generalities about conservation — the species that are in danger of extinction in Venezuela, recommendations for collection of species, and a code of ethics for collectors." These are all subject — or parts of a single subject — that I have written about several times in the past, and this time I did not expect to find myself losing much time over a repeat.

Lexicographers have little trouble in agreeing on the meaning of "conservation" as it pertains to fauna and flora. They use such phrases as "the act of keeping free from depletion," "wise management of natural resources," "official supervision of rivers and forests," "the act of conserving flora and fauna," "preserving, guarding, or protecting a river, forest, or natural resource," and so on.

It seems unlikely that many people would disagree with these generalized definitions of this important word "conservation." But when it comes to individual orchid species and individual orchid enthusiasts, like myself or you or our friends, we frequently have our own favorite species that we would like to see given special protection against depredations by others. However, at the same time, we tend to turn a blind eye when it comes to tolerating "mild attacks" on these species by ourselves — occasions when we tell ourselves that it surely cannot do much harm if we remove just one small piece of a plant.

Many small leaks, however, can end up emptying a bucket. And who can tell at what point the leaks become irreparable? As the Scots say, "Many a mickle makes a muckle," and many hands each picking a few plants can — and often do — "pick a muckle." This is well exemplified by the so-called "orchid safaris," when each person collects only one or two plants. But when the safari has passed on, the area where it has been is left stripped of all desirable — and many only half-desirable — species.

It is now so long since I have been in close contact with the places where we once found many interesting species that I no longer am able to give any reliable estimate of which Venezuelan species are now endangered by such overcollecting. In any case, I think it might very well be difficult to get an unbiased, unanimous verdict from any large group of orchid-minded individuals as to which species they consider truly endangered and what measures they think should — or *could* — be enforced to protect them.

But here is one highly important general objective upon which all of us surely must agree as basic, and this is the need to conserve *complete habitats*, and in particular our tropical forests.

For many years, ecologists and conservationists have been loud in their warnings that these forests are of supreme importance to the whole world and not solely to the nations that own them. Unfortunately, while individuals are turning an occasional blind eye to the collection of a rare species, whole governments and governmental entities, which certainly cannot plead ignorance, are turning a deaf ear to these warnings.

The Amazon Basin, we are told, comprises one-fifth of the land area of this planet and contains one-fifth of its fresh water and one-fifth of its forests. How severely these forests are threatened can be seen from information published by World Wildlife International:

> In 1984, tropical forests throughout the world were destroyed equivalent to three times the size of Switzerland (i.e., nearly 50,000 square miles or 130,000 square kilometers). Already half the forests have gone, the speed of destruction is accelerating, and we will have lost forever the Earth's greatest storehouse of plants and animals, perhaps our most valuable natural resource for the future.
>
> Growing on extremely poor soil, the forests replenish themselves in a perpetual cycle between plants and ani-

[1] Originally appeared in *A.O.S. Bulletin*, Vol. 54, October 1985, pages 1189-1193

mals, each living off and fertilizing the other. Remove the trees, and the nutrients are rapidly lost. With the forests go the plants and animals. After that, erosion begins, and the whole area becomes a wasteland.

The real cause is a combination of ignorance, shortsightedness, and increasing consumer demand — ignorance on the part of those who believe that tropical forests can be replaced by agriculture, the shortsightedness of those who are prepared to surrender their heritage, and the consumer demand for timber on the part of the developed world.

As long as we remain blind to this rate of destruction, shrug our shoulders, and do nothing, there is no hope. And as long as governments consent to the headlong exploitation of natural resources, there is no hope.

In the face of these last few words, what is one to think of a note that has just appeared in the *New Scientist* for February 1985 that tells us that Brazil is contemplating destroying with herbicides *more than 2,000 square kilometers* of rain forest for a new hydroelectric dam near Manaus? That is almost 10 times the area of forest already destroyed, amid much criticism, for the Brazilian Tucuri Dam on the Tocantins River.

We now see, from a Reuter's News Service report (*Daily Journal,* March 21, 1985) on an International Conference on Climatic, Biotic, and Human Interactions in the Amazon, held in São Paulo, that 5-10% (i.e., about *100,000-200,000 square miles*) of Amazon forest have been eliminated in the past 20 years — a rate that is accelerating — and that "Much research is urgently needed into the long-term consequences." Coming on top of the figure for the new Manaus dam quoted above, we may be permitted to ask how much more forest will have disappeared from fire, ax, and bulldozer before this research is finished?

But whatever the answer is, it is surely clear that mankind is just not fit to "manage and conserve" the vital resources that Nature has unwisely placed in its care. Faced with the general attitude on the part of the "owners" of these forests that they are responsible to no one for what they do to them, it is obvious that the future is dim and that our heirs will be left to face the consequences.

In the meantime, it may seem ridiculous to bother ourselves over the loss of a few orchid species. But bother ourselves we must if there is to be any chance of achieving some constructive and halfway permanent good. Every new national park created in any country is at least slowing down this process of destruction and, thus, increasing the chances that somehow something really effective will be achieved before it is altogether too late. This brings us on to the question of Venezuela's record in protecting its fields and forests by means of such national parks.

The answer to this is that the Venezuelan record is good, at least insofar as the *creation* of such parks is concerned. National parks and national monuments (small areas of specialized interest) comprise 8% of Venezuelan territory.

But a good record for the *creation* of national parks does no more than express the legislators' good will, and, as with many other projects, this must be followed by *maintenance* if the original investment is not to be wasted. In the case of the national parks, this maintenance is expressed largely in the form of *policing*.

There is little doubt that some unauthorized removal of individual plants goes on within national park boundaries, and it is difficult to see how this can be suppressed completely unless by an extremely costly increase in the number of "police" allocated to the job. And where the park not only covers remote areas, such as parts of the Canaima National Park that reaches to the Brazilian border, but is also the legitimate home of indigenous Indians, there is no doubt that some collecting goes on for roadside sale to passing tourists. Thus, if one had reliable data (which one does not), certain species might be found really to be in danger.

However, regrettable as such piecemeal activities may be in revealing a gap in the defenses of any national park, there is no doubt that the existence of such parks — and their policing by land and, at times, by helicopter — has put an end to the former commercial destruction of their forests for lumbering and urbanization. Guatopo National Park is a fine example of this. Before it was declared a park, it was under heavy attack from these two prime enemies of forest conservation and was only rescued in the nick of time thanks largely to the efforts of William Phelps, who pushed for — and finally obtained in March of 1958 — the creation of this park of 92,000 hectares to conserve its rich flora and fauna.

But despite these words on the effectiveness of national parks in protecting areas from commercial exploitation, this protection weakens drastically where urban development actually borders on a park. This already has happened in the case of the Avila National Park, an 85,000-hectare preserve created in December 1958 to protect the flanks and summit of the Avila Range that forms the barrier between the Caracas Valley to the south and the sea to the north. Both flanks of this park reach down to already-populated zones, and the Commander of the National Guard, which is responsible for policing the area, is reported to have said that 1,800 *ranchitos* (slum-type constuctions) have been built recently within the park limits on the seaward side and 7,000 *ranchitos* on the Caracas flank. Politically, it will be most difficult to eject those already occupying park territory, but the Governor of Caracas, according to a statement recorded in the press on April 1, 1985, had declared that his office has specific instructions to prevent further homesteading. Fortunately, April 1 does not have the same connotations in Spanish as it does in English!

Enough now has been said to highlight the precarious position of the tropical forests of the world, but this problem fades into insignificance if one looks at the basic factor behind these dwindling forests and behind many other of this world's present ills. This factor is the well-known one of the population explosion. Unlike the lemmings, whose inherited instincts drive them to commit mass suicide when their numbers grow too crowded, man's only instinct is to go on and on, adding to his numbers without control.

The World Health Organization (WHO) has published figures showing that the world's population increased by 1,394,932,000 inhabitants (or nearly 46%) in the 20-year period from 1960 to 1980 — nearly 70 million per year. Viewed in Venezuelan terms, that's an increase equivalent to the population of the city of Caracas every two weeks!

Is it surprising, then, that the tropical forests are taking a beating?

As for the future, WHO estimates that for the period of 1980-2000 we may anticipate a further increase of more than 1,500,000,000 (nearly 47%) in developing regions, and 150,000,000 (just under 7%) in developed areas. Naturally, these estimates do not say just how these increases can be dealt with. Every nation is by now well aware of the dangers inherent in this explosion, and in some regions — naturally the better-developed ones — slow improvement is being achieved through advice on family planning or where the average person can see and appreciate the advantages of a small family in terms of maintaining a better standard of living. But this education is a slow process. In the meantime, even though there has been some slowing over recent years, the population continues to climb at a horrific rate.

Tables 1-4 summarize some frightening statistics on population for all who may be interested. Read them and weep!

Table 1. 1983 World Health Organization Statistics on World Population.

	Year	Population	% of Increase	% of Population
World population	1960	3,037,215,000	—	—
	1980	4,432,147,000	45.9%	—
	2000	6,118,850,000	38.1%	—
Developing Nations:	1960	2,092,307,000	—	68.9%
	1980	3,300,809,000	57.8%	74.5%
	2000	4,846,690,000	46.8%	79.2%
Developed Nations:	1960	994,909,000	—	31.1%
	1980	1,131,339,000	19.7%	25.5%
	2000	1,208,502,000	6.8%	20.8%

Table 2. 1973 United Nations World Population Projections.

Year	Total	Developing Nations	Developed Nations
2000	6,515,000,000	4,061,000,000	1,454,000,000
2025	9,202,000,000	7,502,000,000	1,700,000,000
2050	11,228,000,000	9,392,000,000	1,836,000,000
2075	12,120,000,000	10,245,000,000	1,875,000,000

Table 3. 1983 World Health Organization Population Statistics for Latin America.

Year	Population Estimate	% of Increase	% of World Population
1960	215,731,000	—	7.1%
1980	363,704,000	68%	8.2%
2000	565,747,000	55%	9.2%

Table 4. 1983 World Health Organization Population Statistics for Venezuela

1. 1979 population: 13,500,000*
   A. Ages 0-14: 5,693,000
   B. Ages 55 & Over: 978,000
2. National density: 19 persons/km²
3. 80% of total population urban.

* Estimated 1985 population of Venezuela in excess of 17,500,000

Index to Names of Orchidaceae

(Boldface numbers indicate pages where illustrations appear.)

Aa hartwegii, 264, **265**
Acacallis cyanea, 19, 66, **66**
Acineta alticola, 138, **140**
  erythroxantha, 138
  superba, 16, 75, 84, 138
Ada aurantiaca, 98-99, **99**
Altensteinia fimbriata, 192, **193**
  rostrata, 117-118, 192
Anguloa clowesii, 157-158, **157**, 160
  ruckeri, 157-158, **157**, 160
  uniflora, 157, **159**, 160
Apatostelis garayi, 238-240, **239**
Aspasia variegata, 19, 75
Barbosella cucullata, 75, 231-232, **232**, 242
  fuscata, 231
  orbicularis, 231-232, **232**
Batemannia colleyi, 75, 239
Beadlea lindleyana, 26
Bifrenaria aurantiaca, 192-193, **193**
  longicornis, 19
  maguirei, 38, 44, 105-107, **106**
Bletia purpurea, 16, 26
  stenophylla, 26, 75
Bollea hemixantha, 52, **110**, 110, 111
Brachionidium brevicaudatum, 118, **119**
  floribundum, 118
Brassavola cucullata, 75
  martiana, 75, 239
  nodosa, 75
Brassia bidens, 75, 219-221, **220**, **221**, 225
  caudata, 75
  glumacea, 26, 75, 220
  keiliana, 21, 75
  lanceana, 42
  verrucosa, 220
  wageneri, 75
Bulbophyllum exaltatum, 118, 120
  meridense, **9**
Campylocentrum micranthum, 75
  schneeanum, 121
  tyridion, 121
Catasetum barbatum, 75
  callosum, 16, 75
  costatum, 188, 190, **191**
  discolor, 75
  longifolium, 6, 189, 190-191
  macrocarpum, 16, 23, 26, 75, 188, **189**
  pileatum, 16, 75, 187-188, **189**
  planiceps, 75
  sanguineum, 9, 188, **189**
  splendens, 16, 188
Cattleya gaskelliana, 13, 22, 75, 136, 161
  jenmannii, 161-163, **162**, **163**
  labiata, 13, 22, 136, 161
  lawrenceana, 16, 22, 75, 161
  lueddemanniana, 13, 22, 75, 136-138, **137**, 161
  mossiae, 13, **14**, 21, 22, 75, 136, 161
  patini, 16, 22
  percivaliana, 13, 22, 75, 136, 161
  violacea, **15**, 16, 19, 22, 75
Caularthron bicornutum, 26, 42, 75
Chamelophyton kegelii, 6, 75
Chaubardia surinamensis, 109
Chaubardiella tigrina, 99, 111, **115**
Chondrorhyncha flaveola, **47**, 48, 49, 112
  rosea, 112
Chrysocycnis schlimii, 193-194, **193**
Chysis aurea, 147, **150**

Cladobium violaceum, 26, 75
Cleistes moritzii, 198
  rosea, 16, 26, 61, 198-199, **199**
  stricta, 198
  tenuis, 38, 198
Clowesia warscewiczii, 42, **45**
Cochleanthes discolor, 112, **113**
  flabelliformis, 112
  marginata, 48, 112
Comparettia falcata, 16, 26, 75, 261-262, **263**
Coryanthes biflora, 7, **11**
Cryptarrhena lunata, **9**
Cycnoches chlorochilon, 5, 16, 23, **25**, 26
  loddigesii, 16
  maculatum, 16, 26
Cyrtidium rhomboglossum, 147-148, **149**
Cyrtopodium cristatum, 16, 26
  engelii, 195
  glutiniferum, 6, 140, **140**, 195, 196-197, **196**
Dichaea histrio, **193**, 194
  kegelii, 194
  morrisii, 75
  muricata, 75, 194
  picta, 75
  swartzii, 194
Diothonaea megalospatha, 148, **151**
Dipteranthus obliquus, 21, 120-121
  planifolius, **9**, 75
Dressleria dilecta, 187
Duckeella alticola, 56, 60, 64
Dunstervillea mirabilis, 6
Elleanthus amethystinus, 166, **167**
  arpophyllostachys, 166, **167**, 217
  capitatus, 195
  caravata, **165**, 167-168
  graminifolius, 39
  norae, 64, 166-167, **168**
  oeconomicus, 166, **169**
  sphaerocephalus, 166, 195
  wageneri, **167**, 168
Eltroplectris roseo-alba, 26
Encyclia ceratistes, 23, 26
  chacaoensis, 23, 26, 75
  cordigera, 16, 23, 75
  diurna, 23, 26
  fragrans, 26, 56, 75
  livida, 26
  vespa, 59, 208-209, 241, 245
Epidendropsis violascens, 61
Epidendrum agathosmicum, 75
  attenuatum, 75
  calamarium, 42
  ciliare, 16, 23, 26, 75
  compressum, 75
  coriifolium, 75
  coronatum, 75
  cristatum, 75
  deltoglossum, 23, 26
  dendrobioides, 38, 60, **62**
  densiflorum, 26
  difforme, 75
  elongatum, 60, 75, 237
  ferrugineum, 75
  garcianum, 138-140, **139**
  halatum, 239
  heterodoxum, 75
  huebneri, 76
  ibaguense, 76

  latifolium, 132, **133**, 241, 245
  leucochilum, 76, 208, 211-212, **212**
  lindenii, 76
  longicolle, 241, 245
  manarae, 6
  minus, 241, 245
  montigenum, 60, 237
  moritzii, 76
  nocturnum, 26, 33, 38, 39, 54, 56, 60, 76, 129-134, **131**, **132**, **134**, 241, 245
  oncidioides, 76
  ottonis, 19
  pachyphyton, **53**, 57, 136
  pamplonense, 208-210, **209**, **210**, 241, 245
  purum, 26, 76
  recurvatum, 20, 26
  rostratum, 136
  sceptrum, 208
  secundum, 26, 54, 60, 76
  serpens, 26, 56
  stamfordianum, 76
  stenopetalum, 76
  strictum, 241
  tigrinum, 208-210, 241, 245
Epistephium duckei, 56
  hernandii, 38, 39
  parviflorum, 38
Eriopsis biloba, **29**, 33, 38, 39, 54, 60
Eulophia alta, 6, 26, 76
Eurystyles cotyledon, 76
Galeandra beyrichii, 20, 26
  devoniana, 76
  stangeana, 19, 76
Gongora maculata, 16
  quinquenervis, 21, 76
Govenia superba, 26, 76
Habenaria alata, 76
  entomantha, 26
  mesodactyla, 26
  monorrhiza, **9**, 26, 76
  obtusa, 26, 76
  petalodes, 26
  repens, 26
  trifida, 26, 38
Hapalorchis cheirostyloides, 26
Hexadesmia dunstervillei, 76, 142, **143**
  fusiformis, 26
  sessilis, 76
Hexisea bidentata, 16, 121-122
  imbricata, 39
Hofmeisterella eumicroscopica, 98
Houlettia lansbergii, 251, 252
  odoratissima, 56, 251, 252
  roraimensis, 251
  tigrina, 21, 251-253, **251**
Huntleya lucida, 76, 110
  meleagris, 110-111
Ionopsis satyrioides, 76
  utricularioides, 76
Isochilus linearis, 26
Jacquiniella globosa, 26, 38, 175
  teretifolia, 26, 39
Kefersteinia graminea, 76, 112, **116**, 243, 267-270, **270**
  sanguinolenta, 26, 112, 267-270, **270**
  tolimensis, 76, 112, **267**, 267-270
Kegeliella houtteana, **9**
Koellensteinia graminea, 76
Lankesterella caespitosa, 76

Index to Names of Orchidaceae
(Boldface numbers indicate pages where illustrations appear.)

Leochilus labiatus, 26, 76
Lepanthes steyermarkii, 6
Lepanthopsis astrophora, 76
　floripecten, 39, 76, 122
　vinacea, 76, 122
Liparis nervosa, 26
　vexillifera, 26
　wendlandii, 26
Lockhartia acuta, 76
　imbricata, 19, 76
　longifolia, 26, 76
Lueddemannia pescatorei, 148-149, **149**
Lycaste fulvescens, 99
Macradenia lutescens, 76
Malaxis caracasana, 26, 76
Manniella americana, 38
Masdevallia civilis, 76
　guttulata, 229-230
　maculata, 76
　minuta, 76
　mooreana, 228
　peruviana, 228
　picturata, 76
　rechingeriana, 76
　sprucei, **228**, 228-230
　striatella, 76
　tovarensis, 16, 76, 140-141, 228, 269
　triangularis, 76, 228
　verecunda, 21
　wageneriana, 76, 140-141, **141**
　wendlandiana, 76, 228
Maxillaria aggregata, 90
　alba, 76
　amazonica, 39, 76
　arachnites, 76, 244
　bolivarensis, 76
　brunnea, 76
　caespitifica, 76
　callichroma, 216-218, **216**, **218**, 244
　camaridii, 76
　chlorantha, 246-247
　conferta, 76, 88
　crassifolia, 76
　desvauxiana, 39
　discolor, 76
　equitans, 68
　grandiflora, 243
　guareimensis, 195
　histrionica, 77
　jenischiana, 77, 84
　lancifolia, 84
　lasallei, 77
　lawrenceana, 77
　lepidota, 243-244, **243**, **244**
　luteoalba, 77, **88**, 89
　macrura, 77, 88
　mapiriensis, 77
　melina, 77
　meridensis, 38, 39, 77, 243
　miniata, 77, 84
　multicaulis, 77
　nigrescens, 77, **88**, 90
　notylioglossa, 39, 77, 87
　ochroleuca, **36**, 89, 195, 245-247
　　var. *longipes*, **246**, 247
　parkeri, 52, 77, 90, 243
　pendens, 38, 39
　ponerantha, 26, 77
　quelchii, 61
　ramosa, 26, 77
　reichenheimiana, **36**, 39
　ringens, 77
　rufescens, 26, 77, 90
　setigera, **88**, 89, 217
　sophronitis, 90
　spilotantha, 16, 49, 77, 195
　splendens, 39, 195, 245-247
　stenophylla, 26, 77
　triloris, 16, 77, 84, 88, **88**, 89, 90, 244
　uncata, 42, 77
　violaceopunctata, 19, 77, 90, 243
　xylobiiflora, 77, 87
Mendoncella burkei, **185**, 186
　fimbriata, **185**, 186
　jorisiana, **185**, 186
Miltonia spectabilis, 99, **100**
　var. *moreliana*, 99
Mormodes buccinator, 26, 52, 77
Myoxanthus ceratothallis, 26, 78
　hystrix, 78
　lancipetalus, 78
　parahybunensis, 78
　reymondii, 6, 78
　uncinatus, 78
Myrosmodes cochleare, 264
Neolehmannia porpax, 77
Notylia bungerothii, 77
　incurva, 77, 175, **177**
　mirabilis, **120**, 122, 176
　peruviana, 77, 175
　platyglossa, 77, 175, **177**
　rhombilabia, 77
　sagittifera, 77, 175, 176, **177**
　wullschlaegeliana, 176-177, **177**
　yauaperyensis, 175, **176**
Octomeria connellii, 59
　deltoglossa, 77
　filifolia, 77
　flaviflora, 235-237, **236**, **237**
　integrilabia, 77
　parviflora, 64, 237
　steyermarkii, 144-146, **145**, 213
　taracuana, 77
Odontoglossum arminii, 56, 195
　constrictum, 77
　hastilabium, 48, **49**, 195
　naevium, 77
Oeceoclades maculata, 26
Oncidium ampliatum, 77
　baueri, 77
　bicolor, 77
　boothianum, 77
　carthaginense, 77
　cebolleta, 19, 23, 26, 77
　cimiciferum, 77
　falcipetalum, 77
　globuliferum, 84, 117, 123, **124**, 195
　hastilabium, 195
　heteranthum, 77
　krameriamum, 257-259
　lanceanum, 16, 77, 250
　limminghei, 257, 257-260, **259**
　luridum, 77
　meirax, 85-86, **86**
　murinum, 77
　nanum, 66, **67**
　nigratum, 33, 56, 77
　nudum, 26, 77
　obryzatum, 16, 77
　papilio, 6, 16, 77, 124, 257-259, **259**
　sanderae, 257-259
　scansor, 195
　sphacelatum, 77
　versteegianum, 257-259
　volvox, 6, 16, 20, 26, 77
　warmingii, 33
　zebrinum, 20, 26, 61, 77
Orleanesia maculata, 77
Ornithocephalus bicornis, **9**, 77, 124, **125**
　gladiatus, 42
Otoglossum arminii, 107, 195
Paphinia cristata, 16, 78, **153**, 154-156, **156**, 204
　lindeniana, 42, **42**, 154-156, **156**
Peristeria aspersa, 42
Pescatorea cerina, 111
　coronaria, 111, **111**
Phragmipedium caudatum, 80-82, 84, 196
　klotzscheanum, 254-256, **254**, **255**
　lindenii, **81**, 82, **83**, 195-196, **196**
　lindleyanum, **9**, 78
　longifolium, 82
Physosiphon lansbergii, 78
Pinelia alticola, 39
Pityphyllum amesianum, 126, **127**
Platystele johnstonii, 6, 126, **205**, 207
　lancilabris, 78, 207
　ornata, 2, 16, 78, 126, 207
　ovalifolia, 207
　stenostachya, 73, 78, **124**, 126, 128, 207
Pleurothallis arbuscula, 78
　archidiaconi, 78
　aristata, 74, 78
　barbulata, 78
　bivalvis, 78
　breviscapa, 78
　cabellensis, 78
　cardiostola, 78
　cardium, 78
　chamensis, 20, 26, 78
　discoidea, 26, 78
　dunstervillei, 179-180, **180**
　endotrachys, 78
　erinacea, 26, 78
　fimbriata, 78
　flexuosa, 78
　galeata, 78
　grandiflora, 78
　gratiosa, 78
　grobyi, 78, 208
　hemirrhoda, 26, 78
　hitchcockii, 78
　immersa, 205, **206**, 207
　ionantha, 78
　lanceana, 78
　lansbergii, 181
　lappiformis, 54, 205, 232
　linguifera, **9**, 181
　loranthophylla, 78
　mentosa, 78
　monocardia, 78
　nanifolia, 54, 232
　nephrocardia, 78
　northenae, 234
　obovata, 78
　pedunculata, 78
　perijaënsis, **233**, 233-234

Index to Names of Orchidaceae
(Boldface numbers indicate pages where illustrations appear.)

picta, 208
phalangifera, 78, 179, 181, **182**
pluriracemosa, 78
polygonoides, 78
pruinosa, 26, 78
ruberrima, 78
rubroviridis, 78
ruscifolia, 26, 78, 180, **180**
sclerophylla, 78, 241-242, **242**
secunda, 78, 179, 180, **181**
semiscabra, 78
semperflorens, 78
sicaria, 26, 78
spiculifera, 239
stenosepala, 180-181, **183**
subtilis, 78
talpinaria, 78
testaefolia, 26
undulata, 84
velaticaulis, 26, 78
vittariifolia, 79
wageneriana, 79
xanthochlora, 79
Polycycnis ornata, 225-227, **227**
vittata, 42, 52, **225**, 225-227
Polystachya concreta, 79
foliosa, 26, 79
Ponera striata, 84
Ponthieva orchioides, 26
racemosa, 26
Polyotidium huebneri, 204, **206**
Porroglossum echidnum, 6, **10**, 203-204, **205**
Psychopsiella limminghei, 259-260, **259**
Psychopsis papilio, 258-259, **259**
Psygmorchis glossomystax, 16, 19, 26, 79, 261-263, **262**, **263**
pusilla, 16, 26, 52, 79
Quekettia pygmaea, 79
Restrepia elegans, 79
lansbergii, 79
Restrepiopsis tubulosa, 79
Rodriguezia leeana, 66, 68, **69**
secunda, 16, 19, 79
Sacoila lanceolata, **9**
Scaphosepalum verrucosum, 6, 74, 79
Scaphyglottis amethystina, 19
huebneri, 79
Scelochilus ottonis, 79
Schomburgkia undulata, 23, **24**, 26, 79
Scuticaria steelei, 6, **99**, 101, 239
Selenipedium palmifolium, 214
steyermarkii, 213-215, **213**, **215**
Sievekingia jenmannii, 149, **149**, 152
Sigmatostalix amazonica, 68
huebneri, 68, **70**
Sobralia candida, 79
cattleya, 6, 95, **96**, 97
decora, 201
fimbriata, 79, **93**, 95, 97
fragrans, 79
infundibuligera, 39, 56, 60, 64, **93**, 95, 97, 167
ruckeri, 222-224, **224**
suaveolens, 79
sessilis, 39, 201, **201**
speciosa, 44
stenophylla, 254
valida, 201-202
violacea, 79, **93**, 95, 97, 200
yauaperyensis, 79, 93, **94**, 95, 97

Solenidium lunatum, 273
racemosum, 271-273, **272**
Spiranthes speciosa, 1, 84
tenuis, 26
Stanhopea eburnea, 79
wardii, 16, 20, 26, 79
Stelis alata, 39, 79
argentata, 79
braccata, 26, 79
crassilabia, 79
cucullata, **9**, 79
fendleri, 79
grossilabris, 79
guianensis, 79
humilis, 79
leinigii, 240
muscifera, 79
obovata, 64
porpax, 26, 79
trichorrachis, 26
tridentata, 79
Stellilabium pogonostalix, **9**
Stenia pallida, 74, 79, 110, 111, **114**
Stenorrhynchos lanceolatus, 26
nutans, 1
Telipogon croesus, 128
Teuscheria wageneri, 79, 101, **102**, 103
Trichocentrum capistratum, 79, 248, 249
cornucopiae, 248-250, **249**
hartii, 249
orthoplectron, 249
pfavii, 250
pulchrum, 248, 249
tigrinum, 250
Trichopilia fragrans, 79, 141
laxa, 84
oicophylax, 141, **141**
Trichosalpinx ciliaris, 26, 78, 84
orbicularis, 78
Trigonidium acuminatum, 19, 42, 79
obtusum, 79, 239
Trisetella huebneri, 228
Trizeuxis falcata, 26, 79
Vanilla planifolia, 3
pompona, 26
Warczewiczella flabelliformis, 266
Xylobium leontoglossum, 6
pallidiflorum, 79
variegatum, 79
Zygopetalum burkei, 33
Zygosepalum angustilabium, 59, 61, **61**, **63**, 64, **172**, 174, 208
labiosum, 79, 170, 171, 174
lindeniae, 19, 42, 107, **171**, 171, 174
tatei, 107, **108**, 171, **173**, 174, 208

280

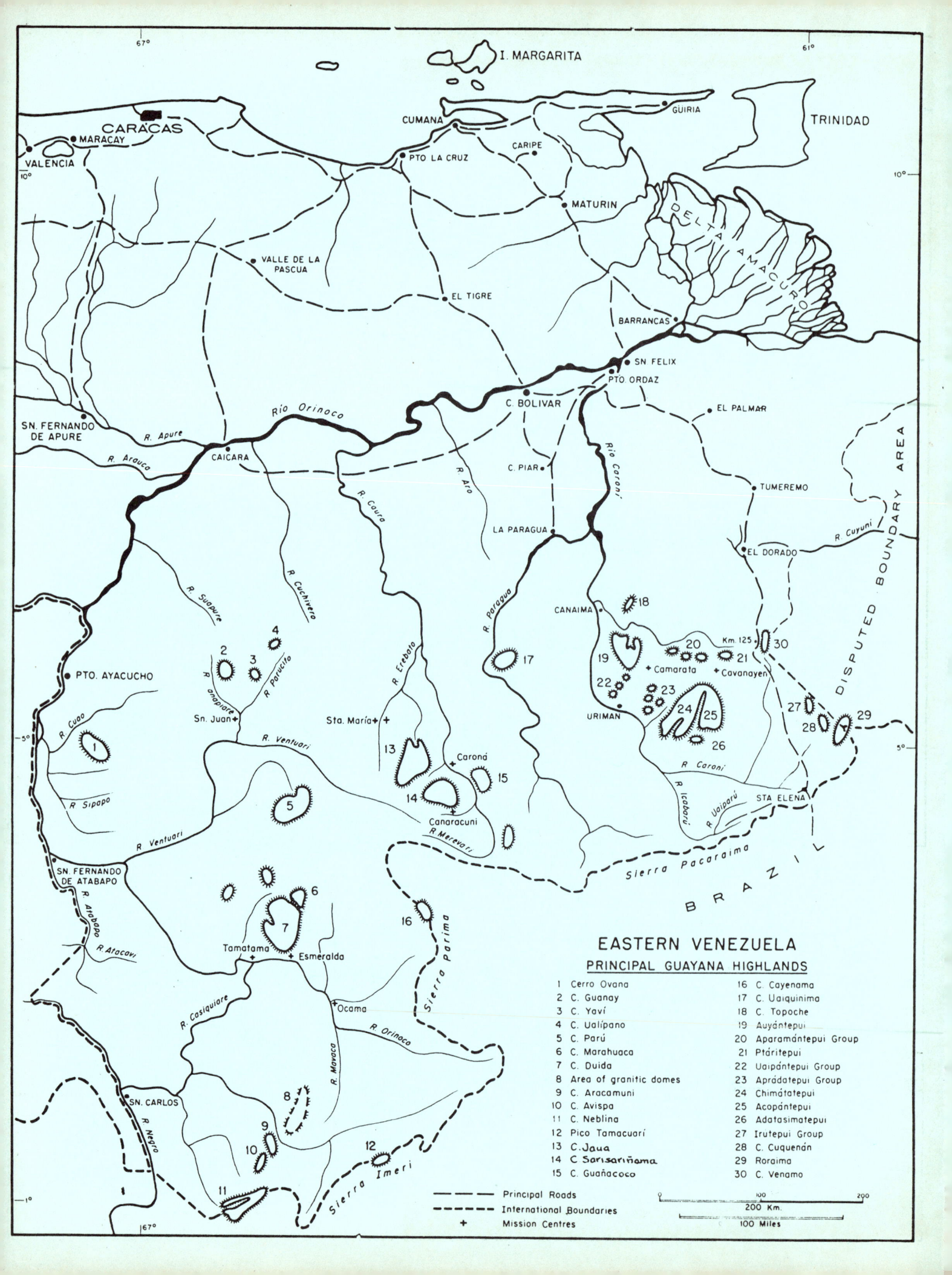

EASTERN VENEZUELA
PRINCIPAL GUAYANA HIGHLANDS

1. Cerro Ovana
2. C. Guanay
3. C. Yaví
4. C. Ualípano
5. C. Parú
6. C. Marahuaca
7. C. Duida
8. Area of granitic domes
9. C. Aracamuni
10. C. Avispa
11. C. Neblina
12. Pico Tamacuarí
13. C. Jaua
14. C. Sarisariñama
15. C. Guañacoco
16. C. Cayenama
17. C. Uaiquinima
18. C. Topoche
19. Auyántepui
20. Aparamántepui Group
21. Ptáritepui
22. Uaipántepui Group
23. Aprádatepui Group
24. Chimátatepui
25. Acopántepui
26. Adatasimatepui
27. Irutepui Group
28. C. Cuquenán
29. Roraima
30. C. Venamo

--- Principal Roads
-- - International Boundaries
+ Mission Centres

200 Km.
100 Miles